A HANDBOOK OF CHRISTIAN MATRIMONY

The Blight of Birth Control and a Fifty Year Battle
for Church Growth
Back to Luther on the Family and Birth Control on
the 500th Anniversary of the Reformation

Herman Otten, Editor

A Handbook of Christian Matrimony

Copyright 2011 © Lutheran News, Inc. All Rights Reserved. No Portion of this book may be reproduced in any form, except for quotations in reviews, articles, and speeches, without permission from the publisher.

Library of Congress Card
Lutheran News, Inc.
684 Luther Lane
New Haven, MO 63068
Published 2011
Printed in the United States of America,
Lightning Source Inc., La Vergne, TN
ISBN # 978-0-9644799-2-0

"No other single force is causing as much measurable hardship in this country as the collapse of marriage" said the cover story, "Unfaithfully Yours" of the July 13, 2009 TIME.

Dedicated to my wife Grace and the Seven from Heaven. She taught about God's Grace in Jesus Christ. May they all continue to teach God's Grace to future generations so we may all rest in Heaven.

Acknowledgements
Thanks to Naomi Finck, Mary Zastrow, Ruth Rethemeyer and Luke Otten for preparing this book for publication and to Pastor Reuel Schulz for editing.

Books Published by *Christian News*

An American Translation of the Bible ($22.95)
Translated by William F. Beck

Bonhoeffer and King: Their Life and Theology Documented in Christian News, 1963-2011 ($11.95)
Edited by Herman Otten

Crisis in Christendom Seminex Ablaze ($16.95)
By Herman Otten

Marquart's Legacy ($5.00)
By Herman Otten

Walter A. Maier - A Man Speaks Missouri and the World Should Listen ($16.95)
By Herman J. Otten

Islam In The Crucible ($8.50)
by R. da Montecroce and Luther

Prayers for The Worship Service ($14.95)
By Arthur J. Clement

Devotions on the Apostles Creed ($9.99)
By Peter Krey

Pass the Salt ($8.99)
by J.B. Romnes

Luther Today ($6.95)
by H. Otten

How To Start Or Keep Your Own Missouri Synod Lutheran Church ($5.00)
by J.M. Cascione

Baal or God ($2.00)
by Herman J. Otten, Ed.

C.F.W. Walther's Pastoral Theology ($8.99)

Luther's Small Catechism (AAT text) ($12.50)

The Christian's Travel Guide to World History ($19.95)
by Henry Koch

Two Rivers to Freedom ($28.95)
by Stella Wuerffel

A Lutheran Catechism on Homosexuality ($2.50)
by Dr. David Kaufmann

Salt, Light and Signs of the Times ($13.95)
By Ronald W. Stelzer

Servant Captains for the Good Ship Missouri ($7.00)
By Herman Otten

Reclaiming the Gospel in the LCMS How to Keep Your Congregation Lutheran ($4.50)
By Jack Cascione

TABLE OF CONTENTS

I.	Marriage	1
II.	Christianity, Children, and Contraception	39
III.	Birth Control	62
IV.	Living Together Before Marriage	180
V.	Divorce and Remarriage	190
VI.	Motherhood	222
VII.	The Christian Family	236
VIII.	Gay Marriage – Homosexuality – Polygamy	267
IX.	Churches Are Dying – Not Enough Children	287
X.	Courting – Engagement	295
XI.	Adultery – Premarital Sex	317
XII.	Over Population	329
XIII.	Weddings	360

FOREWORD

Pastor Herman Otten has contributed more sound theological material on a variety of theological topics for the benefit of the Church during the past couple of generations than anyone else I know. Some of his contributions have been widely appreciated. Some have not. Judging by the looming demographic catastrophe brought about by the birth dearth following the World War II baby boom, most folks have decided that limiting the size of their families is the sensible choice to make. It appears that Pastor Otten's voice in favor of the Church's traditional teaching against contraception has been largely ignored.

People are persuaded to have fewer children when offered something they value more. Commercial consumerism relies on the god of more and more fascinating stuff that passes away with the world. People created in the image of God, redeemed by the blood of Christ, and brought to the saving faith by the Holy Spirit for the enjoyment of everlasting life with God are bombarded by the false promises of this god of materialism. He entertains you. But he gives you nothing of true value. What is at first so very exciting quickly becomes stale and obsolete. You grow older and watch life pass you by. The god of continual acquisition is a false, lying, deceptive god who leaves you empty and alone. Children are the only gift God gives you in this life that you can take to heaven with you. There is no other form of wealth that can compare to the wealth of children. What a tragedy that God's gifts are so universally despised. As Americans play God they show themselves to be very poor gods indeed!

In this volume, Pastor Otten includes many articles from many sources over many years. His pro-marriage and pro-family stance is clear and uncompromising. His conservatism is ecumenical in the best sense of the word as he provides a wide variety of materials from Lutheran, Roman Catholic, and Protestant sources. *A Handbook of Christian Matrimony* is a valuable resource for Christians of all ages.

Pastor Rolf Preus

"And God Blessed Them. . ."

By Rolf Preus
Christian News, April 14, 1997

It was not so long ago – perhaps after the birth of Samuel, our 11th child – that my late father told me, "Rolf, you're a wealthy man." I needed to hear that. One needs a reminder once in a while of what true wealth is. Dad's words came back to me on November 4, 1995, when I was suffering from the shock of his sudden death, and one by one my boys gave to me the comfort of the gospel. They suffered with me, and they sorrowed with me, but not as those who have no hope. Dad was right: I am a wealthy man.

Twelve children! No one is more amazed about this than Dort and I. You see, we didn't plan a single one. We didn't choose to have children. We didn't "let" God give us children, as if He needs our permission. We simply got married. I remember the sermon quite well and have myself preached on that text a number of times. Dad preached on Matthew 6:25-34. Naturally, in true Lutheran fashion, he focused on verse 33, "But seek ye first the kingdom of God and His righteousness, and all these things shall be added unto you."

The same God who reckons to us Christ's righteousness and who thus governs us, not by laws or threats; but by grace alone, is the God who takes care of our bodily needs and who persuades us that life is more than food, clothes, and all the other stuff we spend our time gaining. If you think that you should wait until you can "afford" to have children, you'll never be able to afford it. Dort and I discovered a couple of years ago that we couldn't afford twelve kids. Thank God we already had them! Otherwise, the things that money can buy would have taken the place of children. Our youngest son, Peter, who will be two on May 31, is more valuable than whatever money it costs us to feed him, clothe him, house him, etc.

Rome has an interesting and rather "Catholic" position on birth control. That is, they teach what has been taught for a long, long time. And it makes sense. God most certainly does join sexual intimacy to procreation. This relationship surely ought to be respected. And there is some truth to the Roman Catholic concept of "natural law."

But there are serious problems with Rome's position on contraception, not the least of which is the apparent inconsistency between that and the shameful practice of forced priestly celibacy. You know what the Roman Catholic lady with 10 kids who started using contraception said, don't you? "If you don't play the game, you don't make the rules."

Frankly, I am not persuaded that there is much more difference between following a strict "natural family planning" regimen which includes taking one's temperature before sexual relations and a more "artificial" means of birth control, such as a barrier method to prevent the sperm from reaching the egg. What is more unnatural than to avoid the joys of the marriage bed at precisely those times when God, in his wise "family planning," makes the woman the most desirous of sexual intimacy? The Roman Catholic position on birth control is like the Roman Catholic position on every moral issue: ponderously, depressingly, predictably legalistic. "It's okay to do this if you do it this way, but it's a sin if you do it that way." Right. No wonder Roman Catholics don't believe the teaching of their own church!

Still, at least Rome is capable of a degree of moral discernment, even if it remains captive to scholastic legalism. Most Protestants (and Lutherans) don't even know how to address the subject of birth control from a moral vantage point. This deficiency makes them as legalistic as Rome. If you cannot set down a firm rule which would apply to every situation, such folks simply dismiss the moral dimensions of this issue altogether. I know this because for some strange reason people talk to me about birth control, assuming that I have an opinion on the subject.

One time, several years ago when we only had about 7 children, a Missouri Synod Lutheran pastor sat down next to me at a table as I was enjoying a cigarette with a cup of coffee (a pleasure of which I have denied myself for over four months now and man would I love to have a cigarette!). The man looked at my cigarette and probably smelled my breath (I didn't ask him to sit down next to me) and said to me, "I suppose you think birth control is a sin?" He was really kind of rude. Still I decided to take his question seriously. I have never believed that birth control is necessarily a sin, but I have always believed that it could be a sin. It all depended on the circumstance. This is a far cry from saying that there is no moral compass by which to judge the issue. Clearly, it is a serious matter to seek to prevent the divine creation of new life. "It is He that hath made us and not we ourselves." "I believe that God has made me." To say that birth control is not necessarily a sin is not to say that it is a morally neutral matter. So I had to think about the man's question for while. Then I gave him a one word answer: "Probably." He was annoyed with that answer. He replied, "But smoking isn't a sin?"

Now I didn't start this conversation. But it has stayed in my mind over the years because it illustrates so well the fundamental difference in moral reasoning between the traditional Lutheran and the modern Lutheran. I asked the man if he believes in birth control and if he practiced birth control and he answered yes to both questions. I then explained to him that, while I did not smoke with the intent or desire to kill myself (that being only a possible and very unfortunate side effect of my smoking), he did practice birth control with the desire of thwarting God's creative act in bringing a new life into this world, did he not? Why else do it? Now consider how the standards have changed! We used to believe that a certain course of action was wrong because it would be against our neighbor. "Love does no harm to the neighbor." Now we seem to believe that an action is wrong because it hurts us, that is, the one doing it. So we should love ourselves so much that we don't do harmful things to our bodies! (Like fasting for 40 days and 40 nights? Is that good for your body? Do you think that perhaps Jesus didn't love himself enough?)

Please, spare me lecture on smoking. It's a filthy habit, it stinks, it's expensive, it causes lung cancer, emphysema, heart problems, etc., but I have never met anyone who smoked for the purpose of killing himself. I have never met anyone who practiced birth control who did not do so for the purpose of preventing the divine creation of a human being.

So what do we say about the morality of birth control? We confess that God is the Author of life (Psalm 95:6; 100:3), that He chooses who will be born (Genesis 30:1-3), that children are, objectively, a blessing from God (Genesis 1:28; Psalm 127:3ff; 128:3), that God closes the womb (1 Samuel 1:5), but that He also graciously answers prayers for children (1 Samuel 1:17-20). My wife, Dort, prayed as a little girl that God would bless her with many children. She was moved by the story about Hannah, and how God answered her prayer. God answered Dort's prayer, too. For those Christian women who have prayed that prayer and haven't seen their prayers answered, I can only say that God is faithful and true and that He will, some day, in his own way (not ours) show you that every prayer you prayed was answered.

So what do we say about the morality of birth control? We say such arguments in favor of birth control as those which compare it to insurance against car accidents are offensive on the face of it, for a child is never an accident, and no child ever born was not redeemed by the blood of Christ and a fit object of God's mercy and love. We say that our culture is rotten to the core as it values things that can bring no real happiness while it discards as refuse the broken and dead bodies of millions of unborn children. And we say that it takes a bit of moralistic fine-tuning (to say the least) to claim that it is a mortal sin to destroy the fertilized egg but that it is a morally indifferent matter to do every thing under our power to keep that egg from ever being fertilized, as if man and woman are in control up until the life begins and then we let God take over. And we say that our Lord Jesus is faithful to His words recorded in Matthew 6. My dad preached the truth – and he never even mentioned birth control!

It pains me to see folks who, for whatever reason, stay away from the sacrament of Christ's body and blood, as if it gives them no blessing at all. They just don't want it. What is a pastor to do? To say, but you must go! I don't think so. Certainly not until they regard the sacrament as a blessing! Surely we shouldn't want to turn gospel into law, would we? Let the law be the law and let the gospel be the gospel. Can we do that? It's very difficult.

When it comes to birth control, let us apply God's law. Are we selfish, are we greedy, do we simply want a life centered on things, conveniences, and useless stuff that cannot compare in value to the children God gives? Are our values the same distorted values as these of our godless society which hates God the Father and rejects His only begotten Son? Do we view the "planning" of children as something we as human beings have the right to do, as if we, not God, are the authors of life? Is this not idolatry? If the shoe fits, put it on.

On the other hand, should a woman face a threat to her health if she should bear a child? Should we not care for that woman's health? Should we impose a conscience burden on her? Should we call sin what could rather be the very opposite? Shall we interpret God's law in such a way that it is satisfies whatever legalistic system we have devised? Is that not also idolatry?

Does all this mean that birth control is not a moral issue? Not at all! Precisely the opposite. It means that God doesn't give us a rule book. He gives us His commands and His promises. And He calls on us to apply them to life. And He calls on us to use more moral discernment than that required by a simple "yes" or "no" on the question of the morality of birth control. And above all, He calls us to lay all of our sins on Jesus who bore them for us. He tells us not to look to moral reasoning as that which justifies anyone, but, when we have done all that which was in us to do, to confess before Him our utter unworthiness and total dependence on that righteousness which is ours by faith alone.

To have the righteousness of faith, and to teach that to the children God gives to us, that, my friend, is the greatest joy in life, and the most fervent prayer of every Christian parent, whether with one child or a dozen, is that God will keep our children trusting in the merits of Jesus until they die in peace.

Pastor and Mrs. Rolf Preus with their family of eleven boys and one girl. The photo appeared on page 1 of the August 5, 2002 *Christian News* in its special issue "A Manual of Christian Matrimony, He Her Honor and She His Glory."
In December of 2011 the Preus family had 20 grandchildren and two on the way. Some of the children are not yet married.

Afterword

By Mrs. Rolf (Dort) Preus
From God's Gift to Mankind -
Marriage from the Perspective of a Christian Woman
(Entire essay published in the December 5, 2011 Christian News)

In the Western World, Christianity has enjoyed much freedom and wealth. Christians have had freedom to go to church, study the Bible, and teach the Bible for centuries. So why are the memberships and attendance in faithful Lutheran churches shrinking? It is because Christian parents have not been going to church. It is because Christian parents have not been studying the Bible. It is because Christian parents have not been taking their children to church. It is because Christian parents have not been teaching the Bible with confidence and joy to their children. A wedding ceremony is establishing a 'mission station' by God the Father, Almighty Maker of Heaven and Earth. What God has joined together let no one separate. When God blesses a marriage, God Himself is giving a 'divine call' in the union of Man and Woman within her womb that is one with her husband.

I was always troubled by St. Paul declaring women were saved in childbearing. He seemed to be teaching women earn eternal life by having children. When my children were small, I would read Bible Stories and say prayers with them before kissing them good night. I helped them memorizes their Bible verses and Luther's small catechism. I taught them to pray before and after meals. It occurred to me that I was not only nurturing them in the Word of God, but myself as well. A Christian mother wants to teach about the Savior from sin and death to her children. No Christian mother wants to bear a child to grow up an unbeliever or murderer any more than Eve did. (Genesis 4) Christian mothers want to continue in faith, love and holiness, with self-control because they want their children to have eternal life.   (I Timothy 2:15)

The woman was made special. She was made with a womb to love and honor her husband. The husband is to love and honor his wife as a precious gift from God. Sin destroys this beautiful institution. For the sinful man and sinful woman to have a marriage as one flesh, they must in humility bow to God's Wisdom. In God's Word the marriage is safe, that is God pleasing. When we trust in the Promise of God we look on the marriage as He did when He created Adam and Eve and said 'this was good'. (Genesis 1) The Christian husband treasures his wife's body as if her body is his very own. The Christian wife treasures her husband's body with respect as her very head. In this way, the Christian husband and Christian wife glorify God as our Creator. And if God chooses, He will bless this union, entrusting them with a child. Every child is God's creation formed in the woman's womb by the man's seed. What an awesome and humbling experience for a woman, knowing God, the Father Almighty, Maker of Heaven and Earth is knitting together a child in her womb! What an awesome and humbling experience for a man knowing God, the Father Almighty, Maker of Heaven and Earth is knitting together a child from his seed in his wife's womb! (Psalm 127: 3-5) What a merciful God to consider the man's needs! (Psalm 8) What an awesome responsibility to be entrusted with God's creation! (Genesis 1 & 2)

A young Christian girl needs to understand that she must protect her womb even when she does not know who she will marry. She must protect her womb to honor her husband. She must protect her womb to show respect to her husband. She must protect her womb so their children will hold her husband in high esteem. A Christian woman must protect her womb by seeking a Christian man to be her husband so that the family will be safe in God's Word and Promise for the sake of their children. In this way, her children will rise up and call her blessed. (Proverbs 31:28) What God has joined together, let no man separate. God is committed!

The Christian husband and the Christian wife bring their child to the Baptismal Font to wash away the sins of the child. In this promise in Baptism, Christ, the Redeemer of the World, glorifies God. The Christian husband and the Christian wife nurture their child in the Word of God trusting the Comforter to instill a right spirit in the child so that God is glorified. The child is safe in God's Word and Promise. Where there is forgiveness of sins, there is life and Salvation! God is committed!

PREFACE

The 500th anniversary of Martin Luther's Reformation will be celebrated October 31, 2017. The Church today needs a Reformation far more than it did 500 years ago. *Christian News* has shown for 50 years that today the fundamental doctrines of historic Christianity, the Trinity, the Virgin Birth, Deity, Resurrection, and Vicarious Satisfaction of Christ are denied within all the major denominations.

The chapter on Truth and Doctrine in the author's *Baal or God* published in 1965 shows that direct revelation and the very concept of truth and doctrine are being rejected in the established churches of our day.

Many within churches reject the inerrancy and historicity of the Bible in all matters. They contend that Jesus Christ is not the only way to heaven and that all religions worship the same God, only calling him by a different name. Polls show that most church members, regardless of denomination, maintain they must at least in part work their own way to heaven.

The time has come for faithful Christians throughout the world to unite behind a 21st Century Formula of Concord which reaffirms Luther's scriptural doctrine affirmed in the *Book of Concord of 1580*, but also speaks to the issues of our day such as evolution, higher criticism of the Bible, the J-E-D-P Source hypothesis, universalism, etc.

This *Handbook of Christian Matrimony* shows what the Bible, Martin Luther, the *Book of Concord of 1580*, and the orthodox fathers of The Lutheran Church-Missouri Synod teach about marriage, divorce, living together without marriage, homosexuality, gay marriage, polygamy, motherhood, the family, and extra-marital sex.

The book's major section is on birth control and overpopulation. It includes some of the many articles *Christian News* has published on these issues during the last 50 years.

The section on marriage quotes from the *Concordia Cyclopedia* and *Pastoral Theology* by John Fritz, long used as a textbook in the seminaries of the LCMS. Dr. Kurt Marquart, one of greatest LCMS theologians and scholars during the last 50 years, shows that marriage is not outdated. The preface of Dr. Walter A. Maier's *For Better Not For Worse, A Manual of Christian Matrimony*, is included. It is the best book The Lutheran Church-Missouri Synod's Concordia Publishing House ever published on marriage. CPH refused to give *Christian News* permission to reprint it with current statistics. Today Maier's chapter on "The Blight of Birth Control" is found offensive. Much of it is in this book. During his day, Lutheran Hour speaker Walter A. Maier was the best known Lutheran throughout the world. *Walter A. Maier Still Speaks – Missouri and the World Should Listen*, published by *Christian News,* shows what Maier taught about birth control, marriage, evolution, higher criticism of the Bible, Genesis, war, etc. *He Her Honor and She His Glory*, sold by *Christian News*, is promoted in the handbook.

The three part series "Christianity, Children, and Contraception" by (Chaplain) Brandt Klawitter, a brilliant young confessional Lutheran scholar walking in the steps of such orthodox Lutherans as C.F.W. Walther and Kurt Marquart, deserves careful attention particularly from younger pastors and professors who maintain that the views of the editor of *Christian News* are outmoded.

An overture to the LCMS's 2010 convention titled "Promoting Church Growth by Returning to Luther's and the LCMS's Former and Scriptural Position on Birth Control" was ignored by the LCMS's 2010 convention. A convention committee said the LCMS has never taken a position on birth control. Many articles in the section on birth control show what the LCMS actually said about birth control before the last 50 years. No one has yet refuted Charles Provan's "The Bible's View of Birth Control", which first appeared in *Christian News* in 1988. It is reprinted in the *Handbook of Christian Matrimony*.

LCMS Professor Martin Naumann wrote in "The Tragedy of Birth Control" in 1971: "All children are souls intended for God's kingdom. Any drive for missions is made ridiculous by talk of birth control. As the church is to propagate itself by the power of the Gospel, so are Christians to increase the family of God by increasing in the place where love and missions start – in the family."

The many articles on birth control show that more are beginning to recognize "the blight of birth control" and agree with the position of Martin Luther, John Calvin, Walter Maier, John Fritz, and many other faithful Christian scholars. Note particularly "The Ironic Protestant Reversal – How the Original Family Movement Swallowed the Pill" by Allan C. Carlson. The LCMS's *Lutheran Witness* referred to Margaret Sanger, the founder of Planned Parenthood, as a "she devil." Lutheran Hour speaker Walter A. Maier called contraceptives "the most repugnant of modern aberrations, representing a twentieth century renewal of pagan bankruptcy." Carlson notes that "the average size of Missouri Synod clerical families in 1890 was 6.5." Now it appears as if the average LCMS clerical family is not much more than two. The LCMS's *1964 Lutheran Annual* reports 83,604 children baptized in 1962. The *2011 Lutheran Annual* reports 24,745 children baptized in 2009. Members of the LCMS followed the pattern set by their pastors, practicing birth control and having fewer children.

One of the major problems facing congregations is living together before marriage. This book sets forth the scriptural principles which condemns such "shacking up."

The section on divorce and remarriage answers the question "should divorced pastors be permitted to remain in the pastoral ministry?"

The blessings of motherhood are set forth together with what Luther taught about marriage, family, and children. Gay marriage and homosexuality are shown to be contrary to scripture.

Aaron Wolf, Associate Editor of *Chronicles,* shows that churches are dying due to a lack of babies (or "anemic birth rates").

The principles of courting and dating defended in the handbook and formerly promoted in the LCMS may seem out-dated but they are far more scriptural than the principles followed by many youth today. Haven Bradford Gow calls for a return to moral/sexual sanity.

The fact that overpopulation is a myth is documented.

The section on the wedding service has good advice for all those planning a Christian wedding.

The Table of Contents presents a scope of the essays in this *Handbook on Christian Matrimony*.

Above all, may this handbook lead Christian couples to stop using birth control and let God determine how many children they should have. In recent years as churches shrink in numbers, much is being said about church growth. All kinds of programs are being proposed. If Lutheran Christians practice what Luther taught, as the 500th anniversary of the Reformation draws near, real God-pleasing church growth will follow.

I
MARRIAGE

The Lutheran Church-Missouri Synod on Marriage

From the *Concordia Cyclopedia*
A Handbook of Religious Information with Special Reference to the History, Doctrine, Work, and Usages of the Lutheran Church

L. Fuerbringer, D.D., Professor of Biblical Introduction Interpretation; Theodore Engelder, D.D., Professor of Systematic Theology; P.E. Kretzmann, Ph. D., D. D., Professor of New Testament History and Interpretation and of Religious Education
Editors – in – Chief
St. Louis, MO
Concordia Publishing House
1927

Marriage. "The state of marriage, or wedlock, is the joint status of one man and one woman, superinduced and sustained by their mutual consent, to be and remain to each other husband and wife in a lifelong union, for legitimate sexual intercourse, the procreation of children, and cohabitation for mutual care and assistance." (A.L. Graebner.) In our days, when, as in the days of Noah and in the times preceding, the downfall of the great nations of the world, the factors of a false view of marriage and its relationship and that of sex perversions is so great, the problems connected with the situation can be met in only one way, namely, by stating the principles and truths which are here concerned on the basis of the Word of God, both publicly and privately. The holiness of marriage, the sacredness of the marriage relationship, the fact that marriage is the normal state of the average adult, both from the social and from the hygienic standpoint, the fact that children are a gift of the Lord, the fact that the family is the fundamental unit of the nation: all these truths must be kept before the Christian people of our country, lest the virus of antisocial and anti-Biblical poison enter their hearts and minds.

If marriage is entered into according to God's will, it is done by a valid betrothal (q.v.). This means that the mutual promise of the contracting parties is given only with the full knowledge and consent of the parents on either side, which is to be obtained in advance. Neither children nor parents may make exceptions to this rule, which is based upon the clear ethical teachings of the Bible. The promise must be given by the free will of the persons concerned, since duress or force invalidates a promise if the protest is registered in due time. That the contracting parties have reached the physical age and possess the maturity necessary for the successful carrying out of the prime object of marriage, is not only self-evident, but is also specifically mentioned in the statues of the several states and countries.

The fact that parents give their children in marriage does not signify that the former have absolute power over their children, either in keeping them from getting married or in arbitrarily choosing spouses for them. Marriage is a natural right and therefore cannot be set aside by absolute commands. "There is a consideration which can ratify a marriage to which a parent persistently objects, viz., when such objections is explicitly or implicitly tantamount to a total prohibition of marriage imposed upon a son or daughter, in violation of the word of Scripture. 1 Cor. 7, 2." (A.L. Graebner.) The ideal situation is that pictured in the case of Rebekah and Isaac, Gen. 24, 58; 25, 24, and that of Samson, Judg. 14, 2,3. A physical relationship within the limits fixed by God and by the State will be an impediment to a lawful marriage.

Persons who desire to enter the holy estate of matrimony may not be bound by a previous valid promise, either by a rightful betrothal or by an actual marriage. As a valid betrothal is, in the eyes of God and the Church, tantamount to marriage, a subsequent betrothal while the first is in force does not invalidate the first, but leaves it in full force and binding on both parties. Although the State does not, as a rule, acknowledge the force of a rightful betrothal in the Scriptural sense, such broken promises or their equivalent are often brought up in so-called breach of promise suits. Of course, no person may enter into an actual marriage with a second person while still bound, before God and the state, to a previous spouse. "After a first valid marriage a Christian cannot marry again, unless the first marriage has previously been dissolved with by death or by a divorce which is valid and lawful both before the Law of God and the law of the State." (A.L. Graebner.)

Although mixed marriages, when a person of orthodox confessions marries one of sectarian professions or of no Christian confession at all, are not expressly forbidden in the Bible, 1 Cor. 7, 12-16, they were certainly forbidden to the Jews, and they are discountenanced both in the Bible and in agreement with the experience of earnest Christians. If, in holy wedlock, there can be no common prayer, no common worship in the home, no common churchgoing, there is an element lacking which alone can make for true happiness. And it is a fact that the majority of children of mixed marriages fall away from the Church, if, indeed, they ever become seriously interested.

Marriage is a union "unto one flesh," its avowed object being to give a legitimate and blessed outlet to the sexual impulses given by God to all normal adults. Cp. 1 Cor. 7,3, 4. "The consensus, which constitutes the essence of marriage, must be marriage consent, the willingness of the parties to be one flesh with each other....The refusal to grant such intercourse....is the denial of a right and the neglect of a duty assumed by marriage." (A.L. Graebner.) In this way adultery and other sins are to be avoided, as St. Paul writes 1 Cor. 7, 9. The chief object of such marital intercourse, besides that of avoiding sins against the Sixth Commandment, is that of the procreation of children. Cp. Gen. 1, 28; 1 Tim. 2, 15; 5, 14; Ps. 128; Gen. 30, 1; 1 Sam. 1, 11. 12; Luke 1, 58. "This one fact particularly must be stressed in connection with the perverted views of sex relationship and the contempt of marriage in general, namely, the growing evil of childless marriages by design or of the willful and criminal limiting of offspring, that is of race suicide ....In many cases social ambition or other selfish considerations are the motives for committing sins which are just as heinous as highway murder; for there is not even a difference of degree between snuffing out the faint flicker of life in the worm and shooting down a man in cold blood. . . . Even if we should admit that the unnatural economic conditions of our times, together with the increasing use of luxuries, have had their influence upon women in rendering them less fit to become mothers, no man has a right to set aside God's order as it has been done in the case of thousands of marriages, where people, without valid reason, have deliberately decided not to have children. We might mention, in passing, that the cold-blooded, calculating, mercenary marriages which are becoming so prevalent in our days may often be considered the reason, and the growing number of divorces the result, of the evil of childless marriages." **(The Problems of Adolescence and Youth, 73. 74.)**

Marriage is intended by God to be a lifelong union, "until death you do part." Rom. 7, 2; 1 Cor. 7, 39; Matt. 19, 6; Mark 10, 9. Here it makes no difference whether the one or the other spouse, according to the regular course of nature, later becomes impotent or, as the result of some disease, is no longer capable to performing the prime duties of the married estate. The factor of mutual care and assistance becomes more prominent as the years go by, and the Scripture emphasizes the phase of married life in words of great beauty. Cp. Gen. 2, 18, 20; Eph. 5, 28-33; 1 Cor. 7, 12. 13; Col. 3, 19; 1 Pet. 3, 7. "God wishes to honor it (the state of matrimony) and to maintain and conduct it as a divine and blessed estate, because, in the first place, He has instituted it before all others and therefore created man and woman separately (as is evident), not for lewdness, but that they should legitimately live together, be fruitful, beget children, and nourish and train them to the honor of God." (Luther in the Large Catechism. **Conc. Trigl., 639.)** See Marriage, Annulment of; Ring; Prohibited Degrees; Divorce.

Living In Marriage, Or the Christian Home
From Pastoral Theology
By John Fritz
CPH, 1932

1. Purpose and Importance of Marriage and the Christian Home. -God instituted marriage, by which a home is established, not only for the being, but also for the well-being, of society. The propagation of the human race is not the only purpose of marriage, Gen. 1, 28, but also man's comfort and happiness and well-being, Gen. 2, 18, 24, ("it is not good that the man should be alone"; "a help meet for him"; "be one flesh"), Eph. 5, 28.29.33; 1

Cor. 7, 2, thus making the home the basic factor in human society. The influence of the home either for good or for evil, in its relation to the Church and to the State is immeasurable. The breaking down of the home spells disaster. Because marriage is a divine institution of such great importance, a Christian pastor should not only encourage all of marriageable age to marry, but should also duly instruct his parishioners in reference to the duties of husband and wife, and parents and children, and should carefully watch over the home-life of those whom God has entrusted to his care, Heb. 13, 17.

2. Relations of Husband and Wife. -In order that the home may fulfil its high purpose in this world, there must be a right relation between those whom God holds responsible for the conditions in the home. What this relation shall be God Himself distinctly states in His Word: The husband should love his wife. The wife should reverence her husband. The husband is the head of the wife. The wife shall not usurp authority over her husband, but be in subjection. The husband shall nourish and cherish his wife; he shall provide for, and support, his wife and his family. The wife shall well look after, and manage, the affairs of her household. Eph. 5,22-33; 1 Pet. 3, 1-7; Prov. 31. Since the modern tendency is to take woman out of that sphere in which God has placed her (asking that the word obey be eliminated from the marriage liturgy, removing a woman from the home and from home duties, companionate marriage, etc.), a pastor must warn against such a perversion of God's order. Heathen religions have degraded a woman by not permitting her to enter that sphere of life into which God originally placed her; the modern so-called emancipation of woman degrades a woman by taking her rightful place in life, elevates her to her high position and calling in this world, and assures her a truly happy life.

The sexual relations of husband and wife are spoken of in such passages as Gen. 2,24; 1, 28, 1 Cor. 7, 2-5; Lev. 18,19. "The work of begetting children," says Luther, "is a divine work (eine Kreatur Gottes), good and holy, for it came from God, who has blessed it; and if man had not fallen into sin, this work would have remained a most pure and a most holy work. For even as a man is not ashamed to speak with his wife and to eat and drink with her, since all that is honourable, even so the work of begetting children would have remained a very honorable work. And although even after the Fall the begetting of children is still a natural process, yet the devil's poison has been added thereunto. To wit, the evil lust of the flesh and shameful unchastity, from which arises much that is not good, but utterly sinful, which would not have been so if man had remained perfect. . . Whatever is sinful, however, should be considered apart for the divine work itself, which is good and concerning which the Holy Spirit has not been ashamed to speak." St. L. I, 291. The sex impulse is not in itself immoral, but moral. Man and woman cannot make themselves sexless, for God did not so create them; but God has restricted the exercise of the sex functions to the state of marriage and to such conditions therein as are determined by physical condition, health, occupations, age, etc. as a rule, young healthy people may have sexual intercourse once or twice a week without injury to their health. If people are physically weak or advanced in years, it is preferable not to have frequent intercourse (only two or three times a month). Excessive coitus is said to be a common cause of impotency; it is also injurious to health. When in doubt, a physician should be consulted. Inasmuch as sin has largely perverted it, the sexual desire should be curbed and not excited. A artificial sexual appetite should never be created.

3. Relation of Parents and Children. -Two things a pastor should impress upon married people: 1) That God would bless their marriage with children; 2) That God holds parents responsible for the Christian training of their children.

A husband and a wife should according to God's will become the father and the mother of children. One of God's purposes of marriage is the propagation of the human race. God says: "Be fruitful and multiply and replenish the earth," Gen. 1, 28; Ps. 127 and 128; Fourth Commandment. A Hebrew married woman considered it an affliction to be childless, 1 Sam. 1, 1-20. The Jews had large families; so did our German forefathers. The one, two, or three-children family system is contrary to the Scriptures; for man has no right arbitrarily or definitely to limit the number of his offspring (birth control), especially not if done with artificial or unnatural means, Gen. 1, 28; Ps. 127, 3-6; Ps. 128, 3.4; Gen. 38, 9.10. Such restrictions as uncontrollable circumstances, natural barrenness, or the ill health of wife or husband put upon the number of offspring are the exceptions to the rule. Child-bearing is both a natural and a healthful process, while any interference with natural functions is injurious.

In his mimeographed notes to the students in Pastoral Theology, Prof. Theo Laetsch gives the arguments pro and con in reference to birth control (limiting the number of children by the use of artificial means, by medicines, and by unnatural practices).

I. ARGUMENTS ADVANCED BY ADVOCATES OF BIRTH CONTROL

1. Economic. -Danger of overpopulation.

Malthus, an Englishman, 1766-1834, in 1798 called attention to this danger, due to the fact, as he claimed, that food products increase in arithmetical progression, 1, 2, 3, 2, 4, etc. while mankind increases in geometrical progression, 2, 4, 8, 16, 32, etc. in order to ward off this danger of overpopulation and improve existing conditions, positive limitations, such as wars, epidemics, etc., are not sufficient; the increase of mankind must be stopped artificially. He advised postponement of marriage, and John Stuart Mills advised continence, abstinence, in married life (preventive limitations). Two-children system favored, especially in France. In 1877 the Malthusian league was organized for the purpose of advocating artificial prevention of conception.

2. Hygienic.-Woman's health is broken down by too many childbirths.

3. Biological-The sex urge is a purely biological process, and every man and woman has the right to gratify it and to prevent conception to remove undesirable consequences, just as every person has the right to remove superfluous, undesirable hair, nails, etc.

4. Eugenic. -Not quantity, but quality counts. Quality is improved by

birth control. Mankind, which is now in danger of deterioration, must be regenerated.

5. Social. -Birth control makes for greater marital happiness, better opportunities to enjoy life and attend to social duties, to satisfy cultural demands, etc. Better wages, not so much abject poverty. Children better equipped for life, better chances for education, wealth, etc. Prevention of extra connubial intercourse by married people and more marriages, since marriage without danger of children gives all needed opportunity for satisfying the sexual urge.

6. Expediency.-Rather use contraceptives than resort to abortion or murder of born or unborn children.

II. ARGUMENTS AGAINST BIRTH CONTROL

1. It is sinful.

A. It is wilfully setting aside God's will and command, Gen. 1, 28; 1 Tim. 5,14; 2, 15; Gen. 38, 9,10.

B. It is despising His promises and is depriving oneself of a blessing, Ps. 127 and 128. See texts under C.

C. It is usurping for oneself an exclusive privilege of God, that of giving or withholding children, Ps. 127, 3; Gen. 29, 31-30, 6; 30,22; 33, 5; 16,2; 20,18; Lev. 20, 20. 21; Job 42, 12.13; Luke 1, 58; 1 Sam. 1, 10.11

D. Birth control by means of anti conceptuals, coitus interrupts, etc., is ruthlessly interfering with God's method of creating a living being. Hufeland, one of the most noted physicians of Germany, 1762-1836, says: "the first question undoubtedly is, When does life begin? There can be no doubt that the act of copulation is to be regarded as the beginning of the existence of the future being and that the very first, even though invisible, germ of his being has the same claim upon the care and protection the physician as the alter, fully developed man... A human being is being murdered in its incipiency. I am not going to answer sophistic, even Jesuistic, cavils. I appeal to sane reason and to the pure, unspoiled moral feeling of every man... The product presupposes producing, and if it is wrong to kill the product, then it goes without saying that it is wrong to render futile the act whereby it is being produced, for thereby one actually kills that which is in process of being produced (das Werdende) in its first beginning." Quoted in De Valenti, Die Ehe, biblisch und aortic bleached, page 63.f. This is undoubtedly the Scriptural view. Cf. Ps. 139, 13-16; Job 10, 8-11, especially. 10 (the act of copulation described).

E. Marriage degenerates from a holy estate to mere gratification of carnal lust, Heb. 13, 4; 1 Thess. 4, 4.

2. It undermines the State. It is race suicide.

Even the two-children system will rapidly lead to the extinction of a people, for 10 per cent of all marriages are naturally childless, and unmarried people and childless couples, hence a decrease in population, and the nation will die out. At least four children to a family are needed to prevent this dying out, five children are also needed to bring about an increase in population.

3. It undermines the home.

Parents become selfish, incompatible. Children idolized, pampered, egotistic, self-important, undesirable citizens in many instances. A Supreme Court Justice is quoted as saying: "It is my conclusion that childless homes are responsible for the almost complete absence of real home-life. I cannot help but reach the conclusion that, if our women had children, there would be more happiness and fewer divorces. Presence of children attracts the husband to his home and keeps the mothers from the gossiping neighbours and bridge parties. Absence of children promotes discord. Their presence makes for harmony."

4. It is unnatural and harmful to health

Oscar Lezius, quoted in Lehre and Wehre, 1914, says: "Modern women that are willing, in the interest of decreasing the number of childbirths, to use certain means and force their husbands to do the same thereby destroy their own and their husbands' nerve-power, become hysteric, and shorten their lives. Women who according to the old custom were willing to give birth to five to ten children, to refrain from the use of 'Parisian articles,' and to demand no coitus interrupts from their husbands have every prospect of longer life and the enjoyment of better health than their modern contemporaries, whose renowned cry for the child is often enough satisfied with one birth, who like fallen women (in der Gesinnung von Dirnen) make use of anti-conceptuals, degrade matrimony to the level of unchastely, pass their days in hysteria and nervousness, and make their homes in institutions for the nervous or insane asylums. Women with many children are in middle age much more beautiful than those who have few children and who owe this misfortune not to a hard blow of fate, but solely to an immoral tendency toward the use of anticonceptual means."

Borntraeger, quoted in Lehre and Wehre, 1914: "France has undoubtedly degenerated physically and morally since it has decided for a cowardly and egotistic control of increase of population. It is also a fact that the oldest children are often weaker than the younger. If the latter remain unborn, and if only the oldest children continue the family trunk, degeneration is not to be avoided. Benjamin Franklin was the fourteenth child of his father and the only genius of his family. Today he would not have come into the world. Frederick the Great was the seventh child, and of the older children only one grew up. If the parents of these children had made use of the two-child system, how different would the world look today, and how much poorer would it be!"

Says Borntraeger, quoted in *Lehre and Wehre*, 1914: "That birth control does not improve the quality has been shown conclusively in the example of France, where this system has been in vogue for eighty years and more. In the children of poor France there is evidently physically and ethically a retrogression rather than an improvement as far as the quality of humanity is concerned."

Parents are under obligations not only to provide for the bodies of their children, 1 Tim. 5, 8, and to cultivate their minds, Acts 7, 21.22, but also and especially to bring up their children in the nurture and admonition of the Lord, that is, to give them a Christian training, Eph. 6, 1-4; Ps. 798, 1-8; Prov. 6, 20-22; 22, 6; Deut 6, 1-9. Christian parents dare not shirk nor shift their responsibility of giving to their children a Christian home training. In addition, the best means for the Christian training of children is the Christian day-(parochial) school. If Christian parents consider it necessary to send their children daily to school to learn their three R's (reading writing, and 'arithmetic), it ought not to take much persuasion to convince them that the better school for their children is the school in which the fourth R (religion) is also daily taught, which religious training not only pervades the entire school atmosphere, but gives the proper and necessary basis for the entire life of the Christian and its usefulness in this world, Matt. 6, 33; 20, 25-29, as well as for the Christian's temporal and eternal happiness, 1 Tim. 4, 8. A Sunday-school alone will not suffice. (See chapter on "The Sunday-school.")

Not only the parents, have a duty towards their children, but also the Church. Children are members of the Church, and the Church must look after their spiritual welfare, Acts 2, 39; Mark 10, 13-16; John 21, 15-17. For this purpose the congregation establishes the Christian day-school. Since the pastor is the shepherd of the entire flock, and since much depends upon the Christian training of the children, the pastor has a special responsibility towards them. If necessary, a pastor should himself teach in the church-school; but as soon as possible the congregation ought to call one or more teachers who have been trained for that particular work.

Since the pastor is pre-eminently a teacher, he should not only have a good knowledge of teaching principles and teaching methods (pedagogy and psychology), but be especially trained to teach the doctrines of the Christian religion (Catechism and Bible History) by the method of catechization (question-and-answer method-catechetic).

DIVORCE

There is only *one* Scriptural reason or cause for divorce: *fornication*, Matt. 19, 9. When a party has committed adultery by fornication the pastor shall, if the guilty party appears truly penitent, admonish the innocent party to condone the offense and continue in the matrimonial state with the penitent spouse; but finally he must leave the decision in this matter to the option of the innocent party, and if the latter has applied for, and obtained, a legal divorce, the pastor, sufficient proof thereof having been submitted, cannot, after the expiration of a proper period, refuse the solemnisation of another marriage. The innocent party should be urged to forgive the penitent guilty party especially if the sin of fornication is not known to others and there is good reason to believe that the sin will not be repeated; however, the right to procure a divorce cannot be denied. If, however the innocent party voluntarily continues sexual relations with the guilty party after the sin of fornication has become known to the innocent party, this party thereby waives the right to procure a divorce (condonatio).

Although the Word of God knows of but one rightful cause for the dissolution of marriage: fornication, Matt. 19, 9, there is, according to the plain apostolic statement, 1 Cor. 7, 15: "If the unbelieving depart, let him depart; a brother or a sister is not under bondage in such cases," another cause in which the innocent party may not enact, but will suffer, the dissolution of his or her marriage, to wit, when a spouse deserts the other maliciously, i.e., with the manifest intention of not returning to the abandoned spouse, and will not by any means be persuaded to return. In this case the innocent party, of course after having secured a legal divorce, is, according to the declaring of the apostle, 1 Cor 7, 15, no longer "under bondage," no longer bound to the former spouse (cf. Rom. 7, 1-3) and must not be denied remarriage at a proper time. Desertion is in itself divorce, while fornication is not itself a divorce, but cause for a divorce. In both cases, of course, the necessary legal papers must be procured to establish the fact legally. In a case of desertion the laws of the state must also be consulted; they specify what constitutes a desertion.

Various Aspects of Divorce Cases. –It goes without saying that a divorce may be procured only when fornication (or malicious desertion) can be proved. A mere suspicion of adultery will not suffice, not even as a reason for temporary separation, unless such reason for suspicion has been given *in a most flagrant manner*, in which case a spouse may be justified for the time being to leave the other spouse, as when a wife for the time being returns to her former home or her relatives. -If a married woman has been outraged, that is no cause on account of which her husband may procure a divorce, for as far as her intentions are concerned, she has not been guilty of fornication. - If both parties commit fornication, they are equally guilty and have cancelled each other's right to get a divorce. -If a husband, whatever his reason or purpose may have been (as, for instance, to escape a threat made upon his life), has persuaded his wife to yield to the sin of fornication, he thereby forfeits his right to get a divorce. *Volenti non fit iniuria.* -Sickness of whatever nature (contagious, disgusting, lifelong, even such as prohibits conjugal cohabitation, and insanity) does not break the marriage bond and is therefore no cause for a divorce. Answering the question whether in such case a divorce might be procured, Luther says: "Never! Rather serve God by waiting upon your sick spouse; rather think that God through your sick spouse has given you a holy opportunity to make sure of your heavenly bliss. Blessed are you many times if you accept it as a gift and grace of God and for God's sake will wait upon your spouse. If you say that you cannot remain continent, you are lying. If you will only sincerely wait upon your sick spouse and take it that God has sent unto you that affliction and thank Him for it, let God take care of you."

A Monk Marries

Luther's Wit and Wisdom About His New Estate

Christian News, December 23, 1996

There's a lot to get used to in the first year of marriage. One wakes up in the morning and finds a pair of pigtails on the pillow that were not there before.

If I should ever marry again, I would hew myself an obedient wife out of stone.

I have been very happy in my marriage, thank God. I have a faithful wife, according to Solomon: "The heart of her husband doth safely trust in her" (Prov. 31:11). She spoils nothing for me.

When one looks back upon it, marriage isn't so bad as when one looks forward to it.

Married folk are not to act as they now usually do. The men are almost lions in their homes, hard toward their wives and servants. The women too, everywhere want to domineer and have their husbands as servants.

Of course, the Christian should love his wife. He is supposed to love his neighbor, and since his wife is his nearest neighbor, she should be his deepest love.

When that wise harlot, natural reason, looks at married life, she turns up her nose and says, "Ah, should I rock the baby, wash diapers, make the bed, smell foul odors, watch through the night, wait upon the bawling youngster and heal its infected sores, then take care of the wife, support her by working, tend to this, tend to that, do this, do that, suffer this, suffer that, and put up with whatever additional displeasure and trouble married life brings? Should I be so imprisoned?"

The Devil cannot bear to see married people agree well with each other.

It is impossible to keep peace between man and woman in family life if they do not condone and overlook each other's faults but watch everything to the smallest point. For who does not at times offend?

Some marriages were motivated by mere lust, but mere lust is felt even by fleas and lice. Love begins when we wish to serve others.

The purpose of marriage is not pleasure and ease but the procreation and education of children and the support of a family. People who do not like children are swine, dunces, and blockheads, not worthy to be called men and women, because they despise the blessing of God, the Creator and Author of marriage.

To have a peace and love in a marriage is a gift that is next to the knowledge of the gospel.

In domestic affairs defer to Katie. Otherwise, I am led by the Holy Ghost.

How Do We Know That Marriage Is Not Outdated?

By Pastor Kurt Marquart
From *Lutheran Encounter*, Australian Youth Publication
(*Luther Today What Would He Do Or Say?* pp. 164-165)

"Marriage is totally irrelevant to today's society," a lecturer in sociology claimed at a Melbourne sex education seminar recently, according to a clipping sent in by an Encounter reader.

The sociologist said that "sex could now be considered a normal part of human relationships without being related to marriage or parenthood." This makes very good sense - If man is just an animal, a product of blind evolution, IF, in other words, there is no god and therefore no objective meaning or morality in the universe. Given this starting point, loose views of sex must follow. And since much modern "education" is really a kind of materialistic brain-washing, which assumes that God either doesn't exist or doesn't mater, it is not surprising that "today's society" should hold largely pagan ideas, also about marriage. As the computer people say, put garbage in, and you get garbage out!

But if the God-less view is right, then a lot more than just marriage is outdated! Our sociology lecturer doesn't seem to realize it. He insists that "it is not up to society, your parents, religious groups or anyone else to impose their ideas or hang-ups on you" - and then he cheerfully proceeds to impose his own hang-ups! He adds: "However, sexual relationships should involve respect for the other person."

LOVE, SPIDER-STYLE?

Why? If the universe has no moral rhyme or reason, why must we "respect" humans any more than, say, copulating rats or fleas? If marriage is outdated, why not also "respect"? If nature is all there is, what would be wrong with imitating those female spiders which kill and eat their "husbands" after mating? True, most people mightn't have a "taste" for this sort of thing - and others might even have a taste for marriage; the point is that there would be no sensible moral reason or principle one way or the other. Everything would be just a matter of taste!

And here is where the "sex education" craze makes matters worse as if endless yakking about the physical "facts of life" could take the place of clear moral principles! No wonder one American teenager asked, after he had raped his teacher: "but why not? Didn't she spend the whole year telling us how to do it?" Yes, Mr. Sociologist, why not?

But if there is moral order in the universe - in other words, God - then not only "respect" but marriage itself are far more than just matters of taste. For the Christian the whole thing is settled in Christ. To be a Christian is to trust Christ as Savior and therefore as Lord. But the Christian cannot argue, as his own sinful flesh keeps urging: "Christ; You can be Lord over my whole life except for a few special interests which I must reserve for myself, such as money, sex, politics, and other details like that?!" Yes, I daily fall short of my Lord's will - but the defect is in me, not in Him! It is my sin and evil, not His truth and goodness, that are "outdated"! But His mercies are new every day?

GOD'S GIFT - NOT CAVEMAN'S INVENTION!

The deepest thing that can be said about Christian marriage is that it is a very humble earthly copy of the relation between Christ and His Church (Eph. 5:21-33). Marriage is not something that gradually evolved from Big Bertha's efforts to domesticate "Troglodyte Man"! It was made by God when He made the first woman for the first man. And He Who in the beginning took Eve out of Adam's side, is the same One out of Whose side, on the cross, flowed blood and water, by which His Bride, the Church, is created (I John 5:6-8). This Church, the Temple of God, in turn is made from individual building blocks, "living stones" (I Peter 2:5), who are themselves temples of the Holy Spirit (I Cor. 6:19), and who are to use the gift of sex for its only right and god-given purpose; marriage!

Living for each other like Christ and the Church is impossible for the flesh. Mere romantic love can't do it. But He Who honored that Cana wedding with His very first recorded miracle, that of changing water into wine, as we heard on the second Sunday in Epiphany (St. John 2), gives Himself to His people in His Gospel and Sacrament. By His Spirit and the power of His Resurrection, they are daily enabled to do the impossible; to live as Christians in faith and love.

Let blind, proud, ignorant pagans follow their illusions; their "New Morality" was old and out-dated long ago (Rom. 1:18-32; Gal. 5:16-24). Let them mock, and "glory in their shame" (Phil. 3:19). We Christians take our cue not from the world, but from the Word. And that is never out-dated: "Heaven and earth shall pass away" (Matt. 24:35)!

Marriage Encounter

Christian News, July 9, 1979

"The Theology of Marriage Encounter - We encountered each other, but no encounter with the Almighty occurred" is the title and subtitle of an article in the June 20-27 *Christian Century* analyzing the marriage encounter movement.

Here are a few excerpts from the article:

"Probably the sentence that bothered me most deeply was this oft-repeated one: 'Feelings are neither good nor bad; they just are:'"

The motto of marriage encounter (and 100 other Gestalt-type self-help groups) that 'feelings are neither good nor bad; they just are' is too pat, too easy. Phrases like this are directly related to the family of 'I'm OK, You're OK,' and the problem in marriage seems to me more often to be 'I'm not OK and neither is my spouse.' In the eyes of God, we are not OK - else why bother with the whole salvation-through Christ scheme? The human-potential movement is running aground in society at large. But as is often the case, the church is three or four years behind society, catching up with fads that have begun to dim on the secular scene.

"In the marriage encounter movement as it exists in the churches the world is informing the church about what marriage and true relationship should be and not vice versa. Knowledge gleaned from secular, basically Freudian psychologists is taken to the church in a neat package so that a thin veneer of theological justification can be applied to what is essentially a secular, humanistic viewpoint - no more, no less."

"Marriage encounter, as I experienced it in the Presbyterian version, is long on Gestalt and short on theology. The Christian trappings that surround that movement in the churches seem to me to be just that - trappings. For underneath lies a good dose of 'I'm OK, You're OK' for the layperson (feelings are neither good nor bad; they just are). The horizontal dimension between people seems to have been well thought out; improved marriages are the proof of that. But the theological dimension does not seem to have been sufficiently developed. At no time during the weekend did I hear any reference to Paul's treatment of marriage. A great deal was made of Jesus' appearance at a wedding to change water into wine (this to show that Jesus was especially soft on married couples). But somehow the cutting edge of Christian commitment (Matt. 10:36 'A man's foes will be those of his own household') never comes to light. Convenient passages from the Gospels are occasionally mentioned to feelings, but this device is never really brought off very well. My wife and I were married years ago; we encountered each other significantly during our weekend; but no encounter with anything passing for the Almighty occurred."

Is Marriage Outmoded?
The Northwestern Lutheran, **February 1, 1987**
Christian News, February 23, 1987

"Dearly beloved: Whereas you desire to enter upon the holy estate of matrimony, ordained of God, and to be held in honor by all..." For years these words have preceded the exchange of vows by bride and groom in the Order of Marriage in use in our churches.

These traditional words touch upon two ancient beliefs about marriage. The wording may be somewhat antiquated, but the meaning is clear: Marriage was instituted by God, and it is to be honored. The principles set forth in these words are questioned by quite a few people today. Their question is, are not the thoughts expressed in these words, like the wording itself, antiquated?

A growing number of people in Western civilization seem to think that they are. Many proclaim through their lifestyles that marriage is outmoded. The U.S. Census Bureau reported late last year that 1.9 million couples in this country are now living together outside of marriage. Proponents of this practice commonly dismiss marriage as "just a piece of paper." obviously, marriage is not being "held in honor" by these couples.

One of the reasons why marriage is held in such low regard by many is the development in recent history of effective methods of contraception. Improved contraceptive technique has all but eliminated the fear of one of the natural, but unwanted, consequences of "living together." Contributing to the view of marriage as merely an option for less sophisticated couples is the fact that the procreation of offspring outside of wedlock nowadays does not necessarily carry with it the social stigma it once did. As a matter of fact, it is not uncommon nowadays for celebrities not married to each other unashamedly to acknowledge joint parentage of a child born outside of marriage, thus reinforcing the view that marriage is an outdated relic of ages past.

The demotion of marriage to a low position on the social scale has had some unpleasant side effects. Social critic George Gilder, author of "Men and Marriage," says that the absence of restraints implicit in the marriage bond has resulted in "a growing number of bachelors, giving free reign to their 'instincts,' becoming sexual savages." Syndicated writer Don Feder adds that lack of respect for marriage has also had an effect upon the lifestyles of many young women. He writes of them, "Like their male counterparts, many have become predators, seeking amorous adventures at singles' bars and other spots where the erotically restless prowl." He also attributes the rising rate of alcohol and drug abuse among them to this factor.

Disrespect for the institution of marriage has also contributed to the appalling rate of divorce in this country. It has precipitated an untold number of abortions. It has resulted in an almost incredible number of single parent homes, along with their attendant problems. It has likewise led to widespread promiscuity, and it has been a major factor in the spread of frightening venereal disease.

No one would interpret these facts as evidences of the vaunted enlightenment of society in fact, Feder writes, "if the trend isn't reversed, civilization is doomed. Without the family as its firm center society soon disintegrates."

"... ordained of God, and to be held in honor by all..." Clear facts, to say nothing of scriptural teaching, urge the conclusion that these words in our Order of Marriage do more than perpetuate an outmoded tradition.

Immanuel G. Frey

Ten Rules for A Happy Marriage

The Maranatha, April, 1986
Christian News, May 12, 1986

1. SEEK A CHRISTIAN MATE - 2 Cor. 6:14. Foundation of true love - love of Christ in both hearts - one in spirit, interests, activities. Seek the Lord's leading to the RIGHT MATE - Gen. 2:18; James 4:13-15.

2. KEEP YOURSELF CLEAN -

MORALLY - Ex. 20:14, 7th Commandment 1:27 - unspotted from the world. You want a pure mate; your mate has just as much right to expect purity. Heb. 13:4. Marriage honorable in all. Prov. 31:11 (Virtuous woman) - her husband doth safely trust in her.

PHYSICALLY - Clean dirt (from honest toil) vs. the accumulated type (indicates laziness). No disgrace to get dirty, but a real disgrace to stay dirty! B.O. (lifebuoy soap) halitosis (Listerine)!

HABITS - Tobacco - cigarettes make death 9 times as likely from lung cancer; alcohol - beer, liquor, wine - the drunkard in the gutter would not have gotten there if he had not taken the FIRST DRINK! Reading matter and entertainment - do not poison yourself or your children with filth.

3. DON'T BE LAZY - Husband supports family - 1 Tim. 5:8; Prov. 6:6-11 - "When poverty comes in at the door, love flies out the window." Do little things around the house and yard to keep the home looking respectable. Wife - be a good housekeeper (Prov. 31). House and family cared for. Be a good manager - live within the income - let the Jones' go!

4. BE A GOOD MATE - Face problems together. Learn that "what is good for both is best for each" - unity of the family unit. All for both, indivisible! Be Married, one flesh. Gen. 2:24. Defraud not one another! Cor. 7:5. Keep up the courtship; marriage comes first, lasts long after the children have grown and flown. Many childless marriages are happy ones. Appreciate each other and tell your mate so - often - in many ways. Love each other and practice it. Prov. 3:27k. The three sweetest words in any language are "I Love You." Use this key to happiness often!

5. HAVE YOUR OWN HOME TO YOURSELVES - Gen. 2:24 - Leave father and mother, cleave unto your wife. Not just your own house - move away if need be. Receive good advice courteously but make your own decisions in sweet counsel together.

6. KEEP FROM NAGGNG - Prov. 27:15; 19:14 and belittling - Prov. 14:1-3. You are mates, not antagonists!

7. KEEP FAMILY SECRETS FROM BEING PEDDLED ABOARD - Gossip says: Only two kinds of secrets - "Those not worth keeping and those too good to keep." Titus 2:4; Prov 11:22.

8. DON'T BOTH GET ANGRY AT THE SAME TIME - A soft answer turneth away wrath, Prov. 15:1. It takes two to make a fight!

9. HAVE A CHRISTIAN HOME - 24 hours a day. Children learn by example and neighbours are quick to learn of inconsistencies and hypocrisy. Family devotions. Lead your children to Christ IN THE HOME! Prov. 22:6; Eph. 6:1-4; 5:22, 23.

10. HAVE A SPIRITUAL CHURCH HOME - Where the gospel is preached, lived, and taught, Heb. 10:24; Acts 2:47; 1 Tim. 3:15. Encourage your children to serve the Lord.

Dr. Virgil Arrowood

The Alphabet for A Happy Marriage

Christian News, December 23, 1996

A - Adaptability. Cultivate a taste for each other's tastes.

B - Belief. Trust in God - that He has worked out everything for your good.

C - Church. Seek out that church which is most faithful in teaching all that Christ has commanded. Attend it and it's Bible classes regularly, supporting it with words and deeds.

D - Devotion. Love the Lord, your God, with all your heart and with all your soul, and with all your mind. Don't spare your love for Him or your spouse.

E - Education. Keep growing in the knowledge of the Lord and in understanding your spouse.

F - Finesse. Handle each other with care.

G - Generosity. Don't be stingy with love, or money, or praise.

H - Health. Exercise mentally, spiritually, and physically. Remember not to complain about your troubles, because half of those whom you talk to will not be listening and the others will be glad you're finally getting what you deserve.

I - Involvement. Broaden your horizons and be interested in all the activities of your spouse.

J - Jokes. Laugh at them, and especially be willing to laugh at yourself.

K - Kindness. Never fail to show each other tenderness and sympathy, especially remembering all the kindness God has shown you.

L - Love. Never let your supply run low. God has much of it to give you.

M - Money. Agree before marriage about the division of family income.

N - Need of each other. Make yourself a necessity to your mate.

O - Observation. Notice when your wife has a new outfit or your husband looks particularly spick-and-span.

Q - Quiet. Keep a peaceful home.

R - Respect. Show appreciation for each other's opinions and intelligence.

S - Sportsmanship. Accept the give and take of marriage - always with a smile on your face.

T - Thankfulness. Thank god in all things as all things work together for good to them that love God. From eternity God has designed you for each other he has also designed each card you hold in your hand. Praise Him for all His goodness.

U - Unity. And the two shall become one flesh. Strive for unity with yourselves and with God.

V - Virtue. Pursue that which is good in your lives, with loyalty to each other and your God.

W - Willingness. Be willing to help each other as you give glory to God together.

X - Extra attention. Give more of yourself to the other than you would expect to be given especially when one is down-hearted or sick.

Y - Yes. "Yes" your mate with enthusiasm. Flattery is the oil that lubricates the domestic machinery and makes it click.

Z - Zero. Your marriage will never be zero if you follow the above advice.

Unholy Matrimony
By Paul Walther Neipp
Christian News, December 23, 1996

Historically, words applied to certain basic features of our existence and life often may have a deeper source than we may at first be aware of. Have you ever wondered why marriage is called "holy matrimony" (rather than "holy patrimony")? Since marriage was invented by God (Gen. 1:26-28; 2:18-25) it is easy to see how the word "holy" fits because God is holy (Lev. 19:2; Is. 6:3) and His institution, the family, was and is a sacred institution, designed to fulfill His holy will, the first duty of which was and is to produce children (Gen. 1:28; Ps. 127; 128).

The word "matrimony" perhaps a little etymology will be beneficial. Matrimony is a compound word made up of the Latin word *mater, matris*, (a) mother, plus the Latin suffix *monia*, used to form nouns that mean a resulting thing, condition, or state. Accordingly, matrimony is the estate (status) into which married persons enter, the state of man/male and woman/female be(com)ing husband and wife in order to be(come) father and mother (parents); the condition/state (status) that results in be(com)ing a mother, because that's when a woman/female/wife is entitled to be(come) a mother, a purpose for which she was designed, and to which every normal woman eagerly looks forward. Matrimony thus takes place not to prevent children but to produce children. To prevent children is the exact opposite purpose for which marriage takes place.

Moreover, when God instituted/invented/created marriage, he simultaneously created the family (Gen. 1:28), for mankind would soon cease to exist without the family (= father, mother, and their children). Marriage and family are inescapably inseparable. To deny children is to deny marriage and the family. Genesis 1:28 is a family-oriented statement/order embedded within the marriage relationship/status. Accordingly, no true marriage exists in God's eyes where children are unwanted, or are "planned" (timing and number of offspring) according to the couple's own wishes. Such thinking is a denial of God's sovereignty in the production and-or withholding of children (Genesis 30). God is the only legitimate family Planner.

Adam and Eve were not an end in themselves. Their task was to rule the earth under God, and that requires families (Gen. 1:26-28). Integral to marriage and implied therein are children and the family. The purpose of marriage is (normally) incomplete without children, since God designed Adam and Eve and every couple to "be fruitful and multiply" (Gen. 1:28) during their childbearing years. Couples who overlook/ignore/forsake their responsibility to produce children and reject God's blessing (Gen. 1:28; Ps. 127; 128) rebel against God's created order. ("Okay, God, we have decided if and when and how many children we want, so You can go back to playing God again and fulfill our wishes.") Such a marriage is not true/complete/legitimate marriage since biblical marriage is a package deal (companionship, children, and sexual purity). To deny any one or more of these is to deny marriage according to God's design. How many marriages today must be labeled "unholy matrimony?"

Decline of Marriage

By Phyllis Schlafly
Human Events
June 21, 2010

The decline of marriage is the major cause of the growth of the welfare state. This year we the taxpayers are spending $350 billion to support single moms, and this amount increases every year.

That's only the start of the costs because social problems come out of female-headed households: crime, drugs, sex, teen pregnancies, suicides, runaways, and school dropouts.

The left is content to let this problem persist because 70% of unmarried women voted for Barack Obama for President. They vote for the party that offers the richer handouts.

Marriage Is Hard

The Religious Right Admits It
By Lisa Miller
Christian News, December 7, 2009

Newsweek, October 19, 2009 Excerpt

No one denies that conservative Christians have a marriage problem, a dizzying gap between their articulated ideals and their success in achieving them. According to the Pew Forum, evangelicals are more likely to be divorced than Roman Catholics, Mormons, the Eastern Orthodox, Muslims, Jews, Hindus, and atheists. Of course, every person who utters "till death do us part" and then separates is, in a sense, conceding defeat. But when evangelicals are leading the charge in the marriage movement (and now, the anti-gay-marriage movement) arguing that sacred unions between one man and one woman are good for society because they're good for children, one would hope that they'd have worked out the kinks a little better than the rest of us.

Marriage Counseling

Stop Counseling!
Start Ministering!

Christian News, March 21, 2011

Stop Counseling! Start Ministering! By Martin and Deidre Bobgan. EastGate Publishing, 4137 Primavera Road, Santa Barbara,

CA 93110.

Every pastor, seminary professor, church official, and all supporters of the Association of Clinical Pastoral Education should read this book.

The back cover says:

"Stop Counseling! Start Ministering!

"This book gives reasons why Christian should be opposed to counseling, literally **Stop Counseling! And Start Ministering!** Reasons are revealed why counseling, because it is problem-centered, inevitably involves sinful conversations.

"Central to ministering is helping individuals in need to overcome their fixation on their problems and encouraging them to become Christ-centered on a daily basis.

"This book provides ways of equipping those in need with the truths of Scripture and encouraging them to live the daily life that will be honoring to the Lord and beneficial for meeting life's problems without sinfully talking about them.'"

Martin Bobgan holds four university degrees, including a doctorate in educational psychology from the University of Colorado and heads PsychoHeresy Awareness Ministries. Deidre Bobgan holds an M.A. degree in English from the University of California, Saint Barbara, and is a member of Phi Beta Kappa. They have co-authored twenty books, some published by Bethany House, Moody Press, and Harvest House.

The authors write:

"This book is meant to enable you to Stop counseling! And Start ministering! By helping those in need become more Christ-centered and Word-centered, equipping them with the truths of Scripture, and encouraging them to live the daily life that will be honoring to the Lord and beneficial for meeting life's problems" (7).

". . . biblical counseling is not biblical because it is sinfully problem-centered like the psychological movement" (8).

Oprah and Media Madness

"Complementary to the counseling movement was the rise of media moguls like Oprah and others who capitalized on women's interests by corrupting women's strengths to their own detriment. All of this gave rise to all of life in the United States being viewed through the lens of the psychotherapeutic gospel. At the same time the media madness with its expression and often sinful practices moved into the online availability of almost everything from benign banter to devilish debauchery through such social networking sites as YouTube, Facebook, twitter, and MySpace and through search mechanisms such as Google and Yahoo" (9).

Daily Walk With the Lord

"One of the most powerful spiritual disciplines is an intentional daily walk with the Lord and all that implies" (11).

Stop Counseling

"The entire thrust of this book is to explain biblically, practically, and scientifically why Christians should Stop Counseling! And to provide suggestions for Christians who may need encouragement and guidance to Start Ministering! As a result of reading this book, we pray that you will become totally turned off to psychotherapy and contemporary biblical counseling, which are both sinfully problem-centered, and totally turned on to the traditional biblical ministry that preceded the Johnny-come-lately biblical counseling movement" (12).

Evil Speaking and Jeremiah 17:9 Syndrome

"The Jeremiah 17:9 Syndrome is expressed in evil speaking as counselees engage in tale bearing, speaking ill of others, dishonoring parents as they complain about them, revealing confidences, speaking despairingly of people, telling unsubstantiated stories (gossip), and making rude and disparaging comments" (56).

The Rise of Biblical Counseling

"The biblical counseling movement (BCM) began in 1970 with Dr. Jay Adams' book Competent to Counsel. We were part of the BCM for years until we realized the sinful problem-centered similarity between the BCM and the psychological counseling movement that preceded it. In fact, if the psychological counseling movement did not exist, it is doubtful that the BCM would exist in its present form. Many in the BCM have mimicked much of what is in the psychological counseling movement. The problem-centered format of biblical counseling mimics psychological counseling and mandates lifting the personal veil to private lives. It is the problem-centeredness of both psychological and biblical counseling that is their most common egregious and serious fault as it inevitably involves personal transparency that leads to unbiblical evil speaking about others at the encouragement of the counselors' (32-33).

Facebook and MySpace

"Publicizing one's own private life is now open to every person who has access to a computer. Search mechanisms such as Google and Yahoo enable people to search and find almost anything they want publicly displayed for anyone to see. Not only can people find nearly everything; they themselves can post nearly whatever they want by creating their own web pages, developing blogs, and using sites such as Twitter and any of the various social networking sites like Facebook and MySpace. All one has to do is sign up on a social networking site, present oneself exactly as one pleases through photos and self-descriptions, and publicize one's own private thoughts, activities, and emotions. To further the possibilities of publicizing their private lives, individuals can post videos for public consumption on such sites as YouTube, which is very popular with an estimated ten percent of all Internet traffic going to that site" (44).

"In a society that is 'becoming increasingly exhibitionistic... the Internet has witnessed, under the cloak of anonymity a flood of episodes of self-exposure and public confession in blogs and vlogs' (video logs such as YouTube). Thus the Internet provides the penultimate of the publicizing of private lives and serves as an ever expanding setting for expressions of the Jeremiah 17:9 syndrome (described in the next chapter) with an audience which may be far beyond the environs of one's own networking circle" (46).

A Therapeutic Society

"The United States has privately and publicly become a therapeutic society where private and public trash talk, which was first led by men counselors and later mainly by women counselors, was primarily fueled by female inclinations and interest" (47).

"While these streams of discourse have seriously affected the church, we will primarily pursue the curse of problem-centered counseling and the reasons why it should be stopped" (47).

Narramore and Dobson

"One of the godfathers of the integration of psychology and the Bible was Clyde Narramore. His book The Psychology of Counseling was published in 1960. He was one of the first to promote the wedding of secular psychology with the Scriptures. Narramore's message demeaned the role of pastors, supposedly limited to Scripture in the understanding of the human condition. He promoted the psychological understanding of man in addition to Scripture but downplayed some of the humanistic and psychoanalytic teachings. Narramore's integrationist teaching, along with his Foundation, was a seed bed of the numerous similar teachings that followed. Many of the early integrationists, such as James Dobson, were directly and greatly influenced by Narramore. And, of course Narramore and those that followed him swallowed whole the sinful problem-centered psychological format" (104).

Psychoheresy

"Fifty years ago evangelical Christianity was almost totally devoid of what we call psycho heresy; now it is predominantly embraced by Christian schools at all levels, mission agencies, denominations, and Christians of all persuasions" (105).

His Story (the truth of Jesus)

"However, what one really needs to know about is a person's walk with the Lord. In other words, we want to hear how His Story (the truth of Jesus) has impacted their story. Much greater progress can be made when the purpose is for the fellow believer to grow in knowing and trusting Christ than when the plan is problem-solving through ongoing conversations filled with the Jeremiah 17:9 syndrome. Problems are opportunities for spiritual growth and mutual care among believers. Problems can be used to motivate believers to turn to the Lord Jesus Christ and remember all He has given them: salvation through His death, burial, and resurrection; identification with Him in His death and resurrection; new life in Him; and all they possess in Him to deal with their own problems of living. Our desire is that believers will realize and remember that they are equipped in Christ to live His life and to gain victory in the smallest of problems through Him" (114-115).

Association for Clinical Pastoral Education et al

"It is perplexing to us that, after combing the biblical counseling literature for so many years, there are almost no real biblical counseling sessions on CD or DVD or in writing, and that includes none from the American Association of Christian Counselors, the Association for Clinical Pastoral Education, the Biblical Counseling Foundation, the Christian Counseling and Educational Foundational and the National Association of Nouthetic Counselors" (125-126).

Cross-Gender Counseling

"Should a female counselor strive for rapport and bonding, which would lead to an intimate relationship with a male counselee who is not her husband? Should a male counselor strive for rapport and bonding, which would lead to an intimate relationship with a female counselee who is not his wife? The obvious answer is no! Based upon the absence of any biblical example or exhortation regarding such a relationship, it follows that no such male-female counseling relationship should exist among God's people. Can you imagine the Apostle Paul recommending, endorsing, or utilizing this kind of rapport and bonding in cross-gender counseling"?! (137).

"This vulnerability occurs in both psychological and biblical counseling. In a random sample of members of the American Psychological Association, the *Los Angeles Times* reports:

> "Of the 585 psychologists who responded, 87% (95% of the men and 76% of the women) reported having been sexually attracted to their clients, at least on occasion. Sixty-three percent felt guilty, anxious or confused about the attraction, and about half of the respondents received no guidance or training on this issue."

"*The Harvard Mental Health Letter* reports:

> Research has shown that sexual contact with patients is common and often injurious. Between 7 and 12 percent of psychotherapists (psychiatrists, psychologists, and social workers) admit sexual relations with patients. Therapists who treat sexually exploited patients report that all of them are harmed" (140).

"Cross-gender counseling creates situations that put both men and women at risk and should not be tolerated in the church. Yet it not only exists, but is prolific throughout the church" (147).

Marriage Counseling

"Marriage counseling is big business in the world and in the church. As more and more people have been going to marriage counseling, more and more have become divorced, and this includes professing Christians, who are divorcing at about the same rate as unbelievers. With all the time and money and the great expectations that counseling will help married couples, it is disconcerting to learn that marriage counseling only helps about half of the time, which is similar to sham treatment" (167).

Recovered Memory Therapy

"Recovered memory therapy is especially dangerous as horrific memories are created, experienced, and re-experienced until the newly created false memory is stronger than real memories. Counselees have ended up accusing their families of abuse that never occurred, cutting themselves off from their families, and needing even more therapy to recover from the so-called recovered memories. Thankfully some truth has come forth through memory research and through counselees confessing that these memories were created in therapy. Nevertheless, many lives and relationships have been grievously harmed and even destroyed through recovered memory therapy. But even as these things have come to light, many Christians continue to engage in various forms of inner healing, which combines recovered memory therapy with aspects of the Bible plus hearing Jesus say things never recorded in Scripture.

"Another dangerous form of therapy that sometimes follows recovered memory therapy is for what used to be called multiple-personality disorder (MPD), but now called Dissociative Identity Disorder (DID). In this therapy, the counselor believes that the counselee has hidden identities or 'alters' and therefore seeks to discover these alters and then attempts to help them work together or to merge into one personality" (167-168).

American Association of Christian Counselors

"AACC has a facade of Christianity and often refers to the Bible but is a prime example of psycho heresy at its worst" (182).

The Local Church

"The local church is the place for pastoral care and the mutual edification of all believers, under the authority of the foundation laid by Scripture and as given by Jesus Christ within the mutual ministry of the saints one to another, for the purpose of building up the Body of Christ through mutual encouragement, admonition, confession, repentance, forgiveness, restoration, consolation, and comfort" (201).

"The ultimate goal is to get the individual into a daily walk with the Lord as we discuss in Chapter Ten.

"The default setting for the one who is ministering should be to turn the attention back to the Lord and His Word and the daily walk as soon as possible and as often as necessary" (208).

"Talking about problems often leads to sinful speaking, self-effort, and carnal solutions. In contrast, we desire to help fellow believers to daily remember their resources in Christ, walk daily according to their new life in Him, and daily trust the Holy Spirit to bring forth fruit as they abide in Christ" (212)

CPH Should Update and Reprint Maier's "For Better Not for Worse"

Christian News, December 23, 1990

The Lutheran Church-Missouri Synod's Concordia Publishing House should reprint Dr. Walter Maier's *For Better Not For Worse*. This "Manual of Christian Matrimony" is the best book CPH has ever published on the subject. Some 30 years ago Trinity Lutheran Church of New Haven, Missouri, petitioned an LCMS convention to reprint Maier's manual on marriage, but was told that the statistics were out of date. These could easily be updated. Maier was critical of various psychologists and marriage counselors of his day. Psychologists and marriage counselors of more recent times, who offer anti-scriptural advice, could be quoted rather than those who lived 60 years ago.

Mrs. Maier told us that when her husband first came to CPH with his massive manuscript some at CPH thought it would never sell. It was first published in 1935. We are reprinting here chapter one from the twelfth printing of the third edition of this 600-page book. Maier was the first speaker on the International Lutheran Hour, Old Testament Professor at Concordia Seminary, St. Louis, and editor of *The Walther League Messenger*.

What he says in *For Better Not for Worse* is scriptural and far more helpful than what today's authorities on marriage, like Dr. Joseph Barbour, who has been highly praised by Concordia Seminary and has lectured widely throughout the LCMS on marriage, has to say.

For Better Not For Worse
A Manual of Christian Matrimony

By Walter A. Maier, Ph.D.
Concordia Theological Seminary, St. Louis Editor,
"*The Walther League Messenger*" 1935

PREFACE

When Vera Britain, in her testament of Youth (a volume which stirred at least one university campus "as no other book in recent years"), admits that, while fifteen years ago she would have turned to a prayer book for solace in the bereavement of her fiancé, today she would find comfort in Bertrand Russell's philosophies, her confession typifies the wide revolt against the morality of our Christian faith.

The following pages have been written to record a protest against this growing disparagement of Scriptural ethics and to help stem the onrushing tide which champions the pagan, de-spiritualized interpretation of courtship, marriage, and family relations.

We find a host of counselors today who "look at marriage." The doctor, the psychologist the psychiatrist, the psychoanalyst, the biologist, the anthropologist, the sociologist, the Communist, the radical novelist, the Hollywood strategist - all have beheld marriage with a professional scrutiny; but they have given no trustworthy direction for the attainment of genuine and permanent marital happiness. Too often their overemphasis of the physical, their bias, skepticism, or venom, have remained utterly undisguised.

More than ever before, then, the Church must look at marriage and in the spirit of its Lord and Savoir offer as the basis for all family felicity the truths of divine revelation found within the covers of our Bible. The application of Biblical principles is not only highly concordant with the best results of sociological research, but has been demonstrated in unnumbered homes; for our Christian faith, with its eminently practical endowment, bestows those definite helps for the attainment of the higher happiness in married life: the presence of the redeeming Christian and His renewing Spirit, the strength of His purifying Word, the power of His sustaining Sacrament, and His pledge of answered prayer.

This volume is essentially a code of Christian marriage, drawn from the Scriptures, which would help to make marriage "for better, not for worse"': and it is offered particularly to the mature young people of the Christian Church, those alert, eager young men and women who after their highschool or college years may find themselves confronted by some of the problems which these pages would help solve. For fifteen years it has been my privilege to edit *The Walther League Messenger*, the young people's organ of my Church. Many of the personal questions that have been repeatedly voiced in the extended editorial correspondence of this decade and a half have not only suggested this volume, but have also helped to formulate its presentation. From contact with youth groups throughout the land, from private consultation with students, and from personal inquiries that have been submitted in connection with chain broadcasts I believe that the problems discussed in these chapters are among the major perplexities which confront our young people, and I have endeavored to give the Church's answer in an non-technical, practical manner.

Sometimes, it seems, the study of marriage is restricted to snatched bits of hazy theories or guided by conventions and eclipsed by absorbing, but momentary issues. In other, less complicated days, when Christian marital ideals were uncontested, this neglect may have produced no serious consequences; but today, when every major claim for Christian morality has been fiercely assailed, ignorance of the Scriptural injunctions and disregard of Christ's sustaining power become doubly hazardous. I am convinced that in the broad educational outlines for young people there should be adequate room for the constructive study of marriage blessings and problems. For what is a young woman profited if she can speak authoritatively on Byzantine art, yet has no definite understanding of the high principles of Christian home-life? Or what advantage does a young man enjoy who can quote Homer and Virgil in the original and still is woefully unprepared for the personal issues of the family? The increasing frequency with which courses on marriage appear in the curricula of American colleges shows that even worldly wisdom has been aroused to the necessity of premarital preparation. But since the Church offers more than academic information when it presents the divine will and the help of Heaven, its guidance along the pathway to domestic happiness is doubly imperative. The future of our Church and of our country depends under God, upon stalwart, Christian homes, consecrated Christian families, the exaltation of the Christian doctrines concerning marriage, parenthood, and home. And how can these truths be more effectively inculcated than by a systematic program, designed to make these truths vital, decisive forces in the hearts and lives of our young people?

I gratefully acknowledge the assistance rendered by two members of the Concordia Seminary Faculty, Prof. Th. Engelder, D.D., and Prof. E. J. Friedrich, who read the book in manuscript and offered helpful suggestions and improvements. Pastor Alfred Doerffler reviewed the manuscript, and Miss Harriet Schwenk offered generous assistance in the preparation for printing. The cooperation of Concordia Publishing House deserves recognition.

To the pastors who have answered questionnaires and to all those whose opinions have been sought and generously given, I herewith extend my thanks.

I ask no greater blessing for these pages than that, by the grace of God, they may lead some of tomorrow's fathers and mothers to resolve in their marital relations that whatsoever they do in word or deed they "do all in the name of the Lord Jesus."

Independence Day, 1935

Chapter One
THE CHURCH SUBMIT'S A MARRIAGE CODE

Walking in all the commandments and ordinances of the Lord (Luke 1:6)

"Is marriage worth while?" "Dare we hope for permanent happiness after the honeymoon?"

"How can we help to build a home partnership in which love, camaraderie, and mutual respect will be sustained?"

"Is wedded bliss, the theme on which the serene minds of yesteryear lingered clingingly, an outworn delusion?"

These are questions which keen-minded youth has insistently asked in our days of sagging domestic morals. Surrounded by discouraging influences, – frequent divorce, marital unfaithfulness, many unhappy marriages, and the rankling bitterness of domestic discord, - young men and women pause in survey; and their reaction often betrays a degree of hesitation and uncertainty.

Young people are assaulted by a ridicule of matrimony; they are barraged by appeals for a revolt against marriage; they hear catch-phrases promising a new freedom for a new age. The press, the radio, the stage, the screen, - this quadruple alliance which often helps model their thoughts, – are often confederated in attacking home ideals. And youth cannot altogether escape the impact of newspaper head-lines nor the panderings of erotic novels, which, banned by a wiser generation, are now offered in unexpurgated editions at a few pennies for daily rentals.

YOUTH CONSULTS ITS COUNSELORS

Bewildered young people are putting their questions concerning marriage in the present social order to a host of highly reputed counselors. They have turned to sociologists and demanded a workable code for courtship and married life, achievable principles by which the dreams of romance can be woven into the firmer texture of happy reality; but they have found that Harry Barnes and Havelock Ellis, Schmalhausen and Calverton, and other radicals have advocated extremes which stand self-condemned.

They remember the emphasis which the past years laid upon the physical side of marriage and they hear persuasive voices arguing that physiologists and biologists can outline a clear course to avoid domestic disruption. But with life now concealing few mysteries for our young people, they must come to the realization that a mere knowledge of the body and its functions cannot provide any degree of stability for the inner life.

They have investigated the claims of psychoanalysis, only to conclude that Freudian psychology reduces emotional and spiritual life to a sensual basis.

The faddists of the hour have bid for their support, and youth watch the legislative and congressional battles in behalf of birth control with unusual interest; yet in their hearts they know that Mrs. Sanger's system is anything but the open-sesame to marital enchantment.

With six times as many students enrolled in our colleges as in 1900, the intellectual leaders of tomorrow's America have directed their inquiries to the wisdom enthroned on college campuses. The repeated answers of university radicalism show that the ideals of our intelligentsia are often surcharged with the liberalism of free love.

The promises of radical Socialism have recruited sizable brigades from an anti-capitalistic youth; but Marxism, as it betrays its true identity in the debacle of Sovietism, is revealed as a bleeding delusion.

Professional counselors of the home - and their number is legion - have been approached in this quest for final truth; but too often their theories lead to quicksand.

Youth have stood face to face with their parents and elders, the divinely constituted mentors of their morality; but with their own disheartening example twentieth-century fathers and mothers have often handed their children the stones of stolid indifference toward the scorpions of cynicism.

Disillusioned, they have sought the solution of their problems by taking counsel with themselves. Yet at the First American Youth Congress, held at New York University; August 15-17, 1934, the more conservative element at this convention was radical enough to adopt an official platform declaring birth control desirable from a social point of view and asking for divorce by mutual consent. (Report, p. 17)

In a final appeal, enlightenment has been sought at the altar of God. Youth has knocked at the doors of the Church and said: "In the name of religion tell us, Is marriage worth while?" "Where can we realize our ideals?" "How are we to lay lasting home foundations?" The replies are bewildering; for an ominous list of divorces among the clergy, the attacks on marriage from liberal pulpits, the degradation of wedded life by groups for whom marriage is a less holy and desirable state, have combined to emphasize that even the last prop, religion, has often given way.

Not all religion, however; for as youth stands at the crossroads, Christ's code insists that every pale of pessimism be removed; that we must have done with the carping against marriage. As youth in this second quarter of the twentieth century, analytical in its judgments, challenging its discussions, repeats its questions and demands: "Is the joy of marriage mere myth? If not, how can we find its full happiness?" it becomes the sacred duty of the Church of Jesus Christ to speak with divine authority. Conscious of its everlasting truth it must answer these questions definitely and with constructive solution. It must ceaselessly declare: Holy wedlock, when appraised in the light of Christ's estimate and regulated by His code of marital ethics, is still one of the highest and holiest of all earthly joys.

THE CHURCH'S MARRIAGE CODE

What are these Christian pronouncements on marriage? A large library of conflicting interpretations clamors for recognition; but if the clear statements of the Scriptures are accepted, the code which the Church gives its young people demands the definite endorsement of these basic truths:

1) Marriage is a divine institution, established by God Himself. It is not a social evolution or a heritage from any alleged brute ancestry. As the gift of God, sex, marriage, and family life are holy; and even though disfigured by sin, they should be honored by all men as divine bestowals.

2) Christian marriage is a blessed ordinance, which leads to multiplied benedictions both for those in wedlock and for the race in general. Faithfulness to its requirements, under God, promotes individual and national well-being and progress.

3) Marriage is ultimately the normal state for most people. To exalt intentional abstinence from marriage as more holy and God-pleasing, willfully to spurn wedded life in the pursuit of self-centered ambitions, is to contradict God's wisdom.

4) Christian marriage is monogamous, the union of one man and one woman. Forsaking all others, the Christian husband and wife are to cleave only and always to each other.

5) Christian marriage is established only by free will and mutual consent. Christian children must not be forced to marry any one whom they cannot love. Yet young people are bound to consult their parents and to respect their advice, provided this does not overrule divine will.

6) The marriage union is lifelong, and termination, except by death, always involves a transgression of the Divine Law by the husband or wife or both. Divorce is permitted only in the case of marital unfaithfulness. Malicious desertion breaks the marriage relation.

7) In the choice of a companion for life the decisive factor should not be wealth, physical attraction, higher education, and social position, but common devotion to the one Lord and Savior, the harmony of religious oneness. With the exception of the close degrees of relationship within which a Christian may not marry, there are no restrictions in the choice of husband or wife. A general compatibility of age, culture, and race is normally essential

for sustained happiness.

8) In the Christian family the husband is the representative head before God and man; the wife is the helping companion. The sphere of her highest activity is the home.

9) An avowed purpose of Christian matrimony is the procreation of children. Where this first injunction, "Be fruitful and multiply," is willfully disregarded and artificial means are employed to evade the responsibilities and privileges of parenthood, the full blessings of marriage will be sacrificed.

10) Christian marriage must have a spiritual basis in the reverent acknowledgment of Jesus Christ, the Savior of all men, and in the abiding presence of His comforting and sustaining Spirit. The family altar is to be the effective pledge against shattered promises and broken hearts.

11) Christian marriage must be marked by an intensity of self-sacrificing love. Wedded life characterized by frigid aloofness is not only greatly displeasing to God, but also soon becomes a caricature of the true conjugal devotion.

12) To prepare themselves for these blessings and to meet these high requirements, young people should ask the help of God in leading clean, courageous lives and avoiding all concessions to impurity. Sin poisons their happiness and will rise up later as a spectre of reproach. Only after a careful and prayerful selection of the future helpmate, when all uncertainty has disappeared, should the mutual promise be given in engagement.

These principles are the foundation upon which young people should enter marriage and build their homes. Remove any one of these specifications, and an essential element of happiness is sacrificed. True, every statement in this marriage code has been fiercely attacked, hotly denied, mercilessly criticized, or serenely disregarded by our modern sophistication. Attempts to amend and to broaden are being made every day; but the only standards that have been weighed without being found wanting and that prove their abiding power even in the swift rush of the passing moment are God's ordinances.

The following pages seek to describe the constructive contributions which Christianity makes to married happiness. They have been written from the basic conviction that the mounting marital perplexities of our day can find solution only in remedies that conform to Christ's teachings. The remarkable harmony which exists between these principles and reliable social data will receive conspicuous attention. Contradictory, anti-Christian influences will be discussed and rejected. And with this double appeal - a plea for an appreciation of matrimony, from both the Christian and the social point of view - youth is asked to look at marriage and, reevaluating its sacredness and blessing, to discover the tried and true pathway to individual and family happiness.

The Family In America
Birth Rates Plummeting Around the World
Christian News, November 19, 2007

"More and more people are choosing to have only one child – or none at all. Birth rates are plummeting around the world" says Philip Longman in the July, 2007 *The Family In America*. This is a publication of the Howard Center for Family, Religion, Society, 934 North Main Street, Rockford, Illinois 61103.

Longman is the author of *The Empty Cradle: How Falling Birthrates Threaten World Prosperity*. An earlier version of Longman's essay was delivered as remarks to the World Congress of Families IV in Warsaw, Poland, in May 2007.

Longman concludes his *Falling Human Fertility and the Future of the Family*:

Implications

So this is the new reality of human population. What are the implications? Should we laugh or cry, be thankful or wary?

I hope we can discuss that in greater detail during the question and answer period. Meanwhile, I'll leave you with this one last thought.

You might wonder: Won't persistent, sub-replacement fertility lead to eventual extinction? On current trends, Europe's population, for example, just withers away. But I don't expect current trends to continue indefinitely in Europe or the West in general, for a special reason.

In Asian countries such as Japan, nearly everyone eventually marries and eventually has one child. In Europe, and the West in general, by contrast, there is far more diversity in reproductive behavior. In my generation of Americans, for example, nearly a fifth of us never had children, and another 17 percent had only one.

The high incidence of childless and single-child families in the West has one big implication many overlook. It means a very large proportion of what children are being born are being produced by a small subset of the current population. And who are the people who are still having large families today?

The stereotypical answer is poor people, or dumb people, or members of minority groups. But the more accurate answer is deeply religious people.

To be sure, religious fundamentalists of all varieties are themselves having fewer children than in the past. But whether they are Mormons, Orthodox Jews, Islamic or Christian fundamentalists or evangelicals, devout member of all these Abrahamic religions have on average far larger families than do the secular elements within their society.

In Europe, for example, the fertility differential between believers and non-believers has recently been estimated at 15-20 percent. Though children born into religious families often do not become religious themselves, many do, especially if they themselves go on to have children.

Meanwhile, if childlessness is widespread among the non-religious, the faithful begin to inherit society by default. Total population may fall, perhaps for quite a while; but those who remain will be disproportionately committed to God and family.

Remember Cavitt's Law. "If your parents never had children, chances are you won't as well."

A corollary might be, if you forgot to have children, chances are your descendents won't grow up to be secular humanists.

Remember, too, that another strong finding of sociology, which is also enshrined in European folklore: "The apple doesn't fall far from the tree."

This is the way of the world

Through the broad sweep of human history there are many examples of peoples, or classes of peoples, who chose to avoid the costs of parenthood. Indeed, sub-replacement fertility is a recurring tendency of human civilization. Like today's modern, well-fed nations, both ancient Greece and Rome, for example, eventually found that their elites had lost interest in the often-dreary chores of family life. Here is the Greek historian, Polybius, around 140 B.C, lamenting the fate of his country as it gave way to Roman domination:

"In our time all Greece was visited by a dearth of children and general decay of population...This evil grew upon us rapidly, and without attracting attention, by our men becoming perverted to a passion for show and money and the pleasures of an idle life." By the time of Caesar Augustus, birthrates among Roman nobles had fallen so low that the Emperor felt compelled to enact steep "bachelor taxes" and otherwise punish those who remained unwed and childless. Here's an example of how he felt about the matter.

"We liberate slaves chiefly for the purpose of making out of them as many citizens as possible; we give our allies a share in the government that our numbers may increase: yet you, Romans of the original stock...are eager that your families and names at once shall perish with you."

Needless to say, such exhortations didn't work. Divorce became rampant in Roman society; childlessness increasingly common. When cultural and economic conditions discourage parenthood, not even a dictator—and many have tried—can force people to go forth and multiply. Eventually, the sterile, secular noble families of Imperial Rome died off, and with them, their ancestors' idea of Rome.

But what was once the Roman Empire remained populated. Only the composition of the population changed. Nearly by default, it became comprised of new, highly patriarchal family units, hostile to the secular world and enjoined by faith either to go forth and multiply or join a monastery. Sociologist Rodney Stark has shown that nearly all the spread of Christianity in late antiquity was the result of higher birthrates, and lower death rates, enjoyed by Christians.

With these changes came a Medieval Europe, but not the end of Europe, nor the end of Western Civilization. But secularism and individual freedom went into a long decline.

A section on Birth Control in the forthcoming book of some 500 pages, *Walter Maier Still Speaks - the Missouri and the World Should Listen* mentions Longman's study on declining birth rates. It is reproduced here.

* * *

Chapter VIII
Maier and Birth Control

Missouri and the world should listen to what Maier says about birth control in his *For Better Not For Worse*. Paul Maier in his *A Man Spoke – A World Listened* says that his father's opposition to birth control "is unusual for a Protestant, but part of father's personal persuasions. Among other things, he was worried that such regulated parenthood could induce a dwindling population – an anachronism today with its population explosion. . . ." (p. 160). Paul Maier claims that "in ascribing to birth control an 'antiscriptural bias,' Walter Maier clearly went further than the Bible, which is silent on the matter."

When Maier thundered against birth control, he was doing exactly what the LCMS was doing along with most Protestants of the time, until the liberal Episcopal Church first came out for birth control in the 1930's. Dean John H. C. Fritz of Concordia Seminary in his *Pastoral Theology*, long used in LCMS seminaries as a text-book, took the same position as Maier. Maier said nothing more than what Luther said in the Sixteenth Century. Dr. Tom Hardt, an orthodox Lutheran theologian in Sweden, wrote in his *"The Lutheran Church and Birth Control – The Family in Natural and Revealed Law"*: "The thoroughly affirmative attitude towards fertility is to be found again in the Reformation. 'It is inhuman and impious to reject children disdainfully,' says Luther, who sees in birth control the devil working through the will of human beings to achieve a financially easier way of life" (*Christian News Encyclopedia*, p. 930).

Christian News published a series by Charles Provan which showed that Luther insisted that the Bible opposes birth control. The series is now in *The Bible and Birth Control* by Charles Provan available from *Christian News* for $4.00. Dr. Martin J. Naumann, a professor at Concordia Seminary, Springfield, Illinois in his "The Deadly ABC" took the same position Maier did (*Christian News Encyclopedia*, p. 1437-1438). Other books available from *Christian News* which defend Maier's scriptural position are *Be Fruitful & Multiply* by Nancy Campbell, $12.50 and *Family Man, Family Leader*, $12.50.

The Lutheran Churches of the Reformation in its 1991 convention resolution opposing birth control lists numerous Bible passages (*Christian News Encyclopedia*, p. 3329). It then adds:

"We must maintain and teach the principles relating to this issue, although we allow for exegetical differences and exceptional cases (casuistry), Matt. 28:20; Acts 20:27, such was the united teachings of Dr. Martin Luther and the 'Old Missouri' fathers (C. F. W. Walther, F. Pieper, A. L. Graebner, C. M. Zorn, W. H. T. Dau, J. T. Mueller, W. Dallmann, F. Bente, E.W. A.

Koehler, L. Fuerbringer, T. Engelder, Theo. Laetsch, G. Luecke, W. A. Maier, M. J. Naumann, et al. and LCR founders P. E. Kretzmann, W. H. McLaughlin).

"The reasons given to justify the prevention of conception are often based upon myths, selfishness, materialism, hedonism (love of pleasure), convenience, usurpation of God's prerogative, and humanistic thinking. They generally indicate a distrust of the Almighty God and His Word."

"American Life League Opposes Birth Control – Contraceptive Mentality," a front page story in the July 27, 1998 *Christian News*, reported: "The American Life League (Box 1350, Stafford, VA 22555) continues to oppose birth control and the contraceptive mentality. It is defending the position similar to that held by the Lutheran Church-Missouri Synod, the Wisconsin Evangelical Lutheran Synod, and other Protestant denominations sixty years ago." CN noted that Judie Brown, President of the American Life League, wrote in the July/August 1998 Celebrate Life: "Still as documented in American Life League's *Pro-Life Activist's Encyclopedia*, most Christians refused to accept birth control. Dr. Walter A. Maier, a Lutheran theologian, called it 'one of the most repugnant aberrations, representing a 20th Century renewal of pagan bankruptcy.'"

For Better Not For Worse

Several times the editor's congregation petitioned LCMS conventions to ask CPH to reprint Maier's *For Better Not For Worse*. The Walther Conference also suggested that the book be reprinted. It had been a best seller at CPH. CN was told that CPH would not reprint it because the statistics were out of date. CN argued that the statistics could easily be brought up to date. If no one else would do this, CN would. CN discovered that it was not reprinted because liberals and their sympathizers in the LCMS did not agree with some of the views Maier expresses in *For Better Not For Worse*.

Here are some sections about the book in Paul Maier's *A Man Spoke A World Listened:*"Having laid aside the prophetic role, the core of the book discusses various criteria for a happy marital choice and the central concerns of courtship, engagement, and marriage. A special section is devoted to various marital menaces, especially divorce and, surprisingly, birth control. The author's opposition to artificial birth control is unusual for a Protestant, but part of Father's personal persuasions. Among other things, he was worried that such regulated parenthood could induce a dwindling population – an anachronism today with its population explosion, though in the thirties the birth rate had reached new lows, probably due to the depression. But in ascribing to birth control an 'anti-scriptural bias,' Walter Maier clearly went further than the Bible, which is silent on the matter. Most of Protestantism today would certainly find his objections unwarranted, though some church leaders of the time seconded his position, including, of course, Roman Catholics. Cardinal William O'Connell of Boston wrote his 'approval and appreciation' of Professor Maier's stand on marriage and home life" (p. 160).

(Walter Maier defended Luther's and the Lutheran Church-Missouri Synod's position, at the time, opposition to birth control. Statistics of a dwindling population now show that Maier's fears about a dwindling population were not an anachronism. Philip Longmann, author of *The Empty Cradle: How Falling Birthrates Threaten World Prosperity*, writes in the July 2007 *The Family in America*, a publication of the Howard Center for Family, Religion & Society, 934 North Main Street, Rockford, Illinois 61103: "the ongoing global decline in human birthrates is the single force that will most affect the fate of nations and the future of society in the 21st century." ". . . world population is still growing but the world supply of children is shrinking." "More and more people are choosing to have only one child – or none at all. Birthrates are plummeting around the world." ed.)

A Manual of Christian Matrimony: He Her Honor and She His Glory

Christian News, August 5, 2002

"A third of marriages will end in the first 10 years, survey says." A July 25, 2002 Associated Press story appearing in newspapers through the nation begins: "Washington— one in three marriages will end in divorce during their first 10 years, with certain couples more likely to split up than others, a government survey finds." "People who marry young, have less money, are not religious and whose parents are divorced are more likely to divorce."

"Overall, by age 30, three in four women have been married and about half have lived with a partner outside marriage.

"Those are among the findings of an extensive survey of nearly 11,000 women ages 15 to 44 exploring factors influencing co-habitation, marriage, and divorce. The survey was conducted in 1995 by the National Center for Health Statistics."

"Wedded bliss not a priority for U.S bachelors" a story in the June 22, 2002 *Washington Times* says: "Men can't commit to marriage because they enjoy a sexually active single life in a social climate that doesn't push them to marry." A new report says: "Starter Marriages," in the July, 2002 *Charisma*, says: "These 'icebreaker marriages,' as they are sometimes called, are promoted in the media." The September 2000 issue of *Entertainment Weekly* lists divorce in our 20s as an in thing to do. The headline in *Jane Magazine*'s April 2001 issue boldly proclaims, "Young, Hot and Divorced." Michael McManus writes in the June 27 *Kansas Christian*: "In 1960, 430,000 unmarried couples were living together. By 2000 the number soared 12 fold to 5 million! Only 2.3 million couples marry a year. Thus cohabitation is now the dominant way male-female unions are formed"

Baptist Press recently reported in a story titled "Cohabiting doesn't lead to more committed marriages, study finds:" "*USA Today* reported that more than 5 million unmarried American couples live together and between 50 percent and 60 percent of new marriages now involve couples who have lived together first." "The Year's Most Intriguing Findings, from Barna Research Studies," a December 17, 2001 *Religion Today* story, noted: "Among adults who have been married, born again Christians and non-Christians have essentially the same probability of divorce." "Why aren't young people told these facts about marriage?" A report in the June 15, 2002 *Remnant* says: "Here's a fact that will shock you. Do you realize that the marriage rates for women are at their lowest level in 100 years? As if that weren't enough, one third of young couples today are so brainwashed with materialism that they intend to have no more than one child! This is a mind boggling crisis of faith."

Mona Charen writes in a column titled "Divorce—Living Unhappily Ever After?" In the July 24, 2002 *St. Louis Post Dispatch*: "In the beginning was the myth that children were better off if their unhappy parents divorced. It's better to come from a broken home than to live in one,' they said. And millions of American parents separated. But after several decades had passed, researchers like Barbara Dafoe Whitehead and others showed that divorce was much worse for children than an unhappy home." The June, 2002 *Lutheran Witness* noted: "Statistics that speak of as many as half of marriages ending in divorce. Statistics that say the vows spoken 'for better or worse, for richer or poorer, till death do us part' often have little meaning in the coming years."

Kay Meyer, President, Family Shield Ministries, reports:
"Today's Families Are In Crisis"

"* Households headed by unmarried partners grew by 72 percent during the past decade. "* Households headed by single mothers or fathers increased 25/62 percent respectively. "* Thirty-three percent of all babies were born to unmarried women, compared to only 3.8 in 1940.

"* Cohabitation increased by close to 1,000 percent from 1960 to 1998, and the households headed by same sex couples are soaring."

"Born-again Christians, No More Immune to Divorce Than Others," a January 24, 2002 Religion Today Feature Story," says:

"In the churches, people have a superstitious view that Christianity will keep them from divorce, but they are subject to the same problems as everyone else, and they include a lack of relationship skills," said Donald Hughes, author of *The Divorce Reality* and editor of the Jesus website. 'Just being born again is not a rabbit's foot', he said.

"Hughes says the divorce statistics referred to in his book come from a 2001 Barna Research Poll, which indicated that 33 percent of born again Christians end their marriages in divorce, roughly the same as the general population, and that 90 percent of those divorces happen after the conversion to Christianity. Hughes maintains born again Christians try to foster a public perception that they do not get divorces because of their born again status."

The press has had much to say about the divorce and immorality of clergymen.

"Record warns of dangers of infidelity among leaders" a recent Baptist Press story noted: "ONTARIO, Calif. (BP) —Just as a hidden iceberg destroyed the Titanic after the crew had ignored multiple warnings, lives and ministries of pastors and other church staff are being destroyed at a remarkable rate by sexual infidelity, the president of the Southern Baptist North American Mission Board warned a group of pastors, missionaries, and other denominational leaders."

"Robert E. Reccord also is an author of the book *Beneath the Surface: Steering Clear of the Dangers That Could Leave You Shipwrecked*, published by the Broadman and Holman Publishers division of LifeWay Christian Resources. He shared content from the book during the April 10-13 Connection 2002 conference in Ontario, Calif., the first of the three NAMB-sponsored regional conferences this spring."

"Record cited survey statistics from the book *Men's Secret Wars* by Patrick Means that indicated 64 percent of pastors or church staff struggled with sexual addiction or compulsion. 25 percent admitted to having sexual intercourse with someone besides their wife while married, and after they had accepted Christ. Another 14 percent admitted some form of sexual contact short of intercourse." "Father of Christian Marriage Ministries Says He Plans to Divorce," a report in the March, 2002 *Charisma* says: "The man widely regarded as the father of Christian marriage ministries is filing for divorce from his wife of 42 years and plans to remarry. Ray Moshholder, whose Marriage Plus Ministries (MPM) is credited with saving more than 11,000 couples from divorce, says he is 'ashamed and disgraced.'"

This marriage expert has spoken to marriage seminars across the nation and in 20 countries. He has been endorsed by such Christian leaders as Pat Robertson and Jack Hayford. Millions have heard him on radio and TV.

In some denominations there is little difference in the rate of divorce between clergy and laity. Dr. Martin Scharlemann of The Lutheran Church-Missouri Synod's Concordia Seminary, St. Louis, wrote in the July-August, 1980 *Affirm*: "... in parts of our church body, the number of divorced and even remarried pastors has grown to scandalous proportions."

Church officials were not able to tell CN how many divorced clergymen are on the LCMS clergy roster.

In 1935 the Lutheran Church-Missouri Synod's Concordia Publishing House published Walter A. Maier's *For Better Not For Worse – A Manual of Christian Matrimony*. Maier was a professor at Concordia Seminary, St. Louis, editor of *The Walther League Messenger* and Lutheran Hour speaker. His manual on marriage has long been out of print. 40 years ago Trinity Lutheran Church, New Haven, Missouri petitioned an LCMS convention to ask CPH to reprint the book. Although *For Better Not For Worse* had been a best seller for CPH, Trinity was told that since the statistics were out of date, it should not be reprinted. The editor of *Christian News* suggested that the statistics be updated. In reality the solid scriptural positions Maier took in the book were "out of date" for too many in the LCMS. During the past 40 years *Christian News* has published thousands of stories on marriage, divorce, birth control, the family, counseling, abortion, women, weddings, etc. Some are in *The Christian News Encyclopedia*. The editor during these years has reviewed hundreds of books on the family and related matters.

The best book on marriage the editor has read all these years is *He Her Honor and She His Glory*. *Christian News* has sold hundreds of copies for

$11.95. Congregations have used it as a study manual for adult Bible classes. CN always wanted to print it in a less costly edition. It had to charge $11.25 for each book because of the cost of shipping the book from Australia where it is published. This issue of CN includes the entire book. After each section there is a series of questions prepared by Rev. Robert Hill of Plano, Texas.

The book is still available from *Christian News* for $15.50 plus postage. It is an excellent manual to use for adult Bible class. Give each member a copy. Pastors should give each couple they marry a copy. Parents should give it to their children when they marry.

Some have been critical of *Christian News* because of CNs strong stand against divorce. CN's stand is nothing more nor less than what the Bible teaches. Adultery and desertion are the only scriptural reasons for divorce. A person may be ever so famous, make piles of money, achieve all sorts of awards, become a great athlete, set all kinds of records, and pastor the largest church, but if he gets a divorce for a non-scriptural reason, all the fame he receives means very little. It is far more important for a pastor to be faithful to his wife until death, establish a solid Christian home and have God fearing children who conduct regular family devotions and regularly attend a Bible believing church than to be elected to some high position, receive honorary doctorates, or accumulate any earthly wealth.

Pastor and Mrs. Robert Hill with their children and grandchildren on their 45th wedding anniversary. Photo was on page 1 of the January 10, 2005 Christian News. Pastor Hill is the author of a series of questions for each chapter in *He Her Honour and She His Glory*. The questions are in a special issue of *Christian News* titled "A Manual of Christian Matrimony – He Her Honor and She His Glory", August 5, 2002.

He Her Honour and She His Glory
by V.S. Grieger

$15.50 plus s/h
(available from Christian News,
www.christiannewsmo.com)

II

CHRISTIANITY, CHILDREN, and CONTRACEPTION

Christianity, Children, and Contraception
Part I
by Brandt Klawitter
Christian News, April 12, 2010

Introduction

This chapter, while it will deal with many different issues pertaining to married life, children, and the family in general, will give special attention to contraception. Why debate an issue that seemingly has been decisively settled by the church? After all, the matter has been debated and decisions were rendered. What then is the point of bringing the matter back to the discussion table?

As will be shown in this chapter, the case for contraception is not nearly so "cut and dried" as popular society and even the majority of Christian denominations have led people to believe. In fact, from theological, sociological, and scientific standpoints, the issues have hardly been broached. Instead of being openly debated, though, these issues have been shoved aside into the neglected sidelines of church and society. Even worse, those who would dare to question the authoritative and final ruling of the birth control movement and its ardent allies, are often targets of ridicule, viewed as archaic holdovers from bygone days. After all, what sort of crazy people would still believe that fertility is not an illness requiring implants, shots, surgeries, any number of manufactured devices, and hormone-altering medication? Yes, it is as if there is a war being waged against God's design for life and female biology. After all, what sort of societal misfit would still believe that parenthood with large families is not merely a recipe for global destruction? **On a more p**ersonal level, isn't parenthood just a recipe for poverty, trouble, and enslavement to family? In light of this, one can only conclude that the family and future generations are under attack. Certainly, as one book title quips, "Blessed are the Barren."[1] Needless to say, this chapter will argue that certainly is not the case. If anything, anyone who would laugh at those who still unashamedly value their fertility and their families instead of their fortune and their freedom only proves his ignorance of the actual arguments or his selfishness.

Scripture on Procreation, Fertility, and Children

Throughout Scripture there is an undeniable connection between life and the only true God, the triune God. God is indeed the God of life. From the very beginning when the life-giving Word of God ordered the chaos of creation and caused it to abound with all manner of life, God showed Himself to be the author of life. By the power of His Word, plants and flowers, fish and birds, creeping things and cattle were all brought to life. Through the breath of life given by God, man himself was animated after being sculpted from the dust of the earth. Even more, as much as God's creation teemed with life from the outset of time, God pronounced His blessing and ordinance upon the continuation of life. "Be fruitful and multiply" was His will for the fish of the sea and the birds of the air, for the cattle and creeping things of the field, and even for human life. Indeed, God was saying, "More life! There must be life!"

Even a token glance through the Scriptures will show that this theme does not fade away. God is shown to love and care for all life, whether it be in sparing the fruit trees in times of war, caring for the beasts of burden, providing rain in the deserts, knowing the ways of the animals that man does not even comprehend,[2] noticing the unnoticeable sparrow, clothing the flowers of the field, and yes, especially caring for human life. Certainly, God's will has always been to protect and preserve life. It did not just protect man's ability to breathe, man's physical life, but it also extended to protect man's wife and family, his property and possessions, and even man's reputation is protected by God's commandments.

If this is not enough, God, who alone has authority to give life and to take it, wills that His creatures--yes, even mankind--should live and not die. God wills that man enjoy His gift of life without end. Thus, the incarnation, life, death, and resurrection of the Son of God is the expression of God's providing for and winning back life for those who had doomed themselves to eternal death. In short, there can be no denying that God wills life and He wills it in abundance.

I find it important to introduce this subject of children, parenting, fertility, and such related themes with a discussion of God, because, as G.K. Chesterton rightly notes in *Orthodoxy*,[3] humans have the remarkable tendency of imitating the God (or idol) they worship. Thus, the characteristics one finds in God will ultimately bear human expression. So it also is with the themes of our discussion. If man worships himself as god, and thereby ends up worshipping something that is turned in on itself and its own desires, what impetus is there for man to see the beauty of new life and commit himself to offspring and family? Or, if man worships another creature or creaturely gift instead of the Creator, once again, not only will he be worshipping an idol, but his life will become distorted in accordance with his false deity. Naturally, this also will affect man's attitude toward children. If, however, man knows the God of life and love and sees in God the unbridled desire to give and sustain life, offspring and family take on an entirely different complexion. Indeed, this is the way things actually play out.

At this point, it will be helpful to outline Scripture's teaching as it both advocates, supports, and promotes life and as it defends life from all things that run contrary to it. We have already briefly noted the abundance of life provided in creation. This perfect creation was given the command to be fruitful and multiply. Plants were given seeds and animals were designed to reproduce according to their own kind. In fact, emphasis was placed on the fact that they would do this, each according to its own kind. Thus, as a side note, we see that the Genesis creation account is intrinsically contrary to any notion of macro-evolution. Moreover, this command to be fruitful, to multiply, and subdue the earth was the only positive command given to the man and woman before the Fall. One might say that this combined task of procreating and subduing the earth formed the God-given prescription for human life. While this was frustrated by the Fall, one can see that these vocations are still reaffirmed after it, even though earthly existence became frustrating and difficult (Genesis 3:14-19).

Furthermore, Old Testament teaching, inasmuch as it reflects and expresses God's moral law, shows God's special concern for the continuance of life. Sex was not to be a mere act of which the central importance was man's own self-fulfillment. Rather, it was connected with God's continual creative work in procreation, for which, in fact, it was first intended. While the pleasure associated with sex was certainly never condemned, its use apart from God's divine purposes was strictly forbidden. Leviticus is particularly clear on these matters. Leviticus 18 spells out the basic limits of sexual activity and forbids various unproductive and unnatural sexual relations. Two chapters later, one reads of the severe punishments associated with breaking such commands. Needless to say, one notes the importance of the sexual act before God in the required punishment for rebelling against God's will.

Taking a closer look at the Old Testament's understanding of the proper and improper uses of sex, we must note that one central aspect of the Old Testament's sexual ethic has to do with its understanding of man's seed. The seed was understood as containing life, or perhaps better said, preformed life.[4] In fact, such passages as Jeremiah 4:5, "Before I formed you in the womb I knew you; Before you were born I sanctified you; And I ordained you a prophet to the nations," suggest that there is some sort of existence before God even before a man's conception and birth. Job 10:8-12 also suggests this sort of presence of life before and in the act of conception, even if only in the mind of God, is a real existence. Thus, a voluntary usage or wasting of seed apart from its rightful life-imparting use in normal heterosexual sexual activity was tantamount to destroying life. In other words, it is one thing if God does this through His own ordering of nature. In fact, that is His divine prerogative which He exercises through processes built into His creation. It is another thing, however, if man takes this into his own hands and subverts God's own prerogative so as to exercise his own self-gratifying will. Thus, homosexual acts were forbidden and man/animal liaisons were condemned. Even unproductive heterosexual sexual acts were rejected.[5] Implicitly, too, masturbation would come under divine wrath. If this is understood, then the account of Onan (Genesis 38)[6] falls into proper perspective, as do the sexual regulations of Leviticus 18. Furthermore, castration and deformity of a male's sexual organs led to ritual disqualification, whether connected with priestly service or with animal sacrifice (Lev. 21:17-20; 22:20-22,24-25). This is not to say that involuntarily being this way was considered to be sinful. Rather, this shows that it is not in keeping with God's intention and will for life. It falls short of the perfect wholeness required by God's own perfection.[7]

It should be made clear, however, that Scripture does not say that all sexual activity must lead to conception. Rather, the point is that the giving or withholding of children was something that was viewed as the prerogative of God alone. Therefore what is condemned is the intentional misuse of man's sexuality to serve only his own pleasure and to divorce it from the possibility of its greater life-creating purpose. A simple way to summarize this might be: couples were to know one another—biblically—and if God chose to *bless* them through this with children, then they should thank Him for that blessing. In this day and age of pills, implants, and everything else, the simplicity of it all sounds almost ridiculous! One additional point might be to simply say that men and women should thank God for the gift of sexuality rather than curse the fact that He gave any sort of guidelines along with it. After all, He could have chosen to make life completely devoid of these blessings and pleasures.

If one understands, then, that the marriage-defining one flesh union was not to be separated from its procreative intent, it becomes even clearer why God protects this union in His Law (i.e. 6th Commandment). He protects it because the stability of this life-giving union is pertinent to the offspring that are intended to issue forth from it. Furthermore, God specially protects the role of parents in the 4th Commandment as an added defense of the family.

What is the point of this overall structure? One can safely conclude that God would have His people to be fruitful and multiply that His people might increase. After all, the Scriptural expectation is that God-fearing parents will produce and train up God-fearing children (Dt. 4:9-10; Pr. 22:6). In other words, church growth through the womb is no laughing matter. In fact, to put this more in perspective, each new child is a potential parent, teacher, pastor, missionary, and servant in God's family. Furthermore, the individual families serve as the foundation stones of God's people. It is, first and foremost, in the family that children learn God's Word. It is in the family that children are trained in love, kindness, justice, truth, fairness, and forgiveness. It is in the family that honest labor and productiveness are learned and where laziness and all manner of vice are discouraged. In short, God shows special concern for the family because the family is where disciple-making (through love and discipline) is best accomplished. Thus, we read in such places as Psalm 127 that it is through the womb and the family that God blesses and achieves His purposes. That also helps to explain why God's people in the Old Testament believed fertility to be a blessing and not a curse.[8]

What about the New Testament? After all, arguments are often made that there is a fundamental shift between the familial and sexual ethic of the Old Testament and the New Testament, respectively. After all, hasn't the Gospel abolished not only the Law, but also the purpose and function of sexuality as such passages as Galatians 3:28 suggest. We read: "For there is neither...male nor female; for you are all one in Christ Jesus." What do we make of such passages and what about Paul's encouraging language with respect to celibacy (1 Cor. 7:7-9)? Furthermore, in the Gospels we even hear Jesus' words about forsaking father and mother for His sake.

In answer to these objections, it should first be noted that with respect to Paul's words in Galatians, he is referring to what some have called, "the order of salvation." There is no distinction before God when it comes to faith and the way of eternal life. Baptism is the great neutralizer and faith in Christ is the great equalizer of all mankind. Regarding St. Paul's advocacy of celibacy, we would do well to observe that, while celibacy is encouraged for the sake of service to the Gospel, it is not given as the rule but only as the exception. When it is advocated, it serves a greater purpose and is not an end in itself. In fact, the household tables given by St. Paul in his letters to the Ephesians and Colossians correspond with Old Testament marriage and familial understandings. Moreover, such controversial passages as 1 Timothy 2:11-15 have been historically understood to uphold the Old Testament's valuation of motherhood and the divinely established vocation inherent to womanhood.[9] That is to say, motherhood is given greatest dignity and honor in Scripture (see also Proverbs 31). In fact, St. Paul encouraged this vocation among women within the church and reserved the status of widow for those who had already faithfully fulfilled this calling (1 Timothy 5:3-16).

Finally, did Jesus really abolish family responsibilities and commitments? Certainly, He did say things that seem to shake the very foundations of the family (e.g. Mt. 10:35,37; 19:29). Nevertheless, He Himself was subject to His own parents. In His teachings He not only upheld God's Law, but condemned the scribes and Pharisees for not honoring father and mother in their own teachings and lives (Mt. 15:4-6). Finally, did not Jesus on Calvary show care for His own mother as one of His final acts before death (Jn. 19:25-27)? The point is, the New Testament does not change or overthrow the familial and sexual ethic of the Old Testament. If anything, it upholds and enforces what was established by God in creation, even strengthening the moral force of the ethic in such teachings as when Jesus addresses sexuality and divorce in the Sermon on the Mount.

Scripture on Contraception and Abortion

Thus far in our discussion of Biblical teachings concerning children, fertility, and sexual conduct, we have yet to address directly the topics of contraception and abortion. First of all, the question must be asked, "Does Scripture directly address these topics?" There are many discussions concerning abortion but even proponents of the practice eventually must concede that human life is snuffed out whenever an abortion is performed or induced.[10] I do not believe it is necessary to rehash all of the arguments against abortion. Clearly Scripture reveals that God forms the human being already in the womb and that new life is already present at the moment of conception. Passages such as Psalm 139, Job 10:8-12, Eccl. 11:5, and Jeremiah 1:5 all testify to this reality. Thus, according to Luther's explanation of the 5th Commandment, God requires that we neither hurt nor harm our neighbor (even while he is still in the womb), but that we must help and befriend him in every bodily need. If that were not enough, Old Testament teaching is very clear about protecting the unborn in Ex. 21:22-25 or punishing those who would harm the unborn in passages such as Amos 1:13 ([13]The LORD says this: "For three and four wrongs of the Ammonites I will not change it. Because they ripped open the pregnant women in Gilead in order to enlarge their country). Certainly, any form of infanticide is also strongly condemned by God.

Does Scripture have anything further to say on the matter? Certainly, recent scholarship has had very little to say on the subject of contraception.

In fact, the majority of Protestant Christianity has been so silent on the matter—for almost a century now—that even traditionally conservative church bodies have ruled that the matter of contraception is not clearly addressed by Scripture and, as such, is a matter of Christian freedom.[11] Is this claim really valid?

The implications of this chapter's previous argumentation would certainly argue against this conclusion. As we have already noted, God did not design the sexual act to be divorced from its God-given purpose of procreation and He condemned those acts wherein such a bifurcation took place. Clearly, any act that sets out to impede or prohibit this goal would be included within that prohibition. Thus contraception (meaning that which acts against conception) cannot be viewed favorably if one maintains that the sexual act (and man's seed) is not to be willfully separated from its intended function.

There is more to the Scriptural case against contraception, however. As Bryan Hodge notes in *The Christian Case against Contraception*, it is likely that the New Testament's prohibition of sexual immorality simply reflected the Old Testament's sexual ethic. Thus, passages such as Romans 1:18-32 condemn not only homosexual practices, but may also condemn wrongful heterosexual sexual practices, particularly those that separate sexual activity from the possibility of procreation. This may be the implication of Romans 1:26 where the Apostle writes: "For this reason God gave them up to vile passions. For even their women exchanged the natural use for what is against nature."[12] Hodge does note that the argument is not conclusive. Nevertheless, he argues that if sex divorced from the possibility of procreation can be considered "the natural use", that is, sex focused only upon the couple's intimacy or one's own self-gratification, then there can be no real distinction between either unproductive hetero- or homosexual acts. Nevertheless, if "the natural use" hearkens back to creation and Genesis 1,[13] then there is good reason to believe that this passage is condemning sexual activity that divorces procreation from sexual pleasure and intimacy. This would also explain why Luther considered the practice of contraception to be sodomy.

Before concluding our discussion of Scripture's understanding of contraception and abortion, there is one further possible condemnation of contraception—and almost certainly abortion—in the New Testament's condemnation of *pharmakeia* (potion-making, often translated as "sorcery"). While this term could be related to "a drug used as a controlling medium,"[14] perhaps something like our modern problem with mind-altering drugs, it is more likely that *pharmakeia* is more closely related to the realm of sex and the attempt to either prevent or terminate pregnancy. Probably the clearest New Testament example of this usage is to be seen in Revelation where *pharmakeia* (18:23) is placed in a string of condemnations focused upon sexual immorality (14:8; 17:2; 18:3; 19:2). Then, in 21:8 and 22:15,[15] the two terms are linked with one another. Interestingly, a similar connection exists in the Old Testament where the city of Nineveh received stern judgment from the Lord. "Woe to the bloody city! It is all full of lies and robbery. Its victim never departs...Because of the multitude of harlotries of the seductive harlot, the mistress of sorceries, who sells nations through her harlotries, and families through her sorceries" (Nahum 3:1, 4). While a conclusive case cannot be made, there is good reason to suggest that Scripture is not as silent on birth control as is normally thought. After all, the mixing of potions, both for abortifacient and contraceptive purposes was a known practice of the ancient world.[16]

Notes

[1] Marshall, Robert and Charles Donovan. *Blessed are the Barren: The Social Policy of Planned Parenthood* (San Francisco: Ignatius Press, 1991).

[2] See Job 39-41 in particular for God's knowledge and attention to the animals of the field and birds of the air.

[3] Chesterton, G.K. *Orthordoxy* (London: The Bodley Head, 1957), 122-123.

[4] Note that this is exactly how the writer of Hebrews understands man's seed. In Hebrews 7:9-10, the author points out that in some way Levi was present with Abraham when Abraham paid tithes to Melchizedek. We read: "Even Levi, who receives tithes, paid tithes through Abraham, so to speak, for he was still in the loins of his father when Melchizedek met him." Even more interesting, Abraham was the great-grandfather of Levi.

[5] Note that the (generally—not always) more infertile times of the month for the woman were withheld from sexual activity.

[6] One must conclude regarding Onan's action and punishment that his terrible deed was not simply his unwillingness to give his brother offspring and fulfill his levirate duty. After all, Boaz was not the nearest of kin to Ruth's deceased husband, Elimelech (Ruth 4). Furthermore, if the nearest of kin was unwilling to fulfill his duty, he would not be punished with death for this unwillingness (note also Dt. 25:5-10). Therefore, one must conclude that Onan's terrible sin was not his unwillingness. It is also doubtful that the strict judgment is merely a result of his unwillingness to obey his father in this matter. Rather, "the thing which he did displeased the Lord; therefore He killed him also" (Genesis 38:10). Given the Old Testament's understanding of sex, it seems clear, then, that his effort to thwart the conception of a child through some form of contraception is what merited God's swift and severe judgment.

[7] Note: This might seem to stand in contradiction to Jesus' words in Matthew 19:12, that "there are eunuchs who were born thus from their mother's womb, and there are eunuchs who were made eunuchs by men, and there are eunuchs who have made themselves eunuchs for the kingdom of heaven's sake. He who is able to accept it, let him accept it." William Hendrickson, however, in *The Gospel of Matthew* (Grand Rapids: Baker Book House, 1973), 718-719, explains the passage thus: "The first group consists of those who are eunuchs because of a congenital defect. The second refers to physically castrated men. This deplorable condition was brought upon them by other men...The third class can also be called 'eunuchs,' though the word is now used in a figurative sense. These men are not impotent. They could marry and fulfil all of their responsibilities in that state, if they so desired. Their abstinence from marriage is of a purely voluntary character. They are eunuchs or celibates 'in the interest of the kingdom of heaven.'" Hendrickson goes on to explain that this is not a state established by divine decree and neither is it a state associated with a higher degree of holiness. After all, St. Paul served God as a celibate, St. Peter (and others) served with their wives (1 Cor. 9:5).

[8] See also: Ex. 23:25-26; Dt. 7:13-14; Ps. 128; 1 *Chronicles* 25:4-5; 26:4-5; Hosea 9:10-17; etc.

[9] In "Ordained Proclaimers or Quiet Learners? Women in Worship in Light of I Timothy 2," Charles Gieschen makes the argument that the orders of creation and redemption are not two totally unrelated orders or realms, but that redemption's purpose is that of restoring creation. Thus, in addressing 1 Timothy 2:15, he reaches the following conclu-

sions: "The historical context points to the probability that Paul is affirming childbearing as an important role of women through these words. It appears that some Christians were forbidding or belittling the importance of marriage and procreation in the congregations that Paul is addressing (1 Tim. 4:3). They saw these natural aspects of creation as part of the old fallen order caused by sin. Thus, in light of the overwhelming testimony of Paul elsewhere, one should not understand... 'through childbearing' as the means of salvation but as an important God-ordained role of women established in creation that is not set aside through redemption..." *Women Pastors?* (St. Louis: CPH, 2008), edited by Matthew C. Harrison and John T. Pless, page 86.

[10] Take, for instance, *Abortion: My Choice, God's Grace—Christian Women Tell Their Stories* (Pasadena, CA: New Paradigm Books, 1994), edited by Anne Eggebroten. In this book, a collection of "Christian women" who defend their choice to have had abortions or to support those who have, it is acknowledged with surprising consistency that a person's life was the actual price of the procedure. Nevertheless, the decision is defended for ideological, individualistic, or emotional reasons. Peter Kreeft in *The Unaborted Socrates* (Downers Grove, Illinois: IVP Books, 1983), also offers an insightful look at the idea that the aborted embryo or fetus is somehow not human.

[11] As examples I might mention both the Wisconsin Evangelical Lutheran Synod (WELS) and the Lutheran Church—Missouri Synod (LCMS), though this list might be widened to include all major Protestant denominations. For example, in a 1981 report on Human Sexuality, the LCMS' CTCR made the following statement: "In view of the Biblical command and the blessing to 'be fruitful and multiply' [Gen. 1:28], it is expected that marriage will not ordinarily be voluntarily childless. But, in the absence of Scriptural prohibition, there need be no objection to contraception with a marital union which is, as a whole, fruitful." *This We Believe* (The Lutheran Church—Missouri Synod, 2010), 5. Similarly, in a series titled "The Christian and Birth Control" (*Beginnings*, Feb. 1998), 8-9, WELS Lutherans for Life reached the following conclusions: (1) "A Christian's decision to use birth control is a stewardship issue," and "A Christian married couple can practice some form of birth control. It falls within the realm of Christian freedom and stewardship."

[12] See Bryan Hodge's *The Christian Case against Contraception* (Eugene, Oregon: Wipf & Stock, 2010), 86-90.

[13] Ibid., 90. "It is clear either way that Paul is condemning the sexual act in Romans 1:26-27 because it cannot fulfill the creation mandate "to be fruitful and multiply and fill up the earth" (Gen 1:27). It is also clear that Paul is making direct allusions both to Genesis 1:27-28 and Leviticus 18, which may also allude to the Genesis passage in its use of the term "male" instead of 'Man." Paul purposely uses the words thelus, "female," instead of gune, "woman," and arsen, "male," instead of aner, "man," because these are the words used for the man and woman in the LXX translation of Genesis 1:27." Charles Provan, in *The Bible and Birth Control* (Monongahela, Pennsylvania: Zimmer Printing, 1989), 27-28, reaches similar conclusions.

[14] BDAG. *A Greek-English Lexicon of the New Testament* (Chicago: University of Chicago Press, 2000), 1050.

[15] Note the very close link between idolatry, murder, sexual immorality, and sorcery in these verses!

[16] Hodge. *Christian Case*, 3-11.

Christianity, Children, and Contraception
Part II
Christian News April 26, 2010

Nineteen Centuries of Church History Oppose Contraception

Considering modern Protestantism's general silence or actual approval, both tacit and explicit, of contraception, one would expect to find that the matter was not a subject of discussion throughout the church's history. Yet, such an expectation could not be further from the truth. As has already been shown, God's people, both Old Testament Israel and in the New Testament, held to a specifically procreation-linked understanding of the nature and purpose for sexual relations. Not surprisingly then, this understanding was almost uniformly and unanimously upheld for nearly nineteen centuries of the church's history.

Of course, church history carries neither the authority nor the place of Scripture when it comes to deciding matters of teaching. Certainly, the church has erred from time to time, has struggled with heresy and false teaching, and has been plagued by any number of other problems. Nevertheless, that is not to say that the witness of the historic church should be viewed as insignificant or worthless. In point of fact, the witness of the historic church serves as what some have called a sort of "democracy of the dead." That is to say, through history and tradition generations of the past voice their understanding of the faith to us and offer to guide and steer the church of today. In other words, orthodox Christianity, while it stands on Scripture alone, certainly does not shun the guidance and counsel of its forefathers. In fact, should one find himself to be standing utterly alone on some teaching of the faith when viewed in the broader historical perspective, that should be a cause to question one's own position on the matter. Novelty in theology is almost always a cause for fear and should lead to careful and critical examination of one's own understanding. Remarkably, though, contemporary Christianity has seen little need to even question its unprecedented understanding of sexual relations, contraception, and procreation. Even more, with its general ignorance of history, it has reached the rather arrogant conclusion that it is most unique within all of history in that only now has the having and raising of children become difficult, expensive, burdensome, and as something best avoided.

The church of the late 1st and early 2nd Centuries, in such writings as the *Didache* and *The Epistle of Barnabas* strike out against *pharmakeia* in lists of sins that are said to "destroy men's souls."[17] Once again, the mention of "potion mixing" is most likely linked to the mixing of potions intended to avoid pregnancy or terminate a pregnancy. Moreover, the *Didache* is entirely explicit in condemning any form of abortion. In the same section where *pharmakeia* is prohibited, the author of the *Didache* goes on to say, "You shall not abort a child or commit infanticide."[18] Continuing on through the church's history, Bryan Hodge mentions that such notable leaders as Irenaeus, Justin Martyr, Clement of Alexandria, Cyprian, Lactantius, Cyril of Alexandria, and others came out unanimously in harmony with the Scriptural understanding as they opposed contraception and encouraged sex for the sake of its procreative purpose.[19] Most remarkable within Hodge's survey of church history is a quotation from Epiphanius (AD 315-402), wherein he remarks about the unchristian practices of a Gnostic cult:

"They exercise genital acts, yet prevent the conceiving of children. Not for the purpose of producing offspring, but for the purpose of satisfying lust, are they eager for corruption. To such an extent has the devil deceived these wretched people that they betray the work of God by perverting it to their own deceits. Moreover, they are so willing to satisfy their carnal desires as to pollute each other with impure seed, by which offspring is not conceived but by their own will evil desires are satisfied."[20]

The church's opposition to contraception and abortion did not end there, either. Chrysostom, Jerome, and Augustine[21] are also found among the ranks of those who opposed these practices in the early centuries of the church.

Entering into the middle ages, one will note that the church's stance did not change. Such historic figures as Gregory the Great, Peter Lombard, Thomas Aquinas, and even Geoffrey Chaucer, author of the *Canterbury Tales*, were all uniform in their affirmation that sex should not be separated from its procreative purpose and in their opposition to contraceptive and abortion-causing practices.[22]

The observant reader, though, might quickly point out that the theologians and church leaders mentioned thus far all were prior to the Reformation. Thus, it might be assumed that the Gospel freedom discovered and so fervently defended by Luther and the other reformers allowed for a new and different understanding of sex and its proper function within marriage. However, such an assumption would be false. While the Reformers did oppose the presentation of any sort of merely human teaching as the teaching of God and while it is true that they also adamantly opposed any sort of legalism, whereby the conscience would be made captive to the Law, it is not true that they believed that this nullified the norming function of God's moral law. This moral law they held to be most clearly revealed through the Ten Commandments, though even that Decalogue was a summary of that Law built into creation itself. Thus, the Gospel did not eliminate God's will for human life, but freed man to live according to it. Luther's explanation of the Ten Commandments in both the Large and Small Catechisms clearly illustrate this fact.

Thus we see that the Reformers upheld and taught as binding that which is established in creation and taught by God's word. As an example of this, the Lutheran Confessions ardently maintain and defend marriage (see AC XXIII and *Apology* XXIII). Interestingly, AC XXIII makes no attempt to separate sex from its procreative functions within marriage. It's true that the *Augsburg Confession* and the *Apology* note that marriage is given as an antidote against human weakness. Nevertheless, procreation was not somehow separated from this and other purposes of marriage. In fact, AC XXIII asserts, "God created human beings for procreation."[23] The *Apology* also defends the natural procreative purpose of marital relations, declaring, "First, Genesis 1:28 teaches that people were created to be fruitful, and that one sex should desire the other in a proper way."[24] Even more, the *Apology* points out that despite the claim of its adversaries that "Be fruitful and multiply" no longer applies to the world and its inhabitants, this ordinance can no more be abolished than God's declaration that "the earth sprout vegetation, plants yielding seed."[25] The *Apology* then goes on to affirm the vocation of motherhood when it states, "Paul says that woman is saved by childbearing. What more honorable thing could be said against the hypocrisy of celibacy (that commanded by the church of its clergy and monastics) than that woman is saved by the conjugal works themselves, by conjugal intercourse, by bearing children and the other duties? But what does St. Paul mean? Let the reader observe that faith is added, and that domestic duties without faith are not praised...Therefore, he requires especially faith, through which a woman receives the forgiveness of sins and justification. Then he adds a particular work of the calling, just as in every person a good work of a particular calling should follow faith."[26] In summary, the Lutheran Confessions know of no distinction or bifurcation of the natural ordering of God's creation. Furthermore, they make clear that in opposing this natural order, man is actually fighting against God's own desire for His creation. That was one of the major critiques to the Papal opposition to clerical marriage.

The Lutheran Confessions' understanding of marriage, in both its procreative and antidotal functions, is consistent with Martin Luther's understanding of marriage and marital relations. For example, Luther wrote in his lectures on Genesis (30:22-24), "Most married people do not desire children; in fact, they dislike them and hold that it is better to live without them because they are poor and do not have the wherewithal to support a family. This is true particularly of those who are given to idleness and laziness and flee from the sweat and labor of married life. But the purpose of marriage is not pleasure and ease but the procreation and education of children and the support of a family. This is truly an immense burden, full of great cares and labors. But that is why God created you: to be a husband or a wife and to learn to bear these molestations. People who do not like children are swine, dunces, and blockheads, not worthy to be called men and women, because they despise the blessing of God, the Creator and Author of marriage."[27] Positively stated, then, Luther was an outspoken advocate of the family and children. He understood the family as being the church's nursery where parents raise children for God's Kingdom.[28]

On the other hand, all that opposed God's desire for marriage, the family, and children, Luther also opposed. Although little known in recent years, Luther strongly denounced and condemned contraceptive practices. In his commentary on Genesis (38:8-10), Luther condemns the sin of Onan, not merely on the basis of disobedience or intent, but especially because of his "Sodomitic sin."[29] John Calvin, another renowned reformer, while disagreeing with Luther regarding some teachings of the faith, stood in accord with Luther and the historic church in this respect. In commenting on that same passage, Calvin remarked, "The purposeful spilling of semen outside of intercourse between man and woman is a monstrous thing. Purposely withdrawing from coitus, so that the seed drops on the ground, is twice as horrific. For this is to extinguish the hope of the human family and to kill before he is born the hoped-for offspring. This wickedness is here condemned by the Spirit in the most severe manner possible."[30]

While such statements might strike the modern-day reader as shocking and perhaps even as overly extreme, what is most insightful is the fact that these sorts of statements are actually the norm throughout the church's history (even among Lutherans and other Protestant theologians). The following list of post-reformation theologians who have opposed contraceptive practices is not exhaustive, but it should serve to show the church's uniform stance against such practices. This list includes such men as: Martin Bucer, Abraham Calovius, John Calvin, Franz Delitszch, Johann Gerhard, Martin Luther, Lukas Osiander, Charles Spurgeon, and many, many others.[31] Needless to say, this uniform Christian opposition to contraception (abortion goes without saying) continued into the 20th Century. Nevertheless, it was the societal rumblings of the previous century that ultimately culminated in the drastic change in belief and practice that occurred merely a few decades later.

Social Darwinism, Neo-Malthusianism, Margaret Sanger and the Revolutionary Thought of the 19th and Early 20th Centuries

As we have already seen, the human tendency to shy away from children and towards the isolation of marital (and extramarital) relations simply for the sake of pleasure apart from any procreative purpose, is not a modern phenomenon. This is more or less "par for the course" when it comes to human nature and pagan societies. In essence, then, the Enlightenment-influenced developments of the 19th Century were nothing new. Rather, they were a return to a pre-Christian, pagan worldview. Interestingly, it was this same period of time that also witnessed the return of cremation.[32]

As a brief aside, this chapter's treatment of contraception is somewhat arbitrary. The fact is that this issue is not an issue that enjoys an isolated existence. It is fundamentally connected to various other societal developments. We have already noted a temporal relationship in the reemergence of cremation. Nevertheless, I would argue that the church's change on these two issues is also related to its changed understanding of the relationship between the sexes (note societal and ecclesiastical changes on the role of women in society and particularly in the church), a heightened acceptance of homosexuality, an increase in body mutilation (so-called "body art") in the form of multiple piercings and extravagant tattoos, increased drug and alcohol abuse, increased obesity due to uncontrolled consumption, graphic violence in TV and films, the emergence of "extreme sports" and various forms of "acceptable" violence (MMA, etc.), and an overall devaluation of the physical body. While this might sound odd due to all the attention that is given to health and fitness in society, there is a common thread connecting these negative developments. Namely, the body and the activities related to it are increasingly viewed as merely the domain of human authority and not fundamentally as gifts of God. Thus, one might say that the physical has been devalued and left to abuse while man's freedom and "inner person" have received more and more attention. This correlates also with the rising influence of Eastern thought and religion in Western Society, man's separation from rural life, and a dramatic increase in communication technology (the emergence of "virtual" worlds, etc.) At this rate, we should not be surprised if some day we witness the reemergence of gladiatorial games, infanticide, and any number of now unthinkable practices.

Returning to our subject, what are the roots of the 20th Century birth control movement and the church's monumental change concerning contraception (and abortion, in the case of many denominations)? Bryan Hodge traces the philosophical foundations of this change to the advent, or perhaps reappearance, of various unchristian philosophies.[33] The impact of these philosophies, simply stated, is that they undermined the church's hold on the lives of people and left their minds fertile for the adoption of new ways of thinking their lives to novel ways of living. Thus, the stage was set for the likes of H.G. Wells, Henry H. Ellis, William Inge, Margaret Sanger, and the many other emerging opponents of marriage, family, and, indeed, traditionally free society.

Of course, the most out-spoken advocate for the "birth control" movement in America was Margaret Sanger. One of many children born to a skeptic father and a sickly, Catholic mother, Margaret went on to become the driving force behind the birth control movement (and even Planned Parenthood) in the United States and remained staunchly opposed to the enslaving teachings of the church throughout her life. Of course, positively put, birth control and the emergence of Planned Parenthood could be said to have finally given reproductive freedom to women and to have freed them from the shackles of motherhood, marriage, and their own biology. Nevertheless, there is a much darker side to the birth control movement and particularly of its main leader, Margaret Sanger.

No friend of church, family, or traditional government, Sanger associated freely in the early 1900s with Anarchists, Socialists, members of the Fabian Society, Malthusians, and other such dissident and revolutionary movements prevalent at that time. She was a member of the Rosicrucian Society, involved in occultist Cabalistic practices, had numerous affairs, was finally divorced from her husband for advocating (and practicing) "free love", and was dedicated to the eugenics movement of the early 20th Century, a movement which shared the same scientific and ideological underpinnings as the Nazis, which was a derivation of so-called "Social Darwinism," and which was in league with those who advocated the forced sterilization of the weak and feeble-minded in the United States. If that is not enough, she was once put on trial and fled the country after her paper, *The Woman Rebel*, published articles on assassination and renounced marriage.

Nevertheless, many revere Sanger as something of a secular saint, particularly for her role in spreading the "gospel" of birth control and establishing Planned Parenthood (predominately in the neighborhoods of minorities and those who were societally undesirable). Walter Wangerin of Valparaiso University wrote in the March 2010 Lutheran of the Evangelical Lutheran Church in America: "Margaret Sanger is my sister. For the nation's sake she established the first birth control clinic in the U.S. and was arrested for that audacity in 1916." Yet, despite Ms. Sanger's credentials and her less-than-commendable record, hers is the voice that ultimately preached to and prevailed among American society and its families. Even more, with the global, corporate nature of Planned Parenthood, one might even say that Sanger's legacy has extended far beyond her own lifetime accomplishments. Yes, almost perfectly in step with the creed of Sanger's *The Rebel Woman*[34] and the sort of anti-family, one-world society depicted by her influential friend and lover H.G. Wells,[35] many women have grown independent of marriage, family and motherhood altogether (often in exchange for greater dependence on the state). Even more remarkable in all of this, the church has largely turned a cold shoulder towards some nineteen centuries of pro-marriage, child, and family teaching, only to almost unquestionably embrace Sanger's message of birth control and liberation from traditional norms—and this without the smallest of whimpers.[36]

Notes

[17] Holmes, Michael W. *The Apostolic Fathers: Greek Texts and English Translations* (Grand Rapids, Michigan: Baker Books, 1999), 256-257; 324-325.

[18] Ibid., 256-257.

[19] Hodge, Bryan. *The Christian Case against Contraception* (Eugene, Oregon: Wipf & Stock, 2010), 14-19.

[20] Ibid., 2010), 16. Quotation cited as *Pan* 26.5.2.

[21] One of the questions commonly raised in association with birth control is whether or not the so-called "rhythm method" and other natural ways of controlling conception (aside from abstinence) are valid or not. Hodge quotes St. Augustine as he responded to certain practices of the heretical Manicheans. "Is it not you who used to warn us to ardently look for the period following purification of the menses when a woman is likely to conceive, and during that time refrain from intercourse, so that a soul would not be entangled in the flesh? From this it follows that you do not think marriage is to procreate children, but to satisfy carnal pleasure. Marriage, as the marriage tablets themselves proclaim, unites male and female for the procreation of children...he [who practices the rhythm method of the Manichees] ceases to make the woman a wife, and turns her into a prostitute, who when she has been given certain gifts, is joined to a man in order to satisfy his lust." *Christian Case against Contraception*, 23. Cited by Holmes as *Man.* 18-65.

[22] Ibid., 21-27.

[23] McCain, Paul, ed. AC XXIII. *Concordia: The Lutheran Confessions* (St. Louis: CPH, 2006), 46.

[24] Ibid., *Apology* XXIII, 211.

[25] Ibid., *Apology* XXIII, 211.

[26] Ibid., *Apology* XXIII, 214.

[27] Plass, Ewald, comp. *What Luther Says* (St. Louis: CPH, 1959), 907.

[28] *What Luther Says*, 907. "The best thing in married life, for the sake of which

everything ought to be suffered and done, is that fact that God gives children and commands us to bring them up to serve Him. To do this is the noblest and most precious work on earth, because nothing may be done which pleases God more than saving souls. If the need were to arise, all of us should be ready to die in order to bring a soul to God. So you see how rich in good works the estate of marriage is. God lays souls into the lap of married people, souls begotten from their own body, on which they may practice all Christian works. For when they teach their children the Gospel, parents are certainly their apostles, bishops, and ministers."

[29] Charles Provan cites Luther in *The Bible and Birth Control* (Monongahela, Penn.: Zimmer Printing, 1989), 80-81. Luther refers to Onan and his deed in the following ways: "...the exceedingly foul deed of Onan, the basest of wretches..." "Onan must have been a malicious and incorrigible scoundrel. This is a most disgraceful sin. It is far more atrocious than incest and adultery. We call it unchastity, yes, a Sodomitic sin. For Onan goes in to her; that is, he lies with her and copulates, and when it comes to the point of insemination, spills the semen, lest the woman conceive. Surely at such a time the order of nature established by God in procreation should be followed...He [Onan] preferred polluting himself with a most disgraceful sin to raising up offspring for his brother. Therefore Onan, unwilling to perform this obligation, spilled his seed. That was a sin far greater than adultery or incest, and it provoked God to such fierce wrath that He destroyed him immediately."

[30] Hodge. *Christian Case*, 29. Quoted from Calvin, *Commentaries on Genesis*, 38:8-10.

[31] Ibid., 35-38. Hodge mentions some 120 theologians throughout history who have opposed contraception. Provan (pp. 63-93) also includes a similar list of some 80-plus names from Reformation times to the present.

[32] Schmidt, Alvin J. *Dust to Dust or Ashes to Ashes? A Biblical and Christian Examination of Cremation* (Salisbury, MA: Regina Orthodoxy Press Inc., 2005), 19-21.

[33] In order to avoid an extended philosophical discourse, I want to briefly note that these philosophies, specifically, naturalism, relativism, hedonism, and romanticism, all define human life and values according to human, subjective standards and eliminate the need for any divine, objective norm for human life (i.e. Scripture). Thus, man is left to his own whims and desires which cannot be checked by any outside authority. See *Case Against Contraception*, pages 40-50, for further discussion.

[34] "Rebel women claim the following Rights: The Right to be Lazy. The Right to be an Unmarried Mother. The Right to Destroy. The Right to Create. The Right to Live and the Right to Love." Quoted from Madeline Gray's *Margaret Sanger* (New York: Richard Marek Publishers, 1979), 72.

[35] Michael Perry (editor of this edition of *The Pivot of Civilization*) makes the following comment on Wells' ideas of a World State and universal, coerced population control: "Wells became one of the first scientific writers to advocate global population control—today an all too progressive cause. According to him, controlling births would be how the World State would rid itself of 'rejected' whites and Asians as well as the 'vast proportion of the black and brown races'...At the same time that it was checking 'the procreation of base and servile types.,' the World State would ensure of the procreation of those who were 'fine, efficient and beautiful.' Do not forget that in a Wellsian World State there would

be no place to flee from birth controllers, no distant corner where 'rejected' races and individuals could simply raise a family in peace..." pg. 35.

[36] For further reading on Sanger and Planned Parenthood, I would also recommend George Grant's *Grand Illusions: The Legacy of Planned Parenthood* (Franklin, TN: Adroit Press, 1992), and *Blessed are the Barren* (San Francisco: Ignatius Press, 1991), by Robert Marshall and Charles Donovan. These books are particularly noteworthy as they note the presence and influence of Planned Parenthood in the United States' public school system, its de facto institutionalization by the U.S. government, and its opposition to traditional and Christian family values. Furthermore, they show the harmful side of various forms of birth control, something that is often completely ignored by proponents of sexual freedom and family planning.

Christianity, Children, and Contraception
Part III

Christian News, May 3, 2010

Christianity's Response to Such Social Developments

Not only was the church's minimal response to Sanger and company remarkable in its general absence, even more remarkable is the church's general complicity in the rise of Planned Parenthood and the overall approval given to contraceptive methods. This stems from at least three different factors. First, there is no doubt that Planned Parenthood and its forerunner publication, *The Birth Control Review*, targeted the church to implement its contraceptive, racist, and anti-family programs. Along these lines, George Grant writes the following about Sanger's racist birth control tactics through her "Negro Project" among that particular population:

"In order to remedy this 'dysgenic horror story' (referring to the 'problem' of 'careless breeding' among this race), the project aimed to hire three or four 'Colored Ministers, preferably with social-service backgrounds, and with engaging personalities' to travel to various Black enclaves and propagandize for birth control. 'The most successful educational approach to the Negro,' Margaret wrote sometime later, 'is through a religious appeal. We do not want word to go out that we want to exterminate the Negro population and the Minister is the man who can straighten out that idea if it ever occurs to any of their more rebellious members.'"[37]

Of course, this is not the only instance when the birth control movement made great headway through the tacit or explicit support of the church. The second factor for the movement's success via the church was the willing support of church leadership itself. From the movement's infancy, it enjoyed a certain amount of ecclesial support. For example, the prominent English clergyman and eugenist, William R. Inge, Dean of St. Paul's Cathedral in London, was praised by Sanger in a 1921 issue of the *Birth Control Review* as "A Great Churchman on Birth Control." Certainly, when an enemy of the church is praising someone as "a great churchman," red flags should go up.

Nevertheless, such outspoken approval of theretofore unheard of teachings within the church would only increase from its relatively isolated and scattered beginnings. In 1930, the first official "breakthrough" for Margaret Sanger and company occurred (from the perspective of historic Christianity, "breakdown" might be more accurate). At the 1930 Lambeth Conference, the Anglican Church officially sanctioned the use of contraception with the following statement: "Nevertheless in those cases where there is such a clearly felt moral obligation to limit or avoid parenthood, and where there is a morally sound reason for avoiding complete abstinence, the Conference agrees that other methods may be used, provided that this is done in the light of the same Christian principles"[38] This ruling overturned the 1908 verdict of the same council that had banned any such practice. Even more, it was the first breach in the dam long held by Christendom. In relatively short order most major denominations within the United States would assert the same judgment on the matter, casting a blind eye to church history and any traditional exegetical arguments against contraception and the wrongful use of sexual relations.

Some years later Planned Parenthood would even find an unlikely friend in the otherwise conservative Lutheran theologian (LCMS) and ethics professor, Alfred Rehwinkel, through his book *Planned Parenthood and Birth Control in the Light of Christian Ethics*. This book, published by Concordia Publishing House in 1959, helped to neutralize any remaining resistance within the conservative Lutheran Church—Missouri Synod to a once strongly forbidden practice.[39] Considering the fact that the LCMS in official publications as recently as the 1930s had condemned contraception and was also on record for calling Margaret Sanger a "she-devil", this was a most remarkable change.[40]

Even the witness of the Roman Catholic Church in America was undermined and subverted by those within its own ranks. The National Catholic Welfare Council (NCWC), for example, gave up opposition to birth control in the 1960s as Randy Engel notes. She writes: "Up until the late 1950s, the NCWC held the line on birth control and population control. However, by the mid-1960s this opposition had been severely eroded as is evidenced by the official attendance of Murder, Inc., (i.e., Planned Parenthood-World Population) at NCWC Family Life functions…This tragic breakdown within the NCWC on family life issues and sexual morality mirrored the breakdown in opposition to birth control and population control among key American prelates including Cardinals Spellman of New York, Cushing of Boston, Meyer of Chicago, Dearden of Detroit and Krol of Philadelphia, each of whom made his own private 'arrangements' to accommodate State-sponsored birth control programs."[41]

Furthermore, it should be noted that leadership within the Catholic Church harbored the unethical and immoral Dr. John Rock as he performed ex-utero abortions, did chemical steroid experiments (connected with the development of the Pill) upon female mental patients of State hospitals in Massachusetts, and finally performed his most significant research for the Pill on indigent and uneducated Puerto Rican women (against the opposition of the Puerto Rican Catholic community, but with the support of key United States Catholic leaders). Engel writes about this dangerous, poorly performed, and unethical research:

"At the end of the well-publicized trials, during which only 132 women out of hundreds recruited for the study stayed with the Pill for a year or more, Rock pronounced the Pill to be both safe and effective. He labeled the oral steroids 'natural and physiological.' The mass media also pronounced the Pill to be safe and effective. Equally gullible Catholics at Notre Dame and Catholic University in Washington, D.C. joined the Malthusian chorus—the Pill was safe and effective. Meanwhile, the Puerto Rican authorities quietly buried the bodies of three women who had died from the Pill. Local physicians struggled with the serious complications that many of the women had suffered while on the potent drug."[42]

The third, and perhaps most important factor in all of this, was the behavior of the clergy themselves. After all, if the clergy of a church stand firm on a particular issue and live according to that particular teaching, the church is much more likely to withstand attacks from without and within. Nevertheless, it seems clear that the church's clergy did not maintain the church's opposition to contraception when the church came under attack. In an article titled "Children of the Reformation: A Short and Surprising History of Protestantism and Contraception," Allan Carlson makes the harsh indictment that it was Protestantism's clergy that failed to hold the line against contraception and which failed to maintain its own high standard for the Protestant family (and particularly the pastor's family).[43]

In his article, Carlson traces the family size within the clergy of the Anglican Church. He notes, for example, that "as late as 1874, the average Anglican clergyman in England still had 5.2 living children. In 1911, however, just three years after the bishops had condemned contraception, the new census of England showed that the average family size of Anglican clergy had fallen to only 2.3 children, a stunning decline of 55 percent. The British Malthusian League—a strong advocate of contraception—had a field day exposing what it called the hypocrisy of the priests."[44] Obviously, one does not have to have any sort of an advanced degree to note that if the clergy do not believe and practice something themselves, the people will not be long in following. Furthermore, the 1930 Lambeth Conference only proved that clergy and churches have the remarkable propensity to justify and sanctify their own errant practices with "official church rulings."

Carlson does not stop his critique with the Anglican clergy, though. He next turns his attention to the clergy of the Lutheran Church—Missouri Synod. He notes: "In the very conservative Lutheran Church—Missouri Synod, the average pastor in 1890 had 6.5 children. The number fell to 3.7 children in 1920, 42 percent below the 1890 number...During the 1930s, the Missouri Synod quietly dropped its campaign against the Birth Control League of America." Carlson then goes on to say that in the 1940s Alfred

Rehwinkel concluded that "Luther had simply been wrong. God's words in Genesis 1:28—'Be fruitful and multiply and fill the earth'—were not a command; they were merely a blessing, an optional one at that."[45]

Alan Graebner notes similar developments within the general membership of the Lutheran Church—Missouri Synod in an essay titled "Birth Control and the Lutherans." Of particular interest is a graph he includes which charts the correspondence between the Missouri Synod's own baptismal rate (roughly equivalent to whatever its birth rate might have been) and the overall birthrate within the United States from 1910 to 1970.[46] The overall correspondence between the Missouri Synod and American Society, in general, is astonishing. The only real difference is that whether or not the United States' birthrate increased or decreased, the Missouri Synod always averaged a slightly greater baptismal rate than the American birthrate. The conclusion, though certainly not scientific, is that despite Missouri's outspokenness against societal developments, it was very much influenced by them. Even more, in light of Carlson's article, this was likely linked with the unwillingness of the Missouri Synod's own clergy to practice what they advocated. Such contradictions between teaching and practice can also be seen in the Catholic Church.[47]

The Christian, Abortion, and Birth Control in the 21st Century

In recent years, the Christian discussion concerning birth control has largely centered around which methods are acceptable and which are not. This chapter has argued that such questions are actually not the correct questions for Christian couples to be asking. Rather, in light of the teachings of Scripture and the church's long-held understanding of sex and its proper purpose, Christian couples might do well to ask themselves if they should actually be engaging in any contraceptive practices whatsoever.

Nevertheless, human nature always desires to want to know the boundary of what is still acceptable and what is too far—this as opposed to asking what is most God-pleasing and striving in that direction. It is with that in mind that I am including the following brief discussion on what birth control methods might be allowable and why.

First of all, we should note that birth control essentially begins with the premise that pregnancy is a bad thing (whether generally or for a period of time). Thus, the better alternative to pregnancy is temporary or permanent barrenness and sterility. This is the basic message of all birth control methods. Some declare that the biology of a woman's body must be chemically altered. Some promote the medically and ethically questionable practices of prescribing medicine and chemical-altering procedures (i.e. implants, shots, etc.) to otherwise healthy women with the intention of eliminating the "illnesses" of fertility and womanhood. Other methods target the man's seed and seek to poison it, kill it, and otherwise prevent it from doing what God created it to do. Such words as "spermicide" help to clarify how evil these swimming gametes must be. Of course, many of these methods are neither guaranteed to stop the overly aggressive seed from finding the target of its desire nor can they completely stop the egg that has somehow managed to be released despite an apparent chemical conspiracy against it. Thus, a backup plan becomes necessary, one that can thwart implantation of the now-fertilized egg (i.e. a unique human life). Pretty much every chemical method (including the Pill) has the built-in ability to end pregnancy in this way. While I will admit that this point is greatly debated, for those still debating the merits of this or that form of birth control, consider the following about chemical birth control (i.e. the Pill):

• John Wilks concludes in his article, "The Impact of the Pill on Implantation Factors—New Research Findings": "Some may seek to discount the interceptive/ abortifacient capacity of the pill. For three reasons, this would be a scientifically precarious position to adopt. First, I am of the view that the preceding evidence (of his article) strongly argues the case in favor of the pill possessing an interceptive/abortifacient capacity...Second, even researchers view as the new arena of 'contraceptive' research the interrelated system of implantation factors...Third, and most tellingly, the abortifacient capacity of the pill is recognized by those who support abortion. Consider the following, taking from the *Guttmacher Report*. 'The best scientific evidence suggests that ECP's [emergency contraceptive pill] most often work by suppressing ovulation. But depending on the timing of intercourse in relation to a woman's hormonal cycle, they—as is the case with all hormonal contraceptive methods—also may prevent pregnancy either by preventing fertilization or by preventing implantation of a fertilized egg in the uterus.' Need any more be said?"[48]

• Walter L. Larimore, M.D. makes a similar conclusion in "The Abortifacient Effect of the Birth Control Pill and the Principle of 'Double Effect.'" He writes: "Finally, based upon the principle of double effect, it appears reasonable to conclude that the Pill should not be used or recommended to those who believe life begins at conception unless and until the Pill is proven not to be an abortifacient...Until such proof is available, one way or the other, the Pill should be considered a possible cause of death to pre-born children. It is reasonable to hypothesize that if the Pill was in development today and if the pre-born child was considered truly human under the law, then it would be unlikely that the FDA would allow the Pill to be approved for public use until the manufacturers had studied and established whether or not the Pill causes the death of pre-born children."[49]

I will reiterate the fact that the abortifacient nature of the Pill is a matter of debate. Nevertheless, the concern about the Pill's exact mechanism of preventing conception/ending a pregnancy and the likelihood of the same occurring, should be reason enough for Christian couples to question use of the Pill and, perhaps even better, to avoid it all together.

Thus, for those who still insist that they have to have "sexual freedom" within marriage or otherwise (or should we call this "slavery to desire?"), they are left with taking temperatures and charting days on a calendar or are relegated to using some sort of a barrier method. Why? Once again this is because the possibility of conception is something that is seen as a curse and not as a blessing.

Interestingly enough, abstinence is thought to be simply too lofty a concept for us highly-developed humans these days. We are taught in school that it is impossible to practice. "Enjoy yourself, but be safe," is the message.

In the church's endorsement of birth control and its own obsession with better marital sex the distinct impression is also given that self-control is utterly impossible for men and women. A professor even told me once that the basic problem with my thinking (for mentioning that the church needs to revisit the issue of birth control) is that I'm an idealist. The implication is that anyone who is not married is prone to the grave error of idealism. "Experience" must be our true guide in such matters. He confirmed this by continuing, "You see, the basic problem is that men don't have enough self control." I have since wondered if this reality should cause us to return more to prayer and perhaps put in a special order for the fruit that the Holy Spirit has neglected so much in recent decades (see Galatians 5:22-23). We might also ask, if married couples are considered unable to practice self-control, is it any wonder that unmarried youth show the same tendency?

Conclusion

This chapter has argued that the church of the 20th Century, by and large, abandoned both Scripture and the historic church's understanding of procreation, sex, and contraception. It has attempted to further show that not only has the church turned away from its own Scriptural norm, but it has embraced pagan and unchristian practices and understandings relating to these issues. Most remarkably, Christians seem wholly unaware of this fact. The church's indictment of being 'ahistorical' (unaware of and disconnected from its own history) seems to be of little concern. It might further be argued that this is only one area wherein the historic church's understanding of life, family, the body, and God's will with regard to these matters has been largely forgotten.

Where does that leave us? I would argue that it is high time that Christians begin to reexamine these issues, not in the light of recent doctrinal resolutions by this synod or that denomination, but in an honest return to the teachings of Scripture and perhaps in also allowing the "democracy of the dead" to help guide our thinking. After all, while contemporary Christianity may feel that it is presently in good company—if one considers that of Margaret Sanger, H.G. Wells, and such figures to be such—contemporary Christianity certainly is not able to make the claim that it stands in good company within the wider scope of history. In fact, one would get the idea that we stand relatively isolated. That is, unless being associated with pagan ways of life and errant Christian sects makes for edifying companionship.

Notes

[37] Grant. *Grand Illusions*, 97. The quotations are taken from Linda Gordon's Woman's Body, Woman's Right: A Social History of Birth Control in America (New York: Penguin Books, 1976), 332-333.

[38] Hodge. *Christian Case*, 49. Quoted from Resolution 15 of that conference's proceedings.

[39] Rehwinkel, Alfred M. *Planned Parenthood and Birth Control in the Light of Christian Ethics* (St. Louis: CPH, 1959).

[40] This reference was found quoted in Alan Graebner's essay, "Birth Control

and the Lutherans" as printed in *Women in American Religion* (Philadelphia: University of Pennsylvania Press, 1980), 237.

[41] Engel, Randy. *The Rite of Sodomy* (Export, Pennsylvania: New Engel Publishing, 2006), 558-559.

[42] Ibid., 694-696.

[43] Carlson, Allan. "Children of the Reformation: A Short and Surprising History of Protestantism and Contraception." *Touchstone* (May 2007), 24. Carlson writes: **"Please note: As in England, so in America, the change in clerical family behavior came before the change in doctrine."**

[44] Ibid., 20-25. Alan Graebner in "Birth Control and the Lutherans" (250-251) also notes this Missouri phenomenon and traces the gradual decline in clergy family size up until 1950 at which time the average pastor's family was down to only three children.

[45] Carlson. "Children of the Reformation," 24.

[46] Graebner. "Birth Control," 247.

[47] Marshall and Donovan. *Blessed are the Barren*, 170-171.

[48] Pharm, John B. "The Impact of the Pill on Implantation Factors—New Research Findings" *Ethics & Medicine* 16:1, 2000, 20-21.

[49] Larimore, Walter L. "The Abortifacient Effect of the Birth Control Pill and the Principle of 'Double Effect' *Ethics & Medicine* 16:1, 2000, 28-29. See also: : "Using the Birth Control Pill Is Ethically Unacceptable" an essay by Walter L. Larimore, M.D. and Randy Alcorn, M.A. included in the book *A Reproductive Revolution: A Christian Appraisal of Sexuality, Reproductive Technologies, and the Family* (Grand Rapids: Eerdmans, 2000), 179-191, edited by John F. Kilner, Paige C. Cunningham, and W. David Hager; Alcorn, Randy. *Prolife Answers to Prochoice Arguments* (Sisters, Oregon: Multnomah Publishers, 2000), 329-342.

Mrs. Walter A. Maier, wife of the Lutheran Hour speaker with Pastor Otten and six of the Otten children at the dedication of the Maier study at the Concordia Historical Institute, St. Louis, Missouri, May 25, 1981. Photo from p. 131 of *Walter A. Maier Still Speaks - Missouri and the World Should Listen.* Published by Lutheran News in 2008. Dr. Walter A. Maier wrote *For Better Not For Worse* mentioned on pp. 25, 26, 33, 34, 37, 63, 84, 102, 103, 153, 235, 245, 248 311-313, and 366 of this book. Dr. Maier was the most public opponent of birth control in the Lutheran Church – Missouri Synod.

III

BIRTH CONTROL

Real Church Growth
Promoting Church Growth By Returning To Luther's And The LCMS's Former And Scriptural Position On Birth Control

Overture Submitted to 2010 Lutheran Church-Missouri Synod Convention

Whereas, Most major Protestant denomination along with the Roman Catholic Church and Orthodox Church until the 1930s opposed birth control; and

Whereas, The Bible prohibits birth control (see "Nine Reasons Why the Bible Prohibits Birth Control" by Charles Provan, *Christian News*, February 28, 1988, reprinted in *The Bible and Birth Control*); and

Whereas, Martin Luther strongly condemned birth control. Luther in his comments on Genesis 38:9, 10 (American Edition, p. 21): "Accordingly, it was a most disgraceful crime to produce semen and excite the woman and frustrate her at that very moment. He was inflamed with the basest spite and hatred. Therefore he did not allow himself to be compelled to hear the intolerable slavery. Consequently, he deserved to be killed by God. He committed an evil deed. Therefore God punished him," and

Whereas, John H. C. Fritz in his *Pastoral Theology*, long used as a textbook in LCMS seminaries, shows that birth control "is sinful." "It is a willfully setting aside of God's will and command, Gen. 1,28; 1 Tim. 5:15, 2,15; Gen. 8, 9, 10." (p. 177); and

Whereas, Lutheran Hour speaker Walter Maier in a chapter titled "The Blight of Birth Control" in his marriage manual "*For Better Not For Worse*" shows that Birth Control is sinful and contrary to the Bible (pp. 377-421); and

Whereas, A major factor in the decline of church growth is the ever decreasing size of the families of pastors and church members; therefore be it

Resolved, That the 2010 convention of the LCMS declare that the LCMS still accepts the scriptural position of Martin Luther on birth control and the position long promoted in the LCMS by such orthodox LCMS theologians as John H.C. Fritz, Walter Maier, Martin Nauman, Theodore Laetch and many others.

Trinity Lutheran Church,
New Haven, Missouri

LCMS convention took no action.

This overture was not considered at the LCMS's 2010 convention. A convention committee said the LCMS has never taken a stand on birth control. This book shows that the LCMS, prior to the 1950s, strongly opposed birth control.

The Bible's View of Birth Control
By Charles D. Provan
Christian News, February 29, 1988

Many Christians today have not even considered the question, "What does God think of birth control?" It is a question "too stupid to even consider" in the eyes of most. After all, birth control is an American social custom, practiced by most married couples in our country, and in most "civilized countries," too.

But just because Americans think birth control is morally acceptable does not make birth control right in the eyes of God. Our study here will seek to lay a solid Biblical basis for opposition to birth control. You may be surprised to find that the Bible does in fact say quite a bit about this widespread custom – all of it negative. What we say here should not be viewed as a new idea, for it is a fact that the Christian church, since its inception, has consistently opposed birth control as a great evil. This opposition continued quite strongly down into this present century, when birth control carried the day. Some theologians spoke out against the limiting of children by Christians until fairly recent times. And now, opposition to birth control is almost dead. We hope this article will help to rekindle it, and lead to God bestowing many blessings upon his people: wonderful children!

Before you begin, please be aware of the fact that this paper quotes quite a few Scripture verses which mention sexual matters. We have not used these verses to offend people, but have used them to illustrate various points in our argument. Please do not become upset. Rather, understand that the Bible speaks plainly of these matters. Many do not realize that all the members of Israel, including children, were commanded to hear the entire Mosaic Law. This law contains many blunt sexual matters, matters about which all Israel was to be informed. And this is why we feel free to talk about them, in a proper manner.

Some may think that we quote the Old Testament too much. However, we do not feel bad about this, since the New Testament itself contains some sixteen hundred references to the Old Testament. Further, the Church of Christ is "built upon the foundation of the apostles and prophets," as Paul says in Ephesians 2:20. In addition, in 1 Corinthians 5:1, Paul gets his rules on sexual matters right out of the Mosaic Law (Lev. 18:8), and he was writing to converted Gentiles! As Martin Luther says, God gave us His holy Law "to keep men from open outbreaks of sin" and to "teach us the works which are really pleasing to God." (*Small Catechism*, Question 159).

All Scripture quotes are from the *New American Standard Version of the Bible*. A few of the verses we have cited are margin translations of the same version.

Reason Number One
Be Fruitful and Multiply – (Genesis 1:27-28)

Genesis 1:27-28
"And God created man in His own image, in the image of God He created him; male and female He created them. ²⁸And God blessed them; and God said to them, 'Be fruitful and multiply, and fill the earth, and subdue it; and rule over the fish of the sea and over the birds of the sky, and over every living thing that moves on the earth.'"

Christians should take note of the fact that the first listed command to mankind was "Be fruitful and multiply." This command is repeated over and over again in the Bible (for instance, Genesis 9:1 and 35:11). Our point is this: this is a command of God, indeed, the first command to a married couple. Birth control obviously involves disobedience to this command, for birth control attempts to prevent being fruitful and multiplying. Therefore birth control is wrong, because it involves disobedience to the word of God. Nowhere is this command done away with in the entire Bible; therefore it still remains valid for us today.

Martin Luther had this to say in regard to Genesis 1:28: "He has created male and female and has blessed them that they might be fruitful." (*Luther's Works*, Vol. 5, p. 329)

On this same occasion Luther said, ". . . fertility was regarded as an extraordinary blessing and a special gift of God, as is clear from Deut. 28:4, where Moses numbers fertility among the blessings. 'There will not be a barren woman among you,' he says (cf. Ex. 23:26). We do not regard this so highly today. Although we like and desire it in cattle, yet in the human race there are few who regard a woman's fertility as a blessing. Indeed, there are many who have an aversion to fertility and regard sterility as a special blessing. Surely this is also contrary to nature. Much less is it pious and saintly. For this affection has been implanted by God in man's nature, so that it desires its increase and multiplication. Accordingly, it is inhuman and godless to have a loathing for offspring. Thus someone recently called his wife a sow, since she gave birth rather often. The good for nothing and impure fellow! The saintly fathers did not feel like this at all; for they acknowledged a fruitful wife as a special blessing of God and, on the other hand, regarded sterility as a curse. And this judgment flowed from the Word of God in Gen. 1;28, where He said; 'Be fruitful and multiply.'" "From this they understood that children are a gift of God." (*Luther's Works*, Vol. 5, p. 325).

In Matthew 19:1-9, Jesus was questioned by the Pharisees concerning marriage and divorce. The Pharisees allowed divorce for a multitude of stupid reasons. Jesus corrected their view by calling their attention to Gen. 1:27 and 2:24, telling the Pharisees that if they wanted to see what God expected in a marriage, they should get their rules from the way God set up marriage in "the beginning." Please note that marriage as invented by God "in the beginning" was set up to "be fruitful and multiply" – NOT to "be sterile"!

Many today will say, "But I cannot afford to have lots of children, and so I must practice birth control. If I don't, I will be poor, and my children will be stuck in grinding poverty." Listen to what Martin Luther has to say on this subject: "Although it is very easy to marry a wife, it is very difficult to support her along with the children and the household. Accordingly, no one notices this faith of Jacob. Indeed, many hate fertility in a wife for the sole reason that the offspring must be supported and brought up. For this is what they commonly say: 'Why should I marry a wife when I am a pauper and a beggar? I would rather bear the burden of poverty alone and not load myself with misery and want.' But this blame is unjustly fastened on marriage and fruitfulness. Indeed, you are indicting your unbelief by distrusting God's goodness, and you are bringing greater misery upon yourself by disparaging God's blessing. For if you had trust in God's grace and promises, you would undoubtedly be supported. But because you do not hope in the Lord, you will never prosper." (Luther's Works, Vol. 5, p. 332)

We Christians worship the great and powerful Lord who created the entire world. Can we truly believe that if we obey Him in this matter of being fruitful and multiplying, He will desert us? This idea is truly foreign to the Bible. God is not obligated to give us a Cadillac, but He promises to give us food and clothing and shelter. Ps. 37:25 says, "I have been young, and now I am old; yet I have not seen the righteous forsaken or his descendants begging bread." And Jesus says in Matt. 6:33, "But seek first His kingdom and His righteousness; and all these things shall be added to you." Our dedication to God should be that of Daniel's three friends, who said, ". . . our God whom we serve is able to deliver us from the furnace of blazing fire; and He will deliver us out of your hand, O king. But even if He does not, let it be known to you, O king, that we are not going to serve your gods or worship the golden image that you have set up." (Dan 3:17-18)

Reason Number Two
Children Are A Blessing From God: The More the Better
(Psalm 127:3-5, 1 Chronicles 25:4-5 and 26:4-5)

Psalm 127:3-5

"Behold, children are a gift of the Lord; the fruit of the womb is a reward. [4]Like arrows in the hand of a warrior, so are the children of one's youth. [5]How blessed is the man whose quiver is full of them; they shall not be ashamed, when they speak with their enemies in the gate."

1 Chronicles 25:4-5

"Of Heman, the sons of Heman: Bukkiah, Mattaniah, Uzziel, Shebuel and Jerimoth, Hananiah, Hanani, Eliathah, Giddalti and Romamti-ezer, Joshbekashah, Mallothi, Hothir, Mahazioth. [5]All these were the sons of Heman the king's seer to exalt him according to the words of God, for God gave fourteen sons and three daughters to Heman."

1 Chronicles 26:4-5

"And Obed-edom had sons: Shemaiah the first-born, Jehozabad the second, Joah the third, Sacar the fourth, Nethanel the fifth. ⁵Ammiel the sixth, Issachar the seventh, and Peullethai the eighth; God had indeed blessed him."

According to Holy Scripture in Ps. 127:5, "How blessed is the man whose quiver is full of them." Children (and the more the better), are a blessing from God. What this has to do with birth control is plain to see: birth control seeks to prevent children from being conceived, thereby preventing children from being born. This act prevents blessings of God from being given to people. If some would say: "Those kinds of blessings I don't want," recall the story of Esau in Gen. 24:29-34. God gave Esau a blessing (his birthright), and Esau sold it to his brother Jacob for a bowl of stew! Genesis says that by this act Esau "despised" the blessing of God. What does Hebrews 12:16 have to say about Esau? It says that Esau was "a godless person . . . who sold his own birthright for a single meal." Some Christians today have been so influenced by our godless materialistic culture that their view of children is the same as that of the world: "children are an economic drain –they make you poor – they limit economic progress – they prevent women from reaching their potential." This is not what the Bible says. The Bible says in 1 Chron. 25:5 that "God gave fourteen sons and three daughters to Heman" "to exalt him." (It does not say, "to degrade him" or "to make him disgustingly poor," which is what our modern birth control advocates might have written, had they and not the Holy Spirit been in charge of writing the Bible!) The Holy Sprit also wrote in 1 Chron. 26:4 that "God had indeed blessed" Obededom by giving him eight sons! Planned Parenthood or some of our modern so-called "Christian Sex Manuals" might have used Obededom as a horror story for "overpopulation."

By the way, I have heard of people who say that they have a "quiver full of children" by having three or five children "because back in ancient times that was how many arrows soldiers carried in their quivers." I am not aware of the source of this amazing and ridiculous viewpoint, which may be overthrown "out of the mouths of babes and sucklings." Just go up to a little boy or girl and ask them this question: "If you were a soldier, and you were going to be in a battle with the fierce enemy, how many arrows would you put in your quiver?" The answer will be "piles and piles of arrows" or "bunches and bunches of arrows." So children can interpret Ps. 127:45 better than people who already are in favor of birth control. "Like arrows in the hand of a warrior, so are the children of one's youth. How blessed is the man whose quiver is full of them. . ." That passage obviously means that the more children a believing couple has, the better. The number of children with which a couple is blessed should be determined by God, not birth control. Dr. Luther had this to say concerning Ps. 127: "This passage (Gen. 9:1), moreover, leads us to believe that children are a gift of God and come solely through the blessing of God, just as Ps. 127:3 shows. The heathen, who have not been instructed by the Word of God, believe that the propagation of the human race happens partly by nature, partly by accident, especially since those who are regarded as most suited for procreation often fail to have children. Therefore the heathen do not thank God for this gift, nor do they receive their children as the gift of God." (*Luther's Works*, Vol. 2, p. 132) If Martin Luther were alive today, would he not disapprove of many Christians who view children as a bad thing, and so practice birth control to prevent God from sending more blessings to them? If God wanted to bless Christians by sending them a house to live in, would people practice "house-control" and refuse the house? We think not. And we are not aware of any people who would turn down God if he wanted to reward them with money, either. But when it comes to children, Christian principles change as if by magic! But truly Scriptural principles do not change at all. Therefore we Christians should willingly receive the blessings which God has for us, and not try to prevent them.

Reason Number Three
Childlessness Is An Unfortunate Thing
(Hosea 9:10-17, Exodus 23:25-26, Deuteronomy 7:13-14)

Hosea 9:10-17

"I found Israel like grapes in the wilderness; I saw your forefathers as the earliest fruit on the fig tree in its first season. But they came to Baal-peor and devoted themselves to shame, and they became as detestable as that which they loved. [11]As for Ephraim, their glory will fly away like a bird – No birth, no pregnancy, and no conception! [12]Though they bring up their children, yet I will bereave them until not a man is left. Yes, woe to them indeed when I depart from them! [13]Ephraim, as I have seen is planted in a pleasant meadow like Tyre; but Ephraim will bring out his children for slaughter. [14]Give them, O Lord – what will Thou give? Give them a miscarrying womb and dry breasts. [15]All their evil is at Gilgal; Indeed I came to hate them there! Because of the wickedness of their deeds I will drive them out of My house! I will love them no more; All their princes are rebels. [16]Ephraim is stricken, their root is dried up, they will bear no fruit. Even though they bear children, I will slay the precious ones of their womb. [17]My God will cast them away because they have not listened to Him; and they will be wanderers among the nations."

Exodus 23:25-26

"But you shall serve the LORD your God, and He will bless your bread and your water; and I will remove sickness from your midst. [26]There shall be no one miscarrying or barren in your land; I will fulfill the number of your days."

Deuteronomy 7:13-14

"And He will love you and bless you and multiply you; He will also bless the fruit of your womb and the fruit of your ground, your grain and your new wine and your oil, the increase of your herd and the young of your flock, in the land which He swore to your forefathers to give you. [14]You shall be blessed above all peoples; there shall be no male or female barren among you or among your cattle."

When God decided to punish the corrupt nation of Israel some twenty-six hundred years ago, how did he do it? He prevented conception, pregnancy and childbirth, and killed the children who survived. God views childlessness or fewer children than possible as a negative occurrence, something which he uses as a punishment. Doesn't it say a lot about our dying and impotent culture, which welcomes birth control (with its resultant few or no children) as a "great scientific achievement" and a "blessing to mankind?" Birth control brings about a lamentable catastrophe according to the Bible!

Commenting on Genesis 17, Luther had this to say about sterility, ". . . saintly women have always regarded childbirth as a great sign of grace. Rachel is rude and exceedingly irksome to her husband when she says (Gen. 30:1): 'give me children, or I shall die!' She makes it clear that she will die of grief because she sees that barrenness is a sign of wrath. And in Ps. 127:3 there is a glorious eulogy of offspring: 'Lo, sons are a heritage from the Lord the fruit of the womb a reward (that is, a gift of God).' Surely it is a magnificent thing that children are a gift of God! Therefore Hannah laments so pitiably (1 Sam. 1:10), and John's aged mother Elizabeth leaps for joy and exults (Luke 1:25): 'The Lord has taken away my reproach.' Thus when the world was still in a better state, barrenness was considered a sign of wrath but childbirth was considered a sign of grace. Because of the abuses of lust, however, this remnant of the divine blessing gradually began to be obscured even among the Jews, just as today you could find many greedy men who regard numerous offspring as a punishment. Saintly mothers, however, have always regarded this gift – when they are prolific – as a great honor, just as, conversely, they have regarded barrenness as a sign of wrath and as a reproach." (*Luther's Works*, Vol. 3, p 134-135)

Moving on to the other Scripture passages in our list, we can see that God promised great blessings to Israel, among them (Ex. 3:25-26) the negating of sickness, miscarriages and barrenness. Christians and heathen both view sickness as bad, and Christians view miscarriages (at least caused miscarriages, that is, abortions) as bad. But when it comes to deliberately causing one's own sterility (whether temporary or permanent, via birth control), most Christians unite with the heathen and declare sterility a good thing! As for Moses, he clearly views sickness, miscarriages and sterility as bad.

Deuteronomy 7:12-13 is even more direct. Moses says, "God will love you and bless you and multiply you; He will also bless the fruit of your womb . . . You shall be blessed above all peoples; there shall be no male or female barren among you . . ." Once again we see barrenness, male or female, as a bad thing. Since barrenness is bad and undesirable, so is birth control, since birth control is temporary or permanent sterility.

Yet, in our culture, barrenness is "no big deal," and people are always attempting to tell sterile couples that "everything is all right." But everything is not all right! Listen to what Martin Luther had to say, commenting upon Rachel's' great desire to have children: ". . . from this it is clear that the very saintly women were not lustful but were desirous of offspring and the blessing. For this was the cause of envy in Rachel, who, if she had been like other women whom our age has produced in large numbers, would have said: 'What is it to me whether I bear children or not? Provided that I remain the mother of the household and have an abundance of all other things, I have enough.' But Rachel demands offspring so much that she prefers death to remaining sterile. I do not remember reading a similar statement in any history. Therefore she is an example of a very pious and content woman whose only zeal and burning desire is for offspring, even if it means death. Thus above (Gen. 16;2) Sarah also showed a similar desire for offspring. And in both this feeling is decidedly praiseworthy. 'If I do not have children, I shall die' says Rachel. 'I prefer being without life to being without children.' . . . Consequently, she determines either to bear children or die. Thus later she dies in childbirth. This desire and feeling of the godly woman is good and saintly . . ." (*Luther's Works*, Vol. 5, p. 328)

Reason Number Four
The Onan Incident
(Gen. 38:8-10, Deut. 25:5-10)

Genesis 38:8-10

"Then Judah said to Onan, 'Go in to your brother's wife, and perform your duty as a brother-in-law to her, and raise up offspring for your brother.' [9]And Onan knew that the offspring would not be his; so it came about that when he went in to his brother's wife, he wasted his seed on the ground, in order not to give offspring to his brother. [10]But what he did was displeasing in the sight of the LORD; so He took his life also."

Deuteronomy 25:5-10

"When brothers live together and one of them dies and has no sons, the wife of the deceased shall not be married outside the family to a strange man. Her husband's brother shall go in to her and take her to himself as wife and perform the duty of a husband's brother to her. [6]And it shall be that the firstborn whom she bears shall assume the name of his dead brother that his name may not be blotted out from Israel. [7]But if the man does not desire to take his brother's wife, then his brothers wife shall go up to the gate to the elders and say, 'my husband's brother refuses to establish a name for his brother in Israel; he is not willing to perform the duty of a husband's brother to me.' [8]Then the elders of his city shall summon him and speak to him. And if he persists and says, 'I do not desire to take her,' [9]Then his brother's wife shall come to him in the sight of the elders, and pull his sandal off his foot and spit in his face; and she shall declare, 'thus it is done to the man who does not build up his brother's house.' [10]And in Israel his name shall be called, 'The house of him whose sandal is removed.'"

Judah had several sons. The oldest son, named Er, had been married, but was killed by God before he had any children. In accordance with the law of God in Deu. 25:5-10, Judah told his next son Onan to marry Er's widow, so as to produce a child who would carry on Er's name.

However, Onan was unwilling to father a child for his deceased brother, so "when he went in to his brother's wife, he wasted his seed on the ground." A few words later we read, "But what he did was displeasing in the sight of the Lord; so He took his life also."

Examine the above verses and ask yourself this question: "What did Onan do in the verses?" The only thing Onan did was "wasted his seed on the ground." That is what made God angry. If there wasn't such a stir at this obvious conclusion we could drop the matter here, but we can't do so, because those who defend birth control have come up with alternatives which suit their views. We shall now review three alternate explanations, and show why they are untenable.

Alternate No. 1: "Onan was killed by God for disobeying his father, not for wasting his seed."

Rebuttal: According to Scripture, God has decreed that the marriage of a son ends any mandatory obedience to his father. Genesis 2:24 says, "For this cause a man shall leave his father and his mother, and shall cleave unto his wife; and they shall become one flesh." So, if Judah had authority over Onan, his authority ended when Onan got married to his brother's widow. Therefore God did not kill Onan because he disobeyed Judah, because according to the Word of God, Onan did not have to obey him.

Alternate No. 2: "Onan was killed by God because he didn't show love for his brother by having a child. He should have had at least one child before practicing birth control, and then God wouldn't have been angry."

Rebuttal: Deuteronomy eliminates this reason as a possibility, because it says that regardless of man's motives for refusing to raise up seed for a dead brother, the man is not to be put to death. He is to be humiliated only (shoe pulled off, face spit on, etc.). Onan was put to death for what he did, while the man in Deut. 25 was not.

As we compare the two Bible texts (Gen. 38:8-10 and Deu. 25:5-10), we need to ask, "What did Onan do that the man of Deut. 25 didn't do?" The difference in conduct will explain the difference in the penalty meted out by God. And the difference is that while Onan wasted his seed, the other man didn't! Suppose the man in Deut. 25 thinks exactly as Onan, saying to himself, "I don't want to raise up seed for my brother," and yet doesn't waste his seed? What happens to him according to the law of God? – Humiliation only, regardless of his unloving thoughts.

Alternate No. 3: "Well, Onan must have been killed because he lied to Judah."

Rebuttal: There is no proof that he lied to anyone. The Scripture is silent as to what Onan said to anyone. And we ought not "go beyond what is written," as the apostle Paul says in 1 Cor. 4:6. The Holy Spirit says what Onan did, then it says that God killed him for what he did. And what he did was "waste his seed on the ground." Onan was killed because he "wasted seed." Therefore, birth control is automatically condemned, because all forms of birth control have as their goal the wasting of seed.

Some may say to themselves as they read this, "Why, this is just a Roman Catholic custom, and so may be discarded." But, dear readers, this is not so. Space restrictions prevent us from listing quotes from all the leaders of the Christian faith who agree with our interpretation of the Onan incident. We will here list the comments of Martin Luther and John Calvin, the founders of the Reformation, two pastors not known for advocating "mere Roman Catholic customs," as everyone knows.

Commenting on Genesis 38:8-10, Luther says, "Then Judah urged his son Onan to take Tamar for his wife to raise up seed to his brother. Moses here uses the Hebrew word *'jabam,'* which we find also in Deuteronomy

25:5 and which properly means 'to marry in order to beget children for the deceased brother.' This was a very disagreeable duty and many sought to escape it, as we read in Ruth 4:1ff., for it is indeed hard to live with a woman whom one does not love to continue the inheritance of the brother, and to submit oneself to ceaseless toil and labor in his interest. Therefore Onan, unwilling to perform this obligation, spilled his seed. That was a sin far greater than adultery or incest, and it provoked God to such fierce wrath that He destroyed him immediately." (*Luther's Commentary on Genesis*, p. 250-251).

Luther on another occasion commented on the very same passage: "But the exceedingly foul deed of Onan, the basest of wretches, follows. (Here Luther quotes Gen. 38:9-10) Onan must have been a malicious and incorrigible scoundrel. This is a most disgraceful sin. It is far more atrocious than incest and adultery. We call it unchastity, yes a Sodomitic sin. For Onan goes in to her; that is, he lies with her and copulates, and when it comes to the point of insemination, spills the semen, lest the woman conceive. Surely at such a time the order of nature established by God in procreation should be followed. Accordingly, it was a most disgraceful crime to produce semen and excite the woman, and to frustrate her at that very moment. He was inflamed with the basest spite and hatred. Therefore he did not allow himself to be compelled to bear that intolerable slavery. Consequently, he deserved to be killed by God. He committed an evil deed. Therefore God punished him . . . That worthless fellow. . . preferred polluting himself with a most disgraceful sin to raising up offspring for his brother." (*Luther's Works*, Vol. 7, p. 20-21).

Several years ago I purchased Calvin's *Commentary on Genesis*, to find out what Calvin thought of the Onan incident. Much to my surprise, when I opened to Genesis 38:8-10, I discovered that Calvin's comments on this pivotal birth control passage were omitted by the editor for a reason he did not state. I was subsequently able to locate a Latin copy of Calvin's *Commentary on Genesis*, and the omitted section was graciously translated into English by the late Dr. Ford Battles, the translator of Calvin's Institutes. Calvin's comments are as follows:

"Besides, he (Onan) not only defrauded his brother of the right due him, but also preferred his semen to putrefy on the ground, rather than to beget a son in his brother's name. V. 10 The Jews quite immodestly gabble concerning this thing. It will suffice for me briefly to have touched upon this as much as modesty in speaking permits. **The voluntary spilling of the semen outside of intercourse between man and woman is a monstrous thing. Deliberately to withdraw from coitus in order that semen may fall on the ground is doubly monstrous.** For this is to extinguish the hope of the race and to kill before he is born the hoped-for offspring. This impiety is especially condemned, now by the Spirit through Moses' mouth, that Onan, as it were, by a violent abortion, no less cruelly than filthily cast upon the ground the offspring of his brother, torn from the maternal womb. Besides, in this way he tried, as far as he was able, to wipe out a part of the human race. If any woman rejects a fetus from her womb by drugs, it is reckoned a crime incapable of expiation and deservedly

Onan incurred upon himself the same kind of punishment, infecting the earth by his semen, in order that Tamar might not conceive a future human being as an inhabitant of the earth." (Calvin's *Commentary on Genesis* 38:8-10, translated from the Latin)

Reason Number Five
Death Penalties for Sexual Offenses
(Leviticus 20:13, 15, 16, 18, Genesis 38: 8-10)

Leviticus 20:13
"If there is a man who lies with a male as those who lie with a woman, both of them have committed a detestable act; they should surely be put to death. Their blood guiltiness is upon them."

Leviticus 20:15
"If there is a man who lies with an animal, he shall surely be put to death; you shall also kill the animal."

Leviticus 20:16
"If there is a woman who approaches any animal to mate with it, you shall kill the woman and the animal; they shall surely be put to death. Their blood guiltiness is upon them."

Leviticus 20:18
"If there is a man who lies with a menstruous woman and uncovers her nakedness, he has laid bare her flow, and she has exposed the flow of her blood; thus both of them shall be cut off from among their people."

Genesis 38:8-10
(Listed under Reason Four)

The Old Testament mentions about twenty or so death penalty offenses. The New Testament says that these examples are in the Old Testament to help Christians find out what pleases and displeases God (1 Corinthians 10:1-10; verse 6 says, "Now these things happened as examples for us, that we should not crave evil things, as they also craved.") Many of these offenses are related to sexual matters. These forbidden sexual relations may be divided into two categories: 1) sexual offenses forbidden because of whom the potential or actual sexual partner is (for example, adultery, incest, etc.) and, b) offenses which are forbidden because of the act itself.

It is this second group on which we intend to focus. These offenses are evil no matter with whom they are committed. They are perversions, evil in themselves. A listing of these offenses is as follows:

    1)   Male homosexual intercourse (Lev. 20:13)
    2)   Male/Animal bestiality (Lev. 20:15).
    3)   Female/Animal bestiality (Lev. 20:16)
    4)   Intercourse with a menstruous woman (Lev. 20:18)
    5)   Withdrawal (Wasting Seed) (Gen. 38:8-10)

These sexual offenses are always wrong if done intentionally. (We say this because No. 4 and No. 5 may occur accidentally, as the Bible says — Lev. 15:24 and Deut. 23:10-11).

In any case let us get to the point of this section, which is this: What is common to all these five sins? The answer is: they are all sterile forms of sexual intercourse. Male homosexuals can't produce children from homosexual activity. Neither can bestiality or menstruous intercourse. Withdrawal is meant to be sterile, and is, most of the time. In all cases the seed is wasted.

So we can see that the reason that these sins are condemned by God is because they are almost 100% sterile, and oppose the command of God to "be fruitful and multiply." We are not finished however, because further examination will be useful. Let us now compare some unusual cases of Old Testament jurisprudence.

Unusual Case No. 1: Male homosexuality vs. female homosexuality
Leviticus 20:13

"If there is a man who lies with a male as those who lie with a woman, both of them have committed a detestable act; they shall surely be put to death. Their blood guiltiness is upon them."

The reader will note that we have included no verse on the execution of female homosexuals. This is because there is no penalty prescribed for lesbian activities in the Old Testament. This of course does not mean that lesbianism is OK with God—it just means that there is no civil penalty. (Similar cases would be coveting or lusting.) So we see that male homosexuals are to be executed, but female homosexuals are spared.

Some attempt the explanation that, "Well, God is just nicer to girls." We would reply that God in the Old Testament has nothing against executing female evildoers, as is evident from the fact that God has decreed the death penalty for: female murderers (Gen. 9:6), female sorcerers (Lev. 20:27), female idolaters (Deut. 13:6-9), females guilty of bestiality (Lev. 20:16), female adulterers (Lev. 20:10), etc. in fact, we are not aware of any sin for which God kills guilty males but spares guilty females, except in the case of homosexual activity.

Is this a mistake? Is the Bible inconsistent? The answer, of course, is "No." The New Testament states that the Old Testament death penalties are just in the eyes of God. Hebrews 2:2 states that in the Mosaic Law, ". . . every transgression and disobedience received a just recompense. . ." The Bible prescribes death of the male homosexual and life for the female because only the male homosexual wastes seed, which once again shows that wasting seed is an awful thing in the eyes of God.

Unusual Case No. 2:
Female/animal intercourse vs. female homosexuality
Leviticus 20:16

"If there is a woman who approaches an animal to mate with it, you shall kill the woman and the animal; they shall surely be put to death. Their blood guiltiness is upon them."

Here we have another comparison of different sexual sins similar to the previous example. Women who mate with animals are to be killed, while women homosexuals are to be allowed to live. And what can account for the difference? Again we see that the only explanation of the above law is that the difference is in wasting seed. In female bestiality, the animal's seed is wasted. In female homosexuality, while sin is indeed committed, no seed is wasted.

So ends our examination of Old Testament perversions and their penalties. We may observe that all sterile sexual acts are forbidden, unless (as we have said) they happen accidentally. Therefore, since the very purpose of all methods of birth control is to make the sexual act sterile, they are forbidden too.

Reason Number Six
Castration as a Blemish
(Leviticus 24:19-20; 21:17-20; 22:20-22, 24-25)

Leviticus 24:19-20

"And if a man injures his neighbor, just as he has done, so it shall be done to him: [20]fracture for fracture, eye for eye, tooth for tooth; just as he injured a man, so it shall be inflicted on him."

The Lord laid down a judicial principle for Israel in the above verses: every crime committed against a person was to be punished by an equal penalty against the criminal. It is not here our concern to explain the present day application of this particular set of verses – suffice it to say that inflicting an "injury" on a fellow human being is clearly sinful. We intend rather to focus in on the world "injure," which occurs in both verses. The word in Hebrew is "mum," which means "blemish."

If you examine the various verses in which this word occurs, you will find that the Scripture contains listings of different types of blemishes. They are:

Leviticus 21:17-20

"Speak to Aaron, saying, 'No man of your offspring throughout their generations who has a defect shall approach to offer the bread of his God, [18]for no one who has a defect shall approach: a blind man, or a lame man, or he who has a disfigured face, or any deformed limb, [19]or a man who has a broken foot or broken hand, [20]or a hunchback or a dwarf, or one who has a defect in his eye or eczema or scabs or crushed testicles.'"

Leviticus 22:20-22, 24-25

"Whatever has a defect, you shall not offer, for it will not be accepted for you. [21]And when a man offers a sacrifice of peace offerings to the LORD to fulfill a special vow, or for a freewill offering, of the herd or of the flock, it must be perfect to be accepted; there shall be no defect in it. [22]Those that are blind or fractured or maimed or having a running sore or eczema or scabs, you shall not offer to the LORD, nor make of them an offering by fire on the altar to the LORD. [24]Also anything with its testicles bruised or crushed or torn or cut, you shall not offer to the Lord, or do in your land, [25]nor shall you accept any such from that hand of a foreigner for offering as the food of your God; for there are corruptions in them, they have a defect. They shall not be accepted for you."

Note that in addition to blindness, crippleness, broken limbs, eczema and running sores, there also occurs bruised or crushed or torn testicles! God here declares that damaged or destroyed testicles are a bad thing. We think that all would agree that the lists in the above verses are bad things; we have never seen anyone declaring the great benefits of being crippled or blind, or of having running sores! Once again, though, exceptions are made for birth control.

We are told in the news media and in sex manuals about the "quick and easy, virtually foolproof method of birth-control – vasectomy." Once again, what is a bad thing in Scripture is a "good thing" in our culture. But we Christians should seek to find out what the Bible says, not what the latest point of view is. And the Bible says that anyone who gets a vasectomy is injuring himself, something forbidden by the Bible.

Take a look at Lev. 22:24. This verse forbids offering defective animals to God, but it says more than that – it forbids the castration of animals. We see from numerous Bible passages that God cares about animals; this is a protective law for them.

The animal laws in the Bible speak louder than the letter of the law. The Old Testament declares God's love for animal life in passages such as Ps. 104:10-27 and Pro. 12:10, but the New Testament amplifies them. For example, Jesus says that if God cares for little birds, how much more does he care for humans (Matt. 6:26). And Paul says that if God wants animals fed for work they do (Deut. 25:4), then God surely wants pastors paid for the work that they do (1 Cor. 9:9-10).

Likewise, if a destroyed or damaged reproductive system is a blemish for animals, how much more so for human beings made in the image of God! Therefore neither permanent sterility (vasectomies) nor partial sterility (condoms) is permissible. Castration destroys the seed before it is made. Birth control destroys the seed after . . . it is only a matter of timing, and both do the same things, namely, waste seed. (Tubal ligation, which is merely female castration, is by implication forbidden also.)

We see that the Scripture points to the evil of castration in Deut. 23:1, "No one who is emasculated, or has his male organ cut off, shall enter the assembly of the Lord." If a person who was a eunuch involuntarily was not allowed to be a full Israelite, what would God's view be towards someone who did the awful thing to himself because he wanted to prevent God from sending children into the world?

Another law which is even more pointed is Deut. 25:11-12: "If two men, a man and his countryman, are struggling together, and the wife of one comes near to deliver her husband from the hand of the one who is striking him, and puts out her hand and seizes his genitals, then you shall cut off her hand; you shall not show pity." This law is easy to comprehend. To stop a man who is fighting with her husband, a lady grabs her husband's opponent by his sexual organs. What does God say to do with her? Do you reward her? Do you commend her for saving her husband? No. Rather, the civil authorities are commanded to take the woman and cut off her hand. They cannot cancel the punishment or change it. The woman gets her hand cut off whether she hurt the man or not.

We can observe that God is extremely angry with such a woman. If there is a fight and the woman grabs the man's hand or foot, she suffers no punishment, but if she grabs his sexual organs, she gets her hand cut off. God is, by these verses, showing that interfering with the sexual organs is strictly forbidden. And these verses become a proof text for forbidding birth control, because birth control prevents the sexual organs from carrying out their duties, just the same as grabbing the sexual organs in a fight has the potential to do. If God forbids the potential on pain of getting the hand cut off, how much more does God forbid the actual?

Reason Number Seven
Seed as Semen or Children
(Hebrews 7:9-10)

Hebrews 7:9-10
"And, so to speak, through Abraham even Levi, who received tithes, paid tithes, [10]for he was still in the loins of his father when Melchizedek met him."

If a person looks up the word "seed" in the Old Testament, an interesting fact appears. Namely, the Hebrew world "Zerah" is used of human seed in two different ways: 1) semen (as in Gen. 38:9 and Lev. 15:12, 32), and b) children or people after birth (as in Gen. 46:6 and Lev. 22:13).

Some may say, "So what does that prove? The word 'house' can be used of a man's building or of a man's family. Likewise, just because the word for semen and offspring is the same word, this doesn't prove that they are the same."

To oppose this view we have reason and Scripture. First, the reason that Scripture uses the same word for semen and children is because all humans at one time existed in semen form. Without semen, no children are possible. So, viewing children as a continuous process, we can see that the word "seed" applies well to both stages of human life, before and after conception. Second, what is the reason that most methods of birth control seek to prevent the seed from uniting with a female egg? Is it not to prevent the birth of real people who may result from the semen produced by the sexual act? (Obviously, birth control does not seek to prevent the birth of imaginary babies! Imaginary babies do not need prevention!) Third, the Scripture in Hebrews 7:1-10 proves the subservience of the Levitical priesthood to the prophesied Melchizedek priesthood of Christ by using the following logic: Levi is less than Abraham, and Abraham is less that Melchizedek – therefore, the Melchizedek priesthood of Christ as (prophesied by Ps. 110) is greater than the Levitical priesthood of the Mosaic Covenant. During the argument of Hebrews, there occurs the following statement (7:9-10): "and, so to speak, through Abraham even Levi, who received tithes, paid tithes, for he was yet in the loins of his father when Melchizedek met him."

Note that Hebrews says that Levi, in some real (not imaginary) way was in the loins of his great-grandfather (!) Abraham. Now, if Abraham had practiced birth control and "succeeded," would he not have eliminated the real person Levi who was born some hundred years later, according to this verse?

Those who practice birth control should realize that what they are doing not only eliminates semen (which nobody seems to be concerned with), but also eliminates future people. These eliminated people exist in the loins of those who practice birth control, and are subsequently destroyed by birth control.

We have encountered people who disagree with the above view because of what the Bible says about predestination. Such persons reason like this: "Well, God decides who will be born on earth. Therefore, if I practice birth control and God gives me two children that must be how many children God wants me to have. Therefore, since nothing can hinder God's mighty will, birth control is OK."

To counter this objection, turn to God's Word to Sennacherib the King of Assyria (Isaiah 37:21-19). Sennacherib had invaded and destroyed Judah, as God himself had ordained long before the event (37:26). Yet does this fact of predestination show that Sennacherib's conduct was morally defensible? Absolutely not, as one may see from reading Isaiah 37:28-29. God was angry with Sennacherib for his ungodly conduct, even though God preordained the event! This is, needless to say, a mysterious concept, but it should be apparent that predestination does not justify forbidden conduct. It is not without reason that Moses says in Deut. 29:29, "The secret things belong to the Lord our God, but the things revealed belong to us and to our sons forever; that we may observe all the words of this law."

As further proof that our view of birth control does not contradict the Biblical doctrine of predestination, we now quote from the writings of John Calvin, who, as we all know, surely believed in predestination:

"The voluntary spilling of semen outside of intercourse between man and woman is a monstrous thing. Deliberately to withdraw from coitus in order that semen may fall on the ground is doubly monstrous. For this is to extinguish the hope of the race and to kill before he is born the hoped-for offspring. This impiety is especially condemned, not by the Spirit through Moses' mouth, that Onan, as it were, by a violent abortion, no less cruelly than filthily cast upon the ground the offspring of his brother, torn from the maternal womb. Besides, in this way he tried, as far as he was able, to wipe out a part of the human race. If any woman ejects a fetus from her womb by drugs, it is reckoned a crime incapable of expiation and deservedly Onan incurred upon himself the same kind of punishment, infecting the earth by his semen, in order that Tamar might not conceive a future human being as an inhabitant of the earth." (*Calvin's Latin Commentary on Genesis* – 38:10).

Regardless of predestination, Calvin condemns birth control as the murder of future human beings. As we have before stated, God's secret purposes do not justify conduct which the Word of God forbids.

Reason Number Eight
The Natural Function of Women
(Romans 1:25-27)

Romans 1:25-27

"For they exchanged the truth of God for a lie, and worshiped and served the creature rather than the Creator, who is blessed forever. Amen. [26]For this reason God gave them over to degrading passions; for their women exchanged the natural function for that which is unnatural, [27]and in the same way also the men abandoned the natural function of the woman and burned in their desire towards one another, men with men committing indecent acts and receiving in their own persons the due penalty of their error."

God here says that cultures which reject the worship of God are punished by God "giving them over to degrading passions." The road to these degrading passions begins when men and women exchange "the natural function of women for that which is unnatural." This is stated in Romans 1:26-27. What is the ultimate end of rejecting the "natural function of women"?—Homosexuality and other like perversions.

What is this "natural function" of women? Is it scrubbing the floor? Is it washing clothes? No, for men can do these things. The natural function of women is bearing children. All biological differences between men and women point to this conclusion. The physical differences between men and women are as follows:

1) Women menstruate; men don't
2) Women produce milk; men don't
3) Women have uteri; men don't
4) Men have male sexual organs; women don't

Note these differences. What are these differences for? So women can bear children. There is nothing else that can be described as the "natural function of women" other than childbearing. If you say that the natural function of women is sexual intercourse, not childbearing, then why do women have breasts if not to feed babies? If childbearing is not the natural function of women, then why did God add all that "unnecessary" equipment which enables women to bear children" for it is readily apparent that breasts and uteri are unnecessary for a woman to engage in sexual intercourse.

It is evident that when God made woman, He did not add unnecessary parts. As Paul says in 1 Cor. 12:18, ". . . God has placed the members, each one of them, in the body, just as he desired." For what purpose did God give women uteri? So women could have intercourse? No, but rather that women could receive the seed from intercourse and nurture it. For what purpose did God give women breasts? So men could stare at them? No! Rather, so women could nurture the children which God gives to them. So it is apparent that sexual intercourse is but the means to accomplish the natural function of women, which is childbearing and if this is true, then birth control is opposing the natural function of women.

Once again we quote from Martin Luther: "Moses numbers fertility among the blessings. 'There will not be a barren woman among you,' he says (cf. Ex. 23:26). We do not regard this so highly today. Although we like and desire it in cattle, yet in the human race there are few who regard a woman's fertility as a blessing. Indeed there are many who have an aversion for it and regard sterility as a special blessing. Surely this is also contrary to nature. Much less is it pious and saintly. For this affection has been implanted by God in man's nature, so that it desires its increase and multiplication. Accordingly, it is inhuman and godless to have a loathing for offspring."

(*Luther's Works*, Vol. 5, p. 325)

Reason Number Nine
Childbirth and Salvation For Women
(1 Timothy 2:13-15)

1 Timothy 2:13-15

"For it was Adam who was first created, and then Eve. ¹⁴And it was not Adam who was deceived, but the woman being quite deceived, fell into transgression. ¹⁵But women shall be saved through the bearing of children if they continue in faith and love and sanctity with self-restraint."

Here we have a "strange passage," according to most people today. "It can't mean spiritual salvation," say some.

If you look up the verses in Paul's letters which contain the word "saved" (the same one that is in vs. 15), you will find that every time Paul uses the word he is referring to spiritual salvation. Is Paul then saying that women can earn salvation by childbearing? By no means. Salvation cannot be earned or merited. Salvation is by grace and not by works.

What Paul is saying may be summarized as follows: If a woman is truly saved, she will prove her faith and her salvation by pursuing good works, which are (according to Jesus) inevitable for a true Christian. The pathway of teaching doctrine to husbands or ordering them around is not open to women. The pathway of obedience, which leads to eternal salvation, is (for married women) accompanied by childbearing if possible. Lest a woman think that the childbearing itself will save her, Paul adds that a woman bearing children will be saved if she continues in "faith and love and sanctity with self restraint."

Paul's statement is paralleled by that of Jesus in Matthew 19:17, "If you wish to enter into life, keep the commandments". Christ says the same thing again in Luke 10:25-28. "And, behold a certain lawyer stood up and put Jesus to the test, saying, 'Teacher, what shall I do to inherit eternal life?' And Jesus said to him, 'What is written in the Law? How does it read to you?' And he answered and said, 'You shall love the Lord your God with all your heart, and with all your soul, and with all your strength, and with all your mind; and your neighbor as yourself.' And Jesus said to him, 'You have answered correctly; do this, and you will live.'" Jesus is not preaching salvation by law or works. He is teaching that if a person is truly a Christian, good works will accompany him to eternal life. (It is not even possible to obey the moral law unless one is truly a Christian anyway.)

Paul is saying that the pathway to salvation for married women includes godly childbearing. Those who reject childbearing (when they are married) reject the good works which Paul says accompany salvation.

To demonstrate that we are not teaching "salvation by works," we will now quote Martin Luther and John Calvin, who unswervingly defended salvation by grace alone. Let us see how they interpret 1 Timothy 2:15.

Martin Luther on 1 Tim. 2:15:

"¹⁵'SHE WILL BE SAVED.' That subjection of women and domination of men have not been taken away, have they? No. The penalty remains. The blame passed over. The pain and tribulation of childbearing continue. Those penalties will continue until judgment so also the dominion of men and the subjection of women continue. You must endure them. You will also be saved if you have also subjected yourselves and bear your children with pain. 'THROUGH BEARING CHILDREN.' It is a very great comfort that a woman can be saved by bearing children, etc. that is, she has an honorable and salutary status in life if she keeps busy having children. We ought to recommend this passage to them, etc. She is described as 'saved' not for freedom, for license, but for bearing and rearing children. Is she not saved by faith? He goes on and explains himself: bearing children is a wholesome responsibility, but for believers. To bear children is acceptable to God. He does not merely say that bearing children saves: he adds: if the bearing takes place in faith and love, it is a Christian work, for 'to the pure all things are pure (Titus 1:15).' Also: 'All things work together,' Rom 8:28. This is the comfort for married people in trouble: hardship and all things are salutary, for through them they are moved forward toward salvation and against adultery . . . 'IN FAITH.' Paul had to add this, lest women think that they are good in the fact that they bear children. Simple childbearing does nothing, since the heathen also do this. But for Christian women their whole responsibility is salutary. So much the more salutary, then is bearing children. I add this, therefore, that they may not feel secure when they have no faith." (*Luther's Works*, Vol. 28, p. 279)

As for John Calvin, his comments on our Scripture passage are as follows: "¹⁵BUT SHE SHALL BE SAVED. The weakness of the sex renders women more suspicious and timid, and the preceding statement might greatly terrify and alarm the strongest minds. For these reasons he modifies what he had said by adding a consolation . . . Paul, in order to comfort them and render their condition tolerable, informs them that they continue to enjoy the hope of salvation, though they suffer a temporal punishment. It is proper to observe that the good effect of this consolation is twofold. First, by the hope of salvation held out to them, they are prevented from falling into despair through alarm at the mention of their guilt. Secondly, they become accustomed to endure calmly and patiently the necessity of servitude, so as to submit willingly to their husbands, when they are informed that this kind of obedience is both profitable to themselves and acceptable to God. If this passage be tortured, as Papists are wont to do, to support the righteousness of works, the answer is easy. The Apostle does not argue here about the cause of salvation, and therefore we cannot and must not infer from these words what works deserve; but they only shew in what way God conducts us to salvation, to which he has appointed us through His grace. THROUGH CHILD-BEARING. To censorious men it might appear absurd, for an Apostle of Christ not only to exhort women to give attention to the birth of offspring, but to press this as work religious and holy to such an extent as to represent it in the light of the means of procuring salvation. . . whatever hypocrites or wise men of the world may think of it, when a woman, considering to what she has been called, submits to the condition which God has assigned to her, and does not refuse to endure the pains, or rather the tearful anguish of parturition, or anxiety about her offspring, or anything else that belongs to her duty, God values their obedience more highly than if, in some other manner, she made a great display of heroic virtues, while she refused to obey the calling of God. To this must be added, that no consolation could be more appropriate or more efficacious than to shew that the very means (so to speak) of procuring salvation are found in the punishment itself. (*Calvin's Commentary*, Vol. 21, p. 71)

Summary

Dear readers, we hope we have adequately demonstrated the great importance attached by God to being fruitful and multiplying. God views sterility as bad and large numbers of children as good. It is a great sin to destroy the seed God gives to you. Instead of destroying your future children by practicing birth control, you ought rather to consider the weight of the Scriptures which have been here presented, and adjust your conduct accordingly. Who can tell what great blessings God has for you, blessings which will prove to be of far greater worth than a vacation trip or a fancy car, or any other material things which will fade away.

In closing, let us heed the words of the Apostle Paul, who said in 1 Corinthians 6:19-20: "... do you not know that your body is a temple of the Holy Spirit who is in you, whom you have from God, and that you are not your own? For you have been bought with a price: therefore glorify God in your body."

About the Author
Biography

Charles D. Provan, the son of Dr. and Mrs. Charles A. Provan, was born in 1955. Though raised in a Christian home, he was not converted until December of 1974, while attending Bob Jones University. During the height of the "Lordship Controversy," a fellow student at the University gave Charles some "underground" Reformed literature which was then banned on campus: *Today's Gospel*, by Pastor Walter Chantry, along with *The Lordship Controversy*, by Arend ten Pas. Reading this literature (humanly speaking!) led to his conversion.

Transferring a short while later to the University of Pittsburgh, Charles "dropped out" to work at a printing shop south of Pittsburgh. He later purchased this business, and has been there ever since. Subsequently he met his wife Carol, whom he regards as a gift from God, as the book of Proverbs says in Proverbs 19:14. Chuck and Carol have been blessed by God with four children: Matthias ("gift of God"), Nathaniel ("gift of God"), Susanna ("Lily") and Tobias ("God is good"). Another blessing is currently on the way!

A firm believer in the Lordship of Christ and the supremacy of the Church of Christ, Charles compiled the book *"The Church is Israel Now"*, which demonstrates that faith in Christ (not race!) is the determining factor for membership in the true Israel of God, which is the Church. Charles remains grateful to Chalcedon, led by Rev. Rousas Rushdoony, for publishing his book. He hopes it (along with his own writings) will strengthen the Church of Christ and deal a blow against Dispensational negativism, false racialism and other forces which result in the weakening of the Church.

Response to Article on Birth Control
Please, Don't Get "Mad"

Christian News, February 28, 1988

The publication of a photo of the family of Rev. and Mrs. Rolf Preus and seven of their eight boys on the front page of January 4, 1988 *Christian News* brought a number of questions.

Here are some:

Are you trying to tell us to have more children? How come you have seven children? Don't you believe in birth control? How can a pastor with a large family expect to get many calls? What is Rolf Preus' secret to have only boys? What does the Lutheran Church teach about birth control? What has it taught in the past?

Christian News has published some articles on birth control. A few of them are in the *Christian News Encyclopedia* in the section on "population." They include: "the Deadly ABC" by Professor Martin Naumann, and LCMS professor who taught at Concordia Seminary, Springfield, Illinois; "Contraception Kills Millions;" "Artificial Birth Control Held as Cause of Rising Divorce Rate;" "Zero Growth Brings Problems;" "Jose Espinosa's Medical View on Contraception;" "The Myth of Overpopulation;" and "The Tragedy of Birth Control."

Volume III of the *Christian News Encyclopedia* will have more articles on birth control, including some which show that certain (not all) forms of birth control actually are abortions.

Charles Provan, the author of this week's lead article, "The Bible's' View of Birth Control," was one of those who asked about our views on birth control. CN had favorably reviewed his The Church Is Israel Now, which demonstrates that faith in Christ (not race) is the determining factor for membership in the true Israel of God, the Church. Last week CN published his "Some Reasons to Doubt Whether the State of Israel Is a Fulfillment of Bible Prophecy." Mr. Provan asked if we would publish an article he was planning to write on what the Bible teaches about birth control. He has found that many conservatives do not want to discuss the subject. We urged him to send us the article and reminded him of our policy of allowing critics opportunity to respond. We asked him how those who support birth control, particularly conservatives, respond to his position. According to Mr. Provan, "They just get mad." We ask our readers not to get "mad" at Mr. Provan but to read his article and then let us know where he has misrepresented the scriptural position.

We are also publishing a summary of some material on birth control presented by Mr. Larry Marquardt of the Wisconsin Evangelical Lutheran Synod.

We are reprinting the section on marriage from the *Concordia Cyclopedia*, published by The Lutheran Church-Missouri Synod's Concordia Publishing House in 1927 and edited by professors at the LCMS's Concordia Seminary, St. Louis. A section from Dr. John H.C. Fritz's *Pastoral Theology*, long a standard textbook in the LCMS, is included. *Pastoral Theology* was published by Concordia Publishing House in 1932.

Dr. Walter Maier in his marriage manual, *For Better Not For Worse*, has a section which argues that birth control is contrary to Scripture. Years ago our congregation petitioned the LCMS to reprint this great book on marriage. When Maier was editor of *The Walther League Messenger*, this LCMS youth publication took a firm stand against birth control. Dr. Maier published photos of a good number of large families. This issue of CN includes photos of the families of some of those who have contributed articles to *Christian News*. Several of the pictures appeared a good number of years ago in CN.

Please don't get "mad" at Provan and Marquardt. Answer them. Has Provan misrepresented what the Bible teaches? Has he quoted Luther and Calvin out of context? Has Marquardt misrepresented the former position of the LCMS, or the position of Fritz, Maier, Engelder, Kretzmann, Fuerbringer, etc.?

Dr. Paul E. Kretzmann says in his *Popular Commentary on the Bible*, published by the LCMS's Concordia Publishing House in 1923, that "The modern criminal limiting of offspring is a blasphemous perversion of God's order of creation" (comments on Genesis 8, p. 21, vol. I).

"Wattenberg Warns of Growing 'Birth Dearth,'" the lead story in the December 1987/January 1988 *Family Research Today*, says: "Three decades after the height of America's 'baby boom,' the United States is caught in the throes of an unprecedented 'birth dearth.'

"So concludes American Enterprise Institute scholar Ben Wattenberg, whose recent book, *The Birth Dearth*, states that Americans are not bearing enough children to reproduce themselves over an extended period of time.

"During her childbearing years, the average woman in the United States now bears 1.8 children. For middle-and upper- income women, the figure is only 1.3 births.

"If birth rates remain below the 2.1 level needed to replace population, Wattenberg believes America's economic prosperity and political influence will steadily decline as an aging population gropes to survive with shrinking domestic markets and a dwindling pool of productive workers.

"Wattenberg believes the birth dearth's negative impact on the quality of life in America will extend far beyond the economic realm, 'I believe most people —men and women— who freely decide not to have children will probably live to regret it,' he states. 'More importantly, I believe those who unwittingly arrange their lives in ways that reduce their chances to have children will live to be even more sorry.'"

It should go without saying that the Christian sympathizes with those Christian couples who through no fault of their own have not been blessed with children.

Women seem to think that women who have many children will lose their beauty and in general will be in poorer health than those who have fewer children by practicing birth control. Dr. John H.C. Firtz in the section from his **Pastoral Theology** which we are reprinting in this issue quotes with approval a writer who observed: "women with many children are in middle age much more beautiful than those who have few children and who owe this misfortune not to a hard blow of fate, but solely to an immoral tendency toward the use of anti-conceptual means."

Eleven children, 42 grandchildren, and 12 great-children, haven't kept Rev. and Mrs. Adalbert Oesch from keeping active. Pastor Oesch who will be 89 in August, may be the oldest Lutheran Church-Missouri Synod pastor who is still serving as the full time pastor of a congregation. If he lives to the year 2,000 he says he'll have lived in three centuries. Mrs. Oesch still accompanies him on many of his calls, and often does the driving. He continues to read several chapters each day in the Greek New Testament and also in the Latin Vulgate. Pastor Oesch told us he never believed in birth control. He defends the position taken by the LCMS in former years and by such theologians as Dr. Walter Maier Sr.

It is true that one reason we have at times published pictures of large Christian families is to encourage others, particularly young pastors, to have, God willing, many children. Pastors should set a good example to their congregations. Official denominational publications, which reach hundreds of thousands, should encourage larger families.

Several years ago we suggested that when LCMS youth leaders plan youth conventions and rallies they should consider inviting a mother like Mrs. Robert Preus to speak. Far too many of the women who speak to church gatherings of all kinds have few children. The Wisconsin Evangelical Lutheran Synod should have Mrs. John Parcher (18 children), Mrs. Larry Marquardt (12 children), or Mrs. Peter Prange (nine children) speak to youth gatherings. Far too many of the women who write books about raising children have only a few themselves. We asked Mrs. Juergens whether she ever considered writing a book about bringing up a family. Her answer was an immediate "no." She said she certainly doesn't have all the answers, and besides is far too busy. Perhaps someday we can get one of those mothers with many children to write a book on bringing up a large Christian family. Hopefully it would get many of our Christian youth to recognize that large families are indeed a blessing from God. A change in attitude towards having large families could help solve many "church growth" and "recruitment" for the ministry problems.

Years ago Dr. Maier asked readers of the LCMS's *Walther League Messenger* to send in photos of large Christian families for publication. CN is issuing the same call some 50 years later. Send us your family photos . Perhaps one of you readers has more than the Parcher 18 children or the Oesch's 42 grandchildren.

A Quiverful of Concern
Christian News, January 20, 1992

The Bible and Birth Control, by Charles D. Provan, Zimmer, 1989, 97 pp., paper, $10.95. [Zimmer Printing, 410 West Main Street, Monongahela, Pennsylvania 15063, U.S.A.] (Now available from *Christian News* for $4.00)

You will have had this experience, I am sure: You come across a book on a subject which interests you but which you have never really gone into thoroughly. As you read the book, you feel a growing sense of excitement as you become convinced that the author is unfolding truth - truth which perhaps you believed at the back of your mind but did not know why you believed it.

This reviewer can still remember this great sense of thrill when in the early 1970s he read for the first time *The Myth of Over-Population* by Rousas J. Rushdoony. If you have never read this brief but powerful work then I urge you to do so soon! Rushdoony brilliantly exposes the intellectual poverty and sheer atheism of the lobby which screams at us that all our problems are due to there being too many people on planet Earth.

It was that book which set me wondering if the birth control lobby was wrong at the personal as well as the global level. When the church history of the twentieth century comes to be written, surely godly historians will marvel at the way in which evangelicals allowed the world to write their agenda and took on board so much worldly thinking. Thus I came to the present book with a sense of expectation - and in most respects I was not disappointed. There are excellent and thought-provoking lead-ins, such as the "Birth Control Quiz," the commendatory preface from a pastor whose mind had been changed by the book, and a telling quotation from the Puritan Joseph Hall (1574-1656), who said: "I remember a great man coming into my house at Waltham and seeing all my children standing in the order of age and status, saying, 'These are they that make rich men poor,' But he straight received this answer, 'Nay, my Lord, these are they that make a poor man rich; for there is not one of them whom we would part with for all your wealth.'"

If you agree with Hall's approach to children then you will enjoy this book. If you do not agree, then I beg you to read it because your thinking cannot yet be as biblical as Hall's. Charles Provan sets out to prove that Christians should totally oppose the theory and practice of birth control in any form whatsoever. He explains that this is not a modern, eccentric view, but one which has good historical support. Much more important, he believes that it has good biblical support, and his first chapter, "Nine Reasons Why the Bible Prohibits Birth Control," contains some very thorough and stirring exegesis of some difficult O.T. and N.T. passages which challenges modern atheistic thought patterns. If you do not agree with him, you must answer Scripture with Scripture when one is confronted with texts such as 1 Chron. 24:5 & 26:5 (look them up!), one is forced to think, "who is right - the inspired writer or me?" Much growth in grace begins with "Maybe I have been wrong here."

In the second chapter, "Two Alternative Viewpoints on Birth Control and Their Rebuttals," he answers the sort of questions which will arise in our minds as, perhaps reluctantly startled by the exegesis in chapter one, we begin to think of arguments to support our espousal of various forms of contraception. His repeated emphasis on those passages of Scripture which speak of children as a great blessing from the Lord are very convincing. His even heavier emphasis on the statement that all "wasting" of semen is sinful is harder to accept –though he does argue his case very thoroughly. He is consistent in opposing both natural and mechanical methods of birth control.

His third and final chapter, "Protestant Theologians and the Onan Incident" is less satisfying. It consists of numerous quotations from theologians of different centuries and churches in support of the author's thesis. One could skip this and still benefit greatly from the first two chapters.

There are weaknesses in the book. Chief among these is an unnecessarily bombastic and aggressive style. It is surely unwise thus to antagonize those you are seeking to convince – a fault all too common in modern Reformed writers. He also leaves many quite major questions unanswered. I would love to have asked him if he believed that as all waste of semen is sinful, then intercourse between man and wife during pregnancy should be avoided. He is also free and insensitive to the needs of women who would love to have children, but cannot. It is also a pity that we are nowhere told who Charles Provan is or what his church credentials are – though one assumes he is a Lutheran pastor. However, I do agree with the commendation from a well-respected name, John Gerstner, which appears on the back cover: "A most interesting and thoughtful work on a much neglected theme."

Humphrey Mildred
Elder, Bellevue Baptist Church, Edinburgh, Diakrisis, Spring, 1991.

Protestants Condemn Birth Control
Christian News, May 11, 1992

The Bible and Birth Control by Mr. Charles Provan, available from Zimmer Press, Monogahela, PA 15063 continues to receive favorable reviews. Publications which support birth control have ignored it. Mr. Provan was recently invited to speak to the convention of a major pro-life organization. Several months ago he was interviewed on a California station on birth control. Mr. Provan defends the position taken by Martin Luther and formerly by most major denominations, particularly The Lutheran Church-Missouri Synod.

Below is a review from the May, 1992 *Reflections, The Wanderer Review of Literature, Culture, the Arts*. Most of the material in Provan's *The Bible and Birth Control* originally appeared in *Christian News*.

THE BIBLE AND BIRTH CONTROL
By Charles D. Provan
Zimmer Press, Monongahela, PA 15063; paper; 1991.

What a delightful character this author is – simple but wise, learned in biblical studies but ingenious, humbly reproducing attacks on him in *Christian News* but rebutting them with charity.

Charles D. Provan appears to be a layman from Donora, Pa., probably a Lutheran because most of the quotes are from Lutheran writers.

His book is unique - a condemnation of contraception from Protestant sources. Most of the argument centers around the story of Onan in Genesis, 38, 8-10. The dispute about why Onan was struck down by God has gone on for centuries. Onan was obliged by Levirate law to marry his brother's widow to raise up offspring in his brother's name but he refused to do this. Instead "he spilled his seed on the ground." Therefore the Lord slew him because "he did a despicable thing."

Was this because he would not have a child by Tamar? Or was it because he resorted to coitus interruptus (withdrawal), the oldest form of birth control? The constant Christian tradition has been that the abnormal sexual act was the main thing that God condemned –"onanism" is the standard theological term for contraception.

Provan agrees with this exegesis and points out that all Christian churches were united in this view until the present century. This is supported by several quotations from Martin Luther and John Calvin. The related moral fault is the rejection of childbearing and trust in God.

"God is not obligated to give us a Cadillac," he says in his homely style, "but He promises to give us food and clothing and shelter."

As the argument unfolds the difficulty Reformed churches have with predestination and complete reliance on Scripture (*sola scriptura*) becomes obvious. They have no assistance from tradition or a teaching Magisterium. The sufficiency of grace and faith for salvation is stressed, and the concept of childbearing as a "good work" is rejected.

To show that times really do not change, Luther (d. 1546) wrote: ". . . most married people do not desire offspring. Indeed, they turn away from it and consider it better to live without children. . ."

And there is a statement from Calvin (d. 1564) which is of extraordinary interest in the modern world: "If any woman ejects a fetus from her womb by drugs, it is reckoned a crime incapable of expiation. . ."

In a most valuable historical chapter the author quotes briefly from 69 Protestant theologians from the Reformation to the present day, all condemning birth control; and he lists by name 35 others. It is a common mistake to believe that only Roman Catholics reject contraception (and abortion). This admirable author may not realize it but his book gives hope to all working for ecumenism. Unfortunately, there is no mention of natural family planning which would solve all his difficulties while remaining ethically acceptable.

H.P. Dunn, M.D.
Gaithersburg, Maryland

(The *Bible and Birth Control,* by Charles Provan is available from *Christian News* for $4.00.)

The Overpopulation Explosion Myth
Down With Birth Control
Christian News, March 3, 2003

Until the 1930s just about every major Christian denomination condemned birth control. Children were viewed as blessings from God. The Lutheran Church-Missouri Synod's official publications, and its youth publication, *The Walther League Messenger*, opposed birth control. John Fritz's *Pastoral Theology*, long a standard textbook used at LCMS seminaries by all future LCMS pastors, teaches that the Bible opposes birth control. When the Federal Council of Churches (now National Council of Churches) came out for birth control in 1931, Lutheran Hour Speaker and *Walther League Messenger* Editor, Walter Maier, wrote in *The Walther League Messenger*, May, 1931: "Harebrained sociologists may applaud the recent lapse into paganism of the F.C.C." Maier wrote in the May 1944 *Walther League Messenger*: "The Christian, of course, remembering the repeated divine injunctions, 'Be fruitful and multiply,' welcomes as many children as the all knowing heavenly Father bestows."

Unfortunately, during the last 40 years, *Christian News* has been one of the few religious publications which still defends the position which almost all denominations took until the 1930s and which the LCMS took until the 1950s.

Some of the articles on birth control, population, and children in *The Christian News Encyclopedia* are "The Lutheran Church and Birth Control – The Family in Natural and Revealed Law" by Dr. Tom Hardt (pp. 930-931); "Zero growth brings problems" by M. Stanton Evans, p. 1435; "Contraception Kills Millions," by Rev. Paul Marz; "'Artificial Birth Control' Held Cause of Rising Divorce Rate,"; "Jose Espinosa's Medical View on Contraception," p. 1435; "The Deadly ABC," by Dr. Martin J. Naumann, pp. 1437-1438; "From Diapers to Diploma," by Reuel Schulz; "The Tragedy of Birth Control" by Martin Naumann, p. 1439 (reprinted in this issue of CN); "Birth Control—Why Are They Lying to Women?" J.C. Espinosa, M.D., p. 1439; "Birth Control Pill Harmful to Health," Haven Bradford Gow, p. 1444; "Birth Control Methods and Abortion," Larry Marquardt and Darald Gruen, p. 1783; "Silent Abortion, p. 1783; "Why Pro-Lifers Should Oppose Birth Control," American Life Lobby, p. 1886; "God Save the Family," Rolf Preus, p. 1887; "Not Enough Children," p,. 1887; "Birth Control and the Population Explosion," p. 1887; "Consider the Landon Story," p. 1888; "The Bible's View of Birth Control," Charles D. Provan, pp. 1888-1892; "Overpopulation," p. 1888; "*Christian News* and Birth Control," p. 1889; "The LCMS on Marriage:" from the *Concordia Cyclopedia*, p. 1893; "The World's Worst Killer," p. 1894; "Arguments Against Birth Control," from *Pastoral Theology*, John H.C. Fritz, Concordia Seminary, St. Louis, pp. 1894-1895; "Is American Life Lobby Opposed to Birth Control?", Judie Brown, President, American Life Lobby, p. 1897; "Views Expressed by Dr. Walter A. Maier in *Walther League Messenger*," p. 2633; "Down With Birth Control –

Leave the Number of Children in God's Hand," p. 3328; "Birth Control," position paper of the Lutheran Church of the Reformation, p. 3329; "The Planned Parenthood Deathtrap," pp. 3328-3329; "Fr. Marx Reports on Worldwide Low Birthrate," p. 3330.

A helpful book could be written on birth control and the "population explosion" by simply compiling all the articles on those subjects in the *Christian News Encyclopedia*. LCMS officials do not consider it appropriate to use the CNE. Professors act as if it is unscholarly to study and quote from an encyclopedia edited by someone they refuse to certify.

Reprinted here from the February 3, 2003 *The Report* (British Columbia, Canada) is "The unfolding extinction of Western Europeans shows the fallibility of the infallible." The authors, commenting on "the population explosion," write: "The experts, we are told, were dead wrong, and the problem is the precise reverse. There's a critical threat all right, but it stems from too few babies, not too many, and the process is rapidly reaching a point of no return." "The greatest incentive for having children comes from the belief that they constitute a precious gift from God. No God means no children, which is why birth rates follow church-attendance rates downward. But failure to recognize God also entails divine judgment, as surely as effect follows cause. In this century, we may discover to our sorrow just what that means."

Concordia Theological Monthly, August, 1931

Edited by Concordia Seminary, St. Louis, MO
Theological Observer

Birth Control in the Light of the Bible.-In *Christianity Today* the Rev. J. H. Gauss, D.D., Dean of Brookes Bible Institute, St. Louis, publishes an earnest warning against the sin of "birth control." The matter deserves careful attention. He writes: -

"The reports of a committee appointed by the Federation of Churches on birth control have been made public. Undoubtedly thousands of thinking people are sadly perplexed and some justly indignant at the majority report approving the use of 'contraceptives' in marital relations; also undoubtedly other thousands will be encouraged to resort to the use of such means to indulge sexual lust without marriage or, if married, without incurring the care of children.

"The majority report refers to the Church and the Bible as 'silent upon the subject' and intimates that such silence gives consent or at least does not forbid. Its reference to the Bible is quite misleading, though doubtless unintentionally so. The Bible is not as silent as the report implies. Read Gen. 1, 26, 'multiply,' and again after the Flood, Gen. 9, 1, 'multiply'; 1 Chron. 4, 27, Judah's superiority to Simeon, Simeon's tribal family did not 'multiply'; Ps. 127, 3-5, many children a matter for congratulation as an expression of God's favor; Prov. 31, 28, the 'virtuous woman's 'household' consists of 'husband' and 'children'; 1 Sam. 2, 21, Hannah's answered prayer is followed by the birth of 'three sons and two daughters.' Zech. 8, 5 promises that the streets of Jerusalem shall one day be full of boys and girls at play. 1 Tim. 3, 4 sets forth the fitness of one for the office of bishop as having 'one wife' and being the father of 'children.' 1 Tim. 5, 10 states as a condition that an aged widow receive aid from the church that she has 'brought up children,' and v. 14 directs that 'younger women marry, bear children, guide the house, give none occasion to the adversary to reproach.' 1 Cor. 7, 14 declares God's special interest in a Christian's children. Eph. 6, 4 commends fathers to bring up children for God. Mark 10, 14 records the Savior of our race welcoming children to His blessing and a large place in the kingdom of God. Most truly did the heathen women say to the Christian missionary, 'Yours is a God that cares for little children.'

"God instituted marriage and that for birth of children, and that according to the physical laws He had created in man; true, not as a means for gratifying selfish passion resulting in births too frequent for the health of mother or child, yet not avoiding such births by use of 'contraceptives' to prevent them.

"Birth denial is not birth control, but sinful, selfish refusal to fulfil God's purpose in marriage.

"True birth control, or abstinence, is God-fearing, marital self-control, as we are taught in 1 Cor. 7, 5.

"Not a child, but 'children' are necessary in God's ideal family on earth. Such ideal families are vital to our race, to every nation, to our nation, to the Church of Jesus Christ. Let us not live lower than beasts, but as men, being spirits, created in the 'image' of God, with bodies made in the 'likeness' of God.

" 'Ye are bought with a price; therefore glorify God in your body and in your spirit, which are God's,' 1 Cor. 6, 20. 'Your whole spirit and soul and body be preserved blameless unto the coming of our Lord Jesus Christ. Faithful is He that calleth you who also will do it,' 1 Thess. 5, 23. 24."

J.T.M.

A Study in Biblical and Dogmatic Theology

By C.H. Little, D.D., S.T.D., 1933, Professor of Dogmatic and Systematic Theology in the Evangelical Lutheran Seminary of Canada, Waterloo, Ontario

Christian News, May 20, 2006

Chapter Twenty-Six
RACE SUICIDE

This is a question that is very much to the front in our day. It is usually referred to as "birth control," and is advocated by those who, on the basis of hygienic marriage, would limit the procreation children to the "physically fit," and would arbitrarily fix the number of children of such parents to suit the pocketbook and purse, so as to allow them freedom and enable them to keep up their social relations and retain their proper position in society.

As far as it is a mere humanitarian scheme advocated by such as would breed humans just as men breed horses and cattle, there would be no room for its discussion here. But the idea has caught hold also of the Church; and men and women, here and there, are making propaganda for this cause, and a Lutheran woman is one of its most strenuous advocates. It is well, therefore, for us to be clear as to the teaching of Scripture on this subject. God instituted marriage in the very beginning of human history it was the first institution that He gave man. "And God blessed them, and said unto them, Be fruitful and multiply and replenish the earth." This command of God still holds good and will continue to do so until the consummation, when the saved shall be equal unto the angels, and shall neither marry nor be given in marriage.

Marriage may accordingly be defined as the indissoluble union of one man and one woman, according to the divine institution, entered into by mutual consent, for the begetting of offspring and for mutual assistance in life. And this is still the purpose of marriage. For this reason we have exhortations and counsels given in the New Testament Scriptures to both parties to this contract. Saint Paul says, "I will therefore that the younger women marry, bear children, guide the house." And again, "She shall be saved in childbearing, if they continue in faith and charity and holiness with sobriety." And to men he says, "Husbands, love your wives, even as Christ loved the Church, and gave Himself for it." To this Saint Peter adds, "Likewise ye husbands dwell with them according to knowledge, giving honor unto the wife as unto the weaker vessel, and as being heirs together of the grace of life; that your prayers be not hindered."

This idea of marriage is regarded as old-fashioned by many in our day. The deep, intimate relationship which it involves is lightly regarded. It is looked upon by some as the satisfaction of the desire for mere companionship for the elimination of the loneliness of the single state. Some men would limit the number of children to one or two for social reasons. Many women enter into marriage with no intention of bearing children or of assuming the obligation that marriage naturally entails. And frequently everything that can be done to prevent the bringing forth of offspring is utilized.

There seems to be, on the part of many, no disposition to regard marriage as a school of discipline, but rather to look upon it as one vast honeymoon with no burdens or duties attached to it. Childless homes, which were once the exception and incurred reproach, are now looked upon by many, particularly by the women, as the ideal of married life. They scoff at the words of the Psalmist, "Lo, children are an heritage of the Lord; and the fruit of the womb is His reward" (Psalm 127:3), And men are also found who jeer at the words, "Thy wife shall be as a fruitful vine by the sides of thine house:

thy children like olive plants round about thy table. Behold, that thus shall the man be blessed that feareth the Lord" (Psalm 128:3, 4).

Too many desire to have the joys of married life without taking upon themselves its responsibilities. Saint Paul indeed says, "Let the husband render unto the wife due benevolence: and likewise also the husband hath not power of his own body, but the wife. Defraud ye not one the other, except it be with consent for a time, that ye may give yourselves to fasting and prayer; and come together again, that Satan tempt you not for your incontinency."

Many married couples are quite ready to follow the injunction as far as it forbids the defrauding of one another, but are quite willing to defraud the Lord in the matter by artificially preventing the natural results of their coming together. This is assuming a function that does not belong to them and renders the guilty of fornication within the marriage relation. Their action thus becomes a direct transgression of the Sixth Commandment and incurs its penalties.

Race suicide, or birth control, is a sin and a crime, and should not be tolerated in the Church. It destroys the sanctity of marriage and defeats the purpose for which it was given to men by their Creator. It will as surely as any other sin bring down upon those who commit it God's wrath and condemnation.

Dialogue
Jose Espinosa's Medical View on Contraception

From the February 13, 1977
THE NATIONAL CATHOLIC
REGISTER
Christian News, February 21, 1977

Dr. Jose Espinosa is a practicing surgeon in Cleveland and a teacher at the medical school of Case Western Reserve University. He lectures widely on euthanasia, but here discusses with the Editor his early endorsement of contraception, and tells how he changed his mind. Dr. Espinosa, a native of the Canary Islands, did his undergraduate work at Columbia University and his medical studies at the University of Madrid.

(Editor) Riley: You're a pro-life doctor at this point and you've expressed your belief in the teaching of *Humane Vitae*, but if I'm not mistaken there was a time when you were handing out contraceptives with great abandon.

Espinosa: That's correct. My turnabout on contraception came as a result of my involvement in the pro-life movement. After getting into the pro-life movement in 1972, I started to see things from inside the anti-people mentality of the contraceptionists.

The mentality of contraception views pregnancy as something to be avoided at all costs, almost as a disease. I started to feel that this is a total lack of faith in God and man: man can't take care of the problems that may arise from people, and God has created too many people. I started to see how, if you view the child in the womb as a contraceptive failure, it is very easy to try to remedy that "accident" by abortion, to say: "Well, all I'm going to do is to remedy a contraceptive failure." I realized I was not preventing abortion, as I thought I was doing in one of the local free clinics by giving contraceptives to young girls. I had been saying "I'm doing this because I'm a pro-lifer, I want to do all I can to prevent abortions." However, I saw after a while that I was not preventing abortion, I was leading people to it.

I also realized how this change from contraception to abortion had been given by two respectable organizations. The American Medical Association started after the Supreme Court decision of 1965 to say that doctors should be permitted to give out contraceptives. After the abortion decision the AMA again went ahead to say that abortion is a medical procedure even for non-medical reasons, and doctors should do it because doctors now are technicians. The same thing happened with Planned Parenthood, more rightly called by some 'Planned Barrenhood.'

Riley: Also called by some, 'Murder, Incorporated'. . .

Espinosa: Their first approach was that contraception would cure everything. As recently as 1963 there was a nice pamphlet by Planned Parenthood which says that contraception is not abortion, and that abortion kills the child. It says the child has begun to live; abortion endangers your health, may render you sterile, or may cause your death. Now, of course, Planned Parenthood has branched out into the abortion field for years. That opened my eyes to the danger.

Riley: Doctor, I would like to see a clinical psychological study, or at least a very carefully-controlled psychological study, of the difference in psychodynamics between real contraception and what we call natural family planning.

Espinosa: Natural family planning has to do, and I believe this position comes out of true natural law, well understood, with a truly non-violent principle of doing no violence to nature, to our nature. I take this idea from Van Kaam.

Riley: Dr. Adrian Van Kaam. He's a Dutch Holy Ghost Father, I believe.

Espinosa: We should not pollute the environment; we should not pollute our own bodies by pills and manipulations of nature which are unhealthy, as I found out with the Pill which I was prescribing at times. There natural family planning comes in, in the sense that if you are obedient to your nature, and you want to beget a child, you know when conception is more likely to occur, and if you don't want to beget a child that particular moment in the proper context, you just avoid making use of sex which could give rise to a child at that particular moment in the proper context, you just avoid making use of sex which could give rise to conception and another child.

Riley: I suppose this respect for nature, which is part of the psychology of natural family planning prevents the couple from looking upon the child as another disaster.

Espinosa: Correct. We like to talk about surprise pregnancy rather than contraceptive failure, which is such a terrible thing. The moment we think of our brother or sister as somebody's contraceptive failure, we're really denying all our theology and all our belief in an almighty wise Creator who loves us so much that He creates us.

Anyway, natural family planning lets us act something else out, which is chaste love. That is respectful presence to other human beings: I can love somebody but I don't have to have sexual relations with that other person all the time, as so-called modern thinkers are trying to say. Chaste love concludes the trio of poverty, obedience and chastity, which are still the rungs of the ladder by which we can transcend our nature.

Riley: How does the ordinary Christian practice poverty if he happens not to be a poor person?

Espinosa: The poverty I am talking about is in the context of ecology, the wise use of things, neither destroying the environment nor the body with which we have been endowed. I saw this very clearly with the use of birth control pills, especially with the use of IUDs. Women, for example, at the age of 16 who, due to the fact that they had been taking the Pill for a while, have developed diseases that will be with them for the rest of their lives. Like cystic changes in the breast, which have caused their breasts to age prematurely, and they have lumps and are afraid of cancer. Again, nobody told them that this could happen to them.

Riley: How did this philosophical conversion to see the principles of the Catholic tradition against contraception – how did this natural conversion affect your religious view?

Espinosa: Well, it made me proud and almost happily surprised that the Church is right. I attended a very interesting meeting earlier this year at which Sydney Callahan addressed the Newman Center at Case Western Reserve University. She talked about new aspects of sexuality. Now since sexuality is as old as man, I wanted to know what the new aspects might be. The new aspects turned out to include how we have to have contraception. . .

Riley: It's part of the Christian life.

Espinosa: . . . and the Pope is wrong.

Riley: The Christian tradition is wrong.

Espinosa: . . . and marriage till death do you part was the Christian teaching only when people were living to the age of about 35. Of course now that people live longer it doesn't mean forever.

Anyway, I got up at the end and told her that the true Christian, Catholic position is one that arises from respect for nature, not its manipulation – which is first of all unhealthy and also a faithless position, a denial of our beliefs.

It's frustrating to see people who just haven't been enlightened. A lot of them have been saying: "Look how the Church said the earth doesn't move around the sun." That wasn't a theological question to begin with, yet they downgraded the Church's position that way. Happily, I now find myself in tremendous agreement with the Church's position. I now see how much wiser she is than I thought – after so many people were bad-mouthing her teaching, her supposed lack of knowledge about marriage and sexual matters.

Riley: You thought the Church was short-sighted, but it has turned out to be very farsighted.

Espinosa: Yeah. And those people like Sydney Callahan – she considers herself a progressive, but I think she just hasn't come back to the right position.

Riley: It's very unfortunate that many people have to discover through sad experience that the Church has been pointing out the right path in sexual matters. They discover it only by rushing down a false path, and tripping, and getting themselves bruised.

Espinosa: My fear is that many of them have not found out yet. I don't know how they are going to realize that they have Protestantized themselves. These people call themselves Catholic, but don't waste any opportunity to downgrade the Magisterium and the Pope. Why don't they become Druids? Or join any Christian church that might be more to their liking? As I understand it the Methodists are talking about a liturgy of divorce.

Riley: I'd be interested in knowing some of the clinical problems that arise from the use of contraceptives.

Espinosa: Aside from the ones I already mentioned, teenagers, because of the effect of estrogen, have a 400 per cent increase in stroke, heart attack, high blood pressure, and cancer of the uterus. If they get cancer, it grows quicker with the birth control pill. There are a host of complications – even gallstones. The IUD of course causes infection, causes abortion.

The IUD is called by man a contraceptive but it is not. It produces abortion. That's the problem with the Pill; at least 50 percent of the time the Pill does not produce the lack of ovulation. That is supposedly the mechanism: there is no ovum to enable conception to take place. What actually happens if conception does take place is that the lining of the uterus has been so changed that the child cannot continue to develop and will fall out as a degenerate – fall out as an early abortion. The Pill is 50 per cent of the time an abortifacient. The newer pills are low-dose because of the problems with estrogen, which can cause heart attacks and high blood pressure, strokes and cancer. Most of the time they do not prevent ovulation from taking place.

Riley: Doesn't the IUD sometimes provoke an abortion when the child is fairly well formed?

Espinosa: Yes, there is a case of a girl who had a miscarriage, at 6 months. The child died. In this particular situation the girl faced the fact, and grew in faith. She returned after she saw what was happening. If women who had IUDs could see the destroyed child they would probably refuse to use one. The child is so small. That is how these women often have longer and more painful periods. If they could see the results, they would probably abstain from them.

There is one called the Dalkon Shield which was supposed to be the most efficient in preventing the development of the child, and was finally removed from the market after 43 women died from it. The mechanism of death is an infected miscarriage because the IUD creates a local inflammatory reaction inside the uterus and a bigger incidence of infection. That's why you have an infected miscarriage, and that's why these women died.

Riley: You say that every IUD creates a low-grade infection? That in itself is almost enough to bar the use of the IUD.

Espinosa: They are uncomfortable. There is a new type which contains hormones in order to make it more tolerable. Hormones make the uterus not so cramped, and may decrease some of the bleeding. Another problem with the IUD is that women who wear IUD devices have more chance of an ectopic pregnancy, a pregnancy outside the uterus. This is a dangerous situation. Usually the tube ruptures. This causes the death of 300 out of 100,000 women, and happens more so with the IUD. Some of these studies are from England.

The contraceptive mentality has been so well accepted because of the tremendous propaganda in an industrial society. Natural family methods are the underdogs because there is nothing to sell. People who make money in this industry would do everything in their power to make sure that natural methods are not accepted.

Yet some of the pills have been withdrawn from the market. The so-called sequential contraceptives which were supposed to be more "natural" because they had estrogen in the first part of the period and estrogen and progesterone in the second part were taken off the market when it was proven they caused more heart attacks, more strokes, more cancer than any others. I thought that would be the fate of all contraceptive pills.

Riley: But they're still at the corner drug store, selling by the millions.

Espinosa: I find it interesting that the IUD was developed by camel drivers. Camel drivers didn't want the camels to give birth in the desert, so they put rocks inside their uterus. The contraceptionists got the idea from that: well, they do it on camels, why not on women?

Funny thing, our government is pretty careful about animals, is pro-animal. DES –diethylstilbestrol – is the morning after pill. You can't use it on cows – its use was prohibited – but you can still use it on women.

In the early '50s it was used to prevent miscarriage. Women who used to bleed in early pregnancy would be given these pills, and the bleeding would stop. Now It's been discovered that the children that were inside these women at the time, who now are in their late teens or early 20s, have developed cancer of the vagina, cancer of the neck of the womb, which is extremely rare. It also caused congenital deformity of the children that were born. If it is a boy, the boy has a good chance of not being able to beget children. It it's a girl, she can get early cancer.

The drug had been given to cows to make them grow faster and put on weight so that you could make more money from your investment in cattle. However when all the problems it creates were discovered, its use was prohibited – in cows. But women still can use it.

Of course they do say if it doesn't work by causing an early abortion of the child, then you should go get an abortion because the child may get cancer or may be deformed in some way.

Riley: They have an answer for everything, don't they? Never at a loss for a way out.

Espinosa: These manufacturing companies – a very good industry making pills taken by 2 million women – have created a condition which 90 per cent of these women suffer from: an uncomfortable vaginal discharge. Of course that's fixed by another medicine which they're going to sell you.

Riley: They get them both ways. But I'm surprised the ecological movement seems to be leaving out people. Aren't we part of the landscape?

Espinosa: Oh, we're all very ecological, all right.

I remember seeing a marvelous view near the Shenandoah from several thousand feet high. There, big as life, was a sign saying how magnificent this view must have been when the settlers arrived before the view was spoiled by all those houses down there. But when I looked down, I could see six or seven houses in a panorama that stretched maybe 20 miles. I said, "My God, are trees better than people?"

Riley: What the people who put up that sign don't realize is that some of the world's most beautiful scenery is largely man made. Take Italy: the hilltop towns of Tuscany and Umbria, the valleys with the lonely farmhouses and the vines, the villages along the lake of Como and Lago Maggiore.

Espinosa: All with the church at the top, like in Spain.

But many who are in the ecology movement see man as something opposed to nature. Very often he is, as in the Pill and in all that destruction. But man, when he acts according to nature, gives nature its true meaning and fulfillment. We are God's most beautiful creation. We're the flowers in God's garden.

Christian News and Birth Control
Christian News, June 13, 1988

"The Bible's View of Birth Control," the lead article in the February 29 *Christian News* has been severely criticized by some and highly praised by others.

We published it even though we did not entirely agree with what the author said about the Old Testament and animals. Our *Christian News Encyclopedia* has a few articles on birth control .

Several Roman Catholic Right-to-Life groups commended CN for its position on birth control . This issue includes a guest editorial on the matter.

The Couple to Couple League, 3621 Glenmore Avenue, Box 111184, Cincinnati, Ohio 45211 has published some excellent material on abortion and birth control. Interested readers should write for a list of their publications.

Father Paul Marx, President of Human Life International, 7845 Airpark Road, Gaithersburg, Maryland 20879, wrote to us:

"My sincerest congratulations for your article in *Christian News* from Monday, February 29, 1988. I am referring to Charles D. Provan's 'The Bible's View of Birth Control.' It is just what I have been looking for.

"I always knew that Martin Luther was very strong on children being a blessing from God and I loved the many quotes that Provan pulled out. Give him my sincere appreciation and thanks.

"You may be aware that today only Poland and Malta and Ireland of all developed countries are reproducing themselves. All the other countries are dying out. The wealthier and more educated, the fewer children the people tend to have in every country. The whole of Europe, the whole of the Western world, is dying out including the USA and Canada. That is why Christians should be emphasizing the blessings of children."

"I wonder to what extent Lutherans are interested in natural family planning. It strikes me that, while parents have to be generous before God, there may come a time when they could limit their progeny for health and other reasons. But this should be done with abstinence, not the interference of contraception, and surely not sterilization and least of all abortion."

"Birth Control and Christian Discipleship," a 38 page pamphlet. The Couple to Couple League sent to us shows that at one time many churches strongly opposed the use of contraceptives. It notes that in 1931 the Anglicans and the majority of a committee of the Federal Council of Churches endorsed "the careful and restrained use of contraceptives by married people," at the same time admitting that "serious evils, such as extramarital sex relations, may be increased by general knowledge of contraceptives."

The Washington Post reacted (March 22, 1931): "Carried to its logical conclusions, the committee's report, if carried into effect, would sound the death-knell of marriage as a holy marriage institution by establishing degrading practices which would encourage indiscriminate immorality. The suggestion that the use of legalized contraceptives would be 'careful and restrained' is preposterous."

Dr. Walter A. Maier, professor at the LCMS's Concordia Seminary, St. Louis, is quoted: "Birth control, as popularly understood today and involving the use of contraceptives, is one of the most repugnant of modern aberrations, representing a 20th century renewal of pagan bankruptcy." Here are just a few quotes from Maier found in *The Walther League Messenger*, an LCMS youth publication: "America's danger is not over-population, but an interpolation, which grows the more serious the longer and the more insistently the advocates of birth-control assert themselves" (November, 1925).

"It may not be inappropriate in connection with approaching Mother's Day to suggest that what the nation needs, among other things, is more mothers and better mothers. Harebrained sociologists may applaud the recent lapse into paganism of the Federal Council of Churches of Christ in America in coming out for birth control, they may endorse the increasing incursions into the business world on the part of married women; but level-headed students of human affairs deprecate this menace to motherhood and agree with the recent utterance of Mme. Ernestine Schumann-Heink: 'Motherhood is the most sacred thing in the world. The modern woman does not feel the great sacred emotion. All that is important in her life is the lipstick, jazz and bridge. She does not want children.'" May, 1931

"Birth control is being urged by Dr. Norman Haire, of Paris, as a means of eliminating defectives from human society. This French physician states that the ignorance of poor people 'gives rise to the breeding of an enormous number of mentally and physically defective beings for whom the wealthier classes are obliged to contribute for maintenance.' There are just two fundamental errors in arguments of this kind. In the first place, not all defective children are the offspring of poor parents, and then, many children of poor parents, who have been blessed with large families, have risen to eminent heights of success. Benjamin Franklin, for example, was the youngest of seventeen children.

The Walther League Messenger, April, 1925.

We have compiled a list of many more quotes vs. *birth control* in *The Walther League Messenger* and the LCMS's *Lutheran Witness* before these publications were taken over by liberals.

"Contraception Is the Root Cause of Euthanasia"

Christian News, November 25, 1991

"We must openly insist that legalized abortion and euthanasia directly result from our acceptance of contraception which in turn results from our loss of trust in the Providence of God" says Professor Charles Rice in "Contraception Is the Root Cause of Euthanasia" in the November 21 *Wanderer*. According to Professor Rice, "We are not sliding down a slippery slope toward euthanasia. We are there. It is long past time to reject the failed pragmatists, both clerical and lay, of the establishment pro-life movement and to insist on an uncompromising advocacy of the truth on contraception as well as on euthanasia."

Professor Rice says: "The 1930 Anglican Lambeth Conference approved a limited allowance of contraception. It was the first time that any Christian denomination had ever declared that contraception could ever be objectively right. James Douglas, editor of The London Sunday Express, responded that 'Lambeth has delivered a fatal blow to marriage, to motherhood, to fatherhood, to the family, and to morality.'"

Theologians of The Lutheran Church-Missouri Synod, which until recent years had always opposed contraception, said about the same thing.

Rice adds:

"A major contributor to the triumph of euthanasia is the established pro-life movement itself, including the American Catholic Church. That movement has argued since Roe v. Wade, not for the prohibition of abortion, but for its restriction with exceptions for various cases, e.g., life or health of the mother, rape and incest, etc. this tactic implicitly affirms the pro-death principle that innocent life is negotiable. The establishment pro-life leaders debate not whether, but which, innocent human beings may be legally killed. They should not be surprised at their importance in opposing euthanasia. They mean well. But where they owed leadership in a fight for the right, those spokesmen, clerical as well as lay, have offered scandal by their compromise and they have led the movement to defeat after inevitable defeat."

Dr. Walter A. Maier–Birth Control

Christian News, April 14, 1997

Christian News
Rev. Herman Otten
PO Box 168
New Haven, Missouri 63068
Dear Rev. Otten:
I want to thank you for publishing the pamphlet entitled "Everything You Never Wanted to Know About Birth Control," written by myself and il-

lustrated by my wife. The information contained in the pamphlet is not known widely enough. If it were, then Christians who call themselves pro-life would not still be employing these methods to control their family size.

It may interest you to know that my wife and I are Missouri Synod Lutherans and my pastor, Rev. Ferd Bahr, brought your reprint of our pamphlet to our attention. It is my hope that our Synod will be constant in its strong pro-life stand and condemn the use of any "contraceptive" which actually aborts. In addition to this, I hope our pamphlet or something similar to it, can be disseminated on a Synod-wide basis so that our pastors can be equipped to inform their congregation members about the murderous effects these devils and drugs have on tiny pre-born children. This would be especially timely in premarital counseling situations. The thought of "silent abortions" happening unbeknownst to Christian women while they work, take care of their children, or even worship in your churches is a thought that saddens and sobers me.

In addition to my study on abortifacient birth control, it has amazed me to learn that Protestants of all stripes, including Lutherans, were opposed to all forms of contraception, well into this century. No protestant denomination accepted birth control or contraception until 1930 when the Anglicans did such. One of the Missouri Synod greats, Dr. Walter Maier, professor of theology and Lutheran Hour speaker, wrote a scathing attack on birth control in his book *For Better Not For Worse* in 1935. But somewhere along the line, the Missouri Synod along with all other Protestant denominations began to either actively promote birth control, or silently accept it, thus changing in a matter of a few decades a belief that had been held in all of Christendom for 1,900 years.

The Psalmist write in 137:3-5: "Behold, children are a heritage from the LORD the fruit of the womb is his reward like arrows in the hands of a warrior, so are the children of one's youth. Happy is the man who has his quiver full of them. . ." if Christians would but take this passage at face value and ask for faith to believe that what God is saying here is true, then "the blight of birth control" as Dr. Walter Maier terms it, would cease to be a disease upon the churches of today.

Maranatha!
Jon Valentine

(The January 13, 1997 *Christian News* reprinted "Everything You Never Wanted to Know About Birth Control" by Jon and Maria Valentine and "The Protest of a Protestant Minister against Birth Control" by Rev. Matt Trewhella. Published by Protestants Against Birth Control, Box 07240, Milwaukee, Wisconsin 53207. For more information see the sections on Birth Control and Population in the *Christian News Encyclopedia*, particularly pages 1886-1898.)

For Better Not For Worse
The Blight of Birth Control
By Dr. Walter A. Maier
(pp. 377-421, pp. 407-412 reprinted below).

ITS ANTI-SCRIPTURAL BIAS

To pass over other objections to birth control, – objections so weighty that these sections of the Federal Penal Code make it a criminal offense, punishable by five years in jail or a fine of $5,000 or both, to send through the mails or through other common carriers "any article, drug or medicine, or any obscene, lewd, or lascivious publication intended for preventing conception," – we come to the basic objection, which, if all other argumentation were swept aside, would be a complete denunciation. We refer to the evident indictment of birth control contained in the statements of Scripture.

The majority report of the Committee on Birth Control appointed by the Federal Council of the Churches of Christ in America states that the Church and the Bible are "silent upon the subject."

This is a bold statement. When the first human parent pair was created, the divine command enjoined: "Be fruitful and multiply and replenish the earth" (Gen 1:28). After the Deluge, when the world was to take its second start, the blessing for Noah and his sons again required them to "be fruitful and multiply and replenish the earth" (Gen. 9:1). In Ps. 127:3 we read:
Lo, children are an heritage of the Lord,
And the fruit of the womb is His reward.
The picture of the ideal home is described in Ps. 128:3:
Thy wife shall be as a fruitful vine by the sides of thine house,
Thy children like olive-plants round about thy table.
In Prov. 31:28 children are mentioned as part of the virtuous woman's household. If it is objected that these are Old Testament passages, attention is called to these utterances of the New Testament: 1 Tim. 5:10, where it is stated that those aged widows who "brought up children" received support from the church; 1 Tim. 5:14, where the apostle directs the younger women (the widows "to marry, bear children"; 1 Cor. 7:14, which illustrates God's gracious interest in His children's children; and particularly Mark 10:14, where the Savior of the race utters His memorable "Suffer the little children to come unto Me." In spite of extended argument not a single passage can be adduced from Scripture which even in any remote way condones birth control; and no one acquainted with the Bible should hesitate to admit that it is a definite departure from the requirements of Scripture. Se Gen. 38:9, 10.

THE ATTITUDE OF MODERN CHURCHES

A magazine writer calls attention to the significant fact that many leaders of the clergy, far from frowning on birth control, as the Bible does, recognize it as "essential to the welfare of society." The Federal Council of the Churches of Christ in America has officially endorsed birth control. Liberal preachers glory in urging it, and the 1934 annual convention of the Young Women's Christian Association approved a plan whereby local associations would work for laws permitting dissemination of birth-control instruction. The extent to which the clergy participates in spreading this information may be seen in the Maternal Health Association of Missouri, which spreads across its letter-head the notice that it is "affiliated with the American Birth-control League." On the advisory council of this association are the Rte. Rev William Scarlett, D.D., bishop of the Episcopal diocese of Missouri; the Rev. Arnold H. Lowe, Presbyterian and past president of the St. Louis Church Federation; the Rev. John W. MacIvor, former head of the Federation and pastor of the largest Presbyterian church in St. Louis; Rabbi Ferdinand M. Isserman of Temple Israel; the Rev. Ivan Lee Holt, former national president of the Federal Council; the Rev. George Rowland Dodson, Church of the Unity; the Rev R.W. Adair, executive secretary of the Good Will Industries, St. Louis.

To assist Protestant pastors in advising young married couples, the Federal Council of Churches, through its Committee on Marriage and the Home, has issued a pamphlet entitled Safe-guarding Marriages. On page twenty-nine it deliberately counsels the clergymen of its constituency: "For the protection of the health of the mothers and of the children and for the best interests of the family he [the pastor] may want to take up the question of the spacing of pregnancies and of making parenthood voluntary rather than merely accidental. The husband and wife may well be cautioned against postponing parenthood too long. At the same time a word needs to be said about the obligation of welcoming the child if one should come at a time when the parents would not have planned it, since no method of birth control is entirely dependable in all cases. The minister will do well to counsel the young people to avoid unsatisfactory and dangerous methods of birth control. He may well urge the use of the most authoritative books dealing with this matter, and better still, that the couple seek the advice of a physician who is skilled in this subject."

To show how these attitudes permeate congregational life, the instance of the Second Baptist Church of St. Louis may be cited. At the morning service of Sunday, January 13 1935, the pastor asked his audience to vote on this question: "Is it your Christian conviction that adequate scientific information concerning conception and contraception must be made legally and inexpensively available to all married people in order to permit the development of a race of people capable of establishing the kingdom of God?"

Apparently the congregation at this liberal church was not large; but it was birth-control-minded; for fifty-nine ballots answered, "Yes"; two, "Uncertain"; and none, "No." (*St. Louis Globe-Democrat*, January 15, 1935.)

Protesting in the open forum of The Living Church (Episcopal), a New Jersey pastor thus summarized the consequences of the resolution accepted by the General Convention of the Episcopal Church in Atlantic City, by which the dissemination of birth-control information was endorsed: "The result of this resolution is that we now have priests who openly sponsor birth control, open their parish-houses to such meetings and addresses by leaders of the movement." (January 5, 1938.)

Such pronouncements cannot decide the issue. No church attacks on the divine gift of children and the nobility of parenthood can justify birth control. As a matter of fact, however, the great body of Christians throughout the world is deliberately opposed to it. The Roman Catholic Church has repeatedly voiced its uncompromising denunciation. The Lutheran church is definitely arrayed against birth restriction. As for the action of the Federal Council of the Churches of Christ (a procedure that will help to speed up the disintegration of this body), insistent voices of religious leaders all over the country have been raised against this arbitrary pronouncement.

THE CHURCH'S POSITION

The Church must maintain its emphatic avowal of Christian marriage as God's institution for the propagation of the human race. It must insist that, whenever the divine command "Be fruitful and multiply" is evaded for selfish purposes and through the employment of methods suggested by birth control, divine displeasure is invoked.

This does not mean that the Church establishes an orthodox minimum and insists upon families of ten or twelve children. It has no doctrine of human mass production, nor does it champion the Canadian "$500,000 maternity marathon," started by the extraordinary will of bachelor Charles Vance Millar, Toronto brewer and horseman. He offered a half million to the mother in his city bearing the most children within a decade. Neither does the Church declare that children must follow in rapid succession without sufficient interims for maternal recuperation and infant care. Nor is the health of the mother to be disregarded in the establishment of the family. Her constitution must not be ruined nor her body broken by excessive childbirth. In all of these considerations the Christian principles of love and forbearance must be actuating impulses.

Young couples sincerely concerned over the thought of abnormally large families and the resultant inability to provide adequate means of the cultural growth of their children, should not permit themselves to be disturbed by the alarmist literature of birth-control propaganda. Instead let them consider these five fundamental facts:

First of all, the specter of a prodigal nature that spawns out children and that almost mechanically brings babies year after year in uninterrupted succession is not the picture of nature as it exerts its influences in our lives. There are limits to fertility which are regulated by mysterious factors. The mere physical chances of extraordinarily large families in the average home today in an age that has notable natural trends toward an increase of sterility) are small, particularly in view of the prevalence of late marriages. In England, Doubleday, Pell, Sutherland, and others have presented strong evidence to show that human fertility is reduced as prosperity, comfort, and intellectuality increase.

Then it dare not be overlooked that "children are an heritage of the Lord," the gift of His rich and undeserved mercy. Thousands of Christian couples have learned by sad and personal experience that this heritage has not been theirs, and even with intense desire and fervent prayer they have been denied the rich blessings from which other short-sighted couples flee in aversion. No child comes into the world without the will and direction of God, and every child born into a Christian home is under all circumstances to be welcomed as the embodiment of a divine benediction.

In the third place, it should be emphasized that there may be certain unobtainable, if not infallible, means that will help regulate the size of a family. Christian physicians can offer sound advice in emergencies confronting honest young couples who spurn the artificial methods of birth control. The Church has never protested against the employment of those means which the course of nature itself seems to provide, unless their employment is a selfish attempt to evade the responsibilities of parenthood.

The Church also calls attention to continence, self-denial, and restraint. While this often imposes a hopeless struggle on those without the spiritual forces of Christianity, those who take recourse to the power of effective prayer find a sustaining ally in their faith.

Finally, the Church says that in the infrequent and exceptional conflicts between childbirth and maternal health the Christian conscience must seek pastoral advice and the counsel of a Christian physician.

With all this, unusual consideration must be extended to those who have not received the heritage of the Lord from their heavenly Father. No finger of scorn should be pointed at them, no whispers of suspicion raised behind their backs. They should receive the sympathy which Scripture extends to its Hannahs and Sarahs. In their own lives there should be no diminution of heart-deep prayer to the Father above, who "doeth all things well," that the happy gift of parenthood may be theirs. If this blessing is permanently withheld from them, they may find solace when, beholding a helpless infant, orphaned and deprived of parental love and the full opportunities of an unfolding life, they look beyond to see the great Friend of children as He lifts His arms in benediction and tells them: "Whoso shall receive one such little child in My name receiveth Me" (Matt. 18:5).

Let's Rethink Our Numbers
Protestants Against Birth Control

Jon Valentine
Christian News, January 29, 1996

Every group that is trying to right a wrong in our society quotes statistics to back up their claims. Jews, attempting to stem the tide of anti-Semitism, always refer back to their six million brothers and sisters, and six million others, who were so brutally exterminated in the Nazi regime's Final Solution. Vietnam veterans, advocating their plight and remembering their friends, remind us of the 58,000 who perished in the rice patties and jungles of South East Asia. Likewise, women's groups point to the number of domestic violence incidences in America and children's advocates regularly quote the number of child abuse cases. The pro-life movement is no different, in that we too regularly quote statistics, particularly of the number of dead pre-born children. This is certainly not a bad thing. It helps us, and the rest of the public, to understand the enormity of the abortion holocaust. You're all familiar with the statistics: thirty million dead since Roe v. Wade; 1.5 million dead a year; 4,500 dead a day; 187 dead an hour; 3 dead every minute; one dying every 18 or 19 seconds. These are grim statistics. These are horrible statistics. They reflect the truth that not only does abortion kill children, but abortion kills children on an almost incomprehensible scale. The figures are staggering if you let yourself think about it. It saddens me to tell you that these figures are wrong, very wrong. If we as pro-lifers are going to stand by the statement that life begins at conception, and if we are going to be honest with ourselves, we have to change our statistics. I wish I could say that these statistics were inflated, but they're not. They are severely understated. What am I talking about? I am referring to the problem of abortifacient birth control. Such methods as the Pill, the IUD, Norplant and Depo-Provera, normally thought of as only contraceptives, are truly abortion-causing. This means that they produce the same result as the physician's suction machine, saline solution or curettage: a dead baby. Until the mainstream pro-life groups incorporate abortifacient death counts into their annual statistics of the number of dead pre-born children, they have lost their credibility, because they fail to stand up for all pre-born children.

So how bad is it? Well, because of the earliness of the abortions, many women employing abortifacient methods of birth control abort before they even know they are pregnant. This is because the new human life is ended before it even has a chance to implant on the lining of the uterus. Therefore, it is impossible with absolute certainty to document the exact number of these abortions, but then again, our statistics on surgical abortions are also only estimates, as we know that not every abortion in America is reported. However, we do have some information that will help us. We do know approximately how many women are using abortifacient forms of birth control in America. We also know the approximate rate that these methods fail, and allow ovulation to occur. We also know the chances of fertilization occurring in an ovulating woman engaged in an average amount of "unprotected" (for lack of a better term) sexual activity.

With this knowledge, we come up with some ghastly figures. Extremely conservative estimates regarding the Pill tell us that there are 588,000 abortions annually as a result of this method.[1,2] There are good reasons to believe this figure is much higher. We can figure out that the IUD causes approximately 1,116,900 abortions annually.[3,4] A conservative estimate tells us that Depo-Provera produces 1,200,000 annually and Norplant gives us 2,250,000.[5]

Friends, these estimates are probably too cautious, but even with these numbers, if we add in surgical abortions, our annual death count as a result of abortions in America is 5,154, 900. That is nearly three and a half times more than the number of abortions we previously thought. To break that down, that means 14,123 babies die everyday; 588 dead ever hour; ten die every minute; and one baby dies ever six seconds. God only knows how many children have perished since Roe v. Wade but I think it would be safe to say that our 30 million figure could at least be doubled and probably tripled. Today's greatest offenders, Norplant and Depo-Provera are relatively new. So it would not be correct to add in those statistics for 22 years. However, we know that the number of users of the Pill and the IUD have been declining recently, so our present abortion totals for those two methods would be even greater annually in the past.

However, it would be wrong of me to end this article on such a depressing note. We are the people of God, the Author of Life and Truth. As the pro-life movement, we must take this new knowledge, and instead of giving up in despair, take these truths to others so that the word gets out. We must lovingly confront our friends and family members who are using such methods. This is very difficult. I know, because I have done it recently. We must inform our pastors. Do you realize that there are Christian women who are on the Pill or the IUD who may be unknowingly and silently aborting children right in the sanctuaries of our churches? Once we are informed, how can we let this continue? I pray that God would give us the grace and strength to not be silent. If we choose to ignore this and continue our silence and willful ignorance, then the Church is no different from the world, and we have no moral authority whatsoever, to tell the unbeliever not to get a surgical abortion.

Footnotes
1 Infant Homicides Through Contraceptives, Eternal Life, P.O. Box 787 Bardstown, KY 40004, (1994) p. 24.
2 Beginnings, Pharmacist for Life, Vol. XI No. 2, p. e.
3 Ibid.
4 Infant Homicides Through Contraceptives, pp. 24-25.
5 Ibid., pp. 25-26.

"The Tragedy of Birth Control"

By Prof. Martin J. Naumann, D.D. (March 31, 1971)
Concordia Seminary, Springfield, Illinois
Christian News, January 16, 1978

It is difficult to convince people of right and wrong concerning something universally accepted. There is therefore a point of no return in the morals of a people or individual where it seems senseless to call to attention that something is radically wrong. As, for instance, in the case of birth control the discussion is not anymore whether it is right or wrong to practice birth control, but only how it might best and most efficiently be done and whether or not the state or the schools engage in furthering it.

It is therefore only to the person that still is bound by the Word of God that we can address ourselves in regard to this question. Nor will it be possible to talk of this matter before establishing the basis for a judgment of right and wrong in all matters of right and wrong. In the area of birth control there are a number of scriptural principles that must be stated and confirmed on the basis of study of God's Word.

The area basic to all considerations involving the life of men in general and in particular is anthropology. What is man? Man is a creature of God created in His image. What is the image of God? At least a part of God's original creation is still precious even after the fall. Man lost righteousness and holiness and yet God gives His Son for man's rescue. What is man? He is a creature responsible to God for his life and living. What is life? Here we must speak of it not biologically but theologically. Man has a Life in God from eternity to eternity. God and man stand in relation as individuals. Man is alone responsible to God. God sees each man alone.

Being created in God's image is to be able to speak to God when spoken to by God. Responsibility is the ability to answer and the duty to answer. Man answerable to God is man in the image of God. There is no person that God has not seen or planned in His providence from eternity and whom God does not want in eternity. The free will of man cannot inhibit God's plans, but God's providence does not inhibit man's free will in external matters and in matters leading him away from God to hell. The fact that we are not able to harmonize in our mind the relation between the providence of God and the free will of man does not give us a right to act as if we were not responsible or as if God could be blamed for our mistakes. We simply and in faith accept both realities: the providence of God and the free decisions of man.

The dilemma of man is that he cannot see God in the framework of his own logic. The problem is expressed in the familiar question of election: *Cur alii prae aliis*? Why (are) some (saved and) not others?

If man is fully responsible, and if man's life is one bounded by God's eternity, and if potentially every person born into this world is an heir of everlasting life, and if this is true of all children born into this world, where does man get the authority to decide which of his children (potentially speaking) is to be born into this chance of everlasting life God intends for all men?

We realize that modern man decides right and wrong mainly on the basis of utilitarian and pragmatic thinking. Man does not consider moral right and wrong. For man today everything is useful or useless, good or harmful, beautiful or ugly, but never right and wrong in the moral sense. This is the ethic of man in general and in particular in our day. This is **situation ethics**.

All the arguments for birth control, even those brought by the "churches" are on the basis of self-service, i.e. self-preservation. Even the talk of love and service to mankind is only a pretense of love, a sham, a shield for self-service.

Count all the reasons given for birth control: health, life, education, fortune, room to live, better facilities for man, etc., not to speak at all of the refusal to undergo the rigors of bearing and raising children.

All the sad state of humanity, the starvation in over-populated portions of the world, etc., are the result of the sins of mankind. Poverty in one spot accuses the prosperity of another. Lack of food and clothing is an accusation against the profligacy of the overdressed and over-fed.

It is in the Christian congregation, if at no other spot in the world, that the truth of God's will and commandments must be clearly seen. All children are souls intended for God's kingdom. Any drive for missions is made ridiculous by the talk of birth control. As the church is to propagate itself by the power of the Gospel, so are Christians to increase the family of God by increasing in the place where love and missions should start - in the family. Raise the average size of the Lutheran family and you would have a natural and God-given increase of the church without counting the souls won by the preaching of the testimony among unbelievers.

On the other hand, neglect the doctrine of God's will and the immortality of man and you will not only make mission work ridiculous (except in a social sense) but will cause offense among those who are to learn responsibility to God above all.

Any method of birth control and abortion is immoral no matter what the circumstances might be, except where man must weigh in a responsible way one life against another. Only the gravest concern for the life of a living soul can justify a Christian's contemplation of birth control as a good way of serving mankind.

The extreme result of utilitarian thinking is evident in the attempted extermination of useless, harmful, burdensome existences as practiced by the NAZI government that killed not only many Jews but many incurably ill, insane, etc. as well.

The duty of one human to the other is to provide an environment in which all may have life. It is not for us to limit life in order to make the enjoyment of the environment more pleasant for the fewer number. (e.g. U.S. surplus foods could keep alive any increase in the world population; besides, this would be good for a civilization like ours whose two major problems seem to be overweight and lack of parking space!)

(This unpublished editorial was transcribed from the personal notes of Dr. Naumann by the Rev. Jeffrey C. Kinery, Pastor of Grace Evangelical Lutheran Church, Brownwood, Texas).

QUESTIONS CONCERNING ABORTION AND BIRTH CONTROL

1. Is it good to let a discussion on abortion and birth control start without a firm theological foundation concerning God's created orders?

2. Is it Christian to answer questions about these controversial subjects from a pragmatic and utilitarian point of view?

3. Can we speak of God's will without considering the **family** (the marriage relationship and the parent's and children's relationship) an **order of creation**?

4. Can a Christian let the exception allowed by the Mosaic Law for the "hardness of the heart" be valid for him and his own heart (reborn)?

5. Has not the hard-heartedness of man brought in the deplorable situations we are facing in our sick society?

6. Does not the finger of Christ pointing to Genesis ("from the beginning") imply that the "putting asunder" must be applied in all areas that concern the creative orders? (For instance putting asunder what God has joined together in **marriage** as well as in **parenthood**.)

7. Is it a Godly marriage which on the one hand enjoys the highest evidence of unity of the flesh in sexual intercourse, but on the other hand refuses to recognize God's order of creation as an intended reason for this union?

8. Is not something essential eliminated from marriage and intercourse when the potential life is eliminated?

9. What is the similarity between "putting asunder" the mother from the child in abortion and the separating of potential parents from their children by contraceptive measures?

10. When is a marriage responsibility faithful to God as well as to the personal relations between the spouses? Is contraception unfaithfulness to God?

11. If the absence of children does not, in principle, call into question the full meaning and purpose of marriage, is it not called into question if the willingness to have children is lacking, and moreover is lacking most of the time?

12. Is the push for "planned parenthood" and "abortion" a war of the present generation against the unborn generation?

13. Is the so-called population bomb to be made harmless by acts against God's created orders of marriage and family?

14. Can a Christian allow his "calculated" need for "security" (prosperity, egocentrical emphasis) to take precedence over confidence and faith in God?

15. Does the present ease of contraception or abortion present responsible Christian spouses with a new and stronger temptation to misuse and, thereby, often destroy their marriage?

Is American Life Lobby Opposed to Birth Control?

Christian News, May 14, 1984

A special statement of position by Judie Brown, president of American Life Lobby. This statement has been approved by an editorial review committee which included Lutheran, Presbyterian, Roman Catholic and Baptist members.

Is America Life Lobby opposed to birth control? This question arises every once in a while. Briefly, our position is opposition to all forms of birth control which kill an already formed human life or which encourage promiscuity or abortion. Birth control, and opposition to it, requires scrutiny on several fronts. The official position of American Life Lobby, therefore, cannot be a simple "yes" or "no."

A. Birth control – what is it? When one hears "birth control" or "family planning" or "contraception" one imagines a married couple seeking counseling in the planning of their future family. Whether this planning is due to physical, economic or social reasons - the birth control decision within a marriage is an extremely private one. Many married couples choose the pill or the IUD as the preferred method of "Birth control" without realizing that each of these methods actually performs, always or at least at times, in a manner which kills a brand new human life.[1]

Once an egg is fertilized, you know, there is a new person in existence, someone who has been created by the loving act of intercourse between a man, a woman and the Lord – the giver of life. This brand new person takes a journey from the fallopian tube to the wall of the uterus, so that he or she can attach to the wall of the uterus and thus accept nourishment from the new mother in order to continue the growth process. Just as the brand new baby depends upon the milk of his mother's breast or the formula prescribed for nourishment, in the very same way this brand new person within his mother's womb requires sustenance. When the process of the child's actual attachment to the wall of the uterus is in any way stopped, automatic abortion occurs and the brand new person dies. Intentional? probably not – but abortion occurs just the same.

The pill, at times, and the IUD, almost always acts to irritate the fragile wall of the uterus. The wall becomes inflamed, the new human person cannot attach him or herself, and death occurs at once! Therefore, American Life Lobby opposes all methods of birth control which interfere with the growth of a brand new human being. American Life Lobby is absolutely and totally opposed to the pill and IUD.

Q.: If the pill only acts at times (depending on dosages) to take a new life, why oppose it absolutely?

A.: I would not fire a weapon into a clump of bushes if I heard a noise and could not determine whether I had heard an animal or a person. I would give human life the benefit of the doubt and not fire! In the same way, because I cannot tell when the pill will kill, I should not use it at all.

B) Birth control for teens- how about that?

American Life Lobby is absolutely opposed to all forms of birth control for unmarried teens (emancipated minors living at home, and those not yet married – some of them, you know, are not kids!) If we as Christians are to practice what we believe, then we cannot turn the Christian attitude aside when working with a teen who is "going to do 'it' anyway!" We owe that child an attitude of firmness, resolute understanding-and an education on the values of chastity and self-respect.

Too often, it is much easier to "let the teacher take care of it," or "let the doctor tell her the facts" or "give her the pill and she will at least be protected."

What errors these are! What damage is done in a young person's life! What an example this must be to them of: "Rules are only for some, but not for me – not in this case. I guess I can forget what the Bible school teacher used to say about fornication. After all, my parents don't care."

Thus, American Life Lobby is opposed to any birth control material being provided to the unmarried – be they adolescent or even adults.[2]

Teaching with regard to matters as personal and delicate as human sexuality belongs within the home- the parent or parents teaching the children. For anyone else or any agency developed with taxpayer money to provide guidance, counseling and particular methods of birth control to a youngster is for us as parents to abrogate our God-given responsibility.

Q.: American Life Lobby published material with regard to the so called "contraceptive mentality" – I do not buy that! What about it?

A.: Extensive study into the history of birth control and its effects on society has taught that where birth control is promoted, abortion follows quickly.[3] This is, of course, generally true about our own national history. Look at, for example, the struggle of Margaret Sanger (foundress of Planned Parenthood) to publicly promote assistance for the poor, while privately believing that certain races of people and certain economic groups should be totally eliminated to leave more for the rich and elite of society.

Do you think it is only by chance that her organization today encourages adolescent sexuality with birth control (including abortion) as the means?

Do you think it is by chance that Planned Parenthood itself, on the international level, will encourage birth control methods on women who do not even understand the same language as those popping pills down their throat or carrying suction machines into remote areas?

Do you really think that Planned Parenthood means what it says when it speaks of the "family" – or is it an agent for a permanent change in a sterile society where sex is an end unto itself and God is dead?

Is there such a thing as a "contraceptive Mentality"? You must study the history and decide for yourself. American Life Lobby will provide you with the documentation in order to facilitate an informed decision of your own on the question.

Remember, A. L. L. has a moral responsibility to you to educate, not with the teachings of any given religion, not with outlandish opinions, but with facts which we can document because we have the assistance of many Christian clergymen, Jewish leaders, priests, physicians, attorneys and countless others who have "been there" and know firsthand of whence they speak.

C) Personally, you see, I have been there myself.

Today, I wonder from time to time as I yearn to have more children, how many of them were terminated within my womb because I simply got the wrong advice!

In closing, yes, it is a difficult question. For those of us who are married it is very private and agonizing and personal. For those of us who have adolescents it is a heavy responsibility for us who are accountable for their souls.

But learning is an "always" growing experience, and we can either grow from what we learn or we can stagnate by ignoring reality. No one can force us to learn that which we feel might hamper our lifestyle in some way. That is why we have 1.5 million abortions per year in America.

That is why over a third of them are performed on teenagers. That is why we must remain open to new information, to educational material which will broaden our horizon.

In summary, let me repeat the American Life Lobby is:

• Opposed to the pill and the IUD – they kill.
• Opposed to any form of birth control for the unmarried.

- Receptive to the fact that there is such a thing as a contraceptive mentality and that it is dangerous.

We recognize that many Judaeo-Christian traditions accept birth control between consenting adults. A. L. L. takes no position on the personal beliefs.

God gave us a brain, and God gave us His own Son – a sacrifice so great it defies our understanding, but this sacrifice has opened a door for us to enter the Kingdom of God one day. And I believe, while we are here, we must be like little children and try to follow His will.

We will stumble, we will fall, we will even ignore reality for a while – but He will always be there for us. He will always forgive us. That alone makes everything worth the price we pay for defending all of His children– the pre-born, the young, the handicapped, the elderly – every single one.

By Judie Brown, president of American Life Lobby.

Endnotes
[1] *The Pillar of Society*, by Rev. Denis O'Brien (ALL).
[2] *The Best Birth Control for Teens*, by *Womanity*.
[3] *The Pivot of Civilization*, by Margaret Sanger.

A Partial List of Other Resources
Intra Uterine Death, by Rev. Denis O'Brien (ALL)
A Christian Physician and the IUD, by James Upchurch, M.D. (ALL).
The Pill and the IUD, by Couple to Couple League
"Scientists ducking prime moral issue," by John Lofton, *Washington Times*, Jan. 23, 1984.
"The Secular Case Against Contraception," by Anne Stewart Connell, *Wanderer*, March 8, 1984
"The Pill and the IUD Do Kill Babies," *ALL About Issues*, September 1982
Birth Control – Why Are They Lying to Women? By Jose Espinosa, M.D.
Birth Control for Teenagers: Diagram for Disaster, by Ford and Scwartz (ALL)
Affirming Sexual Abstinence, by *Womanity*
Sex Can Be Beautiful, by Lindsay Curtis (ALL) "General, Sex Education Parallel," by Beverly Mead, M.D., *Family Practice News*, Feb. 15, 1984
Planned Parenthood, Contraception and Abortion, by Robert Marshal (ALL)
"Birth Control Pills: The Fine Print," *ALL About Issues*, September 1983
Be Brave and Angry, by Beryl Sutters
Abortion, by Malcolm Potts, Peter Diggory and John Peel
"Pill Inventor Has Regrets," *ALL About Issues*, February 1982
"The U.S. Taxpayer and the Ice Cream Man," *ALL About Issues*, March 1982 *Special Report on Global 2000*, by Julian Simon (ALL).

Procreation
From the *Faithful Word*
Christian News, July 26, 1993

(The following statement was adopted by the Lutheran Churches of Reformation)

God is the creator of all human life (Gen. 30:2; 1 Sam. 2:5-6; 2 Kings 5:7; Acts 17:25, 28) and desires to create spiritual life in all sinful human beings, that everyone come to the knowledge of the truth and be saved (1 Tim. 2:4). Married couples[1] should reproduce in observance of the following Biblical principles:

1. The command of God to be "fruitful and multiply" (Gen. 1:28; 9:1, 7; 35:11; 1 Tim. 5:10, 14; Augsburg Conf. XXIII, #4 & 8, Triglot, p. 61[2], Apology XXIII, #7-8, Triglot, pp. 365-367[3], Catechism 6th Commandment, #207, Triglot, p. 639[4]).

2. Children are a blessing from the Lord (Gen. 1:28; 15:2-5; 17:5-6; 24:60; 334:5; 48:9; 49:25; Lev. 26:9; Deut. 28:4; Josh 24:3; Ruth 4:11-12; Ps. 107:38; 127:3-5; 128:3-6; 147:13; Prov. 5:18; 17:6; Catechism 4th Commandment #105, Triglot, p. 611[5]).

3. It is God who opens or closes the womb (Gen. 16:1-2; 17:15-19; 20:18; 21:1-2; 25:21; 29:31; 30:2-6, 23-24; Deut. 32:18; Lev. 20:20-21; Judges 13:2-3 Ruth 4:13; 1 Sam. 1:10; 2:21; Job 10:8-12; Ps. 22:9-10; 113:9; 139:13-16; Eccl. 11:5; Is. 8:1; 43:1,; 44:2,24; 49:1, 5; 66:9; Jer. 1:5; Luke 1:36-37, 57-58; Heb 11:11).

4. Having children is a good work for Christians (1 Tim. 2 :15; Apology XXIII, #32, Triglot, p. 373[6]).

5. Christians are to be mindful that they are not only to be fruitful and populate the earth, but they are to bring up their children as Christians and thus populate heaven (Prov. 3:21-22; 4:3-4, 20-22; Mark 10:13-16; Acts 2:38-39; Eph. 6:1,4; Heb. 2:10).

6. In Scripture, barrenness is regarded as an affliction (Gen. 11:30; 15:2; 16:2; 18:11-12; 25:21; 30:1,22-23; 1 Sam. 1:2, 5-7, 10-11; Prov. 30:15-16; Luke 1:7, 24-25, 58).

7. There are many examples in Scripture of fruitful parents amongst the godly (Gen. 3:20; 4:1, 25; 5:4, 30:1-24; Judges 13:2-3; Job 1:2; 42:13-16).

8. The Word of God prohibits us to "put asunder" marriage (Matt. 19:4-6), including its purposes (1 Cor. 7:2-5; Gen 2:24).

9. The Bible exhibit's the wrath of God upon those who defy His will (Gen. 38:8-10; Ex. 21:22; Rom 1:18).

10. God desires that we put our trust in Him in all matters, also in His will and ability to provide for the children He gives us (Ex. 23:22-26; Ps. 20:7; 37:25-26; 50:15; 118:8-9; Prov. 3-5; Matt. 6:254-34; Phil. 4:13; 1 Pet. 5:7).

Pastors should counsel families both publicly and privately to observe these principles. The churches and ministers should not take it upon themselves to investigate the private practices of their members (Eighth Commandment). Refusal to reproduce should be treated first by patient instruction and counsel. Nevertheless, when a situation becomes a public scandal, then evangelical discipline is in order (Matt. 18:17).

While we allow for exegetical differences and exceptional cases (casuistry), we must also maintain and teach the principles relating to this issue (Matt. 28:20; Acts 20:27). Such was the united teaching of Dr. Martin Luther and the "Old Missouri" fathers (C.F.W. Walther, F. Pieper, A.L. Graebner, C.M. Zorn, W.H.T. Dau, J.T. Mueller, W. Dallman, F. Bente, E.W.A. Koehler, L. Fuerbringer, T. Engelder, Th. Laetsch, G. Luecke, W.A. Maier, M.J. Naumann, et al) and LCR leaders such as P.E. Kretzmann and W.H. McLaughlin.

The reasons given to justify the prevention of conception are often based upon myths, selfishness, materialism, hedonism (love of pleasure), convenience, usurpation of God's prerogative, or humanistic reasoning which generally indicate a distrust of the Almighty God and His Word.

Notes

[1] The unmarried are not to reproduce, since they are unable to engage in legitimate sexual intercourse.

[2] "God created man for procreation, Gen. 1:28. No man's law, no vow, can annul the commandment and ordinance of God."

[3] "*First*. Gen. 1:28 teaches that men were created to be fruitful, and that one sex in a proper way should desire the other. For we are speaking not of concupiscence, which is sin, but of that appetite which was to have been in nature in its integrity, which they call physical love. And this love of one sex for the other is truly a divine ordinance. But since this ordinance of God cannot be removed without an extraordinary work of God, it follows that the right to contract marriage cannot be removed by statues or vows.

"The adversaries cavil at these arguments; they say that in the beginning the commandment was given to replenish the earth, but that now since the earth has been replenished, marriage is not commanded. See how wisely they judge! The nature of men is so forced by the Word of God that it is fruitful not only in the beginning of the creation, but as long as this nature of our bodies will exist; just as the earth becomes fruitful by the Word, Gen 1:11: *Let the earth bring forth grass, yielding seed*. Because of this ordinance the earth not only commenced in the beginning to bring forth plants, but the fields are clothed every year as long as this natural order will exist. Therefore, just as by human laws the nature of the earth cannot be changed, so, without a special work of God, the nature of a human being can be changed neither by vows nor by human law (that a woman should not desire a man, nor a man a woman)."

[4] "Therefore, He also wishes us to honor it (matrimony), and to maintain and conduct it as a divine and blessed estate because, in the first place, He has instituted it before all others and therefore created man and woman separately (as is evident), not for lewdness, but that they should (legitimately) live together, be fruitful, beget children, and nourish and train them to the honor of God."

[5] "To this estate of fatherhood and motherhood God has given the special

distinction above all estates that are beneath it that He not simply commands us to love our parents, but to honor them. He separates and distinguishes father and mother above all other persons on earth, and places them at His side."

[6] "That woman is saved by the conjugal works themselves, by conjugal intercourse, by bearing children and other duties (?). But what does St. Paul mean? Let the reader observe that faith is added, and that domestic duties without faith are not praised. *If they continue,* he says, *in faith.* For he speaks of the whole class of mothers. Therefore he requires especially faith, by which a woman receives the remission of sins and justification. Thus the duties of the woman please God on account of faith, and the believing woman is saved who in such duties devoutly serves her calling."

Playing at Being God

(Conception, Contraception, Preconceptions and Misconceptions)

Christian News, September 28, 1992

All of the jams and jellies into which people are able to get themselves (and out of which they are all too often unable to extricate themselves) are a result of their playing at being God. They do not play God, for few have the requisite loose marbles to go that far. No, they dabble. However, the depths into which they immerse themselves are stunning in their complexity and span generations with severe consequences.

Our topic: parenthood - life and death abused!
I. Efforts to Avoid Parenthood

A. Contraception (both within and outside marriage) The "cute" description: "those who try to practice birth control are commonly and usually known as parents" testifies to the failure at one point or another of EVERY method devised by man. The Pill is considered the most effective contraceptive. Yet, as sections below detail, it is also a most brutal sterilizer. Some consequences:

1. Nations deprived of their futures by "depopulation."
2. Difficulties or even the impossibility of ever conceiving. On this dreadful consequence, see the article referred to in the section below on Fertility Clinics.

B. Abortion - Nearly half of all abortions are performed on married women. Some have several abortions blotting their records.

1. "Morning after" pill. RU aware of it, or have you been napping in the company of Rip van Winkle?
2. Induced miscarriage
3. Poison (salt solution or other methods)
4. Mutilation (actual dismemberment)

5. Each just as serious and just as much MURDER as the other.

C. Medically approved starvation of "defective" children. The buzz word is "euthanasia." the crime is murder!

II. Efforts to become Parents

A. Infertility clinics

1. Fertility drugs (sometimes resulting in multiple births, twins, triplets, or even sextuplets)

2. In vitro ("in glass") fertilization, resulting in "test-tube babies."

3. Surrogate motherhood, bearing another woman's child by means of either "in vitro" fertilization or artificial insemination. The natural mother thus gives up her own child "for a price!"

In considering infertility clinics we are forced to refer back to one of the major causes of such efforts to conceive, namely, contraception. An article in *U.S. News and World Report*, October 5, 1987, entitled "Desperately Seeking Baby" conveys the magnitude of the problem already on the cover, with the headline "One Out of Six Couples Now Asks: 'WHY CAN'T WE HAVE A BABY?'" are you surprised to learn, from the article itself, although in a most indirect fashion, that contraception is the major cause of infertility? We quote a few sentences to demonstrate this truth: "More and more women are **waiting** till age 35 or later to try to become pregnant, and a fourth of them are failing" (p. 58). "Technology has given people unreasonably high expectations,' explains Shulamit Reinharz, a Brandeis University sociologist. 'Couples **delay** marriage and pregnancy, use contraceptives and stop, and then expect to conceive.' if they encounter an infertility problem, they expect doctors to have the solution. At age 24, a woman reaches the peak of fertility. The longer she **waits** after that, the more likely she is to develop a disease like endometriosis or suffer the effects of infections. The aging process takes its toll" (p. 59). "Many who **wait** are professionals on the fast track – so many, in fact, that infertility is dubbed 'the curse of the career woman'" (p. 59). "And one recent study indicates that up to 88,000 women are infertile because of infections from intrauterine contraceptive devices" (p. 59). "Women on the Pill for eight years or more may have trouble conceiving" (p. 60). "Says Dr. Richard Blackwell, an infertility specialist at the University of Alabama at Birmingham: '**Waiting** to have children is clearly a gamble" (p. 60). "At 33, she's overwhelmed by guilt. 'I think maybe if I hadn't tried so hard not to get pregnant when I was 21 that this wouldn't be happening" (p. 63 - EMPHASIS ADDED).

You see, of course, the immense grief between every line of the page above. How dreadful that according to their own awareness, they cannot have children because they **waited to** have children, practicing one or several forms of contraception, only to foul up their reproductive systems so thoroughly that they may never have children of their own.

B. Adoption

The same article from *U.S. News and World Report* quoted above, also contains these startling statements: "Adoption costs can exceed $10,000, and the wait may stretch up to eight years" (p. 58f). "For every healthy white infant who is up for adoption, there are 100 couples or singles seeking such a baby" (p. 59). "But, with an estimated 100 couples or singles in quest of every available healthy white infant, it's usually a long wait. Georgia's public-adoption agency is just now studying requests made in 1979. Wisconsin's waiting list for adoptive children became so unrealistic that the state agency scrapped it for a lottery. **The baby shortage [is] a result of the Pill and the rise in abortions**" (p. 64—EMPHASIS ADDED).

The supreme blessing which our gracious God fully intends to bestow upon most married couples is refused at one time only to be demanded at another. Everything about marriage and child-bearing has simply become another arena for human intervention, prevention, and invention. Human ingenuity is applied to thwart God's purposes and then reapplied in efforts to undo the dreadful damage that has resulted. Even as we decry abortion, we ought to decry contraception and birth control. It is truly amazing that the creature which considers itself" homosapiens" (literally "man the wise"), in a desperate attempt to indulge in selfish hedonism, stupidly proceeds to bring about his own extinction by means of various popularly practiced abominations (in alphabetical order): abortion, birth control, contraception, euthanasia, feticide, homosexuality, mercy killing, murder and suicide. Since these sins should be variously viewed as either conception prevention, birth prevention, or life prevention, we are staring at death itself, and self-imposed death at that. The prayerful refrain of Psalm 67 comes faintly to our hearing ears, the volume growing ever louder as more individuals pick up the hymn and join the chorus: "Let the people praise Thee, O God: let all the people praise Thee."

From the *Faithful Word*, Lutheran Church of the Reformation.

Rejects Virgin Birth of Christ - Inerrancy of Bible Spong Attacks Catholics: Birth Control Essential

By Patricia Lefevere Special to Religious News Service

Christian News, February 15, 1993

MAHWAH, New Jersey (RNS) - Episcopal Bishop John S. Spong of Newark took a broad swipe at Roman Catholicism in a weekend talk, contending that "nations or religious traditions that refuse to practice or endorse birth control will be declared by world consensus to be immoral."

Spong added "A Christian church of changeless tranquillity is a dead church. It is an idol that offers only illusions, pretending that such things as papal infallibility... are still viable."

In an address to Episcopal leaders attending an annual convention of the Diocese of Newark, Spong also attacked fundamentalists, assaying that biblical inerrancy is also an idol.

Spong has often irritated Catholics with his writings on human sexuality. Spong has also provoked ire by questioning the virginity of Mary, mother of Jesus, and for arguing that the Apostle Paul was a homosexual.

The bishop's latest book, "Rescuing the Bible from Fundamentalism," has offended many conservative evangelical Christians.

Spong said that human survival requires that the church lead in bringing pressure on nations and institutions that oppose world population control and effective family planning.

"Pressure will be applied to bring them into conformity with the new value of population limitations through effective family planning," Spong said.

Although the Catholic Church supports family planning it opposes artificial methods of contraception.

Spong did not specify where pressure would come from, but he did predict that the political boundaries of today's nations will be replaced by regional economic super-states by the middle of the next century.

He believes that such geopolitical units will produce a shift in consciousness, forcing upon the world "a different mode of life." A first step, he said, will be "the move to control the prolific worldwide breeding habits of Homo sapiens."

By contrast, a "living church" is one that understands that "there is no claim of certainty anywhere with which we can anaesthetize our fears. . . Or hide our insecurities" he said. The ability to accept insecurity and uncertainty is "nothing less than the exhilarating power of the gospel," Spong told the convention's 200 clergy and 400 lay delegates.

Spong called upon his Newark diocese, which includes 30,000 Episcopalians in seven counties of northern New Jersey, to be the vanguard of a new world order that will address such ills as pollution, greed, economic disparity and "inhumane living conditions" that exist in much of the world.

The bishop also asked his diocese to join the national debate on available health insurance for all.

Nationalized health care will demand that Christians "face squarely" human mortality and the question of when to reject the use of medical technology and permit people to die, he said.

"Just because the technology exists to prolong the life of infants born seriously premature" and to keep alive an elderly person no matter what the person's "quality of life" is insufficient reason for insisting that the technology always be used, Spong said.

"When the choice is health care for the masses or exotic care for a tiny minority, then we must choose health care for the masses," he said.

Ed. The Episcopal Church is broad enough to accept Spong's anti-Christian theology. Until the 1930s Spong's Episcopal Church and most denominations said birth control was contrary to the Bible. Then evidently the Bible changed.

Why Pro-Lifers Should Oppose Birth Control

1983 American Life Lobby, October 1983
By Paul Marx
Christian News, October 31, 1983

To venture upon this subject is surely a delicate enterprise, like grasping the sharp horned stem of a rose. Some users of contraception truthfully insist that even if they became pregnant they would never abort. Others claim to know people who use contraceptives but have actively fought abortion. Of course, if a pro-lifer is using contraception it is indeed hard for him to admit any possible connection between contraception and abortion. It is even harder for pro-life Pill- or IUD users to acknowledge that they have already chosen abortion.

Wherever contraception and abortifacients have become a way of life, surgical abortion has later been legalized. Wherever permissive abortion flourishes, approximately 75 percent of these operations are done on the unmarried, who keep recording higher and higher rates of venereal disease and illegitimate pregnancy. These stubborn facts alone should give second thoughts to contraception without abortion, without accompanying sexual abuses.

Contraception unleashes the sexual instincts, trivializes sex, deadens love and puts responsibility on gadgetry and chemicals rather than on cultivated human will, which should place the sexual drive at the service of true love and life.

One is starkly reminded of this reliance on technology in German restrooms, where vending machines offer the "anti-baby Kundom."

Exactly What Is Meant

One should not go on with this prickly subject without explaining the difference between contraception and abortion. Contraception keeps ovum and sperm apart, while abortion (whether by drug, device or surgery) ends a reborn life in progress.

Thus, when we speak of contraception we mean the condom; the diaphragm (cervical cap, with gel), and sponge; the various vaginal gels, foams and tablets; and the oldest method, premature withdrawal (coitus interruptus).

All other forms of birth control, apart from the selective abstinence of natural family planning and the complete abstinence of celibacy, are either sterilizing or abortive, at least some of the time. Nor is any method infallible except celibacy (the method I use).

It is now evident from research that no dosage of the Pill always suppresses ovulation (a sterilizing effect).

The "morning-after pill," Depo-Proverb (and the other injectables) and intrauterine devices are clearly abortifacient, in action as well as in intention if the user has just conceived or is about to conceive. The "mini-Pill" (the "progesterone-only pill") is probably always abortive.

The forthcoming French "Four-Day Pill," working at the uterine level, is clearly abortion-inducing.

Today, the IUD is known to be an abortifacient.

It's Dead End

Virtually no money or effort is being spent on developing effective new contraceptives; that avenue has been virtually exhausted. The recently announced vaginal sponge is relatively expensive and inefficient. The resourceful Japanese have manufactured the condom in many colors, some of them fluorescent- but there are only so many colors!

In short, the goal of most modern so-called contraceptive research is to develop abortifacients.

Finally, those who wish to argue against the evidence of the abortifacient properties of all pills and against the clear statements by the Pill developers should consider that any uncertainty about its abortifacient properties would rule out the Pill on moral grounds, for it is immoral to "probably kill." The burden of proof falls on the user.

A Clear Connection

Years ago, as a teaching family sociologist very active in the family apostolate, it was easy for me to recognize the approach of permissive abortion.

For more than 20 years I have fought abortionism. The fight has taken me to 56 countries of the world, where I have most often been sponsored by local pro-life leaders who have opposed abortion intensively.

I have talked to more such people than any other human being on earth, and the vast majority (surely well over 90 percent) share my conviction that widespread contraception leads to abortion-on-demand. These evils are logically related products of the same basic anti-life (if not anti-love) mentality.

Limited War Impossible

Pro-life organizations that oppose only abortion are aiming at only a symptom of sex-run-loose, at "back-up contraception," at "post-conceptive family planning." No one has put that more succinctly than Professor Irving Cushner of UCLA:

"Family planning is the prevention of births, and as birth is the end of a sequence which begins with the sexual urge, then family planning is anti-conception (contraception), anti-nidation (Pill, IUD, injectables and other abortifacients), and the termination of the conceptus if implanted. This is the social role of abortion in the future" (*The Death Peddlers*, p. 122).

It is easy for many people to see that sterilization follows the implementation of contraception, but the anti-life movement does not stop there.

A Complete Assault

Again, in every country of the world a merely physical, biological, organ-recitation, humanistic, public-school, co-ed, group-style sex education never accomplishes the goals it publicizes – never leads to chastity and always promotes venereal disease, illegitimacy and abortion.

Besides, most sex education is really contraceptive and abortifacient indoctrination leading to the anti-life juggernaut we are so familiar with in our morally-underdeveloped, decadent Western world, now dying out for lack of children.

Historical research makes it clear that Margaret Sanger favored abortion from the very beginning of her anti-life campaign.

The same is true of every other leader in the contraceptive movement. As Dr. Bernard Nathanson has explained in his book Aborting America, the American pioneer abortion promoters made the bishops of the Catholic Church the scapegoats of their campaign not only because that church opposes abortion but above all because it condemns contraception.

These promoters correctly assumed that they would have an easy time neutralizing opposition to legalized abortion by convincing many Americans that the Roman Catholic Church's bishops desired to deny them not only abortion but contraceptives as well.

Ill-Equipped to Fight

Of course, the dissent of some Catholic theologians to *Humanae Vitae* and the apparent lack of enthusiasm to seriously promote natural family planning (NFP) did not help matters. Lacking proper religious convictions on the issue, many Catholics fell for the idea that one could practice contraception without inviting into society not only permissive abortion but massive sterilization, out-of-control venereal disease, increased sterility and rampant fornication and adultery.

Maximizing sexual pleasure in and out of marriage is part of the contraception/abortion supporting mentality. The former medical director of International Planned Parenthood Federation has himself openly said that the more one spreads contraception, the more one must make abortion available!

They Won't Listen

One could go on and on providing quotations from the proverbial horse's mouth, but it would do little to convince those who do not wish to be convinced, who practice contraception themselves, who have theologically justified it, and who (sadly) have little or no understanding of the latest methods of NFP.

"A man convinced against his will is of the same opinion still."

School Birth Control: New Promise or Old Problem
Executive Summary
Christian News, January 5, 1987

From American Life League, Inc.

Proponents of the School-Based Comprehensive Health Clinic concept have produced numerous studies purporting to show the success of these clinics in reducing teen pregnancy. However, what their studies really show

– when reviewed in concert with related works on adolescent sexuality – is that the School-Based Sex Clinic (SBC) phenomenon may well be creating greater problems than the ones it sought to solve.

"School Birth Control: New Promise or Old Problem" reviews the highly publicized reports promoting SBC and points out their institutional biases, statistical and procedural errors. The study also brings together results of related public health research to present a more complete picture of the real and potential impact of SBC.

School Health/Birth Control clinic proponents claim that school clinics facilitate close, daily clinic/student contact to ensure contraceptive compliance thereby allegedly reducing the incidence of teen pregnancy. But they do not even address the question of how such contact is maintained during school breaks and vacations.

The premier school clinic in St. Paul, Minnesota, reports that contraceptive continuance among clinic student/clients was 87 percent after four years use - rates matched nowhere else in world birth control literature with the possible exception of the forced birth control program of Mainland China. Yet, the mean age of entrance into the program was 16.2 years and tracking of students does not continue beyond age 18 or graduation.

Among the procedural flaws common to the reports reviewed is that SBC proponents have purposely used teen live birth rates rather than teen pregnancy rates as a yardstick in order to inflate their "successes." An analysis of this substitution shows that reductions in teen birth rates have been achieved by an increase in teen abortion rates – NOT a reduction in teen pregnancy rates. Since this is not the outcome SBC proponents promised, SBC studies routinely ignore or finesse the abortion rate.

Typical of studies that have claimed SBC 'success' is one that purported to show a reduction in teen pregnancy rates in a Baltimore school. Buried in the footnotes, however, is the fact that one-third of the females in the study could not be located for the final survey –an omission that would include all the girls who dropped out of school due to pregnancy.

Claims of cost-benefits – primarily due to saving in welfare and medical benefits to young, unmarried women – continue to be one of the major attractions of the SBC concept. However, SBC proponents universally ignore the downstream economic costs of widespread birth control usage among adolescents.

Studies have shown there is a direct relationship between adolescent birth control usage and increased sexual activity; and there is a well-documented direct relationship between premarital sexual activity and the incidence of venereal diseases. The estimated current economic cost of just one of these diseases -pelvic inflammatory disease, (PID) - is $2.5 billion and expected to increase to $3.5 billion by 1990. Teens between the ages of 15 and 19 now account for over 15 percent of PID cases.

Although often ignored, medical, public health and sociological studies undertaken by birth control proponents, as cited in "School Birth Control: New Promise or Old Problem," clearly document that:

1. Sexually inexperienced adolescents are routinely given birth control, including the pill;

2. The initiation and continuation of sexual activity (both frequency and number of contacts) increases among adolescent birth control users;

3. The use of birth control increases the numbers of those who resort to abortion;

4. Birth control proponents do support legal restraints as effective behavior modification techniques for teen seat belt use and smoking, but denounce requiring parental consent for birth control users;

5. Teens are not adequately warned about the venereal disease consequences of their sexual behavior; Pill use is associated with higher rates of chlamydeous trachoma and subsequent involuntary sterility and pelvic inflammatory disease which cost American teens (aged 15-19) $192,000 in direct medical costs during 1984;

6. Birth control clinics and medical personnel are not a major source of information concerning pill side effects; medical misinformation is routinely given to adolescents about the pill; the pill is prescribed even for young women who smoke; family medical history for cancer is routinely ignored or incompletely ascertained; pill use is promoted in violation of Food and Drug Administration guidelines;

7. School birth control proponents ignore teen contraceptive drop-out, discontinuance and non-start data;

8. As moral guilt inhibits effective adolescent birth control use, moral restraints to sexual intercourse become impediments to a "perfect contraception society;"

9. Birth control professionals, especially clinic counselors, denounce morality and encourage sexual experimentation/promiscuity as this is more compatible with their own life style;

10. There are more out-of-wedlock teen pregnancies in those areas that routinely make birth control easily available to teens;

11. There is no scientific evidence that wanted pregnancies fare better than "unwanted pregnancies;"

12. The long-term economic benefit of non-marital birth is 3.6 times greater than the present value of public assistance costs for an AFDC mother and child;

The current push to implement SBC appears to derive from a much-heralded 1985 study by the Alan Guttmacher Institute, research arm of the Planned Parenthood Federation of America. The study concluded that the "United States leads nearly all other developed nations in rates of teenage pregnancy, abortion and childbearing." The study 'suggested' freer teen access to birth control, emphasis on sex education in the schools and, of course, extensive government promotion and funding of the birth control program.

A study by Jacqueline Kasun, Ph.D., indicated the opposite approach to be more effective. Her study showed that, "states that spend relatively large amounts on government birth control also tend to have high rates of teenage abortions-plus-unmarried births." States which limited teenagers' access to birth control - through reduced funding, as in South Dakota, or requiring parental consent, as in Utah - reduced the rates of teen pregnancy and abortion.

In California, for example, the tremendous growth in state funding for teen birth control programs was accompanied by a soaring rate of teen pregnancies and teen abortions. In 1970 and 1981 California's teen fertility rate was at the same level as the national average. However, as the state boosted its birth control funding to one-fifth of the nation's total, its teen pregnancy rate soared to 30 percent above the national average. California's program, following the blueprint of pro-SBC studies, has been a documented failure.

The problem of SBCs, then, lie not in the execution, but in the basic concept.

A Challenge for Statistical Verity
It Is Time to Publish the Truth

Christian News, December 30, 1996
From the Winter 1996-97 PABC
(*Protestants Against Birth Control*) update.
By Michael Skott

Standing in front of the hospital with Malachi is a humbling thing. For those who have not seen Malachi, they horribly mutilated and dismembered this poor child to "terminate the pregnancy" of his mother.

Shock and anger is on the faces of the hospital personnel as they drive to their parking spots. The sign is four feet square. The photo is computer generated for greatest resolution and clarity. I pray as I stand here. I pray that the health care conglomerate that owns this hospital will repent of surgically killing pre-born children at its sister hospital here in Milwaukee.

This brings me to the point of this article: Why does the Pro-life community, virtually from the top on down, refuse to affirm the humanity of the pre-born children killed by birth control? I say this because we refuse to include their deaths in the yearly U.S. abortion statistics that we publish. Is it because we have no graphic pictures to commemorate their unjust death? The old surgical abortion strategy works even better with the birth control victims: Keeping the victim's bodies "out of sight" insures that, for the most part, they are "out of mind." Yet, in the United States alone, birth control kills 10 million or more pre-born children every year. Because these children are in an embryonic stage of development, they will die unnoticed. Yet these same children are just as complete genetically as any of us.

Lately, it has been encouraging to see more Pro-lifers becoming aware of the chemical holocaust going on in our land. No Roe-Wade decision began this holocaust. It has been going on officially since 1960, when G.D. Searlye marketed the first birth control pill.

Many influential Pro-life people I have talked with all agree on one key point. Birth control cuts deep through the heart of the Pro-life movement. The problem is the church's scandalous widespread use of abortifacient birth control such as the Pill, the IUD, Depo-Provera, or Norplant. They are unanimous in their perception that this has contributed greatly to the church's reticence to confront the surgical holocaust.

Friends, we, as a church, need to confront our own sin before we aim our condemnation at others. Until we begin to love the pre-born that die of starvation caused by abortifacient birth control we are just kidding ourselves if we think God will bless our pro-life efforts. How can He bless us when Christian mothers are starving their own embryonic children to death?

This is a call for all of us in the pro-life movement who publish abortion death counts to confront our church's secret sin. The way to start is to include their deaths in our abortion statistics. Nothing could dramatize their plight more than a chorus of pro-life voices telling the true abortion death counts this January 22. How much better to hear it in Washington, D.C., at the annual march? How great it would be to see it proclaimed in the many pro-life publications that will once again commemorate the infamous Roe-Wade decision date.

Many people in the pro-life movement say we have the cart before the horse! Until we confront the chemical holocaust in our own pews, we will never have the moral ground to successfully confront the abortion holocaust in this country.

The Protest of a Protestant Minister Against Birth Control
By Rev. Matthew Trewhella
Christian News, January 13, 1997

Sunlight was just beginning to break over the darkness of the morning as my wife and I headed toward the entrance of the cold brick-faced building. Fear and apprehension gripped me each step of the way. A thousand questions and thoughts raced through my mind. "How much pain will there be? Why the heck did I ever do this in the first place and maybe I should just leave."

As I entered the door, I figured these were my last moments to bolt and run. I thought back to when I had done something similar six and a half years earlier and remembered the words that blazed across my mind when the procedure began - I will never do this again? Yet there I was, about to have a vasectomy reversal. What could possibly bring a man to the point where he would be willing to go under the knife once again?

Two Unbiblical Beliefs

Only two things could convince a man to get a vasectomy reversal. A. a radical restructuring of his beliefs, or B. a nagging wife. For me it was the former.

In 1985, I held two beliefs which convinced me that getting a vasectomy was fine. The first belief was that God nowhere in Scripture condemns the use of birth control, therefore it must be okay. The second belief was that

God wants us to use "wisdom," therefore in today's economy and because of my emotional make-up it would not be wise for me to have more than two children. I already had two. Both beliefs are unbiblical.

The first belief, that God nowhere in Scripture condemns the use of birth control, so it must be okay, fails to recognize the very first command of God in Scripture. It is found in Genesis 1:28. God says, after creating man and woman, "be fruitful and multiply." This is not a suggestion-it is a command. By virtue of the fact that God commands us to be "fruitful and multiply," he speaks against birth control.

When we use birth control, we are saying, "No, I won't be 'fruitful and multiply!'" We are disobeying god and we are abrogating one of His intents for marriage (en. 2:24).

Some would say that this command no longer applies because the earth is full. This teaching that the earth is overpopulated or may soon be is a humanistic, pagan myth. Christians who teach this display their ignorance and sadly show once again that too often the pre-suppositions of popular 20th century Christianity are the same as the world's. The truth is, all the people of the world standing side by side in a four-foot square area each could fit in the city of Jacksonville, Florida, leaving the rest of the world wide open (Read The Economics and Politics of Race: An International Perspective by Thomas Sowell.)

The second belief, that we must use "wisdom," is nowhere supported by Scripture and reveals our lack of trust in God to meet our needs. If God wants us to "use wisdom" i.e., use birth control, then why is it that whenever people in the Scriptures have many children God declares it is because He has blessed them? In Chronicles 25:4-5, we read that Haman had 14 sons. For what purpose? To financially burden him? No. The Scriptures say God did it to bless him!

God views children as rewards, gifts and arrows from Him (Psalm 127:3-5). He views them as a blessing (Deuteronomy 7:13, 14), and as a sign of His approval (Exodus 23:25, 26). Most Christians would view houses from the Lord as a gift, reward, blessing, or sign of His approval, yet, if they received four or five houses, I highly doubt any of them would say, "Well, we better use wisdom" and begin to practice house-control, not accepting more than two. Obviously, God's view of children is very different from ours.

Historical Teaching

For too long birth control has been looked upon as a "Catholic issue." It is fast becoming a "Protestant issue" however, as Protestant ministers like myself protest the heretical teaching of birth control that is being propagated in Protestant churches. We must understand that the Church, whether Catholic, Protestant or Orthodox, spoke consistently for 1900 years against birth control. Only in the last 75 years have Protestant churches begun to peddle this belief that God thinks its okay or wise for us to use birth control.

Listen to this quote: "The purpose of marriage is not to have pleasure and to be idle but to procreate and bring up children, to support a household. Those who have no love for children are swine, stocks, and logs unworthy of being called men or women; for they despise the blessing of God, the Creator and Author of marriage." Some Protestants might say, "This quote is obviously the mad dribbling of some medieval Pope." It is not. Rather, it is the founder of the Reformation, Martin Luther, who said this. Protestant Christians need to realize that their leaders, like Luther, consistently spoke against birth control up until about 75 years ago.

Who are some of the leaders besides Luther? John Calvin, John Wesley, Robert Dabney, Charles Spurgeon, A.W. Pink, Zacharius Ursinus, Heinrich Bullinger, Cotton Mather, Herbert Leupold, Johann Keil, Franz Delitszch, Matthew Henry, Adam Clark and John Machen, just to name a few. The founder of Planned Parenthood, Margaret Sanger, once stated, "The most merciful thing a large family can do to one of its infant members is to kill it." This does not shock some Christians because they agree with her. "I can't handle more than two." "I can't wait until you grow up and move out." "Will this be your last?" (asked in church after a couple announces they are having a third child; no congratulations, of course?) All of these statements and those like them parade the party line of Planned Parenthood, and are in opposition to our Protestant forefathers.

The time has come for those of us in Protestant Christianity to come to grips with the teaching of Scripture and our historical heritage and begin to follow the teaching of God and our forefathers, rather that the teachings of Margaret Sanger.

Blood in Our Bricks

If you were to list all the reasons why Christians use birth control, you would see that they are the same reasons why a woman aborts her child. The number one reason (according to all studies ever done) a woman aborts her child is because the child is an inconvenience. The child interferes with the mother's (or the father's) pursuit of happiness or possessions. When we use birth control, we are embracing the same anti-child mentality. We are saying that our pursuit of so-called happiness, our pursuit of possessions, is more important than obeying the command of God. The question is, "How can we abrogate God's design for marriage and expect to really be happy?"

In the Church today, we "warehouse" children. We don't want them around us during the church service. Some pastors are advising newly married couples to use birth control the first two years of their marriage so they can have time to get used to each other and have no undue stress added to the marriage. The cause for abrogating God's command to "be fruitful and multiply," is the same as the cause for abrogating His command "you shall not murder" - self-centeredness! One of the main reasons why the Church has failed to act against abortion is because it embraces the same anti-child mentality as those who advocate the murdering of the helpless reborn. We have no God-given right to manipulate God's design for marriage by using birth control. As long as we continue to make "things" our god and as long as we look at children as a diaper bill rather than a blessing from God, we will never see the Church act in mass against baby-murder. God help us to have His view of children and to obey his commands!

Rev. Matt Trewhella is the pastor of Mercy Seat Christian Church in Milwaukee, Wisconsin, and the founder of Missionaries to the Pre-born.

Why Do Christians Use Birth Control?

By Randall Terry
Christian News, October 21, 1991

Have you ever stopped to think why Christian couples use birth control?
"We just got married and we are not ready for kids."
"We want to give quality time to the children we already have."
"We simply cannot afford another child."
"I'd go crazy if we had any more kids."
Do any of these excuses sound familiar to you? Or more to the point, are you using any of these excuses?

When I discuss the notion that we should trust God with how many children we should have, I hear the above excuses again and again, plus a multitude more.

I have heard these excuses before - to the doorstep of an abortion mill.

The dreadful truth is that most of the excuses that women give for having their children killed through abortion are the exact same reasons we give for not having children.

At its core, birth control is anti-child, and I am not only speaking about abortifacients such as the Pill or I.U.D., but any drug or device that prevents us from having children. When we use birth control we are saying, "No, I do not want children."

Is it any wonder that the church cannot stop child-killing? How do we expect to defeat child-killing in the world when we cannot defeat child-rejection in our own minds? Jeremiah said if we run with footmen and grow weary, what will we do with horses?

I cannot be too hard on Christians who use birth control. My wife and I fell into the same trap when we were first married. We were told by all our peers and spiritual leaders that it was the "wise" thing to do. Frankly, we would much rather have a nine-year-old son or daughter than such wisdom.

In an age of Christianity when we constantly talk about faith, trusting God, God supplying our needs, etc, why can't we simply trust God for how many children we have?

When we use birth control, we are cutting short our heritage; we are perhaps short-circuiting entire generations of humanity. Consider this: Mrs. Wesley's thirteenth child, Charles, wrote hundreds of glorious hymns; Mrs. Whitfield's seventh child, George, was the most prominent preacher in the Great Awakening in America; Mrs. Washington's fifth child (fifth out of ten) was our beloved first President.

If Mrs. Washington had been in some of our churches today, after her third or fourth child, half of the women in the church would have told her to get a diaphragm or have her tubes tied! What a tragic loss that would be for all of us.

What do you think when you see a woman with five children? Are you happy or embarrassed? Do you approach her with congratulations or condolences? Do you happily exclaim, "Are these all yours?! What a blessing!" Or do you somberly question, "Are these all yours? You poor thing. How do you do it? I would go crazy."

The horrible reality is that much of the Church today in America is anti-child. We view children as a burden, a nuisance, an interruption in our lives, a drain on our finances, a sapping of our strength, and on and on.

Many Christians can't get righteously indignant about child-killing when in their hearts they sympathize with why some women have abortions.

So what do we do? Hopefully, nobody reading this is on the Pill or using an I.U.D. If you are, stop immediately. They are abortifacients. If you know someone who is using them, be a friend to them and tell them the truth. But, furthermore, if you are using any kind of birth control—stop. Leave the number of children you have in God's hands.

"Oh, but I'll have 10 kids!" I hear someone exclaiming. With all due respect, you don't know how many children you will have. Leah had six, Rachel had two. Sarah and Rebekah had one. The truth is, you simply don't know how many children you will have.

If you have been "sterilized," seek a medical reversal. I recently met a pastor in Oregon who sold his baseball card collection in order to pay for his wife's tubal ligation to be reversed. They are rejoicing in the Lord as she enters her seventh month of pregnancy with a child they almost never had.

One final thought: consider the origins of the birth control movement––Margaret Sanger and Planned Parenthood. Margaret Sanger wanted Christian's (among others) to use birth control. She despised our God and loathed large Christian families. If someone could laugh in hell, she would surely laugh at us.

I would like to quote one of the least popular Psalms of our day, Psalm 127:3-5. "Behold, children are a gift of the Lord; The fruit of the womb is a reward. Like arrows in the hands of a warrior, So are the children of one's youth. How blessed is the man whose quiver is full of them; They shall not be ashamed, when they speak with their enemies in the gate."

These verses clearly proclaim how we should view our children - they are our heritage, our reward. In fact, our children are the only eternal possession we have except for our own souls.

God restore to us a respect, a love and a desire for our most precious possessions – the fruit of our womb.

Randal Terry, the founder of Operation Rescue is President of the Christian Defense Coalition.

Ed. CN regrets that Terry later left his wife and led an un-Christian lifestyle.

Planned Parenthood and Legalized Contraception

Celebrate Life, July-August 1998
Christian News, July 27, 1998

By Jim Sedlak,
Director, Stop Planned Parenthood International (STOPP) -
a division of American Life League

When Margaret Sanger first founded the American Birth Control League (now known as Planned Parenthood Federation of America) in 1916, she had two major problems. Contraception was illegal in the United States, and it was also condemned by every major religious denomination.

Change Church Position

Sanger and her friends set about to systematically overturn the church restrictions against contraception. One of her first allies was Ralph Inge, the very reverend dean of Saint Paul's Cathedral in London, England. Dean Inge became a champion of birth control. Inge's support of Sanger's efforts was documented in Sanger's 1922 book, *The Pivot of Civilization.*

In 1930, at the Lambeth Conference, the Church of England recognized for the first time the use of contraceptives by married couples under certain limited circumstances. It was the first major victory in Planed Parenthood's war to change the morals of the entire world.

This first victory was followed by many others as one church after another began recognizing the use of contraception, first by married couples, and then by single people. In order to advance the whole contraception issue. Sanger and one of her friends financed the development of the birth control pill. This is the device credited with unleashing the sexual revolution of the 1960s.

After the successful launching of the Pill, Planned Parenthood felt it could accomplish anything it wanted. One aftermath of the pill was a study, within the Catholic church on the issue of contraception. Many people within the Church thought that the teaching would be changed. Planned Parenthood was so eager to bring the Catholic church on board that,as later revealed by Vatican officials, it offered millions of dollars to the Vatican if it would recognize the use of contraception as legitimate.

Planned Parenthood was understandably upset when Pope Paul VI issued *Humanae Vitae* and confirmed that the Church had no intention of changing its stand on the use of contraceptive devices.

Legalization of Contraception

While changing the minds of many churches, Sanger and her friends also fought to get laws against the sale and distribution of contraception overturned. Planned Parenthood's first major victory in this battle came in the mid-1940s when the postal authorities stopped enforcing the Comstock

Laws, which prohibited the sending of any sex information through the mail. This change allowed Planned Parenthood to openly distribute information about contraceptives (and also opened the doors to the pornography industry in the United States).

With the ability to distribute sex information through the mail, Planned Parenthood openly worked to change laws against contraception. In 1965, the United States Supreme Court ruled, in Griswold v. Connecticut, that states could not prevent the distribution of contraceptives to married couples. Ellen Griswold was director of the Planned Parenthood League of Connecticut. In 1972, the Supreme Court ruled, in Eisenstadt v. Baird, that states could not prohibit the distribution of contraceptive devices to unmarried individuals.

Thus Planned Parenthood, working in the courts and through the churches, succeeded in bringing us a society that views children as something to be avoided.

The Ironic Protestant Reversal

How the Original Family Movement Swallowed the Pill
By Allan C. Carlson
Christian News, January 17, 2000

American Catholics today represent that branch of Christianity that weighs heavily against contraception, advocating natural family planning in spacing the birth of children, which normally has reaped larger families. Protestants-whether the mainline, ethnic confessional, or evangelical variety-are generally open to contraception, as evidenced at times by the lower number of children born into Protestant families. These dynamics, however, represent an ironic reversal of nearly five hundred years ago, as the Protestant Reformation began in part as a protest against the perceived anti-natalism of the late medieval Catholic church, celebrating a procreation that considered contraception and abortion among the most wicked of human sins and direct affronts to divine ordinances.

As the Augustinian monk, theologian, and "first Protestant" viewed his world in the second decade of the sixteenth century, Martin Luther (1483-1546) saw a Christianity conflict with family life and fertility. Church tradition held that the taking of vows of chastity-as a priest, monk, or cloistered sister-was spiritually superior to wedded life. In consequence, about one-third of adult European Christians at the time lived in religious communities where vows of chastity were the rule. This, Luther claimed, resulted in widespread misogyny, or a hatred of women, reflected in a saying attributed to St. Jerome: "If you find things going too well, take a wife." Clearly, the late medieval church saw marriage and children as hindrances to spiritual work. At the same time, Luther argued that broken chastity vows reflected a breakdown of spiritual discipline. His voice joined lay complaints about certain bishops who kept concubines, monks who caroused in taverns, and priests who preyed sexually on their parishioners without serious rebuke.[1]

In constructing his evangelical family ethic, Luther emphasized Genesis 1:28: "Be fruitful and multiply."[2] This was more than a command; he called it "a divine ordnance [**werck**] which it is not our prerogative to hinder or ignore." As he explained in his *Lectures on Genesis*, Luther saw procreation as the very essence of the human life in Eden before the Fall:

> Truly in all nature there was no activity more excellent and more admirable than procreation. After the proclamation of the name of God it is the most important activity Adam and Eve in the state of innocence could carry on - as free from sin in doing this as they were in praising God.

Adam's fall into sin interrupted this pure, exuberant fertility. Even so, the German reformer praised each conception of a new child as an act of "wonderment... Wholly beyond our understanding," a miracle bearing the "lovely music of nature," a faint reminder of life before the Fall:

> This living-together of husband and wife-that they occupy the same home, that they take care of the household, that together they produce and bring up children-is a kind of faint image and a remnant, as it were, of that blessed living together [in Eden].

Luther therefore elevated marriage to "the highest religious order on earth," concluding that "we may be assured that man and woman should and must come together in order to multiply." He stressed that it was "not a matter of free choice... But a natural and necessary thing, that whoever is a man must have a woman and whoever is a woman must have a man." He called for the emptying of convents, emphasizing that "a woman is not created to be a virgin, but to conceive and bear children." Luther's marital pro-natalism had no restraints; wives, he stated, ought to be continually pregnant because "this is the purpose for which they exist."

With the same enthusiasm Luther called men home to serve as "Housefathers" dedicated to the rearing of children. In a wonderful passage, Luther describes the father who confesses to God: "I am not worthy to rock the little babe or wash its diapers, or to be entrusted with the care of the child and its mother." Luther assures him that "when a father goes ahead and washes diapers or performs some other mean task for his child... God, with all his angels and creatures, is smiling... Because [the father] is doing so in Christian faith."

Luther sharply criticized the contraceptive mentality that was alive and well in his own time. He noted that this "inhuman attitude, which is worse than barbarous," was found chiefly among the well born, "the nobility and princes." Elsewhere, he linked contraception to selfishness:

How great, therefore the wickedness of [fallen] human nature is! How many girls there are who prevent conception and kill and expel tender fetuses, although procreation is the work of God! Indeed, some spouses who marry and live together . . . have various ends in mind, but rarely children.

In short, Luther's fierce rejecting of contraception and abortion lay at the heart of his reforming zeal and his evangelical theology. His own marriage to Katherine von Bora and their brood of six children set a standard for Protestant domestic life that stood for nearly four hundred years.

Departing from the Family Way

Were he alive today, however, Luther would have discovered that his Protestant heirs in both America and Europe had departed from the family way, embracing contraception and abortion as compatible with Christian ethics by the 1960s. Protestant leaders condemned Pope Paul VI's opposition to both acts in the 1968 encyclical, *Humanae Vitae*, as an attempt to impose "Catholic views" on the world. Although mainline Protestant leaders clearly lead the charge, their evangelical counterparts are not far behind. A month after the pope issued his encyclical, an evangelical symposium sponsored by *Christianity Today* and the Christian Medical Society came to the defense of contraception and, in some cases, abortion: "The Christian physician will advise induced abortion only to safeguard greater values sanctioned by Scripture. These values should include individual health, family values, and social responsibility."[3] Billy Graham, himself a father of five children, also took issue with the pope's letter citing the "population explosion," stating, "I would disagree with it . . . I believe in planned parenthood."[4] Five years later, Southern Baptist voices even defended the 1973 Roe v. Wade decision that legalized abortion. W.A. Criswell, for example, claimed: "I have always felt that it was only after the child was born and had life separate from its mother that it became an individual person."[5] Moreover, few Protestant voices raised opposition in the 1960s and early 1970s to the massive entry of federal government into the promotion and distribution of contraceptives, nationally and worldwide.

How a central pillar of the evangelical Protestant ethic was reversed so completely is a complex question, only partially answered by the historical record. The first formal break came within the Anglican Communion, or the Church of England, with the clergy themselves leading the way. In 1911, the neo-Malthusian advocates of population limitation celebrated the results of England's new census, showing that Anglican clergymen had on average only 2.3 children (well below their 1874 figure of 5.2 children) as clear evidence of deliberate family limitation. The census added fuel to the arguments of dissident clergymen that a solution to England's poverty problems must include the birth of fewer children. Pressures culminated at the Anglican Church's 1930 Lambeth Conference, where delegates heard an address by birth-control advocate Helena Wrighton on the advantages of contraception for the poor. On a 193 to 67 vote, the bishops approved a resolution stating that in those cases where there is such a clearly felt moral obligation to limit or avoid parenthood, and where there is a morally sound reason for avoiding complete abstinence, other methods may be used, provided that this is done in the light of the same Christian principles.⁶

Protestant response to the Lambeth motion on this side of the Atlantic was initially mixed. While the Committee on Home and Marriage of the Federal Council of Churches issued a statement in 1931 defending family limitation and urging the repeal of laws prohibiting contraceptive education and sales,⁷ several member denominations, particularly the Southern Methodists, Southern Presbyterians, and Northern Baptists, protested the committee's action and declaration, claiming the committee had no authority to represent them on the subject. The Southern Presbyterians even withdrew their membership in the Federal Council for the next ten years because of the statement. The council eventually moderated its position, declaring after World War II that "for the individual family, there is nothing more satisfying, even though it may involve real sacrifice, than to have at least three or four children."⁸

What would become the mainline National Council of Churches in 1950, however, became increasingly hostile to the Christian nuclear family, sponsoring the 1961 North American Conference on Church and Family. Setting a radical theme, keynote speaker J.C. Wynn of Colgate Divinity School dismissed existing Protestant books and pronouncements on the family and sexuality as "depressing platitudinous" and "comfortably dull," a regrettable "works [based] righteousness." A second keynoter praised the conference for its intent to merge Christianity with new insights from the sciences, a mighty symbol of the readiness of the churches to ground their policy formation in objective, solid data." Other speakers formed a veritable "Who's Who" of sexual radicalism. Lester Kirkendall said that America has "entered a sexual economy of abundance," where contraception would allow unrestrained sexual experimentation without the burden of children. Wardell Pomeroy of the [Kinsey] Institute for Sex Research explained how the new science of sexology required the abandonment of all old moral categories. Psychologist Evelyn Hooker praised the healthy sterile lives of homosexuals. Planned Parenthood's Mary Colderone made the case for universal contraceptive use, while colleague Alan Guttmacher urged the reform of America's "mean-spirited" anti-abortion laws.⁹

Not a single speaker spoke in the spirit of the old Protestant pro-natalist ethic. Indeed, Luther's ethic now stood as the chief enemy. The conference endorsed development of a new evangelical sexual ethic: one "relevant to our culture," sensitive to the overpopulation crisis, and grounded in modern science. Several member denominations eventually compiled. In 1970, a task force encouraged what is now the Presbyterian Church (U.S.A.) to reject the old "taboos and prohibitions" and to give her blessings to "mass contraceptive techniques," homosexuality, and low-cost abortion on demand. The same year, the Lutheran Church in America fully embraced contraception and abortion as responsible choices. Finally, in 1977, the United Church of Christ celebrated the terms "freedom," "sensuousness," and "androgyny," and declared free access to contraception and abortion as matters of justice.

Even large denominations outside the Federal and National Council orbit stumbled. The Lutheran Church-Missouri Synod, a conservative, older ethnic church body committed to a defense of pure Lutheran orthodoxy, is a case in point. As late as 1923, the synod's official publication, The Witness, was still keeping faith with Luther, accusing the Birth Control federation of America of spattering "this country with slime," and labeling birth-control advocate Margaret Sanger a "she devil." A popular 1932 volume on pastoral theology directly paraphrased Luther in stating that "women with many children are in middle age much more beautiful than those who have few children." In addition, Walter A. Maier, the founding preacher of the popular Lutheran Hour radio program, called contraceptives "the most repugnant of modern aberrations, representing a twentieth century renewal of pagan bankruptcy."

Paralleling the Anglican experience, however, the average size of Missouri Synod clerical families fell from 6.5 children in 1890 to 3.7 children by 1920. The overall synod baptism rate declined from 58 baptisms per one thousand members in 1885 to 37 in 1913 and 25 in 1932. By the late 1940s, a leading Missouri Synod professor of theology, Alfred Rehwinkel, said that Luther had simply been wrong; the Genesis phrase, "be fruitful and multiply," was merely a blessing, not a command. Rehwinkel even defended Margaret Sanger with a sympathetic history of family planning. By 1964, the synod official held that problems of poverty and overpopulation should help guide thinking about family size.[10]

Why Protestants Sold Out

These historical episodes beg the question, **why**. The easiest answer might be to point to the multiple revolutions of the last two hundred years—–industrial, urban, scientific, and democratic—as creating an overwhelming pressure for accommodation that no religious institution could fully resist. The very existence of *Humanae Vitae*, however, gives a counter example of a religious body that has mounted a fierce opposition to the spirit of the age. That a Roman pontiff would lead the opposition—often painfully alone—to contraception at the end of the twentieth century is no small irony. Perhaps the Catholic hierarchical mode, reserving final decision on matters of faith and morals to a bishop whom Catholics believe is the successor of Peter, has proved more resilient in the face of modernity than the Protestant reliance on individual conscience and democratic church governance.

Or perhaps Luther would simply acknowledge that his old enemy, "that clever harlot, Natural Reason," had come back in a new guise at the second millennium's end. By natural reason, he meant the wisdom of the world, unformed and unregulated by the divine witness of Holy Scripture. As he "quoted" this beast back in 1522:

> Alas, must I rock the baby, wash its diapers, make its bed, smell its stench, stay up nights with it, take care of it when it cries, heal its rashes and sores, and on top of that care for my wife, provide for her, labor at my trade, take care of this, and take care of that,. . . Endure this and endure that . . . ? What, should I make such a prisoner of my-

self?[11]

Today, these same sentiments might be found on the lips of "the Playboy philosopher," the "female eunuch," or the "sexologist" at a conference sponsored by the National Council of Churches. Luther well understood the nature of human sin and the power of fallen reason to twist words and science to its ends. He would be disappointed by the near-collapse of his evangelical family and sexual ethic; he probably would not be surprised.

Not all Protestants in this troubled age have neglected the legacy of Luther. Scattered bands rooted in Anabaptism-including the Hutterites and the Amish – have kept 'natural reason' and the modern world at bay by the cultivation and defense of separatist, rural identities. Ever open to the transmission of new life, their families are large and their marriages are relatively strong. Pockets of fundamentalists have also held more tightly to a positive view of fertility. A 1958 survey in the South Appalachians found that 81 percent of "fundamentalists" believed birth control to be "always" or "sometimes" wrong compared to only 40 percent of "non-fundamentalists." In 1980, the Southern Baptist Convention adopted a resolution raising serious questions about birth control that echoed a 1934 resolution against pending congressional legislation that had aimed to relax federal restriction to the interstate shipment of contraceptive devices and information. More recently, Protestant renewal movements count many couples, including many home schoolars that reject contraception and welcome the children that God sends, in his time. These communities may very well remain faithful to the authentic evangelical family and sexual ethic created in the sixteenth century. Their documented growth at the end of the twentieth century may be the sign of a better, more family-centric time ahead.

* * *

Dr. Carlson holds a Ph.D. in modern European history. His most recent book is *The New Agrarian Mind: The Movement Toward Decentralist Thought in Twentieth Century America*, just published by Transaction Books-Rutgers University. A lifelong member of what is now the Evangelical Lutheran Church in America and father of four children; he is president of the Howard Center for Family, Religion and Society in Rockford, Illinois.

Endnotes

[1] On the background to the creation of the Reformation family ethic, see: Steven Ozment, *When Fathers Ruled: Family Life in Reformation Europe* (Cambridge: Harvard University Press, 1983), ch. 1 and 2.

[2] This discussion of Luther comes primarily from three of his works: "Lectures on Genesis"; "The Estate of"; and "An Exhortation to the Knights of Teutonic Order That They Lay Aside False Chastity and Assume the True Chastity of Wedlock"; in *Luther's Works* (Philadelphia: Muhlenburg Press, 1962), 45:18, 39-42, 118, 133, 154-55; and *Luther's Works* (St. Louis: Concordia Publishing House, 1964), 4:304.

[3] "A Protestant Affirmation on the Control of Human Reproduction," in *Birth Control and the Christian: A Protestant Symposium on the Control of Human Reproduction*, eds. Walter O. Spitzer and Caryle L. Saylor, (Wheaton, Illinois: Tyndale House, 1969), p. xxvi.

[4] "Pope Faces Birth Control Crisis," *Christianity Today*, August 16, 1968, p. 42.
[5] "Abortion: A Death Blow?" *Christianity Today*, February 16, 1973, p. 48.
[6] See: Richard Allen Solowary, *Birth Control and the Population Question in England, 1877-1930* (Chapel Hill: The University of North Caroline Press, 1982), pp. 91-111, 233-255.
[7] "Birth Control: Protestant View, Full Text of Federal Council Report," *Current History* 34 (April 1931): 97-100.
[8] Cited by C. Gregg Singer, *The Unholy Alliance* (New Rochelle, New York: Arlington House, 1975), p. 179.
[9] Elizabeth Stell Genne and William Henry Genne, eds., foundations for *Christian Faith Policy: The Proceedings of the North American Conference on Church and Family, April 30-May 5, 1961* (New York: National Council of Churches of Christ in the U.S.A., 1961).
[10] Alan Graebner, "Birth Control and the Lutherans: The Missouri Synod as a Case Study," in *Women in American Religion*, ed. Janet Wilson James (Philadelphia: University of Pennsylvania Press, 1980), pp. 229-249.
[11] *Luther's Works*, 45:39.

From Family Policy, September-October 1999, Family Research Council.

An Appeal to Protestants: Don't Disregard *Humanae Vitae*

Celebrate Life, July-August 1998
Christian News, July 27, 1998

The undeniable focus of this issue of *Celebrate Life is Humanae Vitae* - a Catholic document. But the teaching it expresses - that artificial contraception is sinful in the eyes of God - is not exclusively Catholic. It is based on God's Word, and it is a teaching that was almost universally endorsed by all Christians until 1930.

A historical perspective may be useful. It was in 1930 that the Anglican Church, at its Lambeth Conference, reversed its long-held opposition to artificial contraception by declaring that "where there is a morally sound reason for avoiding complete abstinence, the Conference agrees that other methods [of avoiding parenthood] may be used."

In the United States the National Council of Churches quickly followed in 1931 with its own reversal, endorsing "the careful and restrained use of contraceptives by married people" - even as it admitted that serious evils, such as extramarital sex relations, may be increased by general knowledge of contraceptives."

Still, as documented in American Life League's *Pro-Life Activist's Encyclopedia*, most Christians refused to accept birth control. Dr. Walter A. Maier, a Lutheran theologian, called it "one of the most repugnant of modern aberrations, representing a 20th century renewal of pagan bankruptcy." To Methodist Bishop Warren Chandler, "the whole disgusting [birth control] movement rests on the assumption of man's sameness with the brutes."

Even the *Washington Post* railed against the decision: "Carried to its logical conclusion, the committee's report, if carried into effect, would sound the death-knell of marriage as a holy institution by establishing degrading practices which would encourage indiscriminate immorality. The suggestion that the use of legalized contraceptives would be careful and restrained is preposterous."

In the years since 1930, society has changed. Churches have changed. The Word of God, however, has remained constant through the ages. Among the many Old Testament passages we might cite is Psalm 127:3 – "Children are a heritage of the Lord: and the fruit of the womb is his reward." In the New Testament, Jesus admonished the disciples for trying to keep a group of children away from Him. Instead of rejecting children, the Lord welcomed them: "He took them up in his arms, put his hands on them, and blessed them" (Mark 10:16).

If God loves children this much and wants to bless us with them, why do we think that we can refuse this blessing? Using the Scriptures as our source of faith and practice, we will arrive at the same answer that the Catholic Church has never abandoned-we must control our sexuality, yes; but not our fertility.

Protestant pro-lifers should not eagerly reject this teaching as "Catholic." Rather, all good Christians should prayerfully search the Scriptures, following the advice taught in 1 John 4:1 - "Believe not every spirit, but try the spirits whether they are of God."

This is not to say that those who practice birth control do so purposely in opposition to God's will. Perhaps they simply lack a full understanding of God's teaching in this crucial area. It is our hope that this issue of *Celebrate Life* will contribute to a greater understanding of God's Word. When you are humbly kneeling before the throne of grace and asking for the guidance of the Holy Spirit you will see that God's intended blessings are not to be thwarted by man's chemicals and compounds. May God lead us all into His truth!

The Empty Promise of Contraception

What Four Decades on the Pill Has Conceived
By Teresa R. Wagner
Christian News, February 7, 2000

In June, Japan moved one step closer to legalizing what was introduced into the United States nearly 40 years ago, the oral contraceptive safe enough for Japanese women. While the decision was hailed by feminists, physicians, and pharmaceutical companies as one that will push the Asian economic powerhouse into the modern – meaning Western–world, the pending legalization of the Pill by the government of Tokyo may be more ominous for this traditional and family-centered country than public officials realize. As reflection and deliberation tend to be in short supply in the public policy decision-making process, Japanese government officials probably did little to assess what the Pill has conceived on this side of the Pacific Ocean. Had they carefully looked at the legacy of the Pill in the United States, they might have thought twice before embracing this seeming wonder of medical technology. The American experience with the Pill, and with contraception in general, tells a complex, but nevertheless revealing, story. Since 1960, when the Pill was introduced, and since 1965, when the Supreme Court limited the ability of the states to regulate contraceptive sales, public accessibility to contraceptive drugs and devices has increased dramatically among married and single Americans alike. In the old days, accessibility to contraceptives was largely limited to vending machines that dispensed condoms in seedy public bathrooms. Today, federal and state programs, led by Title X of the Public Health service Act and title XIX of the Social Security Act (Medicaid), spend more than $715 million annually promoting and distributing contraceptive drugs and devices under the guise of family planning to women, specifically teenagers.[1] Not only are Americans now far more familiar with contraception, but also the advent of sex education in many public schools includes explicit instructions on contraceptive technique. According to Donald Critchlow, approximately 80 percent of all adults in the United States now practice some form of contraception, including sterilization.[2]

The widespread acceptance and use of contraceptives has occurred in part because many in the medical and public health field perceived during the 1970s and 1980s that contraception was the answer for the rising rates of out-of-wedlock pregnancy, abortion, and illegitimacy, especially among teenagers.[3] While this perception may have been reasonable 25 years ago, the record a generation later suggests that the heavy dose of contraception pitched on the American public since then has not reduced those rates, but actually intensified the problem. According to the U.S. National Center for Health Statistics, out-of-wedlock births jumped dramatically from 202,000 in 1957 to 1.3 million in 1994, the same period during which contraceptives became commonplace in America. Relative to all births, the portion of out-of-wedlock births increased from 4 percent in 1950 to 24 percent in 1987.[4] The number of abortions continued to climb during the 1970s and 1980s, rising from an estimated 744,600 abortions in 1973 to an estimated 1,608,600 abortions in 1990.[5] The actual numbers may even be higher, given that not all state health departments collect or report abortion data, while others provide only partial data.[6]

Nor has the country experienced a decline in unwanted pregnancies. Family Planning Perspectives reports that one-half of all pregnancies in the United States today remain "unintended" as 18 percent of couples who use condoms and 12 percent who take the Pill become pregnant within two years.[7] Data compiled by the Alan Guttmacher Institute, the research arm of Planned Parenthood, confirmed that reality, finding that nearly 50 percent of women seeking abortions were using some form of birth control.[8] In addition, whatever declines in adolescent pregnancy, abortion, and birth rates have been documented between 1988 and 1995 have occurred because of the increased number of teenagers choosing to postpone sexual relations, not because of increased contraceptive use, according to the Consortium of State Physicians Resource Councils.[9]

The Failure of Contraception

One reason contraception has not been able to significantly reduce rising illegitimacy and abortion is that contraception has not been nearly as reliable or effective as its promoters and marketers have led Americans to believe. Not only is contraception less effective than originally assumed,[10] but abortion is now demanded precisely because contraception - which Americans were told would eliminate the need for abortion - fails. As the National Abortion Reproductive Rights Action League claims: "The need for abortion will never go away until we . . . can achieve . . . better access to more effective contraception."[11] Indeed, the United States Supreme Court reaffirmed the right to abortion in the 1992 Planned Parenthood v. Casey decision on the same grounds: "Abortion is customarily chosen as an unplanned response . . . to the failure of conventional birth control. . . [People have organized intimate relationships . . . in reliance on the availability of abortion in the event that contraception should fail]."[12] Even in its most reliable form, the oral contraceptive, birth control has not altered biological reality: sexual relations continue to result in pregnancy. In fact, the Pill today prevents even fewer pregnancies than it prevented 30 years ago. Originally, the Pill was designed to suppress ovulation through a heavy dose of a synthetic estrogen component and added progesterone. Consequently, today's Pill produces three fertility-related actions, of which one alters the uterine lining so that women cannot sustain newly conceived and developing life, prompting an early abortion. In this respect, the current oral contraceptive acts more like an abortifacient than a true contraceptive, resulting in more actual pregnancies than are recorded and therefore factored into evaluations of the Pill's effectiveness.[13] Technical difficulties, however, are not the main factors that have contributed to the failure of contraception. Contraception in general, and the Pill in particular, fueled nothing less than a revolution in the way Americans understand human sexuality that directly reinforced the very pathologies that contraception was meant to contain. While failing as a matter of biology to prevent pregnancy, contraception ironically succeeded in separating sex from children in the minds of most Americans. Even as millions of women faced unplanned pregnancies or suffered abortions, the contraceptive mentality took hold and persists to this day.

In the days before the Pill, human sexuality was more than simple orgasmic pleasure. It also required a coherent understanding of human nature and family relations. Sex and children were so closely linked that those who chose to ignore that ontological reality did so at great risk: the risk of bearing children. Human sexuality was considered a sacred gift, binding husband and wife together. Whether or not spouses consciously intended children - who were also considered sacred gifts - sexual intercourse by its very nature, as George Gilder notes, anticipated or celebrated progeny.[14] Widespread contraception, however, helped to render this older vision obsolete, offering the grand illusion that one could engage in sexual relations without considering children. Reinforced by popular magazines, music, motion pictures, and television programming, the contraceptive mentality has so effectively persuaded Americans that children need not result from sex that many Americans remain psychologically unprepared for what is now called an "accidental pregnancy." As Janet Smith of the University of Dallas has observed, teenagers and often even health clinic workers wonder, "How did this happen?" when faced with a pregnancy.[15]

The Distortion of Human Sexuality

While some Americans, particularly Roman Catholics and Mormons, have fought hard to resist the contraceptive mentality, the dominant, public culture in American no longer upholds the view that sexuality is a gift to be shared exclusively between husband and wife anticipating or celebrating children: Sexual relations outside the context of marriage have become a societal norm. Notwithstanding a popular abstinence movement that has emerged in primary and secondary schools as an alternative to sex education, the new norm is reflected in the findings of the National Marriage Project of Rutgers University: more than half of young American women not only lose their virginity by age 17, but also are sexually active for eight years before getting married. The same study also discovered that nearly 50 percent of Americans between the ages of 25 and 40 years have at some point set up housekeeping with a member of the opposite sex outside marriage.[16] Even among conservatives who publicly champion traditional values, pre- and extramarital sex is more common than assumed. As Danielle Crittenden of the Independent Women's Forum writes; "The most politically conservative young women I know - women who say they oppose abortion and yearn to marry and have families - would never disavow their right to sleep with whomsoever they please."[17]

By severing the connection between children and sexuality, the contraceptive mentality has fostered new visions of human sexuality. No longer accepted or received as a gift, sex is now demanded as a constitutional right. No longer viewed as a mystery, latent with meaning, sex is now considered a bodily, medical function like eating and drinking; no longer considered a marital privilege, sex is now considered a recreational activity for all. Sex now exists for the benefit of the individual, for personal satisfaction therapy, and enrichment. Self-fulfillment, not self-giving, stands at the heart of the new ethic. Provided sex does not "hurt" anyone, sexuality itself carries no moral dimension invoking transcendent questions of right and wrong aside from the legal claim that all persons have a right to engage in sexual acts. Consequently, legal, religious and social conventions that seek to maintain traditional sexual norms are perceived as repressive limitations of that right —whether between individuals of the same sex, between unmarried individuals, or even between teenagers. As columnist Richard Cohen of the Washington Post recently framed it: "Mature, responsible people are entitled to an erotic life. It is preposterous to suggest that it should be saved for marriage."[18]

The new ethic has not thrown out all the rules, but has rather adopted another set. Modern moralists, in contrast to traditionalists, insist upon the elements of consent and privacy. Consent is the sole moral prerequisite; privacy means that society cannot and should not attempt to impose any norms regarding sexual conduct, which theoretically occurs in private. Reaction to the President Clinton and Monica Lewinski scandal from many commentators and media representatives is illustrative. As Bill Press wrote in the *Washington Times*: "The President had sex . . . and denied it. So what? [Lying about sex . . . As long as it's between consenting adults, has never been prosecuted]."[19]

The Contraceptive Culture Unfolds

The ethic of consent and privacy would never have been possible without the Pill, which provided the focus of legal and constitutional claims about the right to privacy in the 1965 Supreme Court case, **Griswold v. Connecticut**. Once the contraceptive right to sex was established, additional sexual rights followed, including the right to divorce through no-fault divorce, beginning in California in 1970, and the right to abortion in 1973, in Roe v. Wade, which was based upon the same rationale of privacy discovered in the Griswold case. Now, almost all sexual conduct except forcible rape (because it lacks consent) is fair game, or is at least on its way to becoming legitimate. While illegitimacy, abortion, adultery, and divorce constitute the first wave of the contraceptive culture, homosexuality, pedophilia, "consensual" incest, necrophilia, and bestiality may be the next. Already, homosexuality enjoys public acceptance unimaginable just 30 years ago. A growing number of Fortune 500 companies now offer employment benefits to homosexuals on par with married couples; courts have even awarded homosexual couples parental rights over children.[20] The series "Ellen" may have been forced off television after the main character identified herself as a lesbian in April 1997, but the incident, like the Oscar winning 1993 film, "Philadelphia", reflects the long standing and formal acceptance of homosexuality in Hollywood.

The advance of pedophilia is less known. An essay published last year in the Journal of the American Psychological Association not only called for the abandonment of the pejorative term, pedophilia, in favor of the more value neutral phrase, adult-child sex, but also called for the removal of pedophilia form the catalogue of psychiatric disorders. Sexual relations between adults and children, the essay claimed, are "far less damaging" than previously thought.[21] Although the American Psychological Association and the American Psychiatric Association have since denounced the essay, observers have noted that the normalization of homosexuality began exactly the same way.[22] The age of consent has already been lowered in Canada to age 14 for heterosexuals. While the consent age in Holland is 16, in some cases 12 year olds can consent to sexual relations. Although initially defeated, an effort was launched earlier this year to lower the age in Great Britain.[23] As minors have historically been deemed unable to consent to anything legally, such efforts to lower the age of consent indicate either that the promoters do not accept this long-standing legal doctrine or do not care that consent be obtained. In keeping with the modern notion of sex, advocates for a lower age of consent argue that minors have the same right to sex as everyone else and claim that the legal creation of an age of consent violates that right.[24]

Both pedophilia and incest have made recent appearances in novels and in motion pictures as well. Filmmakers remade "Lolita" in 1998, a movie that celebrates a man's relationship with a 12-year-old girl. Based upon the 1955 novel by Vladimir Nabokov, "Lolita" is now popular reading material in English classes throughout American colleges and universities.[25]

In 1997, Random House published *The Kiss*, Kathryn Harrison's account of a daughter and father who begin a sexual relationship after meeting as adults.[26] While Americans may continue to harbor instinctual reservations about pedophilia and incest, these examples suggest that such perversions, as well as homosexuality, are simply by-products of a culture that separates sexuality from children. If privacy and consent are the only moral components left to control sexual reactions, all manner of sexual behavior will be acceptable. In essence, the entertainment and publishing industries are pressing very logical questions: If sexuality has nothing to do with marriage and children, what is wrong with "consensual" incest and why not "consensual" pedophilia?

The Denigration of Life

As the contraceptive promise has persuaded them that they can engage in sex without children, Americans are now considering the reverse of that paradigm: bearing children without sex. This development may represent the most tragic outgrowth of the contraceptive culture. While contraception has sought to suppress fertility, no corresponding panoply of services called reproductive technologies, including in vitro fertilization, has emerged to help those couples who want conception, not contraception. Originally intended to help create life and to fight disease, these sophisticated services are assumed to be pro-life, yet they often constitute new assaults upon human life, involving the blatant destruction of human beings in both the embryonic and fetal stages. For example, some scientists are now experimenting upon and actually killing the surplus embryos from in vitro fertilization clinics under the guise of stem cell research. Consequently, reports of frozen embryos, discarded blastocysts, as well as the destruction of some lives within the womb in order that others may live (called fetal reduction) are commonplace. Books and articles about surrogate mothers, ownership of human embryos, and the rights of a widow to her deceased husband's sperm are also numerous.[27]

Because of the speed with which new technologies have become available, and because of their promised benefits, Americans have not reflected upon the ethical questions they raise. Cloning is perhaps the only reproductive technology to which the public has registered resistance; 32 efforts have been introduced in 17 states to regulate human cloning and Michigan has banned all forms of it.[28] On the other hand, none of the three bills introduced into Congress in 1998 that would have prohibited some type of human cloning passed. To what extent Americans can, in the long run, resist the promises of cloning is not clear, as no one has yet framed a compelling argument against it.

Leon Kass of the University of Chicago has developed a case against human cloning, contending that it will transform starting a family into a manufacturing process, will reduce children to products, and will put family relations into disarray.[29] While these points have merit, they are not compelling in the present contraceptive culture: Families are already very much in disarray; in vitro fertilization has already transformed starting a family into a manufacturing process with children as the products. For good or bad, Americans now blithely accept most reproductive technologies and therefore may not be persuaded that cloning is wrong on these grounds. The initial resistance to cloning can probably be attributed to residual public distaste. Early efforts to normalize homosexuality also provoked an emotional reaction, but that negative response receded once Americans grew accustomed to the idea and become familiar with homosexuals. The ambivalence toward human cloning may very well foreshadow a similar course, just as many Americans have grown more comfortable with homosexuality, in vitro fertilization, and frozen embryos.

Like the relationship between contraception and abortion, the relationship between reproductive technologies and embryo experimentation confirms the larger link between human sexuality and human life (children). While in vitro fertilization does not necessarily lead to embryo destruction – just as contraception does not necessarily lead to abortion – the mentality to manipulate or destroy human sexuality clearly can lead to a mentality to destroy or manipulate human life. Indeed, the United States in the late twentieth century has experienced unprecedented denigration of human life, not only through the rise of infanticide (including abortion), euthanasia, and assisted suicide, but also in the area of child abuse, teen suicide, substance abuse, criminal activity, and medical experimentation upon the disabled. These examples of increased violence against the human person have occurred alongside the advent of widespread contraception. Contraception, of course, is not the sole culprit behind these ills. The denigration of human life is largely the product of secularism, which denies and neglects the role of a personal God within the world and consequently within the human person. Human beings, the Creator's crowning achievement and the embodiment of the sacred on earth, become casualties along the way. Yet secularism's most insidious affront to human life has come within the realm of human sexuality in the form of contraception. By seeking to remove children from sex, contraception has taken the sacred out of sex. This degradation of human sexuality has encouraged the degradation of human beings to which human sexuality is biologically linked. Therefore, to the degree contraception represents the manipulation and mistreatment of sexuality – the means – it has contributed to the manipulation and maltreatment of human beings – the end.

Responding to the Contraceptive Culture

Reversing the effects of the contraceptive culture will not be easy. Many have promoted sexual abstinence, encouraging young people with the same chorus that first lady Nancy Reagan sang in her war against drugs, "Just say no." While the abstinence campaign has value, its ability to challenge the contraceptive culture is limited. By focusing solely on sexual purity in marriage, the campaign unintentionally plays into the hands of the sexual revolutionaries, in particular homosexuals who now seek legitimacy by saying they, too, affirm marriage and purity. The abstinence and purity campaign also obscures the extent to which traditionalists have made peace with contraception—welcoming without reservation contraceptive use in marriage—making them vulnerable when asked: "Heterosexuals engage in sexual relations without children; why not homosexuals?" As Ramesh Ponnuru observes in *National Review*, many conservatives are reluctant "to spell out their case against homosexual conduct because it would condemn the practices of most heterosexuals."[30] Even if they were able to respond to such arguments, conservatives face significant hurdles in the nation's courthouses, which, since the 1965 **Griswold v. Connecticut** decision, have generally sided with those seeking to advance the modern sexual agenda. This puts traditionalists, especially those with religions informed convictions, at a strategic disadvantage. Traditional or religious arguments simply do not carry weight with a legal establishment that is more enamored with modern procedural notions of rights and privacy than with ontological discussions about the nature of human sexuality.

Given these cultural and legal realities, how should traditional Americans respond to the contraceptive culture? For starters, conservatives need to develop a more coherent and compelling philosophy of human sexuality, one that looks at sex not narrowly as a right for married couples to enjoy, but as a divine gift that goes hand-in-hand with the divine gift of children. They need to recognize that tying sexuality exclusively to marriage can only work when sex is equally connected to children. In doing so, conservatives may need to think more critically about contraception, acknowledging that the same convenience that the Pill may provide for married couples has at the same time wreaked havoc in the broader culture. This does not necessarily mean that all conservatives must accept the Roman Catholic distinction between "artificial" contraception and "natural" family planning, but they should at least be open to the merits of the Catholic affirmation of children over contraception as a serious alternative to the sexual pathologies of the age.

Armed and chastened with more coherent understanding of human sexuality, conservatives could achieve more in the political and legal realms, where they face an uphill battle. As no federal law currently forbids cloning, efforts to create the first human clone continue apace; homosexual activists continue to press for greater rights and recognition; and Title X of the Public Health Act and Title XIX of the Social Security Act, which was modified by a predominately Republican Congress since 1994, remain the law of the land. While contraception is no longer a legal issue, Planned Parenthood succeeded in securing contraceptive coverage for the Federal Employee Health Benefits Plan in the 105th Congress and is currently lobbying Congress to mandate contraceptive coverage as a benefit in all health insurance plans.[31]

The proposed federal mandating of contraceptive health coverage may be a battle not worth fighting at this time, since many health plans in the corporate and private sectors already cover oral contraceptives. However, the issue provides an excellent opportunity to start questioning the presumed desirability of contraception, not simply in medical insurance, but also in Title X, Title XIX, and congressional appropriations for the United Nations and its Population Fund, which dispenses contraception in global doses. At the same time, the seemingly minor issue of framing contraception as a medical health benefit is far more revealing than it appears. Contraceptive literature has for years typically referred to the woman as a patient, to fertility as the condition or sickness, and to contraception as the prescription or medication. On the other hand, courts have increasingly found that infertility is a disability for which health plans must also provide treatment.[32] The question remains: What precisely is the disease or disability that needs treatment?

This ambivalence about fertility reflects the ambivalence about women, to whom most contraception is directed. While the Pill and other devices have been successfully marketed as offering emancipation and increased control for women, the alleged freedom comes with a high price: tampering with a woman's natural condition of health and inherent fertility. At a deeper level, this ambivalence reflects the ambivalence about the identity, role, and status of women in American society, the ultimate contradiction of the contraceptive culture. Coupled with all the unintended pathologies contraception itself has conceived in America, this reality may not encourage Japan to rethink the pending legalization of the Pill. On the other hand it might sound the alarm needed to waken Americans to the fundamental realities of "the birds and the bees" to which nearly four decades on the Pill have anaesthetized them. Americans might then be able to direct their sexual passions toward truly productive ends, conceiving once again not only children, but also a culture where children, more than the sexual act that reaps them, inspires the human imagination.

* * *

Mrs. Wagner, a domestic policy analyst, joined the Family Research Council in 1998. A philosophy graduate of St. Michael's College at the University of Toronto, she earned a law degree with honors from the University of Iowa and a master's degree in European history from Washington University in St. Louis. Her essay was prepared with the research assistance of Katherine Ann Steers, a Witherspoon Fellow at the Family Research Council this past summer.

Family Policy, September-October 1999

Endnotes

[1] Jacqueline Darroach Forrest and Renee Samara, "Impact of Publicly Funded Contraceptive Services on Unintended Pregnancies and Implications for Medical Expenditures," *Family Planning Perspectives 28*, No. 5 (September-October 1996): 188-195.

[2] Donald T. Critchlow, *Intended Consequences: Birth Control, Abortion, and the Federal Government in Modern America* (New York: Oxford University Press, 1999), p. 10.

[3] Rochelle A. Ruretsky, M.D., and Victor C. Strasburger, M.D., "Adolescent Contracep-

tion: Review and Recommendations," *Clinical Pediatrics 22* (1983): 337-34; and M. Zelnick and J.F. Kantner, "Sexual Activity, Contraceptive Use and Pregnancy Among Metropolitan Area Teenagers 1971 to 1979," *Family Planning Perspectives 12* (1980): 230-237.

[4] *Statistical Abstract of the United States: 1998* (Washington: U.S. Bureau of the Census, 1998), chart 101, p. 81; and "Infant Mortality by Marital Status of Mother," *Morbidity and Mortality Weekly Report 39*, No. 30 (August 3, 1990): 521.

[5] Stanley Henshaw, "Abortion Incidence and Services in the United States, 1995-1996," *Family Planning Perspectives* 30, No. 6 (1998): 263-270, 264. See Table 1: Number of Reported Abortions, 1973-1996.

[6] Janet E. Gans Epner et al., "Late Term Abortion," *Journal of the American Medical Association 290*, No. 8 (1998): 725-720.

[7] Haishan Fu et al., "Contraceptive Failure Rates: New Estimates from the 1995 National Survey of Family Growth, *Family Planning Perspectives,* 81, No. 2 (1999): 56-63. See Table 1, p. 60.

[8] Stanley K. Henshaw, "Unintended Pregnancy in the United States," *Family Planning Perspectives 30*, No. 1 91998): 24-29.

[9] *The Declines in Adolescent Pregnancy, Birth and Abortion Rates in the 1990s: What Factors Are Responsible?* (Rahway, New Jerseyk: The Consortium of State Physicians Resource Councils, 1999).

[10] Alan O. Otton "Contraceptive Problems Cause More Pregnancies," *The Wall Street Journal*, May 25, 1993, p. B1.

[11] National Abortion Rights Action League, "An American Right at Risk," June 1999, .

[12] Planned Parenthood v. Casey, 505 U.S. 833, 856, (1992).

[13] *The Physician's Desk Reference*, 53rd ed. (Montvale, New Jersey: Medical Economics Company, 1999), p. 2222; Nicholas Tonti-Filippini, "The Pill: Abortificaient or Contraceptive?" *Linacre Quarterly*, February 1995, pp. 5-28; and Marc A. Fritz et al., "The Effect of Oral Contraceptive Pills on Markers of Endometrial Receptivity," *Fertility and Sterility 65*, No. 3 (March 1996): 484-488.

[14] George Gilder, *Sexual Suicide* (New York: Bantam Books, 1975), pp. 33-38.

[15] Janet Smith, "*Humanae Vitae*: Part II," lecture delivered at the University of Notre Dame, June 1991.

[16] David Poenoe and Barbara Dafoe Whitehead, *The State of Our Union: The Social Health of Marriage in America* (New Brunswick: National Marriage Project, 1999).

[17] Danielle Crittenden, *What Our Mothers Didn't Tell Us: Why Happiness Eludes the Modern Woman* (New York: Simon & Schuster, 1999), p. 36.

[18] Richard Cohen, "The Abstinence Candidate," The Washington Post, June 24, 199, p. A27.

[19] Bill Press, "All About Sex," *The Washington Times*, July 29, 1998, p. A21.

[20] Andy Soltis, "New Jersey's Gay Couples Win the Right to Adopt," *The New York Post*, December 18, 1997, p. 5.

[21] Bruce Rind et al, "A Meta-Analytic Examination of Assumed Properties of Child Sexual Abuse Using College Samples," *Psychological Bulletin 124*, No. 1 (1998): 22-53.

[22] Robert H. Knight and Frank V. York, *Homosexual Activists Work to Lower the Age of Sexual Consent* (Washington: Family Research Council, June 1999).

[23] Dirk Kruithof, "Dutch Law on Ages of Consent Since 1991," Dutch Association for the Integration of Homosexuality, ; Joe Woodward, "Victims at Last," *Alberta Re-*

port/Western Report, June 12, 1995, p. 28; and Terence Neilan, "Lords Defeat Gay Sex Bill," *The New York Times*, April 15, 1999, p. A10.

[24] Mark Blasius, "Sexual Revolution and the Liberation of Children,".

[25] Vladimir Nabokov, *Lolita*, Second Vintage International Edition (New York: Random House/Vintage Books), 1997.

[26] Kathryn Harrison, *The Kiss* (New York: Random House), 1997.

[27] For example, see Julia Duin, "Brave New World of Cloning Spawns Ethical Nightmares," *The Washington Times*, May 19, 1999, p. A2.

[28] Clarke D. Forsythe, "Human Cloning and the Constitution," Valparaiso University *Law Review* 32, No. 2 (Spring 1998): 469-541.

[29] Leon R. Kass, "The Wisdom of Repugnance," in *The Ethics of Human Cloning* (Washington: American Enterprise Institute Press, 1998), pp. 3-59.

[30] Ramesh Ponnuru, "Sexual Hangup," *National Review*, February 8, 1999, p. 42.

[31] Senate Bill 1324, Equity in Prescription Insurance and Contraceptive Coverage Act, introduced June 10, 1999. For Planned Parenthood's lobbying efforts in support of the legislation, see its recent newspaper advertisement, "The Ol' Boys' Double Standard... For Fair-minded People It's a BITTER PILL,' in *The Washington Post*, June 25, 1999.

[32] Randy Kennedy, "U.S. Agency Says Employer Should Pay for a Woman's Infertility Treatments," *The New York Times*, April 29, 1999, p. B1.

Down With the Pill and Contraception
Hating Babies, Hating God

Christian News, June 2, 200

"Christian opposition to infanticide and contraception is part of a larger commitment to life" says *Chronicles* editor Thomas Fleming in the June, 2003 *Chronicles*, "A Magazine of American Culture." "Man in the Image of Man - Cloning, Abortion, Contraception, Eugenics" are the words on the front cover of the latest issue of *Chronicles*.

Judie Brown, president and co-founder of the American Life League, writes in the June *Chronicles*:

"The unavoidable truth, however, is that the precursor to abortion is contraception, which encourages people to behave in a manner contrary to God's will. Contraception presented man with the empty promise of sexual fulfillment with no strings attached - instant gratification without long-term responsibility."

"Contraception, however, often failed to meet its promised goal of preventing the creation of new life. These failures were defined as 'unplanned pregnancies' and it became desirable to seek the 'termination' of those human beings. Eventually, that termination was granted the protection of law."

Aaron D. Wolf, a church historian and assistant editor of *Chronicles*, writes in an article titled "Hating Babies, Hating God - Caveat Contraception":

"When I sat down to write this article, Google reminded me that, when it comes to the issue of contraception, the stakes are very high. To check the date of publication of Dr. Charles Provan's important work *The Bible and Birth Control*, I typed 'Charles, Provan, Bible, Birth Control' into the mother of all search engines. As fast as my dial-up connection could react, I was confronted with a paid advertisement, spawned by my search criteria, for Ortho Evera; also known as The Patch, the bastard offspring of The Pill. I followed the line and immediately recognized the happy contraception from the ubiquitous television ad, who lifts her baby-T to show, just above her panty line, the flesh-colored patch, which stands up to the ravages of both shower and swimming pool as it pumps norogestromin and estradiol into her erstwhile fertile (healthy) body. The Patch, claims the commercial, is for women who just do not have the time to worry about taking a pill every day."

"From 1517 to 1930, however, no Protestant denomination or group ever permitted the practice, and it was Protestant state legislatures across the country that made the trafficking of contraceptives illegal until the Supreme Court intruded in Griswold v. Connecticut paving the way for Roe v. Wade."

Wolf quotes Martin Luther:

"The exceedingly foul deed of Onan, the basest of wretches... is a most disgraceful sin. It is far more atrocious than incest and adultery. We call it unchastely, yes, a sodomitic sin. For Onan goes in to her, that is, he lies with her and copulates, and when it comes to the point of insemination, spills the semen, lest the woman conceive. Surely at such a time the order of nature established by God in procreation should be followed. Accordingly, it was a most disgraceful crime... Consequently, he deserved to be killed by God. He committed an evil deed. Therefore, God punished him."

Wolf adds:

"John Calvin agreed, calling Onan's act 'double monstrous' and tantamount to a 'violent abortion' in which the 'offspring of his brother' was 'torn from the mother's womb' and "cast on the ground." Similar natural-law arguments were made by John Wesley, the great Baptist Charles Haddon Spurgeon, and Reformed commentator Matthew Henry, among countless others.

"The Anglican Church became the first Protestant body to sanction the use of contraception, although it took great pains to emphasize that contraception should only be used by married couples. Still the 1930 Lambeth conference's declaration rejected natural law in favor of the law of 'good intentions'. Contraception was deemed permissible 'where there is a clearly-felt moral obligation to limit or avoid parenthood.'"

"Conservative Protestants were horrified by Lambeth. T.S. Eliot said that it was an un-Christian experiment to remake society, and Lutheran Hour speaker Walter A. Maier called it 'one of the most repugnant of modern aberrations, representing a 20th century renewal of pagan bankruptcy.' The Missouri Synod pointed to St. Augustine's warning 'Contraception makes a prostitute out of the wife and an adulterer out of the husband' and noted that so-called "Companionate marriage had been termed 'licensed prostitution.'"

Charles Provan's *The Bible and Birth Control* is available from *Christian News*. Much of the book first appeared as articles in *Christian News*. Some of the other articles *Christian News* has published on Birth Control and Population are in the *Christian News Encyclopedia*. *Christian News* is one of the few non-Roman Catholic religious publications which still defend the scriptural position taken by Martin Luther and the Lutheran Church-Missouri Synod, until recent decades, against contraception.

Make Love and Babies
Christian News, November 19, 2001

"Make Love and Babies" in the November 12, 2001, *Christianity Today* takes about the same position towards birth control which was formerly held by the Lutheran Church-Missouri Synod and before that by most denominations.

Authors Sam and Bethany Torode write: "The contraceptive mentality says children are something to be avoided. We're not buying it." "Artificial contraception appears to alter the language of the body. Regardless of our intent, it seems to send a message: 'I am not giving myself completely to my spouse' or 'I will not accept my spouse in his entirety.'"

"We've heard it said that since artificial birth control is not explicitly forbidden in the Bible, it's fine for Christians to use it. But the contraceptive mentality – treating fertility as an inconvenience, danger, or sickness seems to go against what the Bible has to say about the goodness of creation and children. The Bible teaches us to approach sexual intimacy and the possibility of conception with awe and reverence. The womb is the place where God forms new life in his image, not a frontier to be invaded and conquered."

"We have read many stories from Christian couples who gave up artificial contraception - none regret it."

Some of the articles CN has published on birth control are in the *Christian News Encyclopedia*. One series of articles in CN by Charles Provan opposing birth control have been published in a book on birth control. CN highly recommends the book. Dr. Walter Maier in his marriage manual published by Concordia Publishing House opposed birth control. CN tried without success to get CPH to reprint Maier's marriage manual.

Open Embrace - The Bible and Birth Control
Christian News, August 5, 2002

Open Embrace. A Protestant Couple Rethinks Contraception. By Sam and Bethany Torode. Foreword by J. Rudziseski. William B.

Eerdmans Publishing Company. Grand Rapids, Michigan, 1992.

Christian News is one of the few Protestant publications which has opposed birth control for almost 40 years. CN has defended the position taken by Scripture, Martin Luther and the orthodox fathers of The Lutheran Church-Missouri Synod. Both LCMS and WELS no longer oppose birth control. Several decades ago most churches still opposed birth control.

Lutheran Hour speaker, Dr. Walter Maier, in his *Manual of Christian Matrimony, For Better Not For Worse*, Concordia Publishing House, 1935, has a chapter titled "The Blight of Birth Control." Some of the subtitles are: "Shrinking Families, The Overpopulation Bugaboo, Prevention of Infant Mortality, Retardation of Child Development, Elimination of Unfit, The Physical Penalty, An Outrage Against Nature, A Moral Degradation, A Divorce Stimulus, A Menace to National Prosperity, Its Anti-Scriptural Bias, The Church's Position."

Now some Protestants are beginning to reconsider the pro-birth control position. Note "Being Fruitful" reprinted below from the July 11, 2002, *Washington Times*. This report mentions *Open Embrace - A Protestant Couple Rethinks Contraception*. Another good book which shows that the Bible and Martin Luther opposed birth control is *The Bible and Birth Control* by Charles Provan. Some years ago chapters of this book appeared in *Christian News*. It should be read and answered by theologians in the LCMS and WELS who are now supporting birth control.

Being Fruitful
Evangelicals see biblical directive to 'make love and babies'

By Robert Stacy McCain
The Washington Times, July 11, 2002
Christian News, July 22, 2002

Sam and Bethany Torode oppose contraception. They say it interferes with the "one flesh" nature of marriage declared in the Bible. No one can accuse the Torodes of failing to practice what they preach. Their son Gideon was born almost exactly nine months after their November 2000 wedding.

"We don't waste any time," says Mr. Torode 26, of South Wayne, Wis. He and his 21-year old wife are expecting their second child in February. The Catholic Church condemns contraception as "intrinsically evil," but the Torodes are not Catholic. They are part of a new generation of young Protestants who disdain birth control and favor larger families.

"A lot of people grew up without realizing there was an alternative to the dominant contraceptive lifestyle," says Mr. Torode, art and design editor of Touchstone, a Christian magazine.

In their new book, "Open Embrace: A Protestant Couple Rethinks Contraception," the Torodes declare they want a "passel" of children, and they are not alone. Christian Internet sites such as www.quiverfull.com advocate large families based on Psalm 127:5: "As arrows are in the hand of a mighty man; so are children of the youth. Happy is the man that hath his quiver full of them."

Many evangelical Protestants in the pro-life movement have large families. Tennessee pro-life activist Charles Wysong and his wife, Brenda, have 15 children; Arkansas state Rep. Jim Bob Duggar and his wife, Michelle, have 13; Virginia home-schooling leader Michael Farris and his wife, Vickie, have 10.

The evangelical journal *Christianity Today* began questioning family limits in 1991, asking, "Is Birth Control Christian?" In 2001, the magazine ran an article by the Torodes: "Make Love and Babies," along with a rebuttal by Eastern College biblical studies professor Raymond Van Leeuwen.

"To suggest that birth control is evil or perverse," Mr. Van Leeuwen wrote, "because it undermines God's sovereignty is to underestimate God's sovereignty and reject our responsibility to serve Him wisely."

The Christian Research Journal took on the topic in a 1996 article by Michigan Theological Seminary professor Wayne House. "Many [couples] are more than willing to enjoy sexual relations with no procreation responsibilities, yet the [biblical] text indicates that childbearing is a very real part of the purpose of God in creating male and female," he wrote.

It was not until the 20th century that Protestant churches endorsed birth control. Martin Luther and other early Protestant reformers "believed in abundant fertility," says Allan Carlson, president of the Howard Center for the Family, Religion and Society in Rockford, IL. "He condemned contraception and abortion in the strongest possible terms. Specifically, he thought [God's blessing for Adam and Eve in Genesis 1:28] to 'be fruitful and multiply' . . . was a divine command."

Prior to the 1900s, Mr. Torode says, most Protestants opposed birth control for the same reasons expressed by Pope Paul VI in his July 1968 encyclical *"Humanae Vitae."*

"They believed contraception would increase promiscuity and encourage adultery by separating sex from procreation," he says.

But after the Church of England approved birth control at its 1930 Lambeth Conference, "all Protestant denominations went on to endorse contraception, except for a few groups like the Amish," he says. Protestants "were following the spirit of the age. They were influenced by people like [Planned Parenthood founder] Margaret Sanger."

By the 1980s, acceptance of birth control was so widespread that tubal ligation - surgical sterilization of women, now America's No. 1 contraceptive method - became routine for women after having two or three children. "After my mom had my [younger] sister, who is her third child, the nurse actually prepped her for a tubal ligation without her consent, but the doctor intervened - he was a Christian, too," Mrs. Torode says. "My mom was pretty groggy . . . and she didn't even know what was going on."

The Torodes endorse the Natural Family Planning (NFP) practices advocated by the Catholic pro-life Couple to Couple League, but most Americans don't know about NFP because the medical community almost unanimously endorses artificial birth control, Mr. Torode, says. "It's so hard to get honest information. It's hard to find doctors who encourage large families."

"The national trend toward smaller families has had profound consequences," Mr. Carlson says. Out-of-wedlock births-33 percent of all U.S. babies last year were born to unmarried women - have become a troubling statistic, partly because the marital fertility rate has declined by more that 40 percent in the past 45 years.

Marital fertility is "the most important indicator of social health," Mr. Carlson says. "It's important because it embodies two critical measures of social health: the desire of young adults to marry and to procreate new life."

The Torodes base their opposition to artificial birth control on Genesis 2:24:

"Therefore shall a man leave his father and his mother, and shall cleave unto his wife: and they shall be one flesh."

"God created marriage, sex and children to go together," Mr. Torode says. "There's the concept of the husband and wife becoming one flesh. And children are a gift that God bestows on that union. Contraception puts up a barrier in the middle of the union."

"We believe that husband and wife should hold nothing back from each other," he says, "and children are pretty much the natural result of that kind of love."

The Toroders' love began with a whirlwind courtship after 18-year-old college sophomore Bethany Patchin published an August 1999 article arguing that Christians should not kiss before marriage.

Her article in Focus on the Family's online journal Boundless (www.boundless.org) prompted Mr. Torode to reply with a letter that accused Bethany of trying to "drive young Christian men mad with desire" by boasting she had never been kissed. She now admits there was perhaps "subconsciously" some truth in his charge.

After exchanging e-mails, the two met in January 2000. They were engaged that May and married six months later.

Mr. Torode now laughs at the irony of his letter to Boundless: "I can see the love letters pouring in now, from saps all over the country, proposing to poor Miss Patchin. Never underestimate reverse psychology," he wrote then.

"Then I wound up being the sap that fell for it," he says now, "because we did get married and we didn't kiss until our wedding day." When the couple looked for books about contraception, they found that few modern Protestant authors had addressed the topic -so they decided to write their own book.

"We're not trying to impose our views on others," Mrs. Torode says: "We're just putting an alternative out there, because a lot of people don't even realize all the options they have."

CN's Suggestion for "Church Growth"

Christian News, June 27, 2003

Christian News has long been critical of the theology of some Church Growth leaders. CN has published more than enough information on the Church Growth movement to fill a good sized book. Some of it is in the *Christian News Encyclopedia*.

One sure method of "Church Growth", which CN has promoted ever since it began in 1962, is having children. CN is one of the few non-Roman Catholic publications which still takes the same position toward birth control and having children which almost all churches took prior to the 1930s. CN has published photos of and stories about many large Christian families. Of course, God does not bless all families with many children. Those who have not been blessed with a spouse or those who have some physical disability are still God's children and can serve Him.

This issue includes "Strength in Numbers – Steve and Debbie Armour meet the challenges of raising 12 children with rewarding results." The article appeared in the May, 2000 *Today in Mississippi*.

The June 12 *St. Louis Post Dispatch* published a story about Annabelle Neske, the mother of 16 children, who recently spoke at Fort Zumwalt South High School. The story said in part:

"Sixteen children is a family larger than a football team. And as the hour went by, Neske explained how it all happened.

"The plan had been to have no more than five children, she says, adding that the birth-control rhythm system obviously didn't work. She also explained that she is a Roman Catholic.

"I'm here to talk about family, and as you can see, I have a lot to talk about,' she said with a smile.

"Later, Neske talked frankly about her pregnancies and childbearing and what having so many children did to her reproductive system. She also spoke of how her children would stay close to one another and how they loved one another. That's when they need you, and you need them,' she said, referring to their formative years.

"It was a candid talk, straightforward, a la Dr. Ruth.

"We lived on what he made,' she said, referring to late husband, St. Louis police lieutenant Robert Charles Neske, 'and you can do it. There were times when we didn't have a telephone.'

"Annabelle Ebel is Neske's maiden name, and she moved here from Detroit when she was 6 months old. Her father was a timekeeper at an auto plant and later became a comptroller for the old Boyd's Department Store.

"Even though Neske had a degree as a registered nurse from the old St. John's Mercy Hospital, then on Euclid Avenue, she never worked in nursing. 'I didn't want anyone else raising my children, so they can blame me, or praise me,' she said.

"The spacing was sometimes 11 months to three years apart,' she said.

'As for people's reactions, I probably didn't pay much attention. We just lived our own life in a big place, on an acre of ground, and we mostly stayed home. We did things together, although their dad took the boys fishing and hunting.

"You have a reputation with a large family, but we just went about our business.'

"The Neskes got by with one bathroom on the second-floor, a half-bath on the first-floor and an old shower with a toilet in the basement. That was great for the boys, who always went to the basement,' she said. 'We didn't seem to have problems.'

"Eventually, her 16 children went off to a wide range of jobs and activities. Now it looks as if her grandchildren are doing the same; she travels quite often to see them. Last month, she flew to watch a grandson graduate from the University of Maine at Farmington. His father, Richard, went to West Point and recently retired as an Army colonel.

"The average size of her children's families – just four."

"I always told my children to get yourself as much education as you can, and do what you want to do,' Neske said. 'I never compared one to the other. So I let them follow their own instincts, and that may give you a little heartache for a while.'

"But like one said, 'Mom and Dad, I'll have my degree before I'm 30.' I let them do what they liked, and let them be who they are—all individuals.'

"When the class ended, several students approached Grandma Neske for a hug."

Christians and Birth Control

June 26, 2004
Jay W. Shutt
334 High street
Hamlet, NC 28345

Herman Otten
Christian News
New Haven, MO

Dear Mr. Otten,

I have written a manuscript about why Christians should not use birth control. It is titled What Will You say on Judgment Day About Birth Control? This is an extremely sensitive subject, and, as yet, no publisher is interested or will take the chance on publishing it.

Mr. John Stormer of Liberty Bell Press said you might be interested in helping me get this message before the Christian community.

John stated in his note that birth control use among Christians might be the leading cause of problems in the church since the early 1960s when the use of the "pill" was legalized. I fully agree. Any help you can offer will be appreciated. Thank you so much for your time and consideration of this matter

Yours in Christ,
Jay W. Shutt
(Ed. CN does not have space for the entire essay. Readers interested in the rest of the essay may write to the author.)

Luther Criticized the Contraceptive Mentality
Luther's Enduring Words
Medieval advice fit for families

The Washington Times, July 8, 2004
Christian News, August 8, 2004

Sixteenth-century Christian reformer Martin Luther's writings on marriage and the family profoundly influenced European culture – and addressed many of the issues that are on the public agenda today, says Allan C. Carlson, president of the Howard Center for Family, Religion and Society in Rockford, IL.

The following are excerpts from Mr. Carlson's lecture about what he called "Luther's sexual revolution," delivered Friday in Washington at the Family Research Council.

The late medieval church held arguably conflicting views of women. Formally, the Virgin stood as the model of devotion, of honor and emulation. Informally, there were also signs of certain misogyny, a curious distrust of women . . . by an emphasis on their supposed inferior nature.

Regarding marriage, the late medieval church held two possibly inconsistent views. On one hand, the church held marriage to be a Christian sacrament, a divine mystery, a channel of God's sanctifying grace.

On the other hand, the church also projected the message that the spiritual status of a celibate priest, monk or nun was superior to that of a married lay Christian. Canon law casts marriage as an obstacle to a life based on prayer and wholehearted fellowship with God.

To enter marriage and to bear . . . children . . . were somewhat inferior Christian acts, less than holy. The sexual act itself, even in marriage, stood as unclean, sinful, degrading.

Marriage did enjoy [limited] regulation by the late medieval church. Generally, government was not involved, but divorce was prohibited. Church marriage courts dealt with issues of annulment and then the inevitable disputes. The problems within this . . . regulatory system were accumulating.

To begin with, the late medieval church maintained a long list of impediments to marriage, most of which could be overcome in the early 16th century by payment into the right . . . coffers. Accordingly, cynicism over the institution of marriage grew.

Martin Luther's approach to marriage, family and sexuality cut through this world as a hot knife through butter. Appearing at times to be astonishingly modern, even scientific in his insights, Luther ultimately wrote his argument on his reading of Scripture.

Luther, let us remember, was himself a . . . monk, an ordained priest and a prominent professor of theology at the University of Wittenberg. The principal and historically significant thrust of Luther's thought . . . defined a unique, evangelical interpretation of family life.

Luther [rejected] mandatory celibacy as unbiblical and unnatural. For Luther, God's words in Genesis 1:28, "Be fruitful and multiply," represented more than a command. It was what he called a divine ordinance . . . which it is not our prerogative to hinder or ignore. The reformer [also] emphasized Genesis 2:18.

Luther declared, "Whoever will be a true Christian must grant that the word of God was true and believe that God was not drunk when he spoke these words and instituted marriage."

For it was not a matter of free choice or decision but a natural and necessary thing, that whatever is a man must have a woman and whatever is a woman must have a man. . . Regarding the sexual act . . . through marriage sex became a moral good, an expression of God's will. This was the heart of Luther's sexual revolution. . .

Luther . . . criticized the contraceptive mentality that . . . was found chiefly among the well-born, the wealthy, the nobility and princes. Also he linked contraception and abortion to selfishness.

Luther also understood that marriage was the best protection against the scourge of sexual disease . . . "The benefit not only of the body, property, honor and soul of the individual, but also to the benefit of whole cities and countries in that they remain exempt to the most terrible plagues that have befallen lands and people because of fornication."

The married state . . . was pleasing to God and precious in his sight. . .

A woman is not created to be a virgin, but to conceive and bear children. Similarly, God called the men to serve as Christian . . . fathers. Luther . . . concludes that there is no higher office, state, condition or work than the state of marriage. Luther also casts man and woman as fully equal in dignity and authority [and] marriage . . . a true partnership of work, procreation and child care.

Whatever a husband has, his wife has and possesses in its entirety. If the wife is honorable, virtuous and pious, she shares in all the chores and . . . duties and functions of her husband.

In short, Luther's version of sexual egalitarianism could be expressed only through the bond of marriage. The husband and wife in becoming one flesh found true equality.

So, Luther elevated parenting as a task of responsibility, and in so doing re-energized the Christian home as an autonomous Christian sphere. "There is no power on earth that is nobler or greater than that of parents," stated the reformer. . .

In the Protestant home, father and mother would share the duties of child rearing to an unusual degree. Inspired by Luther's message on family, publishers turned out dozens of editions of so-called house-father books, 16th century self-help [guides] for dads. The goal was to instill in children the true controls necessary to an ordered life.

Luther argued that within clear scriptural guidelines, personal freedom should be granted . . . Luther constantly maintained that true Christian freedom . . . could never degenerate into idleness or wickedness. . . [and called] for greater freedom to marry. . .

Luther never extended this freedom to marry to two people of the same sex. For him it [would have been] an inconceivable, horrific act contrary to the very order of God's creation . . .

How might we judge the success of Luther's family ethic? [It] cast marriage as the highest order and calling on earth. It softened and redirected, while not eliminating, patriarchal leadership. It spiritually and culturally elevated motherhood and homemaking, and it celebrated procreation and large families [and] encouraged . . . family autonomy and freedom that refocused adults' lives around the tasks of child rearing.

What about . . .Christian Families

A.L. Barry, President, The Lutheran Church—Missouri Synod
Christian News, April 14, 1997

Greetings to you in the name of our Lord Jesus Christ. Christian families face enormous pressures in our world today. It is important that they have a good understanding of what God intends for the family and how they best can respond to the many challenges that confront them.

What does God say about families in His Word, the Bible?

In the beginning, God created men and women to live together with one another as husbands and wives, and through their marriages to bring children into the world. We read in Genesis 2:22-24: "The Lord God made a woman from the rib He had taken out of the man, and He brought her to the man. The man said, 'This is now bone of my bones and flesh of my flesh; she shall be called "woman," for she was taken out of man.' For this reason a man will leave his father and mother and be united to his wife, and they will become one flesh." Our Lord Jesus Christ affirmed the divine institution of marriage during his earthly ministry (Matthew 19:5).

Through the Apostle St. Paul, the Lord revealed that Christian husbands and wives are to love and serve one another, modeling before the world the love Christ has for His bride, the church. In Ephesians 5, St. Paul wrote: "Submit to one another out of reverence for Christ. Wives, submit to your husbands as to the Lord. For the husband is the head of the wife as Christ is the head of the church, His body, of which He is the Savior.

"Now as the church submits to Christ, so also wives should submit to their husbands in everything. Husbands, love your wives, just as Christ loved the church and gave Himself up for her to make her holy. ...In this same way, husbands ought to love their wives as their own bodies. He who loves his wife loves himself. After all, no one ever hated his own body, but he feeds and cares for it, just as Christ does the church—for we are members of His body.

" 'For this reason a man will leave his father and mother and be united to his wife, and the two will become one flesh.' This is a profound mystery—but I am talking about Christ and the church. However, each one of you also must love his wife as he loves himself, and the wife must respect husband"(Ephesians 5:21-33).

In this powerful description of marriage, there is no room for husbands to "lord it over" their wives, nor for wives to disregard their husband's role of "headship" in the home. The key is mutual submission to and love for one another, modeled after Christ's love for the church, and the church's submission to Christ her Lord.

Parents are to provide discipline to their children with love and compassion, doing what is best for their children. We read in Ephesians 6:4: "Fathers, do not exasperate your children; instead, bring them up in the training and instruction of the Lord." And children are to honor and obey their parents, as the Lord commands, "Children, obey your parents in the Lord, for this is right." "'Honor your father and your mother'—which is the first commandment with a promise— that it may go well with you and that you may enjoy long life on the earth" (Ephesians 6:1-3).

What are some of the cultural trends impacting families?

As we review what the Bible has to say about families, we quickly realize how far many of our cultural trends are from God's will for families.

Christian families are bombarded by signals which contradict God's Word. Popular culture, through movies, music, magazines, books and especially television, inundates us with wrong messages. The signal is sent that a sexual relationship outside of marriage, or before marriage, is perfectly natural, or that even a homosexual lifestyle is merely an alternative to "traditional" marriage. Children are led to believe that being disobedient and disrespectful to parents is normal, even amusing, or that the elderly are to be viewed as a burden, or subjects for humor. So much of popular culture appeals to humanity's most sinful inclinations, and encourages them in a barrage of images and words.

The pressure on our children—particularly our teenagers—to do whatever is necessary to be "popular" among their friends is sometimes difficult for parents to understand and appreciate. Our young people are often caught up in destructive lifestyles and behaviors, encouraged by popular music which encourages rebelliousness and disdain for life and the dignity of their fellow human beings. As our teenagers grow older, they are given the impression that "living together" without marriage is perfectly acceptable. How tragic it is when their own families do nothing to resist this behavior.

Men in our culture are encouraged to indulge their lusts and selfish desires. So little respect or attention is given to the man who wishes to be a faithful husband or father. How many children today grow up without a loving and responsible father in the home? The horrendous consequences of this trend will only become greater as we move into the future.

Women too are pressured to take a dim view of what God has given them. They are pressured to view childbearing as less than fulfilling, something perhaps only to be tolerated, and not to be enjoyed as a gift from God. They too face temptations to disregard God's expectations for them when they are wives and mothers, or to view marriage as something to be abandoned when it becomes inconvenient for them.

Yes, we surely do recognize that popular cultural trends often convey messages totally contrary to our Lord's Word and His will for Christian families. This needs to be recognized and resisted.

What can a Christian family do to deal with the challenges of our day?

Openly facing the issues is the first step. Pretending that problems do not exist will certainly not help. Nor will it do for a family simply to hope that they will not be faced with problems. Ignoring reality will not make it go away.

It is crucial for Christian parents to spend both quality and quantity time with their children. Reading with their young children, discussing the questions they have and being there to support and encourage them is extremely important.

Husbands and wives need to take time out of busy and hectic schedules to simply talk to one another, discussing the needs they have and the problems they are experiencing, working together to grow in their love for one another, and for their children.

More importantly, Christians need to pray for the Lord's blessing on their marriages and families, asking God to forgive them for their sins and failures as parents and spouses, and then turning to the Lord's mercy through their Savior Jesus Christ.

Christian families need to make every-Sunday worship an absolute priority. As families are gathered by God around His Word and Sacraments, they receive forgiveness, life and salvation—the strength they need to cope with the challenges of daily life.

What role do daily devotions have in the life of the Christian family?

One of the most important things a family can do is spend time together in the Word of God.

Key ingredients for the family's devotional time are the Scriptures, the hymnal and the Small Catechism. These are excellent resources for meaningful time together in the Word of God.

Parents should begin reading and reciting the chief parts of the Small Catechism with their children when they are very young, helping them learn the Lord's Prayer, the Ten Commandments and the Apostles' Creed, and then working on the explanations, building as time goes on.

Parents need to discuss their faith with their children, pray with them and in love encourage their children to do what is right, not hesitating to say "no" when necessary. And always, parents will want to be for their children a model of the Heavenly Father's love in Christ Jesus our Lord.

How can parents help their children resist temptations?
Parents often overlook the very important role they play simply by the way they themselves handle life. Parents can provide important role models for their children.

If a man constantly displays a harsh and fierce temper at home, uses foul language and acts disrespectfully toward his wife, it is little wonder why his son would grow up with similar attitudes and behaviors. If a woman constantly gripes and points out every fault, again, there is little surprise when her children do the same when they grow up.

Christian parents need to model the faith, both to their children and others around them. St. Paul wrote that a Christian marriage is to be an image of Christ's love for the church. This is both an awesome responsibility and a joyous privilege.

May God bless our families richly with His loving mercy, strengthening them as they seek to love one another and serve their Lord and Savior.

Be Faithful and Multiply
By David Klinghoffer
Christian News, June 4, 2007

When our twin boys were born last week here in Seattle, it struck me that my wife and I were implicitly registering a dissent from the secular liberal value system of most Seattleites, as from that of the residents of America's other biggest left-leaning cities. Jacob and Saul are our fourth and fifth babies. This damp, tree-loving city is lushly green but largely sterile. Seattle is America's second-most childless city, just behind San Francisco. It is also the chief metropolis of the country's most unchurched region, the Pacific Northwest. People tend to have dogs rather than kids. The correlation between holding secular liberal views and preferring not to reproduce has been noted elsewhere, but not adequately explained. The data come from a juxtaposition of the red-and-blue quilted electoral map of the 2004 election with information from the National Center for Health Statistics and the 2004 General Social Survey.

Arthur Brooks, a professor at Syracuse University's Maxwell School of Public Affairs, writes in *The Wall Street Journal*: "If you picked 100 unrelated politically liberal adults at random, you would find that they had had, between them, 147 children. If you picked 100 conservatives, you would find 208 kids. That's a 'fertility gap' of 41 percent." David Brooks notes in *The New York Times* a "spiritual movement" of "natalists," but offers no insight into why exactly a spiritual perspective much more than a secular one would encourage reproduction. After all, secularists and liberals love their children too. Certainly, conservative culture is imbued with scriptural values more than liberalism is. And the Bible not only lends strong support to conservative beliefs, but takes an insistently strong pro-natalist stance. This could be part of the explanation.

God likes babies. Noah, whose family alone survived the deluge that engulfed the rest of humanity, was given the commandment of populating the world: "Be fruitful and multiply and fill the land" (Genesis 9:1). Isaiah taught that God made the world with reproduction uppermost in mind: "He is the God, the One Who fashioned the earth and its Maker; He established it; He did not create it for emptiness; He fashioned it to be inhabited" (45:18).

Of course, plenty of secularists have children, too. If asked why they choose to do so, and with no less enthusiasm than that of their religious neighbors, they would say: "I love children." "I want to give my love to a child or children." "I want to nurture a human being, and see him grow and thrive." These are all beautiful and sincere sentiments. But not one of them would be unexpected coming from a would-be pet owner looking for a dog or cat to care for. No, I am not saying that secularists see their children as pets, nor that the traditionally religious always make better parents. But the absence of an additional religious imperative for child-raising makes it understandable that liberals reproduce less often. Just as pet ownership is optional, so too is having children if the only reasons for doing so are those cited above.

It's also possible to have too many pets, and the neighbors will chastise you for this. A staple of local news stories, frequently posted on the Drudge Report, is the eccentric person with way too many pets: There was the lady in Clearwater, Fla., with 100 cats, which led police to condemn her house as a public nuisance. Florida was also home to a man in Ocala charged with animal cruelty for keeping 300 cats. And so on. Just so, families with five or more children can expect to be reproached by strangers in supermarkets and on sidewalks, wanting to know, "Don't you think you've had enough already?"

The religiously motivated are undeterred because, unlike liberalism and secularism, a biblical worldview sees children as having a role besides that of the recipient of parental affection and nurture. These adorable little tikes have the glorious task of being transmitters of an ancient tradition to posterity. The Bible teaches this in connection with the Exodus from Egypt. "And you shall tell your son on that day, saying 'It is because of this that the Lord acted on my behalf when I left Egypt'" (Exodus 13:8). In Deuteronomy, Moses advises: "And these matters that I command you today shall be upon your heart. You shall teach them thoroughly to your children and you shall speak of them while you sit in your home, while you walk on the way, when you retire and when you arise" (6:6-7).

Just as your Internet access depends on countless other computers being linked to yours, the link between generations is stronger depending on how many children you have. This is of special relevance for Jews, of all denominations. I've written before in this space about Jewish fertility and how it is impacted by worldview. As the statisticians Antony Gordon and Richard Horowitz have shown, every 100 Reform Jews will be reduced within four generations to only 10 Jews. Every 100 Conservative Jews will be reduced to 29. In the struggle between rival worldviews that characterizes modern times, the Hebraic view is on the ropes, under constant attack from secularism. As in war, the number of soldiers on the ground matters no less than the qualities of the combatants. A Jew who believes in Judaism cannot have too many children.

David Klinghoffer, a senior fellow at the Discovery Institute, is the author of the forthcoming "Shattered Tablets: Why We Ignore the Ten Commandments at Our Peril" (Doubleday).

A Threat to Our Very Way of Life
By Aaron D. Wolf
Christian News, January 14, 2008

Here's a heresy for you. A grave danger is lurking among us, caused by certain people who are spreading lies-and in the name of Christianity! So grave is this danger that it threatens our very way of life. And, as one of our great leaders once said, "The American way of life is not negotiable."

We are, of course, talking about the threat of babies, and the strain that having them puts on us as Americans, particularly white people. Thanks to the Industrial Revolution, the Managerial Revolution, and the World Wide Webolution, the world has changed, and we just cannot have unrestrained marital sex and produce large, unruly families like we did in days of yore, back when land was cheap, a man could earn a living for his wife and children, and those children (because of the slave labor they endured) were considered an economic asset. Today, we live by a higher standard:

Chattel-children are a thing of the past, and plasma televisions are considered economic assets. Women are no longer bound by the constraints of having multiple children; no career in business. House speakering, or freedom spreading; and nothing to do but keep a house and clothe and feed children and husband. In today's non-negotiable America, a woman can create a company called Baby Einstein, which produces educational enrichment (babysitting) DVDs for children ages six months to three years old; sell the company to Disney for a secret all-cash amount (reportedly $25 million); then be recognized in the gallery during the President's State of the Union Address as a "talented business entrepreneur." You've come a long way... Lady!

Now, there are the naysayers out there who point out that, yes, according to estimates just released by the CIA's *World Factbook*, women in the United States are actually reproducing slightly below replacement level (2.1). These nabobs are just ignorant of the facts and lack the optimism that makes America great. After all, thanks to the influx of Mexican immigrants (they are the most fertile, followed by non-Hispanic black African-Americans, followed by Asian-Americans), we have gained one one-hundredth of a baby per woman (2.09, up from 2.08 in 2005), and we are closing in on communist North Korea, where Comrade Kim has sat right on the replacement level for two years in a row. Watch out, Argentina (2.16) And South Africa (2.2)!

Then again, the ninnies point out that this downward trend in having babies is affecting our churches as well. They point to a 2005 study by three researchers (Michael Hout of the University of California-Berkley. Andrew Greeley of the University of Arizona, and Melissa Wilde of Indiana University) that indicates that the massive decline in every Protestant denomination in the United States can be explained by declining fertility rates. According to their study, the fact that fertility rates among more conservative denominations are now the same as among the Mainline liberals explains why conservatives can no longer claim that they are growing (while the Mainlines are shrinking) because of their conservative stance on abortion, homosexuality, etc.

Nonetheless, we cannot let these startling statistics cause us to lose sight of reality: The threat of babies is as real today as it was 85 years ago, when Margaret Sanger, the founder of Planned Parenthood, wrote *The Pivot of Civilization*, in which she clarified that,

> As a social program, birth control is not merely concerned with population questions ... It looks for the liberation of the spirit of woman and through woman of the child. Today motherhood is wasted, penalized, tortured. Children brought into the world by unwilling mothers suffer an initial handicap that cannot be measured by cold statistics. Their lives are blighted from the start.

In his Introduction to Sanger's *Pivot*, Mr. H.G. Wells declares that the threat of babies is at the heart of a clash of civilizations: the Traditional or Authoritative Civilization versus the Creative and Progressive one. The former

> Rests upon the thing that is, and upon the thing that has been. It insists upon respect for custom and usage; it discourages criticism and enquiry. It is very ancient and conservative, or, going beyond conservation, it is reactionary...

Said the Ancient Civilization - and it says it still through a multitude of various voices and harsh repressive acts: "Let man learn his duty and obey." Says the New Civilization, with ever-increasing confidence: "Let man know, and trust him."

Certain men, however, cannot be trusted, particularly a group of "Christians" who deny the menacing threat of babies, and who claim that they are doing God's will by having children. They belong to something called the Quiver-Full Movement, which takes its name from Psalm 127:

> Lo, children are an heritage of the LORD: and the fruit of the womb is his reward. As arrows are in the hand of a mighty man; so are children of thy youth. Happy is the man that hath his quiver full of them...

In their primitive understanding, they read this to mean that a "man" will be "happy" if he has many "children" - and that this "reward" comes

from "the LORD."
But they don't stop there: They also insist that birth control is a sin - a ridiculous notion easily dispelled by the theologians of all major Protestant denominations decades ago. Of course, the nagging nincompoops are right about one thing: During the oppressive days of the authoritative Civilization, every theologian, from Augustine to Aquinas, Luther to Calvin, Wesley to Spurgeon, condemned contraception as a sin against natural law - a rejection of the obvious purpose (though not the only benefit) of post marital sex.

From *Chronicles*

Margaret Sanger and The Pivot of Civilization
A book review by Brandt Klawitter
Christian News, February 22, 2010

Sanger, Margaret, edited by Michael W. Perry. *The Pivot of Civilization in Historical Perspective*. (Seattle: Inkling Books, 2001), 279pp. http:// www.InklingBooks.com/

Before seeing the name "Margaret Sanger" and looking askance at this book review, allow me to point out that this book is much, much more than a simple reprint of Margaret Sanger's original book published in 1922. In fact, Margaret Sanger's book forms only the final third of this entire volume. The rest is comprised of the essays and writings of such influential forerunners, contemporaries, or opponents of Sanger as H.G. Wells, G.B. Shaw, Theodore Roosevelt, Charlotte Gilman, Victoria Woodhull Martin, G.K. Chesterton and others, all of whom help to put Sanger's writings in historical perspective.

But, why is it important to be knowledgeable about Margaret Sanger? The answer is simply that she was the driving force behind the birth control movement in the United States. Of course, positively put, birth control and the emergence of Planned Parenthood finally gave reproductive freedom to women and freed them from the shackles of motherhood, marriage, and their own biology. Nevertheless, there is a much darker side to the birth control movement and particularly of its main leader, Margaret Sanger.

No friend of church, family, or traditional government, Sanger associated freely in the early 1900s with Anarchists, Socialists, members of the Fabian Society, Malthusians, and other such dissident and revolutionary movements prevalent at that time. She was a member of the Rosicrucian Society, involved in occultist Cabalistic practices, had numerous affairs, was finally divorced from her husband for advocating (and practicing) "free love", and was dedicated to the eugenics movement of the early 20th Century, a movement which shared the same scientific and ideological underpinnings of the Nazis and which was in league with those who advocated the forced sterilization of the weak and feeble-minded in the United States. If that isn't enough, she was once put on trial and fled the country after her paper, *The*

Woman Rebel, published articles on assassination and renounced marriage.

Nevertheless, in many eyes Sanger is revered as something of a saint, particularly for her role in spreading the "gospel" of birth control and establishing Planned Parenthood (predominately in the neighborhoods of minorities and those who were societally undesirable). Yet, despite Ms. Sanger's credentials and her less-than-commendable record, hers is the voice that ultimately preached to and prevailed among American society and its families. Even more, with the global, corporate nature of Planned Parenthood, one might even say that Sanger's legacy has extended far beyond her own lifetime accomplishments. Yes, almost perfectly in step with the creed of Sanger's *The Rebel Woman*[1] and the sort of anti-family, one-world society depicted by her influential friend and lover H.G. Wells[2], many women have grown independent of marriage, family and motherhood altogether (often in exchange for greater dependence on the state). Even more remarkable in all of this, the church has largely turned a cold shoulder towards some nineteen centuries of pro- marriage, child, and family teaching, only to almost unquestionably embrace Sanger's message of birth control and liberation from traditional norms—and this without the smallest of whimpers, even in such traditionally conservative churches as the LCMS.

So, why read this book? If you want to understand the roots of our own sex-saturated, family-distorting and -destroying modern society, you'll have to explore how we actually arrived at where we are today. Unquestionably, Margaret Sanger, the rise of Planned Parenthood, changing societal attitudes, and the failure of churches—particularly their clergy—to offer anything but the weakest of resistance to such anti-family and anti-marriage developments (an exception should be made for the Roman Catholic Church's official position), all are part of the story. This book is not the easiest to read, but the time and effort spent in working through its material are certainly well-invested.

Notes

[1]"Rebel women claim the following Rights: The Right to be Lazy. The Right to be an Unmarried Mother. The Right to Destroy. The Right to Create. The Right to Live and the Right to Love." Quoted from Madeline Gray's *Margaret Sanger* (New York: Richard Marek Publishers, 1979), 72.

[2]Michael Perry (editor of this edition of *The Pivot of Civilization*) makes the following comment on Wells' ideas of a World State and universal, coerced population control: "Wells became one of the first scientific writers to advocate global population control—today an all too progressive cause. According to him, controlling births would be how the World State would rid itself of 'rejected' whites and Asians as well as the 'vast proportion of the black and brown races'...At the same time that it was checking 'the procreation of base and servile types.,' the World State would ensure of the procreation of those who were 'fine, efficient and beautiful.' Do not forget that in a Wellsian World State there would be no place to flee from birth controllers, no distant corner where 'rejected' races and individuals could simply raise a family in peace..." pg. 35.

Real Sexual Revolution Began With Contraception
by Joseph Sobran
The Bare Bodkin
Chronicles, April 2010
Christian News, April 12th, 2010

Nearly a century ago, G.K. Chesterton wrote of "the modern and morbid habit of always sacrificing the normal to the abnormal." Today the very word *normal* is almost taboo. Perish the thought that there is anything abnormal—let alone sinful, vicious, perverted, abominable, sick, unhealthy, or just plain wrong—about sodomy. (Unsanitary? Let's not go there.)

As one T-shirt legend puts it, "I'm proud of my gay son." Sure you are, lady. I'll bet when he told you, you blurted, "O darling, you make me so proud!" I mean, like, who wouldn't? And then you went out and bragged to all the neighbors.

And do you enjoy picturing what he and his "partners" do together? If you're curious, you can probably get the idea from a DVD. Just go into an "adult" DVD store and ask where the anal-sex section is. This should make you just burst with maternal pride.

Let me lay my cards on the table. I'm what they call homophobic, and I believe God loves me just the way I am. He may even regard homophobia as one of my finer qualities. To a much lesser degree, I'm also lesbophobic. I realize that lesbianism is also a form of sodomy, but that strikes me as a rather technical point, because, in my rather limited experience, it doesn't involve the sort of repulsive practices male sodomy does. How often have you heard of a lesbian dying of AIDS?

This is hardly the place to discuss sexual practices in clinical detail. Such discussions are freely available, indeed unavoidable, elsewhere. To add to them here would be, as the old saying has it, carrying coals to Newcastle.

But I digress. (I wondered when you'd notice.) Most people realize that God made two sexes. Even the phrase *gay and lesbian* is an attempt to ape the natural symmetry of nature's (two and only two) sexes. Male and female homosexuality are only superficially parallel; in fact, they are wholly different and dissimilar maladjustments. The male brand is madly promiscuous and indiscriminate; the female brand tends to be monogamous. This will surely be borne out by the upshot of the craze for same-sex "marriage"—an absurd contradiction in terms if ever there was one. (You might as well expect two bulls, or two lions, to form a lasting union.)

We are witnessing what might be called the eclipse of the normal—an eccentric phase of modern history in which huge numbers of people feign ignorance of what is perfectly obvious. The polite taboos on calling abortion "killing" and sodomy "perversion" are mere symptoms of this; Barack Obama, with his sycophantic solicitude for "gays," is typical of the modern liberal mind-set. "Who is to say what is 'normal'?" is now thought to be an insoluble conundrum.

Well, who is to say that, in all the fantastic abundance of nature, there are only two sexes? Or is that another tough one? After all, members of some species of marine life can even change sexes. It's clear that anybody who can't answer such questions just doesn't want them to be answered. All sane people know the answers, and it's a waste of time arguing with a man who pretends not to know, even if he's the president of the United States. This nonsense has been going on far too long.

Who could have imagined, a generation ago, that organized Sodom would achieve such cultural and political power in the United States? And so soon, at that! "We are all sodomites now," exults Andrew Sullivan, and he has a point, at least a semantic one. The word *sodomy*, as he notes, used to comprise all sexual perversions, including contraception within marriage. The real sexual revolution came to pass quietly, when contraception became generally accepted as a legitimate part of marriage. After that, it became hard to argue against virtually any sexual practice, inside or outside wedlock, short of rape. The revolution in morals occurred almost before anyone noticed it. And today it is taken for granted.

Few of us can now remember how sternly nearly all Christians disapproved of birth control before 1931, when the Anglican Church opened the floodgates with a few seemingly innocuous exceptions in certain cases of hardship. By now the old standards of chastity have melted away like ice in August. In today's terms, they are well-nigh incomprehensible.

Modern man is thoroughly cut off from his past. He and his ancestors would be total strangers to each other. The essential problem is a new form of hypocrisy in which we all feel pressure to affect ignorance of things everyone used to know—and which most people still do know.

To put it bluntly, our moral standards would horrify our forebears. They would gasp in disbelief at the things we now accept as normal, for the simple reason that any civilized society would recognize those things as highly abnormal.

This article first appeared in the issue of Chronicles: A Magazine of American Culture.

Lutheran Witness Says Birth Control Not Sinful

Christian News, February 8, 1993

"Birth control, of itself, cannot be called sinful" says the Question and Answer column in the February, 1993 *Lutheran Witness*. Martin Luther and the LCMS formerly said that birth control was sinful.

Dr. John Fritz writes in his *Pastoral Theology*, a textbook long used in the LCMS and published by the LCMS's Concordia Publishing House, that "The Jews had large families; so did our German forefathers. The one-, two-, or three-children family system is contrary to the Scriptures; for man has no right arbitrarily or definitely to limit the number of his offspring (birth control, especially not if done with artificial or unnatural means, Gen. 1, 28; Ps. 127, 3-6; Ps. 128, 3.4; Gen. 38,9.10. Such restrictions as uncontrollable circumstances, natural barrenness, or the ill health of wife or husband put upon the number of offspring are the exceptions to the rule. Child-bearing is both a natural and a healthful process, while any interference with natural functions is injurious."

Fritz's *Pastoral Theology* includes a statement by Concordia Seminary Professor Theodore Laetsch which lists the "Arguments Advanced By advocates of Birth Control" and then "Arguments Against Birth Control." Dr. Walter Maier, first Lutheran Hour speaker in his *For Better Not Worse*, published by the LCMS's Concordia Publishing House, took a strong stand against birth control. Most denominations until the early 1930s opposed birth control. Then they found new "insights" in the Bible. For a defense of the LCMS's former stand against birth control see the sections on birth control and population in the *Christian News Encycopedia*.

Larry Marquardt
Founder - Christian Life Resources
Strong Opponent of Birth Control
Christian News, December 8, 2008

The November/December, 2008 *Clearly Caring* (WELS) says that "The roots of Christian Life Resources can be traced to Mr. Larry Marquardt (died June 2001), from Illinois, who founded this pro-life and pro-family agency. When this organization started, it was originally named Lutherans for Life. It later became WELS Lutherans for Life, and in 1999 it was renamed Christian Life Resources."

Larry Marquardt was elected to the Board of Regents of Concordia Teachers College, River Forest, Illinois. However, he left the LCMS because of its toleration of theological liberalism. Marquardt was a solid, friendly and likable confessional Lutheran. He was a Bible scholar, serving on the revisions committee of An American Translation of the Bible. He was long active in pro-life causes and well informed about world affairs, including Israel.

Some of Marquardt's articles are in the *Christian News Encyclopedia*. A family photo with eleven children is on page 32. CN noted that he was chairman of Lutherans for Life (p. 36). He was a founder of Balance Inc. which published Affirm (p. 1200). A photo of Marquardt with some other members of the AAT Bible Versions Committee meeting at Camp Trinity, New Haven, Missouri is on page 1671 (CN, August 7, 1978). An Overture Marquardt presented to the Wisconsin Evangelical Lutheran Synod is on pages 1892-3. It was published in a special issue of *Christian News* on birth control. Marquardt's overture included documents showing that ancient church fathers, the Lutheran Church-Missouri Synod, Walter Maier, John H.C. Fritz, the

LCMS's *Concordia Cyclopedia*, and others opposed birth control.

Christian News is one of the few religious publications which still defends the position most of Christendom took opposing birth control until the resolution of the Anglican's Lambeth Conference in 1930.

The lead article in the February 29, 1988 *Christian News* was "The Bible's View of Birth Control" by Charles Provan. It is now in Provan's *The Bible and Birth Control* available from *Christian News*, ($4.00 plus $2.00 s/h). Provan defends Luther's position which today is ignored even by many confessional Lutherans. The front page of the February 29, 1988 *Christian News* pictures a Christian family of 20. CN has frequently published the photos of large families. Walter Maier did the same thing in the Walther League Messenger, the LCMS's youth publication he edited.

A major reason churches are declining is because of small families.

Northwestern Publishing Booklet Supporting Contraception

Christian News, April 26, 2010

The Wisconsin Lutheran Synod's Northwestern Publishing House has just published *Birth Control*, a 22 page pamphlet by Jeanne B. Fehlauer. www.nph.net. The WELS along with most denominations, at one time, opposed birth control. Part I. "Christianity, Children, and Contraception" (*Christian News*, April 12, 2010) noted:

"As examples, I might mention both the Wisconsin Evangelical Lutheran Synod (WELS) and the Lutheran Church-Missouri Synod (LCMS), though this list might be widened to include all major protestant denomination. For example, in a 1981 report on Human Sexuality, the LCMS' CTCR made the following statement: 'In view of the Biblical command and the blessing to 'be fruitful and multiply' [Gen. 1:28] it is expected that marriage will not ordinarily be voluntarily childless. But, in the absence of Scriptural prohibition, there need be no objection to contraception with a marital union which is, as a whole, fruitful.' This We Believe (the Lutheran Church–Missouri Synod, 2010), 5. Similarly, in a series titled 'The Christian and Birth Control' (Beginnings, Feb. 1998), 8-9, WELS Lutherans for Life reached the following conclusions: (1) 'A Christian's decision to use birth control is a stewardship issue,' and 'A Christian married couple can practice some form of birth control. It falls within the realm of Christian freedom and stewardship.'"

Northwestern's "Birth Control" says:

"If couples would like a more thorough explanation of the various methods of contraception, they should consult their obstetrician or gynecologist. Another source for information on birth control and motives is the publication *The Christian and Birth Control* (Milwaukee: WELS Christian Life Resources, 1999). WELS Christian Life Resources has the expertise to advise couples on how various forms of birth control work and are happy to discuss these matters."

Reproduced in this issue is "An Overture to the WELS - Publishing Biblical Guidelines on Sexual Relations", an overture by Larry Marquardt, to a WELS convention. Marquart had been a member of the Board of Control, Concordia College, River Forest, Illinois and the AAT Revision Committee and Lutheran Bible Society. He was instrumental in founding Wisconsin Lutherans for Life. Neither Wisconsin Lutherans for Life nor the WELS ever attempted to show where Marquardt's *On Sexual Relations* opposing birth control is in error. It was simply ignored just as the writings of Martin Luther, Walter Maier, John Fritz, Martin Naumann and other orthodox Lutherans are ignored today, even by most conservatives.

The WELS' Lutherans for Life accepted and approved Marquardt's support, but not his views on contraception.

A Line in the Sand
Review by Brandt Klawitter
Christian News, February 22, 2010

Hodge, Bryan C. *The Christian Case Against Contraception* (Eugene, Oregon: Wipf & Stock, 2010), 285 pp.

I have to admit that the statement "drawing a line in the sand" puzzles me. After all, it seems that anything having to do with the beach and sand is by nature rather transient and temporary. But maybe, just maybe, that's really how we mean to use the phrase. After all, most of us have seen a good number of lines drawn in the sand during our lifetimes. There have been promises made by politicians. The line was drawn. Government will really be cleaned up this time. Right. Or a little closer to home, the line was drawn with that New Year's resolution. This year was to be the year. Fortunately, we've managed to forget now that it's February. Yes, there is even that old file folder of lines that were formerly drawn by the church. It bears the simple label: "what we used to teach." Yes, these have all been "lines in the sand", each in their own way. Fortunately or unfortunately, however, lines drawn in the sand these days are subject to the laws of the tide. The line reaches its limit as the next tide washes over. Conveniently, we are left free to redraw those lines as we wish sometime in the future.

"The historic church believed that the line surrounding contraception and the proper use of sex concerned itself with such grievous matters as idolatry, sexual immorality, and murder."

What do we make of it, though, when the tide has come and gone and somehow the line is still there, clearly marked in the sand? A first reaction might include some small amount of puzzlement, perhaps followed by a tentative test with the flip-flop to see whether the line can be done away with. What if it can't, though? What if tide after tide washes over the line and it remains there on the shore—a little wet, perhaps some flotsam and jetsam resting here and there, but completely intact?

I raise the question about a line drawn in the sand for various reasons. First, with the modern devaluation of words and truth, we might do well to question our use of this currency. Perhaps we have contributed in some way to the cheapening of promises and the declining value of "one's word." Second, it seems to me that there is an area of life where the tide has come and is beginning to recede, and yet a line remains clearly in view. With his new book, *The Christian Case Against Contraception*, Bryan Hodge simply directs our attention to this phenomenal reality.

I had originally thought that I'd credit Hodge with being bold enough to have drawn this line himself. Upon further reflection, though, it became obvious to me that this isn't exactly the case. After all, the point of his book is to show that the line drawn by the church in opposing contraception has always been there and is actually the line drawn by Scripture. In fact, by employing the four disciplines of theology (historic, exegetical, systematic, and practical), Hodge makes very compelling arguments that what has actually happened for the last 100+ years is that society has convinced the church to cover up this line. In essence, it has sought to turn the church back towards a pagan and hedonistic lifestyle. Moreover, through naturalistic thought, situational ethics, emotional and experiential argumentation, individualism, questionable and novel exegesis, a loss of historical perspective, and a distorted Christian worldview, shovelful upon shovelful of sand has been heaped upon the now almost concealed line.

Every once in a while, though, it happens that someone reads bits of Luther, or perhaps Calvin, and in doing so they seem to notice evidences of an ancient demarcation. Moreover, from time to time it is observed that men like C.S. Lewis and G.K. Chesterton were aware of this once well-known line. From their account of things, it appears that this line vehemently opposed birth control, contraception, and the limitation of life (Hodge mentions some 120 other well-known theologians throughout the church's history who advocated this same line). Yes, from time to time semblances of this line have emerged as men and women are struck with the far-fetched and almost fantastic idea that sex is (and should be) linked to procreation, that fertility is a natural and good thing, and that God wants couples to "be fruitful and multiply." Yes, it even appears that God loves babies and desires that humans (as bad as we are according to some population-control advocates) have children. Indeed, sections of this once-known line seem to show forth through even the thickest layers of modern sterile- and often self-centered thought. But could such an old-fashioned legend of a line in the sand actually have any validity? Could our forefathers have really known the proper line without the help of modern science?

As unlikely as we may believe it to be, Hodge argues that those who have come before us throughout the church's history weren't actually stupid. In fact, it seems that they read Scripture a great deal and might have even had a better understanding of it, the God who inspired it, and the ethic that corresponds to it than we often demonstrate today. If anything, Hodge believes that it is we, and not they, who have erred. Furthermore, he also contends that the historic church greatly revered this once well-known line for most serious and significant reasons. Their reasons? They believed that the line surrounding contraception and the proper use of sex concerned itself with such grievous matters as idolatry, sexual immorality, and murder. In other words, the historic church confessed that to cross this line was to do what is an abomination before God Almighty. Oddly enough, now such line-crossing is merely a matter of "sexual freedom" and is regulated only by one's own prerogative to determine when and if there should be children. I guess that makes modern-day Western Christendom something of an anomaly. Yes, in ignoring this well-attested line, we have boldly proceeded where "lesser" saints have feared to tread.

Where does this leave us? When faced with such a fork in the road, there seem to be two general choices. One can pat himself on the back for his novel way of life and proceed unabated, or one could actually try to assess the situation and explore God's Word—perhaps God actually does have something to say about contraception and such related matters. Of course, this might just lead to a change of course—something that was once known in some circles as "repentance."

But why use such strong language? After all, as Christians we're basically good people, are we not? Such things as searching the Scriptures in search of God's will, sin, confession, repentance, and other archaic holdovers certainly can't apply to us these days! Here's another thought, though. What if, just what if Bryan Hodge's arguments (generally those of the historic church) have any merit? What if it turns out that he isn't drawing his own arbitrary line in the sand and that he's not just condemning contraception because of his own personal preference for large families? What if it turns out that the line he reminds us of in *The Christian Case against Contraception* is a line not drawn by man in the shifting sand, but in stone by the finger of Him who etched His will into tablets on Mt. Sinai and who has traced that same will upon the surface of the human heart at Creation? What if...Well, I suppose we could just shrug our shoulders and continue on as we are. After all, who ever heard of religion having anything to say about one's sex life? Good grief. Hasn't God heard of privacy and human freedom? On the other hand, there might actually be the option of humbling ourselves before God and submitting to His Word. It's a thought.

Notes on the book: *The Christian Case Against Contraception* offers a comprehensive and systematic approach to the question of birth control and contraception. While Hodge writes from an Evangelical background (the reader will note many references to covenantal theology), he does so in a straight-forward, thought-provoking manner that seeks to engage all Christians on this topic and particularly those of his own background. Even more, by devoting a great deal of attention to the exegetical questions surrounding contraception, Hodge presents the most extensive case for life and procreation that I have yet come across. In other words, Hodge argues that

Scripture's discussion of the matter of contraception does not begin and end with Genesis 38(:9-10), *"And it came to pass, when he went in to his brother's wife, that he emitted on the ground, lest he should give an heir to his brother. And the thing which he did displeased the Lord; therefore He killed him also."* Indeed, that would seem to be pretty shaky ground if that were the extent of the argument. It isn't, though. The argument presented by Hodge is grounded in Creation, reaffirmed in Old Testament law, and comprises the expectation and norm for God's people, both of the Old and New Testaments.

Beyond this, Hodge also takes on the arguments of the opposition point by point. What about a couple that's just not ready for children? What about financial considerations? What about health? What about the idea that sex is legitimate when viewed solely with respect to physical gratification and apart from any procreative intent? Yes, one by one Hodge takes these questions up and provides answers. Certainly, his answers might make many of us squirm and cause us to rethink what we do and why. Even more, his answers (if applied to our lives) might lead to a style of life which might be, negatively put, "frightening and reckless." Yet, it could also be that these answers would lead the church back to something much more positive. Perhaps it might lead us back to something simply called "living by faith"— even if that means living a life that does indeed seem somewhat out of our control and only within God's control.

In conclusion, I am not a professor (and probably never will become one due to my repeated appearances in CN). Nevertheless, I had the thought as I read through this book, "Wouldn't it be great to go through this in a class? Wouldn't it be great to sift through the exegetical arguments, examine the church's history, and to carefully consider the philosophical questions under discussion?" I couldn't help but think that that certainly would be a wonderful study. While I'm not sure that we'd necessarily want to know what we might discover, I'm also reminded of a thought-provoking statement I recently came across. It simply declared that the most adventurous thing a man can do these days is to have a family. Yes, with societal, financial, and personal factors all poised against the family, with so many voices questioning why one should bind himself to one woman and why he (and she) should limit their offspring according to the dictates of personal preference and convenience, how wildly adventurous would it be to simply leave such matters to God? Interestingly enough, it is Hodge's contention that in similar circumstances throughout history, the church has chosen to do just that.

50th Anniversary of the Pill

Christian News, May 3, 2010

"50th Anniversary of the Pill" is the cover story of the May 3 *TIME*.

Some forty years ago Peter Krey wrote in *Christian News* in an article titled "The Glory of Motherhood": "We hear and read a great deal about the prevention of motherhood. Leading men and women of our day advocate birth control and whole church bodies have endorsed it. What shall our attitude be? It should not take a Christian long to find the answer. A little clear thinking should soon tell him that prevention of motherhood runs contrary to the benediction and will of the blessed creator: 'Be fruitful and multiply.'"

The July 2010 convention of The Lutheran Church-Missouri Synod is being petitioned to reaffirm Martin Luther's and the LCMS's former opposition to birth control.

The May 3 *TIME* says:

"The Pill at 50: Sex, Freedom and Paradox

"In May 1960, the FDA approved a new oral contraceptive. Somehow we are still fighting about it half a century later—whom it helped, whom it hurt, what it meant and why it mattered."

By Nancy Gibbs

"There's no such thing as the Car or the Shoe or the Laundry Soap. But everyone knows the Pill, whose FDA approval 50 years ago rearranged the furniture of human relations in ways that we've argued about ever since.

"Its supporters hoped it would strengthen marriage by easing the strain of unwanted children; its critics still charge that the Pill gave rise to promiscuity, adultery and the breakdown of the family. In 1999 the Economist named it the most important scientific advance of the 20th century. . .

"In 1960 the typical American woman had 3.6 children; by 1980 the number had dropped below two. For the first time, more women identified themselves as workers than as homemakers. 'There is a straight line between the Pill and the changes in family structure we now see,' says National Organization for Women (NOW) president Terry O'Neill, 'with 22% of women earning more than their husbands. In 1970, 70% of women with children under 6 were at home; 30% worked. Now that's roughly reversed.'

"Today more than 100 million women around the world start their day with this tiny tablet. So small. So powerful. But in surprising ways, so misunderstood."

"But well into the modern age, contraception met with unified opposition from across the religious spectrum, Protestants and Catholics, Western and Eastern Orthodox. Sex, even within marriage, was immoral unless aimed at having a baby. Fear of pregnancy was a powerful check on promiscuity — and information about contraception was treated as the equivalent of pornography. In 1873 Congress passed a law banning birth control information as obscene."

"The Mothers of the Pill

"The driving force to change all this was a woman born in Corning, N.Y., in 1879 to a Catholic mother and a father who carved angels and saints out of marble. When her mother died at the age of 50 after 18 pregnancies, she confronted her father over her mother's coffin and charged, 'You caused this. Mother is dead from having too many children.'

"Margaret Sanger went on to train as a nurse and as early as 1912 was dreaming of a 'magic pill' that would prevent pregnancy. She coined the phrase birth control in 1914, the year she was arrested for mailing her magazine the Woman Rebel, an outlaw tract with its discussions of contraceptive use. She jumped bail and fled to Europe but returned two years later and opened the nation's first family-planning clinic in a squalid tenement section of Brooklyn. Arrested again, she served 30 days. But she did not stop."

"In the years that followed, Sanger provided the ingenuity and energy to drive the birth control movement, and Katharine Dexter McCormick provided the capital. The movement gained momentum during the Depression, when limiting the size of families became practically a matter of survival. America went from 55 birth control clinics in 1930 to more than 800 in 1942, the year Sanger's Birth Control League changed its name to the Planned Parenthood Federation of America."

"Thirty states still had laws against promoting birth control — so for its early life, the Pill existed only undercover. But there was a sudden epidemic of menstrual irregularity among women across the U.S.

"In 1959 the pharmaceutical firm G.D. Searle & Co. applied to the FDA for approval of the Pill, which would be marketed as Enovid. On May 9, 1960, the FDA gave its blessing. 'Approval was based on the question of safety,' said associate commissioner John Harvey, noting that 'our own ideas of morality had nothing to do with the case.'"

"In 1962, when Pope John XXIII convened the Second Vatican Council, many lay leaders and clergy anticipated a relaxation of restraints on family planning as part of a general liberalization of church teaching. By the time his successor, Pope Paul VI, appointed a commission to study the issue two years later, roughly half of American Catholics were already practicing birth control. Leaked reports of the commission's findings suggested that nearly all its theologians and a majority of the Cardinals favored changing the church's teaching on the immorality of contraception — but the following year, Paul VI issued his encyclical *Humanae Vitae*, in which he sided with the minority. The teaching against contraception stayed in place. Hundreds of American theologians issued a statement that this was not an infallible teaching and that Catholics could in good conscience dissent. In any event, it was too late to reverse the trend; by 1970, two-thirds of Catholic women were using birth control, more than a quarter of those used the Pill."

"In 1964, *TIME* declared that the 'second sexual revolution' was built on the message that 'sex will save you and libido make you free.' Open-mindedness was the new normal; the pursuit of pleasure overtook the pursuit of happiness. As Methodist bishop Gerald Kennedy of Los Angeles put it, 'There is more promiscuity, and it is taken as a matter of course now by people. In my day they did it, but they knew it was wrong.'

"But just because the arrival of the Pill coincided with a liberalization of attitudes does not mean the Pill caused it. The Pill hadn't yet been invented, after all, when the Kinsey Report was published in 1953, asserting that half the women studied had had sex before marriage and 1 in 4 had committed adultery by her 40s."

"Backlash

"Opposition to the Pill among conservative Catholics was consistent from the beginning, but it was only after it had been in widespread use for years that some conservative Protestants began rethinking their views on contraception in general and the Pill in particular. 'I think the contraceptive revolution caught Evangelicals by surprise,' observes Albert Mohler, the president of the Southern Baptist Theological Seminary. 'We bought into a mentality of human control. We welcomed the polio vaccine and penicillin and just received the Pill as one more great medical advance.'

"But beginning in the 1990s, many conservative Christians revisited the question of what God intends in marriage and pondered the true nature of the gift of sexuality. The heart of the concern, in this view, is that using contraception can weaken the marital bond by separating sex from procreation. The ideal of marriage as a 'one-flesh union' places the act of intercourse, with the possibility of creating new life, at the center of the relationship. 'Go back a hundred years,' Mohler says. 'The biblical idea you'd have adults who'd intend to have very active sex lives without any respect to the likelihood of children didn't exist. And it's now unexceptional.' This is not to say that everyone has an obligation to have as many children as possible; Mohler has two, not 12, he notes, and as long as a couple is 'not seeking to alienate their sexual relationship from the gift of children, they can seek to space or limit the total number of children they have.' But the ability to control human reproduction, he says, has done more to reorder human life than any event since Adam and Eve ate the apple."

Margaret Sanger's *The Pivot of Civilization* was reviewed in the February 22, 2010 *Christian News*.

PROTESTANT FAMILY OF TWENTY

PSALMS 127:5
"Happy is the man who has filled his quiver with them..."

Consider the Landon story. Ten boys in the Armed Forces pp. 240-242. Christian News February 28, 1988.

The Delbert E. Landon Family of Broadway, Ohio. Left to right, top row, are: Madaline, Virginia, Delbert, Robert, Wilton, Marie. Second row: Gerald, Grayden, Carrol, Minta holding Patricit, Charles, Marion, Nellie. First row: Paul (Pearl was stillborn), Mary, John, Ronald and James.

IV

LIVING TOGETHER BEFORE MARRIAGE

What's Wrong With Livin' Together Before Marriage?

Christian News, April 7, 1986

Living in a self-centered, pleasure-oriented society, young Christian couples find it increasingly difficult to uphold the true, Biblical standards of righteousness and morality in our land. The frequency of couples living together today apart from the marriage bond is alarming, and the flippancy of their attitude to do so is even more frightening. "Well, what's wrong with living together before marriage anyway?" they ask. "It's our life!"

Since you asked an honest question, let us look at the answer on the basis of God's inspired Word.

1. God calls it sin. Fornication is defined as "sexual intercourse between unmarried persons." There are many specific Bible passages which soundly condemn fornication as immoral. (See 1 Corinthians 6:9, Ephesians 5:3, Hebrews 13:4).

2. The proper place of sex in God's good design of marriage is to consummate the marriage bond and thereafter to serve as a means of conceiving children and enjoying marital intimacy. Any deviation from this model is a violation of God's law with serious consequences.

3. Christians call Christ their Master. They submit to Him as Lord. Therefore, they do not and can not do exactly as they please. "Do you not know that your body is a temple of the Holy Spirit within you, which you have from God? You are not your own; you were bought with a price. So glorify God in your body" (1 Corinthians 6:19-20).

4. Sex without the binding commitment of marriage cheapens both the sanctity of sex and the sacredness of marriage. It also cheapens oneself and the other person involved. Love without commitment is not really love at all, but rather lust.

5. All violations of God's standards of morality carry consequences with them. Some of the many consequences of the sin of fornication are misplaced trust, unplanned pregnancy, "forced" marriages, venereal disease, and difficulty in adjusting within marriage with the greater risk of eventual divorce. In addition, there is the negative Christian witness which this lifestyle presents to the world.

God's standard is clear, and it is still best. "Let marriage be held in honor among all, and let the marriage bed be undefiled; for God will judge the immoral and adulterous' (Hebrews 13:4).

Have you fallen into the trap of sexual intimacy before marriage? If so, don't despair, for there is still hope. Jesus Christ died to save sinners and forgive them of sins against the Sixth Commandment, as well as all others.

So recognize your sin in the light of God's Word. Repent of it and confess your wrongdoing to God. Be assured, that when you confess your sin to Him, He is faithful and just to forgive you your sin and to cleanse you from all unrighteousness. Seek the Lord and His strength

to live a sanctified life, dedicated to a loving Lord. There's no life more glorious!
—Wayne A Bernau (Concordia Tract Mission)

Where We Stand

The Northwestern Lutheran, July, 1986
By Mark E. Braun
Christian News, October 13, 1986

*Come live with me and be my love
And we will some new pleasures prove
Of golden sands and crystal brooks
And silken lines and silver hooks*

*There's nothing that I wouldn't do
If you would be my POSSLQ*

No, it's not the furry little creature that digs in your garbage at night. POSSLQ is an acronym of **P**ersons of the **O**pposite **S**ex **S**haring **L**iving **Q**uarters.

The number of U.S. couples who cohabit without marriage has more than tripled since 1970. A study by the Office of Church in Society (ALC) estimated that 40% of Lutheran couples live together before their wedding day.

And it's giving the church a headache. George W. Cornell, religion editor for the Associated Press, wrote last fall: "Handling matrimonial cases has become a growing, knotty problem for the churches as a result of the increased number of couples who live together before they seek church marriages. That situation upsets the traditional church concept of marriage as consummated by sexual union, since the tie now often is sealed before it's made, leaving pastors to puzzle about their role in the reversed sequence."

How is the church to react? The American Lutheran Church, in a 1984 report, says the Christian tradition "is challenged and affronted by the privatized decision to cohabit" without the rite of marriage, yet it pleads for "a climate of openness," and even asks, "If a couple believes that legal marriage is not the answer, can the church recognize and bless a committed, covenant relationship apart from governmental regulation? Can a churchly ceremony for such relationships be developed?" The United Church of Canada announced that "sexual morality has to keep up with the social sciences." The Church of England, in a new booklet entitled, "Foreword to Marriage," wrote, "It has to be recognized that sex before marriage in this day and age is quite common."

Confused? Scripture says: "Flee from sexual immorality... God will judge the adulterer and all the sexually immoral." Church reports, however, tell us times are changing and ask if we can write liturgies to accommodate the changes.

The Savior didn't say, "Go into all the world, and 'create a climate of openness' for all people." He said, *"Repentance and forgiveness of sins will be preached. . ." Repentance is possible only when there is awareness of sin.* Forgiveness is to be spoken only to sinners who repent.

In the opening verses of John 8, Jesus gives us a model for dealing pastorally with POSSLQs. The Pharisees presented him with a woman caught in the act of adultery. Jesus didn't disagree with the commandment. *The Church must continue to call extramarital cohabitation sin.* Yet he did not allow her accusers to judge themselves more righteous than she, and he told her, "Neither do I condemn you." *The church must continue to announce forgiveness to penitent sinners.* Jesus added, "Go now and leave your life of sin." *The church must continue to look for fruits of genuine repentance.* Can a couple repent of sinful cohabitation, yet continue living in that sin? Isn't it more in keeping with true repentance that a cohabitating man and woman either *separate* or *marry*?

Is it the easy way to handle this question? No. Will some people misunderstand our actions? Most likely. Can there be extenuating circumstances? In some cases, yes. Is there another preacher down the street only too happy to condone living together without marriage? Usually. But is the Savior's method the right thing to do? Clearly. And, ultimately, is it the most loving thing to do?

Absolutely.

If you agree that this is true,
Then do not be a POSSLQ

Living Together: The Modern Trend

By Rev. Glen Huebel
Messiah Lutheran Church, Keller, Texas
Christian News, June 26, 1989

Living together before or instead of marriage has become an acceptable practice today even in a significant segment of the Christian community. The cover story of the May, 1989 *Lutheran Witness* focused upon this very issue and indicated Lutheran pastors everywhere are finding this to be a severe problem.

It seems, however, that "church weddings" have not gone out of style. Couples who have long discarded the Sixth Commandment of God still consider it important to be married in a religious ceremony, in a church building, by a Christian pastor. When asked why, they usually respond that they want God's blessing and they just wouldn't "feel right" about getting married in a civil ceremony by a state official.

How should the Christian church respond to this new situation? On the one hand we do not want to alienate people who are legitimate prospects for the gospel. On the other hand, we do not want to participate in a shameful mockery of God's Word, using His sacred name as a mere "religious ornament" for society. The Christian pastor today is often faced with just this dilemma.

My thoughts on this subject have evolved during my eight years of ministry as a number of cases have come my way. The elders and I have discussed congregational policy on several occasions. I would like to share some of these thoughts with you, the congregation, since I am but the voice of the congregation in my official capacity. This is a community problem and we need to face it as a community under the Word of God.

I. Living Together Outside of Marriage is a Sin.

When I was a teen, the norms were beyond debate. Though not everyone lived according to them, they were fairly clear. The sexual revolution changed all that. A poor old woman in California has been successfully sued for discrimination because she refused to lease her apartment to an unmarried couple as a matter of principle. The courts have thus far concluded that the couple's "right" to live together (though it is against state law) supersedes the woman's "religious convictions." So acceptable has this practice become that it is revolutionary now to **oppose** it.

This acceptability factor has perhaps penetrated the youth of the church more than we would like to admit. We may no longer assume that our youth (and adults for that matter) understand "living together" to be a wrong and sinful practice. I have become painfully aware of my false assumptions in counseling several outside couples who have come to me for a wedding ceremony. Most of these young couples were already living together and all of them had at least one "confirmed Lutheran" partner. When I confronted them with their sin, they usually responded with genuine shock that I should be so narrow-minded and archaic. It was almost as if they could not believe that some pastors still teach the "old-fashioned" way.

This experience has led me to the conclusion that the church's teaching today is either way off base or it is not clear at all. The church seems to be giving the impression that while we may not wholly embrace extra-marital or pre-marital sex, we certainly don't condemn it as sinful, nor do we call for REPENTANCE. It may be that our gentleness is being misinterpreted. And it may be that this is the impression many pastors INTEND to give. I don't know. But we must deal with the situation as it is. The more acceptable a sin becomes, the more loudly and clearly the church must speak against it.

Living together outside of marriage is ADULTERY. It is condemned by God and His wrath is threatened against those who defy His commandment. "Marriage is honorable in all, and the bed undefiled, but whoremongers and adulterers God will judge." (Heb. 13:4) "But fornication and all uncleanness let it be not once named among you as becometh saints. . . Let no man deceive you with vain words" for because of these things comes the wrath of God upon the children of obedience" (Eph 5:3, 6). This testimony of God's Word must be clearly taught against the Devil, the World and our flesh.

II. Indiscriminately Marrying Those Who Live Together is Confirming an Error.

Like most pastors, I used to marry those couples who cohabitate on the reasoning that we want to encourage and help them toward "making things right." Since we want them to seal their union with marriage, we ought to do what we can to foster it.

This reasoning has become less convincing with time and experience. It may have been perfectly valid a few decades ago, but I am not convinced it has validity today. I do not generally find today that "making things right" is even part of the motivation for cohabitating couples to get married. Quite the contrary. "Making things right" implies that they may have done "wrong" in living together, a sin that they steadfastly refuse to acknowledge. Marriage for them is just another step in their original plan which began with a "trial period" (cohabitation). By complying with their wishes for a Christian wedding, are we giving our blessing to this whole perverted belief about sex and marriage? Are we really "making things right" or are we superficially covering a sin for our own comfort? The Bible says, "Rend your hearts and not your garments" (Joel 2:13). God calls us to REPENTANCE – not to a superficial covering of sin. In the present context where God's Sixth Commandment is trampled, we may be "partaking of other men's sins" by giving religious sanction to the sinful practices of our culture.

III. Couples Who Live Together Should Express REPENTANCE Before Seeking and Receiving God's Blessing Upon Their Marriage Through a Christian Wedding.

Since it is obvious that the wedding itself is no longer a statement of repentance, the pastor must be assured that the couple confesses wrong and sincerely desires to walk in the way of the Lord by entering properly into the marriage relationship. The sincerity of confession must be confirmed by SEPARATING until the wedding takes place. This alone will clear the church of condoning sin before the world. This has not been a popular policy so far, but it is one which clearly testifies to the truth of God's Word against the errors of the world.

Of course, when repentance does take place, it is a time of great rejoicing in the Church. In such cases we gladly apply the great Gospel promises of forgiveness through Jesus Christ. The couple is absolved and the marriage may begin with a clear slate and the assurance of God's blessing.

I share all these thoughts with you because we must stand together in confessing the truth. We must also apply the Word to ourselves and our children as we do to others. This may cause tension, difficulty, and family strife at times, but for the sake of eternal souls and in obedience to God's command it needs to be done. We are not called to acquiesce to our culture. We are called to transform it by the power of the Gospel. May God enable us to speak in faithfulness and love for the salvation of souls.

Numbers Show Cohabitating Hurts
By Cheryl Wetzstein,
Washington Times, October 5, 2009

In Iceland, 66 percent of babies are born out of wedlock. In Sweden, it's 55 percent, in Norway, 54 percent and in Denmark, 46 percent.

Why should Americans care? We're not the same culture, and our unwed birthrate is not even 40 percent yet.

The answer is that as unwed cohabiting takes over a culture, it alters the culture in ways big and small.

Cohabiting is escalating in America. Do we really want our culture to become like Europe's?

To see the big picture, one must look at places where cohabiting is ingrained. Sociologist David Popenoe, former co-director of the National Marriage Project, did so, in a 2008 essay.

Europe's acceptance of cohabiting is clear, Mr. Popenoe said in "Cohabitation, Marriage and Child Well Being." A 2006 AC Nielsen global survey, for instance, asked 25,000 people if they agreed with the statement, "I consider a stable, long-term relationship just as good as marriage." More than 75 percent of Europeans said yes, compared with 50 percent of Americans.

One of the first results of widespread cohabiting is a reduction in the marriage rate.

In Europe, "with nonmarital cohabitation being the primary generating factor," many nation's populations have gone from being the most married in modern European history to the least married, Mr. Popenoe said.

Cohabiters also are more likely than married couples to enter and leave relationships, regardless of the presence of children. Thus, unwed childbearing and single parenting become more common. A massive 2006 British study, for instance, found that nearly half of cohabiting parent couples had split up by their child's fifth birthday; in Norway, children of cohabiters were found to be more than twice as likely to face parental breakup compared with children of married couples.

These fragmented families often need social support, so widespread cohabiting reinforces the need for expensive government (i.e., taxpayer-funded), cradle-to-grave welfare systems.

Other international findings about cohabiters are that they are "less serious" about their relationships, "less satisfied" with their relationships, and more prone to domestic violence, child abuse and lower incomes than married couples, Mr. Popenoe noted. Moreover, even with fewer marriages, many European countries have rising divorce rates.

And Mr. Popenoe hardly touched on Europe's dismal fertility rates. In essence (with cohabiting as one of many reasons), many European countries are looking at birth dearths. Millions of European women are having one or no babies.

Despite such unsettling outcomes, cohabiting is permeating the American culture.

Cohabiting supporters, such as John Curtis, author of "Happily Un-married, Living Together & Loving It," and the Alternatives to Marriage Project, defend cohabiting as normal, modern and even a right, since marriage isn't suitable for everyone. The Alternatives to Marriage Project, as one might expect, offers a bounty of positive advice, resources and suggestions about living together.

But there is no getting away from the mountains of research that call for caution about cohabiting.

My view is that if cohabiting is benign or good for couples and children, all this should be reflected in the outcomes — cohabiting adults should be famous for staying together, happily and faithfully, raising their children, prospering and growing old together. Think millions of Goldie Hawns and Kurt Russells.

Instead, the reality of U.S. cohabiting is more fully witnessed in America's black and Hispanic neighborhoods, where cohabiting has almost fully replaced marriage. Anyone who says cohabiting is not playing a major role in the repeated cycles of poverty, antisocial behavior and family heartache just isn't living in the real world.

And discussions of birthrates, marriage rates and welfare programs don't even get into the most important reasons America should fully resist widespread cohabiting. Cohabiting hurts.

Cheryl Wetzstein can be reached at cwetzstein@washingtontimes.com.

The Sin of Cohabitation
Christian News, December 20, 2010

"Among the poor, cohabitation rarely produces fairy tale endings," a column in the November 18, 2010 *St. Louis Post Dispatch* by Colleen Carroll Campbell says:

"In many ways, their protracted courtship, casual cohabitation and plans for a splashy wedding to formalize a union already forged make Will and Kate, the British royals, the quintessential post-modern couple. Many college-educated, upper-middle-class men and women today follow a similar path to the altar, finding and moving in with Mr. or Mrs. Right long before they wed.

"For these men and women, marriage comes at the end of a long list of 'to-dos' that trump it: seeing the world, securing advanced degrees, climbing the career ladder, buying a home. Earlier generations regarded such goals as things you achieve while married, with the help and companionship of your spouse. Today, marriage increasingly is seen as the reward that comes at the end of all that striving. It is the big, white bow you tie atop all the professional accomplishments, financial stability and sexual intimacy you and your future spouse already have experienced."

Lutheran Church-Missouri Synod President Matthew Harrison writes in "Second Thoughts About Living Together", available from *Christian*

News for $1.00:

"7. What's the big deal with living together? Society has accepted it.

"First, the Church doesn't accept a practice just because society has accepted it. Jesus tells us that society will often be diametrically opposed to the Christian way of life. Jesus said:

"John 15:18-19
If the world hates you, know that it has hated me before it hated you. If you were of the world, the world would love you as its own; but because you are not of the world, but I chose you out of the world, therefore the world hates you.

"It should be noted that society has not always accepted cohabitation. Prior to the sexual revolution of the 1960s, living together was frowned upon. That is because the influence of the Christian faith was much stronger in those times. Cohabitation was commonly called 'living in sin.'

"Do non-Christians have much trouble with two people living together or having sex without marriage? Yes, some do. However, the majority of our popular-culture (television, movies, music), which regularly ridicules Christians and religious values, has little trouble with it. So you see where the acceptance of living together and having sexual relations without the benefit of marriage come from--this sinful world. These ideas don't come from Christ.

"It is obvious from the many, many references to 'sexual immortality' in the letters of the New Testament that pagan society had accepted it too. Jesus and St. Paul opposed it."

Why Wait

Rose Publishing, Inc. 4733 Torrance Blvd., #259, Torrence, CA 90503, publishing many excellent Christian pamphlets on a large variety of subjects, lists these Biblical reasons for not living together before marriage and no sex outside of marriage. It's pamphlet "Why Wait" begins:

In a world where celebrities and sports stars brag about their sexual conquests, and where TV and movies portray fun, no-consequence sex, are there any reasons to wait until marriage to have sex?

Yes, there are a lot! There are biblical reasons, health reasons, and emotional reasons to wait. Here are a few.

BIBLICAL REASONS

Sex was God's idea first. He created it! The Bible tells the story of God creating the world, the plants, the animals, and the first man. The Bible says that God saw that it was not good for Adam to be alone. So God created Eve, Adam's wife. God's first command to them was to "be fruitful and multiply" – to join together in sexual union. Sex is God's invention. It was designed for having children, of course, but it's also intended to be a pleasurable act that unites a husband and a wife together in love. If God invented sex, then it might be worthwhile to know how he wants us to use it.

1. **Sex is a beautiful gift from God and is reserved for marriage.** Marriage is a public commitment between a man and woman, and sex belongs to marriage only (Hebrews 13:4).

2. **Having sex with a person creates a kind of "oneness" that God intended for marriage only.** This oneness is not just physical – it's emotional and spiritual too. God created sensuality in a loving marriage to build intimacy and trust, and to bond the couple (Genesis 2:24; 1 Corinthians 6:16).

3. **The Bible says we should not be sexually immoral.** The word used in the Bible is "fornicate," which means sexual intercourse other than between a husband and wife (Acts 15:20).

4. **To be respected by others.** A person who loves you will respect and support your desire to stay pure (Proverbs 3:3-5).

5. **To have a clean conscience and no worries.** If you save sex for marriage, you don't need to worry about sexually transmitted diseases or pregnancy. You also won't need to worry about the embarrassment of seeing former sexual partners at church, school, or work (2 Corinthians 1:12; Hebrews 13:18).

6. **To respect yourself.** Some people promise marriage, love or commitment just to get sex, and then back out of their promises. Many people have sex with people they would never marry (Proverbs 5:3-12).

7. **To grow as a Christian and be holy.** You cannot grow as a Christian if you are having sex outside of marriage (1 Thessalonians 4:3).

8. **To be like Jesus.** Jesus was the most loving and "healthy" person in history. He was tempted in every way we are, but did not sin (Hebrews 4:15). Jesus loved all kinds of people and had a reputation for being kind to sexually immoral people. He forgave them and said they should stop sinning (Luke 7:48; John 8:11).

9. **To have a good life.** If we love and obey God, he will give us peace of mind and will work out the circumstances in our lives, even out troubles, for good (Psalm 37:4-9; Romans 8:6, 28).

10. **The Bible says we should run away from sexually immoral situations.** When you feel yourself being tempted, get away! (1 Corinthians 6:18).

11. **To keep a good reputation.** Having sex outside of marriage hurts your good name. No one wants to be considered "cheap" or the kind of person who takes advantage of others or uses people (Ephesians 5:3).

12. **To be clearheaded when you are making important decisions.** When you are in a relationship you need to have a clear mind. Sexual activity can distort your thinking and cause you to make poor choices (Proverbs 5:22-23; 6:25-26).

V

DIVORCE AND REMARRIAGE

Divorce No Longer Ends a Career
Clergy Divorces: The Number Increases But It Merely Follows National Average

By *Religion News Service*, March 19, 1976
Christian News, March 29, 1976

BOSTON (RNS) - Paul's advice to Timothy about church leaders being "married only once" notwithstanding, clergy divorces are increasing.

With the increase, has come better acceptance on the part of congregations of divorced clergy, even as divorced lay people also increase in numbers and acceptance.

"There was a time when if a clergyman divorced, it was pretty much the end of his career," said the Rev. T.C. Whitehouse of the Massachusetts Conference of the United Church of Christ. "A congregation is more likely now to take a (divorced) man," he added.

Statistics are not readily available, partly because different denominations keep records in different ways, but the Unitarian Universalist Association appears to have among the highest divorce rates among ministers.

David Pohl, UUA ministerial placement director, said one-in-three is "conservative and a very rough estimate."

He added, "Sometimes you look around and wonder who hasn't been through it." He said the high UUA rate may happen because the liberal denomination has "less of a taboo associated" with divorce.

Though denominational clergy divorce rates vary, they do seem to be growing, and have prompted some concern.

A special committee of synodical presidents of the Lutheran Church in America is examining guidelines for dealing with their clergy who divorce, now estimated at a little more than 2 percent of the denomination's nearly 8,000 pastors.

The 1975 General Assembly of the United Presbyterian Church called for a study of the denomination's clergy pension plan to determine whether spouses of divorced ministers are being treated unfairly.

The Rev. Tom Gallen of the ministries council of the New England Southern Conference of the United Methodist Church traced the changes which have taken place in his denomination in the last decade:

"Six to eight years ago if a man (or a woman) was divorced, it was tantamount to giving up a parish," he said. Now, he added, "unless there's been real congregational involvement with complications, the chances of a pastor being asked to surrender his or her orders is not very high."

He cited one case in which "the congregation has allowed the family to stay in the parsonage while the minister got an apartment. That wouldn't have happened before. It's kind of unique."

For United Methodists and Episcopalians, say their New York information officers, the attitude toward and the disposition of cases of divorced clergy depend to some degree on the attitude of the bishop involved.

Episcopalians are faced with a surplus of clergy so they find that a factor in attitudes toward divorce, according to the Rev. Donald Bitsberger, past-chairman of the ministry council of the Massachusetts diocese "There's such a surplus of clergy now that anything that's question marked may eliminate a person. It's a buyer's market."

The Rev. Roscoe Robison, president of the American Baptist Churches of Massachusetts, said the women's liberation movement has caused some of the changing attitudes toward divorced ministers.

"It is a new day in which husbands and wives are finding new identities," he said. Congregations are no longer able to get "two for the price of one" when calling a minister.

Divorce is not just a phenomenon among Christian clergy; some Jewish leaders are aware of more divorced rabbis.

"There used to be a time when rabbis didn't get divorced; it didn't look nice," said Rabbi Samuel Fox, president of the Massachusetts Council of Rabbis. "Hebrew tradition is not against it, but people wouldn't accept it. It would ruin his career if he did."

Views are changing, he added, noting four divorces involving rabbis in the Boston area in the last two years. That, he said, is "most unusual. You hardly used to hear of one."

On the Rocks
By David Virtue
From *The Province*, June 19, 1976
Christian News, September 6, 1976

Ministers' marriages are breaking down at an alarming rate and denominational hierarchies are increasingly concerned that the split-ups are causing widespread problems inside and outside congregations.

While church officials would like to keep the issue hidden and no one will come out with actual statistics on the subject, the problem did surface in the news recently.

The immediate past moderator of the United Church of Canada, Very Rev. Dr. Bruce McLeod, now chairman of the Ontario Human Rights Code review committee, resigned from the chairmanship of his church's division of World Outreach. He was at the time working in a village for abandoned children in Costa Rica.

In letters to the present moderator, Dr. Wilbur Howard, and the general secretary, McLeod said he was influenced in his decision by the fact that he was planning a separation from his wife.

While spokesmen for various churches in Vancouver say the rate of separation and divorce among men of the cloth is rising, it is still lower than among other professionals such as doctors and lawyers.

However the whole issue is taking on a new twist.

Whereas in the past if a clergyman's marriage was on the rocks, he would usually struggle on with the unhappy situation out of a sense of duty or fear of scandalizing the flock. Today all this is changing.

With new public openness apparent in all avenues of morality, clergymen are feeling less restrained in hiding their shortcomings behind the pulpit.

Grounds for separation range from mental cruelty to adultery, and not a few men have found the "other woman" in their own pews.

As well, not a few ministers have declared themselves to be homosexuals with the result that gay churches have begun to spring up in different parts of North America.

Rev. Roy Bell, pastor, First Baptist Church, believes the true pressures are exaggerated and he doubts whether the minister is in any different position from a top-ranking executive, but admits that the minister has more access to the opposite sex in company with doctors and university teachers.

Christianity Today, an influential evangelical publication, recently ran an article by Rev. Andre Bustanoby, titled *The Pastor and the Other Woman*. In it Bustanboy cited the fact that more than 30 graduates of a seminary with which he was involved had marriages which were "on the rocks because of affairs with women in their churches."

He said this was a problem confronting every denomination and the minister "who errs sexually" does not start out with sexual encounter on his mind, but, like men in other professions, starts out to build his faltering ego on the admiration of others.

Rev. David Hawkins, Anglican chaplain to Vancouver General Hospital, says the minister is more often than not a lonely, isolated man at the top who has no peer group relationships.

A further problem heightening divorce amongst clergy is the women's lib movement which has given the pastor's wife a new sense of her own worth.

No longer is she viewed just at the pastor's wife, placed in a churchy box. She is rejecting the traditional role of "unpaid curate" and when her children leave home she will go out to look for a job on her own. Furthermore, she is demanding more time from her husband and more warmth from the marriage as she views how others live.

From a practical point of view it's very difficult financially for clergymen to get a divorce, remarry and pay support for the first wife, even if they leave the church, as most do, either voluntarily or forced out.

Stigma Attached By Parishioners
Divorce Rate Among U.S. Clergy Is Rising

By George R. Plagenz
From *The Rocky Mountain News*, Denver, Co., Sat., Aug. 27, 1977
Christian News, September 5, 1977

The woman had been going to her pastor for counseling about her deteriorating marriage when the bomb fell.

The pastor was getting a divorce!

"It was like finding out your doctor had just died of the disease he was treating you for," said the shocked woman.

Divorces among the clergy are on the upswing, but the trend is still new enough that many parishioners find themselves thrown by it.

"Attitudes toward clergy divorces are changing," said a Methodist pastor who was divorced in 1970. "But there is still a long way to go before the stigma against the divorced minister is removed."

After his 18-year marriage broke up, this pastor resigned his pulpit. Most denominations report an increase in the number of divorced clergymen. Fundamentalist denominations have the lowest incidence. Only 2 percent of Southern Baptist clergy have been divorced.

AT THE OTHER end of the scale are Unitarian Universalist ministers. One out of every three (33 percent) has had a broken marriage.

There are no statistics available on whether it is the ministers or their wives who initiate the majority of clergy divorces.

Women's lib is blamed in many cases where clergy wives want out.

"As a minister's wife, I couldn't be myself," said one ex-lady of the manse who left. "I was never introduced as just Mary Jones. It was always, 'Mary Jones, the pastor's wife.' I was never free to be me."

Other clergy wives get fed up with the lifestyle of the parsonage which, they complain, breeds loneliness.

They are talking not only about the 60 and 80 hour work weeks which keep their husbands away from home most of the time but also about the fact that there is little chance to make close friendships.

"YOU CAN'T BE buddy-buddy with any one family in the church," explained a minister's ex-wife. "You have to try to be the same with everybody."

An even bigger problem is said to be "the other woman."

A seminary professor was quoted in an evangelical magazine as saying he personally knows of 29 graduates of the seminary whose marriages are in trouble because they are having affairs with women in their churches.

These are all ministry-related problems, however, and may not constitute the major reasons for clergy divorces. Marriage counselors generally are of the opinion that most ministers' marriages which break up go sour for the same reasons other marriages end in failure.

"People will have to realize that ministers are human beings with human problems like everyone else," said one counselor.

DIVORCE, DIFFICULT for anyone, is said to be especially painful for ministers.

"Divorce is equated with failure," said a member of the Untied Methodist Church's Board of Ministry, "and ministers are programmed to be high achievers. They hate failure."

But many divorced clergy feel their experience makes them better marriage counselors.

"I understand what troubled couples are going through," said a divorced minister who is now a professional counselor. "I've been through the heartache. People know that what I say to them about marriage has weight to it."

'Artificial Birth Control' Held Cause of Rising Divorce Rate

By *Religious News Service* - (10/25/77)
Christian News, October 31, 1977

MINNEAPOLIS (RNS) - A Roman Catholic bishop has blamed the use of artificial birth control methods for the nation's rapidly-in-creasing divorce rate and for unhappy family life.

"The fact that a couple can sever procreation from intercourse has left the door wide open to infidelity," Auxiliary Bishop Paul V. Dudley of the Archdiocese of St. Paul-Minneapolis wrote in a letter to the Minneapolis Star.

He was commenting on a widely-distributed press report about the large percentage of Roman Catholic couples who now use contraceptive methods forbidden by the Church.

Bishop Dudley said both Catholics and non-Catholics need to consider "the intimate connection between contraception and the fact that individuals often feel free to engage in intercourse at any time, within and outside of marriage, with one or with multiple partners."

"Moreover," he asked, "isn't this 'freedom' an aspect of the increased permissiveness that we see in our society, with the attendant ills of pornography and perversion?"

"For these reasons - among many others - I would like to urge all of us, Catholic and non-Catholics, to return to an authentic appreciation of the constant teaching of the gospels concerning the true value of the disciplined role of sex within and without marriage."

"Once these authentic teachings are recognized and appreciated, even the birth control dilemma can be solved readily and quite naturally," Bishop Dudley said. "For now, I speak of a means of planning and spacing births through the use of some of the new, breakthrough Natural Family Planning methods that medical science has recently been able to offer us.

"These methods replace the old rhythm method by offering the women informed certainty on a day to day basis concerning her regular cycle of fertility and infertility. And it is my hope that all Christians and non-Christians will take the time to learn these methods. Our office of Family Life Commission, 226 Summit Ave., St. Paul, Minn., 55102, will be happy to make referrals to appropriate Natural Family Planning teaching centers."

Divorce and Remarriage
By Samuel H. Nafzger
From *The Lutheran Witness*, June 1982
Christian News, June 21, 1982

Statistics indicate that failed marriages are increasingly common in church circles and even among pastors, whose divorce rate has quadrupled since 1960. Clearly, our society is experiencing a divorce epidemic of staggering proportions. Its full consequences are yet to be realized.

As a result, Lutheran Christians are increasingly facing extremely complex and sensitive questions about divorce and remarriage.

The Holy Scriptures teach that the marriage estate did not result from human social experimentation or some chance, evolutionary development in history. Marriage is a divine institution. (See Gen. 2:18-25).

While the single state may also be God pleasing (Matt. 19:12), through marriage the Creator provides for the needs of the crown of His creation, for companionship and love in a relationship that extends to the intimacy of sexual intercourse (1 Thess. 4:4-5; 1 Cor. 7:5). Through this marital union of husband and wife God desires to carry on His continuing creation of the human race (Gen. 1:27). And ever since the fall into sin, the institution of marriage serves under God's ordinance as a channel for human passion in a permanent relationship of fidelity and love (1 Cor. 7:9).

Christians should never be hesitant to refer to the marriage estate as holy and God-pleasing (cf. Eph. 5:21). Moreover, sexual intimacy within marriage is God-ordained. The Creator's beautiful gift of sex is abused, however, when sexual intercourse takes place outside of the marital union in adultery and fornication. The Scriptures explicitly and repeatedly condemn these actions as contrary to God's will and therefore sinful (Ex. 20:14; 1 Cor. 6:9-10; 16-20).

When the Pharisees came to Jesus with questions about divorce and remarriage, our Lord, after quoting words from Genesis 1:27 and 2:24, says: "So they are no longer two but one. What therefore God has joined together, let no man put asunder" (Matt. 19:6). Marriage is the God created union of one man and one woman that is to be ended only by the death of one of the marriage partners (1 Cor. 7:39; cf. also Mark 12:25).

On this basis, Jesus answers the Pharisees. Divorce, destroying that which God Himself has joined together, is always contrary to His intention for marriage. Moses permitted divorce, says Christ, only because of sinful humanity's "hardness of heart... From the beginning it was not so" (Matt. 19:8; cf. Deut. 24:1-4).

Are there then no Scriptural grounds for divorce? Jesus says: "Whoever divorces his wife, except for unchastity, and marries another, commits adultery" (Matt. 19:9; 5:32). Luther, the orthodox Lutheran theologians of the 16th and 17th century, and our fathers in the Missouri Synod have interpreted these words of Jesus to mean that the act of adultery breaks the unity of marriage. When this takes place, the offended partner has the right, but not the command, to secure a divorce. Certainly the party sinned against should be willing to forgive the party guilty of infidelity, and in many cases the marriage can be preserved.

Moreover, St. Paul does not contradict Jesus' words, when, speaking to a completely different situation, Paul states: "If the unbelieving partner desires to separate, let it be so; in such a case the brother or sister is not bound" (1 Cor. 7:15). The apostle recognizes that desertion by one spouse (an unbeliever) breaks the marriage union. In such a case, the remaining spouse (a Christian) is not guilty of "putting away" his marriage partner if he proceeds to secure a legal divorce.

A person acts in direct opposition to Jesus' command that no one put asunder that which God has joined together, if he or she divorces his or her spouse for any other reason than adultery or desertion. This is true even when both marriage partners may decide to dissolve their union by mutual agreement. Christian love therefore requires that such individuals come under church discipline.

About the remarriage of those who have divorced their spouses, Jesus says, "But I say to you that everyone who divorces his wife, except on the ground of sexual immorality, makes her commit adultery, and whoever marries a divorced woman commits adultery. (Matt. 5:32). The interpretation that best takes account of what Scripture says here and elsewhere about remarriage (see Matt. 19:9; 1 Cor. 7:10ff) is this: That person who has secured an unscriptural divorce and marries another, commits adultery. He who marries such a person also commits adultery. But neither the marriage partner innocently put away, nor the marriage partner who has divorced his or her partner because of adultery or desertion, is included under this prohibition. Such individuals are free to remarry.

May those who have secured unscriptural divorces ever remarry with God's blessing? The Scriptures teach that both the one who puts away his spouse, except for unchastity, and the one who marries such a person, commits adultery.

But also here we must remember that in Christ there is forgiveness for ALL sins, including the sin of putting asunder that which God has joined together. To be sure, genuine repentance necessarily includes the desire for reconciliation. When reconciliation is impossible, however, because the former partner has either remarried or is unwilling to be reconciled, then remarriage becomes a possibility.

A word of warning needs to be issued against the sin of getting an unscriptural divorce, intending later to become penitent in order to remarry. "Do not be deceived; God is not mocked (Gal. 6:7).

May God grant that, fearing and loving Him, "We may lead a chaste and decent life in word and deed, and each love and honor his spouse" (*Small Catechism*).

LCMS District Urged to Remove Divorced Clergymen From Pastoral Ministry

Christian News, February 25, 1980

Most major denominations have thus far done little about the rising number of divorced clergymen which is plaguing most churches. While in former years denominational officials took action against clergymen who divorced their wives for a non-scriptural reason (the Bible teaches that adultery and desertion are the only valid reasons for a divorce), divorced clergymen are now often being permitted to remain in the pastoral ministry.

The Lutheran Church-Missouri Synod formerly was among those denominations which would not allow a divorced clergyman to continue in the ministry if his divorce was not scriptural. However, the current administration is permitting one of its top executives, who lectures all over the LCMS on marriage and divorce, to continue in his influential position inspite of his being divorced (see the November 12, 1979 *Christian News*, p. 10).

Voices of protest against the tolerant policy toward divorced clergy of the current administration are beginning to be heard in the LCMS. A pastor in the LCMS's Texas District is asking the district to "strongly encourage the District President to remove from the pastoral office the man who obtains a divorce."

Not all of the synod's officials are in accord with the new tolerant approach toward divorced clergymen.

After acknowledging that "The members of our congregations are generally pleased and grateful for the dedication to the Lord, the zeal for service, love for souls, the faithfulness and effectiveness to ministry which most of our pastors have demonstrated," a leading official of the LCMS said in a public essay last year: "At the same time, however, we are hearing in Synod that increasing numbers of our pastors are having problems in their personal lives which prevent them from functioning ably and effectively as ministers of the Gospel. . . Adultery, divorce, and drunkenness among the clergy are on the rise, and frequently those guilty of sin are allowed to remain in office despite their obvious disqualification before God and His people for continuing professional ministry."

Rev. Robert W. Hill, pastor of Faith Lutheran Church, Plano, Texas, has presented the following memorial to the 1980 convention of the synod's Texas District:

WHEREAS, Divorce is becoming more commonplace among the clergy within The Lutheran Church-Missouri Synod despite the clear words of our Lord Jesus Christ, "The two shall be one flesh. Wherefore they are no more two but one flesh. What therefore God has joined together let not man put asunder." (Matthew 19:5, 6); and

WHEREAS, The Scriptures say that "A bishop must be blameless, the husband of one wife." (1 Timothy 3:2); and

WHEREAS, The Scriptures require this qualification for bishop (pastor): "One that ruleth well his own house, having his children in subjection with all gravity, (for if a man know not how to rule his own house, how shall he take care of the church of God?)" (I Timothy 3:4); and

WHEREAS, Divorce is one evidence that a man is not ruling well his own house, and remarriage makes him the husband of more than one wife: and

WHEREAS, Divorce in the families of the clergy brings heartache and sorrow to God's faithful laity and is a scandal (a death trap) to the young and weak, that is, those whose marriages are already faltering, contributing to the divorce epidemic in our churches as God said to David, "By this deed you have given great occasion to the enemies of the Lord to blaspheme," (II Samuel 12:14); and

WHEREAS, The relationship of the Christian husband and wife is directed by God to be a living testimony of Christ and His selfless, sacrificing love for the Church, and the Church's response of love, loyalty and obedience to Christ, a message which is central to the pastor's total ministry, a testimony which is never perfect even for a pastor and his wife, but is totally destroyed when divorce occurs (Ephesians 5:22ff); and

WHEREAS, The sinful flesh knows only the curbing power of the Law borne out of fear and is strengthened in this power by publicly dealing with this sin (I Tim. 5:20) so that each of us in ministry to our Lord take more seriously the directive of God's Word, "Flee fornication," (I Corinthians 6:18), "Flee youthful lusts," (II Timothy 2:22); and

WHEREAS, The Gospel of forgiveness through the redeeming death and resurrection of our Lord Jesus Christ is the means by which the Holy Spirit makes us new creatures in Christ and frees us from the dominion of sin, (II Corinthians 5:17; I Peter 2:24); therefore be it

RESOLVED, That the Texas District in Convention urge those pastors having marital problems to seek the counsel of a fellow pastor, the circuit counselor or the District President before the situation is irreconcilable; and be it further

RESOLVED, That the Texas District in Convention urge the pastors of the District to daily and lovingly lead their wives and children into the Word of God as a reflection of Christ's loving leadership of His Church (Ephesians 5:25ff) by which the marriage is strengthened and the armor of God is put around the whole family so as to resist the attacks of Satan (Ephesians 6:10ff); and be it further

RESOLVED, That the District President work with the congregations in exercising church discipline with those pastors who have committed adultery and manifestly sin in seeking a divorce, that they may repent and that they may be reclaimed as brothers in Christ, (Matthew 18:15ff); and be it further

RESOLVED, That the Texas District strongly encourage the District President to remove from the pastoral office that man who obtains a divorce; and be it further

RESOLVED, That for instances where divorce occurs despite all of the efforts that a pastor can put forth to save his marriage, or when there is evidence of genuine repentance, that a commission be set up to help these men obtain employment in some other area of the church besides the pastoral ministry.

LCMS Divided on Divorced Clergymen

Christian News, April 7, 1980

Should clergymen who have secured an unscriptural divorce be permitted to remain on the clergy roster of The Lutheran Church-Missouri Synod? Pastors and leaders in the LCMS are divided on the question. The LCMS's current administration has been permitting some clergymen with unscriptural divorces to remain on the synod's roster, although the LCMS has officially always maintained that adultery and desertion are the only scriptural reasons for divorce.

Last year *Christian News* revealed that the LCMS's executive on Marriage Education and Counseling Seminars had gotten a divorce for unscriptural reasons. This executive recently retired. Some conservatives also maintain that the leaders of the LCMS should not allow the LCMS clergyman, who heads Parish Leadership Seminars, to lecture all over the LCMS and remain on the LCMS clergy roster, because of the circumstances of his divorce, his support of Evangelical Lutherans in Mission, and promotion of historical criticism. *Christian News* has written several times during the past few years to both of these divorced clergymen, but they have refused to answer CN. Both are supposed to be authorities on marriage and divorce.

Parish Leadership Seminars also conducts seminars on the subject.

The February 25 CN published a resolution being presented to the LCMS's Texas District convention by Rev. Robert Hill of Plano, Texas, to the 1980 convention of the Texas District. Rev. William Singleton, the pastor of Grace Lutheran Church, Lamar, Colorado, took issue with the resolution in a letter which was included in an article published in the March 10 CN, p. 24. Pastor Singleton noted in his letter that he was a 1977 graduate of Seminex who entered the LCMS last year through a colloquy.

CN wrote to Pastor Singleton on March 3:

"Thanks for your letter of February 27 which just arrived.

"The Bible only recognizes adultery and desertion as valid reasons for a divorce. This is the position we have always taken and it is the position of The Lutheran Church-Missouri Synod.

"Did you hold the position you now take on divorce when you were approved for the LCMS ministry? Were you asked whether or not you now believe the theological position of Seminex is contrary to Holy Scripture?

"Please be assured that I believe that there certainly is forgiveness for any repentant sinner. If a truly penitent person has gotten an unscriptural divorce and a reconciliation is still possible then he should go back to his spouse. If a pastor has a scriptural divorce, then he should be permitted to continue in the ministry, although it may be best to take a call elsewhere. Of course, each situation is different and must be dealt with on an individual basis."

Rev. Robert Hill wrote to Pastor Singleton on March 24:

Dear Brother Singleton,

Since it was my resolution to which you speak in the letter to *Christian News* as printed on March 10, 1980, I am replying to your letter.

You have charged me with being legalistic. Is it legalistic to seek and follow the wisdom and guidance God gives us in His holy Word? Even our confessions recognize the need for guidance by the law of God? "On account of this Old Adam, who inheres people's intellect, will and all his powers, it is necessary for the law of God constantly to light their way lest in their merely human devotions they undertake self-decreed and self-chosen acts of serving God. This is further necessary lest the Old Adam go his own self-willed way," (Formula of Concord, page 480, Tappert).

Unless we rely on the direction of God's Word we have only the wisdom of man. To rely upon the wisdom of man apart from the Holy Scriptures is to follow the way of humanism. You speak about making the wrong selection for a mate, and ask the question, "Should they live forever with the consequences of that mistake?" Such a question ignores the clear direction of God's Word, "What God has joined together, let not man put asunder," (Matthew 19:6). When in our human wisdom you would allow that a mistake be rectified by divorce, do you realize that you have eliminated sin. When you eliminate sin you are ruling out the need for a Savior. When we make our own rules we don't need forgiveness for breaking them. Forgiveness is needed when God's law is broken. Forgiveness therefore affirms that God's law and his order for marriage are good.

Now if you say that a mistaken choice be made right by divorce, then human wisdom would concoct all manner of devices, such as trial marriages. Instead of fulfilling people's lives as this humanistic notion would purport to do, more lives will be emptied of any real marital joy and security as more young people either in statement or practice enter into marriage on a trial basis. God's order through your human wisdom is destroyed, and your human wisdom is shown to be foolishness (Romans 1:22).

Nowhere in Scripture will you find it a sin to remain together in marriage. By suggesting this, you are denying the power of Christ to forgive the real sins within marriage and work the healing that brings harmony and peace. You who purport to defend the Gospel have forgotten that our Lord who said, "Neither do I condemn you, go and sin no more," provided within that forgiveness the power to begin "putting aside sin."

You charge us with the arrogance of having infinite wisdom. It seems to me that when one leaves the directions of Scripture to base his action merely on human feelings, he then is arrogating to himself wisdom above God's wisdom.

Let's look again to the Scripture. When we feel we have made the wrong selection for a mate, (1) first we recognized the sin of even thinking to set aside God's order, and trust in forgiveness provided by Jesus Christ; (2) then when the going is tough, we draw strength from our Savior who also said, "take up your cross,' and we look to the Savior upon whom His bride, the church, brought suffering indescribable; (3) pastors in particular, who proclaim the love of Christ for an often ungrateful and unlovable church (this is the Gospel), will seek to demonstrate the message they proclaim in showing love in a difficult marriage; and (4) when one makes a foolish choice in marrying, the Gospel which forgives also says, "God will turn this foolish choice for your good," (Romans 8:28).

You indicate that I have no "sensitivity to the real suffering of divorce." You seem to have forgotten that the source of all suffering is sin. As long as God's commandments are ignored such suffering will increase. If by speaking of forgiveness we negate God's commandments we will lead man more into sin and the pain of human conflict. If a pastor continues on in his ministry after public sins are committed for which there is no evidence of repentance this will lead others (he is an example to the flock) into the same sins which in turn bring misery and suffering. Praise God that He offers forgiveness to every sinner, but the sinner who goes on defying God's commandments will also go on in misery.

Finally, you implied that removing a man from the pastoral office means we do not forgive him. It is interesting to me how "the world in this generation is wiser than the children of light." If a bank president were convicted of embezzling large sums of money, he would hardly be accepted back as the president of such an institution . The world knows better. The customers would go to another bank. The pastoral office is of greater importance than a bank president and carries far more responsibility, yet our practice has been where one shows himself unfaithful to his own wife or incompetent to lead his own family he either stays on as the shepherd of that flock or soon moves on to another parish. When a pastor has gotten a divorce, his ministry is hurt. His leadership will be damaged. We have the example of David's public sin:

1. He failed to discipline his own son (II Samuel 13:21).

2. He failed either to confront Absalom for his sin or forgive him (II Samuel 14:24).

3. His own son did not hold him in respect (II Samuel 15).

4. His chief captain did not obey him (II Samuel 15).

5. David by this public sin sowed seeds that later brought division in the kingdom following Solomon's death (II Samuel 19:9-10).

I contend that we can forgive the man and remove him from that high office at the same time, just as certainly as I can forgive my son for a traffic violation and forbid him to drive at the same time.

In my proposed resolution I referred to David's sin by which the prophet had said, "By this you have given occasion to the enemies of the Lord to blaspheme." Nathan the prophet also said, "The Lord has put away thy sin." As comforting as this was to David, this Gospel did not remove the fact that "the sword shall not depart from your home," or, "I will raise up evil against you out of your own house," (II Samuel 12). The Gospel rather was a comfort in these sorrows and consequences that David brought upon himself. When they occurred the assurance of God's forgiveness refreshed him and upheld him. For whatever consequences follow our sins our comfort is not that things will return as they were in our lives but that God will enable us to carry on despite the consequences of our sins.

In our Savior's Name,
Robert W. Hill

Lutherans Departing From God's Standards
Clergy, Public Attitudes on Divorce, Remarriage Surveyed
Christian News, Monday, June 23, 1980

Carol Stream IL - (From the Lutheran Council in the U.S.A.) - What do Lutheran pastors and people think about divorce and remarriage? According to a Gallup Poll conducted for *Christianity Today*, the Evangelical biweekly headquartered here, Lutheran pastors are most likely (61 percent) to consider divorce something to be "avoided except in an extreme situation."

Lutherans in general, however, are most likely to consider divorce "Painful, but preferable to maintaining an unhappy marriage." That answer (of three options) was chosen by 54 percent of the general Lutheran sample, and 36 percent of the pastors. Thirty-eight percent of the general sample chose the response most popular with the pastors.

Few Lutherans (1 percent of the pastors, 6 percent of the public sample) said divorce is something to be "avoided under any circumstances."

Compared with other Christian traditions identified in the poll – Evangelical, Roman Catholic, Protestant, Southern Baptist, Baptist and Methodist – the Lutheran public was most likely (except for Methodists) to consider divorce preferable to continuing in an unhappy marriage and least likely (with the Methodists) to counsel avoiding divorce under any circumstances, or to advise avoiding divorce except for an extreme situation. Among the clergy, Lutherans were least likely to advise against divorce in any situation, most likely (except for Methodists) to consider it preferable to maintaining an unhappy marriage and least likely except for Methodists) to advise avoiding it except in extreme situations.

Given four options concerning remarriage after divorce, a majority of the clergy polled (59 percent) called it "acceptable if reconciliation to the former mate is not possible, regardless of the reason."

That was also the most popular (38 percent) response of the Lutheran public. Second most popular among that group (31 percent) was to consider remarriage after divorce "always acceptable," a position 12 percent of the pastors agreed with.

The second most popular pastoral response (25 percent) was to label post-divorce remarriage acceptable "only in cases of desertion or adultery," a position agreed to by 12 percent of the Lutheran public.

The other possible response –"remarriage after divorce is acceptable only in cases where the former mate is dead" – was selected by 14 percent of the Lutheran public and less than 1 percent of the pastors.

Comparatively, Lutherans were most likely to accept a second marriage if reconciliation is impossible, regardless of reason, and least likely (except for Methodists in the case of the sample of the public) to consider remarriage acceptable only if the former mate is dead.

Ed. The only valid scriptural reasons for divorce are adultery (Matthew 19:9) and desertion (1 Cor. 7:15). Orthodox Lutherans teach that the innocent party in a divorce case may remarry. The guilty party may remarry if true repentance is shown and reconciliation is no longer possible. It is a great tragedy that officials of major Lutheran church bodies are allowing clergymen with unscriptural divorces to remain in the ministry. Laymen argue that "if the pastor can get by with an unscriptural divorce why can't I."

Churches Dealing With Divorce More Openly as a Fact of Life

By Religious News Service
Christian News, September 22, 1980

With a tripling of the divorce rate in the last generation - to the point where there is one divorce for every two marriages in America - Christian churches have begun noticeably shifting in attitude.

From quiet and reluctant acceptance of an unpleasant fact of life, they have begun to acknowledge the trend and deal with it openly.

A tendency to move away from ostracism of divorced persons in favor of welcoming them into church life began initially among Protestants and has more recently been emphasized among Roman Catholics.

One new development in the field - divorce liturgies - indicates that Christians are actively promoting the recognition that failure of a marriage is a tragedy that should be dealt with by the entire church community.

Divorce liturgies were initially greeted with expressions of shock and outrage. A chapter on rituals with the divorced that appeared in a United Methodist study book on rituals published in 1976 generated a good deal of controversy both inside and outside the denomination.

Dr. Hoyt Hickman, staff executive of the church's Section on Worship, clarified the situation two years later by explaining, that the volume "was not a book of rituals but a study book about the meaning and importance of ritual. The chapter entitled 'Rituals and the Divorced' was an essay on reconciling ministries with persons who are already divorced, illustrated with descriptions or excerpts of services actually done in several local churches."

In 1978, England's United Reformed Church adopted a service for married people who wish to be released from their marriage vows. It was endorsed for use on an "experimental basis" after a legal divorce has been obtained, and was prompted by the finding that half the marriages conducted by the United Reformed clergy involved persons who had been divorced previously.

The service contains four sentences of a "Prayer for release" in which both the man and woman express regret for the failure of the marriage. It also includes a prayer by the minister that God will grant "forgiveness for any wrong you have done, release from vows you have made sincerely and regret to have broken, and guidance and help that you may keep faith in any vows you make in the future."

A rationale for divorce liturgy is set forth in the introduction to the text of one such ritual that has been prepared by the Rev. David H. Benson, an Episcopal priest, and Sherrill H. Akyol, a professional counselor.

They write that "many are horrified and assume that a liturgy means rejoicing about the fact of divorce. Such is a misunderstanding of what this liturgy is about. In the recognizing of divorce it is the laying of the fracture before God - with its best examined self-consciousness - and experiencing the healing grace. What is celebrated and cause for great joy is the reconciliation of person(s) to self, community and God as well as the community experiencing once again the living God who cares and remains faithful to us in all our circumstances."

An unusual liturgy has been written by three Episcopalians to help children understand and accept the divorce of their parents, entitled, *A Service of Affirmation, When Parents are Separating*. It was prepared by the Rev. Frederick Bender, a priest; Dr. David Ulrich, a marriage counselor; and Faith Whitfield, a social worker.

The parents promise not to speak ill of one another, and then separately vow to continue their fundamental responsibilities for the care and education of the children. They tell their children that they are "entitled to this relief of our vows only as we accept our basic responsibilities for you and each other."

Mr. Bender said he was "uneasy" about the use of the term "entitled," but said that "when I see division go on in a family because a couple is going to toughen it out. . . Then I must say I'm not going to stand up there and argue with them."

In 1977, Pope Paul VI approved a request from the U.S. Catholic bishops removing the penalty of excommunication imposed against divorced U.S. Catholics who remarry without church approval. The stricture had been in effect since 1884 and the U.S. was the only country to retain such a ban.

A year later, the Vatican's International Theological Commission recommended that the church give "full pastoral care" to divorced and remarried Catholics, even though they may not receive the sacraments of Matrimony and Holy Communion. The commission stressed that "these Christians are not to be excluded from the action of divine grace and still have a bond with the church."

The Rev. James J. Young, the priest who has been at the forefront to the church's ministries to divorced Catholics in the U.S., says the work is "becoming institutionalized" and is now "an accepted part of the family life apostolate." From the first group of divorced Catholics in the U.S., which he started in Boston in 1971, the movement has grown to 700 such groups in the National Association of Divorced and Separated Catholics.

Meanwhile, Catholic annulments of marriage have risen dramatically. The Rev. Donald Heintschel, executive coordinator of the Canon Law Society of America, says 27,670 annulment cases were settled in 1978, the last year for which statistics are available. That was over 60 percent more than the previous year's figure of 17,190.

An annulment is a church declaration that a "true" marriage never existed in the first place, and frees the parties for a new union with full sacramental blessings.

Annulments under a reformed procedure are now being granted in the church on "psychological grounds," similar to criteria in civil divorce.

The Rev. Dennis J. Burns, who heads the matrimonial tribunal in the Boston archdiocese, points out that until the early 1970s, psychological grounds had been limited to cases of insanity. The grounds have been so broadened that he advises that "divorced Catholics who were not granted annulments years ago should consult their priest and ask to have their case reviewed."

In 1978, the General Synod of the Church of England narrowly defeated a proposal to permit divorced persons to remarry in the church. The vote was denounced by the provost of Bradford, the Very Rev. Brandon Jackson, who asserted that millions of persons had turned their backs on the church because of its position on the matter.

Noting that many Protestant denominations and even other Anglican churches around the world have permitted the remarriage of divorced persons, he asked, "Who can say that they have destroyed the Christian witness to lifelong marriage?"

Dr. Donald Coggan, who was Archbishop of Canterbury at the time, suggested that the English Church might eventually adopt the system used by the Anglican Church of Canada, which reviews divorce cases through committees made up of three lay people and three clergy, who then recommend to the diocesan bishops whether couples should be married if one or both of the partners has been divorced.

Scripture scholars have found Jesus' teachings on divorce to be problematical. In Matthew 19, some scholars argue that the ban on divorce and remarriage does not apply universally. But in Mark 10 the prohibition is flat, with no exceptions stated.

Pope John Paul II chose the Matthew account last year in an address reaffirming the Catholic Church's strict position on divorce. He stressed that the passage means that "Christ does not approve of what Moses allowed because of people's hardness of heart. Instead he goes back to the arrangement made by God, which the Book of Genesis links with the state of innocence. That arrangement, therefore, is still valid, in spite of a man's loss of that first great innocence.'"

Most Protestants have combined Jesus' teachings on divorce with other New Testament passages on the subject to reach a more flexible position. This was illustrated in a 1979 book entitled, *The Asundered*. It was written by the Revs. Robert and Myrna Kysar, a United Methodist and a Lutheran Church In America minister, respectively.

The Kysars, who themselves had been divorced, concluded on the basis of their study of several biblical passages that "divorce is a violation of God's intent for marriage and that divorce is always a human failure, a human sin, because it violates the purpose of God in creation."

At the same time, they said, "the message of the gospel is that there is forgiveness for human failure and there is opportunity for rebirth. We interpret that to mean that in some cases remarriage is an opportunity for a new life."

In the technical sense of the word, sin means a falling short of the mark. Viewed from this perspective, the churches continue to stress that divorce is a sin. But as in dealing with other sins, they are moving beyond a simple attitude of condemnation and working to bring the sinners into reconciliation with the Christian community.

—Darrell Turner

Clergy Divorce

Christian News, February 15, 1982

"Clergy Divorce Spills into the Aisle" is the title of an important article in the February 5 *Christianity Today*. The CT article by Robert J. Stout says that "Lyle Schaller believes the divorce rate for ministers has at least, quadrupled since 1960. G. Lloyd Rediger's statistics point out that 37 percent of the clergy with whom his organization works are seriously considering divorce; based on precedent, 15 percent will dissolve their relationship. Over 60 percent of this population deal with problems serious enough to make divorce a distinct possibility. David and Vera Mace bring the current situation into perspective when they write: 'The clergy has remained in a state of supposedly blissful obscurity... until now... broken clergy marriages have now... become an issue to be reckoned with, and ecclesiastical officials are addressing themselves to the perplexing task of formulating policies for appropriate action.'

"There appears to be little doubt that there has been a recent trend toward divorce among clergy of all denominations. Like it or not, we have a tiger by the tail. There may be a strong desire to 'let go' or to ignore it, but it is obvious the problem will not just go away. It should command the attention of the church; it cries out for workable solutions."

CT says that one church leader believes the reasons for the upward trend in clergy divorce are: "(1) the greater acceptance of clergy as people – the stigma previously associated with divorce is no longer a threat; and (2) the tension and pressure of today's society exerted on the life of the pastor, his wife, and family."

CT says that "Women's lib has, and will undoubtedly continue to have, earthquake-force power on relationships." ". . . one often hears this comment: I've had it with the role of Mrs. Pastor! I just want a more normal life for myself and family.'"

"There is just no way a pastor can be at his or her peak if there is a running battle going on at home. If he is torn between his inner convictions, and strong demands of family, the results may be chaos, conflict, and possible breakdown."

CT says that "Another contributing factor is infidelity. There is little doubt that there is a percentage of women who consider the sexual conquest of a pastor a goal worth pursuing."

"A potpourri of clergy wives' complaints include too little personal time together; less freedom than the majority of families to move or stay in the community of their choice; less remuneration than other professions with similar educational requirements. ('Perks' such as car allowance; rent-free, church-owned housing; and occasional discounts narrow the gap. But a sense of dissatisfaction may still permeate parsonage families.)"

* * *

"Divorces among pastors is a relatively new issue" says the February 3 *Lutheran* of the Lutheran Church in America. The LCA paper adds: "Not too many years ago divorced pastors were almost automatically asked to resign from the ministry. Divorce carried a stigma within the church that it no longer does.

"Currently in the Illinois Synod approximately 10 percent of the active pastors have been divorced. Many are serving parishes. Some stayed where they were when the divorce took place. Others went on leave from a call before being called to a new parish."

* * *

Conservative Roman Catholics have been protesting against the liberal annulment policy of the Roman Catholic Church in the U.S. An AP dispatch in the January *6, 1982 New York Times* noted that "Last year, church figures said, there were an estimated 77 annulments in the United States for every one in 1968. Americans get 70 percent of all annulments granted by the Roman Catholic Church."

John J. Mulloy, a Roman Catholic lay theologian says in the February 11 *Wanderer* that "These figures strongly suggest that the Catholic Church in the United States has already seceded from Rome on this matter so central to Catholic moral teaching and sacramental life. Is there any other way to interpret such lopsided figures but to recognize that the church in this country has broken loose from Rome's jurisdiction on this matter, and is going its own way in an effective dismantlement of the Sacrament of Matrimony? And all of this has occurred within 13 years – from 1968 to 1981."

Mulloy writes that "By the exercise of the magic wand of annulment by a diocesan tribunal, you are told that you were never really married in the first place – most Catholic marriages aren't real, you understand – so you are now free to marry again with the blessing of the Church. It is all very cozy and convenient. The party who gave up Catholic wife or husband to live with someone else in a civil marriage, simply anticipated Church authorities in having decided that his or her first marriage was not valid. The Church courts follow obediently in the path set for them by those who have no respect for the Catholic Church or the Sacrament of Marriage – and this is spoken of by the canonists as showing 'pastoral concern.'"

The Roman Catholic theologian says that "it is clear that almost any marriage can be annulled if the canon lawyers on the court will have it so. . . If the tribunal wants a marriage annulled, it will be annulled."

* * *

LCMS and Divorce

"There was a time when any pastor or teacher of Synod who was divorced almost automatically removed himself from Synod's roster as being no longer qualified for the position he held" say Dr. Martin Scharlemann in the February-March, 1982 AFFIRM.

The retired Concordia Seminary, St. Louis, professor adds: "Today there are more than 200 divorced pastors on the clergy roster! District Presidents are very upset by this scandalous violation of the requirements set forth in the *Pastoral Epistles*. And well they might be! For how can such divorced (and even re-married!) persons serve as 'examples to the flock'?"

The Holy Scriptures only allow remarriage for the innocent party in a divorce case. Some pastors are now arguing that they have a valid reason to get a divorce and remarry even if their wife has not been sexually unfaithful. They find some comfort in the way the New International Version translates Matt. 19:9. "I tell you that anyone who divorces his wife, except for marital unfaithfulness, and marries another woman commits adultery" (also Matthew 5:32). Even some conservative Reformed scholars, who are concerned that this translation leaves the door open for unscriptural divorces, take issue with this translation. An American Translation correctly translates: "I tell you, if anyone divorces is wife, except for adultery, and marries another, he's living in adultery." "But I tell you, anyone who divorces his wife except for her being sexually unfaithful, makes her a partner in adultery. And also the man who marries the divorced woman is living in adultery." (Matthew 5:32).

Unfortunately, some go too far when they argue that a pastor should never marry more than once. In case of the death of his wife, a pastor may remarry.

Marriage, Divorce & Remarriage
Christian News Encyclpoedia, p. 1285, 1286

Marriage, Divorce & Remarriage In the Bible. **By Jay E. Adams. Phillipsburg, New Jersey, Box 817 08865. 1980. 99 pages. Paper, $3.50.**

Jay Adams should need no introduction to our readers. We have frequently recommended his books on counseling and related matters. With the exception of his Reformed views on double predestination, we have found almost all of his writing thoroughly scriptural. What he writes about marriage, divorce, and remarriage is scriptural and is almost exactly what graduates of orthodox Lutheran seminaries were taught before the liberals took over.

Commenting on engagement and marriage, Adams says:

"We must now turn to the important matter of engagement in the Bible. Today in our quite different culture, most Christians have little or no understanding of what a biblical engagement was like, and what it involved. Modern practices must not be read back into the biblical account.

"Engagement, for us, is often a trial period. Many look on it as officially going steady with some intent to marry. There is nothing really binding about it. In effect, it was the first step of marriage. In the engagement the marriage covenant was made, and an engagement could be broken only by death or by divorce (Deut 22:23; Matt. 1:16-24).

"An engaged person who willingly entered into illicit sexual relations with another did not incur a fine, but (as in adulterous relations after marriage) was put to death (cf. Deut. 22:23 N.B., the engaged girl is called the 'wife' of the man to whom she is engaged). Indeed, contrary to the views of some, there is every biblical reason for referring to illicit sexual relations during engagement as nothing less than adultery.

"In contrast to an engaged person, the single individual who entered into illicit sexual relations underwent a lesser penalty (Deut. 22:28, 29). The point, therefore, to keep in mind is that engaged parties were given the same penalty as married persons (cf. Deut. 22:22). No distinction whatever was made.

"The same usage that we noted in Deuteronomy 22:23, where we see that engaged parties are referred to as husband and wife, occurs consistently elsewhere in the Scripture, confirming the high view of engagement that persists (cf. II Sam. 3:14; Matt. 1:19). In the last cited passage, Joseph is plainly called Mary's 'husband,' even though it is explicitly said that they had not come together in sexual union (Matt. 1:25).

"A few additional comments on the events recorded in Matthew 2 might be helpful. Matthew tells us that Joseph had decided to divorce Mary secretly (v. 19). Probably by this time divorce had come to replace stoning. Possibly, under Roman law, punishment by stoning for this offense was not allowed. Some, however, conjecture that stoning was rarely, if ever, used (perhaps that was involved in what Jesus called the 'hardness of men's hearts' that he said influenced Moses). The facts regarding this substitution (or change) are not clear. But because in that very verse Joseph is called a "just man" (plainly a commendation of his contemplated action), it seems evident that (at that time, anyway) God did not look with disfavor either on the substitution of divorce for stoning or, N.B., on the idea of divorce itself for illicit sexual relations. This interesting fact has implications that bear upon later considerations.

"But, for now, notice that the marriage which began with engagement (and required a divorce to break) did not begin with a sexual union (Matt. 1:25) and had to be ended by divorce.

"All these facts make it as clear as can be that marriage is fundamentally a contractual arrangement (called in Mal. 2:14 a marriage 'by covenant') and not a sexual union. Marriage is a formal (covenantal) arrangement between two persons to become each other's loving companions for life. In marriage, they contract to keep each other from ever being lonely so long as they shall live. Our modern wedding ceremonies should stress this point more fully than they do" (13).

Adams writes that:

"When wives vainly attempt to fight loneliness by substituting children (especially a son) for husbands, or when husbands try to do so by burying themselves in business (or busyness), they err greatly. Under God, a husband and a wife must put one another first, before all others, and all activities. Only in that way will children be free to leave home without heartache when the time comes. And, the marriage will grow.

"The relationship between parent and child is established through birth (or adoption); the relationship between husband and wife, by covenant promises. Blood may be thicker than water, but it should not be thicker than promise. This contrast between the temporary parent-child relationship and the permanent husband-wife union once again forcefully points up the uniqueness of marriage in God's plan for human beings.

"Since this description of marriage focuses on covenantal companionship it is obvious that one must cultivate companionship. A marriage lacking companionship is headed toward misery or divorce. All that jeopardizes companionship must be avoided; whatever promotes it must be cultivated" (20).

The author observes that "There are many wrong attitudes in the conservative churches about divorce and divorcees. From the way that some treat divorced persons, you would think that they had committed the unpardonable sin. Let us make it clear, then, that those who wrongly (sinfully) obtain a divorce must not be excused for what they have done; it is sin. But precisely because it is sin, it is forgivable. The sin of divorcing one's mate on unbiblical grounds is bad, not only because of the misery it occasions, but especially because it is an offence against a holy God. But it is not so indelibly imprinted in the life of the sinner that it cannot be washed away by Christ's blood" (24). "Divorce can be, had been, is being and will continue to be forgiven by God. His church, therefore, dare do no less" (25).

According to Adams, "The modern view of separation is an anti-biblical substitution for the biblical requirement of reconciliation or (in some cases) divorce. These two options alone are given by God. Modern separation settles nothing; it amounts to a refusal to face issues and set them to rest" (33).

Adams observes that the concept that divorced persons may be "still married in God's eyes" is repugnant. God has called this state of two sinfully-divorced believers *agamas* (unmarried) by our rationalizations; let us not put together what God has separated! The facts are plain: a divorce breaks marriage obligations belonging to marriage and rights and privileges of marriage do not pertain to divorced persons" (43).

Adams says in a footnote commenting on 1 Cor. 7 that "the believer could not remarry the unbelieving partner (unless he/she should become a Christian) since to do so would violate another biblical command to marry 'only in the Lord' (v. 39). A believer must not marry an unbeliever, even if the unbeliever is a former spouse!" (48).

In a chapter on "The Exceptional Clause," Adams writes:

"We have seen already that while God did not institute divorcee, he (nevertheless) regulated it. I shall look at the point again in chapter 11. We discovered that God hates divorce, not as a process but because of its sinful causes and many of its devastating consequences. All divorces, in one way or another, are caused by sin; but not all divorces are sinful. In the last chapter, for instance, we examined a case in point - the divorce of a mixed couple (believer/unbeliever). The Bible legitimatized such a divorce after every attempt had been made by the believer to maintain the marriage to his unbelieving spouse. But if that spouse adamantly refuses to go on with the marriage, he is required not to stand in the way of a divorce (I Cor. 7:15). This divorce is reluctantly granted after all attempts to avert it have failed. The effect of that divorce, we noted, was to free the believer of all marriage obligations as well as any obligation to remarry that unbelieving former spouse. He is free to remarry another.

"Now we turn to the exception clause in Matthew, chapters 5 and 19, by which Jesus made it plain that there is one ground on which believers might divorce a spouse – fornication (or sexual sin). In this case, however, no requirement to divorce the other is laid down. Note well, at the outset, that Jesus acknowledged one, and only one, ground for divorce among believers: *porneia* ('fornication,' or 'sexual sin') (51).

The author adds:

"Though some equate adultery and fornication, it is altogether wrong to do so. Frequently one hears the exceptional clause misquoted: 'except for adultery.' But, as we have seen, that is wrong. While in the context of Matthew 5 and 19, adultery is in one's mind as he reads the exceptional clause, the clause itself does not place the emphasis (at that point) upon the effect of sexual sin (adultery), but upon the sin itself – the act by which one violates his marriage covenant. In both Matthew 5 and 19, Jesus' permission to divorce a spouse is based on the violating act (sexual sin, *porneia*) not on its effect (adultery).

"Why does Jesus focus on the act? Because He wants to cover all the possibilities. He declares fornication (sexual sin) to be the ground upon which one may serve a bill of divorce because fornication covers incest, bestiality, homosexuality and lesbianism as well as adultery. To speak of adultery only, might tend to narrow the focus too much.

"Most modern translations translate *porneia* with words like 'sexual sin,' thus avoiding much of the confusion. All the sexual sins condemned as fornication are included" (54, 55).

According to the author, "All persons properly divorced may be remarried" (86). There is no law in the Bible which says that the guilty party must remain unmarried. Adams writes:

"Let's talk about this so-called 'guilty party' a bit. Loraine Boettner is absolutely right when he says, 'There is no law in the Bible which says that he must remain unmarried.'

"Clearly, God allowed the marriage of David and Bathsheba to stand even though both of them had been guilty of adultery, and David of murder as well. No more sordid beginning to a marriage could be imagined. Yet,

God blessed that marriage in time because forgiveness was granted, the past was cleansed, and the future was cleared for God's blessings (cf. II Sam. 12:13; Psa. 51; esp. v. 2). If this marriage, which at its inception was knee-deep in sin (David didn't' repent until after the marriage), could be blessed by God to the bringing forth of the Messiah, why do we say that some persons who are forgiven and cleansed before marrying, cannot expect God to bless their marriage because of sin in their past?

"Now, someone will say that this makes forgiveness too easy and will encourage divorce. I do not honor that argument any more than Paul did in Romans. Divorce, wrongly obtained, is sin – a heinous offence against God and man. I am not encouraging divorce any more than God encouraged robbery, adultery, homosexuality, lying and murder by declaring that such sins are to be totally forgiven in Christ and put into the past (I Cor. 6:11). Repentance, when genuine, is like David's repentance (Ps. 51, 38, etc.); it is not treated lightly as a gimmick. A repentant sinner recognizes the serious nature of his offense and is not only grateful but produces fruit (change) appropriate to repentance. In any discussion of divorce or remarriage we must be careful to preserve the integrity of two biblical truths.

"1. Sin is heinous.

"2. Grace is greater than the most heinous sin (Rom. 5:20).

"So, we have seen that (1) remarriage after divorce is allowed in the Bible and that the guilty party—after forgiveness-is free to remarry" (95).

The rapid rise of divorce among clergymen, even some who consider themselves conservative, and the publicity given to the divorce of such "born again" Christians as Anita Bryant, Terry Bradshaw, and JoJo Starbuck shows the great need for some sound scriptural guidance with regard to marriage, divorce, and remarriage. This book by Jay Adams is about the finest we have seen on the subject.

Barna Study: Christians More Likely to Experience Divorce Than Others

Christian News, January 17, 2000

(RNS) A news study by the Barna Research Group in Ventura, Calif., says that born again Christians are more likely to go through a marital split than non-Christians.

Using statistics drawn from a nationwide survey of nearly 4,000 adults, the Barna data show that 11 percent of the adult population is currently divorced but that 25 percent of all adults have experienced at least one divorce during their lifetime.

Among born-again Christians, 27 percent are currently or have previously been divorced, compared with 24 percent among adults who are not born again.

Surprisingly, the Barna Report said, the Christian group whose adherents have the highest likelihood of getting divorced are Baptists. It did not specify any particular denomination. It said the only group to surpass Baptists were Christians associated with non-denominational Protestant churches.

"Of the nation's major Christian groups, Catholics and Lutherans have the lowest percentage of divorced individuals - 21 percent. People who attend mainline Protestant churches, overall, experience divorce at the national average of 25 percent.

From Both Conservatives and Liberals
Why Little Protest vs. Unscriptural Divorce?

The essay by Belinda Luscombe in the May 3, 2010 *TIME* comments on divorce. It mentions that Larry King is about to get unhitched for the eighth time. Elizabeth Taylor "has also hatched and dispatched eight unions"; the same for Mickey Rooney and Zsa Zsa Gabor. The official record holder had 23 ex-husbands. *TIME* says that "Evolution favors the alpha-male serial monogamist who bonds with a mate until she gets old and is replaced by a more fertile one. Other primates change partners all the time."

TIME concludes:

"Then again, perhaps we should just leave the serial splitters alone. There's a little of Liz and Larry and Linda in every couple; we are all occasionally convinced that we married the wrong person. If King has taught us anything- I mean anything apart from how to wear suspenders with a straight face-its that there are plenty of people to marry. The real question is whether you can make it work with the one you end up with."

A major reason why both liberals and conservative leaders in the Lutheran Church-Missouri Synod say very little against unscriptural divorce may be that unscriptural divorced millionaires who have left their wife and children for a younger woman have funded both liberal and conservative causes. They would never fund *Christian News*.

CN's position on marriage and divorce is stated in Luther's Small Catechism with An American Translation text, pp. 69-72. This is still the best catechism to use in both adult and children's classes. It was first published by the LCMS's Concordia Publishing House and for decades was used by many LCMS churches. The 230 page catechism (hardcover) is available from CN for $12.50 plus s/h.

Reprinted below is the section on the Sixth Commandment:

MARRIAGE AND PURITY

Do not commit adultery.
What does this mean? We should fear and love God that we may lead a chaste and decent life in word and deed, and each love and honor his spouse.

61. What is marriage?

Marriage is the *lifelong union of one man and one woman into one flesh.* Marriage was *instituted by God* and is entered into by *rightful betrothal,* or engagement.

[141] - And so they are no more two but one flesh. Now, what God has joined together man must not separate. Matt. 19:6.

Bible Narratives: The institution of marriage. Gen. 2:18-24.-The angel calls Mary, who was engaged to Joseph, Joseph's wife and calls Joseph her husband. Matt. 1:19, 20, 24.

62. What does God forbid in the Sixth Commandment?

A. God forbids the *breaking of the marriage vow* by unfaithfulness or desertion. He permits the innocent party to procure a divorce when the other party is guilty of fornication.

[142] - What God has joined together man must not separate. Matt. 19:6.

[143] - If anyone divorces his wife, except for adultery, and marries another, he's living in adultery. Matt. 19:9.

[144] - God will judge those who sin sexually whether single or married. Heb. 13:4.

Bible Narratives: David committed adultery with the wife of Uriah. II Sam. 11.-Herod took his brother's wife. Mark 6:18.

B. God also forbids all *unchaste and unclean thoughts, desires, words, and deeds.*

[145] - Out of the heart come evil thoughts, murders, adulteries, sexual sins, stealing, lies, slanders. Matt. 15:19.

[146] - Anyone who looks at a woman to lust after her has already committed adultery with her in his heart. Matt. 5:28.

[147] - Sexual sins, anything unclean, or greed shouldn't even be mentioned among you. This is the right attitude for holy people. No shameful things, foolish talk, or coarse jokes! These aren't proper. Instead give thanks. Eph. 5:3, 4.

[148] - We're ashamed even to mention what such people do secretly. Eph. 5:12.

Bible Narratives: Potiphar's wife, with lust in her heart, cast her eyes upon Joseph. Gen. 39:7-12.-Samson committed fornication. Judg. 16:1.

63. What does God require of all of us in the Sixth Commandment?

We should lead a *chaste and decent* life in thoughts, desires, words, and deeds.

[149] - Stay away from the desires of your body, because its appetites fight against the soul. 1 Peter 2:11.

[150] - Keep your minds on all that is true or noble, right or pure, lovely or respectable, on anything that is excellent or that deserves praise. Phil. 4:8.

[151] - Don't say anything harmful but only what is good, so that you help where there's a need and benefit those who hear it. Eph. 4:29.

64. What must we do to lead a chaste and decent life?

In the fear of God we must -

A. *Fight to overcome* all impure thoughts and desires with God's Word and prayer, work and temperance;

[152] - How could I do this great wrong and sin against God? Gen. 39:9.

[153] - Create a clean heart for me, O God. Ps. 51:10.

[154] - Don't look at wine when it is red, when it sparkles in the cup and goes down smoothly. Finally it bites like a snake and stings like an adder. Your eyes will see strange sights, and your mind will say confused things. Prov. 23:31-33.

B. *Flee and avoid* every opportunity for unchasteness.

[155] - Flee from sexual sin. I Cor. 6:18.

[156] - Flee from the lusts of young people. II Tim. 2:22.

[157] - Don't you know your body is a temple of the Holy Spirit, Whom God gives you and Who is in you? You don't belong to yourselves. I Cor. 6:19.

[158] - My son, if sinners tempt you, don't be willing to sin. Prov. 1:10.

Bible Narrative: Joseph resisted the temptation of Potiphar's wife and fled from her. Gen. 39:7-12.

65. What does God require of married people especially?

God requires married people to *love and honor each other*, the husband his wife as *his God-given helpmeet* and the wife her husband as *her God-given head*.

[159] - As the church obeys Christ, so wives should obey their husbands in everything. You husbands, love your wives, as Christ loved the church and gave Himself for it. Eph. 5:24, 25.

The Divorced Pastor
By David Cloud, Fundamental Baptist Information Service
Christian News, January 2, 2006

"A bishop then must be blameless, the husband of one wife ... One that ruleth well his own house, having his children in subjection with all gravity; (For if a man know not how to rule his own house, how shall he take care of the church of God?)" (1 Timothy 3:2, 4, 5).

"If any be blameless, the husband of one wife, having faithful children not accused of riot or unruly". . . (Titus 1:6).

Neither as being lords over God's heritage, but being ensamples to the flock" (1 Pet. 5:3).

There is a great controversy over the matter of the pastor's marital standing, whether or not he can be divorced and continue in the ministry, yet God has made it clear that He intends for the pastor to be a man who is above average. He cannot do things other Christians might be able to do. The pastor must be "blameless" in some very clearly defined areas of his life.

We know this is not speaking of any sort of perfection. The Bible doesn't say the pastor must be perfect; it says he must be blameless. There is a big difference! The requirement of being blameless does not mean that the pastor must fit everyone's idea of what a pastor should be. That would be as impossible as attaining sinless perfection! Some believe a pastor must never smile; others feel he must always smile. Some are convinced he must always dress formally; others believe he should be informal. Some want their pastors fat; others want them skinny. Some want them scholarly; others feel a studious man cannot meet the needs of the common folk. Some want the pastor to spend all his time in visiting church members; others want him to spend all his time in soul winning. Some want a pastor who loves sports; others feel it is wrong for a pastor to have such interests.

It is impossible for a pastor to be blameless by human standards, but that is not what God requires. He must be blameless by the standards that are set forth in the Scriptures.Let us examine those standards in light of whether or not a divorced man is qualified to be a pastor.

I. THE PASTOR MUST NOT BE DIVORCED BECAUSE HE MUST BE BLAMELESS IN HIS REPUTATION BEFORE MEN

"A bishop then must be blameless ... Moreover he must have a good report of them which are without; lest he fall into reproach and the snare of the devil" (1 Timothy 3:2,7).The first thing to consider is that the pastor must be blameless in his reputation before men. A divorced man, no matter what the cause for the divorce, does not have the spotless reputation a pastor must have. His divorce is a handle that the devil can take hold of to injure the work of God. The blemish of divorce will be used against his ministry and against the church. It will hinder the ministry. And since the church's testimony is far more important than the feelings or ambitions of any individual, divorced men should refrain from pastoral positions.

What if the divorce were for the cause of fornication? It appears in Christ's teaching in Matthew 19 that divorce might be allowable for such a cause. "And I say unto you, Whosoever shall put away his wife, except it be for fornication, and shall marry another, committeth adultery..." (Matt. 19:9). Even so, divorced men do not have an unblemished reputation in the eyes of men. It is the nature of divorce that some respect is lost, no matter what the cause. It is a rare divorce, anyway, which is not caused, at least in part, by both parties—even if it were only in the matter of neglect.

What if the divorce occurred before the man's conversion? Is he not forgiven? Certainly he is; yet he has, by his divorce, done permanent damage to his freedom to hold offices in the church. Forgiveness does not necessarily mean a person will avoid consequences for past sin. A man who, in a drunken condition before salvation, has an accident and loses a limb, will be handicapped the rest of his life even if he gets saved. King David was forgiven for his sin with Bathsheba, but he suffered for the rest of his life as a consequence of this sin. (The fact that David was not removed from being king does not mean that a pastor can remain in office regardless of what he does. The office of king in Israel was a matter of lineage and was very different from the office of a pastor in the church.)

This applies to the person who was divorced before his conversion. The sin is forgiven and he can enjoy the manifold blessings of the Lord, but scars will remain throughout his earthly life. One consequence is that he is restricted as to the type of office he can hold in the church.

II. THE PASTOR MUST NOT BE DIVORCED BECAUSE HE MUST BE AN EXAMPLE OF GOD'S PERFECT WILL

"The elders which are among you I exhort ... be ensamples to the flock" (1 Peter 5:1, 3).The second thing to consider is that the pastor is to represent God's perfect will before this world. If the pastor is not a pattern for God's will, there will be no pattern, and standards among God's people will fall to the level of the world. This has happened repeatedly and we see it all around us today.

What is God's will in this regard? The Word of God clearly says that God opposes divorce. "For the Lord, the God of Israel, saith that he hateth putting away..." (Mal. 2:16). "And unto the married I command, yet not I, but the Lord, Let not the wife depart from the husband: but and if she depart, let her remain unmarried, or be reconciled to her husband: and let not the husband put away his wife" (1 Cor. 7:1-11).

God only allows divorce because of the hardness of human hearts; it has never been God's perfect will. "He said unto them, Moses because of the hardness of your hearts allowed you to put away your wives, but from the beginning it was not so" (Matt. 19:8).Since the pastor should be in the business of upholding God's perfect will he must not be a divorced man, no matter what the cause of the divorce. In many parts of the world divorce is no longer looked upon as a bad thing. In some states in America a divorce can be obtained almost as easily as a driver's license! Some pastors in the United Methodist Church have begun performing divorce ceremonies to help remove "the guilt and stigma" associated with divorce. This is wrong.

We should be kind to those who suffer divorce and love them with Christ-like love, but the world also needs to see that God takes divorce seriously, even if society and apostate denominations do not.

What does God say about the marital bond? "Wherefore they are no more twain, but one flesh. What therefore God hath joined together, let not man put asunder" (Matt. 19:6).If these truths cannot be seen in the marriages of our church leaders, where will they be seen? If a pastor tries to warn against divorce and remarriage, yet he himself is divorced and remarried, how seriously will people listen?

Believers need to see God's will in the lives of their leaders. Can a divorced man truly set forth the right standards for young people (or older people, for that matter)? Will they listen to him and take him seriously as he tries to teach them what God thinks about marriage?

The institution of marriage is under fierce attack. God's people need to see that a successful Christian family marriage is possible. Where are they going to see that, if not in their pastors?

III. THE PASTOR MUST NOT BE DIVORCED BECAUSE HE MUST PREACH THE WHOLE COUNSEL OF GOD

Third, the pastor must not be divorced because he has to preach the whole counsel of God, and if he has a broken and crippled marital status, he is not in a position to preach some things with complete authority. People tend to discount preaching when it is done by a man who has serious blemishes in relation to the things he preaches.Christians are continually having marital problems serious enough to lead to divorce if not corrected. A pastor must be a man who can share with them God's perfect will for marriage. He must be able to exhort couples to avoid divorce, to stay together and work things out by God's grace. His own marital life must back up his exhortations. Otherwise his counsel will not have much effect. He must be a man who has demonstrated in his own marriage that God's plan and God's grace are sufficient for holding a home together. A divorced man simply cannot do this.

BUT GOD HAS CALLED ME

I have heard men say that God would not allow them to get out of the ministry after their divorce, that God had called them and His calling is without repentance.

I don't believe God operates contrary to His Word. When He lays down standards for the pastorate, He is not going to lead a man to go contrary to them.

Our feelings about God's will are very undependable.

"The heart is deceitful above all things, and desperately wicked: who can know it?" (Jer. 17:9).

"He that trusteth in his own heart is a fool..." (Prov. 28:26).

We can easily be led astray by one's feelings in regard to God's will. We must therefore depend upon what the Bible plainly says and not what we feel.

Many women are absolutely convinced that God has called them to be pastors. They feel so strongly about this that they would rather die than quit. You can quote the Scripture to them all day long and it has no effect, because they are living by their subjective experiences.

Yet they are wrong. If they are saved, they will be ashamed at the judgment seat of Christ because of their disobedience to God's Word; but in this present hour they are utterly self-deceived, entirely convinced that God has called them to pastor.Likewise, many men who feel that God has called them to pastor aren't qualified to do so and are flying in the face of clearly defined Scriptural teachings.

A wise man or woman will be content to be what God has truly called him to be, not what he would like to be. "For I say, through the grace given unto me, to every man that is among you, not to think of himself more highly than he ought to think; but to think soberly, according as God hath dealt to every man the measure of faith" (Rom. 12:3).A man's calling needs to be tested by the Word of God. If I am not qualified to do something, I should not do it, no matter how much I desire to do it.

A CALL TO PREACH IS NOT NECESSARILY A CALL TO PASTOR

A man might argue, "God has called me to preach, therefore I must be a pastor," but the call to preach is not necessarily the call to pastor. A man does not have to be a pastor to have an effective preaching ministry. He can preach on the streets. He can preach from house to house. He can preach in jails and nursing homes. He can preach in the highways and byways.

Let me give my own testimony. I know that God has called me to preach. I believe I have a teaching prophetic gift and ministry–not foretelling, but forth telling. The prophets of Israel spent most of their time preaching about Israel's sin and calling God's people to repentance. I believe God has called me to this today. I believe my calling is referred to in Romans 12:6– "Having then gifts differing according to the grace that is given to us, whether prophecy, let us prophesy according to the proportion of faith."The major verses God has laid upon my heart in regard to my preaching ministry deal with a prophetic type of ministry.

For example, the ministry of "Way of Life Literature" is based upon Proverbs 6:23 – "For the commandment is a lamp; and the law is light; and reproofs of instruction are the way of life."

The ministry of "O Timothy" magazine is based upon 1 Timothy 6:20 – "O Timothy, keep that which is committed to thy trust, avoiding profane and vain babblings, and oppositions of science falsely so called."

The section in "O Timothy" called "Digging in the Walls" is based upon Ezekiel 8:7-10 –"Then said he unto me, Son of man, dig now in the wall ... And he said unto me, Go in, and behold the wicked abominations that they do here. So I went in and saw..." God specifically laid these verses upon my heart as these ministries were started. All of these have to do with speaking against error and upholding the old paths. This is what God has called me to do, and it is what I am qualified and gifted to do. I know that God has not called me to be a pastor, but he has definitely called me to preach.

The fact that a man has a burden to preach does not mean that God has called him to be a pastor. He might be an evangelist, a prophet, or a teacher. There are four types of ministry gifts mentioned in Ephesians 4:11. Romans

12 also mentions four – prophesying, ministry, teaching, and exhorting.

It is common today to use the term "called to preach" synonymously with the call to the pastorate, but the two are not necessarily the same. The man who is "called to preach" might be called to be a pastor, or he might not be. Not only must a man's calling be tested by the Bible, but it must also be tested by the church. This is what ordination is all about. It is the church's recognition of God's call upon a man (Acts 13:2-3). If a spiritual church does not think God has called a man to a certain ministry, he would be unwise to push himself forward in that thing. As Charles Spurgeon said to his Bible students,

"I have noted ... that you, gentlemen, students, as a body, in your judgment of one another, are seldom if ever wrong. There has hardly ever been an instance, take the whole house through, where the general opinion of the entire college concerning a brother has been erroneous. . . . Meeting as you do in class, in prayer-meeting, in conversation, and in various religious engagements, you gauge each other; and a wise man will be slow to set aside the verdict of the house" (C.H. Spurgeon, Lectures to My Students).

The counsel given by the apostle regarding marriage is fitting in this matter of God's calling: "But every man hath his proper gift of God, one after this manner, and another after that. . . . Let every man abide in the same calling wherein he was called" (1 Cor. 7:7, 20).

A divorced man should, for honor's sake, be content to serve outside of the office of the pastorate–for the honor of that office and for the honor of the church of Jesus Christ. If you are called to preach, preach on, brother, but don't be a pastor unless you are qualified.

"My brethren, be not many masters, knowing that we shall receive the greater condemnation" (James 3:1).

Ed. CN has lost support because of its strong stand against divorce. Today many pastors are divorced. Only those who have a scriptural divorce should remain pastors of congregations. The only scriptural reasons for divorce are adultery and desertion.

VI

MOTHERHOOD

The Glory of Motherhood

By Peter Krey
Christian News, March 3, 2010

From *Devotions on the Apostles' Creed - Why I Am A Christian and Other Writings.* by Peter Krey. ($9.99 plus $3.50 s/h)

Gen. 3:20

Adam called his wife Eve. This was the greatest tribute he could have paid her. No other name could have been more fitting for the name Eve means "living". Adam saw clearly that woman's greatest glory would be that for which she was created and for which she was peculiarly fitted by the Creator - the bearer of human life. From Eve's body would come a race that would fill the earth.

What is true of Eve is true of every mother. Every mother is a bearer of life. And what is more wonderful than life, human life, human beings ? To bring such precious life into this world is a privilege of motherhood?

1.

Every person who comes into this world is a work of divine omnipotence. "I believe that God has made Me, that He has given me my body and soul, eyes, ears and all my members, my reason and all my senses" - and let us not forget all this is given chiefly by our mothers. A mother is God's handmaid. By her God does a work that He does nowhere else in heaven or on earth. He created new human beings for this earth, new souls for heaven and immortality. Is not that a great honor and distinction that God has bestowed upon woman? What greater honor could He bestow upon her? Therefore also the holy women of old of whom we read in the Bible greatly desired this honor and prayed that God bestow it upon them. And so it is for every godly woman today. Every Christian wife will surely want God to bestow this honor upon her; for what greater honor and glory could she desire?

She might aspire to become a great educator or doctor or lawyer or business woman. Nearly all positions are open to women today at least in this country. But what would all such honor and glory be in comparison with the honor that God bestows upon her - that of childbearing and motherhood. Motherhood is woman's greatest glory. Here she is in a field all her own, doing work for the Lord.

Without motherhood this earth would soon be an empty and dreary place. Without motherhood it would not be long before there would be no man to till the soil, no man to rule and govern and subdue the earth, no man to preach the glad tidings of salvation; indeed, no people at all on earth.

The nation, the people,or the church that despises and frustrates motherhood is doomed to oblivion. There is nothing more wonderful and miraculous in this world than a mother who nourishes new life under her heart. But so calloused are we and so indifferent toward such wonderful works of God that we regard it but little. Sadly, many women in our day would rather not have God bestow this honor upon them. Yes, many are ashamed of motherhood when everyone ought to praise God for His wonderful work.

Why is motherhood avoided and looked down upon so much in our day? Why do so many women today glory in a career, in good dress and good looks or in the preservation of their youthful complexion? But the glory that is of God, motherhood, they despise or do not want. Is it not because their judgment is perverted, because they prefer pleasure and ease to the burdens and responsibilities of motherhood? But it ought to be clear to every one that there can be no honor and glory without burdens and responsibility. No one can hold a position of honor without corresponding burdens and responsibilities.

Women who refuse motherhood cast aside the glory that is of God, the honor that God has bestowed upon her, choosing instead the vanity and flattering glory of men and fashion. Motherhood is woman's greatest honor and glory bestowed upon her by the Creator. Therefore at all times we ought to respect motherhood and talk about it only with the highest respect and esteem, gratefully praising God.

2.

Motherhood is woman's greatest glory. It is also her greatest oppoortunity for service to humanity. In no other place can woman wield such great influence or accomplish so much good than in the state of motherhood. Therefore, we read in our text that Eve is the mother of all living. That is to say, Eve chose motherhood as her career. She was, according to her husband Adam's words not only to give life to new human beings, but also to be a mother to them, to nourish them and bring them up to take their place in the world and the church. That Eve was such a mother is evident from the story of her sons. She had a wayward son Cain, it is true, but she also had Abel and Seth who became the fathers of a long list of distinguished and God-fearing men who kept alive the divine promise of deliverance from sin and death, man's only hope, by calling upon the name of the Lord as we read, all of which would not be if EVE had not brought up and trained her children in the ways of God's Word.

Motherhood is woman's greatest opportunity to serve God and mankind. Motherhood brings with it the privilege and the responsibility to bring up, to nourish and train the coming generation to become useful citizens, faithful friends, helpful neighbors and godfearing men and women who will carry on the work of God's kingdom here on earth and be heirs of the world to come. What more important work can a woman do in this world than that? In what field of activity could she wield a greater influence?

Who can calculate the influence that a mother has on her sons and daughters for better or for worse? Bad men have blamed their mothers for their fall into sin and more than one great man has said "all that I am I owe to my mother." One of our own great poets, as quoted by Lincoln, truly said "The woman that rocks the cradle rules the world." Because she to a greater extent than any one else implants or can implant in the heart of her child the principles that will govern its future conduct. As a mother a woman has the opportunity to instill into the receptive hearts of little souls the incorruptible seed, the Word of God, which lives and abides forever and is able to save their souls. The Word of God, the songs, the prayers that our mothers taught us, are never forgotten. They are our companions on the way; they come to our rescue in the sinking flood; they give us new courage in the fray and we find in them sweet comfort when we need it most. What a precious influence and value can a mother not be to her sons and daughters! If she keeps their confidence even when they grow older they can seek her advice concerning the problems of life. What wonderful opportunities mothers have to accomplish things of lasting worth.

Some women may be great artists, some may be capable business executives, some may be excellent teachers, some give themselves to the service of the sick and unfortunate, but the woman who is a good mother does a greater and nobler work. We may well get along without women artists and actresses, women painters and teachers, women executives and physicians, but our race, our country, our church would perish without mothers who bring up their children in the fear of the Lord. No woman can aspire to a higher calling than that of motherhood. No other calling affords her greater opportunities to serve God and humanity. May every mother realize this and thank God for having become a mother and strive to make the best of the opportunity that motherhood gives her. "Many daughters have done virtuously, but thou excellest them all." Prov. 31:29.

3.

But our text presents one more thought which must not be overlooked. We read "and Adam called his wife's name Eve." It was his wife whom Adam called living, the mother of all living. She was to be the mother of all, living as his wife - that is in holy wedlock. For God the Creator had brought Eve to Adam and united them and blessed them with the blessing "Be fruitful and multiply." According to God's ordinance, motherhood is to take place within wedlock, not outside of wedlock. Motherhood outside of wedlock is contrary to God's ordinance and is a transgression of His holy will.

Before I conclude there remain a few pertinent questions with regard to motherhood that should be answered according to God's word.

We hear and read a great deal these days about the prevention of motherhood. Leading men and women of our day advocate birth control and whole church bodies have endorsed it. What should our attitude be? It should not take a Christian long to answer. A little clear thinking tells him that prevention of motherhood runs contrary to the benediction and will of the blessed creator: "Be fruitful and multiply." Let us strive to live in the fear of God. According to Christian knowledge and good sense we should ask God daily to keep us from burdening our conscience with that which is contrary to his will. And if in weakness we fail or have failed, then let us repent not doubting the forgiving mercy of our heavenly Father and striving not to offend him again.

Sometimes God withholds the blessing of motherhood. That is a great cross to a godly woman. What to do in such a case we may learn from the Godfearing women of the Bible. Sarah, Rachel, Rebecca, Hannah and Elizabeth were for some time denied the privilege of motherhood. What did they do? They bore their cross patiently and they prayed to God for the blessing of motherhood. God heard them. Sarah in her old age became the mother of Isaac. Rebecca after twenty years became the mother of Jacob and Esau; Rachel, after years of waiting, gave birth to Joseph and Benjamin; Hannah became the mother of Samuel; Elizabeth gave birth to John the Baptist.

Sometimes a mother is blessed with many children in quick succession. Then very often the whispering of evil tongues come to her ear who say: "It's a shame. It's too much. Why doesn't she do this and why doesn't she do that?" That is a grievous thorn in the heart of such a mother. Let such a mother remember that those who speak evil of her are not speaking against her but against God for "Children are an heritage of the Lord; and the fruit of the womb is His reward." And let her commit her case unto God her heavenly Father in prayer - who will not leave her nor forsake her and her children.

At times God permits a woman to become the mother of an imperfect child, a child who is mentally or physically handicapped. That is a great sorrow. Such a mother is apt to think that God is punishing her. But that is not the case. If she is a Christian mother she shouldwell recognize that God is merely testing her patience and obedience. Let such a mother submit herself to God's will even if she cannot understand, not doubting that also in caring for such a child she is doing a holy work and serving God. Let her take comfort in this thought that all such imperfections are due to sin, not her sin always, but sin in general and when sin is abolished in the resurrection of the dead, such imperfection will afflict her child no more.

(Read *Angel Unawares* by Mrs. Dale Evans Rogers.)

Ed. From *Devotions on the Apostles Creed - Why I Am A Christian And Other Writings*, by Peter Krey, published by Christian News. 300 pages. $9.99 plus $3.50 s/h.

This book contains some of the hundreds of devotional articles Christian News published by Peter Krey, one of the finest devotional writers of the 20th century. CPH refused to publish his writings. A major reason was that he defended Christian News and wrote for Christian News.

Blessings Abound
Christian News, June 6, 2000

(Heading—Recommended by Grace Otten who said CN should enlarge the type and fill an entire page with this letter by Pam Regentin in the Spring 2000 *Adorned in Godliness*, 4359 Woodworth Drive, Mt. Hood, Oregon 97041)

Dear Friends,

Finally, the Spring 2000 issue of AiG is complete. I won't give you my list of excuses for its great tardiness (well, okay, maybe one of the excuses: my computer was out of commission for over three weeks!) but I rejoice that this Spring issue made it into your mailbox before the first day of summer!

I will try to be more timely with the Summer issue despite the fact that our baby is due at the end of June and my attentions will be directed elsewhere.

Everyone knows that being pregnant is a unique and special time in a woman's life. There is one aspect of it, though, that only mothers (and fathers) of large families really know. That is the need to deal with the different reactions of people when they hear the news of your pregnancy and when they thought you were "done" making your family. We want to convey the message that we view each child as a blessing and that if a pregnancy occurs, as a surprise or not, we accept it with joy and thankfulness as a blessing from God. Some people make this a challenge for us.

For example, a second pregnancy and birth is greeted with comments about how "complete" your family is now, especially if you have a boy and a girl (as we did). Some people assume that with two children, you now have the "perfect" family! A third pregnancy is welcomed mostly with joy but usually without all the fanfare of the first two. It is much quieter in its progression and completion. After you have had three children, subsequent pregnancies take on the new challenge of addressing comments and questions from friends and strangers alike about how and why this came to be and "Are you done now?" I know from talking with other mothers of many that I am not alone in the way I handle these situations.

For one thing, we may become selective in whom we choose to announce the upcoming birth. We're happy to talk about it with friends and family whom we know will share our excitement and joy and be understanding of our feelings of inadequacy. When it comes to those who may not share our excitement, sometimes it's easier to let the "Grapevine" handle a lot of the announcements, knowing that *eventually* everyone will know; that way any embarrassing moments, inappropriate questions or comments of a "stunned" nature may be headed off at the pass with time to think about what to say. When we do meet, I feel a responsibility, regardless of how I may be feeling that day, to convey a message of joyful thankfulness and love for children in response to any rude comments about having "another" child.

Many people really do think that couples are in complete control of building their own families, when in reality, there is only one Builder. Man proposes but God disposes. It is God who opens and closes the womb. A couple may decide they want to have two children, or a dozen! But God is the one who will ultimately give or not. Our responsibility is simply to accept His gracious will for our lives and our families and to trust that "the will of God is always best" (Hymn 517 TLH).

"Six children! I don't know how you do it! I can barely handle one!" Is an oft-heard comment. Well, I didn't just wake up one day with six children. It was a gradual progression. First I learned to "handle" one, then two, then three. I actually anticipate that the sixth will be much easier than the first if only because I have so many helpers and I've done it before. So I know what to expect. My first-born is age seventeen, an anxious and eager nanny-to-be. Two more children cook, clean and do laundry already. What the youngest siblings don't do yet, they are about to learn to do! With the workload shared among many there "should" be more time to enjoy the baby!

The biggest difference between "then" and "now" is that early in our family life there were several young children, all needing much hands-on care and only Mom to handle the work of daily life. Today, with older children, there are many activities to clutter our calendar. Each child has his or her own interests and that makes for very full days. It can be a challenge to schedule all the meetings, outings, music lessons, and sports practices in addition to home, school and church responsibilities.

Above all, the answer to *"How can you do it?"* is that God gives us grace to do all that we need to do.

Another thing people say is that they could never afford to raise so many children. Again, God provides what is needed. Not always what is *wanted* does God provide, but always what is *needed*. Those ridiculous and astronomical figures purported to be the amount of money needed to raise a child to adulthood are exaggerated, in my opinion. It IS still possible to live on one income; we've done it for seventeen years. We have learned to be frugal as all large families do.

The final comment that must be dealt with by mothers of many is that which usually comes from a non-Christian acquaintance or even a stranger. Once in a while the news that we have more that the average 1.8 children elicits a response that is said as though we are selfishly and single-handedly overpopulating the planet. This attitude deserves a ready answer. While pregnant with a sixth child and living in the very liberal state of Oregon (a place full of earth worshipers) and after all the hoo-haw about the arrival of the six billionth person on Planet Earth, I am especially aware that I need to be ready to counter the opinion that the world is overpopulated and being "destroyed" by humankind. Did you know that the members of the Zero Population organization actually believe the ideal number for the earth is half a billion! I'd like to know which five and a half billion they'd choose to eliminate and how they propose to do it!

I believe that it is up to Christian families to spread the message to the world that children are a blessing and to be ready with a gracious and joyful answer that each child is to be welcomed with thankfulness as a gift from God.

God bless you!
Pam
* * * * * *

What Luther Says about . . . Women

Woman unexcelled – if she stays in her sphere

Men are commanded to rule and reign over their wives and families, but if woman, forsaking her position (*officio*), presumes to rule over her husband, she then and there engages in a work for which she was not created, a work which stems from her own failing (*vitio*) and is evil.

For God did not create this sex to rule. For this reason domination by women is never a happy one. The history of the Amazons, celebrated by Greek writers, might be advanced against this view. They are reported to have held the rule and to have conducted wars. But I believe what is told of them to be a fable. To be sure, the Ethiopians choose women to be both queens and princesses, in accordance with their custom, as the Ethiopian queen Candace is mentioned in Acts 9:27; but this is stupid of them. . . There is no divine permission for ruling by a woman. It may, of course, happen that she is placed in the position of a king and is given the rule; but she always has a senate of prominent men according to whose counsel all is administered. Therefore even though a woman may be put in the place of a king, this does not confirm the rule of woman; for the text is clear. "Thy desire shall be to thy husband, and he shall rule over thee" (Gen. 3:16). Woman was created for the benefit (*usum*) of man, that is, for the prudent and sensible training of children. Everyone does best when he does that for which he was created. "A woman handles a child better with her smallest finger than a man does with both hands (*Fäusten*)." Therefore let everyone stick to that work to which God has called him and for which he was created.

Temptation
Man's temptation is to flee the responsibility and authority that is his.
Woman's temptation is to usurp the responsibility and authority that is the man's.

A Mother's Day Message
101 Reasons For Having Children!
Above Rubies, Nancy Campbell
Christian News, August 5, 2002

I receive constant complaints from mothers telling me how hurt they are by the negative comments they receive from family and friends when they share the news that they are going to have another baby. "God gave you a brain, didn't He?" or "Oh No, not another one!" and so on. One *Above Rubies* reader wrote to me, "....I can't understand why people think children are such burdens that they'd only want one or two, and then suggest to me that I stop at that number also....I've sometimes joked with my husband that I could write a book of all the one liners people say and title it, "*101 Reasons Why Not to Have Any More Children.*"

This gave me a wonderful idea. But I decided to dwell on the positive rather than the negative. I asked our readers of *Above Rubies* to share why they love having children. I received so many answers, so here are "*101 Reasons Why Mothers Love Having Children.*" Many of these reasons were reiterated over and over again by different mothers.

1. We love receiving gifts and blessings from God.

2. Why would I ever want to turn down one of God's blessings?

3. We not only want to receive gifts from God for ourselves, but we want to give more gifts to the world. Every child God gives us is a gift to the world.

4. It's so exciting to see whom God will send to bless us each time.

5. It's an honor for the Lord to use my womb again.

6. I love being "with child."

7. I love to see what God thinks of next. I believe each child is a precious and unique thought, with vast possibilities, straight from our Heavenly Father. It's the most exciting thing in my entire life to give birth and see the new little person. There is nothing that moves me as much as seeing the birth of a baby.

8. I love to behold the handiwork of the Lord as a new little miracle comes forth.

9. The birth of a baby is the ultimate fulfillment of love between a husband and wife. Each child is an unbreakable bond between a father and mother.

10. It is amazing to think that each child is a part of me and my beloved husband.

11. God said to Jeremiah, "BEFORE I formed you in the womb I knew you..." God is the One who will form my future children. If He knew Jeremiah before conception, then He knows all my children before conception, yes, even the children who haven't yet been formed. I don't want to refuse children God has chosen.

12. I'd love another baby because to choose not to is like saying NO to God. I want to say YES to God and His will for my life.

13. I'll have more people to love.

14. I'll have more hands to help.

15. I'll have more babies to nurse and therefore less risk of breast cancer.

16. I feel so blessed that God wants to reward us again.

17. I look upon each child as an incredibly beautiful jewel. Each one takes on a different loveliness and I can't wait to see the next jewel arrive.

18. Another baby in the family makes my other children so happy.

19. I love to see the faces of my children as they see a new brother or sister for the first time.

20. Babies teach the older children so much about caring for little ones, being kind, protective, and unselfish.

21. Children brighten up the home. They make life interesting.

22. I become a better mother with each child I have.

23. Children teach me patience.

24. My children think I'm beautiful no matter how I look.

25. The more children we have, the more they entertain one another.

26. There's always someone around to visit with, play with, pray with, or read to.

27. It's just as easy to cook for ten as it is for one!

28. More children give us the opportunity to have our faith increased as we see God meet our daily needs.

29. You have your own cheering squad in whatever you do.

30. The more children we have, the more impact we have upon the world.

31. We want to establish a godly dynasty that will continue down the generations to come.

32. We want to raise another soul for Jesus.

33. We desire to raise up a standard for God in this evil day.

34. More children releases more of Christ in our home.

35. Because babies are the most irresistible treasures on earth.
36. There is nothing like a new baby in the house.
37. There is no occupation more rewarding than motherhood.
38. Because I am fulfilling the only career that is eternal! Every other career will be left behind when we leave this earth, but I can take my children with me into glory. My children are eternal souls who will live for ever.
39. Parenthood is investing in eternity.
40. Children are like arrows which we send to places where we will never be able to go.
41. We want to fill our quiver.
42. Because of the people who might be reached for Christ through this child.
43. I want to increase the 'salt' and 'light' proportion in the world!
44. We're forming our own orchestra to make music to the Lord.
45. Having and raising children aids in sanctification of us parents.
46. Having children helps to develop in us the godly character of servanthood.
47. My children help me surrender the selfish desires of my flesh.
48. Parenthood allows us to experience the kind of love our Heavenly Father has for us.
49. In an era when so many individuals condone the denial, or taking of life - we want to give life - for life is sacred.
50. We don't want to deprive our parents of their "crowning glory" (Proverbs 17:6). We want to bless them with grandchildren.
51. Our children are my teachers. I learn sweet things from them every day.
52. I'm replenishing the earth with godly seed.
53. I want to be obedient to God's Word to "Be fruitful and multiply."
54. My children are my friends and my brothers and sisters in the Lord. Now who can have too many of these?
55. I have a passionate love for babies.
56. I just love being a mother. I love being pregnant. I love giving birth and I love breastfeeding.
57. I love the sweet smiles, the delightful giggle, the soft baby to cuddle.
58. Jesus said that when we welcome a little child into our home and family we are actually welcoming Him. I don't want to spurn Jesus.
59. We want our children to have the riches of many relationships with brothers and sisters. When we are no longer living, our children will have each other for encouragement, fellowship and a sense of family.
60. The more children we have, the more our love is multiplied.
61. We still have an empty seat in our van, and we'd like to fill it!
62. Our children are all so wonderful, who could resist another one?
63. God says that children are a reward and we believe Him!
64. Children are the most precious gift of marriage.
65. We get lots of experience in sharing and communicating.
66. Children help me see my daily dependence on God for His wisdom and strength.
67. I love to feel a precious life within my womb.

68. Large families are FUN! And we love having fun.

69. In a large family, the children and teenagers don't want to go out to find entertainment because they are lonely and bored – there is already fun and entertainment at home. A new baby reminds me of how Jesus came into the world.

70. To be open to more children shows our present children that we love them. How can our children understand the love of God if we have the attitude that a certain number of children is too many?

71. More children help to grow the church.

72. I want to rear strong soldiers for the Lord.

73. I'll be able to spend eternity with my children.

74. My body was created for this purpose.

75. Family celebrations – birthdays, holidays and Christmas – are even more wonderful with a new baby in the house.

76. Hope for mankind is expressed in the miracle of a baby's birth. Wherever there is life, there is Hope.

77. Babies are sweet, cuddly, adorable and have so much potential. It's like planting seeds in a flower garden - a beautiful bouquet for the future.

78. There will be more people to pay for social security benefits.

79. I want to yield my womb as a living sacrifice to God.

80. To prevent menses and enjoy the nursing hormones of prolactin and oxytocin. My most enjoyable and peaceful times are during the absence of menses during pregnancy To give a sweet testimony to a lost world.

81. Babies remind us how wonderful and how creative our God is.

82. We are training a godly generation that will cover the earth with the Gospel and prepare the way for Jesus' return.

83. Younger children teach the older children how to be helpers. By the time they are old enough to be married and have children of their own, they'll be prepared for raising them.

84. I want another arrow for God's army.

85. I love to feel a precious new life moving within me.

86. I would hate to stand before God on Judgment Day and have to answer why I rejected the children He had ordained for our family.

87. Our children have taught me the value of relationships and the shallowness of the world's value system.

88. I trust God in all other areas of my life so I want to trust Him in the area of having children too.

89. It sure is nice to kiss and smell a little one again. Their scent is so sweet.

90. Babies are also a blessing to other people. They sure love to hold and cuddle mine. Since my siblings have stopped at two children per family, I want to supply them for my parents' and everyone else's pleasure.

91. Our horizon and interests are constantly widened. Each child is born with a different destiny upon his/her life. Each child has different gifts. As we encourage our children in their varied gifts we constantly learn new things ourselves. Our children will often take on ventures and interests that we would never have dreamed of. Parenthood is not confining, but enlarging.

92. Babies are future dish washers!
93. Babies are a lot more entertaining than TV.
94. We're helping to build the kingdom of God.
95. So I can buy cute baby and children's clothes, even if it's at yard sales.
96. I'll be able to spend eternity with my children.
97. Children teach me to become a servant, and that's what Jesus wants us to be. Jesus Himself said He came to serve rather than to be served.
98. To be convicted of sin and the need for repentance, as I observe my sinful nature in my children's sinful natures.
99. The more children we have, the more we will be blessed when we are older. Instead of being lonely, we will have many children and grandchildren around to entertain us, bless us and care for us.
100. Raising up a godly seed is laying up treasure in heaven.
101. Having children causes us to depend upon God moment by moment!

After reading all these wonderful reasons, wouldn't you like another baby?

* * *

This article is reprinted from, the study manual, *God's Vision for Families*.

GOD'S VISION FOR FAMILIES
What the Bible Says About Having Children
By Nancy Campbell

This manual goes into the Word of God to see what God says about having children. How many should we have? Does the Bible have anything to say on this subject? Order the manual to check out. You'll get lots of surprises. Every married couple needs to study this manual together. It also has questions for personal meditation or group discussion at the end of each chapter.

Unliberating Women

WESTERN STANDARD, February 13, 2006
Christian News, November 28, 2005

We've spent 30 years convincing women that having kids isn't a priority. It's too late to tell them we've changed our minds

The government of France has launched what can only be described as a "frantic appeal" to women to have more children. It was careful, however, not to phrase it quite this way. "We must do more to allow French families to have as many children as they want," said the prime minister. The problem, as he well knows, is that too many French women do not "want" to have any children, or perhaps just one. Since stabilizing the population requires that couples produce an average of 2.1 children, France has a problem.

Not just France has a population problem, says a spokesman for the Institute for Population Development in Berlin. All Western Europe is facing a "real crisis." Its average birthrate is 1.5 children per family, with Italy, Spain and Germany at 1.3. REAL Women of Canada reports that Asia is even worse off, with the Japanese rate at 1.28, Taiwan's at 1.22, and South Korea's at 1.19. The Canadian rate, about 1.5, is the lowest in history. The U.S. rate, due chiefly to Hispanic immigration, much of it illegal, is holding at just above 2.

But for France, the problem is particularly dangerous. True, the national birthrate is 1.9, far above the European average. But that's because of France's Muslim ghettoes, where families of five and six children are not uncommon. The problem is to persuade native-born French women to produce native-born French kids.

So now France fervidly advances the ideal of the three-child family. The government will donate $1,176 when a third child is born, pay an additional $1,060 a month for a year, plus the $164 a month paid for the first two children. Tax deductions will be doubled for a third child. Railway fares will be cut 75 percent for the three-child family.

Will this solve the problem? It will not—no more than the please-have-kids programs advanced by Quebec are solving it, or prior programs advanced in France. It will fail for three reasons:

First, no amount of money can adequately compensate a woman for the burdens imposed by a multi-child family. Even with a helpful husband, it involves a 16-hour workday and a seven-day work week for years on end. If any employer demanded this, he could be jailed. Why anyone would want to become a mother is baffling, were it not for a single mysterious factor. It seems to be a matter of instinctive need, a sense of human responsibility, of purpose in life—or even a love for children, particularly those she brings into the world herself. How could a man know?

Which raises the second explanation. Governments all over the western world, and particularly the idiotic ones we've had in this country, have spent the past 30 years using every device of propaganda to rid women of this instinct. They must have careers, women were told, always with the innuendo – often bluntly stated—that a life largely spent raising little kids was a life wasted. They must achieve independence, something children, by their very existence, destroy. They must assume the "important roles' in society, meaning that "mere motherhood" is a retreat into "unimportance."

"The enemy of the 'liberated' woman," said the particular woman I married (who raised six kids and had four of them in five years), "is not the man, it's the child."

Finally, we have "liberated" couples from the "holy deadlock" of lifetime marriage commitment. We have made divorce easy. We took away all the legislative support, which governments once provided to reinforce marital stability. We did it with the highest of motives. We always do everything, however insane, with the highest of motives. But in so doing, we sentenced women with three or more kids to a probable lifetime of poverty if the marriage failed, which is statistically ever more likely. So no, said the woman, she would not have children. Now we must suddenly reverse ourselves. We must tell her that everything we've been telling her for 30 years is mistaken. Motherhood was her vocation, after all. She will reject this, I think. She will conclude that we are being governed by lunatics. And you know, I believe she will be right.

Where Are Mothers?

TIME'S 100 Most Influential People In the World

Christian News, May 12, 2008

The cover of the May 12 *TIME* features *TIME*'s 2008 list of the 100 "Most Influential People in the World."
The list includes some women, but mentions nothing about their being mothers. Time's managing editor says in the May 12 *Time*: *"TIME's* 100" IS NOT A LIST of the smartest, the most powerful or the most talented – it is a thoughtful and sprightly survey of the most influential individuals in the world."
Ever since we began in 1962, CN has promoted the importance of motherhood and solid Christian families. CN has repeatedly said that the most influential women in the world have been the mothers of the great men in history.
Some 80 years ago Dr. Walter Maier noted in his *For Better Not For Worse – A Manual of Christian Matrimony*, a best seller which CPH has refused to reprint, that the "woman attains the highest ideals when, forsaking the roar of business, the mud slinging of politics, and the clash of other careers, she marries, settles down to make a home, proves herself a helpful wife, and cheerfully assumes the responsibilities and blessings of motherhood."
This is not to say, of course, that a God-fearing Christian woman, who has not been able to find a Christian man to marry, can not be a great and faithful servant in God's kingdom. When preaching a sermon on Mother's day, this pastor generally, in one way or another, attempts to make this clear.
Some of the many articles CN has published on motherhood, marriage and families are in the *Christian News Encyclopedia.* CN has repeatedly promoted *He Her Honor and She His Glory*, an excellent Christ-centered pre-marital and marriage counseling book. The May 12, 2008 Christian News has "Nailing Down Jello Or Replying to Mrs. Feminist's Mother's Day". Charles Provan responded to a leading LCMS promoter of allowing those who support women pastors to remain on the LCMS clergy roster. She defends the position on women taken by Voices-Vision, Jesus First, DayStar, David Benke and Jerry Kieschnick.

VII

THE
CHRISTIAN FAMILY

Luther on Marriage, Family, Children

Pastor Herman Otten,

Luther Today, What Would He Do Or Say? pp 43,44

Most of us are familiar with the high rate of divorce in America and throughout the world. Hundreds of books and scores of magazines are being published on the family, marriage and the raising of children. The White House has held conferences on the family. 1980 was designated as the "Year of the Family." All sorts of programs have been established by various churches to strengthen the family. A good number of pastors have even left the ministry to become full time marriage counselors. Some of these "marriage experts" haven't always followed what the Bible says about divorce in their own lives.

Christians have a tremendous heritage and guide for a successful marriage and family first of all in the Holy Scriptures. Next to the Holy Scriptures, one of the best sources for guidance for a sound marriage and Christian home can be found in the writings of Martin Luther. Read the 25 pages on marriage in Plass's anthology *What Luther Says*. What tremendous practical advice Luther offers. *Christian News* has sold many copies of *He Her Honor-She His Glory*, a book which promotes Luther's view of marriage. ($15.50)

Neelak Tjernagel, a Luther scholar, observes in "Luther Still Lives - In His Concept Of The Home":

The hospitality, the joy and the whole life of Luther and his family in their Wittenberg home illuminate his theology. He and his family had found salvation, not in what they could do for God, but what God, in Christ, had done for them. Their joy and gratitude for that great blessing led them to prayers and songs of joy, to love for others and generous hospitality to everyone in need. The picture and example of Luther's home remains an important legacy of the Lutheran Reformation. We remember it fondly in this 500th anniversary of his birth (1983).

A celebration of the 500th anniversary of Martin Luther's birth gives us an opportunity to recall many of the achievements and contributions of the great Reformer. Not least of these is the example of Christian life, especially as we see it in his home. The Black Cloister was to become a showcase of all the best characteristics of a Christian home. An endless stream of visitors came to see the great man. Kings and princes, lords and ladies, the strong and the weak, the rich and the poor, many of them unemployed, disabled, disconsolate; they all came away enriched and enlivened by the vicarious experience of Christian family life pulsing in the precincts of a defunct monastery.

What these visitors saw, first of all, was a man and woman who lived together, holding each other in high honor, each living as equal persons, each fulfilling joyfully the obligations and the responsibilities of their chosen roles. Few of the embellishments of romantic love were in evidence, for certainly they had not married out of the prompting of a love affair. Something deeper and more fulfilling developed between them as they grew in mutual esteem and dependence on one another. People were drawn to the Luther home out of respect and admiration for the German hero. They were immediately made aware of Katherine's role because, unlike the usual practice, Luther's wife was not kept out of the sight of visitors. Nor did Martin exclude her in discussions of theology and contemporary issues. Visitors found no atmosphere of gloom and austerity in the Cloister. It was a happy home enlivened by good humored banter as when Martin called Katherine his "rig," his "chain," the "boss," the "martyr of Wittenberg," and the "mistress of Zuehlsdorf," the farm they had bought to provision their home. Once when Luther was downcast and in a bad mood Katherine, asked him: "Is God Dead?"

The management of money and the family resources was beyond Luther's interest and capability. The generous hospitality shown to visitors at the Cloister would have been impossible without Katherine's shrewd business sense and managerial skill.

A remarkable feature of life at the Black Cloister was the fact that Martin and Katherine actually lived, and even ate, with their children. They were not, as was the case in most homes of families of substance, exiled to the care of servants and nannies. The children, and all the members of that large household, played games, sang together, and enjoyed many other forms of merriment. Joyful laughter was the characteristic of a house that had formerly seen the long faces of the monks who had lived their solemn and quiet lives within its confines. (Lutheran Sentinel, May 1983)

Luther stressed the importance of family worship. Today we can't overemphasize the importance of family devotions, Bible reading, hymn singing and good conversation in the home on theological, political and social issues. Consider the wealth of information in Luther's Table Talks. The talk that goes on in Christian homes should be more than just about the weather and sports.

The *Lutheran Witness* noted:

"Do statistics tell anything? Consider the following from the U.S. Census Bureau as noted in the March 24, 1980 Marriage and Divorce:

Although nationally one out of three marriages currently ends in divorce, those who have church weddings and attend church regularly beat the odds by one in 50. But for couples who have married in the church, attend regularly and have family worship, only one in 1,105 ends in divorce." *Lutheran Witness* January, 1951.

The Break Up of the Family

By Haven Bradford Gow
Christian News Encyclopedia, p. 3844

Rutgers University scholar David Popenoe points out that "during the past 25 years, family decline in the U.S., as in other industrialized societies, has been both steeper and more alarming than during any other quarter-century in our history... Today's societal trends are bringing to a close the cultural dominance of the traditional nuclear family – one situated apart from both the larger kin group and the workplace, and focused on procreation. It consists of a legal, lifelong, sexually exclusive, heterosexual, monogamous marriage, based on affection and companionship in which there is a sharp division of labor (separate spheres), with the female as full-time housewife and the male as primary provider and ultimate authority."

Dr. Popenoe adds: "During its heyday, the terms family, home, and mother ranked extraordinarily high in the hierarchy of cultural values."

Dr. David Popenoe's observations are buttressed by a new study from the U.S. Census Bureau, which reveals that the traditional family is in decline, with a decrease in households headed by married couples and an increase in the number of families headed by women without husbands.

In 1970, 87 per cent of all family households in the United States were headed by married couples; by 1990, the number had decreased to 79 percent.

In 1970, 5.5 million households were headed by women without husbands; by 1990, the number had doubled to 10.9 million.

How pervasive is the breakdown of the traditional family? To answer that agonizing question, we must reflect on the following statistics:

1. Divorce is widespread: From 1901 to 1987 divorce increased more than 700 percent in this nation. One in 3 first marriages now culminates in divorce.

2. Twenty-five million children return from school to a home with no parents around to provide love, care and guidance; the parents are at work or out socializing.

3. One in 5 babies is born out of wedlock, an increase of 50 percent during the past decade.

4. There was a 157 percent increase in unmarried people living together during 1970 to 1980.

5. Each year 2.5 million children are the victims of domestic violence.

6. Twenty million children live with at least one parent addicted to alcohol.

7. More than one million children run away from home each year.

8. More than 25 percent of all children in the United States now live in a single-parent household.

According to Dr. Malcolm Hill, president of Tennessee Bible College, the breakdown of the traditional family results from their rejection of orthodox Judeo-Christian morality: "Years ago, moral principles and high ethical standards were taught. Our Founding Fathers came to this country for religious freedom and to build a nation based on God and the Bible. The books they used for learning were geared to high moral principles and Biblical ethics. The first-grade readers had to do with honesty, right-dealing, purity of life, the sanctity of the home, the world God made, and many other principles taught in the Bible."

Unhappily, we find today that "Secular humanists, atheists, agnostics, evolutionists, and vain philosophers have led our youth down the road to despair. Our young people have been taught - and still are being taught - that they are nothing more than glorified apes. They have been told that there is no set standard for right and wrong."

The repudiation of extra-personal and extra-legal moral standards has contributed to pernicious personal and social consequences: "Crime is at an all-time high, families are falling apart, and cheating and underhanded dealings seem to be the American way of life. Immoral sex activity is no longer clearly wrong, but a matter of the way one views the situation. The movies show our young people how to murder, drink, use drugs, and be sexually impure, as well as how to lie, steal, rob, and use a gun. This thinking is channeled into the living rooms across this nation. What is its influence on our society? All one has to do is look around. Wrong is no longer wrong and right is no longer right."

America's moral and spiritual crisis consists not simply in widespread transgressions but also in the repudiation of extra-personal and extra-legal moral standards. We always have had violations of traditional Judaic-Christian moral standards, but until today, the standards themselves were not seriously questioned.

Clearly, America is suffering from moral and spiritual disorder. And the only way to rectify this tragic state of affairs is through a resuscitation of religious faith and commitment. Confucius said it this way: "if there is righteousness in the heart, there will be beauty in the character; if there is beauty in the character, there is harmony in the home; if there is harmony in the homes, there will be order in the nation; when there is peace in the nation, there will be peace in the world."

Christian News Encyclopedia, p. 3844.

Consider the Landon Story

Ten Boys in the Armed Forces
Christian News, February 28, 1988

The Landon name is French Huguenot in origin. The French Huguenots were expelled from their native land to find life in Protestant countries where 'new birth' did not mean 'death.' Even in these Protestant countries difficulties arose between creeds as Protestant desired to rule Protestant, so the Landon name came to America. It is here the free exercise of religion gave new birth to life and freedom. My grandfather, Delbert, and my grandmother, Minta, passed the Protestant heritage to my father, Wilton, who joined the ranks of Gnesio Lutheranism (the results of an LCMS clergyman and his witness). Now, I am a member at Prince of Peace – WELS, 530 McNaughten Road, Columbus Ohio 43213 where the heritage continues and the faith is passed on to others.

When birth control and abortion, interfaith marriage and fellowship, and doctrine and life are no longer issues, consider The Landon Story and remember where you read it. There is no finer PRINT in the English speaking world based on FACT than CHRISTIAN NEWS.

A Lutheran for Life,
Michael Landon

Editor's note: The Landon family received special recognition from the President of the U.S. for giving 10 sons to the U.S. Armed Forces in WWII. Gerald was killed in Germany. The following story appeared in the *Columbus Dispatch* and the *Marysville Journal Tribune* in 1937.

* * *

If you think you have a long list of Christmas gifts to buy, consider the list of Mr. and Mrs. Delbert E. Landon of Broadway.

Mr. and Mrs. Landon have seventeen children. As a matter of fact, had the Landons resided in Ontario they would have shared in the $500,000 prize offered for the largest number of babies born within a period specified in a will.

Although there have been many mouths to feed and much clothing to buy, Mr. Landon has never accepted any public assistance. Even in good times it is a problem to raise a family of that size, but Mr. and Mrs. Landon have met financial needs in good times and bad through their own efforts.

The children not only have a heritage of parents who overcome all obstacles by their industry, but the family is one of the healthiest in the state.

Dr. E.J. Marsh, general physician of Broadway, must take a bow along with the Landons. He is believed to have set an Ohio record by attending at the birth of fourteen consecutive children of the family.

Mr. and Mrs. Landon were married in January, 1915. There have been eighteen children born to them and only a twin has died.

Of the 17 living children, 16 are at home and the eldest, Mrs. John M. Schafer, lives at 151 Highland Avenue, Columbus.

The family of 18 persons lives in a six-room home in Broadway, and comprises about 6 per cent of the village population. The Landons own their home.

Father Drives Bus

Mr. Landon, age 44, has always made a living for his expanding family, mostly by working as a farmhand until recent years, when he bought a school bus on time, paid for it, and through the school year earns from $65 to $85 per month transporting children to Taylor rural school in Broadway. Incidentally, 10 of his own children are in this school, but don't have to use the bus.

Before school, after the morning trip and after the evening trip, Mr. Landon most likely will be found working in the village or at some nearby farm, doing any kind of task demanded of him.

Bakes Daily

The mother, now 43 years old, is said by I.C. Plummer, chief of the Ohio bureau of vital statistics, to be probably the youngest mother of 17 living children in the United States. Every week day and Sunday, Mrs. Landon bakes eight large loaves of bread, and every Monday, Wednesday and Friday she washes clothes, regardless of the weather. Only in the last year has she had an electric washer; before that she labored by hand at the washtubs.

Mr. Landon is thoroughly individualistic and proud of his independence. Even in the depths of the depression and ever since, he has spurned all offers of relief, be it from township, county, state or federal sources. Surplus commodities also were rejected. Landon said he could take care of his own, and he did.

Free of Sickness

In Broadway and the surrounding countryside the Landons are well known and respected. Many farmers and business men have advanced credit or cash to help Mr. Landon get ahead. They always are paid, either in work or money. Mr. Landon is in demand among farmers to supervise or assist in the fall butchering.

"The family has been remarkably free from sickness in the 15 years I have been their physician," says Dr. March. "Nothing serious in all that time. Doctors all over Ohio and the state department of health have been intensely interested in this family, and I don't blame them. Of the 14 births I attended, one was dead on arrival. The other 13 were bottle babies which is unusual."

Teeth Perfect

Dr. Homer C. Brown, chief of the division of dental hygiene of the Ohio state department of health, personally made a check of the children's teeth, and said 14 of 16 had practically perfect teeth. He found only one cavity in 16 mouths.

Dr. Shong Rothermund of the state department made a physical examination of the children prior to the arrival of the latest baby a year ago and declared he found only one defect, and that one was on Paul Lynn, twin of the child that was stillborn.

Two children, Robert Lee, age 18, and Wilton Allen, age 17, were born while the family lived at Marion, and the rest arrived while the family lived in Union County, in or near Broadway.

Visits of the stork to the Landon home in the 22 years of their married life have fallen only a little short of being annual. Birth dates show arrivals in 1915, 1917, 1919, and then one baby each year until 1930 with the exception of 1928. The twins arrived in 1930, and more came singly each year through 1936.

Pastors and Laymen Need Role Models for
Establishing Christian Homes

Father and Mother of 1992

Christian News, June 1, 1992

Comments made by Vice-President Dan Quayle (CN, May 24, p. 19) about TV sitcom character Murphy Brown contributing to the deterioration of American family values by glamorizing illegitimacy have received widespread publicity. "DAN RIPS MURPHY BROWN" was the full-page headline of the *New York Post*. The full-page headline of the *New York Daily News* was: 'QUAYLE TO MURPHY BROWN: YOU TRAMP! Veep: TV's unwed mom symbol of U.S. woes."

The Vice-President is correct. TV has contributed to the deterioration of American family values. Some 40 million are estimated to be watching Murphy Brown every Monday evening. *Christian News* has often published statistics showing how far our nation's youth and adults have departed from the standards God sets forth in His Word, Holy Scripture. Already thirty years ago we noted that situation ethics and the new morality, which is really the old immorality, promoted by liberal churchmen, would help lead to the downfall of our nation. The divorce rate and the rate of youth and adults who condone and practice sex outside of marriage, illegitimacy, abortion, homosexuality, etc. keep climbing. CN has regularly said Americans would be much better off if they watched less TV.

"In Defense of a Little Virginity," a full page advertisement in the May 21 *Washington Times* by "Focus on the Family" says that "The federal government has spent almost $3 billion of our taxes since 1970 to promote contraceptives and 'safe sex' among our teenagers. Isn't it time we asked, what have we gotten for our money? These are the facts: . . ." The ad in the *Washington Times* then lists statistics showing the tremendous rate of growth of sexually transmitted diseases.

The ad rightly says that "There is only one safe way to remain healthy in the midst of a sexual revolution. It is to abstain from intercourse until marriage, and then marry and be faithful to an uninfected partner. It is a concept that was widely endorsed in society until the 1960s. Since then, a 'better idea' has come along . . . one that now threatens the entire human family."

Many clergyman act like wimps when it comes to speaking out in plain language against immorality as did God's prophets of old. They promote the "better idea" of condoms.

Thousands of churchmen find it difficult to condemn immorality and champion God's standards because their own homes and values have disintegrated. Their children do not set a good Christian example and many have even departed from the Christian faith.

Clergy divorce in most denominations continues to rise. The press has been filled with all sorts of stories about clergy divorce, sex pervertion and homosexuality among the clergy. Even the leaders of such conservative denominations as The Lutheran Church-Missouri Synod in recent months have been exposed as covering up some flagrant cases of immorality. Pastors guilty of adultery and sex perversion have been kept on the clergy roster.

When the Lutheran Church-Missouri Synod several years ago held a national youth convention in Washington, D.C., we suggested that instead of inviting some prominent liberals and feminists, the LCMS leaders responsible for the youth program should invite a full-time mother and homemaker like Mrs. Robert Preus, to speak to the LCMS youth, particularly the girls. Our Christian young women should be shown that their highest calling is still being a mother and homemaker. There is nothing wrong with having babies within marriage. Girls need a role model such as Mrs. Preus, the mother of ten and soon to be the grandmother of 44. They don't need as role models most Hollywood actresses, who may have been divorced or had babies out of wedlock, or some ranting feminists constantly griping about inequality and the lack of women's rights in the U.S.

It should be noted, of coarse, that God does not bless every woman with a husband, or a man with a wife, or parents with children. Throughout history single men and women, such as the Apostle Paul, have been great Christian heroes and fine Christian role models.

Comments we made about Dr. Preus when he was removed, primarily because of LCMS President Ralph Bohlmann's long vendetta vs. Preus, were in an editorial, "The Preus Record," appearing in our special "PREUS SACKED" issue of CN. There we noted that one of the most important contributions the Preuses made to the future clergy of the LCMS was the example they set as a father and mother. This is why we have nominated them as "FATHER AND MOTHER OF THE YEAR." No home is perfect, but the homes of far too many pastors, professors and church officials have not been very good examples for future pastors to follow.

What a tragedy it is that LCMS President Bohlmann and all five of his vice-presidents have spent hundreds of hours and hundreds of thousands of dollars to remove Dr. Preus from the LCMS, accusing him of impenitence of sin, being a liar, and guilty of unchristian conduct. Dr. Preus is not only one of the greatest confessional theologians of the last 30 years, but the Christian home life and devotional life he and Mrs. Preus have led all these years show that they well deserve a FATHER AND MOTHER OF THE YEAR AWARD in the same year the LCMS president and vice-presidents have been able to get the membership of Dr. Preus in the LCMS terminated.

We became acquainted with the older Preus children when Dr. Preus invited us to his home for dinner in 1957, the year he began teaching at Concordia Seminary, St. Louis. Daniel, the oldest child, was about eight at the time. We were impressed how Daniel and the other children could sing solid Lutheran chorales at devotions following dinner. Since then Pastor Daniel Preus has written a few hymns and poems. The LCMS could use as one of its vice-presidents a young experienced pastor, who is not only a confessional theologian like his father, but who also recognizes the importance of solid family life for all the homes of the LCMS.

Years ago the LCMS took the lead among U.S. denominations in emphasizing the importance of solid Christian homes, home devotions, the sanctity of the marriage vow, and moral purity among both youth and adults. Anyone who doubts this should read the Walther League Messenger during the years that it was edited by Dr. Walter Maier Sr. Read Maier's *For Better Not for Worse*, Fritz's *Pastoral Theology*, and the LCMS's official publications during the early decades of this century. Families, such as the Preus', were featured and promoted in the *Walther League Messenger*, the LCMS's youth publication. The time has again come when LCMS official publications should be pleading in no uncertain terms for a return to God's standards of morality, particularly for our youth. CN invites the LCMS's *Lutheran Witness* to nominate Dr. and Mrs. Robert Preus as FATHER AND MOTHER OF THE YEAR. If the charges of President Bohlmann and his vice-presidents are shown to be false and Dr. Preus again becomes a member of the LCMS, the *Lutheran Witness* should not listen to what President Bohlmann says about nominating Dr. and Mrs. Preus as FATHER AND MOTHER OF THE YEAR.

An Honor to Honor Our Father and Mother
By Pastor Daniel Preus

Our Father in Heaven who made us,
Who gave to us each life and breath,
Throughout all our life has sustained us.
Preserved us from harm and from death.
His kindness can hardly be uttered;
The blessings which come from His hand
So exceed all the needs of His children
In ways we cannot understand,
That as we consider His favor,
We look for a way to express
Our hearts' deepest thanks and devotion
To Him Who His children does bless.

So we praise Him for father and mother
For through them He has given us life.
Through them He has clothed and protected
And spared us from trouble and strife.
Through them He has guided and led us
Toward a glorious future that's sure
As they showed to us Jesus, the Savior,
Son of God on the cross to endure
All our guilt and our shame and transgression
Our sorrows and griefs as His own
That we, by His great intercessions,
As the children of God might be known.

Our Savior has graciously told us,
"The righteous shall shine as the sun."

What joy to a father and mother
Whose family and home were begun
In the name of the Father who loves us,
His Son who has given us life,
The Spirit who comforts and leads us
In the midst of all sorrow and strife,–
What joy to you, Father and Mother
To know that your children shall be,
Like the sun in the heavens above us
Shining eternally!

"Honor your father and mother,"
The law of our Lord does command.
"Honor your father and mother"
And you shall live long in the land.
Should such a commandment distress us
Or cause us to fret and complain?
Should such an injunction cause anger,
Make us grumble in bitter disdain?
No, to honor our father and mother
Is an honor for children who know
Christian parents as one of the greatest
Of treasures our God can bestow.

To Mom and Dad on Mother's Day, 1990
–By Daniel Preus

The Profession of Motherhood—
Rolf Preus Makes Good Sense
"Have More Children"
Christian News, April 14, 1997

The lead story in this week's special issue on families reports on the recent World Congress of Families held in the Czech Republic. Neither the secular nor religious press have given the congress the publicity it deserves.

CN is using its extremely limited means to send this issue to just about every church in the Lutheran Church-Missouri Synod, the Wisconsin Evangelical Lutheran Synod, and the Evangelical Lutheran Synod because of the excellent Declaration on Families of the World Congress of Families. It is our hope and prayer that it will at least persuade Lutheran pastors and teachers to have more children and encourage young married couples in their congregations to have more children. The fine statement on families in this book by LCMS President A. L. Barry adds some important Christian emphases to the Declaration.

"World Congress of Families Launches Counterrevolution," a report on the Congress in the conservative Roman Catholic April 3 *Wanderer* concluded: "Perhaps from among all the descriptions of any prescriptions for the state of the family today offered by the 61 speakers, the best and simplest (and simplicity is paradoxically complex) was offered by Dr. Margaret Ogola, a pediatrician from Kenya, who said, 'Have more children.'"

The declaration adopted by the congress noted that "there is no profession that has a higher status than motherhood."

The program of the congress listing the 61 speakers notes how many children each one has. One has nine, two have eight and several have seven. None have as many as the 12 of Pastor and Mrs. Rolf Preus, the author of "And God Blessed Them. . .", or the 18 of Pastor and Mrs. John Parcher. Pastor Parcher has contributed articles to CN for some ten years.

An article by Charles Provan, "The Bible and Birth Control", in the *Christian News Encyclopedia*, pp. 1889-1896, includes the pictures of some families: The Charles Provan family, 4 at the time, but next month expecting number 9; the Dr. Robert Taylor family of 7 children; the family of Dr. and Mrs. Robert Preus of 10 children and now about 45 grandchildren; the Harold Juergen family of 10 children; the family of Pastor and Mrs. Adelbert Oesch of 11 children; the Peter Prange family of 9 children; the Larry Marquardt family of 12 children; the Paul Lehenbauer family of 6 children; the Gene Oesch family of 6 children; the Gerald Otte family of 6 children; the Herman Otten family of 7 children; the John Parcher family of 18 children; and the Delbert Landon family of 18 children.

Decades ago the Lutheran Church-Missouri Synod's *Walther League Messenger* published the family photos of large families in order to encourage young couples to have more children.

Of course, God does not bless all couples the same way. Some of our fine Christian youth are never even able to get married. God blesses them and uses them in other ways in His kingdom.

Unfortunately, many church couples are too self-centered to have many children. They claim they cannot afford children.

Pastor Rolf Preus writes: "Dort and I discovered a couple of years ago that we couldn't afford 12 kids. Thank God we already had them! Otherwise, the things that money can buy would have taken the place of children. Our youngest son, Peter, who will be two on May 31, is more valuable than whatever money it costs us to feed him, clothe him, house him, etc."

Preus says that no one is more amazed than he and his wife that they have 12 children. He writes: "You see, we didn't plan a single one. We didn't choose to have children. We didn't 'let' God give us children, as if he needs our permission. We simply got married."

CN knows of some missionary families who were paid only a few hundred dollars a year and yet had many children.

Grace and I and thousands of other Lutheran pastors and laymen in the past had the same attitude as Rolf and Dort Preus. We simply got married and didn't plan just when and how many children we wanted. When Grace had to give up being a deaconess in Iowa when she moved to Missouri after the wedding, we simply took for granted that we would get by on my $250 a month salary. She would be the homemaker. She did teach for a year when a teacher in our local school had to resign in the middle of a school year and no substitute could be found. Of course, she also spent many volunteer hours in the office of *Christian News*, which was in our home, mailing out *Christian News* and taking care of the business end of the paper she helped begin.

When Grace did not get pregnant after three years, we started making plans to adopt a Native American child. Then seven children came in ten years. She did the best she could from the salary I received from a small, poor congregation which could not even afford medical and hospital insurance until our fourth child. Much of the clothing was used. Sometimes the children still mention how they had to carefully swallow the whole grain wheat soup or the beet soup from mom's garden. She butchered old leghorn chickens she bought for five cents a pound. There was no money for any vacation the first 16 years or funds for such "luxuries" as eating out, soda and beer, or a new or second car. The children called one car we bought for $300 an orchestra because of all the strange noises. About the only thing that worked properly was the cigarette lighter which we didn't need. Yet we were able to use that car for about a year to take care of congregational, CN, and family work.

One critic, who thought that certainly the editor of a weekly newspaper, the author of a book which had been printed in over 100,000 copies, must surely have a large income, was surprised to discover how frugally CN operated. The long distance phone calls at the time were only around $50 for an entire year. The editor wrote letters rather than phoning.

Many other pastors in the past had even less to live on and yet they never used poverty as a reason not to have children. Our family qualified for free school lunches but we wanted no government handouts.

CN hopes and prays that congregations all over the LCMS will present overtures to their district conventions this year or to the LCMS convention next year to adopt some statement on the family similar to the Declaration on Families of the World Congress of Families, adding the distinctive Christian and Lutheran emphasis in "What About Christian Families" by LCMS President A.L. Barry. It certainly would be more wholesome for any church body for its congregations and pastors to spend more time discussing the issues covered in the 'Declaration on Families of the World Congress of Families' than to waste so much time on relatively insignificant matters.

Some 30 years ago Trinity of New Haven, Missouri, petitioned the LCMS to reprint Dr. Walter Maier's *Manual on Christian Marriage, For Better Not For Worse*. It was a best seller at CPH. The excuse that the statistics are out of date is invalid. They could easily be updated by some confessional Lutheran theologian who is in accord with the principles Dr. Maier sets forth on marriage and the family. This issue of CN quotes from Maier's manual on marriage and the family. CN has sold hundreds of copies of *He Her Honour, She His Glory*, a book many consider to be the best book on Christian marriage published in recent years. It is available from *Christian News* for $15.50. The cost is fairly high since it has to be shipped from Australia. If CN had the funds, it would print it in this country and see that it was circulated in thousands of cities all over the U.S. With the ever rising rate of divorce, even among the clergy, including those who are considered conservatives, it is just the kind of book our churches and nation need.

The Christian News Encyclopedia includes some of the thousands of articles CN has published during the last 35 years on issues covered in A Declaration of the World Congress on Families. It's unfortunate few know CN exists.

P.S. Rolf, many had some doubts about your orthodoxy because of your smoking. At least you didn't pollute your home with that filthy smoke. We are glad that the "stubborn" boy is finally listening to his mother. Keep it up. She was right all along.

"Conservative and Confessional"
Do Not Have Too Many Children
Christian News, May 12, 1997

Normally I do not write letters to papers, etc., but I wanted to tell you how much I enjoyed your April 14, 1997, "*Christian News.*" The topics were varied, but the centering on the topic of children was important.

My wife and I have 5 wonderful children. Psalm 128 is true: "Your wife will be like a fruitful vine within your house; your sons (and daughters) will be like olive shoots around your table. Thus is the man blessed who fears the LORD." My wife and I see our 5 gifts from God not as a burden but as a blessing. Like Rolf and Dort Preus, Betsy and I are wealthy. I wouldn't change it for the world.

Yet, I find something disturbing in all of this. The world and the organized church often frown on those of us with many children. I expect this of the world, but the organized church? Those who feel the need to tell me they are "Conservative and confessional" in their faith are often the loudest in telling us we have too many children. Often my wife and I have tried to plan a social gathering in our pastoral circuit to include children. We are told quite bluntly that "children are not welcome!" "It is nice just to have the pastors and wives come to enjoy a quiet dinner," we are told. What about the pastor's children? Wouldn't they like to get together with other clergy children and just talk?

I find a disturbing trend in the organized church. Often people speak with words about their conservative and confessional faith – but there is very little living of this faith. Children, in the opinion of even some conservative Christians, are "expensive, loud, noisy, smelly, a hassle, etc." Have we lost sight that children are probably the most wonderful gift God can give us? What about the laughter, deep spiritual insights, companionship, love (real simple agape!), and the friendship children can bring? Sure they are noisy and loud–sure they smell at times – sure they make you tear your hair out at times! Guess what–so did we when we were children!

As far as expensive, yes, children are expensive. We held off for 17 years before my wife finally had to work outside the home. She does not have a college education, so "good" jobs are few. We are now like most American families and we miss home cooked meals, and Mom being there when the kids come home. I find it interesting that I have eight years of college and yet cannot afford to support my family. I work for the organized church. Districts have salary guides which are very helpful. But, have you noticed there is nothing in the salary guides to make local congregations think of pastors with large families? Rolf and Dort Preus mentioned in an earlier issue of "*Christian News*" that they are fortunate to have been able to allow Dort to stay at home. I can only figure out this means they have had congregations paying salaries which allow them to do this. Most do not. Most will say, "Well, you didn't have to have 5 kids."

We have had invitations from Christian people to events (weddings, district or circuit happenings, etc.) where the invitation themselves state that children are not included in the invite. OK, this is not a problem, but then don't expect people who have children to come! Some Lutheran congregations (as in Arizona) do the same thing – letting people know that children are not welcome in their congregations. Some of these congregations do not even build their buildings with facilities for Sunday school, etc. "Let the little children come to me"?

I wish the organized church would practice what we confess. The world would see a much better example of what the Christian Faith is really all about. I guess, like the world, people in the church see success as having an important job, a title, or degrees attached to your name, a fancy house, car, boat, etc. I wonder if I will be a success in this world? I guess I will be if on that great Day of YHWH Elzbieta and the 5 children are standing next to me in the presence of our LORD.

Thank you for your issue of April 14. I enjoyed it.
In His Service,
Carl and Elzbieta Noble
Pastor, St. John's Ev. Lutheran Church, Lansing, IL

Opposing Cloning – Commending Barry and World Congress of Families

Missouri Church Asks LCMS to Adopt Lutheran Statement on Families

Christian News, April 14, 1997

Trinity Lutheran Church of New Haven, Missouri, is asking The Lutheran Church-Missouri Synod and the Missouri District to oppose the cloning of humans, to adopt a Lutheran statement on families, to commend "A Declaration on Families of the World Congress on Families" and LCMS

President A.L. Barry's "What About Christian Families?" Both documents are published below:
The New Haven, Missouri church on April 8 adopted this resolution:

A Declaration on Families

Whereas, Reports of cloning sheep, monkeys and possibly human beings, have filled the media; and

Whereas, The Bible teaches that the Holy Trinity, the only true God, is the creator of all; and

Whereas, A "Declaration on Families of the World Congress of Families" which met March 19-22 in the Czech Republic (report in the April 14 , 1997 *Christian News*), noted in part:

1. "Marxist and totalitarian regimes have intruded into and diminished family life interfering with its normal operation and functions."

2. "In many democratic countries, cultural revolutions, materialism and sexual permissiveness have resulted in a destruction and denigration of moral values, thereby producing hedonistic societies in which extramarital relationships, adultery and divorce proliferate, leading to widespread abortion, illegitimacy and single parent children."

3. "Many methods of reproduction biotechnology, such as gene manipulation, in vitro fertilization and cloning can threaten marriage, the family morality and religion."

4. "WE DECLARE that communities in harmony with human nature exhibit common traits in custom and law that include:

–Recognition of religion as a common, necessary foundation of family life;

–Affirmation of marriage as a lifelong covenant between a man and a woman and the only legitimate province for sexual intimacy;

–Recognition that there is no calling that has a higher status than motherhood;

–Encouragement of the extended family as a source of added security and continuity for humanity;

–Celebration of conception and birth of children;

–Welcome of large families;

–Respect for the dignity of human life from conception to natural death;

–Respect for the distinctive traits of manhood and womanhood as biologically determined and not as socially constructed;

–Respect for the right of families to ownership of private property, productive land, shelter and capital."

Whereas, Lutheran Church-Missouri Synod President A.L. Barry recently sent to the congregations of the LCMS a pamphlet in which he says that "One of the most important things a family can do is spend time together in the Word of God."

"Key ingredients for the family's devotional time are the Scriptures, the hymnal and the Small Catechism. These are excellent resources for meaningful time together in the Word of God.

"Parents should begin reading and reciting the chief parts of the Small

Catechism with their children when they are very young, helping them learn the Lord's Prayer, the Ten Commandments and the Apostles' Creed, and then working on the explanations, building as time goes on.

"Parents need to discuss their faith with their children, pray with them and encourage their children in love to do what is right, not hesitating to say 'no' when necessary. And always, parents will want to be for their children a model of the Heavenly Father's love in Christ Jesus our Lord"; therefore be it

Resolved, That Trinity Lutheran Church petition the 1997 convention of the Missouri District and the 1998 convention of the Lutheran Church-Missouri Synod to commend the Declaration of Families of the World Congress of Families and to adopt a Lutheran statement on families incorporating the fine Christian approach in President Barry's "What About Christian Families?"

Trinity Lutheran Church
New Haven, Missouri
President Rick Kloppe
Pastor Herman Otten
Adopted at Voters' Meeting
April 8, 1997

*See "No Cloning Around" by Dr. John Drickamer, *Christian News*, March 17, 1997, and "Cloning Body and Soul" by Pastor Jack Cascione, *Christian News*, March 321, 1997.

Declaration on Families of the World Congress of Families

Christian News, April 14, 1997

WHEREAS, we the delegates at this World Congress of Families place our trust in God and His guidance in our deliberations; and

WHEREAS, the delegates at this Congress have come together from all parts of the globe recognizing the present profound world crisis as is demonstrated by the decline of families in many countries both as the prime social unit and as the greatest contributor to the well-being, stability and moral values in those countries; and

WHEREAS, Marxist and totalitarian regimes have intruded into and diminished family life, preventing its normal operation and functions; and

WHEREAS, in many democratic countries, cultural revolutions, materialism and sexual permissiveness have resulted in a destruction and denigration of moral values, thereby producing hedonistic societies in which extra-marital relationships, adultery and divorce proliferate, leading to widespread abortion, illegitimacy and single-parent children; and

WHEREAS, the United Nations, its N.G.O.s and agents, have pursued dangerous philosophies and policies that require population control, limitation of family size, abortion on demand, sterilization of men and women and have sought to persuade Third World countries to adopt such policies; and

WHEREAS, this world crisis now involves well-recognized demographic implosions which, if unchecked, will ultimately lead to the extinction of entire nations and their cultures; and

WHEREAS, those policies of Marxism, neo-Marxism, totalitarian welfare states and economic consumer capitalism which have forced mothers into the work force, have thereby deprived children of the proper benefits of full and continuous maternal care; and

WHEREAS, the structures and family policies of modern societies (including their taxation systems) tend to weaken family life and discriminate against large families; and

WHEREAS, we recognize and pay tribute to those developing nations which, despite poverty and economic hardship, have retained strong family-centered systems; and

WHEREAS, we, the delegates at this Congress, realize that the need to confront these problems has become a matter of extreme urgency; therefore

WE DECLARE, the family to be a man and a woman bound in a lifelong covenant of marriage, as ordained by God, for the purpose of (1) providing support, protection, love and companionship for both husband and wife; (2) satisfying of male-female sexuality; (3) welcoming and nurturing of children; and (4) the continuation of the human race; and

WE DECLARE, the natural family holds fixed characteristics rooted in human nature. The complementary nature of men and women is rooted in the psychological and physical differences between the sexes. The love of parents for their children, also rooted in human nature, uniquely qualifies parents to rear their own young. Children, for their part, innately long for a direct bond with their parents in whom they place their trust. Parents and their children constitute a unique natural community that is necessary to human spiritual, moral and intellectual development; and

WE DECLARE, that the family is the first social unit, and it holds primacy over all manmade communities, economic entities and governments; and

WE DECLARE, that the family is the most important of all social units and holds primacy above all governments, institutions, the United Nations and other communities and that political theories and systems which place governments, their officials, institutions, or other communities in a position of supremacy over the family are to be condemned and opposed. The Universal Declaration of Human Rights of 1948 (and Amendments) recognize as inviolable the rights of families, parents and children to protection from state intrusion; and

WE DECLARE, that all political theories and systems which elevate "the state" or a social class or "the collective will" to a position of supremacy are to be deplored and condemned; and

WE DECLARE, that those philosophies which elevate the abstract "individual," thereby encouraging social fragmentation, are to be deplored. Radical individualism, often thought to expand liberty, has instead resulted in the consequent loss of liberty; and

WE DECLARE, that many methods of reproductive bio-technology, such as gene manipulation, in vitro fertilization and cloning, can threaten marriage, the family, morality and religion; and

WE DECLARE, that policies which undermine the family erode the bedrock of society, thereby undermining the very source of their own authority. Such policies include:
- Subverting the legal and religious status of traditional marriage;
- Using population control and abortion as a vehicle of state policy for any social, economic, political or other reason;
- Establishing policies that create gender or generational war, setting husband against wife, wife against husband or child(ren) against parent(s);
- Maintaining state school systems that focus education on state ends and neglect or oppose parental rights and re sponsibilities;
- Providing state welfare systems that undermine intact families, discourage the presence of fathers and impose coercive tax policies that force both parents to work full time outside the home;
- Funding and promoting contraception, abortifacients and sterilization programs that promote immoral behavior;
- Funding or promoting sex education/indoctrination programs that have been shown to increase promiscuity, sexually-transmitted disease, unwanted pregnancy, illegitimacy and teenage pregnancy;
- Creating state policies that give encouragement to non-marital cohabitation, homosexual unions and single parent ing as the norm in society.

WE DECLARE, that communities in harmony with human nature exhibit common traits in custom and law that include:
- Recognition of religion as a common, necessary foundation of family life;
- Affirmation of marriage as a lifelong covenant between a man and woman and the only legitimate province for sexual intimacy;
- Recognition that there is no profession that has a higher status than motherhood;
- Encouragement of the extended family as a source of added security and continuity for humanity;
- Celebration of the conception and birth of children;
- Welcome of large families;
- Respect for the dignity of human life from conception to natural death;

- Respect for the distinctive traits of manhood and womanhood as biologically determined and not as socially constructed;
- Respect for the right of families to ownership of private property, productive land, shelter and capital;
- Encouragement for family businesses and enterprises without interference or state intrusion;
- Recognition that husband and wife have the sole responsibility for deciding the size of their family using non-abortifacient, natural and morally acceptable family planning;
- Recognition that a fundamental biological need of infants and small children is the full attention of their mothers with fathers also sharing parental responsibilities;
- Encouragement of an economic climate and taxation policies in which the family wage may prevail; thereby allowing parents, especially mothers, to take full care of their children;
- Recognition of the social value of marriage and the value of the presence of dependent children and aged parents in the home;
- Proscriptions against the commercialization of sexuality and the promotion of promiscuity and pornography.

WE DECLARE, that there is eternal hope arising for the knowledge that the destruction of human family relationships can never be complete; that love and mutual aid between family members are among the strongest of innate human motives and spring up in each generation; and that, while many persons in our age have been confused or misled, we can yet celebrate that so many yearn for the restoration of the family to its central place in natural and loving communities.

TOWARDS THESE ENDS WE CALL on all governments and the United Nations to promote policies supportive of the traditional family. We dedicate ourselves and our organizations to creating and sustaining communities that will protect and support family life. We pledge to establish ongoing structures of cooperation and communication that will defend the entity of the family and all its members in the millennium ahead.

This declaration was the work of a committee headed by Dr. Jean Garton (USA, member of the board of directors LCMS, and former president of Lutherans for Life. She is the author of *Who Broke the Baby* and has written and lectured widely on issues related to education, the family, and human life) and Charles Francis (Australia, former member of the Victorian State Parliament, lecturer and trial lawyer), with the advice and contribution of the delegates.

World Congress on Families

By Sarah Boniek Bachmann
Waldistrasse 41
8134 Adliswil, Switzerland

Christian News, April 14, 1997

"How many legs would a dog have," asked Mr. Lincoln, "If you called his tail a leg, too?" The man he addressed answered, "Five, of course," to which Mr. Lincoln replied, "No! Calling it thus, does not make it so."

This pertinent exchange was reported by Professor Lynn Wardle in his address to the recent World Congress of Families as he spoke on the topic of legal claims for same-sex marriage being a departure from true marriage. Professor Wardle was one of more than 50 prominent advocates of the importance of Family who addressed hundreds of delegates from around the globe. They were gathered to discuss ways to restore the institution of Family as central to societal, governmental and individual wellbeing.

The World Congress of Families met in Prague in the Czech Republic on March 20-22, 1997. The idea of the Congress was born a few years ago in a meeting between Dr. Allan Carlson, president of the Rockford Institute on American Culture in Illinois, and Ivan Schevchenko, a Russian philosopher, artist and musician laboring on behalf of the natural family and the unborn child. With the support of various individuals and organizations, their vision took form, until they assembled more than a dozen family-oriented organizations from six continents to contribute their wisdom and insights to the Congress. These organizations included, besides the Rockford Institute, Alianza Latinoamericana para la Familia, The Australian Family Association, The Chesterton Institute of Canada, The Civic Institute of the Czech Republic, The Family Center of Croatia, the Family Research Council of the USA, the Orthodox Brotherhood of Scientists and Specialists of Russia, Verein zu Foerderung der psychologischen Menschenkenntnis of Switzerland, and the World Association for Family and Education of Mexico, and others.

The aim of the congress was to set forth an honest definition of Family, and to address the problems facing the institution of Family with workable solutions, not only at the family level but also in the realm of national and international policy. The congress especially wanted to counterbalance the proclamations and aims of the United Nations' conventions. The definition of Family as set forth by the Congress is "a man and a woman bound in a lifelong covenant of marriage for the purpose of the continuation of the human species, the rearing of children, the regulation of sexuality, the provision of mutual support and protection, the creation of an altruistic domestic economy, and the maintenance of bonds between the generations."

The Family Should See America
Christian News, August 5, 2002

After the editor's first year at Concordia Seminary, St. Louis, his father took our entire family to Europe. We were gone 3 ½ months. The trip took 10 days each way. We slept in a crowded three-decked dormitory. These conditions did not bother us. During the day we had great fun all over the boat. Brother Walter and I biked through northern Germany and Holland on 50 cents a day for meals and a dormitory room in some youth hostel or under a hay rack in a field.

Later Dad let eight of us youth use the Volkswagen omnibus he had while in Europe in order to travel through Switzerland, Italy, France and Austria. While the editor was referred to as "Hitler" for insisting that the group follow the schedule so that we could see as much as possible, years later they thanked him for getting to see so much for so little. We generally slept outside and bought our food in markets.

The editor thought it would be great if he could take his own children to Europe but Grace disagreed. She said it was more important to first see America. "When the children are older they can pay their own way to Europe." She traveled through Europe alone when she attended the Fourth Assembly of the Lutheran World Federation in Helsinki in 1963. During the editor's first 16 years as the pastor of a small church and father of a large family there never were funds for a vacation. This all changed in 1979 when a friend, working through Dr. John Baur, a member of Trinity, New Haven, got the family going on their first trip. Miriam, our oldest daughter, tells about this in the first section of the report she wrote on the family's exactly 10,000 miles to the last frontier, Alaska. The rest of her report is a day by day account of the 27-day trip through Canada and Alaska.

The editor encourages all young families, particularly the families of pastors, to see America when their children are still young and you do not have to take along hairdryers and all sorts of other "unnecessary" equipment. The Otten family tented in just about every state in the nation, including Alaska. The only states we missed were Hawaii and Maine.

The 10,000-mile trip to Alaska, the Pacific Northwest and Canada, plus a 400-mile ride on a ferry through the Northwest inland passage cost $3,000. This included all meals for nine and the $1,400 it cost for the van and its nine passengers on the ferry.

This is about what some touring companies charge per person for a ten-day trip to Alaska. Dad again was a "Hitler" as he got the family out of the tent each morning at 5 a.m. The family jogged on many trails throughout the U.S. and Canada. After reading Miriam's day by day account of the five trips the Otten family took to see America, some have urged CN to publish a book on how to see America for less. A person sees so much more when tenting in state and national parks. The children found most of the evening lectures by rangers fascinating even if some of them spouted the usual evolutionary nonsense.

The long driving miles seemed much shorter for the children because

Dad generally always read them a book on the area through which the family was traveling. He read several of the books of the *Little House on the Prairie* series, books by National Geographic on the various states, books on the Constitution, Declaration of Independence, Eskimos, Indians, etc.

While driving through the Northwest he read *Dr. Bessie* by Dr. Alfred Rehwinkel and then *Salt, Light and the Signs of the Times – An Intimate Look at the Life and Times of Alfred (Rip) Rehwinkel*. This is before the book was published by CN. The children sat around Dr. Albert Schwermann, who with Dr. Rehwinkel, helped found Concordia, Edmonton. They listened with careful attention as he told them about the opening of Western Canada.

On a trip through Perry County, Missouri and then on to the Smokies, the editor read Stella Wuerffel's *Two Rivers to Freedom*, which tells about the founding of the LCMS in a fascinating way. It should be reprinted. Grace and the children would not let him stop even after 12 hours of reading. *(Christian News reprinted Two Rivers to Freedom in 2011 and it is available for $28.95 at www.christiannewsmo.com).*

Indeed, young families should see America together!

(See Appendix A p. 393-396, for photos)

The Family, Health and Physical Fitness

Christian News, August 5, 2002

Surveys show that when parents set a good example by following a regular exercise and physical fitness program their children will follow the pattern.

When CN began in 1962 one of its minor goals was to get clergymen to stop smoking and get rid of the "dunlap" (the belly dun lap over the belt) disease. In recent years CN has said little about smoking since many other publications have publicized its harmful effects.

CN highly recommended Kenneth Cooper's book (*Aerobics*), when it first appeared almost 40 years ago. Some of the many articles CN published on health and physical fitness are in *The Christian News Encyclopedia*. The simple formula of the Creation Health Society was often mentioned in CN: Health Fitness = (+) nutrition (+) exercise (+) rest (-) stress (-) drugs (-) pollution, where (+) means optimal, and (-) means minimal. The true Christian has the advantage of another factor, namely, (+) prayer, Bible reading and Christian fellowship. Optimal nutrition is the scriptural creationist practice of eating foods as close as possible to the way God created and intended them to be to fuel the bodies He created for us.

Dr. David Kaufmann, who has been "the teacher of the year" at the University of Florida, is the primary author of this formula. He will be leading a "Health is Wealth" weekend at Camp Trinity, New Haven, Missouri, September 5-7, 2002. For information call Camp Trinity, New Haven, Missouri,

573-237-2073. Kaufmann is also the Secretary of the Creation Research Society. He has lectured in several countries, including Israel and Russia.

CN has been publishing a series of columns by Dr. Kaufmann titled "Adventures in Christian Stewardship:" 12 Preventive Practices You Can Do to Avoid the Nursing Home, Hospital and Hospice So You Can Serve Christians and Your Fellow Man Right Up to Your last Breath.

The congregations of the LCMS's Missouri District's Washington Circuit will hold a circuit forum on Sunday, September 8, Camp Trinity beginning at 2 p.m. Dr. Kaufmann will speak on "Health Fitness for Pastors; How to Preserve Your Quality of Life So You Can Serve Christ and Your Fellow man Right to Your Last Breath on Earth."

Dr. Kaufmann will speak at 9 a.m. at Trinity Lutheran in New Haven on "Is Evolution a Fact, Law, Theory or None of the Above." At 10 a.m. he will speak on "Creation: The Cornerstone of the Gospel." Kaufmann was a member of the CPH Board of Directors for 12 years and then he was elected to the LCMS's Board for Higher Education.

The Washington Circuit has also invited Dr. Wallace Schulz, Lutheran Hour speaker and Second Vice-President of the LCMS's, to speak at the circuit forum.

Some 20 years ago the editor and his family visited with the Kaufmanns in their home in Gainesville, Florida. Dr. Kaufmann helped inspire the children with his fitness trail and program. Now they built a physical fitness center at Camp Trinity and are working on a fitness trail.

All of the Otten children went on to participate in high school sports. Four were All-State. Several played on winning college teams. Miriam was the National College Marathon Champion in 1988 and now with three children still has her eye on the Olympics. Ruth came in first in her division in an Iron Man Distance Triathlon (2.4-mile swim, 112-mile bike, and 26-mile run). Three of them will again be participating in the Wild Onion Urban Challenge course this September in Chicago, a 24-hour race which includes running, canoeing, scootering, biking, orienteering, rappelling, climbing the Sears Tower, roller blading, etc.

During their early years the children ran 3 ½ miles every day to town to get a ride to Washington where they attended a Lutheran school. Before they went to school they went "running" with Mom and Dad every day on an air strip. Each one had to run or walk a certain number of laps, according to age. When 5 p.m. rolled around, the children came to the office, a room upstairs in the parsonage, saying it was "playtime." During the summer months the children went swimming with Mom and Dad. Each one was supposed to swim a number of laps according to his/her age.

The editor had little time to attend many of the childrens' ball games. He thought it was more important to get them interested in a lifetime program of physical fitness.

Now almost all of them and their spouses continue biking on the scenic roads surrounding Camp Trinity. Many of them use the weight equipment in the physical fitness center attached to the CN and Camp Trinity office.

If the editor had his life to live over again he would make certain changes as far as a fitness program is concerned. He would have started lifting weights already during high school years and entered triathlons shortly after college days. Swimming, biking, and running are better and more fun than just running alone. The novice does not have to start with an Iron Man Triathlon. Almost every busy pastor has time at least for one or two triathlons a year. That is all it takes to inspire a person on as he trains. If you know a race is coming up, you have an added incentive to push just a little harder.

As a person ages, he should at least take a good vigorous half hour walk several times a week. God gave you your body. Keep his gift in as good a condition as possible so that you can continue to serve right up to your dying day.

(The WELS pastor, who edited this book, rides his Schwinn exercycle for 15 minutes twice a day, listening to classical music or watching TV news (not Oprah)!

Family Man, Family Leader - Biblical Fatherhood as the Key to a Thriving Family

Christian News, January 5, 2004

Family Man, Family Leader -
Biblical Fatherhood as the Key to a Thriving Family
By Philip Lancaster. *Vision Forum*, San Antonio, Texas. 2003. 330 pages. Available from *Christian News* $13.50 plus S/H.

Every father should read this book. The back cover of *Family Man, Family Leader* says: Beyond Feminism, Back to Biblical Patriarchy. What this country and the Church need now are a few good men – husbands and fathers who are willing to love and lead their households with manly resolve and Godly vision. We are experiencing a national crisis of manhood. Absent a revival of fatherhood, we can expect to see an ever-increasing rise in the numbers of effeminate boys and masculine women, and the total breakdown of the Christian family. We need family men who are strong leaders.

"For more than ten years, Phil Lancaster has been a prophet of hope, calling fathers to their rightful duties as family prophets, priests, protectors, and providers. He has emerged as one of the most articulate and theologically sound defenders of the biblical family. Through his magazine *Patriarch*, Phil has reached thousands with the vision necessary for family revival. In *Family Man, Family Leader*, Phil lays the biblical foundation necessary for men to turn their hearts to home and change the world, *Family Man, Family Leader* presents the vision of biblical household leadership and addresses the many practical issues necessary to achieve victory as a man." Douglas W. Phillips, President, *Vision Forum*.

Philip Lancaster writes: "What is so earth-shaking about a man turning his heart to his family? It is the movement of a father's heart out of the sphere of immediate, temporal, and self-centered concerns toward the sphere of long-range, even eternal, concerns. A man who shares God's priorities sees in his children his (and his wife's) most important mission in life. He sees in them the foundation of many generations, generations which he can shape for God, and which God can use to shape history, through the power of Christ and His gospel" (6).

"When a father makes his family his top priority, it is inevitable that the hearts of his children will be turned to him. There is no generation gap when fathers do their job. Quite the contrary. There is a solid generational bond. How can a child turn against his father when their hearts are bound together? For that child to rebel would destroy his own heart as well as his father's. With the heart of the children won to their father and their father's God, the cause of Christ in the world can go forward through the generations. There is no speedier path to fulfilling the Great Commission gave Jesus to his followers: to make disciples of the nations.

Back to the Bible

"I am truly encouraged by the evidence that God is moving millions of fathers to be family-centered. However, I am looking for indications of the other 'turning' that marks a time of true revival: returning to God's Word, the Bible, as the source of wisdom for how to live in a way that is pleasing to God.

"Now millions profess belief in the inerrancy of God's inspired Word and intend to live by its teachings. But the fact is that, despite such professions of high regard for the Bible, few demonstrate this by practicing what the Bible says in day-to-day life. There are not even many evangelical Christians who read Scripture with regularity, much less spend time in serious study of the Book or applying it to daily life" (6,7).

"The church is in a sad state today. Never mind the mainline denominations that have long-since abandoned biblical faith; we're talking about the Bible-believing church. Here, too often, we see much ado about nothing. There is talk of revival without the reality. The church today measures its success by the numbers on its rolls, the size of its offerings, or the volume of its worship bands-rather than by the holiness of its members. "When was the last time you heard of a church rebuking members for gossip, admonishing men for the immodest dress of their wives and daughters, or excommunicating a member for adultery? Today's evangelical church may take a strong stand on fundamental doctrines like the divine nature of Christ and the inspiration of Scripture, but too often it denies Christ and His inspired Word by not practicing a true Christian lifestyle. The pattern of life of most Christians is so much like the world around them that they blend right in and cannot serve as salt and light.

"The family, too, is in decline among Christians. Believing fathers generally fail to play their God-given role as the spiritual leader of their families. Christian fathers in times past led their families in twice-daily family worship. Today most Christian fathers reinforce the pervasive humanism of our culture, denying the practical relevance of God to the lives of their children by failing to worship Him together with their families in the home.

"Christian mothers too often neglect their home-centered role for the empty promise of fulfillment in the workplace, while they warehouse their children in daycare centers. Parents send their children to secular schools where God is outlawed, and they allow them to watch trashy movies and listen to vile music-and hanging out with those who do the same. After years of training in the ways of rebellion through godless schooling, debauched entertainment, and peer association, Christian parents are somehow surprised when their teenagers rebel, forsaking the God of their fathers"(12,13).

"To be truly Christian men we must get back to the Bible and to the God of the Bible. The goal of this book is to present the foundations of biblical patriarchy as revealed in God's Word. After a brief look back in history to discover how men and their families have fallen so far since colonial times, we will look at what the Bible teaches about manhood and fatherhood, with particular emphasis on how God the Father and Jesus Christ are models for the Christian man.

"The goal of this study is to restore what has fallen and 'raise up the foundation of many generations.' It is to rediscover the long-lost knowledge of the Bible as it relates to men and their primary calling in the home. It is to equip men with food for study and meditation so that they 'will have good success' as they work to turn their hearts toward their families.

"My immediate hope is to build on the promise of the Christian men's movement and of home schooling and help them both to carry through to long-term fruitfulness. That will only happen as we get back to the Bible and back to biblical patriarchy"(20).

The State Becomes Father

"So the state has become the father to the nation, and men have allowed it. We can't simply blame the politicians and judges, though they deserve blame. Fathers by the millions have been passive in the face of the ongoing assault against their families. Someone has called it 'responsibility drift.' Men have been glad to relieve themselves of some of the burdens of fatherhood, and the state has been only too happy to take them over" (37,38).

Feminized Churches and Doctrine

"First, instead of standing up and challenging the direction modern society has taken, *the church has acquiesced to the culture at every turn.* In the liberal denominations this has taken the form of accommodating feminism and embracing whatever new idea the God-haters have come up with, to the point where they are now in the process of embracing practicing sodomites and considering them for the ministry instead of calling them to repentance and offering them the forgiveness of God and His grace to live a new life. The mainline churches have simply followed the cultural drift, accepting the ideology du jour with fawning gusto" (42).

"The second way the church has been part of the problem instead of the solution in the cultural drift is that *it has largely abandoned the virile doctrine of the early church and the Reformation.* Instead of the Bible's masculine doctrine of salvation in which an initiating God acts with efficacious love to draw His chosen people to Himself, much of the church now proclaims a passive God who offers His love but would not think of imposing His love on His bride. The pallid Jesus stands at the door and knocks, hoping we'll let Him in. God is no longer presented as the very archetype of masculine power and love. This kind of feminized doctrine has contributed to the proliferation of feminized men who stand fearful even before their wives. If God is feminized, what chance do Christian men have?" (pp.43,44)

Christ-like Men

"Perhaps it will be easier if they come to see more and more examples of the other truth about a father's calling-that he is the servant of his house. Ms. Ireland said she'd never seen a master who was also a servant. Maybe not. We need to provide her and other doubters many examples of such men and of such homes. In other words, the world needs to see Christ-like men and God-centered homes-homes where the cross tempers the exercise of real authority" (124)

"Men need to rediscover what it means to be a man instead of a woman. We need to re-learn how to be a father like the Father. Adding psychological band-aids to the disease of emasculated manhood will not be enough. Prescribing a list of behavior modifications for fathers to employ in the home will not bring the healing our families and nation need. "Central to our whole project is the matter of fathers turning their hearts toward their children. In the first chapter we noted the hopeful signs of home education and the Christian men's movement. Both seem to have moved many men in the direction of making the home a higher priority. But we also noted the need for these initial movements back home to become well grounded in the Bible.

"Unless Christian men self-consciously ground their behavior on the Bible's view of their identity and their callings, there will be no long-term family renewal. This will involve study, and it will involve a costly commitment to a new way of life" (126).

Promise Keepers

"I may not have attended any Promise Keepers rallies, but I have read the literature of the Christian men's movement. I have been struck by one consistent trait in the dozens of such books I have read: they almost always hedge in their discussions of the father's role as leader" (154).

"A father is the head of his house, its lord, its master, its ruler. Yes, this leadership is indeed softened by love and made merciful by the cross, but it is true authority. It is the power to command and direct. It carries with it the responsibility for the course of the home. Truly, the buck stops with fathers since they are in charge. They make the final decisions in the household. This is what the term 'leadership' means" (159).

Use of Time

"In too many Christian homes today there is no rational control of the schedule. Families are tyrannized by the urgent demands of school, church, youth groups, sports teams, field trips, birthday parties, part-time jobs, and on and on it goes. It is common for families to be so busy with seemingly good activities that they have no time left for the best: quiet family times for conversation, reading, worship, play-the stuff of which memories are made and by which unbreakable bonds of love are woven.

"The policymaker in the home can have some of his greatest influence by taking charge of the family schedule. He should determine when the members of the family arise in the morning and when they retire at night, at least until the children are nearing adulthood. He should decide when they worship together and when they eat. He should lay down the rules that will determine in which of the out-of-home activities the children can participate.

"Above all else, he must guard against the insane busyness that characterizes modern family life. If things are out of control and the family members simply meet each other coming and going, he is the one who must call a halt to the rat race and establish time priorities that will build and bind rather than fragment his family"(171).

Father as Priest

"One of the greatest tragedies in Christian homes today is the spiritual malnutrition of wives and children. When a person is starving physically we can see it in their gaunt faces and swollen bellies. If we were to put on our 'spiritual glasses' we would see that the children in many a Christian man's home look like those in a 'Feed the Children' documercial-they are starving for spiritual food. (We will deal more with the spiritual provision when we look at the father's roles of prophet and priest)" (182).

Protection

"He must keep a constant eye out for danger and take steps to defend his wife and children when necessary. The cry of men on the sinking *Titanic*. 'Women and children first,' appropriately expresses godly priorities. It is a man's job to pay any price necessary, including his own life, to defend women and children, especially his own household" (183).

Education

"Scripture does not even use the word 'education' to describe the process of training children for adulthood. That word, as we use it, is freighted with connotations of schooling, academics, and training of the mind-a very narrow Greek and Western concept of training (rationalism views man's mind as his supreme faculty).

"Those who are informed by a biblical and Hebraic perspective would say that true 'education' is discipleship. It is a process of training the whole person, not just the mind. The goal is not a mind stuffed with facts; the goal is a changed person.

"The heart is the most important part of a person 'for out of it springs the issues of life' (Prov. 4:23). The purpose of life is to love God with the whole heart (Deut. 6:5); and this purpose is realized in children as parents have God's Word engrafted in their own hearts and then impress that Word on their children (6:6,7). Fathers are to say to their sons, 'Let your heart retain my words; keep my commands, and live' (Prov.4:4)" (195).

The Rod

"Christian fathers will physically restrain their children from sin through the appropriate use of force. Feminized men will agonize over their right to do this and will be more concerned for the child's body than for his soul. One sure sign that fathers' hearts are being turned to their children will be when they give the rod its proper place within the home. And what these dads will find is that there is no surer way to win the hearts of their sons and daughters than to demand their obedience and enforce their authority through the loving use of corporal punishment.

"Following the Lord's prescription for dealing with sin is often an act of faith. Our own confused sympathies for our children and the natural inertia that hampers any decisive action in most of us will make us hesitate to use the rod consistently. But as we keep the goal in view, we will be motivated to obedience in this area. Biblical discipline produces good fruit. 'Now no chastening seems to be joyful for the present, but painful; nevertheless, afterward it yields the peaceable fruit of righteousness to those who have been trained by it'" (Heb. 12:11) (208).

A Father's Chief Duty

"As James W. Alexander in *Thoughts on Family Worship* wrote, regular, even daily (or twice daily), family worship is simply an historical fact among godly families in all ages and places. This gathering of the whole family for the purpose of worship, Bible reading, and prayer is a conscious, corporate ritual. It is a specific, intentional gathering to acknowledge God together in addition to thanks offered at meals or bedside prayers. While the church gathers weekly to worship the Lord, the family assembles daily for that highest of all human endeavors.

"Both Old and New Testaments contain abundant evidence that family devotion is assumed as the lifestyle of the godly" (226).

"From the early church to Reformation times in Switzerland, France, Holland, Scotland, and elsewhere, to the colonial days in America, indeed up to our own century, the institution of family worship is an ever-present evidence of a vital faith within the home. During times of spiritual health, family worship was the rule among Christian households, not the exception" (227).

"Q: Is it necessary for the father himself to lead the family worship?"A: Yes! Although leadership does not mean that he does everything. Dad should take the initiative to establish the practice and set the time; he should take charge of the worship time itself. During worship, he may have others read or pray; he may even disciple an older son by letting him lead the whole worship at times; but the father should retain clear control of the family worship time. When the children are grown and away from home, their memories of their father should include hearing his voice reading the Bible to his gathered flock and lifting them all up to God in prayer" (233,234).

Getting Wives Out of the Workplace

"A vital social effect of a return to patriarchy will be that married women will leave the workforce and return home. In an earlier chapter we mentioned how men allowed the civil government to take over so many of the functions that previously were performed by families: child care, education, welfare, care for the elderly, healthcare. In a patriarchal renewal these functions must be reclaimed by families, and as the domain of family government increases, civil government will shrink" (282).

"I recognize the challenge involved here. Since the whole structure of our society has changed in the last two hundred years to accommodate the new economic order, which tends to fragment the family into the workplace, schools, and other institutions, any progress made at restoring family functions will involve sacrifice, but must be done nonetheless.

"The warehousing of babies and young children, in disease-infested institutions under the care of strangers, is one of the saddest side effects of sending mothers into the workforce. With mother home there is no need for the daycare center, and the little ones are provided with the best possible care by the person God designed to be their primary caregiver. When the wife is home during the day, it also becomes possible to think of caring for an elderly parent who may need companionship or supervision. This is one of the chief ways in which children can honor their parents. 'But if any widow has children or grandchildren, let them first learn to show piety at home and to repay their parents; for this is good and acceptable before God' (1 Tim. 5:4).

"A mother at home is able to teach her children, thus fulfilling the mandate of Deuteronomy 6:6-9. The educational process was one of the first family functions ceded to the state, and its recovery by the family is one of the most costly commitments a father and mother can make in terms of time and energy. But reclaiming the educational role is probably the most effective step parents can take to revitalize their family and make sure that the Christian faith is passed along to the next generation"(283).

Christ Is The Focus, Not Patriarchy

"The inherent danger of being people with a cause is that we lose sight of our Cause. Biblical patriarchy is not the meaning of life for the Christian. Christ is. 'For to me, to live is Christ...' (Phil. 1:21). Biblical patriarchy itself is not the secret for rebuilding our families, churches, and nation. Christ is. It is horrible to think that while focusing on the ingredients of a wholesome and biblical way of life, we may lose sight of the one who is the only source, guide, and goal of the Christian life, Christ himself" (303). Urge fathers, particularly fathers who still have children at home, to read this book.

VIII

GAY MARRIAGE - HOMOSEXUALITY - POLYGAMY

The Conservative Case For Gay Marriage
By Brandt Klawitter
Christian News, January 25, 2010

The January 18, 2010 *Newsweek* cover story, "The Conservative Case for Gay Marriage," by Theodore Olson, poses an interesting dilemma for morally conservative citizens of the United States. Namely, it asks the question, what reason is there to deny homosexuals equal rights in the civil realm at any given level—including the right to marry one another? After all, and this is the basic issue, what right does Christianity (arguably the chief advocate of conservative mores within the conservative community) have to impose its beliefs in the civil realm?

While such a statement coming from a conservative Christian may surprise you, I think the honest answer to this question must be, "It does not have any business imposing its beliefs in the civil realm." In fact, I think it is rather presumptuous and ignorant on the part of Christians to believe that their worldview is and should be the worldview of the United States. After all, short of such a claim being clearly established in the U.S. Constitution, who said that any particular ideology or religion has the right to control the public schools, define marriage, or to structure society at large? Naturally, that criticism could and should be leveled at secular humanism, the 'de facto' religion of our nation. Nevertheless, I do find it presumptuous of Christians to act like they own the United States. In fact, such an attitude and desire to control the nation based on any sort of a moral majority is likely to ultimately prove disastrous not only for Christians, but for all who love and cherish freedom. If the will of the majority determines what is right or not, what happens when the majority changes?

So, what about "The Conservative Case for Gay Marriage?" While you might have been thinking that I was about to support Theodore Olson's argument, let me point out that I do not. "The conservative case" (i.e. Theodore Olson's case) is actually just as weak as any moral majority's attempt, based on some majority vote, to claim the United States as its very own personal property. In other words, Theodore Olson's case comes down to a grab for power. Even worse, it is a grab for power based on subjective definitions and poorly presented facts and interpretations. Take, for instance, his description of marriage. He writes, "Marriage is one of the basic building blocks of our neighborhoods and our nation. At its best, it is a stable bond between two individuals who work to create a loving household and a social and economic partnership...Marriage requires thinking beyond one's own needs. It transforms two individuals into a union based on shared aspirations, and in doing so establishes a formal investment in the well-being of society." (48) This language, while seemingly right on the surface, is actually very problematic in its vagueness. The fact is, not only does its vagueness allow for homosexual marriage, it actually could be used very easily to make the case for man/boy or woman/girl marriages, too. After all, might not such couples also share aspirations and be capable of forming a stable bond?

Of greater concern, however, is a second question, namely, who gave Mr. Olson the right to define what marriage actually is or is not? Did science allow him such liberties? Did God speak to him? Does he represent the will of the entire nation or the voice of absolute truth? Was it the constitution itself (and its proper interpretation) that led him to such a conclusion? In order to answer this question, we'll have to further analyze his article.

One component of his "case" is that of critique. He critiques the arguments of his opponents as being too "traditional," self-contradictory (as in the requirement that marriage be connected with procreation when many heterosexual marriages fail this test), or as simply weak. Naturally, comments could be made on all these points, but these critiques deserve neither the time nor attention required to argue against them.

Mr. Olson not only offers critique but he also appeals to the authority of science as a basis for his claims. He writes, "Science has taught us, even if history has not, that gays and lesbians do not choose to be homosexual any more than the rest of us choose to be heterosexual. To a very large extent, these characteristics are immutable, like being left-handed." (52) While this statement is, at best, a distortion of half-truths and, at worst, a flat-out lie, I also don't want to take issue with him about this statement. If science were the ultimate authority to which he appealed in his argument, I would be more than happy to review scientific findings and to point out that homosexuality has also been shown by studies to be a learned and aberrant behavior. It all depends which studies one chooses to look at! But, alas, science is not Mr. Olson's ultimate appeal.

What is, then? While it's easy to miss, Mr. Olson's ultimate appeal is higher than science. It is also loftier than simple logic. His ultimate appeal, though very brief, is a divine appeal lodged in the words of the Declaration of Independence. "We hold these truths to be self-evident, that all men are created equal, that they are endowed by their Creator with certain unalienable Rights..." Did you catch that? In quoting that document, he has claimed to both rightfully interpret our nation's Declaration of Independence and he has also claimed to have the correct interpretation of natural law—an appeal to the divine, you might say.

That begs the question: does Mr. Olson really know the will of the divine and the true intentions of our founding fathers? That would, in fact, seem to be the case as his appeal is (and must be) to some sort of divinely ordered natural law in our nation's founding documents. What's interesting is that, while any other person who makes this appeal is subject to scrutiny, he is claiming to somehow be the arbiter and chief prophet of the Creator's will, that is, of some sort of natural law. Such a claim begs the question: what wonderful tradition of religious history does Mr. Olson represent and what is his proof that gay marriage is, in fact, in accord with the intentions of our nation's founding fathers? Unfortunately, Mr. Olson doesn't seem interested in clearly making such a case--perhaps because nearly the entire tradition of natural law stands in opposition to his actual argument. No, if Mr. Olson were really interested in natural law and the Creator, one would expect that his argument might be somewhat different.

So, what is my point in all of this? Two things come to mind. First, it must be clearly stated that it isn't the government's job to make our nation a Christian nation. Christians (and any interest group) play a very dangerous game when they look to the government to fulfill such a role, a role which doesn't rightfully belong to it. Rather than fighting to assert their will through some sort of moral majority, it would be much better to fight for truth and integrity in law-making and in the interpretation of law. Whether that includes or excludes homosexuals from marriage is not the ultimate concern (though I can't imagine how it would include them). The ultimate concern is in protecting liberty and our own constitutional form of government. Otherwise, a moral majority is simply exercising a form of tyranny that may easily be turned against it.

My second point is simply to point out the hypocrisy in Olson's attempt to win this argument based on some sort of claim to the Creator and natural law. And he would be the one to rob his opponents of this very same claim? How pathetic.

Two Peas in a Pod

Rome and Homosexuality – The LCMS and Evolution
Christian News, March 14, 2011

The Roman Catholic Church officially opposes homosexuality. A story on page one of the March 14, 2011 *Christian News*, reports that the cover up of homosexual priests guilty of sex abuse continues to grow within the Roman Catholic Church. Homosexual priests are not removed from the Roman Catholic Church. Only those who complain about Rome's toleration of homosexuality are frowned on and get into difficulty with the hierarchy.

The Lutheran Church-Missouri Synod officially opposes evolution. Yet no LCMS pastor or professor who promotes evolution has ever been removed from the LCMS clergy roster. The LCMS's Council of Presidents some years ago even appointed Dr. John Gergeley, one of the most outspoken evolutionists in the LCMS, to the LCMS's Commission on Theology and Church Relations. During the LCMS's first hundred years there were no evolutionists on the LCMS clergy roster. Today the LCMS's top officials take no action vs. any evolutionist on the LCMS clergy roster. Only those who filed charges of false doctrine against an evolutionist on the clergy roster are frowned on by the LCMS's bureaucracy and those who support the bureaucracy.

Christian News for decades has documented the fact that there are evolutionists in the LCMS's Concordia University System.

Commenting on an LGBT (Lesbian, Gay, Bi-sexual, Transgender) event at Concordia University, Chicago, mentioned in "Stop Hating Homosexuals" (*Christian News*, March 7, 2011), Pastor Tim Rossow writes on a March 5 posting on John the Steadfast:

"This is now the second sad time in two years that Dr. John Johnson

(President of Concordia University, Chicago) has avoided strong leadership and instead allowed faculty members to wrongly establish theological and cultural standards for the university in clear violation of Biblical morality. In 2009 President Johnson endorsed faculty members signing a petition in support of the terror-bomber, humanist and pagan William Ayers all in the name of academic freedom. The Concordia University system is spinning out of control. A passionate pursuit of size and influence on the culture is blurring our Concordia vision. May the Lord have mercy on us."

During the last 50 years CN has published hundreds of articles showing true love to homosexuals by insisting that homosexuality is a sin and that unrepentant homosexuals who continue in their sinful lifestyle are going to Hell. CN has shown that there are liberals in the LCMS and its Concordia University System who want to change the LCMS's official opposition to homosexuality. Yet the fact that evolutionists are tolerated in the LCMS and its schools is even more devastating than tolerance of homosexuals.

Time to Show True Love to Evolutionists

Hopefully, the organized conservatives who oppose *Christian News* will nevertheless support the charges of false doctrine which CN has filed vs. one of the most outspoken evolutionists in the LCMS. It is time for the organized conservatives to show true love to the evolutionists in the LCMS and Synod colleges to show true love to students being misled by the evolutionists and true love to God and His Word by filing charges of false doctrine vs. evolutionists on the LCMS clergy roster and the LCMS officials who refuse to take any disciplinary action vs. the evolutionists. All the evidence the organized conservatives need is in *A DAYSTAR READER*, Dr. Matthew Becker, editor.

Episcopalians Promote "Queer Theology"

Radical Love Knows No Boundaries, says Cheng, in First Published Introduction to Queer Theology from Seabury Books
Religion Press Release Service

Christian News, April 4, 2011

(New York, NY)—Contextual theologies have developed from a number of perspectives—including feminist theology, Black theology, womanist theology, Latin American liberation theology, and Asian American theology—and a wide variety of academic and general introductions exist to examine each one.

However, *Radical Love*, by Patrick Cheng and newly published by Seabury Books, is considered to be the first introductory textbook on the subject of queer theology. If early responses are any indication, the new title will be well received for years to come in academic and church communities struggling with issues of gender and inclusivity.

"Radical Love—a love so extreme that it dissolves our existing boundaries! What concept could be more liberating for a culture like ours, where lives are crucified on rigid binaries like male, vs. female, us vs. them, straight vs. queer? *Radical Love* is an excellent introduction for beginners and an excellent synthesis for more advanced readers," said Virginia Ramey Mollenkott, author of *Sensuous Spirituality and Omnigender*, among many other books.

"Patrick Cheng's *Radical Love* is not only an excellent introduction to LGBT theology but an important contribution to the discipline of theology and the life of the church. It is a must read for anyone who cares about the health of the church and theology today," added another early reviewer, James H. Cone, distinguished professor of systematic theology at New York's Union Theological Seminary.

In this lucid and compelling introduction, Cheng provides a historical survey of how queer theology has developed from the 1950's to today and then explicates the themes of queer theology using the ecumenical creeds as a general framework. Topics include revelation, God, Trinity, creation, Jesus Christ, atonement, sin, grace, Holy Spirit, church, sacraments, and last things, as seen through the lenses of LGBT theologians.

"Patrick Cheng's *Radical Love* is an excellent introduction to queer theology. It is readable and nuanced, a marvelous teaching resource," said Carter Heyward, author of *Keep Your Courage: A Radical Christian Feminist Speaks* and Professor Emerita of Theology, Episcopal Divinity School, New York.

Kwok Pui Lan, who teaches theology and spirituality at the Episcopal Divinity School and is the author of Postcolonial Imagination and Feminist Theology, published one of the first reviews of *Radical Love*, saying, "One of the strengths of the book is that it touches on all major doctrines of Christian theology: revelation, trinity, creation, sin, atonement, church, saints, sacraments, and eschatology (the last things). It showcases the breadth of the theological output of queer theologians. The book includes further study questions and a lengthy bibliography. It will be a very good resource to be used in the classroom and in church and small groups."

A variety of other scholars and professionals have previewed *Radical Love*, and endorsed it, as follows:

"This book is a clear, accessible and exciting analysis of Queer Theology. Cheng perfectly captures both the challenge and the rootedness of Queer Theology."—Professor Elizabeth Stuart, Pro Vice-Chancellor, University of Winchester, UK

"I would characterize Cheng's notion of 'radical love' as 'wild grace' with which mainstream theology has yet to wrestle. This is a good text for introducing queer theology to undergraduate and graduate students."—Rev. Dr. Bob Shore-Goss, Senior Pastor/Theologian, Metropolitan Community Church in the Valley, North Hollywood, CA

Patrick S. Cheng is assistant professor of historical & systematic theology at Episcopal Divinity School, Cambridge, MA. Cheng holds a B.A. from

Yale College, a J.D. from Harvard Law School, and a Ph.D., M.Phil., and M.A. in systematic theology from Union Theological Seminary in New York. He is an ordained minister in the Metropolitan Community Church.

The new book can be ordered through any Episcopal, religious, or secular bookstore; through any online bookseller, direct from the publisher by calling 800-242-1918 or by visiting www.chu rchpublishing.org.

Founded in 1918 and headquartered in New York City, CPI is the publisher of official worship materials, books, and music for the Episcopal Church, plus a multi-faceted publisher and supplier to the broader ecumenical marketplace. Publishing imprints include Church Publishing, Morehouse Publishing, and Seabury Books. Additional CPI divisions include Morehouse Church Supplies, a provider of church supplies, ecclesiastical furnishings, and vestments, located in Harrisburg, PA; and Morehouse Education Resources, which produces lectionary-based curriculum, faith formation programs, plus e-publishing resources and services, in Denver, Colorado.

Homosexuality Is At The Root of Rome's Sex Abuse Crisis

Christian News, March 14, 2011

"New revelation of child-molesting Catholic priests in Philadelphia" on page one of the March 14, 2011 *Christian News*, reports from Philadelphia: "Three weeks after a scathing grand jury report accused the Philadelphia Archdiocese of providing safe haven for as many as 37 priests who have been credibly accused of sexual abuse or inappropriate behavior toward minors, most of those priests remain active in the ministry." Similar reports have come from all over the world. Yet the homosexual friendly media generally fail to report that most of those abused are adolescent males and not girls.

"Homosexuality Is at the Root of Rome's Crisis" in the May 3, 2010 *Christian News* is just one of scores of articles in *Christian News* about homosexuality in the priesthood. "Cardinal Bertone Says... Homosexuality Is At The Root Of The Crisis" in the April 22, 2010 Roman Catholic *Wanderer*, reproduced in the May 3, 2010 *Christian News* said: "The Vatican's number two official, Secretary of State Tarcisio Cardinal Bertone, said April 12 that the Church's problem with pedophile priests has not been caused by celibacy, but by homosexuality."

The story in the Roman Catholic paper concluded: "A report on the U.S. sex abuse crisis, done at the behest of the U.S. Conference of Catholic Bishops in 2004 by the John Jay College of Criminal Justice, found that the vast majority of victims in priest sex abuse cases were adolescent males."

Father Richard John Neuhaus, a hero of CPH's Paul McCain and some of the LCMS-organized conservatives and hyper-euros, covered up the tremendous homosexual crisis in Rome. CN has documented the fact that Neuhaus praised a leading homosexual in Rome. CN has not only opposed

Neuhaus for rejecting the inerrancy of the Bible, justification by faith alone, and promoting universalism, but CN also took sharp issue with homosexual-friendly Neuhaus's views on homosexuality. Yet the organized conservatives seldom exposed Neuhaus's radical attacks vs. historical Christianity, including support of Rudolf Bultmann's demythologizing of the Bible. The "intellectual snobs" simply refused to read the voluminous evidence about Neuhaus presented in CN for decades. Neuhaus was invited to speak at both LCMS seminaries which banned the editor of CN. When Neuhaus died, the *Concordia Journal* of Concordia Seminary, St. Louis, published an article by LCMS Atlantic District President David Benke praising Neuhaus as a great faithful Christian leader.

Now some are critical of what CN's editor said at Concordia University, Wisconsin on February 3, 2011. Here is a section on Rome and homosexuality from pp. 277-279 in *Bonhoeffer and King: Their Theology and Life Documented in Christian News 1963-2011*:

The Worldwide Uprising Against Sex Abuse Within the Church, particularly within the Roman Catholic Church

14. Protestantism, including especially the charismatics, has had its share of sex abusers and adulterous womanizing and divorced clergymen, including the much publicized televangelists. *Christian News* has published many reports about this scandal.

A *Catholic News Service* story in the January 7, 2011 *St. Louis Review* of the archdiocese of St. Louis reports in a story titled: "Milwaukee Archdiocese files for bankruptcy over abuse claims:"

"Milwaukee is the largest archdiocese to file for Chapter 11. The archdiocese of Portland, Ore., with approximately 390,000 Catholics, filed for bankruptcy in July 2004. In February 2007, the Diocese of San Diego, with nearly 900,000 Catholics, filed for Chapter 11 protection."

"Milwaukee Archbishop Listecki wrote that, since the late 1980s, the archdiocese had worked 'to meet the needs of victims/survivors without taking this drastic action (Chapter 11 reorganization).'

"'We have directed increasing resources toward providing financial, psychological, pastoral and spiritual support to victims/survivors. . . . We have spent more than $29 million to cover costs associated with this tragedy,' the archbishop said.

"Since 2002, the archdiocese has sold property, liquidated savings and investments, eliminated ministries and services, cut staff by nearly 40 percent, and put all available real estate on the market in order to provide resources.

"'As a result, we have succeeded in reaching mediated settlements with more than 190 individuals,' Archbishop Listecki said. 'But in the end, our available resources fell short.'"

The primary cause of the great sex abuse scandal in the Roman Catholic Church is its decades long cover up of the tremendous number of homosexual priests, bishops, archbishops, seminarians, and even a Pope. Some Roman Catholic authorities have estimated that as many as 50 percent of Roman Catholic priests and seminarians may be homosexuals. Its difficult to give an exact figure. The September 26, 2005 *Newsweek* reported that "The Rev. Donald Cozzen, in his book, *'The Changing Face of the Priesthood'* estimated that 23 to 58 percent of Catholic clerics have homosexual orientations."

Some 40 years ago my congregation petitioned The Lutheran Church-Missouri Synod to support what the Bible teaches about homosexuality. It is a sin. (Romans 1) Homosexuals should not be permitted to serve as pastors. The LCMS did adopt this position. It actually showed more love to homosexuals than the Roman Catholic Church and all those major Protestant denominations which now permit homosexuals to be pastors and who commune homosexuals. The Bible teaches that homosexuals, who continue in their sinful lifestyle, are going to hell. By refusing to commune homosexuals and have them serve as pastors, the LCMS is showing them true love. We want them to go to heaven. Hopefully, they will repent of their sin if we do not commune them, and then confess Jesus Christ as their Savior from sin and go to heaven when they die.

Christian News has noted for some 30 years that Milwaukee Archbishop Rembert Weakland was a pro-homosexual, who was covering up for homosexual priests. Father Enrique T. Rueda in his *The Homosexual Network – Private Lives & Public Policy,* published by Devin Adair in 1982 and reviewed in *Christian News,* exposed the infamous Milwaukee Archbishop. Liberal churchmen appreciated Weakland's socialist notions and his attack on America's free enterprise system.

"'The Wisconsin Lutheran Synod's Favorite RC, a Homosexual Predator,' Dr. Gregory Jackson --Archbishop Signed $450,000 Agreement to Hush Sex Abuse Claim" was the title of a headline in the June 3, 2002 *Christian News*. The story noted that Gregory Jackson, Ph.D. Notre Dame, S.T.M., Yale, wrote: "Roman Catholic Archbishop Weakland was the featured speaker at Wisconsin Lutheran College, WELS."

The June 3, 2002 *Christian News* reprinted "An Archbishop's Fall from Grace," from the June 3, 2002 *Newsweek.* "A Gay Culture in the Church" and "More cover-ups, more shame", from the June 34, 2002 *U.S. News and World Report,* and "Milwaukee bishop admits he paid off accuser," from the May 24, 2002 *St. Louis Post Dispatch.* "Marty and Archbishop Weakland at Wisconsin Lutheran College" in the June 3, 2002 *Christian News* was a letter *CN* wrote to the presidents of the WELS and ELS about Martin Marty and Archbishop Weakland speaking at Wisconsin Lutheran College.

The June 8, 2009 *Christian News* said in a review:

AMCHURCH COMES OUT
The U.S. Bishops, Pedophile Scandals
and the Homosexual Agenda

Paul Likoudis, the author of this book, writes in a front page story titled "The Shameless Archbishop... Weakland's Self-Revelations Are a Cautionary Tale," in the May 28, 2009 *Wanderer*, a Roman Catholic Weekly:

"Today, we have the spectacle of the former archbishop of Milwaukee, Rembert Weakland, OSB, proudly bragging about his sin, recalling his past sexual affairs with other men and objecting to the Church's teaching that homosexuality 'is objectively disordered.'

"Those are bad words because they are pejorative,' he told The New York Times' Laurie Goodstein in an interview heralding the May 29 release of his autobiography.

"Weakland's public proclamation that he is a 'gay' American and the attention he is drawing to himself with his new narcissistic, tell-all book, *A Pilgrim in A Pilgrim Church*, one Milwaukee Catholic told the *Wanderer*, 'is opening a can of worms. Even worse, it is like he is ripping off all the scabs from the still-festering wounds he left in this Archdiocese.'

Now the Roman Catholic Arch diocese of Milwaukee has become the largest Arch diocese in the nation to declare bankruptcy because the Roman Catholic Church from the Pope down has covered up the tremendous homosexual scandal in Rome and failed to remove homosexuals from the priesthood.

Randy Engel, a Roman Catholic scholar, in her *The Rite of Sodomy - Homosexuality and the Roman Catholic Church* has much to say about homosexual churchmen like Archbishop Weakland. The 1300 page book concludes:

"There can be no question that Pope Paul VI's homosexuality was instrumental in the paradigm shift that saw the rise of the Homosexual Collective in the Catholic Church in the United States, at the Vatican and around the world in the mid-20th century.

"Pope Paul VI played a decisive role in the selection and advancement of many homosexual members of the American hierarchy including Joseph Cardinal Bernardin, Terence Cardinal Cooke, John Cardinal Wright and Archbishop Rembert Weakland and Bishops George H. Guifoyle, Francis Mugavero, Joseph Hart, Joseph Ferrario, James Rausch and their 'ilk'.

"The knowledge that a homosexual sat in the Chair of Peter—knowledge that spread like wild-fire on the 'gay' gossip circuit—would certainly have served as an inducement for homosexual men to aspire to the priesthood and even prompt them to contemplate the unthinkable—a religious order or community composed exclusively of sodomites.

"Most importantly, the long-guarded quasi-secret of Paul VI's homosexual life has, for decades, contributed to the silence and cover-up by the American hierarchy on the issue of homosexuality in general and the criminal activities of pederast priests in particular.

"But it is a secret no longer.

"The final piece of the puzzle has been put in place" (1157).[25]

AFTER SAME SEX MARRIAGE IS LEGALIZATION OF POLYGAMY NEXT?
Christian News, April 11, 2011

"Since the door is open. . . Same-sex marriages give polygamy a legal boost" is the title of a major story in the March 28 *Washington Times*.

"The outlook for polygamy hasn't been this good since Abraham took Keturah as his third wife.

"Plural marriage remains illegal, but it's undergoing an image upgrade as a result of television shows like HBO's 'Big Love' and TLC's 'Sister Wives.' More significantly, it's getting a legal boost from a strange bedfellow: the success of same-sex marriage.

"Gay-rights advocates cringe whenever the connection is made between same-sex and plural marriage, but more than a few legal analysts say the recent gains posted by gay marriage in the courts and state legislatures cannot help but bolster the case for legalized polygamy.

"The federal government and most states define marriage as an institution between one man and one woman. If marriage is redefined to include two people of the same sex, the argument goes, then it can be redefined to include more than two people.

"Critics reject the polygamy comparison, arguing that marriage's definition as a union of two people remains inviolable. They also dismiss the specter of legalized polygamy as a scare tactic used by the traditional-marriage camp to chill public support for same-sex marriage.

"Claiming much deeper roots in human society than gay marriage, plural marriage has been practiced for centuries in nations and cultures across the globe and has ties to both Christianity and Islam. Same-sex marriage is a recent phenomenon confined to the secular West.

"'Unlike same-sex marriage, which has no historical roots and is a new frontier — you can't say the same thing about polygamy,' said Austin Nimocks, attorney for the conservative Alliance Defense Fund, which opposes same-sex marriage. 'There's a cultural underpinning and support for plural marriage, so one could say the case is actually stronger for plural marriage.'"

"What About Polygamy"

by Norman Olson in the March/April Baptist Bulletin, Says:

"**Q. Legalizing polygamy has been in the news lately. If it's wrong, why did so many Old Testament believers practice it? Why did they go unpunished?**

"**A.** In the Dispensation of Innocence, God spelled out His perfect plan for marriage: 'And the Lord God said, It is not good that man should be alone; I will make him a helper comparable to him. . . . Then the rib which the Lord God had taken from man He made into a woman, and He brought her to the man. . . . Therefore a man shall leave his father and mother and be joined to his wife, and they shall become one flesh' (Genesis 2:18, 22, 24; Ephesians 5:31).

"Notice the singular aspect of this plan—a helper, a woman, a man. The passage implies that a man should leave his father and mother and cleave unto his wife one time, except for death (cf. Romans 7:2, 3). But mankind's fall into sin brought all kinds of deviations from God's perfect will, including issues in sex and marriage. Polygamy got its start in the ungodly line of Cain (Genesis 4:16–24). We then read about other perversions of fallen mankind as we continue through the Scriptures, including homosexuality and incest (Genesis 19; Jude 7).

"We view the swinging pendulum of morality over the centuries—from civilizations that were very corrupt, to societies greatly influenced by the Scriptures, such as our own United States. In recent years, however, the spiritual foundation of our country has been under attack. We are witnessing profound changes regarding homosexuality, abortion, prostitution, gambling, pornography, and so on. Signs indicate that things will only become worse.

"I wrote a letter to one of our U.S. senators recently about the repeal of the 'Don't Ask, Don't Tell' policy in the U.S. military. He answered my letter, 'I oppose discrimination based on an individual's sexual orientation.' I would like to respond by asking him what stance he will take when the issues of polygamy, incest, and other perversions come next. I have news items before me that report legalizing these practices is being considered in countries, including Canada. In some countries, they have been legalized already. *Newsweek* reported that 'polygamy activists [are] emerging in the wake of the gay-marriage movement.' Surely we are living in days like those of the judges, when 'everyone did what was right in his own eyes' (Judges 21:25). Our society is reaping a better harvest from at least a couple of generations thoroughly exposed to relativism, lack of Bible doctrine, and 'do your own thing' philosophies.

"Polygamy was indeed practiced by a number of Old Testament believers, including Abraham, Jacob, David, and Solomon. However, we must remember that others did not practice it, such as Adam, Noah, Job, Isaac, Moses, and Joseph and Mary. Practicing polygamy did not make it right. Feeble attempts have been made to explain why God allowed it and didn't punish those who engaged in it: A woman's need for the protection of a man outweighed the prohibition, since there were more females than males in the world; wars resulted in the need for replenishing the population; polygamy was better than divorce. None of these arguments has Scriptural support. The fact is, we do not know just why God allowed polygamy. We do know that it wasn't His design from the beginning. The Bible says that God permitted divorce because of the hardness of people's hearts, not because He approved of it.

"Throughout time, God's long-suffering concerning the innumerable evils of mankind is obvious. We learn of tragedies in our day and wonder, Why, God? Why do You allow such suffering and evil? But then we who know the Scriptures realize that mankind chose to sin and must bear the consequences. It was not God's fault. And we remember that someday all things will be made right. In the meantime, we can trust the sovereignty of God. He knows what He is doing.

"Polygamy has brought much unhappiness to its participants and victims. Accounts of polygamy from Utah in the 1800s reveal a sad chapter in U.S. history. In the Old Testament, Abraham's household suffered due to friction between Sarah and Hagar, and the consequences of his sin have resulted in major world tensions and conflicts today. If you read carefully the accounts of polygamists, you find that polygamy led to their downfall. David and Solomon are prime examples.

"Some people say we should merely let people do whatever they wish, especially when it involves 'religious beliefs.' But the government must protect people from what is destructive. The Biblical formula for marriage—one man, one woman—is under attack and must be protected if we are to continue as a society."

Pope Paul VI, A Homosexual, Right on Birth Control

Christian News, September 1, 2008

"40 Years After. . . .POPE PAUL VI WAS RIGHT AND THE WORLD WAS WRONG" from the August 21, 2008 *Wanderer*, praises Pope Paul VI for his 40 year old Vitae opposing birth control.

The Wanderer observes: "It's interesting to note, by the way, that the 16th-century Protestant Reformers, even as they were rejecting so much of Catholic doctrine, insisted on retaining the Church's condemnation of contraception. It was only fairly recently, beginning with the approval of contraception in 1930 by the Church of England and its Anglican off-shoots, that the Protestant churches began one by one to throw overboard what they previously had taught."

The Lutheran Church-Missouri Synod was the last major denomination to regularly condemn birth control as contrary to Scripture in its official publications and youth publications. Chapter VII on Birth Control in *Walter A. Maier Still Speaks – Missouri and the World Should Listen* shows what the Bible, Martin Luther, the LCMS and Walter Maier taught about Birth Control. Fritz's *Pastoral Theology,* used in the LCMS's seminaries, strongly opposed birth control. Today *Christian News* is one of the few publications which still defends this position. Even the Wisconsin Evangelical Lutheran Church's fine right to life group has caved in. It no longer defends the position one of its founders, Larry Marquardt, took against birth control. CN published what Larry Marquardt wrote about birth control.

While the Wanderer praises Pope Paul VI, it fails to recognize that evidence shows that Pope Paul VI was a homosexual. Randy Engel, a well informed Roman Catholic scholar in *The Rite of Sodomy – Homosexuality and the Roman Catholic Church* (New Engel Publishing https://www.riteofsodomy.com. 1,282 pages, $64.00) shows the tremendous inroads homosexuality has made into the Roman Catholic Church. Some have estimated that about half of today's Roman Catholic priests are homosexuals. Randy Engel presents documentation showing that some prominent Roman Catholic leaders are among the homosexuals. CN has yet to see any refutation of Engel's massive *The Rite of Sodomy – Homosexuality and the Roman Catholic Church.* It is unfortunate that even most Protestant and Lutheran publications have never even mentioned the book. Some editors and bloggers should spend less time with their computers and more time reading important books. The December 17, 2007 *Christian News* included several pages of quotations from the book. Here is part of what is in *The Rite of Sodomy – Homosexuality and the Roman Catholic Church* about Pope Paul VI:

"The 15-year pontificate of Paul VI was marked by a series of unprecedented crises and betrayals as has rarely been seen in the Roman Catholic Church at any point in its 2000 year-old history.

"The betrayals associated with the Second Vatican Council were put into motion by Pope John XXIII, who used his authority to facilitate the restructuring of the ten Conciliar Commissions. Pope John jettisoned all the original schemas drawn up by the Council's Preparatory Commission over a three-year period, save one, the schema on the Sacred Liturgy. Under Paul VI, the original schemas were replaced by new texts in keeping with the planned agenda that had been worked out by Archbishop Montini and the Rhine Group before the opening of the Council" (1147-1148).

"The Unprecedented Fraternization of the Church with heretics, schismatics and other traditional enemies of the Church including Communists, Freemasons, Zionists and functionaries of the so-called New World Order" (1150).

"All of the above mentioned actions associated with the reign of Pope Paul VI had catastrophic repercussions for the Church.

"Also, each in its own way benefited the rapidly expanding Homosexual Collective both within and without the Church during the Post-Conciliar era and each played a role in the paradigm shift in the Church's position on the vice of homosexuality that flowed out of the Second Vatican Council.

"Yet there still remains one further factor that needs to be considered when examining the Homosexual Collective's extraordinary success in colonizing the Catholic Church in the United States and abroad. That is the matter of Pope Paul VI's alleged own habituation to the vice of homosexuality" (1151-1152).

"It is significant that the Homosexual Collective's identification of Pope Paul VI as a homosexual took place long before the subject of homosexuality became part of the American consciousness. In other words, the rumor that Montini was sexually attracted to young men was part of the gossip-line of the Collective long before charges of homosexuality were publicly brought against the pope" (1152).

"The Curtain Comes Down"

"There can be no question Pope Paul VI's homosexuality was instrumental in the paradigm shift that saw the rise of the Homosexual Collective in the Catholic Church in the United States, at the Vatican and around the world in the mid-20th century.Pope Paul VI played a decisive role in the selection and advancement of many homosexual members of the American hierarchy including Joseph Cardinal Bernardin, Teraence Cardinal Cooke, John Cardinal Wright and Archbishop Rembert Weakland and Bishops George H. Guifoyle, Francis Mugavero, Joseph Hart,

Joseph Ferario, James Rausch and their heirs.

"The knowledge that a homosexual sat in the Chair of Peter – knowledge that spread like wild-fire on the 'gay' gossip circuit – would certainly have served as an inducement for homosexual men to aspire to the priesthood and even prompt them to contemplate the unthinkable – a religious order or community composed exclusively of sodomites.

"Most importantly, the long-guarded quasi-secret of Paul VI's homosexual life has, for decades, contributed to the silence and cover-up by the American hierarchy on the issue of homosexuality in general and the criminal activities of pederast priests in particular.

"But it is a secret no longer.

"The final piece of the puzzle has been put in place.

"Our Lady of Fatima, pray for us."

Media Catches Up to Luther On Celibacy, Whoremongers, Homosexuals and Pedophiles

By Rev. Jack Cascione

From *Luther Today-What Would He Do or Say*, pp. 157, 158.

(This writing by Luther is not appropriate for children).

It is 2002 and the media is finally focusing on the problems of the Catholic Church's promotion of celibate priests. Luther raised the issue in 1521. Luther claimed the requirement for celibacy was due to the perversion of the papacy. It has only taken the media 483 years to recognize what Luther wrote in some of his most vitriolic and graphic terms.

Luther wrote that there is nothing holy about celibacy. Rather imposed celibacy is perversion and marriage is holy, because God blessed marriage. Faithfulness in marriage is true chastity.

The introduction of celibacy was promoted by Pope Gregory VII in 1075 AD, who annulled the marriages of all priests. This madness was the result of the Catholic Church's flawed understanding of the "so called" sacrament of ordination. Catholics believe that ordination supposedly turns the priest into the equivalent of a transubstantiated communion wafer. Thus, the "holy priest" must have equally holy sons, who in turn inherit their father's office by divine rite. This is the inevitable direction of today's Hyper-Euro-Lutherans.

Pope Gregory solved the problem by imposing celibacy, thus making all the priests' sons bastards. Within a hundred years, celibacy made the Pope the most powerful man in the world because he now had the right to appoint all priests, bishops, archbishops, and cardinals and thus control all church property.

In answer to the Pope's perversion, Luther wrote: "Answer to the Hyperchristian, Hyper-spiritual, and Hyperlearned Book by Goat Emser in Leipzig-Including Some Thoughts Regarding His Companion, the Fool Murner" (1521) and another writing titled, "Against the Spiritual Estate of the Pope and the Bishops Falsely So Called" (1522).

Luther explains in his Genesis commentary that the sin of homosexuality had not infected the general population in his day as it did in Sodom and Gomorrah. There was a problem with an occasional traveling merchant or soldier, but, of all orders of monks, the Carthusians of Luther's day were notorious for problems with homosexuality.

Luther writes as follows in his Genesis commentary:

Genesis 19:4. But before they lay down, the men of the city, the men of Sodom, both young and old, all the people to the last man, surrounded the house;

Genesis 19:5. And they called to Lot: Where are the men who came to us, that we may know them.

"Moses proceeds with a description of a terrible sin. I for my part do not enjoy dealing with this passage, because so far the ears of the Germans are innocent of and uncontaminated by the monstrous depravity; for even though this disgrace, like other sins, has crept in through an ungodly soldier and a lewd merchant, still the rest of the people are unaware of what is being done in secret. The Carthusian monks deserve to be hated because they were the first to bring this terrible pollution into Germany from the monasteries of Italy. Of course, they were trained and educated in such a praiseworthy manner at Rome." Luther's Works, Volume 3: page 251.

Rather than a problem with homosexuality and pedophilia, in Luther's day, most of the priests kept whores, or their housekeepers, for some unknown reason, would conceive. Luther wrote as follows in "Against the Spiritual Estate of the Pope and The Bishops Falsely So Called" (1522):

"The papal bishops certainly have noble attributes which cost less effort. What are they? They are: to be ignorant; to avoid marriage instead to have little whores, as many as they need; to have a silver cane carried after themselves; to put on a precious hat; to have a big tonsure; to grab many towns and much land within the diocese; to ride fine horses; to hold princely court; to keep "Episcopal officials," LW 39:255.

"Adviser, advise well! Why do these whore-keepers dislike it when young men marry? No doubt because they lose their interest rates. For bishops receive the greater part of all their annual interest rates in almost all religious foundations from nothing but the priests' whores. Whoever wants to keep a little whore must give one guilder a year to the bishop. There is a proverb among them, 'Chaste priests are not liked by the bishop—indeed, they are his enemies.' Who else but a bishop could be a rich tradesman with women in this world? Who would blame the spiritual fathers for permitting whoredom for the sake of money, for selling living bodies of women and for prohibiting marriage, which does not yield money? People make their living in many ways. A merchant sells spices and linen, bishops sell the flesh of whores. How else could they make a living? To top it all, if a priest's maid stumbles over a dishpan and breaks in two, so that one part of her must be carried to baptism, the interest rate increases beyond the annual guilder. The bishop now has a reason to show his mercy by selling a mother to the poor priest. Blessed are the bellies that carry babies! But let the father worry about whether the breasts that are sucked are blessed too. The spiritual bishop has twice received his share from the belly. Are these not noble and dear female bellies, which have to be bought twice a year and which twice become pregnant with money for the spiritual lord!

"My dear, do not think this is a bad reason to motivate these holy spiritual people to forbid the poor priests to marry. Should they not prefer whores to pious wives? A married woman is a shameful and harmful thing; she does not produce a single penny for the most reverend fathers and lords in God. Forgive me this joke, my dear man; it comes not from a joking heart but rather from one made anxious by these very senseless and blind masks. They are completely deprived of all sense, wit, and reason by God's wrath so that pigs, oxen, and asses are smarter than they are. Yet they are spiritual rulers, which is really punishing the world with fools and babes, as Isaiah says (Isa. 3:4)! Do you think they can cite reasons and arguments other than those cited, which are only greed and money? Even if they were cruder than crude asses, they still could not say that God has prohibited marriage to the priests. Indeed, St. Paul instituted it for the priests when he said, 'A bishop should be the husband of one wife, keeping his children submissive and respectful,' I Timothy 3 (2, 4), and Titus 1:6. Do you hear this, you masks and gaping fools? I mean you who are wolves and who subject innocent blood to tyranny. Answer me: what would you like to say or what could you say about St. Paul's statement that a priest should have no more than one wife? How are you going to interpret 'one wife'? As a priest's whore whose belly you sell twice a year? St. Paul means only one wife, not two or more wives as was custom and law in the Old Testament. So if a priest wanted to obey this divine saying, who are you, you blood-thirsty masks, to prevent him? What is your argument? What do you say against it? Why do you elevate yourself above God and his words? Should one worship you unlearned asses more than God?

"The pope prohibited it. What shall I say? My dear asses, if the pope commands you not to honor your father and mother (which he really does) and destroyed all of God's commandments, should you not be the ones to oppose him, risking life and limb for the sake of God's word? Did you not read St. Peter's saying, Acts 4 (5:29), 'One must obey God rather than men? Then you know that all human commandments, even if they were good and useful, are invalid and are no longer binding when they become unbearable. Your own fleshly law teaches you that. You can see that it is impossible for all priests to obey the accursed human law prohibiting marriage. Yet you great insatiable keepers of women still forcibly drive the poor souls into sin for the sake of your accursed greed. You can see and understand that they cannot obey the law, but (you say) they should obey it without any trouble. Oh, you murderers of souls! How shamefully you stain your hands with innocent blood! What an account you will have to render for such tyranny!

"But now it is indeed clear that these human commandments regarding the prohibition of clerical marriage are not human commandments but rather commandments of the devil. Three passages from St. Paul prove it. Two of them are the passages to Titus (Titus 1:6) and to Timothy (I Tim. 3:2) mentioned above, that a priest shall have only one wife. This is God's word and order, (spoken) through St. Paul. That is why whatever is commanded or ordered differently must be the devil's work. For God does not speak against himself or give the lie to his mouth, as all Scripture and all reason must confess. But all reason must also confess that these papal laws are indeed contrary to Paul's divine order. Is all this not clear enough, you silent and blind masks? How can you chafe against that? Are your iron heads and crude minds not ashamed publicly to commanded and force everyone to keep the commandments of the devil contrary to divine order? The third passage is I Timothy 4:1-3, 'Teachers will come with pretensions, teaching devilish doctrines. They will forbid marriages and enjoin abstinence from foods which God created.' See, he himself calls it devilish teaching to prohibit marriage. Nor does he speak here of the Tatians, as the liar of Dresden says. The Tatians did not prohibit marriage; rather, they condemned it as something sinful. But St. Peter speaks here of those who prohibit it rather than condemning it or regarding it as sinful, just as they prohibit food without regarding it as sinful. The pope is doing just that: he does not, like the Tatians, say that marriage is an evil or a sin; again, he does not consider meat, eggs, or milk evil or sin. Instead, he prohibits them in order to make a pretense of spirituality, as St. Paul says here. Thus they speak through pretensions based on the devil's teaching." Luther's Works Vol. 39: pages 289-292.

Family Shield Reports: Thrivent Will Not Support Any Pro-Life Program

Christian News, February 28, 2011

"Thrivent Financial currently has a policy that they will not support any pro-life program or anything to do with Biblical principals related to sexuality. This is, according to them, too controversial. The Board of Directors and I prayerfully encourage Thrivent leaders to rethink this policy. It is unbiblical" writes Kay L. Meyer, Founder, President, and Host of Family Shield in a February 21 Family Shield Ministries News letter.

The Aid Association for Lutherans and Lutheran Brotherhood which formed Thrivent have a long history of financing many groups but refusing to support those who publicly oppose the pro-abortion, pro-homosexual and liberal theological position of those who formed Seminex. (See the *Christian News Encyclopedia* for evidence). Thrivent has told *Christian News* that it cannot support *Christian News* because "*Christian News* is not neutral." CN responded that it is true that CN is not neutral. It has a positive public position. It does oppose abortion, homosexuality, and anti-scriptural theology. It does list the names of liberals, following a pattern set forth in the Bible and the Lutheran confessions.

Bonhoeffer and King - Their Life and Theology Documented in Christian News - 1963-2011 shows that the AAL spent millions promoting Dietrich Bonhoeffer, a liberal Lutheran theologian who denied the deity and resurrection of Christ and insisted the Bible contains legends and fiction. CN sent documentary evidence to the AAL Board of Directors about Bonhoeffer's theology. The LCMS bureaucracy and many conservatives, who have received support from Thrivent, hesitate to protest against Thrivent's policy of not supporting those who publicly oppose abortion and homosexuality.

Those who publicly oppose abortion, homosexuality, and the promotion of theological liberalism by naming the liberals must pay the price. They will not receive support from major insurance companies and foundations who will support liberals and conservatives who do not publicly object to the toleration of theological liberalism within the Lutheran Church - Missouri Synod. Seminarians are taught to "cooperate and graduate." Conservative publications and organizations are taught to cooperate with the bureaucracy and get the money.

Christian News recently wrote to Dr. Addie Butler, a member of the Board of Directors of Thrivent and Dr. Kurt Senske, Chairman, Board of Directors, Thrivent Financial for Lutherans.

September 30, 2010
Dr. Addie Butler, Elective Director
Thrivent Financial for Lutherans
4321 N. Ballard Road
Appleton, Wisconsin
54919-0001

Dear Dr. Butler:
"Thrivent Re-Elects Pro-Lesbian to Board," a story on page one of the May 4, 2009 *Christian News* said: "Thrivent Financial for Lutherans has re-elected Addie J. Butler to the organization's Board of Directors. CN has noted for more than 10 years that Butler, a former ELCA Vice-president, is a pro-lesbian and that she is a member of a homosexual and lesbian group." "Butler was recommended for re-election by the Thrivent Board of Directors."
Homosexuals and lesbians rejoiced at your election.
Are you a lesbian?
Do you believe that practicing homosexuals and lesbians should be permitted to serve as pastors and members of the Thrivent Board of Directors?
Sincerely,
Herman Otten, editor
Christian News

No response

November 23, 2010
Dr. Kurt Senske, Chair-

man
Board of Directors
Thrivent Financial for
Lutherans

Dear Dr. Senske:
Attached is a letter *Christian News* sent on September 30 to Dr. Addie Butler, one of the members of your Thrivent Board of Directors. Dr. Butler has not responded. Some have left Thrivent, claiming that the Thrivent Board of Directors defends Dr. Butler, "a lesbian or lesbian sympathizer." The Thrivent Board of Directors recommended the election of Dr. Butler. Did you support this recommendation? Have you expressed any concern about having Dr. Butler on your board?
Sincerely,
Herman Otten, editor
Christian News
684 Luther Lane
New Haven, Missouri
63068

No response

Concordia Publishing House recently published *The Calling: Live a Life of Significance* by Kurt Senske. CPH's Paul McCain has been enthusiastically promoting the book. McCain wrote in one of his Cyberbrethren blogs:
"Dr. Kurt Senske serves as Chief Executive Officer of Lutheran Social Services of the South (LSS), as Chair of the Board of Directors of Thrivent Financial for Lutherans, and on the Board of Directors of Lutheran Services in America. He holds a law degree from the University of Illinois College of Law, a BS in Business Administration from Valparaiso University, a master's degree in International Relations from Schiller International University in Paris, France, and a PhD in Government from the University of Texas at Austin.

IX

CHURCHES ARE DYING - NOT ENOUGH CHILDREN

Not Enough Children
Christian News, October 21, 1985

"Childless Clergy" in the November, 1985 *Lutheran Women*, published by Lutheran Church Women, Lutheran Church in America, supports clergy couples who are physically able to have children but have decided to practice birth control and remain childless.

The Lutheran Church formerly took a strong stand against birth control. See "The Deadly ABC" by the late Dr. Martin Naumann of The Lutheran Church - Missouri Synod in the *Christian News Encyclopedia* (p. 1437). Also note "Jose Espinosa's "Medical View on Contraception", CNE, p. 436; "The Myth of Overpopulation," CNE, 1438; "The Tragedy of Birth Control" by Dr. Martin Naumann, CNE, p. 1439; " 'Artificial Birth Control' Held Cause of Rising Divorce Rate," CNE, p. 1435; and "Zero Growth Brings Problems" by M. Stanton Evans, CNE, p. 1435.

China's official one-child-per-family policy is producing a generation of spoiled brats whose parents require special instruction in how to cope with them, the Xinhua News Agency has reported.

"In the past five years, newly married couples in Peking actively answered the call of the Communist Party and adhered to the single-child policy," *Peking Daily* said:

"According to the statistics, more than 740,000 young couples had only one child, making up 95.16 percent of the total." Nearly 94 percent of couples married in the first half of 1985 agreed to have only one child, compared with 83 percent in 1979, the paper said.

Lutheran Women and all church publications should be promoting larger families rather than smaller families or childless ones. Pastors should set a good example for their congregations and not remain childless, if they are able to have children.

Dr. Harold O.J. Brown, who has been active in the pro-life movement and is now interim pastor at the Evangelical Reformed Church of Kooster, Switzerland, while he is on leave of absence from Trinity Evangelical Divinity School, Deerfield, Illinois, writes in the "Speaking Out" column in the October 18 *Christianity Today*:

"Feminist Betty Friedan called for a second stage of feminism when she recognized that many women need to invest themselves in marriage and children (as well as in a career) in order to find fulfillment. Yet even Friedan may not be able to stop the forces unleashed by ideological feminism.

Because of abortion on demand and other social forces, Americans are now experiencing the "birth dearth." Although it is not the sole cause for the dramatic drop in U.S. births, the 1.5 million abortions per year tremendously reduce the number of babies.

In the U.S., the average number of children per family has fallen below two. An average of 2.1 is needed for the present adult generations simply to reproduce itself. It is only because the older generation now passing from the scene has fewer members than the present crop of young adults that births still outnumber deaths.

Collective Suicide

The whole developed world faces the same problem. Noted French demographer Pierre Chaunu observes: "The rejection of (marriage and the family) is a recent phenomenon. For the moment, it is limited to the sixth of the world that constitutes the developed nations, the eight hundred million men and women who have decided to commit the strangest collective suicide of history."

There are two dramatic social changes that contribute to this collective suicide: in France and Scandinavia, fewer people marry; in West Germany and the U.S., they marry but often remain childless.

While no Western nation now attains the average 2.1 children per family that is needed to maintain the population, the figures for West Germany are catastrophic: the average dropped to 1.27 children per family. By the year 2020, if present trends continue, the population of West Germany will decline from over 60 million to 30 million.

The United States, France and Switzerland remain comparatively better off. But, says Professor Chaunu, the difference between West Germany on the one hand and countries such as France, Switzerland and the United States on the other, is the difference between imminent population collapse and slow death.

A Biblical Defense For Large Families

By Brenda Weatherly
Christian News, August 5, 2002

Christians have avoided the practice of birth control both for biblical and social reasons throughout history. Couples with many children were highly esteemed in Christian society because a large family was a sign of God's abundant blessings and prosperity in their lives. Why would anyone think that so many children to take care of and feed would be a blessing? Because God told us so: Psalm 127:3-5 says, "Sons are a heritage from the Lord, children a reward from Him. Like arrows in the hands of a warrior are sons born in one's youth. Blessed is the man whose quiver is full of them." Did you know that 75 percent of America's Presidents came from families with five or more siblings? And that Jesus Himself came from a family with at least six siblings (Mark 6:3)? What a drastic comparison to today's 1.8 children per American family!

What has happened to the Christian church in such a short time period that it has changed its views about families so dramatically? I believe Satan, The Deceiver, has crept in and taken control of Christian's minds and warped their ways of traditional thinking. We have forgotten that Satan's main goals are to steal, kill and destroy (John 10:10). In today's culture, instead of being looked down upon for not having children, couples are being criticized for having more that that magical number of "2" children per household. The biggest tragedy is that even the Christian church is alienating themselves from fathers and mothers who choose to let God bless them with a quiver full of children. It is not uncommon for the mother with many young children to hear negative comments from her fellow church members and friends, such as "Don't you know what causes that?" "Why in the world would you want to have so many children?" "Don't you know there's something for that?" or "When are you going to stop having kids?" And when the outward comments aren't made, surely many people are in a state of confusion as to why anyone in their right mind would want to have more than one, two, or even three children.

Satan has caused us to believe a number of lies about birth control and large families. Some of the myths that Satan has implanted in our minds are: 1) God gave us the technology to make and use birth control, therefore birth control must be a good idea and we must take advantage of it, 2) It is financially irresponsible to have more than 1 or 2 children, 3) Having a lot of children is too great a burden for any mother to bear, and 4) Too many children cause stress in a marriage. All of these myths can easily be refuted with Scripture.

Lack of Babies
Churches Are Dying
Christian News, April 16, 2007

"Simply put, in order for there to be babies to baptize, they must first be born. They are not and the churches are dying" says Aaron Wolf, Associate Editor, in the April, 2007 *Chronicles* (928 North Main Street, Rockford, Illinois 61103, www.chroniclesmagazine.org), in an article titled "When Experts Attack - The Church Growth Movement Versus Church Growth."

Wolf continues: "Take one example: In 1961, The Lutheran Church-Missouri Synod baptized 82,000 babies. In 2004, only 33,000 - a staggering decline of 60 percent. And the numbers released in late August for 2005 are worse: Only 31,700 children were baptized (down 1,300)."

"Saffen Rails vs. Otten and His Ilk," in April 16, 2007 *Christian News*, notes that LCMS Professor James Burkee in his Ph.D. thesis for Northwestern University critical of CN editor Otten, writes: "Church liberals, he carped, were legitimizing homosexuality, pornography and contraception. Most major Protestant denominations, he complained, no longer condemned the use of contraception." Burkee then quotes from the CN editor's *Baal or God* published in 1965. *Christian News* is one of the few religious publications which has, during the last 45 years, opposed the birth control movement. CN champions the position taken by Martin Luther, Walter Maier, John Fritz and formerly by the LCMS's *Lutheran Witness* and *Walther League Messenger*. Wolf writes in the April, 2007 *Chronicles*: "For over 30 years, the churches of America have been declining; their numbers, plummeting. Each year, a new set of numbers emerges from the various denominational headquarters, telling the tale. The liberal Protestant mainlines are in the worst shape, as the figures for 2006 to 2007 indicate."

"Their conservative counterparts are not faring much better. The largest Protestant denomination, the Southern Baptist Convention, at 16,270,315 members, reported a slight increase of 0.02 percent. The Lutheran Church-Missouri Synod, down to 2,440,864, reported a decrease of 0.93 percent. Only the Catholic Church, at 69,135,254 members nationwide, managed to buck the trend, reporting an increase of 1.94 percent."

"Researchers who support the Church Growth Movement contradict Warren's enthusiasm, even indicating that there is a deliberate deception going on. Thom S. Rainer writes, 'When I shared with many of the leaders of these congregations that most of the growth in American megachurches the past 20 years had come from transfer growth (Christians moving from one church to another), few were surprised.' Rainer, who is quite sympathetic to the aims of the Church Growth Movement, admits that "Every level of research I have seen on megachurches in the past 20 years, including my own, has pointed to a clear and growing trend: The percentage of American churchgoers attending churches with an attendance of 2,000 or more is increasing. More church attendees are worshipping at megachurches, and fewer attendees are heading to smaller churches."Two things are certain: More and more Americans are flocking to megachurches; and more and more Americans are not going to church at all. In other words, the sheep are wandering off to another pasture, then wandering off a cliff. Barna indicates that a staggering 20 million have gone from megachurches and their veteran impersonators to something they call *homechurch*. Overall, the percentage of Americans attending Christian churches each Sunday has dropped from 20.4 percent in 1990 to 18.7 percent in 2000 - and down to 17.7 percent in 2004. During that same period, the U.S. population has grown by 18.1 percent - more than 48 million people. So the churches are nowhere near keeping up with the overall population. Thus, Thom Rainer notes that '94% of our churches are losing ground in the communities they serve.'"

"'But,' Warner adds, 'simple demographics can account for almost three fourths of the mainline decline.' Could it really be that simple? Yes, say Michael Hout of the University of California-Berkeley, Andrew Greeley of the University of Arizona, and Melissa Wilde of Indiana University: 'For most of the 20th century, conservative women had more children than mainline women did.' In fact, 'Differences in fertility rates account for 70 percent of the decline of mainline Protestant church membership from 1900 to 1975 and the simultaneous rise in conservative church membership. . .'

"And now, conservative Protestants and Catholics have finally caught up. 'Fertility rates are now virtually the same' for the liberal.mainlines and conservative Christians, writes Wagner. Thus, the liberals and conservatives are in the deathbed together, as the trio of sociologists write, for, 'Unless conservative[s] increase their family size or mainline Protestants further reduce theirs, this factor in mainline decline will not be present in the future.'""Blithely, the church's leaders pass over this defect, as a press release from the Missouri Synod indicates: 'In the 1950s and '60s, churches saw a "natural increase" because families were larger, says LCMS Senior Research Analyst, Dr. John O'Hara. Today's families are much smaller, and societal norms regarding religious participation have changed, he said.'"

"Indeed, they have. 'Society's norms' changed, and the American churches have changed right along with them, following the Whore of Babylon to her sure destruction. In 1930, with the Anglican Church's Lambeth Conference, the Church of England caved in to the propaganda campaign waged by the neo-Malthusians and their Babylonian queen, Margaret Sanger, editor of the Woman Rebel and founder of what is now called Planned Parenthood. Eschewing the divine blessing of the Logos uttered on Day Six of Creation. 'Be fruitful,' and the solemn command that followed, 'and multiply,' the Episcopalians spoke their own destruction into existence by transgressing against 2,000 years of unbroken Christian teaching, East and West, Protestant and Catholic. For them, large families were bovine, the fruit of the unrestrained actions of an ignorant people lacking self-control."

"After this self-important celebration of unselfish selfishness, the American churches began to fall, one by one. The old Federal Council of Churches quickly followed Lambeth by not only endorsing but recommending contraception. Mainline acceptance of modern Onanism penetrated the Mainline congregations, and their numbers began to decline. And the conservatives followed a few lengths back. In the 40's, Walter A. Maier of the old *Lutheran Hour* radio broadcast called Sanger a 'she-devil' and denounced the hedonism of liberal mainline Christianity. By the 50's, Prof. Alfred Rehwinkel, a conservative defender of a literal interpretation of Genesis, was celebrating Sanger and encouraging the same 'self-control' that the Anglican demanded in 1930. Rehwinkel's book, in which he lauded Sanger's 'brilliance' and 'God-given talents,' was published under the thoroughly modern title Planned Parenthood, the name Sanger used to rechristen her Birth Control League.

"T.S. Eliot, in his *Thoughts After Lambeth*, wrote:
> The World is trying the experiment of attempting to form a civilized but non-Christian mentality. The experiment will fail; but we must be very patient in awaiting its collapse; meanwhile redeeming the time: so that the Faith may be preserved alive through the dark ages before us; to renew and rebuild civilization, and save the World from suicide.

"A present rates, we won't have to wait too much longer."

Christian News published Ron Stelzer's "*Salt, Light and Signs of the Times - An Intimate Look at the Life and Times of Alred (Rip) Rehwinkel.*" While CN was in accord with most of Rehwinkel's views, CN did not agree with him on what he wrote about birth control in Planned Parenthood published by the LCMS's Concordia Publishing House. Dr. Robert Preus, who was also a professor at Concordia Seminary, St. Louis, where Rehwinkel taught, agreed with Rehwinkel on almost everything except birth control. Some of the articles CN has published on birth control are in the *Christian News Encyclopedia*. CN has promoted large families, often publishing photos of such families. Rev. John Parcher, who wrote many articles appearing in *Christian News*, has 18 children and now around 100 grandchildren. The January 1, 2007 *Christian News* published a photo of Mrs. Robert Preus with 93 of her children and grandchildren.

Large Families Beneficial to Earth
By Claudia Ericson, Fontana
From the *Walworth, Wisconsin Times*, June 3, 1992.
Christian News, October 12, 1992

About the only thing on which I can agree with Kent Johnson's May 20 editorial, "Suffer the Children," is that, yes, it's time to think and act globally to prevent unimaginable human suffering.

Unfortunately, Mr. Johnson advocates one more easy answer or "solution" to all the crises in our world: stop having large families and convince our UN delegates, religious leaders and legislators to help other people world-wide to learn and practice birth control and family planning. Supposedly, we will then reverse the destruction of our natural world, and have adequate food to eat and water to drink.

We could follow Mr. Johnson's short-sighted "remedy:" world-wide birth control to promote the eventual elimination of undesirable large families. However, I wonder if, before we tidy up our world by completely eliminating large families, perhaps we could first learn something from them about the way they need to cooperate in order to live together peacefully and lovingly.

Probably the most obvious thing we can learn is that large families need to share. Regardless of how much or how little my large family had, sharing was a habit, not an option. We shared bedrooms, beds, bathrooms, telephones, clothing, food, living space, toys, friends, parents and the Sunday paper. Because living with a dozen or more people required that we learn to balance our own needs with the needs of others, we also learned to be flexible and adaptable.

Where there were so many others' needs, we had few opportunities to become self-absorbed or overly concerned with creature comforts. When there were small children who needed attention (and, perhaps a clean diaper), we learned patience and sacrifice. When we argued and there weren't enough rooms in which to hide, we learned forgiveness. When many people shared few bathrooms, we learned consideration and thoughtfulness.

With such a variety of personalities living under one roof, we learned to be tolerant and appreciative of each other's differences. When there were a dozen pork chops for dinner and someone unexpected arrived, we shared what we had and learned hospitality. We practiced recycling and conservation long before it was politically correct.

We never went without; we never felt unloved. Our home was people-centered, not thing-centered. The lonely, the friendless, and the unexpected were always welcome in our home and at our dinner table. No matter how full, there was always room for one more. While some of our friends spent little time in their own empty homes, they spent a great deal of time in our full, sometimes-crowded, always boisterous home.

Aren't these qualities ones from which our world could still benefit? And what better place to start than in our own homes, whether our families are large or small? Because the world's crises really have nothing to do with overpopulation by large families, or inadequate food and water.

There is more than enough food and water if we can solve the problems of distribution. And there are not too many people living on our earth – just too many who are greedy, careless and wasteful. We don't need to push birth control and small-family planning; we need to push the idea of responsibility towards each other. We certainly are in a crisis if we use our own greed as a litmus test for how many people with whom we can share our earth.

Sometimes, we seem to forget that how well we take care of ourselves isn't as important as how well we take care of each other. And this all begins at home – and it spreads person to person, family to family, neighbor to neighbor, and country to country, to prevent human suffering.

Pastor and Mrs. John Parcher and their 18 children, 1984. Pastor Parcher was a longtime columnist for *Christian News*. At the time of his death on October 8, 2011 the Parcher's had more than 100 grandchildren.

Mrs. Robert Preus, wife of former president of Concordia Seminary, Ft. Wayne, with 93 of her children and grandchildren, *Christian News*, January 1, 2007.

X

COURTING - ENGAGEMENT

Christian Courtship

Christian News, September 14, 1981

"The days of courtship and romance are the loveliest days in the life of man," declared the pastor. "I have used that word lovely with design," he continued, "for love must be at the root and heart of all courtship and romance it would be a truly lovely experience. Where it is absent and sheer lust or animal passion have their way and sway, the courtship soon degenerates into a horrid experience and definitely blights both body and soul. The highest and holiest kind of courtship is Christian courtship."

With these words the pastor introduced the discussion of courtship to the young people of his congregation. For many years he had followed the practice of setting aside one evening of the year for a very frank and free discussion of matters pertaining to marriage and the home. These meetings were always well attended. The young people loved them and looked forward to them. They were informal meetings. The young people were encouraged to express themselves freely. In previous meetings, divorce, engagement, marriage, personal purity, and other matters related to the home had been discussed. For this particular evening "Christian Courtship" was on the docket. There was plenty of buzz and excitement. It was only natural that the young people showed a keen interest in the subject. Here was a matter which definitely concerned them and yet one concerning which there was much confusion and misgiving. All of them naturally sought the thrill and the satisfaction of a happy romance. It was a basic drive in their lives.

As a result, questions were not slow in coming. And the pastor welcomed the opportunity to answer them. Now, here is about the way the questions ran and the answers which the pastor gave to them.

What Should Courtship Be?

Courtship is a hunting expedition. Stripped of its lacery, it is simply the effort of a man or woman to find a mate for life. You see, the Lord in His infinite wisdom has endowed man with certain mating urges, and when these begin to assert themselves, as the body and mind mature, the natural and normal result is the quest for courtship. Needless to state, these urges are healthy urges. To be sure, they are sex urges; yet they are much more. If properly directed and controlled, these urges make for life's greatest joys and satisfactions. If abused or misdirected, they make for lifelong remorse and regret. Yet every young life seeks courtship and romance. It is his or her normal right.

Now, it should be noted that courtship is always a means to an end, and that end, whether recognized or not, must always be marriage and the home. This very recognition of marriage as the ultimate goal of courtship not only gives direction and meaning to courtship, but also helps guard against certain excesses. Courtship dare never be pursued as an end in itself. If so, it soon degenerates into mere sex satisfaction, or carnal debauchery. Only when courtship is pursued with a view to ultimate marriage will it continue to operate on a high and holy level. And courtship is something more than mere friendship and companionship. To be sure, it is these, but something infinitely higher. It is the steppingstone to the greatest companionship in life, that of man and wife in marriage and the home.

Courtship, at least in the beginning, is little more than an opportunity for two young people to ascertain their fitness for each other with a view to possible marriage. In its further development it is the natural forming and strengthening of that genuine affection and love which is the true basis of all happy marriages. Courtship, then, in its simplest form is mate hunting.

Though bluntly expressed, it's absolutely true. The girl you court has a right to expect, and I believe usually does, that you may want to marry her someday.

This will account for the encouragement or discouragement which she will give to your courtship advances. In all honest courtships both parties should always realize that this may be the first step toward the altar. This very implication makes the "hunt and search" period doubly interesting and significant. And the young man must never lose sight of this as he sets out on his courtship quests. With what veneration and concern he will regard the girl he is courting when he feels that she will probably someday become his wife and the mother of his children! And with what caution and confidence a girl will entrust herself to the young man when she visualizes him as her probable husband and the head of the family! When in addition the young folks look upon marriage as a divine institution, in which God has a tremendous stake, there will be something deeply religious about all of their courtship. They will not overlook the will of God in all that they do and say, but will try to order all of their ways in accord with His Word. Courtship is justifiable only in the light of the marriage to which it may lead. Let me repeat, love and love only, is the key to a truly happy courtship.

Christian and Non-Christian Courtship

There is a difference. It is essentially the same difference that distinguishes the Christian life from the non-Christian life, the Christian death from the non-Christian death. Where deep Christian convictions are lodged in the mind and heart of young lovers, these convictions will definitely affect the entire tone, level, and drift of their courtship. Thus Christians look upon marriage as something divine, in which God plays a vital part, and they recognize courtship as their first step toward this divine institution. Non-Christians know little of this. Christians look upon the body as the temple of the Holy Ghost and in courtship will do nothing to harm or abuse the body, knowing that "the body is not for fornication, but for the Lord, and the Lord for the body." Non-Christians know nothing of this. Christians have a high regard for morality and personal purity and are duty bound to flee youthful lusts. Non-Christians in their giddy whirl of dine, drink, and dance know nothing of this. Christians are guided and moved by Christian love and idealism in their courtship relations. Non-Christians know nothing of this. Too frequently non-Christians know nothing of the promptings of Christian love. Courtship to the non-Christian is frequently an end in itself, and not a noble end at that. But to the Christian it is definitely a stepping stone to something infinitely higher and nobler – engagement, holy matrimony, and the home. Guided by prayer and a conscience enlightened by the Word of God, the Christian is ever mindful of the will of Christ in his courtship and romance. This is also the reason prompting him to seek his courtship among Christians and in a manner inviting Christian sanctions and support. There is, then, a basic difference between Christian and non-Christian courtships. Their standards are different. Their ends and aim are frequently different.

Honor, purity, mutual esteem and reverence, and the desire to promote the health and happiness of the other will always characterize Christian lovers. They will ever strive to keep their courtship hallowed, innocent, and sublime. And they will thrill to the natural development of courtship, first the date, then keeping company, then going steady, then engagement, and finally marriage.

When a young man and a young lady have been keeping company for a while, they are no longer the same as they were before. They are either better or worse. If it is Christian courtship, they are decidedly better in every possible way. If, however, they are mentally, morally, and physically worse as a result of their courtship, they can be sure that theirs is not a Christian courtship. The only courtship worth while is Christian courtship.

What About Dating?

What about it? Well, it is as normal and natural as the air you breathe. Young people should date and be dated. Parents want it. God urges it. Young people need it.

Days of courtship, as you know, are the days of love's young dreams, and they begin with dating. Let the romance-inclined young man seek a date with the girl who in her own way "gave him quiet attention, not so pointed as to alarm, nor so vague as not to be understood." He can ask her in person at the close of the young people's meeting. He can phone her. He, like Isaac, can have another speak for him. He may even blind-date her, but only with caution and the utmost care. He will try to ascertain in advance what pleases her most, the "movie, meal, or merry-go-round," possibly all three, and try to arrange for her pleasure in these preferred areas. The counsel and confidence of his mother will always prove a real help to him in this vital matter.

Courtship is a growing experience and as a result will involve successive dating. The healthiest courtships are not hurried courtships. It is best not to rush matters. Romance has a way all its own and, if left to itself, will soon determine its own timetable, speed, and course.

Needless to state, the days of dating and courtship test youth's character to the utmost. Then the strength or weakness of character are soon revealed. Pity the young man and woman whose fascination for the other is born of weakness of character. Their courtship will soon degenerate into base debauchery. On the other hand, where the attraction is found in the strength of character and the appeal of love, there courtship soon ripens into something noble and beautiful. After all has been said and done, it is character that gives true beauty to courtship.

Christian lovers will at all times be guided by an enlightened conscience and the fear of God in their behavior toward each other. Love will dictate and direct their expressions of endearment. Intimacies reserved for the married and the engaged will never be indulged in by them. They will be ever cautious of what they say and do, lest they endanger the success of their own courtship or that of others, should this particular romance fail.

Let me repeat, love and love only, is the key to a truly happy courtship and romance. The answer to the question how far a man can go when he courts the girl is found in that one word "love." Love will give the proper guidance. Love is beautiful, noble, self-sacrificing, pure, and always seeks the good of the beloved. There is not a selfish note in the song of love. Lust, on the other hand is hideous, base, selfish, impure, and seeks nothing outside itself. It will ever be true: all the fine promises of affection, all the sweet expressions of endearment that are whispered to a girl in the course of courtship are but lies and deceits of the vilest kind if it is lust and not love that prompts these expressions. So by all means date the girl, but date her only in love.

Is It Wrong to Go Out with More than One Girl?

Certainly not if you are lucky enough to have more that one girl "fall for you." And you will certainly try to date a fourth girl if the first three feel disinclined to further romance with you after the first venture. Some would find virtue in going out with but one girl and finding the right one at the very outset. More power to them! We have repeatedly seen instances of love at first sight and a love that definitely blossomed and grew more beautiful with the passing of years. We have seen other "loves at first sight" which were not so good. Someone, we felt, had lost his head at first sight and apparently had lacked the restraint and self-control so indispensable to a truly happy courtship. There is undeniably something like one love, an early love, and the only love with some people, but for the majority of young people, we feel, more than one date, possibly a series of dates, is most advisable and beneficial. So, if one girl somehow or other refuses to be dated by you, do not hesitate to date another. You will, of course, be a gentleman at all times.

When courtship has progressed so far that the young lady has come to believe that the young man has serious intentions of marriage and that the formal engagement is just around the corner, courtship with another girl is positively out of place. It is immoral. There is a point in every courtship beyond which the quest of man for other courtships is a sign of fickleness, selfishness, insincerity.

So, there is nothing wrong in dating several girls successively provided your deportment at all times is what it should be. If your dating flounders the first time, try again.

How About the Religion of the Girl?

Certainly it is character that counts, but the undergirding of character is religion. Morality is a vital part of character and morality without the restraints and inspiration of religion is unthinkable.

If the Lord in His Word repeatedly warns against marriage with pagans, and if experience definitely proves that a divided religion makes for a divided home, then certainly the wise young man will carefully consider the religion of the girl he is inclined to court. If her religion is clearly contrary to his, he should move on. It is true that not all mixed marriages are unhappy, at least not to the human eye; yet it is equally true that not many of them give that measure of wholehearted joy and satisfaction to be found in a home where man and wife kneel at the same altar. Some religions are definitely antagonistic and fanatical. They especially must be shunned. Others are of so passive and spineless a nature as to contribute little or nothing to the spiritual life of the home. Such a religion in a home will prove a positive drag on a spiritually alive Christian. On the other hand, when there is one God, one religion, one altar, and one pastor as confidant and friend, that marriage will enjoy tremendous advantages. Marriages of this type seldom fail. And the secret is largely in the religios unity and the common family worship which it inspires.

Because of the prominence of religion in the successful operation of the home the young man will wisely and tactfully inquire about the religion of the girl he wants to date. If she has a religion which conflicts with his own, he will check his affections and turn them into more promising channels. Despite the rational attitude that love is blind and that its emotions cannot be controlled, it is a matter of common, everyday experience that affections can be stifled or redirected. It is always wise to be alerted for certain friendships and against others. And undesirable friendships which may accidentally bud and eventually flower into engagement and marriage had best be avoided from the very beginning. If you want your courtship unburdened by religious conflicts and your subsequent home life undisturbed by religious bickering and strife, it is best to shun at the very beginning the girl who will not kneel at God's altar with you.

What About That Good Night Kiss?

I know that it took courage to ask this question, and I shall endeavor to answer it in the spirit in which it was submitted. Twenty-five years ago that question would have been unasked. Then lips were guarded as sacred and reserved only for those whose love was definitely sealed in engagement and marriage. Yet in our day the "goodnight kiss" has become all too fashionable, and the girl who will not submit to it is simply out of date and out of luck.

But is she? Is this really a concession she must make in order to rate in the courtship advances of the young man? Frankly, I doubt this. I was happy to note that in a questionnaire recently submitted to approximately 400 students at a Midwestern university fully 60 percent of the students left no doubt as to where they stood in this matter. "If the price I must pay is the virtue of my lips, he'd better think twice before he tries to date me," wrote one young lady. And another asks: "How can anyone enjoy a partner who lives on nothing but mushing and necking?" that was their answer to the "goodnight kiss."

Generally speaking, a kiss shows no moral implications. A goodnight kiss in itself may be neither right nor wrong. Yet under conditions it must be right or wrong. It is right when it is an expression of something honest, noble, and beautiful between man and woman and is done in a manner not offensive to others or harmful to themselves. From ancient times a kiss has been looked upon as a sign and symbol of deep affection between two individuals. It is this between parent and child, husband and wife, and between intimate friends. It must be this, and only this, in courtship. When the lips of lovers meet, it must be the expression of the deepest love, moved by the desire to bind and solidify this love in eventual marriage. It speaks where words fail and seals mutual esteem and friendship.

Promiscuous kissing debases the noble sign of friendship. Aaron Hill was probably right when he said: "She most attracts who longest can refuse." No young man in quest of honest courtship and marriage will find much attraction in lips that have been freely roughed by the passion of others. And if the girl he is wooing is easy and ready to grant un-maidenly privileges and familiarities to him the young man will, and usually does, rightly infer that she has been equally loose and wanton in her conduct toward others. It won't take him long to tire of her and to spurn her.

That should be sufficient on the "Goodnight kiss." Next please.

What About Necking and Petting?

It is with no little reluctance that I touch upon this matter, and yet, being a realist, I feel that I should.

If by petting and necking you mean the passionate foundling of the body, often accompanied by prolonged kissing, on bodily parts of the young man and woman in the course of their courtship, then these terms point to a carnal indulgence as coarse, cheap, vulgar, and sordid, as the very terms themselves would seem to indicate. All passionate embracing and kissing and all impure fondling of the body by would-be lovers is just plain lewd and lecherous. Young people who stoop to such carnal indulgence reveal an extremely low and feeble conception of morality and common decency. These practices of necking and petting in their very nature have but one design, and that is to arouse and satisfy animal passion. And they usually do this remarkably well. If the touch is not sufficient to this immoral end, the support of intoxicating drink and dance is frequently added. Then under the abandon of the moment and the coercion of unrestrained passion, carnal liberties are taken which not only debauch the individual, but linger like a haunting nightmare in the memory. And let no one seek to justify these indulgences in the name of love. They can be understood and honestly interpreted only in the light of lust. They are a caricature of true love and friendships, a coarsening of indispensable ideals, and a shameful cheapening of some of the noblest and most sacred emotions known to man.

No, Christian young men and women who are true to their name will never engage in necking and petting, not even when it would appear mild and conventional. They will be on guard constantly against the temptations of touch, knowing that the sense of touch is usually the most seductive in regard to purity. They will keep themselves clean mentally, morally, and every other way.

Every decent woman should be in a position to ask of a man who pretends to love her that he control himself sufficiently to reverence her honor and safeguard her virtue. And the young man should realize that the body of the young lady, which is the fountain of life, may one day harbor his own child or that of another, and hence he will do nothing to abuse or cheapen that body. Privileges reserved for the married will not be indulged in by the unmarried.

Perhaps I should add that the young lady who hopes to promote her romance through necking and petting has yet to learn a thing or two. Experience proves that such carnal liberties have a tendency to delay marriage if indeed not to cancel it. But let's turn to something less sordid.

Progress of Real Courtship

Every courtship is in a class by itself. No two are alike. For that reason it is difficult to answer your question categorically. Yet there are certain unmistakable signs of growth and progress common to all healthy courtships, and to these I would point briefly.

You are progressing in your courtship when there is a growing preference for the company of each other to the exclusion of all others. This frequently is meant by the phrase "going steady." When either party is inclined to share his or her courtship with a third party, that courtship is not progressing. It isn't even standing still. It is slipping backward.

You are progressing in your courtship when the very thought of spending a few hours in the presence of the other awakens the very best that is within you, when it stirs your boldest emotions, inspires the best of physical appearance, and awakens the "heroic" within you. When your courtship leaves you mentally, morally, and physically low, it is making no headway.

You are progressing in your courtship when it has the growing sanction and support of others, especially your parents. Basically, courtship is a social venture, and when it invites not the approval, but disapproval and even the criticism of those secondarily concerned with it, as are the parents, your courtship apparently is making questionable headway.

You are progressing in your courtship when both minds turn quite naturally to the subject of marriage and two hearts begin to beat as one, as they contemplate the establishment of their home. These are unmistakable signs of fruitful and maturing courtship.

When both minds begin to think more and more as one, pursue the same righteousness, shun the same sins, prefer the same culture, enjoy the same humor, love the same kind of movies, and begin to plan their future as one rather than two entities, then that courtship is progressing. Then the mutual adjustment which lies at the very heart of a ripening romance has definitely taken place. There engagement is just around the corner.

You are progressing in your courtship when the natural urge to possess and to be possessed grips both the young man and woman, when the desire to please the other becomes dominant, and when further life becomes unthinkable except in the company of the other. When a man thinks only of himself and his personal gain in courtship and disregards the happiness and welfare of the other, that courtship is making no headway. In all probability it has not even begun.

Courtship to be truly enjoyed must ever be a growing, expanding, ennobling experience. There is not room for selfishness in real courtship.

How Long Should Courtship Last?

Not too long. If they are normal and natural, courtships have a way of determining their own terminals. In general, I would say, one, possibly two years at the most, should be sufficient. Extremes should be avoided. Conditions vary. An old proverb makes long regrets follow upon short courtships. Alexander Pope points to it in one of his sonnets when he writes; "Men dream in courtship, but in wedlock wake." Certainly, courtship should be long enough to permit the individuals to come to some sort of understanding with regard to those matters which make for a happy marriage. On the other hand, courtships should not be too long. When extended over a number of years, courtships have a way of growing thin and wearing out. A happy medium, possibly a year or two, would be the ideal for a regular and respectable courtship. Within this time lovers will have plenty of occasions to get thoroughly acquainted with each other. But, again said, if left to themselves and not burdened by unusual pressure, courtships will determine their own length, breadth, and height.

With these last remarks the pastor brought his discussion of Christian courtship to a close. All too soon the hour had passed. Despite its sensitive character at times, the discussion had commanded a respectful attention on the part of young people. They thoroughly enjoyed it and were grateful to their pastor for his friendly counsel and fatherly advice. What is more, they could now enter upon the period of courtship with a far greater understanding and appreciation than they had possessed before. He wanted them to enjoy the period of courtship to the fullest.

To them courtship had taken on new meaning and beauty. And as they concluded their meeting with "Praise God, from whom all blessings flow," who will doubt that among these blessings they counted a happy and healthy courtship and romance, moving on into engagement and terminating in a happy home?

E.W.F.
Concordia Publishing House

Why Should A Believer Not Marry An Unbeliever?

By James E. Bellis
Bob Jones University
Backbone, December 1986/January 1987
Christian News, January 12, 1987

The basic principle upon which a believer approaches marriage is found in II Corinthians 6:14: "Be ye not unequally yoked together with unbelievers: for what fellowship hath righteousness with unrighteousness? and what communion hath light with darkness?" I Corinthians 7:39 states about a widow that "she is at liberty to be married to whom she will; only in the Lord."

In Deuteronomy 7:3-4, the Lord declared to Moses about the Canaanites: "Neither shalt thou make marriages with them; thy daughter thou shalt not give unto his son, nor his daughter shalt thou take unto thy son. For they will turn away thy son from following me, that they may serve other gods; so will the anger of the Lord be kindled against you, and destroy thee suddenly."

In this case the future generations of God's people would have been affected, and this principle is still true today. The believer and the unbeliever will have distinct differences in viewpoints about life, which will adversely affect their offspring. The saved person who marries an unbeliever not only faces a life of possible conflict and misery, but also the possibility of seeing his or her children reject Christ.

Moreover, the dedicated believer who marries a lukewarm Christian runs a similar risk. The dedicated believer will create friction when he expends his time, energy and money in God's service. The lukewarm Christian mate will be a weight to hold him back and also a constant source of temptation to cool his zeal. When children come, they will recognize the conflict and become part of it. They will be pulled by both parents and experience frustration similar to those of the children of the Christian and non-Christian. Therefore, it is imperative for a believer to seek a mate who is not only saved, but also equally dedicated to the Lord.

Ten Rules for Selecting a Husband

Christian News, September 24, 1990

At a recent mothers' and daughters' banquet Pastor L. Neuchterlein of St. Joseph laid down ten rules which ought to be heeded by all marriageable daughters. These rules are based on many years of pastoral experience. During a period of some thirty years in the ministry he listened to many confessions of married people. He gratefully admits that in the Christian congregation there still are by far more happy marriages than unhappy ones. This is due to the fact that Christians follow the instructions given them in God's Word.

"If you buy a new car, a new sewing machine, a new refrigerator, the company will give you, free of charge, a book of instructions. You turn to this book very frequently. The Lord has given married people His book of instructions in Ephesians, chapter 5, and at the same time the strength in His Word to follow these instructions, so that the marriage will not be ruined."

1. Marry only the one without whom you cannot be happy. Never just

get married. Don't go merely by money, beauty, or sex appeal.

2. Marry one of your own faith. Bring him to your own faith first. Religious differences, if both are sincere, grow with the years. How much better if both worship together!

3. Preferably one between twenty and thirty years of age. Remember, ideals and tastes change with maturity. As a rule, the man should be somewhat older. (This refers to young people.)

4. One who respects your modesty, never one who tempts you to sin. Womanly reserve in love pays high interest

5. One who has lived a moral life. Not a drinker, gambler, or adulterer. By all means, do not make marriage a reform school. You might be greatly disappointed with the reforming process.

6. One who loves home-life and children. Have that clearly understood beforehand. It is not immodest to speak about this essential matter of a happy marriage.

7. Be careful of one who is stingy, commanding, or jealous. Those traits are very bad and grow with years if not cured by the power of the Holy Spirit. Youthful attractions disappear, but character traits remain.

8. One capable of sacrifice in all relations, religious, marital, financial, or social.

9. As much as possible one on your own level, mentally and socially.

10. One who gets along also with the Un-lovely people, even with his and her relatives, and says: "Thy people shall be my people."

Then, after a lengthier acquaintance and a short engagement, get married even on a very modest income, trusting in the power and grace of Him who instituted marriage.

(Article in *The Lutheran Witness* - 1941)

ENGAGEMENT

Marriage Should Be Honored By All
Christian News, October 5, 1981

Marriage Should Be Honored By All. By Herbert A. Birner. Milwaukee, Wisconsin: Northwestern Publishing House, 3624 W. North Ave. 53206. 1981. 120 pages. Paper.

This is one of the best up to date books on marriage and related matters which we have seen. Parents should read it and then give it to their teenage children. Pastors will find much help, sound advice, and good suggestions for topics at various church meetings, and even wedding sermons. It is the kind of book a pastor could give to those preparing for marriage.

Engagement

Those who reject the authority of God's Word seem to have difficulty answering the question: When Does Marriage Begin." The author says in part: "I am a little unhappy with the NIV translation of this section (ed. Mt.

1). One wonders what the translator had in mind when he rendered verse 18 as follows: 'His mother Mary was pledged to be married to Joseph.' I consider it a rather weak, interpretive translation. This becomes even clearer when we read in v. 20 the rendition: 'Joseph, son of David, do not be afraid to take Mary home as your wife.' The idea of 'taking home' is not in the text, and the words 'your wife' stand in apposition to 'Mary,' leading us to prefer the King James translation. This leaves room for the idea that betrothal was not quite the beginning of marriage - that something was missing or left out.

"Joseph too regarded this betrothal as a husband-wife arrangement. Feeling that Mary had broken her part of the promise to be faithful to him, he had made up his mind to go through the legal channels and obtain a divorce. But once the true facts were revealed he was ready to continue the marriage and validate it by taking Mary to his home. Yet he did not consummate the marriage until after Jesus was born. This leads us to this definition of marriage: marriage in its very essence is a promise that shall not be broken. We feel that it is a definition which stands the test of Scripture.

"Our theologians have tried to say this in various ways. It was often expressed in this way, 'engagement is tantamount to marriage,' that is, equivalent to marriage. President Schuetze and Professor Habeck in their seminary textbook on pastoral theology (Wisconsin Ev. Lutheran Synod) say that consent binds before God. They go on, 'Before God a binding relationship is established when a man and a woman who are free to do so unconditionally promise to live together as husband and wife . . . In view of this, it was often said that before God engagement is the same as marriage. This can be properly understood.'

"Dean Fritz, in his book on pastoral theology, put it this way, 'Not the marriage ceremony nor sexual intercourse, but the mutual consent to be husband and wife established (the marriage). The marriage ceremony is but the public declaration that two persons have consented to be husband and wife, and sexual intercourse is the usus conjugal, which otherwise would be fornication.' Our Wisconsin Synod catechism agrees in a footnote, 'This union is established by mutual consent (Genesis 24. Isaac and Rebekah; Matthew 1:19-24. Joseph and Mary.)'

"A question we must grapple with: Is modern day engagement tantamount to marriage? The freedom with which most couples break an engagement prompts us to ask the question. If engagement means nothing more than an agreement to go steady together, or an agreement after a trial period of going together to marry later, then it certainly is not tantamount to marriage. It is only a part of what one would call 'the courtship.' Again, if an engagement is clandestine (secret or concealed), and no one knows about it except the two who made the agreement, it is hardly tantamount to marriage.

"If engagement is tantamount to marriage then it has to be much more than an agreement to keep one's options open. It has to be an agreement, an understanding, a promise on the part of two people of marriageable age to enter into all the duties and obligations of marriage. Moreover this promise is confirmed and validated by making it public, that is, by revealing it to those whom it may concern: parents, relatives, friends, etc. There are many ways in which this may be done when this is done, and it is so understood by those involved, when in the eyes of God a valid marriage has been established. Yet in our country and others there remains the duty of confirming his promise before one whom the state designates. But more of this later.

"On the other hand, if engagement means nothing more than to go steady together and keep one's options open, then it certainly is not a marriage. All it amounts to is a courtship that may be broken off at any time. Sad to say, even among our Christian people, engagement often means nothing more than going steady.

"We are also convinced that for much of the unbelieving world a marriage does not take place before the binding promises are made before an agent whom the state designates to perform the marriage.

"To determine a definition of marriage, however, we must always return to this thought: The very essence of marriage is a promise that shall not be broken." (pp. 13-15).

Pastor Birner says that "Any sex outside of marriage is adultery."

"Let's talk about courtship and sex. Courtship is not the time to find out whether you are sexually compatible. The commandment that says, 'You shall not commit adultery,' applies. Any sex outside of marriage is adultery. In fact, courtship is the time to ascertain whether your friend is morally clean. How he or she acts towards you should speak volumes.

"It is true that deeply penitent people, who have committed adultery, can make good marriage partners. The question you will have to answer is, 'Can you handle it?' After marriage would you be thinking, 'I wonder if he or she is being faithful to me in view of the former indiscretion?' If you can't handle it, you had better break off the relationship.

"A whoremonger and a strumpet are not going to be changed much by marriage. I beg you, Christian young people, to keep yourselves morally clean for your marriage partner. Don't listen to the false teaching of the world that sexual abstinence is unhealthy. That is not true. Besides, when there is a church wedding and the bride wears white, the couple is making a statement to their fellow church members. They are saying, 'Look, we have saved ourselves for one another. We are morally clean" (p. 21). "He who breaks his promise after becoming engaged is therefore sinning against his fiancé and against God before whom he made the promise" (p. 24).

"There must be a mutual trust that each will be true to the other in marriage. A solid marriage can only be built on such mutual trust, for as we have already shown, marriage in its essence is a promise that must be kept. He who breaks the promise breaks the marriage. He who breaks his promise after becoming engaged is therefore sinning against his fiancée and against God before whom he made the promise. That is why we said that the courtship is the time to determine whether each is morally clean, and a person of his word.

"There should be no impediment, such as physical disabilities, which will render impossible the *consummati* or continued sex in marriage. It may be in order to consult a doctor, as we have already said. He can also warn whether it will be impossible to have children. However, it must be stated that the inability to have children does not invalidate a marriage. One can always adopt children to love.

"I believe that there should be love for children and also, a desire to have children. I am not much given to quoting statistics since one can prove anything one wants to with them, but it said that if a couple lets nature take its course, only one out of ten couples would be childless. Psalms 127 and 128 should be read by couples contemplating marriage. We shall look at these two Psalms later (24).

"In the matter of engagement one should also speak about parental consent. To ask for girl's hand is considered old-fashioned by this generation, but the Fourth Commandment, like all others, never goes out of style. Parents on both sides of the family should be honored by being consulted by their sons and daughters. To ask the hand of a daughter in marriage shows both honor and respect. Parents can give helpful hints. They can point to things that a couple blinded by love cannot see at the moment. The experience of parents in marriage matters should not be ignored."

Church Weddings

Here are some things the author says about church weddings:

"Perhaps this is as good a time as any to discuss the church wedding. Because a wedding is a church function, all the rules which apply to a regular worship service also apply here. The clergyman should be of your denomination; the same also goes for the organist and the soloists who may play and sing at the wedding. Romans 16:17 and other passages on church fellowships ask this of us all. Here it is not a matter of what has been permitted in some other church — or even by a church and a clergyman of our own faith, but what the Lord Himself indicates we should do. Here is a good reason for you to visit your clergyman before you firm up your wedding plans, and listen to him.

"Since a wedding is a church function there are also applications to the music used in the wedding service. Some music is so readily identified with the morals and manners of this world that it is totally unfit for use in a church of any denomination. Music does not rise above its source. Dance hall music remains dance hall music. The works of the rock and pop culture of our day may have some haunting melodies, but their words are so filled with double meaning and hidden innuendos that we cannot permit them in church. At best they are terribly humanistic, glorifying man and woman, and not the Lord whose blessings are being sought in a church service. The lyrics from "Jesus Christ Superstar" which describes the love of Mary Magdalene for Jesus, are sometimes used at weddings, but they present a theology that is totally false and unfit. The opera, Lohengrin, the source of 'Here Comes the Bride,' is the pagan end product of a twisted mind. Yet, how many a pastor has not been faced by a young bride and her mother, who, having heard this music used at another church, insist that they want this music also. This writer has consulted many pastors who have said that for this reason they dread being confronted with a church wedding. Unfortunately, too many brides, trying to have a wedding like their sectarian friends, cannot be objective.

"When there is so much fine church music one wonders why brides so often choose the unacceptable. Music can be used right out of the hymnal. There is plenty of excellent music in the musical anthologies most of our churches and organists have acquired. A large body of good, contemporary wedding music is being published these days, and pastors, organists and choir directors will do well to acquaint themselves with this music, so that they can give good counsel and direct those who participate in a wedding service to music that is fit and gives glory to God" (pp. 33, 34).

"Requests sometimes come for the celebration of the Sacrament of the Altar in the wedding service. Again the request undoubtedly comes because it is seen in other churches, notably the Roman Catholic. If the request comes, your pastor will have to say 'no' for the following reasons: The sacrament is never a private matter between the bride and the groom. When the sacrament is celebrated, the whole congregation should be invited to celebrate it. Because we celebrate close communion, and because people from all faiths are generally invited to weddings, a wedding is hardly the place to celebrate the sacrament. Remember that, in spite of the teaching of the Roman Catholic Church – marriage is not a sacrament' (p. 35).

"It is also the custom in some church bodies that where there is a mixed marriage that the clergyman of the other faith also be invited to participate in the service. Naturally our pastors must refuse to become part of such a ceremony, nor will we invite the clergymen of another faith to participate in our services. That is unionism" (p. 37).

Sex

Pastor Birner has a few things to say about sex:

"I would strongly warn against the practice of withholding sex from one another as a punishment for real or imagined wrongs. Likewise, I would also warn against using sex as a reward to get one's way. All this shows smallness of character" (p. 42).

"Nowhere does the Bible discuss the mechanics of the sex act. Nor do we find it necessary in this work to go into it. If you want more information ask your doctor or someone whose judgment you can trust. It is an act into which husbands and wives can enter joyously with abandon" (p. 43).

Roles in Marriage

In a chapter on roles in marriage Birner writes:

"We suggested earlier that we study Proverbs 31:10ff. If we think that a wife is confined to homemaking activities we will certainly have to shed such preconceived notions. Proverbs here pictures a truly liberated woman. She is no slave of her husband doomed to a secondary position in the economy of the home. In fact it is because of her that her husband prospers and is respected in the community. A wife can make or break a man. In the book of Proverbs Solomon certainly makes no secret of that fact. He should know. His wives influenced his reign and started the nation of Israel on the path to ruin. No wonder the book has so many caustic comments addressed to 'my son'" (p. 58).

Interracial Marriage

Here is what the Wisconsin Synod pastor says about interracial marriage: "Nowhere in Scripture are interracial marriages forbidden. But nowhere in the Bible are they advocated either. So in all honesty we have to say that there is no moral reason why the races may not intermarry" (p. 101).

We regret that the price of this 120 page paperback will probably limit its circulation.

"For Better Not For Worse"
By Walter Maier

Chapter Twenty-Five
"Keep Thyself Pure"
Christian News, December 8, 2008

Create in me a clean heart, O God! Ps. 51:10

"The moment of formal betrothal is time enough for the first kiss." – This is not a maxim from a Puritan copybook nor a motto from the austere days of samplers. Nor is it the pronouncement of a world-weary octogenarian counselor of youth. It is rather the deliberate verdict of one of America's foremost psychologists, a literal quotation from William McDougall's *Character and Conduct of Life* (p. 219).

Few earnestly spoken opinions from eminent sources will evoke more challenge. Yet the principle Dr. McDougall enunciates and the protest which he implies merit the approval of every young life that would scale the highest heights of human happiness.

EXPONENTS OF UNRESTRAINT

The author of Proverbs lists three things too wonderful for himself and four which he knows not (chap. 30:19). This quartet of enigmas includes "the way of an eagle in the air, the way of a serpent upon a rock, the way of a ship in the midst of the sea, and the way of a man with a maid." Commentators have expressed contradictory interpretations in explaining the last and oft-quoted phrase; but whatever its meaning, "the way of a man with a maid," the conduct characterizing the relation between the two sexes, has today become the topic of long-drawn debate.

Those who endorse an unrestrained relation between young people will immediately assert the utter futility of the restrictions which Professor McDougall implies and which the Christian church has always regarded as ideal. We shall be accused of closing complacent eyes upon glaring evidence; we shall be charged with ignorance of modern trends; we shall be labeled as harmless idealists, with a code of conduct which no modern young person takes seriously. Young people themselves will complain that, if they maintain this reserve and refuse to make concessions to the spirit of the day, they will soon be ostracized. Young women, embittered by experience, will declare that young men take altogether too much for granted, insisting on intimacies even at the first meeting. And in answer comes the countercharge that the man who does not bestow his caresses lavishly must face the social blackball.

The First Kiss
"KEEP THYSELF PURE"

Christian News, December 8, 2008

"Will You Marry Me? Courtship Stories You Will Love to Read" in the October 2008 *Above Rubies* has wholesome advice for today's youth. The masthead of *Above Rubies*, Box 68187, Franklin, Tennessee 37068-1687 says: *Above Rubies* is a magazine to encourage women in their high calling as wives, mothers, and homemakers. Its purpose is to uphold and strengthen family life and to raise the standard of God's truth in the nation. The name has been chosen from Proverbs 31:10 AMP. "'A capable, intelligent, and virtuous woman, who is he who can find her? She is far more precious than jewels and her value is far ABOVE RUBIES or pearls.'"

Editor of *Above Rubies* is Nancy Campbell. Her book "Be Fruitful & Multiply – What the Bible Says About Having Children" is available from *Christian News* ($12.50). Jackelynn Eerdelt writes in "Will You Marry Me?": "We saved our first kiss for our wedding day. Our wedding was beautiful, but our marriage is heavenly." "We Saved the Kiss" until our wedding day is the title of a column by Stacie Earley. Kelly Fernandes writes: "Glenn and I married October of 2004 and shared our first kiss at the altar. God REALLY is the greatest romantic!"

What is in the October *Above Rubies* reminded the editor or what Lutheran Hour speaker Walter Maier wrote in Chapter 24, "Keep Thyself Pure," in his marriage manual *For Better Not For Worse*. The first section of this chapter is reproduced above.

The January 14, 2008 CN stated in an editorial "LCMS Youth Poll Shows Need For Solid Christian Education – Maier's Marriage Manual Should be Reprinted – Maier's Youth Publication Restored."

The poll taken of youth at the 2007 LCMS National Youth Gathering shows why the LCMS needs a vast program of solid Christian education beginning in the home. More organizations and meetings are not the answer. Teach, teach, teach, the Bible and Luther's Catechism. Concordia Publishing House should reprint an updated version of *For Better Not For Worse*, a marriage manual by Dr. Walter Maier, and publish a youth publication which takes the same position Dr. Maier took when he edited the LCMS's *Walther League Messenger*. When Maier was editor, it had some 70,000 paid subscribers. Many adults also regularly read it.

The poll shows that almost 50% of all the LCMS youth at the gathering hardly ever study the Bible, more than 40% maintain that pre-marital sex is not always wrong, more than half of the 19 year olds have had pre-marital sex, 35% contend that homosexuality is not always wrong, 14.5% allow for same sex marriage, 25% say they have been drunk during the past 12 months, 17.5% maintain that all religions are the same, 50% support joint worship with all those who call themselves Christians, about half believe women should be pastors, and less than half agree with what the Bible and the LCMS teach about capital punishment.

The Bible and Luther's Catechism should come first. It would also be helpful to send a copy of *Walter A. Maier Still Speaks – Missouri and the World Should Listen* to every LCMS church professor and seminarian.

Youth must be taught that all sex outside of marriage is contrary to the Bible, that homosexuality is a sin condemned in God's Word, that the ordination of women is contrary to what God says in His Word, that Christianity is the only saving faith, that all other religions lead to Hell, that a person is justified by faith alone in the merits of Jesus Christ, and that the Bible is man's only standard of faith and life.

Youth particularly should read these sections in *Walter Maier Still Speaks – Missouri and the World Should Listen*: Chapter VII, "Marriage", "The Liberal Clergy on Marriage," (pp. 115-117); "CPH Should Update and Reprint Maier's 'For Better, Not For Worse'," (pp. 122-127); "The Church's Marriage Code," (pp. 122); "Marriage Ceremony in Modern English – Here Comes the Pride!," (pp. 122- 127). Chapter VIII: "Birth Control" (pp. 128-131).

Dating and Marriage
How Much Can You Tell From a Kiss?
Christian News, July 21, 1996

"How in the world can you tell if you want to marry somebody if you've never kissed them?" Elisabeth Elliot answers this question in her *Passion and Purity* (Published by Fleming and Revell, 1984): "But how in the world can you tell you want to marry somebody just because you've kissed somebody?"

Elisabeth Elliot is one of the best Christian authors of our day. We first heard about her when her husband, Missionary Jim Elliot, was one of the five missionaries killed by the Aucu Indians in the jungles of Ecuador some 30 years ago. We referred to the event in a sermon we preached at the time in the chapel of Concordia Seminary, St. Louis. *The Christian Century* had an editorial titled "Five Missionaries Die Needlessly."

Since then Elisabeth Elliot has written many fine articles and several books.

She writes in *Passion and Purity*:

"Intimacy is not necessary.

"When Abraham sent his servant to find a wife for Isaac, there was no question of any tryouts by means of intimacy. The servant, the third party, had to look her over and assess her worth and suitability. He went to the logical place -- the spring outside the city where the women would come. He prayed silently, watching all the time. He had specifically asked God to give him a sign: The girl whom he asked for a drink would not only give him one, but would then also water his camels. The servant continued 'watching quietly to see whether or not the Lord had made his journey successful.'

"It was Ruth's mother-in-law, Naomi, who made the choice of a husband for her and told her exactly what moves to make. A good portion of the human race has had arranged marriages, and the rate of success of that kind seems to have been far higher than of our do-it-yourself kind. A missionary told me recently of the marriage seminars he is holding for Indians of Northern Ontario. 'You mean they have marital problems?' I asked. (The Indians I worked with in South America never thought of marital problems.)

" 'Do they ever!' he said. 'Ever since they began to follow the white man and gave up arranged marriages.'

"There is not much likelihood that our society will ever consent to arranged marriages. We are stuck with our ill-defined system. Even so, one can learn much about a prospective mate by observation alone."

Martin Luther wrote: "Effort and care on the part of parents are required in order to provide an honest and pious marriage for their children. They should, therefore, seek and look about for a spouse and not imagine that she will come by chance or in a novel and unusual manner from somewhere or other.

"Nor does a young man or girl commit a sin by thinking about his or her future spouse. In fact dinners are arranged in order to get marriageable young people acquainted, social gatherings of respectable folks, and dances, which, if they are decent and modest, are in no ways to be condemned." What Luther Says, Plass, p. 893.

The author carefully observed Jim Elliot on a college campus. She writes;

"Long before I had any reason to think he might be interested in me, I had put him down as the sort of man I hoped to marry. Kissing and holding hands would have added nothing to this conviction (anybody can kiss and hold hands). On the contrary, in fact, it would have subtracted something very important. I wanted to marry a man prepared to swim against the tide.

"I took it for granted that there must be a few men left in the world who had that kind of strength. I assumed that those men would also be looking for women of principle. I did not want to be among the marked-down goods on the bargain table, cheap because they'd been pawed over. Crowds collect there. It is only the few who will pay full price. 'You get what you pay for.'

"Chastity, an outmoded word, the world says, but the truth is it's a Christian obligation. It means abstention from sexual activity. For the Christian there is one rule and one rule only: total abstention from sexual activity outside of marriage and total faithfulness inside marriage, period. No ifs, ands, or buts."

"If your goal is purity of heart, be prepared to be thought of as very odd." Reprinted below from Again, published by the Evangelical Orthodox Church, Conciliar Press, Box 106, Mt. Hermon, California 95401, is an interview of Elisabeth Elliot. We wish every young person would read what she says in this interview.

According to Elliott, the American dating and courtship patterns are in "chaos, absolute chaos" and that "dating has fallen on very hard times." The kind of advice Elisabeth Elliot offers often appeared in youth publication of The Lutheran Church-Missouri Synod, particularly the *Walther League Messenger* when it was edited by Walter A. Maier.

Again asks: "What advice would you give to a young person trying to choose a mate; what are the bottom-line essentials to a good match?"

Elisabeth Elliott: "Number one: must be a Christian. The Bible makes it clear that we don't have an option there."

Face the Facts
Lutheran Sentinel, July, 1992
Christian News, July 13, 1992

The Facts of Life for Young People; By James A. Aderman; Northwester Publishing House, Milwaukee, Wisconsin. 1992. 172 pages. Paper, $9.95.

There has long been a real need for a book dealing with the issues of adolescent sexuality written from a Christian perspective. I know of no other book that is trying to accomplish what Pastor Aderman has done. He has taken a very delicate subject and has handled it in a very straight forward, matter-of-fact way.

John Juern, Ph.D.
Licensed Psychologist
Clinical Director

Face the Facts is a handbook for the personal and sexual "coming out" of early adolescence. Aderman writes accurately and on the level of his Christian audience, creating a very readable blend between personal self-disclosure and teaching. From a physician's perspective, the need for this type of publication is clear. Adolescents are desperate for this information and, especially when it is in a non-threatening written form, they will absorb it. This is a book I will recommend to my patients. This is a book I will give to my children.

Janet C. Lindemann, M.D.
Assistant Professor and Director
Medical College of Wisconsin

Pastor James A. Aderman graduated from Wisconsin Lutheran Seminary. Married in 1972, he is the father of one preteen and two teenage daughters. Pastor Aderman has been very active in synodical youth ministry. He has served as a minister of youth and evangelism, as a member of the Commission on Youth Ministry, and as a speaker at International Youth Rallies. Currently he is editor of *YOUTHINK* magazine, and pastor of Fairview Ev. Lutheran Church, Milwaukee, Wisconsin.

The author explains the purpose of Face the Facts:

"1. That the teens who read this book will grow in their gratitude to God for His goodness and grace, in their appreciation of His wisdom in designing humans as He has, and in their desire to live lives that thank Him.

"2. That the teens who read this book will recognize that the changes they are going through mark the normal path everyone travels to reach adulthood. Everyone's path is different, but that, too, is normal.

"3. That the teens who read this book are equipped to meet the special challenges to sexual purity which grow out of a culture that has made a god of sex.

"4. That the teens who read this book will have a resource of accurate and biblical information that will serve them well from early puberty through early adulthood" (ix).

Aderman repeatedly emphasizes that "God warned us against sexual activity outside of marriage" (83).

The author warns against masturbation (98-99).

Commenting on Abortifacients, IUDs or Intra-Uterine Devices, The Pill, Norplant, The Morning After Pill, Abortion, the author writes:

"None of these methods of stopping pregnancy should be used by Christian husbands and wives, because they result in the murder of the youngest of children. Since life begins at conception, God's Fifth Commandment obligates us to protect life from that point.

"Sometimes Christians use one of these methods for contraception without realizing how it works. Those believers will find great comfort in God's promise, 'There is now no condemnation for those who are in Christ Jesus' (Romans 8:1). God's forgiveness will also motivate them to find an acceptable form of contraception.

"You should also know that the Pill and the IUD are not 100% effective in stopping pregnancy. The Pill has an 11% failure rate. That means if 100 teenage girls are on the Pill and are sexually active, 11 will become pregnant this year. The IUD has a failure rate of almost 11% (And here's something else about the Pill: Researchers have found that young women who take the Pill increase their risk of developing breast cancer) (107-108).

Contraceptives

"There are four principles married couples will want to consider about using contraceptives. The first is that children are a blessing God gives. The second is that God, not humans, determines when children will be conceived. The third is that we are to be good stewards of everything God has given us. The fourth is that everything we do should show our trust in God" (108, 109).

Homosexuality

"First, you need to know that homosexuality is not a sickness that can be 'cured.' Homosexuality is not even something that a person is. It is something a person does. Homosexuality is an activity, a habit, a lifestyle that can be changed" (137).

An excellent book for youth and their parents.

XI

ADULTERY - PREMARITAL SEX

We Need to Return to Moral/Sexual Sanity

By Haven Bradford Gow
Christian News, January 31, 2011

We indeed are living in a sex-crazed, sex-saturated society that has elevated sex (especially immoral sex) into a false god. As Lutheran clergyman/scholar Rev. Scott Blazek observes, "An NBA superstar (Kobe Bryant) can be caught cheating on his wife, but she is considered lucky for now he has to shower her with expensive jewelry to offset his indiscretion. . . . A popular network talk show host (David Letterman) can be targeted for blackmail, but only then, to avoid being blackmailed, does he openly admit to having illicit relationships with numerous members of his staff. (Moreover) the so-called greatest pro-golfer of this generation, (has) admitted to cheating on his wife, having dozens of affairs." It seems all too clear that Judeo-Christian morality has become out-of-date for all too many Americans today.

Today in America, many—young and old—have become obsessed with the false idol of sex. As pointed out by *Designed for Desire: God's Design for Sexuality* (published by RBC Ministries, Grand Rapids, MI), "Sexual obsession occurs (inside or outside of marriage) when we become more focused on temporary physical pleasure than in finding satisfaction in the design and desires of God."

According to Bible scholar Tim Chester, author of *Closing the Window: Steps to Living Porn Free* (Intervarsity), "sex is everything and everywhere. It's used to sell products. The media talk incessantly about the sexual availability. To be 'enlightened' about sex in our culture has become a . . . . euphemism for immorality."

According to Catholic scholar Father Pat McCloskey, author of *Ask A Franciscan: Answers to Catholic Questions* (St. Anthony Messenger Press), one example of our sexual obsession is the widespread availability and popularity of pornography. He says "pornography implicitly denies that human sexuality is a profound gift from God. The Bible teaches us that we must always recognize people as our brothers and sisters loved by God (and) never as mere objects for our pleasure." Indeed, "habitually viewing pornography and accepting the images as normal corrupts a person's understanding of sexuality. Pornography has become an addiction for more and more people who prefer virtual relationships that require no self-sacrifice over genuine relationships."

Indeed, pornography helps create a moral/social climate conclusive to sexual abuse and exploitation. Pornography reduces sex to a plaything, human beings to mere bodies and human bodies to sex machines; it denigrates the sacredness of sex, marriage, family and human life; it transforms sex from a communion of life and love within the sacrament [sic] of marriage to simply a tool of masturbational and voyeuristic gratification.

Even those who contend pornography is harmless must at least tacitly acknowledge the power and influence of words and ideas; otherwise, they never would attend school, go to the library or write letters, articles, books, advertising copy, and TV and movie scripts.

Certainly if the great works of the moral and intellectual giants of civilization can educate, enlighten and inspire, then pornographic works can corrupt by glamorizing and encouraging pernicious ideas and behavior: Ideas, after all, do have consequences.

The Playboy Philosophy and Abortion

By Haven Bradford Gow
Christian News, June 6, 2000

A professor of philosophy and government at the University of Texas, Dr. J. Budziszewski tells us in his new work *The Revenge of Conscience* (Dallas, TX: Spence Publishing) that "The official line is that modern people do not take sex outside marriage seriously any longer; mere moral realists say this is because we no longer realize the wrong of it. I maintain that we do know it is wrong, but pretend that we do not." He adds: [N]o human society has ever held that the sexual powers may be exercised by anyone with anyone, and the recognized norm is a durable and culturally protected covenant between man and woman with the intention of procreation."

The above observation brings to mind the recent controversy in Chicago concerning Hugh Hefner, founding father of Playboy Enterprises, Inc. A bitter controversy has ensued after a city political leader proposed that Chicago honor Hefner by naming a portion of Michigan Avenue after the perennial playboy.

Should the City of Chicago honor Hugh Hefner? Judy Guarr, a pro-life feminist, points out the moral and social harm caused by Hefner's playboy philosophy and lifestyle. "The whole *Playboy* philosophy treats women as things... In this view, women exist only for the pleasure of men, and are to be discarded if they are stupid enough to get pregnant. Abortion on demand is good not because it liberates women, but because it reduces their inhibitions about being somebody's plaything. Treat the unborn child as a person? *Playboy* wouldn't grant that status to the mother – or any other woman."

Pro-life feminist Elizabeth Moore also discerns an intimate connection between the *Playboy* philosophy and lifestyle and the pro-abortion mentality and ethic. Abortion becomes a method of birth control for those who engage in premarital and extramarital affairs and do not want to accept responsibility for their actions.

Clearly, a nexus exists between the *Playboy* philosophy and lifestyle and the pernicious moral/sexual climate permeating society. Hefner, founding father of Playboy Enterprises, Inc., long has recognized that "recreational" sex has been and is an immensely profitable business; thus, in his popular and successful magazine, he has emphasized photos of naked women in sexually suggestive positions and editorials, articles and cartoons trying to provide "philosophical" justification for premarital and extramarital sex, voyeurism, incest, pedophilia, sequential and simultaneous affairs, group sex, oral and anal sex, necrophilism, homosexuality and abortion.

The *Playboy* lifestyle reduces sex to a plaything, human beings to mere bodies and human bodies to sex machines; it denigrates the sacredness of sex, marriage, family and human life, it is a lifestyle designed for insecure men and sexually frustrated women who view sex not as the communion of life and love within marriage, but rather as a mere tool of masturbational and voyeuristic gratification. The results of the *Playboy* philosophy and lifestyle are broken hearts, broken lives, broken homes, broken families.

More Nonsense From *Newsweek*
What The Bible Really Says About Sex
Christian News, February 28, 2011

"What the Bible Really Says About Sex" is the religion feature in the February 14, 2011 *Newsweek*. The subtitle is "New scholarship on the Good Book's naughty bits and how it deals with adultery, divorce, and same-sex love." *Newsweek*'s Lisa Miller writes:

"What does the Bible really say about sex? Two new books written by university scholars for a popular audience try to answer this question. Infuriated by the dominance in the public sphere of conservative Christians who insist that the Bible incontrovertibly supports sex within the constraints of 'traditional marriage,' these authors attempt to prove otherwise. Jennifer Wright Knust and Michael Coogan mine the Bible for its earthiest and most inexplicable tales about sex—Jephthah, who sacrifices his virgin daughter to God; Naomi and Ruth, who vow to love one another until death—to show that the Bible's teachings on sex are not as coherent as the religious right would have people believe. In Knust's reading, the Song of Solomon is a paean to unmarried sex, outside the conventions of family and community. 'I'm tired,' writes Knust in *Unprotected Texts: The Bible's Surprising Contradictions About Sex and Desire*, 'of watching those who are supposed to care about the Bible reduce its stories and teachings to slogans.' Her book comes out this month. Coogan's book *God and Sex: What the Bible Really Says* was released last fall.

"Knust, a religion professor at Boston University, is also an ordained minister in the American Baptist denomination. Coogan, director of publications at Harvard University's Semitic Museum, once trained as a Jesuit priest. With their books, they hope to steal the conversation about sex and the Bible back from the religious right. 'The Bible doesn't have to be an invader, conquering bodies and wills with its pronouncements and demands,' Knust writes. 'It can also be a partner in the complicated dance of figuring out what it means to live in bodies that are filled with longing.' Here, in summary, are the arguments:

"The Bible is an ancient text, inapplicable in its particulars to the modern world.

"In the Bible, 'traditional marriage' doesn't exist.

"Husbands, in essence, owned their wives, and fathers owned their daughters, too. A girl's virginity was her father's to protect—and to relinquish at any whim.

"Those who follow the gay-marriage debate are likely familiar with certain bits of Scripture.

"That which is forbidden is also allowed.

"The Bible is stern and judgmental on sex. It forbids prostitution, adultery, premarital sex for women, and homosexuality. But exceptions exist in every case, Knust points out.

"Knust also argues—provocatively—that King David 'enjoyed sexual satisfaction' with his soul mate, Jonathan. 'Your love to me was wonderful,' laments David at Jonathan's death, 'passing the love of women.'

"Divorce is permitted in the Old Testament—but it's forbidden in the Gospels. Jesus didn't like it: that much is clear. 'Whoever divorces his wife and marries another, commits adultery against her; and if she divorces her husband and marries another, she commits adultery,' Jesus says in the Gospel of Mark. But in Matthew's telling, Jesus softens his position slightly and leaves a loophole for the husbands of unfaithful wives. 'When it comes to sex, the Bible is often divided against itself,' writes Knust.

"Coogan and Knust are hardly the first scholars to offer alternative readings of the Bible's teachings on sex. What sets them apart is their populism. With provocative titles and mainstream publishing houses, they obviously hope to sell books.

"Yet in a democracy, even those who speak 'heresies' are allowed a voice. And whether readers accept Coogan's and Knust's interpretations, the authors are justified in their insistence that a population so divided over questions of sex and sexual morality cannot—should not—cede the field without exploring first what the Bible actually says. The eminent Bible historian Elaine Pagels agrees. To read the Bible and reflect on it 'is to realize that we have not a series of answers, but a lot of questions.'

"The Conservative Case for Gay Marriage" was the cover story of the January 18, 2010 *Newsweek*. CN's response appeared on p. 1 of the January 24, 2010 *Christian News*.

Chapter 15 in the editor's "*Baal or God*" on "The Law of God" (1965) shows what the Bible teaches about sex, including homosexuality. At the time *Baal or God* was published, CN's critics said CN was bringing up unimportant issues which concerned very few. *Newsweek* begins by misusing *Song of Songs*. *Concordia Commentary's Song of Songs* shows what this book actually teaches about sex.

Adultery - The Inconspicuous Silent Sin

There are many more adulterers in the church today than there are drunks. Yes, there are. What is being done about this? NOTHING. What is being said about this? NOTHING. Is the sin of adultery preached against in the churches quite often? NO. WHY. Because adultery in the church has become "common place" among it's members and even it's clergy. That's why.

Drunkenness is a rather unambiguous, obvious sin. This sin is more rarely seen in the churches even though it is very apparent in the community when one is a drunk. THIS sin is preached against in the churches quite often. Churches, especially Baptist churches, think even "moderate" drinking is a "grievous" sin.

Do you know there are more adulterers in the churches than drunks? Do you know that God hates adultery as much, or more, than He does drunkeness? Drunks do not cause others to become willful, habitual sinners, but adulterers do.

Matt. 5:32 "But I say unto you, that whosoever shall put away his wife, saving for the cause of fornication, causeth her/him to commit adultery: and whosoever shall marry her/him that is divorced committeth adultery".

THIS is the ONLY passage in the Bible that speaks of one causing another to sin, except for the verse that speaks of outlandish women causing King Solomon to sin the sin of Idolatry (serving other gods - Nehemiah 10.20).

I know folks who are "proud" of their parents, even though one or the other is living in adultery as "supposed" spouse number 3 or 4. Hardly anyone is speaking out against this sort of lifestyle. Surely not the children of these adulterers, and not the Baptist churches that they attend. NO ONE seems to care.

You may have heard the old saying; "blood is thicker than water". Well- in this case, blood is thicker than obeying God, to the families of these adulterers.

Would these same people be ashamed and embarrassed by these parents if they were community drunks? You bet they would. They would be speaking to them too, about their sin.

Why, many drunks are not nice, friendly, helpful people when they are drunk, and many adulterers are so. Look on the "outward" appearance is what they do. These are Christians, mind you now. They KNOW what God says. Yes they do.

The apostle Paul warns the brethren of looking on the outward appearance of man. He says if we trust that we are Christ's (saved) and we look at others this way (outward) we had better think again. (2 Cor. 10:7). In Matt. 23:27, the Lord Jesus speaks of the "outward" beautiful appearance of Pharisees who are "within" full of dead men's bones and all uncleanness.

It is not so easy for a drunk to "hide" his sin as it is for adulterers; but God knows, and they BOTH will end up in the Lake of Fire. This is not a lake CALLED Fire. This is a lake OF fire.

1 Cor. 6:9 "Know ye not that the unrighteous shall not inherit the kingdom of God? Be not deceived: neither fornicators, nor idolaters, 'nor adulterers', nor effeminate, nor abusers of themselves with mankind.

v. 10 "Nor thieves, nor covetous, 'nor drunkards', nor revilers, nor extortioners, shall inherit the kingdom of God.

v. 11 "And such were some of you: but ye are washed, but ye are sanctified, but ye are justified in the name of the Lord Jesus, and by the Spirit of our God."

And such WERE, (past tense) some of you, the Spirit says. Since they were washed in the Blood of the Lamb and sanctified and justified (saved) THEY AIN'T NO MORE.

If a married person commits fornication this is adultery. If a single person commits fornication, this is illicit sex. Either way, they BOTH committed fornication.

1 Cor. 6:16-17 "What? Know ye not that he which is joined to an harlot is one body? For two, saith he, shall be one flesh. But he that is joined unto the Lord is one spirit.

v. 18 "Flee fornication. Every sin that a man doeth is without the body; but he that committeth fornication sinneth against his own body."

The phrases, "without the body" and "against the body", are difficult for some; but I believe it tells us that other sins, such as drunkenness, have effects "on" the body, but fornication is a sin wrought "within" the body and involves a monstrous denial of union with Christ by union with the harlot or whoremonger (anyone other than the wife or the husband that GOD has joined together.)

Drinking is a "pet peeve" of the church, while adultery is "cast aside" as though it were no problem in the churches.

December 1999-January 2000 CNV News Service Archives. [cnview web site]

More Christians are divorced than non-Christians, concludes Barna Research Group. A survey of nearly 4,000 adults found that 27 percent of born-again Christians have been divorced compared to 24 percent of others. Within the denominations surveyed, Baptists had the highest divorce rate (29 percent) and Catholics had the lowest (21 percent). The rate for nondenominational Christians was 34 percent, while for atheists and agnostics it was 21 percent. George Barna said that the statistics follow a pattern that has existed for some time (*Charisma* News Service, 12/23/99).

Christian Century Opens Door for Sex Outside of Marriage

Christian News, April 4, 2011

"SEX – A Sacramental View," the cover story of the March 22, 2011 *Christian Century* does not say that all sex outside marriage is sinful and contrary to God's Word. Elizabeth Myer Boulton, minister of discipleship of Old South Church in Boston and Matthew Myer Boulton, who teaches at Harvard Divinity School, write in the *Christian Century*:

"When churches do talk about sex theologically, the spectrum of approaches to the subject can seem woefully narrow. On premarital sex, for example, some cast the discussion in terms of 'purity,' 'chastity' and 'saving oneself,' while others frame the question primarily in terms of risk and street-smarts—that is, as chiefly a matter of avoiding unwanted pregnancies and sexually transmitted diseases.

"Meanwhile, according to the Center for Disease Control's 2009 data, nearly half of all high school students (46 percent) reported already having had sexual intercourse, and one third of them reported having had it in the previous three months. Likewise, a recent study by the Guttmacher Institute found that no less than nine out of ten Americans report having had sex before marriage, with similar rates among those who abstained from sex until age 20 or older.

"In other words, by all accounts the world is full of sex before or otherwise apart from marriage. What do North American churches have to say about it? Some call for purity in the face of potential pollution; others for prudence in the face of potential pregnancy or disease. But more often than not, we stammer and stall. We change the subject."

"Above all, reframing sexuality as a sacramental [sic] gift holds the promise of teaching young and old alike that, at its best and by the grace of God, sexual intimacy can be a vivid taste of the loving relationship that God desires to have with us."

"For those who insist that sex always belongs within the sanctuaries of marriage or life partnership, the centerpiece of the case should be neither 'purity' nor 'prudence' but rather the love of God sacramentally [sic] available in and through the best of human intimacy. From this point of view, sex belongs within lifelong, faithful partnerships not for abstract moral reasons, but precisely because in and through sexuality we are meant to taste God's lifelong, faithful love for us.

"For those who insist that under certain conditions sex may properly take place outside of marriage or life partnership, the sacramental [sic] dimensions of sexual life may help clarify those conditions. From this point of view, because God is faithful and sex is sacramental [sic], human sexuality should take place within relational sanctuaries of fidelity and commitment. Because God is love, because God delights in us, because God knows us and calls us by name, human sexuality should always and only be loving, playful and kind—never casual, anonymous or cavalier."

The *Christian Century* has long opened the door for sex outside of marriage and homosexual sex. The November 12, 1979 *Christian News* printed on the front page "No Biblical Sex Ethic Says *Christian Century.*"

The Late Dr. Margaret Mead and Her Legacy

The National Catholic Register, January 28, 1979
Christian News, January 29, 1979

The late Margaret Mead (1901-1978) was one of those personages about whom the media agree to say nothing but good. Even a writer in the (politically) conservative *National Review* paid her the incredible compliment of saying that among the necessities of civilization in which she believed was the sanctity and permanence of marriage.

Dr. Mead, however, must be reckoned among those whose writings contributed most to the disintegration of moral standards in America.

Nominally an Episcopalian and a lecturer in the Catholic University of Fordham, this woman never, in any words I have read or seen reported of her, evinced any realization that there exists a reality beyond the measurable and the observable. Yet she was "expert" in many fields. *Christian News* reports of her, with a fine irony, whether conscious or unconscious, that "she became a scientific generalist with expertise in a number of fields including family life, ecology, culture, education, mental health, and transactional relations." She supported legal abortions and the legalization of marijuana. She did not believe that marriages of the future would be a life time proposition. She of course favored birth prevention.

Dr. Mead's fortune as an anthropologist was made after the publication of her first book, *Coming of Age in Samoa, in 1928.* She made the claim, with surely more pride than deliberation, that it was the first book by a serious professional anthropologist that was understandable by the layman.

The book is readable but its conclusions are not scientific. The last two chapters are mostly propaganda, designed to deliver a blow against the toppling Christian moral standards of the 1920s. The preceding chapters may contain accurate observations about Samoan life. I do not know, but I suspect that Margaret was not wholly objective.

Margaret, in her studies of the adolescent girl in Samoa was very much interested in sex, and she recorded with apparent satisfaction the allegedly easy way in which adult Samoans regarded the relations between people of both sexes in the pre-married years. Pre-marital sex, if we would believe her, carried with it no stigma except – and the exception is significant – for the daughters of chiefs, who were required to be virgins. Abortion seems not to have existed in Samoa, and even illegitimate children were welcomed.

I am not obliged to defend the morals of any people just because they are called "primitives." Many, perhaps all, of those who are called primitives today descend from peoples of more advanced culture. All share with us the liabilities of Original Sin. But among people who have some claim to a primitive view of life, such as the Pygmies of Africa, such renowned anthropologists as the late Fr. Wilhelm Schmidt tell us that many have a clear belief in the unity and goodness of God, the efficacy of prayer and sacrifice, the immortality of the soul, divine rewards and punishments, the indissolubility of marriage, and the imperative of premarital chastity.

Margaret connected two supposed realities of Samoa: The alleged sexual freedom of the young and the alleged absence of neuroses among the Samoans. The one did not follow from the other. We need only shift our sights from the 1920s to the 1970s. In the 70s many young people have grown up without sexual restraints. Are they therefore less in need of the attentions of the psychiatrist? Fortunately for Margaret Mead, her admirers do not force the question.

But *Coming of Age in Samoa* was all that the avant-garde of the Roaring Twenties needed. Soaked with Freudianism, they proclaimed that in Samoa, where there are no sexual taboos, life is healthy. Ergo, we should imitate the Samoans. For the mental, not to say the moral, health of America in the late 1970s, we can give no small part of the credit to the little book, *Coming of Age in Samoa*.

In the last two or three pages of this book (246-248), Dr. Meads doctrinal calm rises to the lyricism of a Phoenician prophetess:

"The home must cease to plead an ethical cause or a religious belief with smiles or frowns, caresses or threats. The children must be taught how to think, not what to think. And because old errors die slowly, they must be taught tolerance, just as today they are taught intolerance. They must be taught that many ways are open to them, no one sanctioned above its alternative, and that upon them and upon them alone, lies the burden of choice. Unhampered by prejudices, unsexed by too early conditioning to any one standard, they must come clear-eyed to the choices which lie before them." Then, on the final page, Margaret wrote the punch line: "But it is unthinkable that a final recognition of the great number of ways in which man... Is solving the problems of life should not bring with it in turn the downfall of our belief in a single standard (p. 247-248)." For "single standard" read the God-given moral law.

* * *

Anthropologist Margaret Mead was posthumously awarded the Presidential Medal of Freedom – the nation's highest civilian honor – during a memorial ceremony this month (January 1979), in her honor. Andrew Young, U.S. Ambassador to the United Nations, representing President Carter, read the official citation that praised Mrs. Mead as a "student of civilization and an exemplary of it."

Mrs. Mead was a frequent speaker at meetings of the World and National Council of Churches. She was an outspoken advocate of women's rights and abortion. Thrice divorced, she rejected Christian standards of morality and advocated trial marriage.

Franklin Delano Roosevelt
Flagrant Adulterer
Christian News, May 12, 2008

During the editor's grade school, prep school, college and seminary days many of his teachers and professors often expressed a high regard for President Franklin Roosevelt. FDR became president the day after the CN editor was born. During his school days the editor did not share the enthusiasm of many of his teachers for Roosevelt. He supported the position taken by Lutheran Hour speaker, Walter A. Maier, toward Franklin and Eleanor Roosevelt, Pearl Harbor, World War II, the bombing of innocent civilians, socialism and communism. Some of this is in *Walter A. Maier Still Speaks*.

During the editor's student days not much was publicized about Franklin Roosevelt's adultery and Eleanor Roosevelt's lesbian lover. Historian Joseph E. Persico has written a new book which should convince even the most ardent admirers of Franklin Roosevelt that he was a flagrant adulterer. Both *Time* and *Newsweek* recently had full page stories on Perisco's book. "The Women the President Loved – New suggestions that FDR's affair with doting Lucy Mercer never ended" in the May 5 *Newsweek* reported:

"In 1931, when Franklin Roosevelt was considering whether he should, and could, run for the presidency, he called in three physicians to advise on his physical capability. They reported that the man who had contracted polio ten years earlier, losing all movement in his legs, was indeed in good health—and, furthermore, that he had 'no symptoms of *impotentia coeundi*.' 'In plain English,' writes historian Joseph E. Persico, 'he could sustain an erection.'

"It is a significant detail for Persico, given the questions he seeks to answer in his new book, 'Franklin and Lucy: President Roosevelt, Mrs. Rutherfurd, and the Other Remarkable Women in His Life'. Did he have an ongoing relationship with Lucy Mercer (later Rutherfurd)? Was it sexual? Was she the only one? His answers to each are yes, undoubtedly, and no.

"The charming, pretty Lucy was employed by Eleanor Roosevelt as her social secretary in 1913. Five years later, a stricken Eleanor discovered a bundle of love letters from Lucy to her husband—at which point, Eleanor wrote, 'the bottom dropped out of my particular world.' She offered Franklin a divorce, but his mother threatened to disinherit him, and his political adviser cautioned that accepting it would destroy his chances of becoming president. FDR returned to his wife, promising that he would never again share the marital bed—or see his lover, who married a man 29 years her senior.

"We have long known that Lucy came back into FDR's life in his White House years (she was with him when he was stricken at Warm Springs). Persico, however, is the first to document, with letters FDR wrote to Lucy between 1925 and 1928, how early Roosevelt began breaking his promise to Eleanor. The contact between Lucy and FDR, he says, was 'almost unbroken' for decades: they spoke on the phone often; she visited him 40 to 50 times in the White House, usually under the name 'Mrs. Paul Johnson'; she was present at each of his inaugurations, and FDR orchestrated 'accidental' meetings while driving through the Virginia countryside. 'If the relationship was simply the shared companionship of old friends,' Persico asks, 'why all the machinations to conceal it?' "FDR had a host of close female companions, who Persico says were the 'oxygen to his soul.'"

"It is hard not to feel indignant on Eleanor's behalf as you trawl through the evidence of her husband's infidelity and need for the admiration of other women—not simply because she is described as physically inferior, but because she is so often cast as a rejected, loveless figure."

Will any of the liberal churchmen who hailed Roosevelt as a Christian, patriotic American and great moral leader now finally recognize and admit the truth?

Solution For Sex Addiction

Christian News, February 28, 2011

"The Truth About Sex Addiction" is the title of a major story in the February 29 Time. The subtitle: "Is it a real disease or an excuse for men to cheat and spend hours on porn sites? The inside story on uncontrollable desire." Time says "Because the desire for sex is so powerfully enfolded in our DNA, the abstinence model for treating sex addiction is usually unrealistic." Sex addicts should be told "Flee from sexual sin" 1 Cor. 6:19. "Flee from the lusts of young people" 2 Tim. 2:22. Tell them about Jesus and forgiveness of sin. "Keep our minds on all that is true or noble, right or pure, lovely or appealing, on anything that is excellent or that deserves praise." Phil. 4:8.

XII

OVER POPULATION

Christians Should Not Fall for the Myth of Over-Population Constantly Proclaimed by Abortion Enthusiasts

Christian News, March 12, 1973

Robert L. Sassone writes in the March *Applied Christianity* that "there is no valid reason why population growth must be limited today or anytime even in the far distant future." He notes that "the trend for more than a generation has been for food supplies to increase one percent faster than the growth of population. Animal and fish protein production has increased faster than food production, so there is now 8 percent more per person than before World War II. There are about 58 million square miles of potential agricultural land on earth, of which only about 15 per cent is used. Of this 15 per cent, only about one-half is harvested in any one year, nearly all of it at yields per acre less than one-half of nations like Mexico and Egypt, which are scarcely technological leaders."

Sassone says: "In regard to oxygen - which some Zero Population Growth people are sure that we are running out of fast - there are more than one million tons of free oxygen in the atmosphere for every living person. That percentage has not changed in the last 50 years.

"What about resources such as coal and oil? They're made of elements arranged in a useful form. At the present rate of use, we have more than enough of these elements to last mankind 900 million years. There is more oil in the ground in three states in the U.S. than the entire world would use in a hundred years. There is more oil in the Arctic alone than could be used by the whole world in a thousand years."

The author, who has written a book entitled "Handbook on Population," concludes: "The problem today in the United States is not population growth but population stagnation."

Birth Control and the Population Explosion

Christian News, March 10, 1986

Liberal churchmen are among those who have defended birth control in part because of their fears of a population explosion. CN is one of the few Protestant publications which has not shared the concerns of these liberals (See the section on population and birth control in the *Christian News Encyclopedia*, pp. 1435-1439).

The UN International Conference on Population in Mexico City in 1984 found that there is no evidence that population growth diminishes economic well-being.

Tom Bethel writes in the March 14, 1986 *National Review*: "In 1970 Paul Ehrlich, Stanford University's renowned specialist in population biology and author of *The Population Bomb* (1968), predicted that famine would be 'directly or indirectly responsible for 65 million American deaths in the decade of 1980-89.'"

Bethel observes that "The Soviet Union exports Communism. The United States exports condoms."

The *National Review* article concludes:

Is there no population crisis, then? Maybe there is. It takes an average of 2.1 children per woman to replace a population over time, not counting immigration. "The key fact of our time," as Ben Wattenberg has written, "is that the important, modern, free, powerful nations of the world are not having 2.1 children per woman. In England, its 1.8; in France, 1.9; in Japan, 1.7; in Italy, 1.6; in West Germany, 1.4. This is the first time in history that a collection of nations – without the stress of war, famine, or disease – has opted not to reproduce themselves."

Even allowing for the unreliability of such forecasts, the populations of several Western European countries are likely either to have declined by the year 2000, or to be stable thanks only to rapidly growing Muslim cohorts in their midst. (In Britain today there are a thousand mosques.) The U.S. population will continue to rise for a while – because of immigration, and the declining death rate (people live longer).

"The U.S. Population is now growing and short of violent disaster will continue to do so for some decades to come," Peter Beckmann of Boulder, Colorado, wrote recently in his always entertaining newsletter, *Access to Energy*. "From this it is often quite wrongly concluded that there is a population explosion in the U.S. This is like fearing a flood because the river level is still slowly rising after the spring run-off, when a look at the dry mountains would reveal that what is really threatening is a drought."

Yield of Farms, Cattle Industry Can Be Increased
Marine Biologist Says Food Problems Stem From Failure To Use Technology

By *Religion News Service* (12/20/73)
Christian News, December 31, 1973

DAYTON, Ohio - (RNS) - Lack of dedication to the use of existing technological competence to attack malnutrition, hunger and pollution, rather than overwhelming numbers, is the cause of what is being decried as the world population problem, according to a University of San Francisco biologist, who is a leader in anti-hunger and anti-pollution programs.

Dr. Francis P. Filice, a director of Dayton-based More Agricultural Production, Inc., takes the view in a report made public here that major ills of society often blamed on population growth actually stem from an "unwillingness" to use available technology "in an unselfish manner."

Citing gains made in the application of conventional agricultural techniques and the development of high-yield strains of wheat and rice, he said it is obvious "that we right now have sufficient technological competence to feed a world population many times larger than the existing one."

Dr. Filice fears that if the public is "oversold" on the question of overpopulation, we will be "blinding ourselves to the real causes and (this) will inhibit our chances of working out solutions."

The "immediately foreseeable potential" in food production from new sources is even greater than the promise of "conventional agriculture," he said.

"We have hardly touched the agricultural use of ponds, lakes and the sea," Mr. Filice said. "The sea represents 70 per cent of our earth's surface and it produces only 1.5 percent of our food."

He said experimental work in Israel and Japan has demonstrated that agricultural efficiency can be increased to 15 times that of our best farm lands by growing plants in water.

The biologist cited research into possible use of algae, and gave as one example the theoretical use of the 212,000 acres of San Francisco Bay.

If the bay were filled and planted in corn, the crop could produce about 60 million pounds of beef. "However, if you used the bay as a place to grow an algae like Chlorella, then fed the crop to beef cattle, you could produce over 800 million pounds of beef in a year."

Turning to the population issue, the California biologist said "curves" graphically indicating growth through history can be deceptive, because "we have no reliable data prior to around 1750." The data from Western Europe and North America are fairly accurate for the last century or so, but even now figures from most of the rest of the world are unreliable, he contended.

From reliable data available, however, it does appear that a decline in the birth rate has been taking place in the West for more than 200 years. If this long "trend" which began before the widespread use of contraceptives, continues, a balance of births and deaths is bound to come, he indicated.

"Certainly there is no sign of an explosive increase in the birth rate," he observed.

Dr. Filice, an expert in marine biology, is associate editor of *Wasman Journal of Biology*; an advisory board member of the University of Pacific marine Station, Dillon Beach; vice-chairman of the San Francisco Industrial Waste Review Board and honorary advisory board member of the Save the Bay society.

His view of the food problem was presented in the M.A.P., Inc. publication, *The Compass.*

Population, Resources, and the Future: Non-Malthusian Perspectives

Edited by Howard M. Bahr, Bruce A. Chadwick, and Darwin L. Thomas (Brigham Young University Press: Provo, Utah, 1972), $3.95 paperbound.

Reviewed by Bruce D. Porter
From the May, 1974 *FREEMAN*
Christian News, May 20, 1974

Ever since Parson Malthus penned his *Essay on the Principle of Population*, prophets of gloom by the handful have denounced childbirth as the source of human woes. In more recent years, however, that handful has multiplied geometrically (and common sense but arithmetically), to make it "common knowledge" that a population crisis of immense magnitude is at the door, about to thrust civilization to its doom.

"In the belief that non-Malthusian perspectives on population are not receiving the attention they deserve," fourteen top scholars are highly critical of "population myopia" - the increasing trend to blame all manner of social maladies on the infants coming into the world. Such a catchall diverts our attention from far more significant problems and creates a convenient scapegoat for erring politicians. Drumming up a crisis may only encourage hasty, possibly foolhardy solutions.

Several scholars challenge the Malthusian premise that resources inevitably run a losing race with population. The food supply, for example, has not only kept pace with the birth-rate, but since the dawn of serious agricultural research in the first half of our century, it has surpassed it, and the Green Revolution is only beginning. If fully developed and allowed to produce, the world's present croplands could support our growing numbers many times over.

The same is true of housing and energy technology. R. Buckminster Fuller contributes an imaginative essay on the potential of engineering to handle increased population at increasing levels of affluence. He maintains that improved technology rather than political organization will ultimately be the key to erasing housing, water and energy shortages.

Certain environmentalists have identified overpopulation and "the exploitive system of capitalism" as the two main sources of our pollution problems. B. Dilworth Gardner of Utah State University convincingly demonstrates that most environmental damage involves public resources and lands, where common ownership eliminates individual responsibly for waste. Contrarily, private ownership of well-defined properties normally works to reduce pollution to negligible amounts. He proposes some unique ideas on using the free market system to control environmental abuses.

Another major assertion of neo-Malthusians has been that high population density is the major cause of crime, delinquency, civil unrest, suicide, and drug abuse. An analysis of demographic patterns dispels this idea. Our urban riots have typically occurred in areas declining in population; the highly crowded countries of England and Holland have among the lowest crime rates in the world. A case can even be made in favor of high density life- that it is good for people, their health and sanitation. The big picture we get is that population is only one of many factors contributing to social problems, and a minor one at that.

"Mass starvation is not made in bedchambers, but in council chambers." The closing essays of the book deal with the moral questions raised by population control. "Coercive programs are incompatible with self-direction and personal freedom." In the realm of living, breathing people, there are values more precious than survival itself.

Should the time indeed come when our numbers reach crisis proportions (and these scholars agree the time is still distant), people will voluntarily bear fewer children. It may frighten some to thus trust humanity's future to the wisdom of free individuals, but a far more foreboding specter is that of a society planned and ordered and limited, but alas! void of the values, dignity and freedom we have come to take for granted.

The Myth of Overpopulation
By Murray Norris
Christian News, November 4, 1974

This talk about the population explosion and its terrible aftermath is dead wrong.

If we gathered up all the 3.5 billion people in this world and stood them shoulder to shoulder, we could easily get them all into Ventura County here in California. In fact, if we gave each of them six square feet to stand in, we could fit every last one of them into the national forest portion of Ventura County and probably still have room for some of them to lie down. This would leave the rest of us in Ventura County, just about the same as we are today since everyone else would easily fit into the national forest areas.

So what is all the noise about?

Someone seems to think we will outrun our resources, have famines and other problems, if we "let the population grow unchecked."

EARTH CAN SUPPORT MORE PEOPLE

But there are a large number of economists, agronomists and others who tell us that many parts of the earth are under populated. And we could easily support 35 - to 40 billion people, or more than 10 times the present population.

Robert Sassone, author of *Handbook on Population* insists that there are no natural resources in danger of complete exhaustion. He offers a $1000 reward to anyone who can suggest a valid reason why we must limit population in the next century.

Sassone points out that all buildings in the world take up .01 percent of the earth's surface, or one-ten thousandth of the surface.

Says Dr. Sassone,

"Every nation in the world that publicly lists its food supply in statistics compiled by the United Nations, has a succinctly large supply (of food).

"The trend, for more than a generation, has been for world food supplies to increase one percent faster than the growth of population. Animal and fish protein production has increased faster than food production, so there is now eighty percent more per person than before World War II."

Sassone says the UN reports that only 15 percent of the potential agricultural land is now being used in this old world. And of this 15 percent, only half is harvested in any one year. So even this could be increased, if there were a true need to do so.

All the farms, roads, buildings, and cities take up only three percent of the earth's surface. And anyone can tell you that our farmers could produce more food on less acreage if they had to.

But what About India?

At last count, the United Nations figured that India has roughly 400 people per square mile. That's fewer people than live on a square mile in Italy. And if you figure only the inhabited portion of Ventura County (not the national forests), there are more people right in Ventura County than in India, by the square mile.

If you really want to see a place where they pack in people, try The Netherlands with 1,000 people per square mile. Or Taiwan with better than 1,200 people per square mile. Both nations export food and have twice to three times the population density of India (or Bangladesh, where there is a famine right now).

England, that tight little isle, has nearly 600 people per square mile.

So what causes famines?

Problems of nature, problems with politicians and government policies that do not favor farmers, cause more famines than nature. And none of them are caused by too many people.

But let's take a closer look at the food situation.

First off, at least three-fourths of the tillable land of this old earth of ours has not been touched with a plow. And of the rest, only a small portion is extensively farmed. American farmers lag behind 17 other nations (some undeveloped) in the production of food per acre.

Even when this food is produced, frequently it cannot be moved from the farms to the dinner table. Governments who fail to give attention to farms, communication and transportation first, frequently find themselves without food in the cities, when it is rotting in the country. India was like this when she first got her independence from England. The government concentrated on industry, and promptly had a famine. Then the government gave attention to agriculture and now has plenty of food.

Those nations who first build up their agriculture and transport don't need to worry about industry or exports.

WHY THE GRAPHS ARE WRONG

Now, it is easy to see that the world population increased from one billion in 1840 to two billion in 1940. And, if you used the right kind of curve, the right kind of graph, you could easily fill up the world by some certain year in the future.

But things don't always go that way.

The mother herring in the ocean lays enough eggs that, if each one of these hatched, the sea would be solid herring eggs in only three years.

It seems that Our Lord commanded - not asked, but commanded - man to go out and increase and multiply and fill the earth. He did this several thousand years ago. But apparently man has been too busy with wars, sex and Playboy bunnies, to heed His command.

And, if it isn't one of these things, a plague or flood comes along to give a break between the war and games.

Our birth rate has been falling since the end of the 19th century – throughout the world. It is people who are living longer who are making higher population statistics.

And now we are killing one baby in three before it is born through abortions – on a worldwide scale.

It not only appears that man isn't producing enough children, but if we use the same graphs used by the people who are predicting too many people, we come up with no babies being born in the world after 1990, and no one in the world after 2050.

BACK TO REALITY

Japan is producing only 00 percent of this replacement population. It is so short of laborers it is importing workers from many other areas such as Korea and Pacific islands. Many countries in Europe are not having enough babies to replace their population. And in many places, it is already affecting – for the worse – their economies. Japan may soon be in the same sort of situation.

Even here in the United States, the birth rate is dropping so fast that we may soon see a drop in the population. About 70 percent of the rural counties are actually losing population. Many areas, even here in California, are seeing bear and beaver, deer and antelope, where they were recently thought to be extinct.

WHAT ABOUT POLLUTION?

Don't more people cause pollution?

A few individuals may cause pollution, but sheer numbers of people do not.

In the words of Dr. Sassone:

"Pollution has been used very effectively by the anti-life forces in the United States as a justification for proposals of dictatorial control of population and the family.

"There is no major kind of pollution that cannot be controlled economically. While it might cost as much as $30 billon to clean the environment, pollution is now costing the public far more in sickness, premature deaths, loss of property value, and loss of recreational areas.

"Pollution is caused by a relatively small number of persons and companies, not by population growth.

POPULATIONS STAGNATION

"The problem today in the United States is not population growth, but population stagnation. Children born a generation ago are not reproducing themselves. History records no single case where population stagnation or decline has had a happy result."

Perhaps people who worry so much about the population explosion might do better to worry about the population concentration in the cities. We certainly could stand a little better planning and layouts in most of the cities I've seen. And when 90 percent of the population tries to concentrate on five percent of the land area of this nation, we have major problems.

However, recently there have been some slight changes, even in this. New York City at the turn of the century had 45,000 people per square mile in its city area. Today there are only 42,000 people per square mile in New York City.

If our industrialists can go over to foreign countries to build factories because labor is cheaper, why can't they build the same factories in the rural areas where living and wages obviously are cheaper?

But, you ask, how about feeding and clothing all these people we now have?

Frankly, the United States doesn't know what to do now with all the food and fiber it is producing on less and less land. Despite the recent "grain shortages" we still see limitations on farming operations. Land is still left idle.

As recently as 1959, there were U.S. Department of Agriculture people who frankly said they wanted at least two-thirds of our farmers to retire because they were producing too much. They had statistics to show that the other third could produce more food than was needed by the entire population and still have enough for exports.

The last figures I saw, we were selling about 60 percent of our wheat crop to Communists and other buyers. And the real problem in Communist countries is the government, not the farmers, when it comes to food production. In Russia, the tiny individual plots that measure less than an acre or two actually account for a third to two-thirds of the produce and other foods, according to best available sources. The huge government-run farms are failing in Russia, not the individual farmer plots.

FALLING WORLD BIRTH RATE

Throughout this nation, hospitals are abandoning maternity wards because there are fewer babies. The birth rate is plummeting to a dangerous level. Our economy is suffering now and will suffer even more if this continues.

But it is the same across the world. Hungary and Romania are dropping in population. Russia is so worried it offers hero medals to mothers of five or six children.

In Vienna, Austria, deaths are exceeding births at the rate of two to one. Two-thirds of Europe is failing to produce enough children to replace the adult population.

The United States faces a time in the very near future when the "Pepsi generation" will be trying to support a fantastically high percentage of older people, with fewer young people coming along to help pay the needs of the oldsters.

Dr. George Carter, a Fellow of the American Association for the Advancement of Science and the American Geographical Society, says that "suppression of these facts (on population downtrends) amounts to scandalous treatment of the data on population."

PEOPLE MAKE NATIONS PROSPEROUS

Carter agrees with Colin Clark, world-renowned demographer, that the more people you have per square mile, the more prosperous your nation. People not only eat, but they think, they work and they produce.

As the population moved out of northern New England, the area has stagnated and declined. The South, with its growing population, attracts industry and increases prosperity.

In East Germany, when they were losing people to the West their economy tottered and faced complete collapse. The Berlin Wall was a savior of that nation's economy because it stopped the people drain.

In his book *Population Growth, Its Advantages*, Colin Clark shows how nations become great because they have large populations as well as other assets. While other nations with the same assets, without a large population, remain backward and even undeveloped.

Despite automation, people will be in demand as long as industries and farmers remain free. Only governmental intervention can change that.

Free industrialists in France and Germany imported Italians, Spaniards, Greeks, and even Arabs to run their machines. But as industrialization around the Mediterranean developed, there were fewer people available.

While there are few people starving, particularly in the African famine now, there are few that starve where the governmental policies allow the farmers a free hand and there is no war going.

Most farmers are not producing at capacity. For instance, an American cow produces about 10 times as much as cows in the Far East. Our chickens produce 4 to 10 times as many eggs.

In the words of Dr. Carter,

"We are too gullible. We are too pessimistic. We are too emotional. We are overly propagandized, as can be shown by the fact that such (population) figures. . . can be multiplied indefinitely."

As for the exhaustion of natural resources of metals and other minerals, Dr. Clark points out that those who write books predicting famine and mineral exhaustion do not even use available figures on our reserves – some of which have more that 500 years supply and none of which is shorter than 20 years' reserve – with more being found all the time.

Concentrating his fire on two books by the Professors Erlich, *Population Resources Environment* and *The Population Bomb*, Clark refutes – item by item – the false claims by the two (man and wife) harbingers of doom.

Taking oil, for instance, there are some 300 to 500 million tons available today, as compared with the "ultimate reserve" of only 76 million tons in 1949. So the actual reserves are really far larger today than they were 25 years ago.

Shortages of fuel today are caused by environmentalists who halted refineries, the Alaskan pipeline, governmental tinkering with prices and other causes not connected with shortages of reserves or availability of oil.

With plenty of resources available, it is only fair to conclude that man is an asset, not a liability. Man's potential increases with each new thought. And new thoughts come only from men.

Obviously the future is quite terrific, if we keep a good supply of homosapiens around.

Rather than cutting back the population, we should be encouraging increases. Perhaps even family allowances could be offered like some of the European countries and Canada.

With more people to tackle the real problems of production and transport, the only limit in the future is the sky itself.

And how high is the sky?

(EDITOR'S NOTE: the writer Murray Norris, is a 29-year veteran newspaper reporter and editor and father of 13 children.)

Overpopulation
Christian News, December 30, 1985

Is the world overpopulated?

A number of years ago *Christian News* sold many copies of *The Myth of Overpopulation* by Rousas Rushdoony. The section on population in the *Christian News Encyclopedia* includes some articles we have published on overpopulation and birth control.

Dean C. Curry, who teaches political science at Messiah College in Grantham, Pennsylvania, shows in the October *Eternity* that the earth is not as overpopulated, underfed, and environmentally depleted as even many Christians think.

Professor Curry writes in part:

"In the realm of public policy there are increasingly few issues on which evangelicals agree. An important exception is found in that class of issues which relates to the world's population and its resources. Most evangelicals accept as truth the idea of an overpopulated, underfed, resource, and environmentally depleted world.

"Fifteen years ago, Francis Schaeffer was one of the first evangelicals to attempt to define a Christian response to the ecological crisis in his now all-but-forgotten book *Pollution and the Death of Man*. In more recent years, evangelical commentators have made the issue of resource scarcity an important item on their agenda of social concerns. Ron Elsdon's *Bent World: A Christian Response to the Environmental Crisis* (InterVarsity, 1981) and particularly Loren Wilkinson's *Earth Keeping: Christian Stewardship of Natural Resources* (Eerdmans, 1980) have been influential in molding evangelical attitudes toward the extent of the environmental crisis, its causes, and its solutions.

"The analysis contained in these and other evangelical responses borrows heavily from the conclusions of the 1972 Club of Rome – MIT report, *The Limits of Growth*, and the 1980 federally funded *The Global 2000 Report* to the President. The general thesis of both these reports is not new. Nearly 200 years ago Englishman Thomas Malthus warned of the dangers associated with the inability of agricultural production to keep pace with population growth. What is new is the sophistication of their methodologies and the urgency of their conclusions. The initial report warned that the world faced environmental – and consequently economic, social, and political – collapse within 100 years. While the latter concluded that in just 20 years (the year 2000) life on this planet will be 'precarious' at best.

"Indeed, the oil and grain crisis of the 1970s seemed to provide incontrovertible evidence that humankind stood on the precipice of ecological disaster. Today, starving Africans, UN population projections, anxieties generated by the backyard presence of nuclear power plants, and a general sense that the by-products of industrialization are, in one way or another, toxic, have even further confirmed what the experts have been telling us. But are the experts right?

"Not every expert accepts the thesis of global limits to growth. In what is certainly one of the best kept secrets of the past 20 years, a study called *The Resourceful Earth*, 29 heavy-weights from the economic and scientific worlds have come together – In their own words, 'out of passion for truth and outrage at bad science' – to fire a broad salvo at practically every conclusion of *The Global 2000 Report*. *The Resourceful Earth* is almost encyclopedic in its breadth. There are chapters on fish yields, global forests, species loss, soil erosion, cropland change, water resources, and many other topics which bear directly on nearly every issue addressed by its more pessimistic predecessors.

"The editors of this book – University of Maryland economists Julian L. Simon and the late Herman Kahn of the Hudson Institute – have long been lone voices decrying the fraudulent (Simon's term) nature of *The Global 2000 Report*. In his 1981 book *The Ultimate Resource*, Simon offered his own personal critique of several aspects of the Global 2000 Report. Now in *The Resourceful Earth* Simon and Kahn have assembled a group of experts to answer point by point the conclusions reached in the Global 2000 Report.

"Kahn and Simon have never been known to mince their words. So in this joint effort they begin their lengthy introduction by writing that *The Global 2000 Report* is 'dead wrong.' Tying together the conclusions of each of the contributions to their study the editors summarized that their sophisticated scientific analyses demonstrate that "if present trends continue the world in 2000 will be less crowded (though more populated), less polluted, more stable ecologically, and less vulnerable to resource-supply disruption than the world we live in now.'"

"First, predictions of population growth rates are notoriously inaccurate and there are good reasons – just five years after its publication – to be skeptical of the projections made in *The Global 2000 Report*. Furthermore, the University of Pittsburgh's Mark Perlman demonstrates that there is no empirical evidence to suggest a correlation between population growth, standard of living, and the availability of natural resources. To quote Perlman, "the growth in number over the millennia from a few thousands of million living at low subsistence, to billions living well above subsistence, is the most positive assurance that the problem of sustenance has eased, rather than grown more difficult, with the years."

"Second, food production has increased dramatically in recent years. Today, and in the future, access to food is dependent not upon the availability of food – for this is no longer a problem in most countries – but upon family income. Where severe food shortages do exist, as in much of Africa, these shortages are the result of inefficient and counterproductive political - economic choices made by the governing elites.

"Third, University of Virginia economist, S. Fred Singer argues, as most of us have already deduced by the lower prices we are now paying for gasoline, that the free market price mechanism has worked well in reducing demand for oil while generating cost-effective substitute energy sources. 'It is clear,' writes Singer, 'that fuel substitutions based on purely economic decisions provide an automatic adjustment to higher oil prices.'"

"Finally, physicists Karl Cohen and Bernard L. Cohen argue respectively for economic and safe nuclear power. The American public's fear of nuclear power, writes Bernard L. Cohen, has been cultivated by the media who constitute 'a group of scientific illiterates, drunk with power, heavily influenced by irrelevant political ideologies, and so misguided as to believe that they are more capable than the scientific community of making scientific decisions.'

"These are strong words. Not all the contributions to *The Resourceful Earth* are so seemingly angry and intense. Yet, one does sense an underlying frustration that pervades the entire book. The contributors' frustration arises from knowing that they too are experts – and in many instances the real experts – and yet their perspective has been all but ignored by both well-intentioned individuals as well as by those who harbor hidden agendas.

"The stakes in this debate are high. None of the contributors to *The Resourceful Earth* argues for complacency. The world's eco-system is indeed fragile and the environmental problems which humankind faces are real. Vigilance is imperative. However, we will only be able to effectively address the environmental problems which confront humankind when we make a sincere attempt to understand the real extent and causes of the problems we face. True compassion begins with honest inquiry."

Pin-pointing problems

Exploding Population Myth
From the May 9, 1976 *TWIN-CIRCLE*
Christian News, May 10, 1976

The American people have been laboring too long under the myth that overpopulation is a problem, says Robert J. Bonsignore, president of the New York Chapter of the Population Crisis Council.

If anything, he says, the emerging problem of this decade and this century is de-population.

Population Depletion
At a recent chapter meeting, he reported that 1.3 million Americans had themselves sterilized in 1974 - a 43 percent increase over 1973.

He notes that this trend, coupled with widespread use of the pill and liberalized abortion laws, all lead to population depletion.

Bonsignore says it's a false assumption that overpopulation is a leading cause of crowding and depletion of resources. Sydney, Australia, has congestion and housing problems and no one can say that continent is overpopulated, he points out.

Nations in Africa, South American and Europe are actually trying to increase population or stave off depopulation, Bonsignore pointed out at the meeting.

Argentina, the size of India, has only 25 million people and much of that land lies fallow for lack of human resources.

Greatest Resource
Bonsignore reminds others that people are a nation's greatest resource and children are our greatest blessing; that without children, there is little future for our society.

Zero Growth Brings Problems

By M. Stanton Evans
From *The St. Louis Globe-Democrat*, June 7, 1977
Christian News, June 27, 1977

WASHINGTON - Does anybody out there remember "the population explosion?"

This was the awful process, it may be recalled, that agitated all our no-growth types for better than a decade. Various self-styled experts kept telling us we were threatened with massive overpopulation. At the rate we were breeding, supposedly we would soon be standing on each other's shoulders, exhausting all our known resources and destroying the environment. It was a dreadful, all-consuming crisis.

As these pronouncements poured out across the years, a handful of dissenters tried to tell us that it wasn't so. The facts, they said, were just the other way around. Since the latter 1950s, the U.S. birth-rate has been steadily falling (from 3.8 per woman in 1957 to 1.8 last year), extending a long-term trend that has been under way since 1800. The true direction of our population figures has been 180 degrees at variance from the warnings of the ZPGers (Zero Populations Growth).

* * *

UNFORTUNATELY, these efforts to discuss the facts were blandly ignored by most political and media types and a host of alleged remedies has been promoted to deal with a nonexistent explosion of people. An extensive crusade for sterilization and birth control, wholesale abortion, extravagant mass transit systems, billions of dollars for public schools and rigid environmental restraints are among the measures that have been promoted by the ZPG brigade.

Only belatedly, after most of the damage has been done, has it been possible to get a reasoned assessment of the facts. A few weeks back both Time and *Newsweek* had informative articles on the long-term decline in the American birth-rate and its potential impact on the future. It was the kind of major media attention that would have been extremely useful back when we were spending billions to cope with a crisis that did not exist, while failing to prepare for impending problems that were, and are, quite real. These latter difficulties are lucidly discussed by James A. Weber in his recent book, "Grow or Die" (Arlington House). This volume not only lays out the facts about our falling birth-rate but shows persuasively that an expanding population is far more desirable than a stagnant or a declining one. "More people," Weber puts it, "can do more things better. This has been the experience of humankind in the past. There is every reason to believe that it will continue to be the experience of all the peoples of the world in the future."

To take the obvious case, a ZPG society is one in which the population gets progressively older. This means that as the years go by there will be increasing numbers of retirees who must be supported by a relatively decreasing number of working taxpayers. One need only consider in this respect the problem facing our Social Security system, which claimed a comfortable margin of 35 workers for every recipient in 1945 but today is down to 3.2 to 1. That ratio of course, is still declining.

* * *

A SIMILAR PROBLEM afflicts the numerous private pension plans that play a central role in our economy. *Newsweek* observes that the pension bill at General Motors has doubled in the past decade and will double again in the next. The ratio of workers to beneficiaries has fallen from 10:1 to 4:1 and within another 15 years will be down to parity. "We're building one (hell) [sic] of a burden for our future workers," says a (profane) GM official.

At the other end of the scale, meantime, we discover that we have over invested billions in elementary and secondary schools and training for teachers who have a hard time finding jobs. Schools that cost us a fortune to build are being closed down across the country, or converted to other uses. And, as Weber comments, there are other costs of ZPG that are hard to quantify but nonetheless important.

A society in which population stagnates loses forward momentum, both psychological and economic. It has trouble accommodating changes in the mix of technology and jobs, since we can't rely on expanding markets to provide the various sectors of our economy with slices from an expanding pie. And per capita costs for social overheads - for example, defense - are relatively higher because there isn't a growing base to provide the necessary revenues.

These are the authentic population problems we confront in the immediate and long-term future. Too bad the self-styled experts on the subject were looking the other way as they developed.

From Diapers to Diploma
Christian News, November 28, 1977

The Planned Parenthood Association has publicized alarming figures clearly designed to discourage childbearing. According to their highly suspect statistics it's supposed to cost from $70,000 to $107,000 to raise a child from diapers to college diploma. The larger figure includes lost earning power of the mother sacrificing her career in order to be "just a housewife."

Although such figures overlook young people working their way through college and in general are patently absurd – a statement I make as the father of five who are being raised satisfactorily even though the Lord has not supplied the $350,000 to $535,00 the Zero Population Growth people maintain we need to rear them – many couples have swallowed the anti-child propaganda poison and are so intimidated that they feel even having one child would demand unbelievable financial sacrifices and interfere too much with their modern American materialistic and pleasure-mad lifestyle.

How sad to hear in premarital counseling even our Lutheran youth claiming they can't afford to think of having children for several years and then to see them drive off in expensive cars to luxuriously appointed apartments with color TV and stereo! Have we parents, pastors, and teachers perhaps become too mired in materialism ourselves that we can't convince our offspring that receiving children as precious gifts of God and bringing them up in the nurture and admonition of the Lord is much more satisfying and God pleasing than piling up property and possessions which so soon rot and rust away?

Wisconsin Synod couples, blessed with fertility, need not feel guilty about bringing children into a world allegedly threatened by the specter of over population, not if they are truly Christian parents and give this sin-corrupted world what it needs most - youngsters properly trained to live their Christian faith, to talk about their Savior, to witness by word and deed to the Gospel of the crucified and risen Lord Jesus.

Christian parents, who seek first the kingdom of God and His righteousness, will surely receive, as Jesus promised (Matt. 6:33), the material things needed to adequately provide for their children from diapers to (high school and/or college) diploma.

Reuel J. Schulz
Northwestern Lutheran, November 13, 1977

Population Controlled
Christian News, February 8, 1993

Whose Choice: Population Controller's or Yours? **By Robert Whelan. Published jointly by The Committee on Population and in the Economy, London and Human Life International, 7845 Airpark Road, Suite E. Gaithersburg, MD 20879 USA. Paperback, 56 pages, $3.95.**

Is family planning the same as population control? Advocates of the latter would have you believe it's identical to the former. But this small monograph concisely strips the bark off that lie. In 1 short chapter, Robert Whelan demonstrates that the population control programs implemented worldwide through the United Nations, World Bank, International Planned Parenthood Federation and others are antithetical to true family planning, which derives from personal freedom, individual circumstances and cultural norms. Population control, on the other hand, is the product of State mandates and bureaucratic impositions.

Using documented examples, this book examines programs ranging from pervasive, manipulative and deceptive population control efforts that integrate contraception, sterilization and aborting into "women's health" programs to the bribery and extortion used in such countries as India; and finally to the brutally coercive forced sterilizations and abortions in China.

It reaches the inevitable conclusion that such programs are anti-woman, anti-family, anti-human life and antithetical to freedom. "Those who advocate population control do not trust parents. They prefer to put their trust in government planners, or international bureaucrats at the United Nations or the Word Bank. These people are supposed to be able to decide how many children parents in Third World countries should have more wisely that the Third World parents themselves" (pp. 46-47).

The author concludes that the population control movement does not spring from concerns about health, freedom or economic benefits—or even from the ecological anxieties and chimeras of fringy environmentalists. Rather, population control is power in its rawest form; it is about imposing the Western neo-liberal vision of the way things ought to be on the rest of the world and its inhabitants. The fact is, notes the author, population growth was regarded as an asset until recent years when Western liberals, using bogus statistical models, began sounding the alarm about to explode.

"The assumption that the world is overpopulated is one of those things which 'everyone knows,'" the author says in his introduction. "There has been such widespread agreement in the media and among public policy makers, that the planet is threatened by a 'population explosion,' and that we in the West should do something about it, that any expression of doubt on the issue is akin to claiming membership in the flat earth society."

In a few short chapters **Whose Choice...?** exposes the deceptive tactics, the bastardization of language, the insincerity, the distortion of facts and figures, the perversion of true feminism and the misuse of government authority by population controllers. Once the cloudy illusions are stripped away, we can clearly see the vultures circling, eager to feed on the remains of a civilization that has assigned the value of human life somewhere below that of animals and plants.

Folks who already suspect that the 'population bomb' is a dude – or more accurately a ruse – will want to have this book in their defense arsenal. The imaginary bomb won't go off but the effort to defuse the illusion is literally killing people, as Whelan demonstrates.

This compact book also is for bomb believers, especially those with a spark of intellectual integrity who are willing to challenge preconceived notions and perhaps even to admit that they have been successfully propagandized and deceived by overpopulation doomsayers.

Vatican's Post-Beijing Conference In Taiwan
Pope Population Myth

THE WANDERER, October 5, 1995
(Special to *The Wanderer*)
Christian News, October 9, 1995

TAIPEI – The demographic myths enshrined in United Nations population control policies were punctured at a post-Beijing population conference sponsored by the Vatican's Pontifical Council for the Family.

Under the direction of the council's president, Alfonso Cardinal Lopez Trujillo, some of the world's leading demographers were brought to Taipei Sept. 18-20. They showed the world that there is no international consensus in the scientific community that state-sponsored population control measures will produce economic benefits.

Indeed, as conference speaker Rosa Linda G. Valenzona of the Philippines stated in her paper on demographic trends in the Asia and Pacific region, sufficient evidence exists "for concluding that governments pursuing a neo-Malthusian family planning program are indulging in unscientific and inaccurate promises.

"There is enough basis for concluding," she added, "that family planning programs are not only immoral because they are anchored on promotion of contraceptive and abortive methods; but also because they will wreak havoc on the demographic vitality of their societies."

The problem countries need to face, she said, is not that of population growth, but rapidly aging populations, accompanied by a shrinking labor force. Policy planners and social scientists must also begin to seriously analyze the impact of contraception and divorce on demographics and also "determine the extent to which family planning proponents have indulged in mind control to poison the hearts and minds of many people."

Unfortunately, she concluded, "most demographers are bootlickers of those who control the huge resources that go into family planning. They are full of intellectual prejudices that close their minds to real facts. There are no economic incentives for undertaking this kind of research and for disseminating this information to counteract the contraceptive mindset that is influencing the attitudes of many families toward childbearing."

Her claims were supported by demographic experts and social scientists from Eastern Europe and Asia, who showed near-vertical declines in national vital statistics on birthrates and marriage rates, accompanying dramatic upsurges in cohabitation and divorce and economic stagnation.

Among the 120 participants at the conference were government officials from several Asian countries, most of the Catholic bishops of India, Asia, and the Philippines, and some of the world's leading demographers: Professor Gerard-Francois Dumont, director of the Institution of Demographic Studies at the Sorbonne; Dr. Irene Kowalska, director of the Institute of Statistics and Demography at the Warsaw School of Economics; Professor Fernando Moreno, sociologist at the University of Chile; and Dr. John Aird of Washington, D.C. a former U.S. and UN census official.

Dr. Kowalska discussed the extremely low population growth in Europe in the context of historical patterns since World War II, and cited numerous recent demographic studies produced by the Council of Europe in 1986, 1991, 1993, and so on, which showed that Europe no longer has enough births to keep pace with deaths.

Though Europeans will not face the fact, Europe is rapidly dying.

With charts and graphs to illustrate her claims, she demonstrated how some Eastern and Central European countries have birthrates so low that the lines are scraping the bottom of the charts, with rates below .5%.

Since 1970, marriage rates have dropped by nearly half, from ten per 1,000 in such countries as Poland, Bulgaria, the Czech Republic, Romania, and Hungary, to less than five per 1,000 in 1993.

Another chart, on "increase" in population, shows most Eastern European countries now in an irreversible population decline, with growth rates from -.2 to -.4.

In Latvia, Estonia, and Lithuania, the statistics are even worse than those for Central Europe.

Asia is equally imbalanced demographically, though not yet the terminal case Europe is. In one of the most remarkable addresses given to the conference, Taiwan's minister of the interior, Dr. Huan Kim-Huei, spoke of his country's experience with strict family planning. It was so "successful" that Taiwan is now promoting policies to raise the birthrate.

"Although our nation has effectively achieved the goal of controlling population growth," admitted the University of Pennsylvania graduate, "an analysis of current birthrates reveals a continuously decreasing rate."

"If the present situation is not corrected, within the next 30 to 40 years, the population growth will reach zero and then will become negative. For this reason, we are now actively implementing a number of population policies aimed at achieving a reasonable rate of growth."

Dr. Dumont presented evidence which showed that the increase in global population in the 20th century was based on increased longevity due to improved health, and not on an increase in birthrates. Furthermore, there is no evidence whatsoever that state population control policies produce economic growth.

To add some moral supports to the scientific analysis of the demographic situation in Asia and Europe, Jaime Cardinal Sin of Manila gave a stirring address, reminding participants that the message they must carry to the world is that "we belong to God; the Maker is the Owner."

We do not belong to ourselves, said the respected prelate, who rallied more than a million Filipinos to protest last year's UN agenda in Cairo.

"Every person is duty-bound to maintain his own integrity, because we are only stewards of ourselves. We must maintain ourselves; we must ensure that we return ourselves intact and improved to our Maker.

"No one is at liberty to damage or mutilate or in any way pollute his or her body, mind, or spirit" or that of another.

What the Pope is Doing

Cardinal Lopez Trujillo recalled the teaching of Popes John Paul II and Paul VI on marriage and social development, explaining that the family is not a privilege given by the state, but a natural framework given by God for life to be respected and maintained.

At Cairo and Beijing, he said, the Church "had to fight against the attempt (knowing well it will not be the last) to put abortion forward as a means of demographic policy invoking this crime as a right!"

He scored the UN for focusing on "extraneous" issues such as "sexual orientation" at Beijing, and contrasted the Church's teaching on the meaning of sexual relations between married men and women and the UN's obsession with sexual pleasure without responsibility.

The human person, he added, unlike animals, cannot be controlled by others, and his body cannot be abused by self or others.

He recalled several addresses by Pope Paul VI, including his Oct. 4th, 1965 address to the United Nations, in which the Pope appealed to the UN to increase the amount of food on the tables of mankind, and not to decrease the number invited to the banquet of life.

Pope Paul VI was right in calling the new restrictive population control policies a "war against the poor," and Lopez Trujillo insisted that Catholics must challenge the popular adage that people should only have as many children as they can nourish and educate.

"Does this mean the poor do not have a right to have any children?," he asked.

Surely, he said, governments have the responsibility to ensure that the poor enjoy the same rights as the rich to marry and have found a family.

Welcome, Baby Six Billion
Christian News, November 1, 1999

"'Events point to return of Christ,' Graham says." A front page article in the October 18, 1999, St. Louis Post-Dispatch reports: "As Billy Graham faces the new millennium, he waits for the return of Jesus to the earth. That's what he told 43,000 people at the Trans World Dome during the closing services of his four evening Greater St. Louis Crusade."

The St. Louis paper noted: "Recent earthquakes in California, Turkey and Taiwan; natural disasters, like the three hurricanes that hit his native North Carolina; and famine in North Korea and the Sudan seem to fit with the biblical predictions", he said. "And things could grow worse with the world population recently passing six billion 'We don't have enough food to feed them; we don't have enough water,' he said."

This issue of CN is reprinting a full-page advertisement which appeared in the October 12 *Washington Times* with the title "Welcome, Baby Six Billion!" The long list of the pro-life and anti-abortion leaders who signed it is included. The subtitles are: "The Population Controllers of the World Would Have Us Mourn the Birth of the World's Six Billionth Person – INSTEAD, WE CELEBRATE! The world's population has doubled since 1960. And humanity has never been so prosperous."

The Christian News Encyclopedia has some of the many articles CN has published since it began in 1962 exploding the "myth of overpopulation" and defending what most churches, including The Lutheran Church-Missouri Synod, formerly taught about birth control.

Joel Belz, publisher of *World*, said in a perceptive column in the October 23 *World* titled "Wrong Again – What the Experts Missed: God Controls the Population Clock:"

"From the macro to the micro last week, world population experts got just about everything wrong.

"Let's concede that sometime this year, the world's population is probably passing the six billion mark. Nobody knows that for sure, of course, since the experts also tell us they don't even know how to produce an accurate count of the people in a typical American city. And in any case, the population mark wasn't reached nearly as soon as the doomsday prophets like Paul Ehrlich said it was going to happen. For the last generation, he's been predicting this would happen early in the 1990s, not in the last quarter of 1999.

"And they missed on the little stuff as well. In their zeal to dramatize the milestone, the experts and their media hacks repeatedly referred to a baby boy born at 12:02 a.m. on October 12 in Sarajevo as the 'official' six billionth person on the earth. What they really meant, of course, was that he was the 'symbolic' six billionth person—precisely the opposite of 'official.' So they got that wrong too.

"But that's exactly what ails these experts. They regularly act as if they know so much more than they really do.

"The biggest surprise for many coming out of October's big turn of the population clock was the almost ho-hum announcement that a frighteningly uncontrollable world population is now miraculously almost under control. It took from the beginning of the human race until 1804 for the worlds' population to reach one billion. The second billion took another 123 years. Then we reached the third billion in 1960, the fourth in 1974, and the fifth just 13 years later in 1987. The sixth billion has taken only 12 years.

"So aren't we about to sink the planet with people? Not so, say the experts. For now, they claim, the curve is turning around. The seventh billion, they think, will take 14 years to be born, the eighth billion 15 years more, the ninth 26 years after that, and the 10th billion full 129 years after that! Some scenarios actually project a shrinking world population—a pattern right now in effect in modern countries like Germany, Greece, and Italy. Indeed, on a worldwide basis, a typical mother right now is bearing only three children during her lifetime as opposed to a figure of six less than a generation ago. Demographers tend to agree that between two and three children per mother is the figure close to that which will ultimately produce a stable population.

"But the fact is the experts really don't know for sure even what that basic statistic is. So many variables affect population that even the most sophisticated and complex models barely touch on future reality. The AIDS epidemic for example, was a totally unknown factor less than a generation ago; now it has a profound impact.

"In the face of such confusion, a Biblical worldview brings to the population discussion three important perspectives:

"First, God-centered thinking brings a cautious modesty and reverence to all projections. It is God who raises people up and sets nations down. His scheme is so much bigger than anything we could possibly reduce to a computer model. Nor dare we ultimately worry that He may have thoughtlessly built a home too small for the human race He planned to inhabit Planet Earth. Yes, our sinfulness has terribly skewed that plan. But God's people should be characterized by confidence that He has a blueprint that works over the long haul.

"Second, God-centered thinking always sees children as a blessing rather than a problem. To be sure, an increasing population—whether within a nation or an individual family—produces new challenges. But in God's scheme of things, those challenges are always better than the alternative. A few dour grouches may see a no-growth world as a better place to live, but the only viable economic models known to the human mind are those that include a growing population. It's part of who we are.

"Third, God-centered thinking takes into account the key role of biblical morality even in such a coldly analytical science as population projection. Some beginning-of-life and end-of-life issues tend to find evangelical Christians speaking with a single voice; they include abortion, AIDS, and euthanasia. The issue of contraception, however, remains perhaps the single biggest moral issue not to be seriously debated among evangelical Christians in our time. That is too bad, since contraception is almost certainly the most influential variable of all in the population equation. (Evangelical Christians shy away from the contraception discussion for at least two reasons: The issue is intensely private, and the stakes are very high. On the one hand, few of us want to give offense to our friends. On the other hand, while a majority of evangelical Christians have clearly become part of the modern contraceptive culture, few relish defending themselves against charges that they have joined a movement that sets aside lives God intended to populate His creation. So evangelicals, even on so basic an issue, apparently seem willing to agree to disagree.)

"Two bits of popular wisdom seemed in order after last week's population milestone: Don't count your chickens until they've hatched. And remember not to holler 'Wolf!' too often."

Population Controllers Got It Wrong

By Sheldon Richman, September 1999
Christian News, November 1, 1999

World population is estimated to be nearing the six billion mark.

In fact, no one knows precisely how many people there are on earth. One would have to have an exaggerated confidence in the record keeping of governments to make such a claim. How reliable are the records-birth and death-of, say, Rwanda? Has anyone counted all the Chinese? Population numbers are soft, to say the least.

The Population Fund's perennial campaign to scare us about the number of people is another unfortunate waste of the taxpayers' money. On its face and out of context, the number six billion says nothing. It is no more scary than saying the sun is 93 million miles from earth. In context the number says nothing disturbing. The population's rate of increase is slowing markedly. Fertility rates have been falling for decades. According to MSNBC, "Since 1992, the United Nations has had to push back its six billion estimate by almost two years."

The Population Fund and its brooding boosters such as Paul Ehrlich and Lester Brown have been predicting disaster from population growth for decades. No set of predictions has been more forcefully falsified. Even Alex Marshall of the Population Fund had to concede, "No one in history thought it would be possible to reach this number with an intact planet; they predicted ecological collapse, famine, and nuclear war, but we are doing rather well and that's an achievement." That optimistic outlook stands in stark contrast to the "authoritative" pronouncements of recent decades. But the statement is flat wrong. Several people knew it was possible for the population to grow without harm: P. T. Bauer and the late Julian Simon are two of them. They told us all along that the idea of the earth's "carrying capacity," which was supposed to make population growth dangerous, failed to take into account the power of human intelligence. With roughly six billion people, the world is a far richer place than it was when the population was one billion. The population catastrophists were just plain wrong.

Alex Marshall could not resist adding to his upbeat statement: "But the other side is that so many people are living in desperate poverty and the population is still growing, mostly in the poorest countries to the poorest families." In fact, people in most places are living longer, healthier lives than ever before. Life expectancy has grown more in the 20th century than in all previous centuries combined. One reason the population grows is that the death rate falls.

One of the myths too many of us live by is that people cause poverty. This is worse than wrong. Poverty needs no cause or explanation. Mankind is born into poverty. It is wealth that must be explained. And by now we should know the cause of that: People!- more precisely, free and enterprising people living, in a regime of private property. Thus it is interference with private property, not population growth, that should be the cause of concern.

The poverty that remains in the world is the result of one thing: government barriers to private property and enterprise. Where people are free to produce wealth, they do so. When government plans, regulates, taxes, mandates, and otherwise meddles with peaceful citizens, it impedes the production of wealth that benefits all. We have too much experience not to realize that.

But political rulers, UN bureaucrats, and anti-population activists insist that population growth is the evil underlying all other evils. To their applause, the dictators of China still force women to have abortions and be sterilized under its one-child policy. Rulers routinely distract attention from their own bad policies by condemning innocent people for having too many children.

There is no limit to the wealth that free people can produce. There is no good reason for governments' interfering with the individual's right to have children. No one who claims to favor human rights can also favor population control.

*Sheldon Richman is senior fellow at The Future of Freedom Foundation in Fairfax, Va., and editor of **The Freeman: Ideas on Liberty** magazine.*

Population Proposition from Putin: Be Fruitful, Multiply

By David R. Sands, *The Washington Times*, May 15-21, 2006
Christian News, June 5, 2006

Russia is losing Russians and on May 10 became the latest European government to offer hard cash to get its women to have more babies.

Saying plunging birthrates and a falling population are Russia's "most acute problem," President Vladimir Putin devoted much of his annual state-of-the-nation speech to proposals to stem the country's mounting demographic crisis.

"We have raised this question many times but in fact have done little," Mr. Putin said, noting that Russia's population has been falling by an annual average of 700,000 in recent years. "We need to reduce mortality, have an effective migration policy and increase the birthrate," he said.

Lawmakers repeatedly interrupted Mr. Putin with applause as he outlined an ambitious and expensive program to reverse a 15-year decline in birthrates. Quoting Russian Nobel literature laureate Alexander Solzhenitsyn, Mr. Putin said solving the demographic problem "is, in a broader sense, saving the people."

As with countries across Europe, average fertility rates in Russia are far below the average 2.1 children per woman "replacement rate" needed to keep the population stable. For a massive country like Russia, a falling population could leave large parts of the country under populated and create a society wide financial crisis as the population ages.a World Bank report projected that Russia's population, which stood at 146 million in 2000, could fall to 100 million by 2050 if present trends continue.

"We have to encourage at least the birth of a second child," Mr. Putin said.

Industrial countries across the globe have tried a range of strategies to counter falling birthrates since the 1980s. Family-incentive programs, so-called "baby bonuses," have been tried in countries such as Canada, Australia and Poland.

France, with a package of "pro-natalist" programs ranging from tax breaks and baby bounties to large-family discounts on museum tickets and subway passes, has seen an increase in fertility since 1993. French women now on average bear 1.9 children during their lifetime, second only to Ireland in the European Union.

Germany also faces an acute problem, where the number of children born in 2005 was the lowest since the end of World War II. Despite new tax incentives and generous maternity-leave programs, the German birthrate of 8.5 births per 1,000 inhabitants last year was believed to be the lowest on the continent.

Carl Haub, a demographer with the Washington-based Population Reference Bureau, said many complex factors — from cultural values to workplace attitudes to patriotism — will affect whether Western societies can reverse the unprecedented fertility decline.

Mr. Putin's cash-based incentives "could have an impact, but nobody expects one simple solution can solve by itself the long-term problem," Mr. Haub said.

The Russian leader's 10-year proposal includes increasing the monthly payment for families having a second child to up to $110, providing mothers with 40 percent of their work salary for 18 months if they take time off to have a baby; bigger subsidies for child care and higher payments for those who adopt Russian babies, and a direct payment to mothers who have a second child of more than $9,000 to be used for mortgage payments, the child's education or the mother's own pension.

Mr. Putin acknowledged his program would require "huge amounts of money."But "the problem of our low birthrate cannot be changed without changing the attitude of the whole society to the family and its values," he

added.
* Michael Mainville contributed to this report from Moscow.
  Ed. Ever since CN began in 1962 it defended the position Martin Luther, the LCMS, and all major denominations took against birth control until the 1930's when liberals took over most of the major denominations. Some of CN"s articles on birth control and population are in *The Christian News Encyclopedia*. CN promoted "The Myth of Over-population" by Rousas Rushdoony when it was first published. Good books on birth control available from *Christian News* are *The Bible and Birth Control* and *Be Fruitful and Multiply*.

Orthodoxy
The Unfolding Extinction of Western Europeans Shows the Fallibility of the Infallible

The Report, Canada, February 3, 2003
Christian News, March 3, 2003

All through our lives, from our distant youth onward, people of our generation have been repeatedly warned of a dire circumstance threatening the world. It was called "the population explosion," and the warnings came from unimpeachable sources—earth scientists, demographers, and economists, men whose authority one dared not challenge. Their message was always the same.

By the 1980s, or at the latest some time in the 21st century, they predicted, vital resources would run out, massive starvation beset the world and people would perish by the millions. The cause of this doom was that the human race was having far too many children. Organizations such as Planned Parenthood, therefore, deployed their forces about the globe, wildly wielding contraceptives and frantically opening abortion mills in a desperate effort to save humanity.

Many took their message to heart. Single men in North America voluntarily opted to be vasectomized, ostensibly to escape personal responsibility for the coming disaster. Parents would announce the advent of unplanned children with undisguised shame. "We may have one, possibly two, but certainly no more," newlyweds would typically vow, convinced that any more hungry young mouths would constitute wanton excess.

But now, it turns out, all this was balderdash. The experts, we are told, were dead wrong, and the problem is the precise reverse. There's a critical threat all right, but it stems from too few babies, not too many, and the situation is rapidly reaching a point of no return.

In Europe, where birth rates are far below replacement levels, the Caucasian race may soon become a beleaguered minority or vanish entirely. Already, workforces cannot be maintained, economies are imperiled, and the most massive migration since the fall of the Roman Empire is replacing the missing Caucasians with Middle-Eastern workers. Since these continue having numerous children, Europe's democracies in the not-very-distant future will yield to Muslim autocracies and her great cathedrals become mosques. Europeans prefer not to talk about this. A French teacher was actually prosecuted for asking her students to calculate the date when France would have a Muslim majority. The newspapers covered the story—but did not reveal their conclusions.

Canada, with a birth rate 15% to 20% below replacement level, also must maintain heavy immigration. U.S. figures are much the same, although complicated by an avalanche of Latino "illegals." Illegal or not, however, they are necessary to the U.S. economy.

Four recent books on the subject are reviewed in the current issue of Touchstone magazine by Leon J. Podles, one of the magazine's senior editors.* The figures he quotes are more startling than ever. To maintain zero-population growth, women of childbearing age must have an average of 2.1 children, but Spain and Italy—lowest in Europe—are now down to 1.2. In Canada, the province of Quebec is a prime contender for the world's lowest birth rate, but the city of Bologna in Italy, at 0.8, probably still retains that title.

And there are other ominous trends. In Vienna, Austria, for example, half the population is single.

The inevitable effects are indeed striking. As our population ages, the proportion of seniors expands while the proportion of people who must support them diminishes. Newcomers brought in to do this job—replacing, in effect, our own non-existent children—will soon constitute a majority. But these replacements may not remain all that keen about providing massive tax subsidies for elderly Caucasians.

Meanwhile, our social planners are beginning to ask themselves why people, especially women, do not want to have children. Here are a few possible explanations:

1. Because for 50 years we have employed every possible instrument of social propaganda to persuade women to embrace careers, which usually limit them to one child or none. 2. Because our entire social apparatus emphasizes material well being as "success," and raising children erodes material well being. 3. Because hare-brained "anti-spanking" zealots work to prohibit effective discipline of children, which makes raising them extraordinarily difficult. 4. Because teachers are encouraged to undermine parental authority in sex-education courses. 5. Because divorce has been de-stigmatized and made into a common occurrence easily acquired, thereby depriving the family of the social support it has received in every previous era. 6. Because wage levels and job opportunities no longer favor heads of families. 7. Because State funding continues to support anti-birth lobby groups, although their efforts are socially detrimental and destructive.

Most serious of all is the pervasive anti-Christian bias of most of the media and at every government level. The greatest incentive for having children comes from the belief that they constitute a precious gift from God. No God means no children, which is why birth rates follow church-attendance rates downward. But failure to recognize God also entails divine judgment, as surely as effect follows cause. In this century, we may discover to our sorrow just what that means.

A Question of Numbers, by Michael S. Teitelbaum and Jay Winter; Hill & Wang, New York. *The Death of the West*, by Patrick J. Buchanan; St. Martin's Press, New York. *World Population Prospects*, United Nations Publications, New York. *The New Christendom: the Coming Global Christianity*, by Philip Jenkins; Oxford University Press, New York.

Mating for Martyrdom

Fending off our own demographic annihilation – the old-fashioned way

WESTERN STANDARD, Canada, February 13, 2006
Christian News, May 29, 2006

Over Christmas vacation, my brother-in-law went to check out the old folks' home my mother-in-law is now considering.
"Very nice, but it's full of old people," he said.
I had to reply, "Get used to it; it's the wave of the future." But I fear that he, like most people, just didn't get it.
Mark Steyn has just published a *Wall Street Journal Online* column, "It's the Demography, Stupid" now making the e-rounds. He's describing the reality that number crunchers like Nick Everstadt, Julian Simon and Ben Wattenberg have been trying to broadcast for almost 20 years; what management guru Peter Drucker called the "collective suicide" of Western civilization through infertility.
If you want to see the great cathedrals, hurry, because Europe is dying of sterility – but its Muslim immigrants aren't. The economic engine that once was Japan is seizing, because they neither breed, nor allow immigration. And North America is rapidly becoming a continent of senior citizens, with plus-65s likely to make up 30 per cent of the population by 2050.
The pundits are waking up, but what of people on the street? Self-absorbed in consumerism, baby boomers have lived as if they're the last generation. They've turned their backs on all of the West's great political institutions, music, art, architecture and literature, because they're so much more liberated and self-expressive, and the achievements of 2,400 years are just so oppressive.
With three million dead from abortions in Canada, 10 times that many in the States—well, I may be naïve, but it seems to me that people who eat their young have a death wish. With the average couple bearing 1.5 chil-

dren, we don't have much hope in the future, because we really haven't invested in it.

There are practical things government could do to encourage people to breed—tax relief being number one. If we had the same child deductions as we did in the 1950s (when average-income parents of four paid virtually no income tax), that might help reverse the trend. But the problems we face, like the growing Islamist threat, are not essentially political, but moral and spiritual.

When a Catholic couple proposes to marry and receives (if possible) proper instruction from their church, they're told that in order to really marry, in fact and not just appearance, they must intend to accept all the children sent by God. Yet the bishops have largely soft-pedaled this for fear of seeming oppressive and sexist. And now there are a lot of DINK (dual income no kids) Catholics walking around, unaware they're not really married. Luther, Calvin and all the great reformers condemned contraception as an abomination, but post-war Protestants still adopted mass contraception in a fit of absent-mindedness. And whatever happens to Israel, North American Jews may vanish within two generations.

For those who have understood the fertility message, there are practical benefits in the form of maturity. They're taken outside themselves. They're forced to plan and look into the future. They're drawn to think of the culture around them and how to ensure a stable home for their children and grandchildren. Yet sheep need shepherds, and people need encouragement. So where are the pastors, priests and rabbis when we need them? If they're commiserating over shrinking congregations, this really is a bad joke.

At this point, I feel qualified to speak only to Catholics. Yet if Canada's 25 per cent Catholic population alone would do its duty, we'd step back from the brink. We Catholics have a lovely document called "Humanae Vitae," issued by Pope Paul VI in 1968, when everyone expected the church to rescind its condemnation of artificial contraception. Instead, the Holy Father prophesied all the social pathologies that would swamp us—pornography, family dissolution, child abuse, sexual deviancy—if we divorced sexuality from procreation. Well, we did, and they did. If you're Catholic, read it. If you're a priest, teach it.

The rot is pretty deep, so we need real witnesses, martyrs. Today that means living the countercultural truths of family fertility at the risk of seeming odd to relatives and neighbors. It's raucous and always on the financial edge; but I prefer such soft and happy martyrdom to a suicide bomb or sharia court.

More Devastating than the Earthquake and Tsunami

"Japan: Leading The Way To Extinction"

The Blight of Birth Control
"The Road to Insanity"

Christian News, March 21, 2011

Both the secular and religious press have been reporting much about the destruction and death toll of the powerful earthquake and tsunami that hit Japan last week. It is supposed to be "Japan's worst disaster since World War II." Christian disaster relief agencies have been pleading for funds. "The Terrible Aftermath in Japan," an Assist News Service story, notes: "Let's pray for our brothers and sisters in Jesus Christ in Japan. Countless believers have lost loved ones and friends. May they experience God's comfort, solace, encouragement, strength, joy, and peace in this difficult season of grief."

Yet a disaster far more devastating than the powerful earthquake and tsunami has struck Japan.

"Japan Leading the Way to Extinction," An article by Dr. Brian Clowes, research manager of Human Life International (www.hli.org.) In the February 24 Wanderer says that "The time to end population control programs and promote larger families is now." The next book by *Christian News* will be "A Manual of the Christian Family - The Blight of Birth Control – A Fifty Year Battle For Real Church Growth."

Dr. Clowes writes:

Do you know any Japanese? Better look fast, because they're an endangered species. According to the United Nations, there are 1,170 fewer Japanese in the world today than there were yesterday. By the end of this year, there will be a third of a million less, and by the year 2050, Japan will have lost nearly 1/3 of its population. Such is the legacy of a country which has so eagerly embraced materialism and the Culture of Death. Japan is invaluable as a demographic laboratory because it is practically a closed system, with almost no emigration or immigration. Its 99% ethnically homogenous population gives us a rare glimpse of what the future holds for the entire world. The problem is simple: Japanese women have virtually stopped having babies. The total fertility rate, or TFR, is the number of children each woman must have in order for a nation to have a stable population. For an advanced nation like Japan, this is 2.1 children per woman. However, Japan's population was the first in the world to dip beneath replacement fertility fully half a century ago (in 1960), and its TFR has continued to plunge, It now stands at an astonishing 1.00 children per woman (less than half that required for replacement), and will continue to decline to .6 children per woman by 2050. When women stop having babies, the result is unavoidable — the nation's population stabilizes, then declines Japan's population peaked at 127.5 million in 2005, and is now one million less. This trend will accelerate until the nation is losing a million people a year within two decades.

x x x

Since 1995, the Japanese government has tried everything to get women to have more babies, including greatly increased child-care benefits, but without any result. In 2006, the "Year of the Dog," former Prime Minister Junichiro Koizumi said that "dogs produce lots of puppies and when they do, the pains of labor are easy." The government even pays for "speed dating." But once you get people addicted to things and tell them for decades that babies are a burden, that they interfere with your wants and your needs, and they are bad for the environment, your nation is doomed. No nation in history has recovered from a total fertility rate as low as Japan's. What may we learn from the ongoing slow motion Japanese disaster? Just as Japan is a closed system, so is the world. Just as Japan's population leveled out and began to plunge, so will the world's, and very soon. This will lead to gigantic economic displacements and suffering on a scale never before known. Yet our population control cartel continues to abort, sterilize, and contracept the people of the world, just as fast as they can. Worldwide demographic trends have the momentum of a supertanker. The world's total fertility rate will hit replacement in just three years. Its population will peak in only three decades and then begin to decline. The time to end population control programs and promote larger families is now. Continuing on the current course is insanity.

XIII

WEDDINGS

The Wedding Service
Christian News, May 3, 1982

"Some Thoughts Concerning Wedding Practices and Services within the Lutheran Church" (pp. 8-10) by Rev. Loren Trapp deserves the careful attention of pastors and all those responsible for planning a wedding service.

We discussed Pastor Trapp's CN article on funeral services with our Bible Class. His thoughts on wedding services and practices could well be reviewed at youth and other congregational meetings. His "The Order of the Wedding Service" is just the kind of service we were hoping would appear in Lutheran Worship. Several years ago we suggested that the new hymnal include a wedding service which would stress congregational participation. We welcome suggestions which any of our readers may have about the wedding service. If Lutheran Worship is ever revised and its serious weaknesses eliminated, it should include a wedding service such as Pastor Trapp suggests. His thoughts on a processional may appear "revolutionary" but it certainly makes far more sense than the traditional parade which most pastors tolerate but probably don't particularly appreciate. All changes should, of course, be done cautiously and with careful explanation, but some things could well be changed when it comes to the traditional wedding service.

Any pastor who has arranged an order of worship for special occasions is welcome to share his work with others by following what Pastor Trapp suggests in his P.S. Please send us a copy and we'll note in CN that copies are available from us or the author for a self-addressed stamped envelope.

Marriage Ceremony in Modern English
Here Comes the Pride!

When The Lutheran Church-Missouri Synod was planning Lutheran Worship we suggested that Dr. William Beck's marriage and baptismal services in Modern English be included and that the introits and graduals would be better understood if Beck's An American Translation were used. This issue includes Dr. Beck's "A MARRIAGE CEREMONY in Modern English" which he gave us some twenty years ago.

Another Lutheran Church-Missouri Synod theologian who wrote many sensible things about marriage and the wedding ceremony was Dr. Walter Maier Sr. His classic *For Better Not For Worse* should still be read by those contemplating marriage. We've reviewed hundreds of books on marriage and the home since we first read Maier's marriage manual, but we still consider his the best. Our efforts to get Concordia Publishing House to reprint it have thus far been unsuccessful.

Below are some things Maier wrote in the May, 1927 Walther League Messenger in an article titled "Here Comes the Pride!" The Messenger was the youth publication of The Lutheran Church-Missouri Synod's Walther League. Maier was its editor for many years. Here is what Maier wrote some 55 years ago:

As you read these lines, then, there are some five thousand homes in which these June brides (and, incidentally, grooms) are planning the details of their wedding. Invitation lists are being made; wedding dresses fitted; trousseaus completed; showers given; honeymoons planned; wedding menus inspected; florists' estimates considered; photographers consulted; bridesmaids instructed; and the one hundred and one (literally) details involved in a modern wedding are being successively considered and arranged.

But it is frequently the case that with all this preparation and emphasis on externals there is little time, and less thought, for the issue which should be of paramount importance in every wedding of Christian young people, — the distinct and reverent Christian keynote to the whole ceremony. It sometimes happens even in Christian circles that the modern conception of a wedding as a fashion show predominates, and that the whole marriage ceremony degenerates into an unwarranted expenditure of money, in which one bridal couple simply tries to outdo the other. Judging by the artificial and extravagant make-up of some ceremonies, we are constrained to exclaim, not "Oh, Here comes the Bride," but "Here comes the Pride." And if in the large circle of our readers there are those bridal couples who have not given sufficient thought to the necessity of making their wedding ceremony an expression of their Christian faith, we write the following lines directly for them, (and indirectly for all of our young people) to show what high principles should direct the arrangements and the ceremonies incidental to a Christian wedding.

It follows from this that under ordinary circumstances the marriage should be performed in the church, before the altar at which the young people pledged themselves to their Savoir. No public hall or hotel salon is good enough for this sacred ceremony. It is possible, of course, to have a Christian marriage consummated in the Sahara desert, or on board a ship, or in a pastor's study, but this should take place only under exceptional circumstances. If it is objected that a church wedding costs too much, we reply that a church wedding in itself need cost not a penny more than the ceremony that is performed before the altar. No crowds need be invited; no dress suits need to be hired; no lavish floral display need decorate the sanctuary; the strains of "Lohengrin" are not especially essential to a church wedding; but in a quiet and reverent manner and in the divine presence of Him who is to be the third in their life-union the young couple can kneel down in the church without incurring the expenditures that will impair their financial standing. And if any of our congregations have the mistaken conception that they ought to charge our young people an exceptional price for the use of the church building on such occasions, it is high time that the members of such congregations stop to ask themselves why they built their churches.

But even more important than the scene of the wedding is the manner is which the wedding takes place. Very specifically we mean that when Christian young people are married, there should be a marriage sermon, even if circumstances make it necessary or advisable to have the ceremony performed at home. The very importance of the event should suggest that at least a few words of Scripture and a short address by the pastor dignify the occasion and bring the necessary encouragement and admonition. And

when the ceremony is performed at the church and guests are invited, there ought to be a prominent place for congregational singing and prayer. How utterly unexplainable is the attitude of so many bridal couples whose wedding festivities last into the wee small hours of the morning and who have all the time the photographer wants for his various poses, but who are too crowded to have a full marriage service, with sermon, hymns, and prayers!
. . .

But a word of warning may be in place that all artificiality should be avoided. An endless, snail-like wedding procession, with an over-dressed male contingent, but with the bride, as well as the brides-maids, parading in the opposite state of dress- all this is hardly the right atmosphere for anything so sacred as marriage. After all, the bride who wins the admiration and respect of all is not the girl whose face has been artificially prepared, whose dress is ultra-extreme and whose bouquet is the largest ever seen in the church. The girl who is not thinking of her face and appearance, but who is asking God to keep her true and faithful and imploring His divine benediction on her future family will make the better wife, the truer companion, the more loving mother.

Marriage is an occasion of joy and, according to our conception, every marriage ceremony should be followed by a social gathering; if not a marriage banquet, then at least a social meeting where friends can get together to express their congratulations and good wishes to the new husband and wife. Many young people make the mistake of omitting this feature from their wedding-day program, and again the excuse is: "It costs too much." But the expense need not be so great that it becomes prohibitive; and we believe that it is better to forego some luxury or non-essential in the equipment of the household rather than to omit this feature, which, as the Scriptures assure us, was blessed by our Savior Himself when He came to the wedding feast at Cana. But such festivities must preserve their Christian character. And dancing is not only contrary to the spirit of the occasion, but must also be anything but welcome to the bride or the groom who sees the newly pledged helpmate swaying around the room in the close embrace of another. If people cannot have a good time without dancing, we question their mentality, not to mention their Christianity. But otherwise, let joy reign supreme. Let there be song and laughter and jokes - not that vulgar, insinuating type of alleged humor which testifies of coarseness and bad-breeding, but the spontaneous speech-making and the wholesome fun which does not militate against our Christian convictions. And no matter how much there is, let the evening close, as all evenings should close, with a prayer and a petition to God.

And then comes the honeymoon! Every young couple, circumstances permitting, should take a wedding trip; and while it is often a wrong sense of economy that rules out such a trip, it is correspondingly an example of extravagance when young people spend so much for this purpose that they have little left for the stern realities of their subsequent household. But a definitely planned trip, which does not involve too great an outlay of money and which does not call for the most expensive hotels and the most exclusive accommodations, will constitute one of the most wonderful and imperishable memories of life.

A wedding which thus does not degenerate into an ostentatious display of clothing and extravagance, but which is consummated with a full consciousness of its sacred importance, will be the gateway, under divine blessings, to lifelong happiness. For the song of a wedded life is usually sung according to the note struck at the wedding. Those who do not hear Christ when He knocks at their door on the wedding day will very often be impervious to His approach when He later would enter their home. But those who take Him as the Third in their union from the very first moment will truly experience what rich blessings this divine wedding Guest continually provides for their home and family.

Walter A. Maier, Sr.

A Marriage Ceremony In Modern English
By Dr. William Beck

Hymn: "Thine Forever, God of Love!" (TLH #338).
The Pastor's prayer (from the heart).
The Pastor's message.
Hymn: "O Perfect Love, All Human Thought Transcending" (Hymn #623, stanza one).

THE MARRIAGE:

Dear Friends:

You are getting married. Everyone should think highly of marriage, and so we listen to what God tells us about it.

God Himself planned marriage when He said:

"'It isn't good for a man to be alone. I will make someone who will be like him and who will help him.' "So the Lord God had the man fall into a deep sleep, and while he slept, He took out one of his ribs and filled its place with flesh. Out of the rib that He had taken from the man the Lord God made a woman, and He brought her to the man. 'Now this is the bone from my bones,' the man said, 'and flesh from my flesh. She will be called woman because she was taken from a man.' That is why a man will leave his father and his mother and live with his wife, and they will become one flesh.' Listen also to what God has ordered in regard to the behavior of a husband and a wife toward one another:

"You husbands, love your wives, as Christ loved the Church and gave Himself for it to wash it clean with water by the Word and to make it holy to have the church stand before Him as something wonderful, without spot or a wrinkle or anything like that; yes, it is to be holy and without fault.

"That is how husbands ought to love their wives, like their own bodies. A man who loves his wife loves himself. Nobody ever hated his own body. Everyone feeds it and treats it tenderly as Christ does the church becaus we are parts of His body."

"You married women; obey your husbands as you obey the Lord, because a husband is the head of his wife as Christ is the head of the church. It is His body, and He saves it."

Hear also what sorrow God has laid on marriage on account of sin: "He said to the woman, 'I will give you much trouble when you are going to have a child, and the birth of a child will be painful for you. You will long for your husband, and he will rule over you.'

"He said to Adam, 'because you listened to your wife and ate some of the fruit of the tree when I had ordered you, "don't eat it," cursed is the ground on account of you. Weary from work, you will eat your food as long as you live. The ground will grow thorns and thistles for you, and you will eat the plants in the field. In the sweat of your face you will eat bread until you return to the ground, because you were taken from it. You are dust, and you will return to dust."

And yet God is pleased with marriage and has blessed it. It is written: "God made man like Himself. He made them male and female. And He blessed them. 'Be fruitful and multiply,' He told them, 'and fill the earth. Control the earth and rule over the fish in the sea, the birds in the air, and every animal that moves on the earth.'

And Solomon says: "If you find a wife, you find a good thing, and the Lord is pleased with you."

And the Psalmist says: "Happy is everyone who fears the Lord and lives in His ways. Yes, you will eat what you produce by the work of your hands. You will be happy and prosperous. Your wife will be in your home like a vine with grapes. Your children will be like olive plants around your table. You see, that is how a man is blessed if he fears the Lord. May the Lord bless you from Zion!"

And so God has made marriage holy and will bless every husband and wife who fear, love, and trust in Him. Christ, whose blood takes away our sins, has made holy even the sorrows of those who believe in Him. In such a holy marriage you now come to be united. And so everyone may know that your promises are sincerely and freely given, it is right that you should declare before God and these witnesses the sincere intentions you both have.

And so I ask you, _____, will you have _____, here present to be your wife? Will you love, honor, and cherish her, and keep with her this bond of marriage holy and unbroken until death separates you? If so, declare it before God and these witnesses by saying, "I will."

(Groom: "I will.")

_____, will you have _____, here present to be your husband? Will you love, honor, cherish, and obey him, and keep with him this bond of marriage holy and unbroken until death separates you? If so, declare it before God and these witnesses by saying, "I will."

(Bride: "I will.")

(The pastor takes the ring and lays it on his book offering it to the groom. The groom takes it and puts it on the 4th finger of the bride's left hand while the pastor says:

Receive this ring as a pledge of married love and faithfulness.
(If there is a ring for the groom, this is repeated for him.)
Join your right hands.
(The pastor lays his hand on their hands and says):
"Now what God has joined together man must not separate." Since ____and ____ have agreed to be one in holy marriage and have declared this before God and these witnesses, I pronounce them man and wife in the name of the Father and of the Son and of the Holy Spirit.

(To the couple: Please kneel.)

(Praying): Almighty God, You made a man and a woman and joined them in marriage, and You tell us that this is like the union of Your Son Jesus Christ with His bride, the church. We ask You, don't let Your holy work be set aside by anything we do. Bless these two, and guide them by Your Holy Spirit that in every way they may do what pleases You and may live together to Your glory. Let the Word of Christ live richly in them, and make their hearts and their home Your home. Let them be united by a love that is in Christ so that they may never feel any change or doubt in their love. Bless them in each other, and give them the forgiveness and patience to bear with one another's faults. Give them success, and crown everything they do with Your mercy. Let even their troubles and pains bring them Your blessing and a real growth in a Christian life. Teach them to come to You with every difficulty and to thank You for every good thing. And when as Your faithful children they have finished their pilgrimage here on earth, give them a home with You in heaven. For the sake of Jesus, Your Son, our Savior and Lord.

(The pastor puts aside the book, lays his hands on the heads of the kneeling couple, and says):
Let us all unite in the Lord's Prayer: "Our Father", etc.
The Lord bless you and keep you.
The Lord let His face shine on you and be merciful to you.
The Lord look kindly at you and give you peace. Amen.
Hymn: "I Am Trusting Thee, Lord Jesus" (TLH #428)
(During the first words of the hymn, the Pastor tells the couple to rise, and they stand prayerfully until the end of the hymn.)

(This form was prepared by Doctor William F. Beck. It is in the language of today. The Bible quotations are from his translation. The hymns are from *The Lutheran Hymnal*.)

* * * * * * * *

SOME THOUGHTS CONCERNING WEDDING PRACTICES AND SERVICES WITHIN THE LUTHERAN CHURCH

By Rev. Loren Trapp, Pastor
St. Paul's Lutheran Church, Whittemore, Iowa 50598
Christian News May 3, 1982

Over the years there have been many books, pamphlets, and articles written about weddings. These publications have covered a wide variety of material ranging from the planning of socially correct weddings through premarital counseling and the preaching of wedding sermons. While some of what is written contains references to the wedding service, quite often we have found that reference to be quite small. In addition, we have not found much available offering to the parish pastor various forms of wedding services in which congregational worship is highlighted. It would seem that there is a great need for this within our church.

In speaking just the other day with a fellow pastor, the comment was made that the LBW contains a wedding service so that now people can be baptized by the book, confirmed by the book, married by the book, and buried by the book. Perhaps it is because of the uniqueness of the latter two and the desire for variety within forms of worship to account for varying circumstances that such services are most difficult to "set up" according to a strict form.

The difficulty that also arises is that we are influenced so strongly by other traditions and by the wishes and desires of the people involved within these services. Since we have shared some thoughts concerning funeral practices and services within the Lutheran Church previously, we turn now to wedding practices and services. We are not claiming to be an authority in this area any more than in the latter, but what we seek to share is an honest attempt to cut through much of what has been written and, especially, to offer some suggestions which would bring the wedding service into the realm of congregational worship rather than what is so generally found today – that of a wedding held within a church building which could just as well be conducted or led by a justice of the peace! We feel that the orders of marriage provided in our present agenda do little or nothing to make the separation that needs to exist and, above all, to make the wedding service an act of congregational worship. The "Short Form" is simply an extension and elaboration of the simplest rite which enables one to enter the church, get the job done, and get out in the shortest amount of time possible! The form for "The Congregation's Participation" has such little congregational participation that one is forced to wonder how it even got its title!

From the outset, we are fully aware that there will be those who will disagree with much, if not all, that is written here. When writing of practices connected with a wedding, it is impossible to cover all of them or to place them in any order of importance. The latter is not our intention, but simply to present some thoughts for discussion. When writing of the wedding service itself, we are fully aware that what we shall present is not the "cure-all" or even "the best possible" way. What is presented is simply the honest attempt to make the wedding service a form of congregational worship as it ought to be. We are sure that there are many who could improve upon that service in many ways. However, considering the normal practices and the usual wedding services that have existed within our church for so many years, it would seem that any effort to bring about some changes is an effort that is greatly needed and long overdue within the church!

Congregational Worship

We had mentioned in our previous article on funerals our great disappointment that such services were not and are not included within the new *Lutheran Worship*. Considering the "Introduction" found on pages 6 and 7 of *Lutheran Worship*, and the stress that is currently being found within our church towards a rich and varied congregational worship experience, it would seem that its a mistake to omit these additional services. Just because these worship experiences are unique in that, in most cases, the congregation assembled is not composed primarily of parish members, these services, nevertheless are very important and very much a part of the worship life of the congregation. Any and every worship service held within the church should be viewed as an important part of the the worship life of the congregation and should not be separated from it! Any other view would place the wedding service within the realm of the church functioning on behalf of the government. While it remains true that the church does indeed have some connection in this respect because of the laws of particular states, yet the church must remain distinctive and true to its character and confession as it carries out that function and adds to it, refining it, as a special worship activity of the Christian congregation.

One area of concern: Which weddings are to be conducted by the pastor? Surely performing weddings like a justice of the peace, that is, performing a wedding for anyone and everyone, should be out of the question. The pastor is a servant of the congregation and not of the state!

In this respect, since the wedding service is an act of congregational worship, the question should be raised, regarding the church affiliation of the couple wishing to be married. While there are those pastors who would hold a wedding service for any couple and justify their actions by saying that it gives them an opportunity to present the Gospel both to the couple and to those assembled, we believe this is a contradiction to their calling as the pastor of the local congregation and a basic denial of the confession of the church. While it is true that we are to present the Gospel whenever and wherever we can, the ambiguous circumstances of the witness that we give could easily denigrate any positive Law/Gospel presentation. In fact, the very opposite might be said, namely, that we are denying the church's very reason for existence and giving further enhancement to the thinking of many who see the church's existence as that of providing a convenient place for baptizing, confirming, marrying, and burying. In short, desiring a wedding to be held in a local church building because it's a wonderful and beautiful place to hold "their" wedding or some such other reason that is equally mundane and sentimental is not sufficient reason to justify the holding of a wedding service and seeking to justify one's actions by claiming to seek to want to present the Gospel in such a situation. One cannot help but wonder if the primary thought, though not expressed and usually denied, is the whole question of "fees received". In past confrontations concerning the same, we have seen many a pastor become quite flustered with the very mention of "fees" to the point that the old adage quickly comes to mind: "Me thinks he doth protest too much!"

The Neo-Christian

Of equal concern is the scheduling of a wedding in which one of the members of the bridal couple is not a Christian and consents to a church wedding only because that's where a wedding should be held or because the fiancee so desires that the wedding be held in a church. Most assuredly this is a difficult situation and there are many areas of concern involving both members of the bridal couple. While we would like to say that the pastor ought to conduct such a wedding service on behalf of the party who is a Christian (also a member of the congregation), yet there seems to be a definite problem involved. Scripture references to the two becoming one flesh, comparing the union of husband and wife with the union of Christ with the Church, and the life, to say nothing about pronouncing them husband and wife in the name of the Triune God – all of this would have no meaning to the non-Christian party. That party would be going through the motions of a "legal" service rather than a Christian wedding service. We doubt that the two can go hand in hand!

The above discussion would seem to raise another question that is often faced by the pastor in connection with the wedding service. What about the participants within the wedding, namely, the bridal party and others? What demands can we place upon them and insist that they follow? This entire area, of course, is one that is quite "tender" and filled with emotions. However, we think it only right to say that all people involved ought to be Christians! It seems inconceivable that someone who is not a Christian could take part in a worship service dedicated to the glory of our Triune God! So that there be no misunderstanding as to whom we are speaking about, we list the following: all members of the bridal party, soloist (if any), the organist, instrumentalists, ushers, and the like. While we realize that there are those who would also insist that the same must be Synodically affiliated, we do not feel that under the circumstances involved such an insistence ought to be made. It would seem that such a prohibition would automatically rule out 99 and 99/100 percent of all weddings. At the same time, to insist upon Christian faith upon the parts of the participants is a necessary requirement. The wedding service remains a worship experience and remains an act of Christians.

"Cute" Wedding Vows

In the further planning of a wedding service, there are many other areas of concern. One of the first that comes to mind is the increasing practice found today of bridal couples writing their own wedding vows. While the practice is not wrong in and of itself, yet our experience has shown that such is often inadvisable. It would appear that so many couples today are more concerned with being "unique", "different", or incorporating something that could be "cute" as they attempt to write those vows and incorporate so many secular ideas and thoughts of what marriage is all about with the result that the vows express little real meaning or substance. Oftentimes the ideas of romantic love tend to be uttered with a great deal of emotionalism that undermines everything else included with the service.

"Obey"

A real concern in the above area is the desire, in the light of "women's lib", to omit or in some way make a substitution for the word "obey" on the part of the woman. While much could be written on the subject, permit us to simply quote from the "Guidelines for Weddings" booklet or pamphlet that is written for use within our own parish: "please do not ask the pastor to omit, eliminate, or remove from the vows spoken the promise on the part of the woman which speaks of obedience. The Apostle Paul clearly speaks of the matter in his letter to the Ephesians, chapter 5: 'Wives, submit yourselves unto your own husbands, as unto the Lord! For the husband is the head of the wife, even as Christ is the Head of the Church!' The vow of obedience is not one of slavery or subjugation, but rather one of establishing the Biblical precept and foundation, namely, that the husband is the head of the household and is responsible to God for all within that household. Any effort to reword that vow in order to make it sound better or less disagreeable isnot an option available to the bridal couple!"

"Till death us do part"

There has come about in recent years another area of concern. Some couples do not wish to use words like "till death do us part" or other such words. Marriage today has come to be viewed as an institution that is no longer under the directive of the Scriptural injunction: "What God hath joined together, let not man put asunder!" Those seeking to write their own vows often come up with such trite phrases as "So long as our love shall last" or some other such thought. Clearly no in harmony with Scripture. Marriage remains a life-long union which God alone is to dissolve or break through death. Such a statement is not meant to disregard or ignore the reality of divorce on Biblical grounds nor the realty of divorce in general However, let us not permit couples to enter into the marriage covenant leaving themselves an "easy out" should they wish to terminate tha covenant! It would seem that we have enough problems in this area withou adding to those that already exist!

Perhaps it seems out of place at this point in our discussion, yet we are compelled to speak our thoughts about some other wedding practices which surely will generate much response from our readers. Quotations of Scriptural passages to support our views or thoughts would be difficult and ver open to challenge. However, we must speak from the heart. We remain dis turbed that many of our pastors and congregations look upon weddings i a very open and liberal way in regards to certain customs of the past. Tack ling the lesser of two evils first, we submit that those divorced are not entitled to the "trimmings" of a "first" wedding. It seems to us that such is greatly out of place and ought to be avoided. Argumentations of the wedding being a "first" for one of the parties does not seem to hold much weight. Nowhere is it decreed that a person is entitled to a wedding with all the trimmings! Most certainly, this does not rule out a church wedding nor a congregational worship experience. It does, however, rule out certain "trimmings" which have come to be associated or connected with weddings in our day and age. No matter how or under what circumstances a divorce occurred, that for the one divorced, a simple, few frills wedding ceremony is fitting. We could enter into the whole matter of sin and its effects, etc., in both this discussion and the next, but have not the time nor the inclination to write a detailed exposition of the same.

"Great with child"

Our views concerning a similar area will be also looked upon as "narrow-minded" and bring much objection. At the same time, we are not hesitant to state that it remains our personal feeling that those who are "great with child" ought to forego the normal "trimmings" associated with weddings today. There are those who would object to the same, arguing that it is the bride who is called upon to suffer in such cases and that the groom its thereby "excused" from consideration. That, however, is not the case. Neither one is more innocent than the other. The old saying holds true, "It takes two to tango!" However, it would seem that to hold or conduct a wedding with all the "trimmings" would be seeking to excuse or ignore the obvious sin and to announce to one and all that it really doesn't matter! This is not to rule out a church wedding nor an act of congregational worship! It is only to say that certain customs have developed through the years that have meaning and, it is our feeling, that they ought not to be discarded or ignored.

Gowns and Tuxedos

In the light of the above two situations, we have had some very wonderful and beautiful worship experiences. In no way was sin ignored, denied, excused, or otherwise put aside. But, as in every worship experience, there are gathered together a group of sinful beings, so we have moved forward both in repentance and in forgiveness to give all praise and glory and honor to our Triune God. No pretense of seeking to excuse or "pulling the wool over others' eyes" was involved! Everyone knew the circumstances (oftentimes they could not be hidden from view)! We simply gathered together after repentance and forgiveness to call upon the blessings of our gracious Triune God and to enter into prayer for His continued love and mercy and forgiveness! Gowns, tuxedoes, and the like do not add to or take away from the worship service in any way! In fact, we cannot help but wonder whether the whole mania that has come to be involved with weddings in our day can be truly justified in the light of Christian stewardship! Perhaps it would be far more Christian and God-pleasing to return to that more ancient form of having the couple step forward within the regular worship service of the congregation and to include in the same the marriage vows without all the "huppla, hurrahs, and unnecessary expense"!

"Lohengrin"

No discussion of the wedding service would be complete without some words directed to music. It ought to be accepted, without question in our circles, that "Lohengrin" by Wagner and the shop-worn Mendelsohn piece are not acceptable for worship music. Though these pieces are somewhat connected with weddings of the past, there are few musicians today who would deny that they are trite and musically inferior! Argue all you will about their meaning. Its obvious that they were not written to the glory of God. One cannot use the argument that the use of every talent gives glory to God. That argument falls flat with regard to notorius non-Christians like Mendelsohn and idol-glorifying Wagner!

Soloists and A Singing Church

How did soloists enter the worship service to the exclusion of congregational singing? We had one member jokingly suggest that, since soloists have become a normal part of many weddings and funerals, perhaps there is a connection. Seriously, we cannot find justification for soloists as substitutes for congregational singing. What about the old adage that the Lutheran church is a singing church? Surely also at weddings (and funerals) the congregation should actively participate instead of being mere spectators. The congregation should assemble to worship the Lord God, to give praise, adoration, and thanksgiving to the God of our salvation. They should not be denied that privilege and opportunity. The old, idea of singing unfamiliar hymns is nothing more that an excuse calling to the foreground the issue of who the couple chooses to invite to their wedding. We find it hard to believe that a Christian couple would invite people to their wedding service who would not be able to join with them in prayer and praise and thanksgiving to the Triune God. To do otherwise would seem to be a contradiction in terms, in reasoning and motive.

"The Lord's Prayer"

At the same time, pastors are often faced with what music is acceptable and edifying within the wedding service if a soloist is used. It seems to me having a soloist sing "The Lord's Prayer" is out of place, no matter how beautiful the music is. The Lord's Prayer is the family prayer of God's church and ought not to be relegated to one person. More often than not, the prayer is lost in either the rendition sung or the competence of the soloist. Prayer should not be listening to beautiful singing, but prayer is always the active participation and response of the worshipper.

Neither can we accept the many types of music often sung by a soloist which seem to idolize and glorify the romantic love of the bride and the groom. Often music is selected or wanted because it has a "catchy" tune or because it has "touched" or "moved" the bridal couple in some way. While we do not deny the "meaning" of such music to the bridal couple, we can in no way accept or condone the use of such music within the wedding service.

We have not gathered in the House of the Lord to glorify man's ideas and thoughts of love, but rather to consider God's love to us poor sinners. Pleas of "this is our special day" ought to fall upon deaf ears in this respect.

Church Choir

In addition to most heartily recommending the use of congregation singing within the wedding worship service, we also highly recommend the use of the church choir. Much fine music is available for such use and need not be limited to those pieces of music written specifically for weddings. In addition anthems or singing a psalm the choir can lead the congregation in hymns. As stated earlier, the congregation has not assembled as spectators (or ought not to have done so), therefore, every effort should be made to involve and include them as Christian worshipers. The use of congregational involvement through vesicles and responses, a psalm, unison prayers and the like is highly recommended. Let us not forget that the congregation is assembled to worship!

We are acquainted with suggested orders of worship for weddings which use The Order of Matins or Vespers and those which provide for Holy Communion within the service. We have no objectionsto these orders of worship if those assembled are fellow members, well acquainted with the the liturgies so the service can proceed smoothly, with joy and praise to the Lord. They most certainly provide a fitting framework around the wedding vows and place the entire service into a form utilizing meaningful and memorable congregational participation.

Holy Communion

We do, however, have some very definite problems with the use of Holy Communion at a wedding service. The problem would be non-existent if those assembled were all members of the congregation or were fellow Lutherans whose participation in the sacrament would be in accord with Synodical guidelines and practices. The fact is, however, that most weddings have many people in attendance who would not be able to partake of the sacrament. Often either the bride or groom is not Lutheran as well as some of the members of the wedding party. The problem cannot be resolved by calling the wedding service "unique" and thereby allowing the practice of "open communion" for this "unique" event. We have seen this done and cannot find any justification for such lax unionism in our theological and confessional position. We have also found that some couples wish to include Holy Communion in an effort to have something different at their wedding. Such a wish clearly is out of order and contrary to our Holy Communion practices. There could be some instances where Holy Communion could be celebrated with great meaning and blessing to the assembled congregation. But generally its use ought to be avoided just as it is to be at many other gatherings which have, in recent years, begun to incorporate its use (retreats, rallies, and the like).

Bridal Procession

Before we turn our attention to the wedding service itself, there are a couple of things very closely connected with that service that ought to be discussed. The first of those is the area of the bridal processional. We cannot help but wonder how this custom found its way into the church as it is so often used today. While many churches have sought to "dim" this custom by having the couples proceed into the church together rather than to have the groom's party waiting at the front of the church for the bride's party to enter one by one down the aisle, still the effect is much the same as putting on a production centering on the bride and turning the wedding from a worship experience to one of a "star" event. It would seem that the wedding then becomes more of a legal occasion taking on the characteristics of a "show" or some other type of entertainment. There seems to be little justification for such "over the top" display..

Our suggestion in this respect is to use the same type of processional music used in festival worship celebrations in our churches. Depending on the individual parish's practice, the use of a crucifer, banner bearers, acolytes, and pastor leading the bridal party (entering by couples and the bride and groom each accompanied by their parents) would be far more desirable and fitting. We would further suggest that this processional take place to a processional hymn rather than a processional prelude, though we would not greatly object to the latter. Such a dignified processional would immediately set the proper tone at the gathering, namely, that all have assembled to worship and that the service is one of worship, praise, and adoration to our Triune God.

Kissing at the Altar

In the same light, we have strong objections to the idea that the bridal party is there to present a fashion show to the assembled congregation. Most certainly it is to be desired that the bridal party present a pleasing "picture" at the front of the church, but that does not mean that we need to permit or condone a member of the bridal party straightening and arranging the bride's dress when she is at the front so that it is properly displayed. Other customs or practices found at some weddings are equally out of place and should be avoided. Simply checking the soles of the shoes of bride and groom can eliminate that common "joke" that still is found occasionally to make a mockery of what is happening. The practice of bride and groom, now husband and wife, kissing at the altar simply is out of place, for who needs to witness the couple in such a private exchange of love and those in attendance do not need to be treated to some passionate display or non-display (depending upon whether they exchange a "peck" or go further). Such practices clearly turn the worship experience into an uncomfortable spectacle.

Wedding Spectators

Surely such changes can be to make within a local parish. People have become accustomed to being spectators at a wedding. Couples have become accustomed to having all the attention focused upon them. Parents do not want to spend all that money and then have all the attention drawn away from their children. It remains our feeling, however, that some healthy edifying changes can be made through a program of education both of the bridal couple and within the congregation. It most certainly will not happen overnight as long as we have many pastors, if not most, who continue to condescend to following and accepting "traditional" or customary practices. It will be most difficult to institute such changes. Present practices did not come into existence in a short time, but evolved through the years. New dignified practices and customs will also take a good number of years to establish. Often it can be accomplished through the celebration of one such wedding service to "break the ice," to demonstrate what a wedding service really can and should be!

Throwing Rice

"No discussion of weddings would be complete without the mention of throwing rice on the bridal couple as they leave the church. Much has been written on this subject in regards to it being a pagan custom and also in regards to its undesirability when so many people throughout the world are starving and hungry so that the waste involved ought to be unthinkable. We most certainly agree with all that has been written in that respect. However, we look at the practice from a different point of view. Anyone who has ever had to clean after a wedding would know what we are talking about. It is an almost impossible task to accomplish. It is because of this latter point that we have a policy at our local parish that forbids the throwing of rice. Past experience provided us with a situation where the dew fell overnight upon some of the rice kernels not completely cleaned up and resulted in a person slipping and falling upon entering the church for worship the following morning. Since the person was seriously injured, it did not take the voters assembly long to institute a "no rice" rule that previously they had stubbornly resisted.

"Camera Bugs"

A word ought to be said also regarding photographers and "camera bugs" in attendance. We have found most photographers cooperative and willing to comply with any reasonable restrictions placed upon them so that they do not disrupt the worship service in any way. The same cannot be said of those in attendance who bring cameras and wish to record portions of the wedding service for posterity. After a number of times in which we were almost blinded by the flashing of cameras from people in attendance, we instruct the ushers to tell those entering with cameras that their use in the service is prohibited and that the pastor and couple will gladly pose for all desired pictures after the service (yes, even if the photographer takes the wedding pictures before the service as is often done today). Occasionally, one or two people will disregard our instructions. We do not hesitate to immediately request that they refrain from the same in order that those assembled may be able to worship the Lord without being disturbed. We are not concerned if they take offense at such instruction. They do not have the right to disrupt our worship. Usually most couples know those "camera bugs" who might be invited and have the opportunity to speak with them earlier, to inform them that they do not want them to disrupt their wedding service.

Baptismal Font

One final thought before we turn to the wedding service itself. While we are aware of the fact that many desire the baptismal font to be placed at the entrance to the nave of the church to remind one and all that they enter to worship their Triune God because of their acceptance through the Sacrament of Holy Baptism, nevertheless, most churches do not have the font so placed. In fact, most churches have a "movable" font that is often stuck in the corner and out of the way when not being used. It would seem that it ought to be moved to the entrance of the chancel so as to be directly in front of the worshippers at all times as a remembrance of that blessed sacrament. We mention this because we also feel that the bride and groom ought to begin the worship service standing at the font, giving the witness thereby that they have been made children of God through the blessed sacrament. Now they are coming before Him as His dear children to speak their vows of faithfulness, one to the other, to seek His blessings upon their life together. To that end, they might well stand at either side of the font (the font between them) as the service begins. We can remember one bride who thought the idea was quite acceptable until she realized that when she progressed further into the chancel the font would partially block out her and her intended from view. To be sure, we were back at the beginning, dealing with old customs and traditions which are most difficult to put aside.

To try to set up a worship service for a wedding is a task that lends itself to much criticism and comment. As stated before, we are not an expert in this field. Furthermore, it is to be doubted that anyone can set up a service that will be accepted by all and that will fit every situation. That might be one argument for the omission of a wedding liturgy from *Lutheran Worship*. However, in light of the fact that many pastors will not take the time nor make the effort to set up such a service and have it printed for use within each wedding service, the inclusion of the same is greatly desired! To distribute little additional booklets would seem to be awkward and since we can be sure that the same will not be available at a really low price, the possibility of worshipers taking such a booklet with them will place the congregation in a situation which continually requires them to replace and purchase more of the same.

What we offer or suggest below for possible use is merely our own attempt to have a wedding service that is truly a worship experience of the congregation and for the bridal couple. It is not to be looked upon as being perfect or even ideal. We are sure that there are many others who could do the same or better. At the same time, we do not want to give the impression that we are able to always use such a service. As stated earlier, old customs and traditions are hard to break and there is a great deal of difficulty in getting couples to consent to a service that requires them to be in the church for more than 15 or 20 minutes. In spite of the above, we still offer the same with a great deal of humility, simply seeking to make an honest attempt in providing an alternative that seems to be greatly needed within our circles. We shall make comments within the following Order of Worship as might be helpful. All hymns listed or suggested are taken from *The Lutheran Hymnal* as it is still most familiar to all.

THE ORDER OF THE WEDDING SERVICE
The Pre-Service Music
The Ringing of the Bell
The Prelude
The Processional Hymn: 39 (other suggestions would be numbers 250, 30, 23, 24, 41)
(We prefer that the processional take place during the singing of this hymn)

P: In the name of the Father and of the Son and of the Holy Spirit. Amen!
C: All Praise and Glory and Honor Be to You, O Triune God, Now and Forevermore!
P: Our help is in the name of the Lord!
C: Who Made Heaven and Earth!
P: O come, let us worship the Lord!
C: He is Our Maker, Our Redeemer, Our Comforter!
P: Glory be to the Father and to the Son and to the Holy Spirit!
C: We Worship You! We Give You Thanks? We Praise You Now and Forever!
P: We have come together this day to share with _____ and _____ as they, with joy, make a covenant one with the other and both of them make a covenant before the Lord, their God. They ask that you, the assembled congregation, rejoice with them now, join your hearts in prayer unto our Triune God as you witness their wedding vows, and remember them often in your prayers from this day forward, that our God would grant them many years of joy and blessing together! To that end, let us join together in prayer unto the Lord, our God!
ALL: Gracious Father, in Your tender mercy look upon this couple and gladden their hearts as Your Son gladdened the hearts of the couple at the wedding at Cana in Galilee. Look in favor upon _____ and _____ and grant that they, rejoicing in all Your gifts, may at length celebrate with Your Son the marriage feast which has no end. Hear this, our prayer, as we ask it in the name of Your Son, Jesus Christ our Lord. Amen
P: Our gracious and loving God has given His command that children are to remain loving and obedient unto their parents who have brought them into this world by the blessings and grace of God. At the same time, our Lord Jesus said, "Haven't you read that He who created them from the beginning made them a male and female? That is why a man will leave his father and mother and live with his wife, and the two will be one flesh!" Therefore we ask the parents of this couple to joyfully and willingly give their consent to this marriage.

_____ has been loved and cherished by his parents who have led him in the way of the Lord. Do they now give him freely and willingly to become the husband of _____, and promise to love them together as their dear children from this day forward? Then declare the same before God and this assembled congregation by saying, "We do promise!"

_____ has also been loved and cherished by her parents who have led her in the way of the Lord. Do they now give her freely and willingly to become the wife of _____, and promise to love them together as their dear children from this day forward? Then declare the same before God and this assembled congregation by saying, "We do promise!"

May the love that you have given to your children ever be an example of the love which they seek to cultivate within their marriage the one to the other; and may your love to them ever be returned in fullest measure so that you will always be enabled to give thanks and praise to our God for His great love and blessing in the precious gifts He gave you in your children. To Him be glory now and forevermore! Amen!

The Hymn of Trust: 393 (a hymn from "The Family" section of the hymnal may be sung at this point instead)

The Psalm: Psalm 118:22-29
P: The stone the builders rejected has become the cornerstone.
C: The Lord Has Done This, and We Think It Is Wonderful.
P: The Lord made this day! Let us rejoice and be glad in Him!
C: Lord, Please Save Us! Lord, Please Give Us Success!
P: Blessed is He who comes in the Lord's name!
C: We Bless You in The Lord's Temple!
P: The Lord is God, and He gives us light. Deck the shrine with branches, adorn the horns of the altar!
C: You Are My God, I Honor You Highly!
P: Thank the Lord!
C: Because He Is Good and Loves Us Forever!
P: Glory be to the Father and to the Son and to the Holy Spirit!
C: As It Was In the Beginning, Is Now, and Will Be Forever. Amen!

The Epistle Lesson: Ephesians 5:21-33

The Holy Gospel Lesson: Luke 6:47-49

The Sermon Hymn: 625 (This hymn will, of course, be chosen to fit the sermon text and the message of the day)

The Sermon (This message need not be the length of a normal Sunday sermon. At the same time, the sermon should both be a collection of pious thoughts and words put together for the occasion, and should contain both Law and Gospel as it applies God's Word to the bridal couple and to the assembled congregation. The book "Join Your Right Hands" [CPH, copyright 1965] has an excellent selection on this subject. The sermon should always have a Scriptural text as its basis! We have attended weddings where the pastor has chosen some nursery rhyme or some other secular writing upon which to speak a few words. We find that practice totally unacceptable! and quite objectionable! It is no wonder that weddings are so often looked upon as something other than a worship service when some pastors are guilty of such things that disgrace their calling as servants of the Word!)

The Marriage Hymn: 621 (any of the hymns in the section "Marriage" could be used here or, perhaps, even a suitable hymn from "The Family" section.)

P: _____and _____, you have come here to be united into the holy estate of marriage, which requires your mutual consent, sincerely and freely given. I ask you, therefore, in the presence of God and this assembled congregation, to express the sincere intent you both have this day.

_____, will you have this woman to be your wedded wife, to live with her after God's ordinance in the holy estate of marriage? Will you love her, comfort her, honor her, and keep her in sickness and in health, and, forsaking all others, keep yourself only unto her, so long as you both shall live? Then declare the same before God and this congregation by saying, "I will!"

_____, will you have this man to be your wedded husband, to live with him after God's ordinance in the holy estate of marriage? Will you love him, comfort him, honor him, obey him, and keep him in sickness and in health, and, forsaking all others, keep yourself only unto him, so long as you both shall live? Then declare the same before God and this congregation by saying, "I will!"

I ask you, _____ and _____, to repeat after me the vows uniting you in holy marriage.

I, _____, in the presence of God and this congregation, take you, _____, to be my wedded wife. I pledge you my faithfulness throughout my life and will never part from you until God parts us through death!

I, _____, in the presence of God and this congregation, take you, _____, to be my wedded husband. I pledge you my faithfulness throughout my life and will never part from you until God parts us through death!

The rings which you now exchange are the symbol to you and to all of the promises that you have now made the one to the other! As you give them to each other, please repeat after me your final vows.

_____, I give you this ring as a sign of my promise, and with this ring I now become your husband in the name of the Father and of the Son and of the Holy Spirit. Amen!

_____, I give you this ring as a sign of my promise, and with this ring I now become your husband in the name of the Father and of the Son and of the Holy Spirit. Amen!

Since you, _____ and _____, have so given your promises before God and this assembled congregation, and have declared already your marriage before God by the promises you have made, I pronounce you to be husband and wife in the name of the Father and of the Son and of the Holy Spirit! What, therefore, God has joined together, let not man separate!

Thy Hymn of Thanksgiving and Praise: 36 (We know of no other hymn so fitting and so meaningful at this point!)

P: My dear Christian friends: Let us turn now to our great and glorious Triune God and pray that He will bless with His grace Mr. and Mrs. _____, now joined together in Christ Jesus.

The Prayers for the Day (Included here is a prayer for the bridal couple, for their parents, for all married couples, and for the assembled congregation. Other special prayers and concerns may also be included.)

The Lord's Prayer (spoken together by all assembled)
    P: We praise You, O God! We give You thanks and glorify You Forever!
    C: Thanks, Praise, and Adoration be Unto You, A Most Holy Triune God, Now and Forevermore!
    P: You are the God of Our Salvation!
    C: In You Do We Trust and In You Is The Hope of Our Salvation!
    P: Let the People Praise You, O God!
    C: Yea, Let All the People Praise You!
    P: Let Us now bless our Lord!
    C: Thanks Be To You, O Lord!

The Benediction

The Recessional Hymn: 15 (Some other hymn or stanza of a hymn containing a doxology may be used here. During the singing of the hymn, the crucifier, banner bearers, pastor, bridal party, and parents of the bridal couple leave the sanctuary.)

"Marriage Candle"

It is to be noted that the use of the "unity candle" or "marriage candle" is not included in the above service. We find little reason for the inclusion of the same. Its inclusion only seems to emphasize a kind of "cuteness" that is based upon emotion rather than real meaning or value within the service.

We also object to those who seek to decorate the chancel of the church further for their wedding by placing ribbons, greens, "whatever" on the candelabra or candlesticks. It seems out of place and should not be permitted. A floral arrangement or two within the chancel should suffice, especially with the "decoration" of the bridal gowns and wedding apparel.

We know that many couples will object to the length of the service suggested above, because a great number of people still look upon the wedding service as a legal ceremony or a quick "in and out" type of gathering. It becomes even more difficult in light of the fact that most Protestant services today require a ceremony of some 10 minutes or less and the fact that a justice of the peace or a judge often operates like Al Capp's legendary "Marryem' Sam". We question such a procedure as a worship experience! It is totally out of place within the church!

We are concerned, also, that in our present time many couples are choosing to hold their wedding services in places outside of the church. While the church building is not to be looked upon as some kind of "magical" place for a wedding, at the same time, weddings in parks, meadows, and elsewhere seem to appear as an effort to follow the present thinking of being unique or different. We are not hesitant to suggest that such weddings ought to be left to judges or justices of the peace to perform. The Christian wedding service is not to take on the characteristics of a "circus". To be sure, a small, private weddingmay be desired or fitting under certain circumstances. There can be no doubt that the pastor ought to be willing to conduct such a wedding on the basis of those circumstances as he seeks to minister to his people according to their needs. Those needs, however, should not pressure the pastor to be "used" as a mere civil servant to fulfill questionable "needs" of bridal couples. There are legitimate circumstances and needs dictating far less than what is suggested above. However, those circumstances are and should be quite rare and the exception to the rule.

Perhaps a further word is in order considering the fact that most couples spend anywhere from three to eight hours or more at a wedding reception that is often quite questionable in terms of its activities. We find it hard to accept that they could reasonably object to a wedding service that provides a real worship experience to those in attendance. Most certainly it becomes a matter of where one places their priorities! Somehow, we have found it to be generally true that the longer and more elaborate the reception, the more the couple sought to "cut" the wedding service down to "bare bones".

Once again we want to thank Brother Otten for giving us this opportunity to offer the above thoughts and ideas. As stated earlier, they are not perfect and certainly will not be accepted by one and all. We have claimed no "divine guidance" for the same, only a humble and honest attempt to generate some discussion and, above all, a review of our present practices. If what we have written causes such thinking, study, and review, then we have accomplished our purpose. To God alone be the glory!

We should note, finally, that we have seen some excellent attempts to bring some order and generate a worship experience for the assembled congregation in the past. Some of these have included a responsive prayer or type of litany by the congregation in place of the suggested prayers for the day. Neither time nor space permits us to include the same. There can be no doubt, that other pastors, couples, and parents are also concerned about the witness given at a wedding service. Certainly, no one way is right and can be called "the best". Any and every effort to lift the wedding service from the depths of secularism to which it has fallen in our day a cause for rejoicing and thanksgiving! May the day come soon that our church realizes and accentuates its distinct and vital Christian witness in this area of the lives of our people!

P.S. Herman, there are many of us pastors who, loving the worship of the church, are involved in writing or arranging special services for congregational worship outside of the normal forms used. Such services are set up for special occasions which generally fall outside of the regular worship services of the congregation (for example: church dedications, organ dedications, anniversary celebrations, and a host of other such services). There is no way that we can expect that you would serve as a clearing house for the same. However, since many of these services are mimeographed for the local congregation and additional copies could easily be run off on plain paper available, would it not be possible to list in a section of *Christian News* the addresses and types of services available to interested readers? A self addressed and stamped envelope should help to disseminate it to those interested in obtaining a copy for their files. It would afford many pastors, not so gifted in writing, to lift the worship life of their congregations. I have seen and used many such Lenten, Advent, and other such worship folders throughout my ministry. All of us pastors get those copyrighted mailing of services (including those from CPH) which leave us "panic-stricken" to use even a portion for fear of violating some copyright laws. Personally, I find such printings to be quite offensive when they cross my desk, for the thought is that the writer is more concerned about the revenue that might be received than about the worship life of countless thousands upon thousands of Christians who might benefit, but cannot afford to pay the price (so to speak) of ordering the same. What I have suggested in both the area of funeral services or wedding services is freely open to one and all to use, or to adapt.

P.P.S. We have used our first article concerning funerals as the basis of discussion for many of our congregational organizations. While we have not found total agreement, we have found it generates much discussion and thinking. Since most of what appeared in that article is common practice in our local congregation, we can hardly wait to discuss the present article, especially since we have not been able to make such "inroads' in that area to this point. We are pleased, however, that we are able to include congregational singing within every wedding here. At the same time, we do use a great portion of the service as it appears as our normal custom. We continue to hope that we might use all of it in the near future. This, by the way, is in a congregation that some 2½ years ago held funeral services without congregational participation other than singing a couple of hymns and wedding services which generally included little of what we have suggested.

Wedding Worship
By John M. Drickamer
Christian News, December 29, 1986

Planning a wedding can be a very trying time for a pastor. Many people have trouble understanding how a Christian wedding is to be conducted because they do not realize that it is worship. Once that fact sinks in, everything else falls into place.

The Bible neither describes nor prescribes the form of a Christian wedding ceremony. There were no church weddings until the fourth century (when Christianity was legalized). Before that (including the time of the apostles) Christians got married before a secular official. Their marriage may have been mentioned in prayer in church. But there was no church wedding.

The Bible does not give specific instructions for conducting weddings. It does give instructions for conducting worship. The New Testament does not authorize the church to perform weddings. It does authorize the church to meet to worship God and hear His Word. A pastor's call does not mention performing weddings, but it does mention teaching, preaching, etc. A pastor has no business conducting a wedding unless a Christian wedding is a specific type of worship. It is not an official, pastoral act if it is secular (worldly).

That a Christian wedding is worship should be obvious to everyone from its contents: praise, Bible reading, the sermon, prayer, the benediction, etc.

It should also be clear from the use of the church building, which has been dedicated for worship, preaching, prayer, etc., not for worldly sideshows. Those who do not want a worship service for their wedding do not want a church wedding, do not intend to begin their married life with the Word of God and prayer, and so do not need to have a Christian pastor conduct the wedding. Let them go to a judge or justice of the peace.

Any non-Christians invited to a Christian wedding may not have the idea that it is a worship service. That only makes it more important to be clear throughout the service that it is precisely a Christian worship service. We should do everything we can to show them that our main concern is not worldly but spiritual, that Jesus Christ is the central Figure in our lives and thoughts. The Gospel should predominate in a Christian wedding for the sake of Christians present, to strengthen their faith, but also for the sake of non-Christians present. It is an evangelistic opportunity in the same way a Christian funeral is often an opportunity to proclaim the Gospel to the unchurched.

The church at Corinth had problems in several areas, including worship. The Holy Spirit addressed these problems through the Apostle Paul. The principles of Christian conduct expressed there apply generally to the whole of life and specifically to the activities of Christians when they are assembled for worship. Among the principles that are especially important for a Christian wedding or any other worship service are that (All Things be done): 1. **to the glory of God** (1 Corinthians 10:31); 2. **for the edification (spiritual instruction and upbuilding) of the people** (1 Corinthians 14:26); and 3. **in a decent and orderly way** (1 Corinthians 14:40).

This principle is well summarized when the Augsburg Confession says that "all ceremonies should principally serve this purpose that the people learn from them what it is necessary for them to know about Christ" (Article XXIV, Die Bekenntnisschriften der evangelisch-lutherischen Kirche Goettingen: Vandenhoeck & Rupprecht, p. 92). This principle is Biblical, as we have seen above. Those who call themselves Lutheran should bend every effort to make church weddings clearly worshipful, and centered on the Word of God.

All disputes about wedding customs will be quickly settled if we ask whether they meet these criteria, especially whether they teach people about Christ. A good example is the kiss that some churches (either not caring about worship or giving in to worldly pressure) permit in the wedding service. Is it done to the glory of God, for the edification of the people, and in a decent and orderly way?

    1)   The kiss is not done to the glory of God but rather directs attention to the beauty, romance, and/or passion of bride and groom. Many people will think at that point in terms of some romantic ideal rather than about the spiritual significance of marriage. In the case of non-Christian guests and even some Christian worshipers (we are still plagued by the flesh!), thoughts may be channeled in a carnal direction. That may not be intended, but it is the result in the minds of some.

    2)   The kiss is not done in an attempt to edify, instruct, or up-

build the people. The exalted, spiritual, Christian understanding of marriage is well expressed in the Word of God and the vows based on it as contained in the worship service in *The Lutheran Agenda*. The love of bride and groom for each other and their willingness to be united for life in holy wedlock are most solemnly testified in the unconditional promises they make. The meaning of a kiss in the wedding service can be at best romance; at worst sexual passion. Some people will see it one way; some will see it the other way. But in no way does it communicate what the Christian wedding service is about.

The concern is that the couple and all others present have their thoughts directed by the worship service to the spiritual significance of Christian marriage, with Christ and His Word at the center of life. A romantic kiss would direct thoughts to a fairy tale, "happily-ever-after" view of marriage. A passionate kiss would direct thoughts to the sexual aspect of marriage, which should remain private and should not be put on public display. The wedding service, as it is contained in our agenda without a kiss, directs attention primarily to marriage as God's institution, made difficult because of human sin, but nevertheless blessed by God in the case of Christians for Jesus' sake. The emphasis on Law and Gospel is necessary for every aspect of the Christian life.

3) The kiss is not **always** done in a decent, seemly, orderly way. A kiss might be done so if it were the holy kiss St. Paul elsewhere mentions (for example, 1 Corinthians 16:20). That would mean a "friendship kiss" (as the Greek word St. Paul used signifies), a brief kiss on cheek or forehead. That is customarily done in some cultures between two men or between two women. It is not the lip-to-lip kiss of a new husband and wife.

Some couples might kiss briefly, but many would make it last, and some would let it become passionate, as experience has shown. No one can deny that that is out of place in worship. The need to avoid the carnal curiosity that would be aroused by a long kiss and the embarrassment that would be caused by a loud kiss are reason enough not to permit the public kiss of husband and wife in a worship service. Even if a kiss were otherwise permissible, the fact that some couples would make it passionate means that no couple should be permitted to kiss in public worship.

Putting the kiss after the benediction is no solution, for the couple is still in front of the congregation. We should not rush to banish all worshipful thoughts simply because we arbitrarily declare the worship service over. The recessional is also part of the service. The couple must not kiss until after they recess. They should not give any appearance that sexual passion overwhelms them and overshadows their devotion to God. If it does, they have a serous spiritual problem in their married life.

Dr. Martin Luther wrote in his *Traubeuchlein* ("Wedding Booklet," which is sometimes appended to the *Small Catechism*): (A church wedding) "also serves the purpose that the young people learn to consider this estate seriously, and to hold it in honor as a divine work and command, and not to pursue their insulting foolishness in connection with it by laughter, mockery, and similar frivolity, as people have previously been accustomed to do, as if it were a joke or a children's game to get married or celebrate a wedding. Those who first instituted the custom of bringing bride and groom to church certainly did not consider it a joke but a very serious matter. For there is no doubt that they wanted to have the blessing of God and common prayer and not to stage some comedy or pagan farce.

"The work in itself well demonstrates the same thing; for whoever requests prayer or blessing from the pastor or bishop certainly indicates thereby (even if he does not say so with his mouth) the danger and need into which he is entering and how much he needs divine blessing and common prayer for the estate which he is beginning, something which is also clearly seen every day in the unhappiness the devil causes within marriage by adultery, disloyalty, discord, and all sorts of misery." (See *Die Bekenntnisschriften der evangelisch lutherischen Kirche*, pp. 529-530).

Since the principle expressed here is clearly Biblical, and since there can be no doubt that it applies to a Christian wedding, we may be surprised that some Christians have difficulty understanding and appreciating it. But we should not really be surprised. The reason is that Christians in this world are still not perfect in their understanding. That is why we all need constantly to be in contact with the Word of God – so that all our attitudes may be in accord with it.

Lutheran pastors should try to instruct their congregations thoroughly about the matter of wedding worship as it applies across the board, to kissing, music, decorations, etc. If all Lutheran pastors would speak with unanimity about these things, it would make weddings much easier for all of us.

Good Advice from Parents to Children
A Letter to You, Paul and Anne, On The Day of Your Wedding, November 26, 1988

Dear Paul and Anne,

As you remember, on the day of your confirmation and again on the day of your graduation from high school, Mom and I wrote you a letter as part of those celebrations and as an additional way of remembering the significance of them. Now on the day of your wedding we would once again like to write you a letter in order to express some of our deepest thoughts on this your special day.

You might remember in your confirmation letter we mentioned that on the evening of the day Mom and I were married, just before we went to sleep, we asked the Lord to be the center of our marriage. We promised to always try and do His will as long as we would live. Since then twenty five years have passed and each day since has shown us how the Lord has so richly blessed us spiritually and materially. Now you have the opportunity as husband and wife to also ask the Lord to be the center of your marriage. You also have the opportunity to promise to remain faithful to Him and to each other. God will answer your prayer just as he has answered ours and Grandma and Grandpa's before us. The Lord is just waiting to be invited into your home and to pour out His blessings upon you. With His presence and blessing, your home can be a forecourt of heaven. Let His love shine through you both toward one another, toward all those you invite into your home, and toward everyone with whom you come in contact. Together look for ways to serve Him in His Kingdom. Be a model and inspiration for others. You might also want to set aside a time each day when you worship the Lord together, in addition to your personal devotions. You will be amazed how the Lord will strengthen you during times of difficulty and trials, how He will rejoice with you when you rejoice, and how He will day by day cause your love for each other to grow even deeper than it is now. He'll also give you the ability to forgive each other when you fail to live up to each other's expectations and if He so chooses someday He will bless your home with the gift of children with whom you can share your love and who will love you both in return.

Anne, we love you so much. We hope you already know that but we want to say it to you again. You are the answer to our prayers. You are so very special and we're just thrilled to have you as part of our family.

In closing, we want you to know how proud we are of both of you and how happy we are that the Lord has brought you together. We rejoice with you on this your special day.

With all our love,
Mom and Dad

Gods Word - The One Thing You Need

Christian News, December 18, 1989

Luke 10:38-41
Sermon at the wedding of Miriam Otten and Randall Hill, September 3, 1989, New Haven, Missouri. By Pastor Herman Otten.

Miriam and Randy, during the past few months you have been busy preparing for this day. You have spent many hours planning your wedding, the rehearsal dinner last night at Camp Trinity with a whole hog, the dinner after the service today, sending out invitations, making dresses, selecting music, flowers, and many other items, baking, cooking, cleaning, mowing grass and even cutting and burning brush. Other couples similarly spend hundreds of hours preparing for their wedding.

Last Sunday I officiated at a wedding here where there were only ten present. There was no music, no elaborate preparations. Yet I told the bride and groom that if they established their marriage upon God's Word, they had the only thing they really needed for a lasting marriage. It is no secret that many marriages which have started with a well planned and beautiful wedding have ended in divorce. *World* magazine recently noted that "Anyone looking at national marriage and divorce statistics and concluding that the United States is returning to 'family values' had better look again. That's the conclusion of two University of Wisconsin researchers who predict that two of three current marriages will break up."

Ten years ago yesterday, there was an AP story in the St. Louis Post-Dispatch titled: "Quiet Hell - Half of U.S. Marriages Called Loveless." It began: "Marriage is a 'quiet hell' for about half of American couples, according to a survey conducted by advice columnist Joyce Brothers.

"Speaking before a convention of the American Hospital Association this week, she said four out of twelve marriages are likely to end in divorce, while another six become loveless 'utilitarian' relationships to protect children, property, shared goals and other goals."

When a couple gets married, members of the family are often asked by those who intend to get them a present: "What do they need?"

Our text tells us how Jesus taught the members of a family about one thing they really needed. Luke writes that Jesus and his disciples came to a certain village where Mary, Martha and Lazarus lived. It may have been Bethany, although many commentators maintain that at this time Mary, Martha, and Lazarus lived in a village on the Samaritan border and only later moved to Bethany.

We find Martha busy directing the affairs of the home, occupying herself with all sorts of household duties and preparing the dinner. Mary, on the other hand, sits down to listen to the words of Jesus. Finally Martha comes to Jesus and says: "Lord, don't you care that my sister has left me and I have to do the work alone? Now tell her to help me." It almost appears that Martha wishes Jesus would be quiet for a while and stop teaching so that Mary could help with the household chores.

Pastors are often told to "keep the sermon at the wedding short" by those who have spent hundreds of hours preparing the dinner and other externals associated with the wedding. Jesus answers Martha: "Martha, Martha, you worry and fuss about a lot of things. But there's one thing you need. Mary has made the right choice, and it must not be taken away from her."

There is a wonderful lesson in this text for every married couple, family, and congregation. Members of Trinity, when you came to church today you noted the five new stained glass windows. This week again some of you spent time installing them. During the past year many of you spent hundreds of hours building this church. Let's never forget that it is possible to have the best planned wedding and the finest church building and yet neglect the one thing which is needed.

What is the "only one thing you need?" God's Word and its message of forgiveness of sins and eternal salvation in Christ Jesus.

God's Word on Marriage

What does God's Word tell us about marriage? God's Word, Holy Scripture, tells us that it was God who instituted marriage. God told Moses to write in Genesis: "The Lord God said, 'It isn't good for the man to be alone. I will make him a helper such as he needs'. . . So the Lord God had the man fall into a deep sleep, and while he was sleeping, He took out one of his ribs and filled up its place with flesh. Out of the rib He had taken from the man the Lord God made a woman and brought her to the man.' This is why a man leaves his father and his mother and lives with his wife, and they become one flesh," (Genesis 2:18, 21-24).

This account is no pious fairy tale. Jesus, who is God, the second person of the Holy Trinity, said it was the absolute truth. Quoting these verses from Genesis, Matthew tells us that Jesus said: "Haven't you read, He who created them from the beginning made them a male and a female?" "That is why a man will leave his father and mother and live with His wife and the two will be one flesh. And so they are no more two but one flesh. Now, what God has joined together man must not separate" (Matthew 19:4-6).

When men reject what God says about the origin of man and marriage and accept the evolutionary notions taught in most schools that man evolved from some primary organism and that originally he had many wives or women had many husbands, is it any wonder that many can so readily break the marriage vow? If marriage evolved and was devised by man then man can dissolve the marriage bond whenever he pleases. Many now agree with a lecturer in sociology who claimed at a sex education seminar that "Marriage is totally irrelevant in today's society." The sociologist said that "sex should be considered a normal part of human relationships without being related to marriage or parenthood."

That makes good sense - If man is just an animal, a product of blind evolution, If in other words, there is no God and therefore no objective meaning or morality in the universe. Given this starting point, loose views of sex must follow. And since much modern "education" is really a kind of materialistic brainwashing, which assumes that God either doesn't exist or doesn't matter, it is not surprising that "today's society" should hold largely pagan ideas, also about marriage. Randy, as you computer people say, put garbage in and get garbage out.

God's Word, the one thing you need, tells us who is the true God. Already in Genesis we find references to the Holy Trinity, the only true and saving God. All other gods are pagan images fabricated by man. The first verses of Genesis mentions "God's Spirit" and God speaking. We read of a plurality in the Godhead. God said "Let us make man in our image, like Ourselves" (Genesis 1:26). The Apostle John writes: "In the beginning was the Word and the Word was with God, and the Word was God. He was in the beginning with God. Everything was made by Him, and not one thing that wa made was made without Him" (John 1:1-3). Who is this "Word" who was there at the creation of the world, who is God and who made all things? John tells us: "And the Word was made flesh and lived as in the tabernacle, and we saw His glory, a glory as of the only Son from His Father, full of love and truth (John 1:14).

Justified by Faith Alone

God's Word, the one thing you need, tells us that after God created Adam and Eve they did not evolve to a higher state, but fell into sin. God's Word declares that "The wages of sin is death" (Romans 6:23). But God still loved man and promised him a Savior from sin. God sent His son Jesus to take upon Himself your sin and the sins of all men. Randy and Miriam, may God's Word alone, not man's philosophy, man's dreams and visions, or human tradition be your only source of faith. Remember that all religions besides Christianity are man-made and religions of the law. They teach that man must work his own way, at least in part, to get to heaven. "Deeds not creeds" is the cry of the hour. "Do good and be good and God will be good to you" is what even many church members say. God's Word, the one thing you need, reveals that the central truth of Christianity, the only true faith, is that man is justified, saved, by faith alone in the precious merits of Jesus Christ, who died and rose again for you and all men.

Many books have been written on marriage. Numerous magazines have all sorts of advice for married couples. All sorts of marriage encounter seminars are being held throughout the nation. We have hundreds of books in our own library on the subject besides bulging files with all kinds of articles on marriage and the family. Yet nothing can take the place of God's Word when it comes to teaching the loving attitude a husband and wife should have toward each other.

Obey and Love

No better advice for husbands and wives can be given than in Ephesians 5:21-33, the scripture lesson you selected for your wedding. Married women are told to "obey your husband as you obey the Lord, because the husband is the head of the wife as Christ is the head of the Church, which is His body that He saves. Yes, as the church obeys Christ, so wives should obey their husbands in everything." God's Word teaches that for married women their highest career is still in the home and, if God blesses the marriage with children, raising their children according to the one thing needful. Miriam, your highest career or ambition in life should not be winning some Olympic gold medal. Randy, there are far more important things for a Christian husband and father than slam dunking a basketball or high jumping seven feet – of course, now you would have to jump eight feet to win an Olympic medal.

Although God's Word tells the wife to obey her husband in everything, it doesn't tell the husband that he is supposed to be some sort of dictator. The Apostle Paul continues: "You husbands, love your wives, as Christ loved the Church and gave Himself for it." Christ loved the church, which means all men, not some building or denomination, so much that He gave His life for the church. Husbands should always attempt to show the same self-sacrificial love toward their wives. All of us will fall short of that goal, but this is the example husbands should strive to follow.

Randy and Miriam, both of you were confirmed before this altar. Here both of you promised to remain faithful to all the teachings of God's Word. However, the fact that you are Christians is no guarantee that you will never have any disagreements and even arguments in your family. In this respect Christian families are somewhat like the families of unbelievers. However, there is a key difference. You know why unnecessary arguments and strife arise. You are still sinners. Yet the Christian knows where he can receive forgiveness of sin. Make regular use of God's Word and His Holy Sacrament, through which you receive God's forgiveness in a very personal way.

Family Worship

How should you use God's Word, the one thing you need? Never think that the knowledge you gained in confirmation class is sufficient. Study His Word the rest of your lives. Conduct family devotions, Bible reading, hymn singing and good conversations in your home on theological, political and social issues. A number of years ago the *Lutheran Witness* included this interesting item:

> Do statistics tell anything? Consider the following from the U.S. Census Bureau as noted in the March 24, 1980 "Marriage and Divorce". Although nationally one out of three marriages currently ends in divorce, those who have church weddings and attend church regularly beat the odds by one in 50. But of couples who have married in the church, attend regularly and have family worship one in 1,105 end in divorce.

One of the frequent arguments against family worship and devotions and families studying the one thing needful is lack of time. Joseph Bayly, author of numerous books, offered a provocative suggestion in "Family Life Together":

> Read the Bible to your children every day, pray with them every day, do other things with them: take walks, play games, read good books aloud. Where will the time come from? Don't have TV. Refuse to rent your living room and all your time - your own, your spouse's, your children's - to pagan hucksters. Ask whether you'd want these people as guests and friends in your home. Whether you'd want your children to grow up under their influence. Is their image of God, the Christian life, the church, the one you want 'sold' to your children?

Television, of course, in itself is not sinful, but neither TV nor anything else should keep your family from the one thing you need, God's Word.

The figures we mentioned from the U.S. Census Bureau showed that the family which together studies the one thing needful remains together as a team. Today many get a big thrill out of participating in a tractor-pulling contest. While such contests do not particularly thrill us (when we hear the roar, we think of blowing up engines and ruining tires) some 40 years ago we did watch horse pulling contests. Any farmer knew that he had to get his horses pulling together if he was going to win the prize. We learned that already when getting our horses to pull a heavy load of hay up hills. If the horses didn't start together and didn't evenly pull the load, first one would jump ahead and then the other and the load would go nowhere.

A husband, wife, and family which regularly gathers around God's Word has a bond which ties them together. They sing:

"Blest be the tie that binds our hearts in Christian love,
The fellowship of kindred minds is like to that above" (TLH #464).

God's Word, the one thing needed, declares: "See how good and pleasant it is for brothers to live in unity!" (Psalm 133:1)

Randy and Miriam, today is a joyous day for you. Yet many here this afternoon can tell you from experience that trials and sorrow enter into every home. There are some here who have lost a loving father, a dear husband or dear wife, a grandson in recent months. Many in our own community this past week mourned the death of an infant, while others were saddened by the loss of a young doctor. Randy, you have experienced grief in your own home. Miriam, in your own family a few weeks ago it looked like a stroke following serious surgery might cast a cloud of sorrow over your wedding day. God's Word, the one thing you need (not a new home, fancy cars, a large bank account, fame or fortune), will give you true comfort when sorrow enters into your home. God tells us in Isaiah: "Don't be afraid -I am with you. Don't look around anxiously - I am your God. I will strengthen you, yes, I will help you. I will support you with My victorious right hand" (Isaiah 41:10). Jesus said: "Come to Me, all you who are working hard and carrying a heavy load, and I will give you rest. Take my yoke on you, and learn from Me - I am gentle and humble-minded - then you will find your rest. My yoke is easy, and My load is light" (Matthew 11:28-30). Peter says: "Throw all your worry on Him, because He takes care of you" (1 Peter 5:7).

Dying People

This week marks the fiftieth anniversary of the beginning of one of the deadliest and most sorrowful events of all history, World War II. Before it was all over, an estimated 50 million died. The fathers of many children, the sons of many parents, and the husbands of many wives all over the world never returned. Death finally enters every home. It will enter your home. We are all dying people. Some of you here this afternoon were members of various athletic teams in college with Randy and Miriam. Some of your coaches are here. Right now most of you are or could be, if you resumed training, at your prime. But soon you'll start going down hill. When I ran home on Friday I saw a runner coming toward me in the distance who ran like a real runner. I thought that I'd better step it up, at least as we pass one another, or he'll really think I'm some old klutz. It was one of you here in the wedding party. There was a time, Miriam, when you always urged me to slow up. Once, as we were running together, you even asked for an umbrella for a shield from the hot sun. Now it's the other way around. Randy, one of the first times you visited us here in New Haven, we played a game of basketball. It was then, as you about broke my finger with a wicked pass, that I realized I was over the hill when it came to playing basketball with college players. Old age, and finally the grave, catch up with all of us.

Miriam, much time was spent designing and making your wedding dress. Yet we all know that such wedding garments do not last. But, if you have the wedding garment mentioned in God's Word, you have the one thing, the heavenly wedding garment, you need which will never fade away.

John writes in Revelation: "Then one of the elders turned to me and asked, 'These people dressed in white robes - who are they and where did they come from?' And I answered him, 'My Lord, you know.' Then he told me, 'They are the people who have come through great suffering, who have washed their robes white in the blood of the lamb. That is why they are before the throne of God and serve Him day and night in His temple, and He who sits on the throne will spread His tent over them. They will never be hungry or thirsty again, and the sun or any heat will never burn them, because the Lamb before the throne will be their Shepherd and will lead them to springs of the water of life. And God will wipe every tear from their eyes" (Revelations 7:13-17).

And so we sing in the hymn:
Behold a host, arrayed in white, like thousand snow clad mountains bright.
With palms they stand. Who is this band before the throne of light?
Lo, these are they of glorious fame Who from the great affliction came
And in the flood of Jesus' blood Are cleansed from guilt and blame.
Now gathered in the holy place, Their voices they in worship raise.
Their anthems swell where God doth dwell, Mid angels' songs of praise (TLH #656, v.1).

And again in another hymn:
Jesus, Thy blood and righteousness My beauty are, my glorious dress;
Midst flaming worlds, in these arrayed, With joy shall I lift up my head (TLH #371, v. 1).

Randy and Miriam, if you follow the example of Mary in our text, you will have the one thing you need, God's Word which tells you about the heavenly wedding garment, Jesus' blood and righteousness. If you always trust in Him and build your marriage upon His Word, then regardless of what may happen in the world, regardless of what sorrow may enter your lives, regardless of death itself, you will be together in heaven for all eternity with all your loved ones, enjoying forever the heavenly marriage feast where Jesus Christ our Savior is the eternal host. God grant you such a reunion at the heavenly marriage feast of the Lamb. Amen.

APPENDIX A
The Family Should See America, p. 257, 258

Great Smoky Mountains, National Park, Tennessee

World's Fair at Knoxville, TN

St. Matthew Lutheran Church, the oldest Lutheran Church in America, where Dad was baptized and confirmed in New York City.

Williamsburg, VA

Blacksmith shop, Colonial Williamsburg

The Minutemen at Lexington

This tent saw us through three of our trips - but first they must figure out how to put it up!

A Tour of America

Mt. Terry Fox, British Columbia

Concordia College,
Edmonton, Canada

On the Mayflower,
Plymouth, Massachusetts

Lake Superior,
Pancake Bay, Canada

The Grand Tetons. It was a long walk - all up hill!

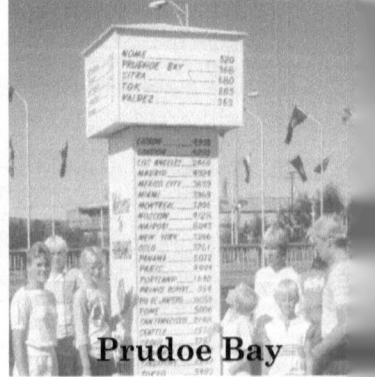

Prudoe Bay

A Tour of America

End of 10K race in Anchorage, Alaska

Mt. McKinley, Alaska

Boarding the S.S. Klondike for tour, Yukon

Continental Divide

Supper time at St. Mary's Campground in Glacier National Park

A Tour of America

Uncle Matt's Cabin at Shepherd of the Hills, Branson, Missouri

On a trail at Hot Springs, Arkansas

Southwest, 1979

↑ Saxon Lutheran Memorial, Frohna, Missouri

The Alamo
San Antonio, Texas →

INDEX

A DayStar Reader - 271
Abortifacient - 46,59,61,97,102,107,121,
    122,126,127,142,255
Abstinence - 6,29,46,53,56,59,91,99,114,
    121,135,139,143,146,147,149,
    284,307, 328
Adams, Dr. Jay - 21,209-213
Adorned in Godliness - 226
Adultery - 3,9,10,38,54,72,73,81,123,
    144,151,154,177,178,183,184,193,
    196-200,204,209,210,212,213,
    215,218,221,244,251,252,261,
    308,318,321-324,328,386
African Americans - 165
Aid Association for Lutherans - 284
Akyol, Sherrill H. - 205
Alfonso Cardinal Lopez Trujillo - 346,348
America - 28,31,35,52,53,56,57,60,61,
    84,100,103,106, 107,111-113,
    123,125,130-132,135,138,141,
    148,149,165,178,186,187,191,
    193,204,206,207,208,218,237,
    240,257,258,265,286,288,290,
    313,318,325,326,332,356,
    393-396
American Association of Christian Counselors - 23,24
American Life Lobby - 89,111-114,121
American Medical Association - 94,149
American Psychological Association - 23,144
An American Translation of the Bible
    (AAT) -171,173,209,214,361
Anarchists - 52,167
Anglican - 57,135,137,193,206,279,280,292
Anglican Church - 56,57,139,151,170,206
Annulment - 4,158,206,208
Anthropology - 109
Arrowood, Dr. Virgil - 16
Augsburg Confession - 49,383
Augustine - 53,167,
Babies- viii,36,77,79,90,105,107,
    114,118,150,152,153,154,155,
    163-166,174,186,230,231,232,
    233,239,241,242,244,266,283,
    288,290,336,337,338,352-354,
    358,359
Bachmann, S. - 256
Bahr, Fred - 102,333
Baptismal Font – vi,376
Baptist Bulletin - 277
Baptists - 136,214,323
Barbour, Dr. Joseph - 25
Barry, A.L. - 160,246,248,250,251,252
Battles, Dr. Ford - 72
Bauer, P.T. - 351
Bayly, Joseph - 390
Beck, William - ,364,366
Becker, Matthew Dr. - 271

Beckmann, Peter - 331
Belz, Joel - 349
Bender, Frederick - 205
Benke, David - 235, 274
Benson, David H. - 205
Bente, F. - 33,116
Bernau, Wayne A. - 182
Birner, Herbert - 305,307,309
Birth Control –ii-iv,vii-ix,6-8,28,33,34,37,
    40,46,47,52-69, 71,72,75-79,
    82-96,99-114,117,119-121,
    123-132,135,137-142,148,151 -
    157,166-168,170-175,177,178,
    195,225,241,247,279,288-290,
    292, 293-295,312,319,330,339,
    343,349,354,358
Birth Control League - 57,104,132,178,292
Bitsberger, Donald - 192
Blazek, Scott - 318
Boettner, Loraine - 212
Bohlmann, Ralph - 244,245
Bonhoeffer and King- Their Life and Theology - 274,285
Bonhoeffer, Dietrich - 285
Bonsignore, Robert J. - 342
Borntraeger - 8
Bradshaw, Terry - 213
Bridal Procession - 373
Britain, Vera - 25
Brooks, David - 163
Brothers, Joyce - 387
Brown, Harold O.J. - 288
Brown, Judie - 34,89,111,114,150
Brown, Lester - 351
Brown, Murphy - 243
Bryant, Anita - 213
Bryant, Kobe - 318
Bucer, Martin - 51
Budziszewski, J. Dr. - 319
Bullinger, Heinrich - 129
Bultmann, Rudolf - 274
Burkee, James - 290
Burns, Dennis J. - 206
Bustanoby, Andre - 193
Butler, Addie Dr. - 285,286
Calovius, Abraham - 51
Calvin, John – viii,50,51,54,71-72,78,80,81,
    84,88,129,151,162,174,357
Camera - 375
Campbell, Nancy - 33,229,233,311
Canada – 90,91,99,144,234,257,258,278,
    339,353,354,355,356,394
Cardinal Bertone - 273
Carlson, Allan Dr. – viii,57,61,133,138,154,
    155,158,256
Cascione, Jack - 252,281
Castration - 42,75,76
Celibacy - 43,50,121,159,273,281
Chandler, Warren - 139

Charen, Mona - 36
Charisma - 35,37,323
Charismatics - 274
Chester, Tim - 318
Chesterton, G.K. - 41,46,167,169,174,256
Children –i-ix,2-9,11,15,16,18,19,28
    33,35,36,38-44,48-55,57,59,61,64-
    70,72, 74,76-93,98-100,102-119,
    123,126-131,133-138,140,142-
    148,150, 152-166,171,172,174-
    177,179,181,184-188,192,193,
    199,202, 205,211,214,217,224-
    234,237-239,241-259,261-266,
    281,283,287291,293,294,297,304,
    305,308,311,313,315,322,325,326,
    331,334,336-339,343-345,348,
    350,352-358, 365,366,374,376-
    378,385-387,389-391
China – 124,345,352
Christian Medical Society - 135
Christian News - vii,viii,33,34,37,38,63,83,
    83-85,87-90,99,102,151,152,153,
    155,171,172,176,179,198,200,
    201,214,226,235,237,241,243,
    248,249,250,251,252,258,270,
    271,273-275,276,279,280,284-
    286,290,292,294,311,321,325,
    339,354,358,381
Christian Research Journal - 154
Christianity Today - 90,135,139,152,154,
193,203,207,289,
Chronicles - 46,66,150,167,169,290
Church Choir - 373
Church Growth Movement - 156,290,291
Church of Canada - 182,192,206
Church of England - 132,135,154,182,
    206,279,292
Clark, Adam - 129
Clergy Divorce - 191,207,243
Clinical Pastoral Education - 20,23
Clinton, Bill - 144
Cloning - 145-147,150,250,251,252,254
Close Communion - 309
Clowes, Brian - 358
Coggan, Donald - 206
Cohabitation - 2,10,35,36,183,185-
    188,254,347
Cohen, Bernard - 341
Cohen, Karl - 341
Cohen, Richard - 143,149
Colderone, Mary - 136
Conception - 6,34,42,44-46,53,59,68,77,
    95,97,103,104,107,116,117,119,
    122,134-136,145,152,230,251,
    254,301,315,362,363
Concordia Cyclopedia – vii,2,83,89,172
Concordia Journal - 274
Concordia Publishing House (CPH) -
    vii,2,25,27,34,37,47,53,56,60,
    83,84,138,152,153,170,214,
    226,235,248,259,274,286,292,
    303,311,312,361,380,382
Concordia University System - 270,271
Condoms - 76,141,243,331

Cone, James H. - 272
Confessional – vii,133,171,172,244,248,
    249,373
Conservation - 166,293
Conservative - 19,28,45,56,57,107,
    120,136,143,151,163,164,166,
    168,178,179,191,208,209,211,
    213,214,243,247,249,268,277,
    285,291,292,321,325
Contraception – i,vi,14,39,40,44-49,51-57,
    60,61,83,86,88,89,93-95,100-
    102,104,111,114,117,118-123,
    125,132-142,145-148,151-155,
    159,167,169,170,172-179, 195,
    254,279,288,290,292,315,345,
    347,350,357
Coogan, Michael - 320,321
Council of Presidents (COP) - 270
Counseling - 19-24,37,102,111,113,184,
    194,200,209,235,344,367
Couple to Couple League - 99,100,114,154
Cozzen, Donald - 275
Creation Museum - 404
Cremation - 51,54
Criswell, W.A. - 135
Curry, Dean C. - 339
Curtis, John - 187
Cushing - 56
Dabney, Robert - 129
Dallmann, W. - 33
Dancing - 363
Dau, W.H.T. - 33,116
Daycare - 262,266
Declaration of Independence - 258,269
Delitszch, Franz - 51,129
Demographers - 346,347,350,354
Depo-Provera - 107,108,126
Didache - 48
Discovery Institute - 165
Dissociative Identity Disorder - 24
Divorce – vii,viii,3,4,9,10,15,27-29,32,
    34-38,42,44,65,83,89,96,144,
    153,158,181,186,190-215,
    217-219,221,234,237-239,243,
    244,249,251,252,278,278,296,
    306,320,321,323,327,347,355,
    35,370,371,387,390
Dobson, James - 22
Doerffler, Alfred - 27
Drickamer, John - 252,382
Drucker, Peter - 356
Drunkenness - 198,322,323
Dudley, Paul V. - 195
Duggar, Jim Bob - 154
Duggar, Michelle - 154
Dumont, Gerard-Francois - 347,348
Earthquake - 208,358
Education - 2,7,11,12,17,20,23,26,29,50,
    109,112,114,122,125,136,141,
    143,157,200,205,250,254,255,
    256,259,263,264,266,273,311,
    325,353,355 ,375,388
Ehrlich, Paul - 331,349,351
Election - 109,163,285,286

Eliot, T.S. - 151,292
Ellen - 144
Ellis, Henry H. - 28,52
Elsdon, Ron - 339
Engagement - 30,34,210,215,295,296,298-
    300,302,303,305,306,309
Engel, Randy - 56,57,61,276,279
Engelder, T. - 2,27,34,84,116
Episcopal Church - 33,104,120,273
Episcopalians - 120,191,192,205,271,
    291,325
Espinosa, Jose Dr. - 83,89,93-99,114
Estonia - 347
Eugenics - 52,150,167
Europe - 31,32,99,135,138,178,186,234,
    257,332 ,336,338,342,347,348,
    353-356
Euthanasia - 93,101,118,119,146,350
Evangelical - 22,116,120,133,134-136,138,
    154,159,175,193,194,203,261,339,
    340,350,351
Evangelical Lutheran Synod - 246
Evangelical Lutherans in Mission - 200
Evans, M. Stanton - 89,288,342
Eve – vi,13,18,80,134,154,179,188,223-
    225,389
Extreme sports - 51
Fabian Society - 52,167
Facebook - 20,21
Family – ii,v,viii,2,5-8,11,13,15-18,25,26,29-
    32,37,38,40,41,43,44,05-53,55-57,
    60,61,70,77,83,85,88,90,91,94,
    95,97,99,101,102,104-106,108,
    110,111,113,114,12-123,125,
    129,133-139,141,142,146-148,
    154,156-160,162,164,167,168,
    171,172,176-178,185,187,191,
    194,14-196,199,202,205-208,219,
    227-232,234,236-239,241-244,
    246-248,250-261,264-266,284,
    288,289,291,293,294,297,300,308,
    311,318,320,325,336,339,341,
    345-348,350,353,355,357,363,
    364,372,378,386,387,389-391,
    393,404
Family Research Council - 139,148,149,
    158,256
Family Shield Ministries - 36,284
Family Worship - 238,261,265,300,390
Farris, Michael - 154
Feder, Don - 15
Federal Council of Churches -
    89,100,104,136,292,
Federal Council of the Churches of Christ-
    100,103,10
Fehlauer, Jeanne B. - 172
Feminists - 140,244
Ferrario, Joseph - 276
Filice, Francis P. - 332
Focus on the Family - 243
Food supply - 333,335
For Better Not For Worse – vii,25,26,33,34,
    37,61,63,84,102,103,153,235,
    245,248,310-312,361

Founding Fathers - 239,269
Fox, Samuel - 192
Frederick the Great - 8
French - 100,122,233,234,240,289,353,355
Freudian - 13,28
Freudianism - 326
Frey, Immanuel G. - 15
Friedan, Betty - 288
Friedrich, Prof. E. J. - 27
Fritz, John - vii,viii,4,33,63,83,84,89,170,
    171,173,245,279,290
Fuerbringer, L. - 2,34,84,116
Fuller, R. Buckminster - 333
Fundamentalism - 120
Fundamentalist - 31,119,138,194
Gabor, Zsa Zsa - 214
Gallen, Tom - 191
Gallup Poll - 203
Gardner, B. Dilworth - 333
Garton, Jean Dr. - 255
Gauss, J.H. - 90
Gay Marriage – vii,viii,19,267-
    269,277,278,321
Gerhard, Johann - 51
Germany - 7,234,241,257,282,289,331,
    338,350,353,
Gibbs, Nancy - 177
Gilder, George - 15,142,149
Gilman, Charlotte - 167
Gladiatorial - 52
God's Word – vi,43,49,58,78,109,139,140,
    159,161,175,181,184,185,199,201,
    216,220,224,225,231,261,262,264,
    283,284,304,305,312,324,378,
    387-389,390-392
Good Will Industries - 104
Gordon, Antony - 164
Government - 32,35,52,55,98,110,125,
    135,140,141,148,158,167,173,186,
    233,234,243,248,253,255,266,
    270,271,277,280,286,319,335,
    345-347,351,352, 355,360,368
Gow, Haven Bradford – viii,89,239,318
Gowns - 371,380
Graebner, Alan - 2,3,33,58,60,61,116,139
Graham, Billy - 135,349
Grant, George - 55
Greece - 32,350
Greeley, Andrew - 166,291
Green Revolution - 334
Griswold, Ellen - 133,144,147,151
Guarr, Judy - 319
Guifoyle, George, H. - 276,280
Guttmacher Institute - 125,141,324
Guttmacher Report - 59
Guttmacher, Alan - 125,136,141
Habeck Professor - 306
Hardt, Tom - 33,89
Harrison, Matthew - 47,187
Hart, Joseph - 276,280
Harvard Divinity School - 324
Haub, Carl - 353
Hawkins, David - 193
Hawn, Goldie - 187

Hayford, Jack - 37
He Her Honor and She His Glory – v,vii,8
    35,37,38,235
Health – iv,5,6,8,17,23,35,52,84,89,91,94,
    99,101,104-106,109,120,124,126,
    135,141,143,147-149,155,163,
    171,176,265,272,298,325-329,
    334,345, 346,348,349,379,380
Hefner, Hugh - 319
Heintschel, Donald - 206
Hendrickson, William - 46
Henry, Matthew - 129,151
Heyward, Carter - 272
Hickman, Hoyt - 204
Hill, Randal - 386
Hill, Robert - 38,198,200,201,203
Hodge, Bryan - 45,49,52-54,60,173-176
Holland - 144,257,265,334
Holy Communion - 205,373
Home Schooling - 154,262
Homosexuals - 74,136,144,146,147,193,
    268,270,274,275,276,277,281,285
Honeymoon - 27,92,363
Hooker, Evelyn - 136
Horowitz, Richard - 164
Hout, Michael - 166,291
Huebel, Glen - 183
Humanae Vitae - 123,132,135,137,139,
    149,154,178,357
Humanism - 201,261,268
In vitro fertilization - 118,145,146,251, 254
India – 335,342,347
Inerrancy - vii,119,120,261,274
Infidelity - 36,37,195,197,208,328
Inge, William R. - 52,56,132
Internet - 21,22,154,164
Interracial Marriage - 310
Ireland - 99,353
Italy – 99,234,257,282,331,335,350,355
IUD - 97,98,107,108,112-114,121,122,
    126, 315
Jackson, Brandon - 206
Jackson, Gregory Dr. - 275
Jaime Cardinal Sin of Manila - 348
Japan - 31,140,148,331,1332,336,337,357,
    358
Jews - 3,6,19,31,69,72,106,110,164,170,357
John Cardinal Wright - 271,280
Johnson, John – 270, 271, 293
Juergen, Harold - 247
Kahn, Herman - 340
Kass, Leon - 146
Kaufmann, David Dr. - 258,259
Keil, Johann - 129
Kennedy, Gerald - 178
Kim-Huei, Huan Dr. - 347
Kinsey Report - 178
Kirkendall, Lester - 136
Klawitter, B. - vii,40,167,173,268
Klinghoffer, David - 163,165
Knust, Jennifer Wright - 320,321
Koehler, E.W.A. - 34,116
Kowalska, Irene Dr. - 347
Kreeft, Peter - 47

Kretzmann, P.E. - 2,34,84,116
Krey, Peter - 176,223,226
Kwok Pui Lan - 272
Kysar, Myrna - 207
Kysar, Robert - 207,
Laetsch, Theodore - 6,34,116,171
Lambeth Conference - 56,57,101,132,135,
    139,154,172,292
Lancaster, Phil - 260
Landon -89,179,240,241,242
Landon, Michael - 241
Landon, Delbert – 241,247,
Larimore, Walter L. - 59,61
Latvia - 347
LCMS's Texas District - 198,199,200
Lehenbauer, Paul - 247
Letterman, David - 318
Leupold, Herbert - 129
Lewinski, Monica - 144
Lezius, Oscar - 8
LGBT - 270,272
Liberalism - 28,163,164,171,285
Likoudis, Paul - 275
Liquor - 15
Lithuania - 247
Little, C. H. - 91
Lohengrin - 308,362,372
Lolita - 145,150
Longman, Philip - 31
Lord's Prayer - 162,252,366,372,380
Luecke, G. - 34,116
Luscombe, Belinda - 214
Luther, Martin – vii-ix,4,5,10,11,33,45,49,
    50,51,53,54,58,63,64,65-69,71,
    72,79,80,84,87,88,99,116,129,
    133,134,135,137,138,151-154,
    158,159,167,170,173,174,197,
    228,237,238,279-283,286,290,
    291, 313,314,354,357,384
Lutheran Brotherhood - 284
Lutheran Church - Missouri Synod – vii,2,
    34,47,56,57,58,63,85,87,101,
    136,152,153,160,171,172,177,187,
    198,200,214,244,246,250,251,252,
    270,275,279,290,291,314,349,361
Lutheran Church in America - 53,136,138,
    191,207,208,288
Lutheran Churches of the Reformation -
    33,115
Lutheran Hour – vii,viii,25,37,61,63,89,102
    137,151,153,171,259,292,311,327
Lutheran Witness –viii,36,100,170,183,196,
    238,245,290,305,390
Lutheran Women - 288
Lutherans – ii,vii,51,58,61,99,102,139,171,
    172,203,204,214,284,285,286,
    287,373
Lutherans for Life - 47,171,172,173,255
Mace, David - 207
Mace, Verna - 207
Machen, John - 129
Macro-Evolution - 41
Maier, Dr. Walter – vii,viii,25,33,34,37,61,
    63,84,85,89,101,103,116,137,

139,151,102, 152,153,170,171-
173,235,245,248,279,290-292,
310,311,312,314
Maier, Paul - 33
Malta - 99
Malthus, Thomas - 6,333,340
Malthusian - 6,57,135,333,346
Marquardt, Larry 83-85,89,171,173,247,279
Marriage Encounter - 13,389
Marshall, Alex - 351,352
Martin, Victoria Woodhull - 167
Marty, Martin - 275
Marx, Father Paul - 99,121
Masturbation - 42,315
Mather, Cotton - 129
Matrimony – i,v,vii,viii,ix,3,4,8,14,17,18,
25,27,30,35,37,38,116,153,205,
208,235,298
McCain, Paul - 53,153,273,286
McManus, Michael - 35
McCloskey, Pat - 318
Mead, Margaret - 325,326
Means, Patrick - 37,
Melchizedek - 46,77
Mercer, Lucy - 327
Methodist - 139,178,191,194,195,203,
204,207,218
Meyer, Kay L. - 36
Miller, Lisa - 19,320
Mills, John Stuart - 6
Mohler, Albert - 178
Mollenkott, Virginia Ramey - 272
Moore, Elizabeth - 319
Moral Majority - 268,270
Moshholder, Ray - 37
Mother's Day – 100,229,235,246
Motherhood – vii,viii,44,50,52,53,100,101,
116,118,160,166,167,168,176,
177,222-226,231,234,235,246,
247,251,254
Mueller, J.T. - 33,116
Mugavero, Francis - 276,280
Mulloy, John J. - 208
Multiple-personality-disorder - 24
Music - 134,143,161,188,228,231,260,
262,273,308,309,356,372,373,
374,385,387
MySpace - 20,21
Narramore, Clyde - 22
Nathanson, Bernard - 123
National Review - 147,150,325,331
Natural Family Planning – ii,88,94,95,99,
121,123,133,147,154,195,196
Naumann, Martin J. – viii,33,34,83,89,108,
110,116,173,288
Nazis – 52,167
Negro Project - 55
Neske, Annabelle - 156,157
Neuhaus, Richard John - 273,274
New International Version - 209
New Testament - 2,43-45,47,48,64,73,74,
76,85,92,103,140,176,188,207,
265,382,
Nimocks, Austin - 277

Noble, Carl - 250
Noble, Elzbieta - 250
Norplant - 107,108,126,315
O'Connell, William - 34
O'Hara, John Dr. - 291
Obesity - 51
Obey - 5,46,66,71,80,82,128,129,161,166,
189,202,216,283,365,370,379,
322,390
Oesch, Adalbert -85,247
Ogola, Margaret Dr. - 247
Old Testament - 25,42-46,48,64,73-77,
99,103,140,176,277,278,283,321
Olson, Norman - 277
Olson, Theodore – 268,269,270
Onan – 42,46,50,54,70-73,78,87,88,151,292
Open Communion - 373
Ordination - 221,281,312
Ortho Evera - 151
Osiander, Lukas - 51
Otte, Gerald - 247
Otten, Herman - 101,157,237,247,252,
285,286,386
Otten, Miriam - 387
Otten, Peter - 404
Parcher, John - 85,247,292,294
Parcher, Mrs. John - 85,247
Parish Leadership Seminars - 200
Paul – v, 3,23,43,44,46,47,50,64,71,76,79,
80-82,92,93,117,120,160,163,
178,188,191,197,213,244,283-
285,323,370,383,384,389
Pearl Harbor - 327
Pedophilia - 144,145,282,320
Perlman, Mark - 341
Persico, Joseph, E. - 327,328
Pharmakeia – 45,48
Phillips, Douglas W. - 260
Physical Fitness - 258,259
Pieper, Francis - 33,116
Pill – viii,57,59,61,89,94,95,97,99,107,108,
114,117-119,121,122,125,126,
130-133,141,142,144,147-151,
176-179,315
The Pivot of Civilization - 54,114,132,166-
168,179
Planned Parenthood Federation of America
-125,132,178
Playboy - 138,319,320,336
Pless, John T. - 47
Poland - 31,99,347,353
Polybius - 32
Polygamy – vii,276-278
Pomeroy, Wardell - 136
Ponnuru, Ramesh - 147,150
Pope - 96,129,135,274,276,280-284,303,
346,348
Pope Gregory VII - 281
Pope John Paul II - 206
Pope John XXIII - 178,280
Pope Paul VI - 132,135,154,178,205,276,
279,280,348,357
Popenoe, David - 186,239
Population Controllers - 346,349,351

Population explosion - 33,34,89,90,135,330,
        331,334,337,342,346,354
Pornography - 133,177,195,255,278,290,
        318,357
Prange, Mrs. Peter - 85
Prange, Peter - 247
Pregnancy - 45,48,58,59,68,87,94,95,97,
        98,118,121,123,124-126,131,141-
        143,149,177,181,189,227,232,
        254,315,324
Preus, Daniel - 244-246
Preus, Dort - v,247,249,250
Preus, Robert – 245,297,292
Preus, Robert Mrs. - 85,244,245,247,293,
        294
Preus, Rolf - i,v,83,89,246,247
Priest -57,104,113,133,134,158,159,205,
        206,560,264,270,273-276,279,
        281-284,320,357,
Promise Keepers - 263
Protestant – i,ii,viii,33,34,45,47,48,51,57,
        63,87,88,102,104,106,126-129,
        133,135-140,151-155,159,166,
        167,172,177,179,203,204,206,
        207,214,240,275,279,290,292,
        330,357,380
Protestants Against Birth Control - 102,
        106,126
Provan, Charles D. – viii,33,47,54,63,64,82-
        89,99,151-153,172,235,247
Psychotherapy - 21
Putin, Vladimir - 352,353
Quayle, Dan - 243
Rabbis - 192,357
Rainer, Thom S. - 291
Rausch, James - 276,281
Reagan, Nancy - 146
Reccord, Robert E. - 37
Recovered Memory Therapy - 24
Rediger, G. Lloyd - 207
Reformation – vii,ix,33,49,51,54,57,61,71,
        88, 90,115,119,129,133,138,237,
        262,265
Regentin, Pam - 226
Rehwinkel, Alfred - 56,58,60,137,258,292
Repentance - 24,175,183,184,185,197,200,
        202,204,213,219,220,233,262,371
Rice, Charles - 101
Richman, Sheldon - 351,352
Robertson, Pat - 37
Robison, Roscoe - 192
Rock, Dr. John - 56
Rockford Institute - 256
Rod - 265
Roe v. Wade - 101,107,108,135,144,151
Rogers, Dale Evans - 226
Roman Catholic Church - 56,63,105,208,
        270,274-276,279,280,309
Rome - 32,208,270,273,274,276,282,340
Rooney, Mickey - 214
Roosevelt, Franklin - 327,328
Roosevelt, Theodore - 167
Rosicrucian Society - 52,167
Rossow, Tim - 270

Rueda, Enrique T. - 275
Rushdoony, Rousas J. - 82,86,339,354
Russell, Bertrand - 25
Russell, Kurt - 187
Russia - 256,259,337,352,353
Sacrament – iv,13,26,158,208,209,281,309,
        318,373,376,390
Saffen - 290
Same-sex marriage - 256,276,277,312
Sanger, Margaret – viii,51-56,60,113,114,
        123,129,131,132,137,154,166-
        168,178,292
Sassone, Robert L. - 330,334-336
Schaeffer, Francis - 339
Schaller, Lyle - 207
Scharlemann, Dr. Martin - 37,209
Schevchenko, Ivan - 256
Schlafly, Phyllis - 19
Schmidt, Alvin - 54
Schultz, Reuel - 89,345
Schulz, Wallace Dr. - 259
Schwenk, Harriet - 27
Searlye, G. D. - 126
Second Vatican Council - 178,280
Senske, Kurt Dr. - 285,286
Sex – vii,2,3,5,6,11,13,19,29,36,42,45,46,49,
        50,58,60,67,76,81,95,100,113,114,
        116,121,122,124,125,133,136,139,
        141-47,149,150,154,155,159,160,
        165,167-169,173-79,181,182,184,
        185,188,189,193,195,196,228,240,
        242,244,254,256,270,273-277,
        296,305,307,309,312,315,317-
        321,323-325,328,336,355,388
Sex Education - 11,12,114,122,125,141,143,
        254,355,388
Shaw, G.B. - 167
Shore-Goss, Bob - 272
Shutt, Jay W. – 157,158
Simon, Julian L. - 114,149,340,351,356
Singer, Fred S. - 341
Singleton, William - 200,201
Skott, Michael - 126
Social Security - 141,147,232,343
Socialists - 52,167
Soloists - 308,369, 372
Solzhenitsyn, Alexander - 353
Song of Songs - 321
Southern Baptist - 37,135,138,179,194,
        203,291
Sowell, Thomas - 128
Spellman - 56
Spong, John S. – 119,120
Spurgeon, Charles - 51,129,151,167,221
St. Jerome - 133
Starbuck, JoJo - 213
Stark, Rodney - 32
State Welfare - 254
Stelzer, Ron - 292
Sterilization - 52,100,122,123,141,154,
        167,253,254,343,345
Stewardship - 47,172,259,340,371
Steyn, Mark - 356
Stout, Robert J. - 207

Stuart, Elizabeth - 272
Tax relief - 357
Taylor, Elizabeth - 214
Taylor, Robert - 247
Television - 143,144,151,161,165,188,
    277,390
Terence Cardinal Cooke - 150,276
Terry, Randall - 130,131
The Bible and Birth Control - 33,47,54,
    63,85,87,88,151-153,172,247,354
The Christian Case Against Contraception -
    45,47,53,173-175
The Epistle of Barnabas - 48
The Kiss - 145,150, Therapeutic Society - 22
Thrivent Financial - 284-286
TIME - 235,327,328,343
Tjernagel, Neelak - 237
Torode Bethany - 152-155
Torode, Sam - 152-155
Trapp, Loren - 361,367
Trinity Lutheran Church of New Haven,
    Missouri - 25,37,63,250,252
Tsunami - 358
Tuxedos - 371
Twitter - 20,21
Ulrich, David Dr. - 205
Unionism - 309,373
Unitarian Universalist Association - 191
United Church of Canada - 182,192
United Methodist Church - 191,218
United Presbyterian Church - 191
United Reformed Church - 205
United States - 20,22,52,55-58,84,125,
    126,132,133,139,140,141,142,146,
    149,165,166,167,170,208,239,
    242,268,276,277,280,289,330,
    331,336,337,338,387
U.S. News and World Report - 118,275
Utah - 125,278,333
Valenzona, Rosa Linda G. - 346
Van Kaam, Dr. Adrian - 94
Van Leeuwen, Raymond - 154
Vasectomy - 76,127
Vision Forum - 260
Von Bora, Katherine - 135
Wagner, Teresa R. - 140,148,291,372
Walter A. Maier Still Speaks - vii,61,279,
    312,327
Walther Conference - 34
Walther League Messenger - 25,26,37,
    84,85,89,100,172,245,247,290,
    311,314,361
Walther, C.F.W. - vii,33,116
Wanderer - 101,114,208,247,273,275,276,
    279,346,358
Wangerin, Walter - 53
Wattenberg, Ben - 84,331,356
Wayne House - 154
Weakland, Rembert - 275,276,280
Wedding - v,ix,13,14,22,37,38,153,155,182,
    183,184,185,187,211,238,247,250,
    305,307,308,309,311,360-364,
    367-378,380-392
Wells, H.G. - 52,53,54,60,166-168

Weber, James A. - 343,344
Wesley, John - 129,130,151,167
West Germany - 289,331
Whelan, Robert - 345,346
Whitehead, Barbara Dafoe - 36,149
Whitehouse, T.C. - 191
Whitfield, Faith - 205
Wilde, Melissa - 166,291
Wilkinson, Loren - 340
Wilks, John - 59
Wisconsin Evangelical Lutheran Synod -
    34,47,83,85,171,172,246
Wolf, Aaron D. - viii,150,151,165,290,352
World Congress on Families - 249,250,256
World War II - i,136,327,330,337,347,353,
    358,391
Wrighton, Helena - 135
Wynn, J.C. - 136
Wysong, Charles - 154
You Tube - 20-22
Young Women's Christian Association - 104
Young, Andrew - 326
Young, James J. - 206
Zero Population - 228,330,344

The Creation Museum Is A Must In A Tour of America

The Creation Museum of Answers in Genesis in Petersburg, Kentucky includes a show titled "Men In White." Kerri Otten in her report of a visit to the museum mentions that her children considered this show the highlight of their visit. It includes a young girl at a fire place in some camp contemplating how the world, mountains etc. got here. It reminded this editor of lectures his family received from many rangers and others in their five family tenting trips during the 1980's which took them to 48 states, including Alaska, and five provinces of Canada. Evolution in one form or another often was promoted as absolute fact in evening lectures at state, national and provincial parks. Had the 27 million dollar creation museum of Answers in Genesis in Petersburg, Kentucky been in existence, it would have been a must on the Otten family tour of America. The family did have books with them which responded to the evolutionists and defended creationism. Yet a visit to the Creation Museum would have been even more helpful. Parents now is the time to see to it that your children get the answers to evolution they often get not only from park rangers but also from teachers and even churches. Photos on this page show some of the many places the editor's family visited. Parents with young children, now is the time to plan a trip to see America, including the Creation Museum.

"Young girl" listening to the "Men in White" at the Creation Museum explaining the truth about creation and evolution.

Peter and Kerri Otten with their children, Lydia, Caroline and Riley at the Creation Museum in Petersburg, Kentucky

From the special Creation Issue from Christian News, August 4-11, 2008

www.ingramcontent.com/pod-product-compliance
Lightning Source LLC
Chambersburg PA
CBHW031401290426
44110CB00011B/231